© Elisa Cicinelli/Index Stock

After decades of ups and downs, of mass hippie infiltration, gentrification, throngs of homeless, and the ongoing shopping boom and bust, **HAIGHT-ASHBURY (left)** still somehow embodies the counterculture. Its streets are gritty. Its residents are, too. And sprinkled throughout are youthful and trendy clothing stores, cheap eats, and enough head shops and tie-dyed T-shirts to remind you that this was once the epicenter of Flower Power.

Like most cities, gentrification continues to encroach on the city's diversity. But the colorful **MISSION DISTRICT (above)** still celebrates its Latin community, especially through its preservation and recognition of its hundreds of murals. For good insight into the Mission District community, take one of the Precita Eyes Mural Arts Center's tours to see 60 murals in an 8-block walk.

First page: top, © Daniel McGarrah/Index Stock; bottom, © San Francisco CVB

© San Francisco CVB

SAN FRANCISCO (above) is so condensed that it's easy to explore multiple areas in one day. I've always marveled that I can run from one end of town to the other in just over one hour.

The Ferry Building Marketplace is filled with artisan foods and throngs clustering at the wine bar or picking through fancy organic products on **FARMERS MARKET (right)** days. But what really lures me here, besides the bayfront view, are the restaurants, where you can find everything from traditional Chinese tea service to gourmet burgers to outstanding Vietnamese food.

© Stephen Saks Photography/Alamy

Whether you walk it, bike it, drive it, or view it from a distance, San Francisco's most famous landmark, the **GOLDEN GATE BRIDGE,** commands attention. The bridge is a visual wonder in itself. But its flanking backdrop of the woodsy Presidio to the south, rugged Marin Headlands to the north, and glistening waters of the Golden Gate below make it downright magical to behold—even for folks like me who've seen it almost daily for more than three decades.

© Cliff House

I'm the first to admit the historic **CLIFF HOUSE (left)** restaurant is a tourist trap. But it's still pretty darned cool. Hunker down near a picture window overlooking the Pacific to see what I mean.

I'm not much of a sports fan, but the **SAN FRANCISCO GIANTS' BALLPARK (below)**, now named SBC Park, is such a beautiful venue that I happily attend games here. With a San Francisco Bay backdrop and killer garlic fries (and other surprisingly good stadium food and wine), watching a game here is an exceptional way to spend some time.

Chinatown is an exotic world unto itself. Sure it's crowded, residents can be apathetic, and you're likely to hear the occasional coughing up and spitting of phlegm. But that's part of what makes Chinatown so great. It's not some shiny Disney version of Asian life but the real deal, complete with **TEA HOUSES (above right)**, killer **DIM SUM (below right)**, the clatter of Mahjong tiles, fabulously cheap and fresh markets on Stockton Street, and, as of late, a more tasteful selection of trinkets along Grant Avenue.

© Lee Foster/Lonely Planet Images

© James Marshall/Corbis

© Bruce Burkhardt/Corbis

© Mark Newman/Index Stock

PIER 39

HARASSMENT OF
SEA LIONS IS
A VIOLATION OF
THE MARINE
MAMMAL
PROTECTION ACT
NO DOCKING

Locals love to loathe PIER 39. But despite the abundance of tchotchke shops, mediocre restaurants, and kitschy attractions, there are some great things about Fisherman's Wharf. And of those things—which include stunning vistas, access to ferries, and fresh Dungeness crab—the **SEA LIONS (above)** that bathe, bark, and splash around are definitely heart-melting fun. Even jaded San Franciscans can't deny their charm.

Of all the city's edible delights, Dungeness crab is my favorite seasonal indulgence. Availability varies from year to year, but the season usually begins in November and ends in April. If you're around during crab season, don't hesitate to feast on the delicacy, whether it's from a sidewalk stand in **FISHERMAN'S WHARF (right)**, a restaurant, or a supermarket—I usually have the folks at the seafood department crack it for me, grab some napkins, and have an alfresco feast along the Marina Green.

© Ed Young/AGStockUSA, Inc./Alamy

San Francisco's architecture is as diverse as its population, but the city is best known for its Victorian houses. Though you can find them in other neighborhoods, it's the strip of **HOUSES ALONG ALAMO SQUARE (right)** that are often ogled for their picture-perfect side-by-side positioning and great upkeep.

The lines to board **SAN FRANCISCO'S CABLE CARS (below)** ensure that most locals don't take them regularly. But on the rare occasion that I manage to get on one, it's an instant reminder of why they are so fun—and romantic, thrilling, and even a little death defying—as they slowly lunge down the city's steep hills. Seriously, this is a must-do.

© Ron Stroud/Masterfile

© Jon Hicks/eStock Photo

© Jerry Alexander/Cephas Picture Library/Alamy

For the past few years I've spent much of my time in **WINE COUNTRY (below),** and here's what I've learned: It is one of the most decadent places I've ever been. (And I've been a lot of places.) Here it's all about great wine, outstanding food, and leisure pursuits like spas, golf, **BIKING (left),** lounging, and, of course, eating and drinking. If the city is fogged in and you're itching for some sunshine, consider driving one hour to Napa or Sonoma to sip your way through a few wineries, plop down at a bucolic restaurant, and linger over a bottle of wine and a ridiculously good meal. It's more than the good life: This is about as good as life gets.

© Charles O'Rear/Corbis

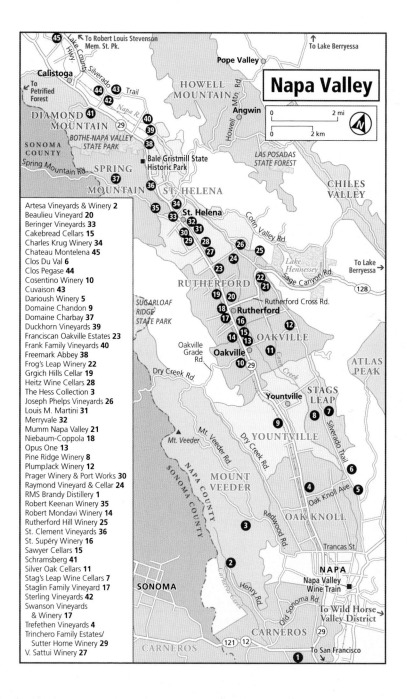

Napa Valley

To Robert Louis Stevenson Mem. St. Pk.
To Lake Berryessa
Pope Valley
Calistoga
To Petrified Forest
HOWELL MOUNTAIN
Angwin
DIAMOND MOUNTAIN
SONOMA COUNTY
BOTHE-NAPA VALLEY STATE PARK
LAS POSADAS STATE FOREST
Bale Gristmill State Historic Park
SPRING MOUNTAIN
ST. HELENA
St. Helena
CHILES VALLEY
Colm Valley Rd.
Lake Hennessey
To Lake Berryessa
RUTHERFORD
Sage Canyon Rd.
128
Rutherford Cross Rd.
Rutherford
SUGARLOAF RIDGE STATE PARK
Oakville Grade Rd.
OAKVILLE
Oakville
Dry Creek Rd.
ATLAS PEAK
STAGS LEAP
Yountville
Mt. Veeder
Dry Creek Rd.
YOUNTVILLE
MOUNT VEEDER
Silverado Trail
Oak Knoll Ave.
OAK KNOLL
Redwood Rd.
Trancas St.
NAPA
Napa Valley Wine Train
SONOMA
To Wild Horse Valley District
CARNEROS
CARNEROS
To San Francisco

Artesa Vineyards & Winery **2**
Beaulieu Vineyard **20**
Beringer Vineyards **33**
Cakebread Cellars **15**
Charles Krug Winery **34**
Chateau Montelena **45**
Clos Du Val **6**
Clos Pegase **44**
Cosentino Winery **10**
Cuvaison **43**
Darioush Winery **5**
Domaine Chandon **9**
Domaine Charbay **37**
Duckhorn Vineyards **39**
Franciscan Oakville Estates **23**
Frank Family Vineyards **40**
Freemark Abbey **38**
Frog's Leap Winery **22**
Grgich Hills Cellar **19**
Heitz Wine Cellars **28**
The Hess Collection **3**
Joseph Phelps Vineyards **26**
Louis M. Martini **31**
Merryvale **32**
Mumm Napa Valley **21**
Niebaum-Coppola **18**
Opus One **13**
Pine Ridge Winery **8**
PlumpJack Winery **12**
Prager Winery & Port Works **30**
Raymond Vineyard & Cellar **24**
RMS Brandy Distillery **1**
Robert Keenan Winery **35**
Robert Mondavi Winery **14**
Rutherford Hill Winery **25**
St. Clement Vineyards **36**
St. Supéry Winery **16**
Sawyer Cellars **15**
Schramsberg **41**
Silver Oak Cellars **11**
Stag's Leap Wine Cellars **7**
Staglin Family Vineyard **17**
Sterling Vineyards **42**
Swanson Vineyards & Winery **17**
Trefethen Vineyards **4**
Trinchero Family Estates/ Sutter Home Winery **29**
V. Sattui Winery **27**

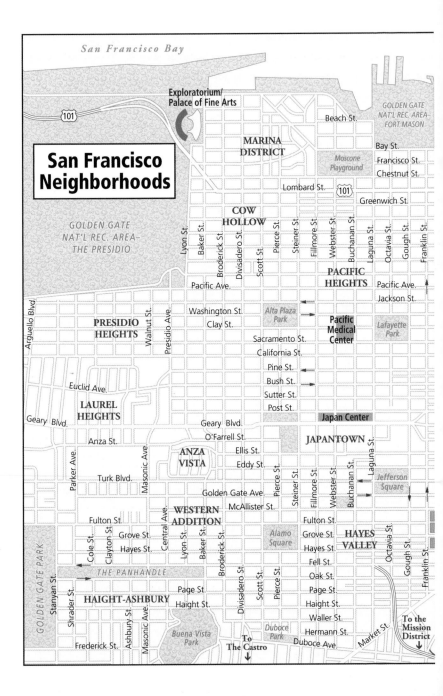

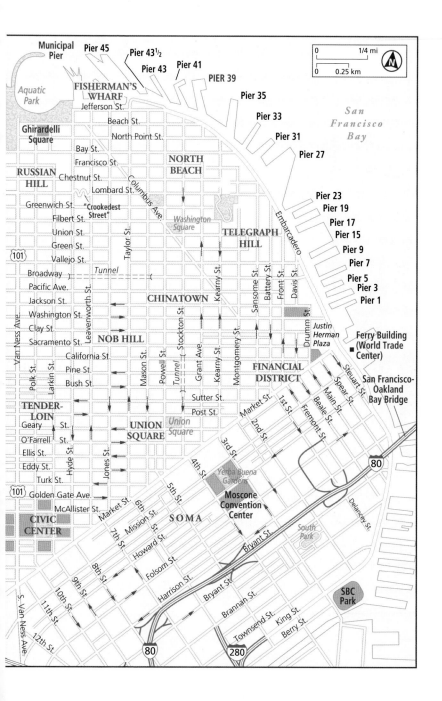

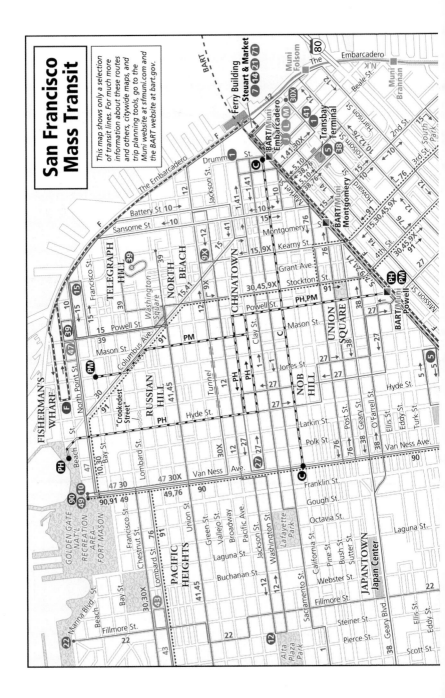

San Francisco
Mass Transit

This map shows only a selection of transit lines. For much more information about these routes and others, citywide maps, and trip planning tools, go to the Muni website at sfmuni.com and the BART website at bart.gov.

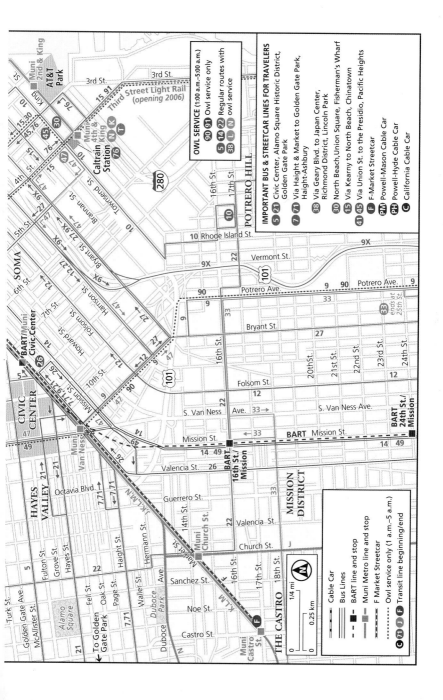

OWL SERVICE (1:00 a.m.–5:00 a.m.)

90 91 Owl service only

15 14 22 Regular routes with owl service

5 14 22
38 L N owl service

POTRERO HILL

IMPORTANT BUS & STREETCAR LINES FOR TRAVELERS

5 21 Civic Center, Alamo Square Historic District, Golden Gate Park

7 71 Via Haight & Market to Golden Gate Park, Haight-Ashbury

38 Via Geary Blvd. to Japan Center, Richmond District, Lincoln Park

30 North Beach,Union Square, Fisherman's Wharf

15 Via Kearny to North Beach, Chinatown

41 Via Union St. to the Presidio, Pacific Heights

F F-Market Streetcar

PM Powell-Mason Cable Car

PH Powell-Hyde Cable Car

C California Cable Car

Muni 2nd & King

AT&T Park

3rd St.

King

3rd St.

Third Street Light Rail (opening 2006)

Muni 4th & King

Caltrain Station

280

16th St.

17th St.

10

10 Rhode Island St.

9X

SOMA

22

Vermont St.

9X

101

Potrero Ave.

9 90 Potrero Ave. 9

90
9

33

33

38 ends at 25th St.

Bryant St.

27

6th St.

7th St.

Folsom St.

Howard St.

Harrison St.

Bryant St.

Brannan St.

Townsend St.

4th St.

5th St.

10th St.

BART/Muni Civic Center

26

16th St.

20th St.

21st St.

22nd St.

23rd St.

24th St.

12

BART 24th St./Mission

CIVIC CENTER

47

49

5

Muni Van Ness

Folsom St.

12

S. Van Ness Ave. 33

S. Van Ness Ave.

14 49

BART Mission St.

14 49

Mission St.

BART 16th St./Mission

Valencia St. 26

Turk St.

Golden Gate Ave.

McAllister St.

HAYES VALLEY

To Golden Gate Park

5

Alamo Square

Fulton St.

Grove St.

Hayes St.

Fell St.

Oak St.

Page St.

Haight St.

Waller St.

21

21

22

7,71

7,71

Octavia Blvd.

7,71 ←7,71

Guerrero St.

14th St.

Valencia St.

Church St.

Muni Church St.

Market St.

J

22

33

MISSION DISTRICT

Hermann St.

Duboce Ave.

Duboce Park

Dubose Ave.

16th St.

17th St.

18th St.

Sanchez St.

Noe St.

Castro St.

Muni Castro St.

THE CASTRO

F

N

K,L,M

1/4 mi

0.25 km

0

0

Cable Car

Bus Lines

BART line and stop

Muni Metro line and stop

F Market Streetcar

Owl service only (1 a.m.–5 a.m.)

5 71 F Transit line beginning/end

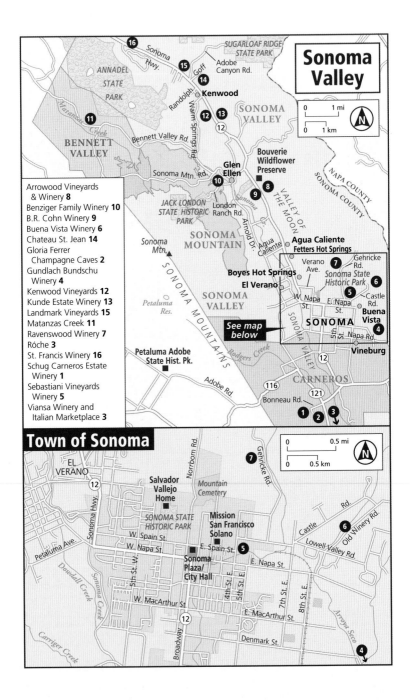

Sonoma Valley

0   1 mi

0   1 km

SUGARLOAF RIDGE STATE PARK

ANNADEL STATE PARK

BENNETT VALLEY

SONOMA VALLEY

Kenwood

Adobe Canyon Rd.

Bouverie Wildflower Preserve

Glen Ellen

JACK LONDON STATE HISTORIC PARK   London Ranch Rd.

SONOMA MOUNTAIN

NAPA COUNTY

SONOMA COUNTY

VALLEY OF THE MOON

Sonoma Mtn.

Agua Caliente Fetters Hot Springs

Verano Ave.   Gehricke Rd.

Boyes Hot Springs

El Verano

Sonoma State Historic Park

W. Napa St.   E. Napa St.

Castle Rd.

SONOMA

Buena Vista

SONOMA VALLEY

Petaluma Res.

See map below

Petaluma Adobe State Hist. Pk.

Adobe Rd.

Bonneau Rd.

CARNEROS

116   121

Vineburg

Napa Rd.

Arrowood Vineyards & Winery **8**
Benziger Family Winery **10**
B.R. Cohn Winery **9**
Buena Vista Winery **6**
Chateau St. Jean **14**
Gloria Ferrer Champagne Caves **2**
Gundlach Bundschu Winery **4**
Kenwood Vineyards **12**
Kunde Estate Winery **13**
Landmark Vineyards **15**
Matanzas Creek **11**
Ravenswood Winery **7**
Róche **3**
St. Francis Winery **16**
Schug Carneros Estate Winery **1**
Sebastiani Vineyards Winery **5**
Viansa Winery and Italian Marketplace **3**

Town of Sonoma

0   0.5 mi

0   0.5 km

EL VERANO

Norrbom Rd.

Gehricke Rd.

Salvador Vallejo Home

Mountain Cemetery

SONOMA STATE HISTORIC PARK

Mission San Francisco Solano

W. Spain St.   E. Spain St.

Castle Rd.

Old Winery Rd.

W. Napa St.   E. Napa St.

Lowell Valley Rd.

Sonoma Hwy.

Petaluma Ave.

Dowdall Creek

Sonoma Plaza/ City Hall

W. MacArthur St.

E. MacArthur St.

Broadway

Denmark St.

Carriger Creek

Frommer's®

San Francisco
2007

by Erika Lenkert

Here's what the critics say about Frommer's:

"Amazingly easy to use. Very portable, very complete."
—*Booklist*

"Detailed, accurate, and easy-to-read information for all price ranges."
—*Glamour Magazine*

"Hotel information is close to encyclopedic."
—*Des Moines Sunday Register*

"Frommer's Guides have a way of giving you a real feel for a place."
—*Knight Ridder Newspapers*

Wiley Publishing, Inc.

About the Author

A native San Franciscan, **Erika Lenkert** divides her time between San Francisco and Napa Valley where she is forever seeking the next best restaurant, hotel room, and fun way to savor the region. She frequently writes *InStyle* magazine's party guides and offers up tasty tips on the region for *Food & Wine* magazine. In her spare time she pays visits to local and national television news programs where she gives entertaining and cooking tips based on her book *The Last-Minute Party Girl: Fashionable, Fearless, and Foolishly Simple Entertaining.*

Published by:

Wiley Publishing, Inc.

111 River St.
Hoboken, NJ 07030-5774

Copyright © 2006 Wiley Publishing, Inc., Hoboken, New Jersey. All rights reserved. No part of this publication may be reproduced, stored in a retrieval system or transmitted in any form or by any means, electronic, mechanical, photocopying, recording, scanning or otherwise, except as permitted under Sections 107 or 108 of the 1976 United States Copyright Act, without either the prior written permission of the Publisher, or authorization through payment of the appropriate per-copy fee to the Copyright Clearance Center, 222 Rosewood Drive, Danvers, MA 01923, 978/750-8400, fax 978/646-8600. Requests to the Publisher for permission should be addressed to the Legal Department, Wiley Publishing, Inc., 10475 Crosspoint Blvd., Indianapolis, IN 46256, 317/572-3447, fax 317/572-4355, or online at http://www.wiley.com/go/permissions.

Wiley and the Wiley Publishing logo are trademarks or registered trademarks of John Wiley & Sons, Inc. and/or its affiliates. Frommer's is a trademark or registered trademark of Arthur Frommer. Used under license. All other trademarks are the property of their respective owners. Wiley Publishing, Inc. is not associated with any product or vendor mentioned in this book.

ISBN-13: 978-0-470-04897-9
ISBN-10: 0-470-04897-2

Editor: Marc Nadeau
Production Editor: Eric T. Schroeder
Cartographer: Liz Puhl
Photo Editor: Richard Fox
Production by Wiley Indianapolis Composition Services

Front cover photo: Cable car going up a steep incline.
Back cover photo: Interior of the Asian Art Museum.

For information on our other products and services or to obtain technical support, please contact our Customer Care Department within the U.S. at 800/762-2974, outside the U.S. at 317/572-3993 or fax 317/572-4002.

Wiley also publishes its books in a variety of electronic formats. Some content that appears in print may not be available in electronic formats.

Manufactured in the United States of America

5 4 3 2 1

Contents

Index   333

List of Maps

An Invitation to the Reader

In researching this book, we discovered many wonderful places—hotels, restaurants, shops, and more. We're sure you'll find others. Please tell us about them, so we can share the information with your fellow travelers in upcoming editions. If you were disappointed with a recommendation, we'd love to know that, too. Please write to:

Frommer's San Francisco 2007
Wiley Publishing, Inc. • 111 River St. • Hoboken, NJ 07030-5774

An Additional Note

Please be advised that travel information is subject to change at any time—and this is especially true of prices. We therefore suggest that you write or call ahead for confirmation when making your travel plans. The authors, editors, and publisher cannot be held responsible for the experiences of readers while traveling. Your safety is important to us, however, so we encourage you to stay alert and be aware of your surroundings. Keep a close eye on cameras, purses, and wallets, all favorite targets of thieves and pickpockets.

Other Great Guides for Your Trip:

Frommer's California
Frommer's Portable California Wine Country
Frommer's California Best-Loved Driving Tours
Suzy Gershman's Born to Shop San Francisco
California For Dummies

Frommer's Star Ratings, Icons & Abbreviations

Every hotel, restaurant, and attraction listing in this guide has been ranked for quality, value, service, amenities, and special features using a **star-rating system.** In country, state, and regional guides, we also rate towns and regions to help you narrow down your choices and budget your time accordingly. Hotels and restaurants are rated on a scale of zero (recommended) to three stars (exceptional). Attractions, shopping, nightlife, towns, and regions are rated according to the following scale: zero stars (recommended), one star (highly recommended), two stars (very highly recommended), and three stars (must-see).

In addition to the star-rating system, we also use **seven feature icons** that point you to the great deals, in-the-know advice, and unique experiences that separate travelers from tourists. Throughout the book, look for:

Finds	Special finds—those places only insiders know about
Fun Fact	Fun facts—details that make travelers more informed and their trips more fun
Kids	Best bets for kids, and advice for the whole family
Moments	Special moments—those experiences that memories are made of
Overrated	Places or experiences not worth your time or money
Tips	Insider tips—great ways to save time and money
Value	Great values—where to get the best deals

The following **abbreviations** are used for credit cards:

AE	American Express	DISC	Discover	V	Visa
DC	Diners Club	MC	MasterCard		

Frommers.com

Now that you have the guidebook to a great trip, visit our website at **www.frommers.com** for travel information on more than 3,000 destinations. With features updated regularly, we give you instant access to the most current trip-planning information available. At Frommers.com, you'll also find the best prices on airfares, accommodations, and car rentals—and you can even book travel online through our travel booking partners. At Frommers.com, you'll also find the following:

- Online updates to our most popular guidebooks
- Vacation sweepstakes and contest giveaways
- Newsletter highlighting the hottest travel trends
- Online travel message boards with featured travel discussions

What's New in San Francisco

As a native and someone who sees the city's evolution on an ongoing basis, I'm still surprised to see just how much San Francisco—a city that doesn't appear to have enough undeveloped space to welcome much in the way of additions—continues to change. Anyone who hasn't been here in a few years will marvel at how much more attractive The Embarcadero waterfront is—not to mention how much more there is to do there. Likewise South of Market (SoMa), which despite a mass exodus of start-up companies after the dot-com bust is an epicenter of city growth from lofts, shops, and restaurants around the ballpark area to the four-star hotels and museums surrounding Yerba Buena Gardens.

WHERE TO STAY Perhaps most important to you and your visit are the changes in the hotel scene. The hottest news is the opening of the **St. Regis Hotel,** 125 Third St. (☎ **877/787-3447** or 415/284-4000). Part historical structure, part brand-new high-rise and all SoMa luxury, it immediately became *the* place to book.

Additionally, last year, many of the city's temporary abodes got face-lifts, which means you'll get a fresher place to lay your travel-weary head. The small rooms are still pricy for what you get at **Hotel Monaco,** 501 Geary St. (☎ **800/ 214-4220** or 415/292-0100), but at least they're draped in all new goods. Downtown's **Hilton San Francisco,** 333 O'Farrell St. (☎ **800/HILTONS** or

415/771-1400), is still gargantuan and convention-y, but now when you close your door and snuggle up to watch a good movie you can enjoy it on one of their new flatscreen TVs. The **Pan Pacific,** 500 Post St. (☎ **800/533-6465** or 415/771-8600), also promises new furnishings in their rooms, which already looked Asian-chic. Good thing **The Maxwell Hotel,** 386 Geary St. (☎ **888/ 734-6299** or 415/986-2000), is about to do major room renovations. The old hotel was showing a lot more than her age. Up the street, **Hotel Beresford,** 635 Sutter St. (☎ **800/533-6533** or 415/ 673-9900), was a good deal before its upgrades scheduled for 2006 and 2007, so once they're completed it can only be better—so long as they don't pass the expense onto guests.

On tony Nob Hill, reigning luxury hotel **The Ritz-Carlton,** 600 Stockton St. (☎ **800/241-3333** or 415/296-7465), is upping the haute hospitality ante with a $12.5-million room update, including 32-inch LCD TVs, DVDs, and CD players, wi-fi, and two cordless phones. As this book goes to press, SoMa's **The Argent Hotel,** 50 Third St. (☎ **877/222-6699** or 415/974-6400), is preparing to throw $30 million toward its rooms and add a new fitness center and restaurant. Also just South of Market, one of my favorite luxury boutique hotels, **Hotel Palomar,** 12 Fourth St. (☎ **877/294-9711**), is sprucing up rooms with new drapes, bedspreads, and carpeting.

Personally, I'm still not sure the rooms at **The Mandarin Oriental,** 222 Sansome St. (© **800/622-0404** or 415/276-9888), needed updating, but they got it anyway—in golds and warm tones. But even if they went with burlap, it'd still be fabulous—their unbelievable views are some of the best in town. Also in the Financial District, the **Hilton San Francisco Financial District,** 750 Kearny St. (© **800/HILTONS** or 415/433-6660), may not be new from the outside, but the interior is a whole other world—and one of contemporary business standards and comfort at that!

In North Beach, sweet little **Washington Square Inn,** 1660 Stockton St. (© **800/388-0220** or 415/981-4220), doesn't have celestial views, but it is giving guests something good to look at—specifically flatscreen TVs along with new bedding.

With all the hotels I stay in for business, I sometimes forget how much thriftier I am when divvying up my vacation money on hotels vs. must-dos like shopping and dining. With that in mind, I added a few great budget options. **Hotel des Arts,** 447 Bush St. (© **800/956-4322** or 415/956-3232), in Union Square, lacks some of the more fancy amenities, but it makes up for it with a great location and low rates for vibrant rooms designed by local artists. **Stratford Hotel,** 242 Powell St. (© **888/504-6835** or 415/397-7080), is another colorful and cheap option in the heart of the Union Square action. New to the book but not new to the city is the **Marina Motel,** 2576 Lombard St. (© **800/346-6118** or 415/921-9406), a cheery option in the Marina with rates that hover around $150.

Something to anticipate: **Radisson Miyako Hotel,** 1625 Post St. (© **800/ 533-4567** [within the US only] or 415/ 922-3200), in Japantown, is under new ownership, and word is they'll say sayonara to mid-level Japanese-style digs for fancier stuff. Stay tuned.

WHERE TO DINE As always, the food scene is hopping, but not always in the right direction. When **Campton Place,** 340 Stockton St. (© **800/235-4300** or 415/781-5555), lost its award-winning chef Daniel Humm to New York City, it also lost its place in this book's dining section. Whether it returns depends on new chef Peter Rudolph. I don't like to dedicate too many pages to super-expensive restaurants, so for one to be included it'd better be fabulous. Is it? Time will tell. I was equally dismayed to hear Fabrice Roux left the **Grand Café,** 501 Geary St. (© **415/292-0101**), to go to the Carnelian Room, which is not in this book because though the views are amazing, the food has been mediocre—and expensive. If Roux keeps the standard he set at the Grand Café in his new celestial digs, you'll see the Carnelian Room listed next year. Meanwhile, the Grand Café made the cut again because talented chef Ron Boyd, who has made lovely food in a number of fine restaurants, including Domaine Chandon in Napa Valley, is now heading up the kitchen.

In previous editions, I've recommended you venture off the beaten path to the Richmond District to dine at Singaporean restaurant **Straits Café.** Now, you don't even have to make an effort if you're staying downtown. As this book goes to press, the restaurant is relocating—and changing its name to Straits Restaurant. Look for it at the newly expanded San Francisco Centre (San Francisco Centre, 845 Market St., Suite 597; © **415/668-1783**). It is expected to open in September 2006—and include a Bloomingdale's!

You won't find **Harbor Village** mentioned in the book this year. The Embarcadero spot for dim sum and Chinese food closed in 2005 after 20 years in business. Ditto North Beach's **Gold Spike,** which closed after 86 years—allegedly due to a landlord dispute. But I have added another North Beach favorite, **Steps of Rome Caffe,** 348 Columbus Ave. (© **415/397-0435**).

However, there are a few great new dining options. On the casual side is **Zuppa,** 564 Fourth St. (© **415/777-5900**), a hip, relaxed SoMa spot for delicious Italian food amid an equally sumptuous environment. At the luxury end of the spectrum is **Ame,** in the St. Regis Hotel at 689 Mission St. (© **415/284-4040**)—the latest restaurant of one of my all-time favorite chefs Hiro Sone and his front-of-house and pastry managing wife Lissa Doumani. They made their name at their other restaurant, Terra, in Napa Valley, which is still going strong, too. Down in Fisherman's Wharf you can't miss the new shrine to sourdough bread, **Boudin at the Wharf,** 160 Jefferson St., near Pier 43½ (© **415/928-1849**). Drop in for a meal, snack, and tour of the working bakery and history of the city in conjunction with this long-standing brand.

After clearing a little room later in the book, I added a few more of my favorite haunts: **Hawthorne Lane,** 22 Hawthorne St. (© **415/777-9779**), a great choice for tasty Contemporary American fare with Asian flare amid upscale but relaxed surroundings, and **Takara,** 22 Peace Plaza #202 in Japan Center Miyako Mall (© **415/921-2000**), a low-key spot for quality sushi and Japanese food.

ATTRACTIONS   After closing for several years so a completely new building could be constructed, the **de Young Museum,** 50 Hagiwara Tea Garden Dr. (© **415/682-2481**), has reopened in Golden Gate Park. I'm thrilled to report that it is an absolutely fantastic museum, from the collection to the architecture to the gardens and cafe with alfresco tables. It's definitely one of the must-dos while visiting the city.

WINE COUNTRY   One of Wine Country's most renowned chefs, Richard Reddington, made a name for himself at Auberge du Soleil, left about 2 years ago, and finally opened his own spot in Napa Valley's quaint Yountville. **Redd,** 6480 Washington St. (© **707/944-2222**), is a sophisticated, expensive affair amid a stark and contemporary dining room. Food lovers should definitely check it out.

1

The Best of San Francisco

Even if you've never been to San Francisco, you probably already have an image of it in your mind. Perhaps you envision cable cars cresting monstrous hills with the glistening bay as a picture-perfect backdrop, neighborhoods of colorfully painted Victorians, small streets lined with swank boutiques, killer restaurants packed with fans of the region's exceptional food and wine, ferry rides across the bay or walks across the Golden Gate Bridge, hippies celebrating free love, or even gay and lesbian couples celebrating a briefly legal union on the steps of City Hall. Regardless of what you expect or imagine, The City by the Bay is all that and more. As the country's most romantic European-style city, which was founded on—and still revels in—the pioneers' boom-or-bust lifestyle and diversity in all things, it really does have a little bit of everything tucked into only 7 square miles. So, what can you expect with a visit? Whatever your heart desires! Like an eternal world's fair, it's all happening in San Francisco, and everyone's invited.

1 The Most Unforgettable Travel Experiences

- **An Early Morning Cable-Car Ride:** Skip the less-scenic California line and take the Powell-Hyde cable car down to Fisherman's Wharf—the ride is worth the wait. When you reach the top of Nob Hill, grab the rail with one hand and hold your camera with the other, because you're about to see a view of the bay that'll make you a believer. Oh, and don't call it a trolley. See p. 151.

- **An Adventure at Alcatraz:** Even if you loathe tourist spots, you'll like Alcatraz. The rangers have done a fantastic job of preserving The Rock—just looking at it is enough to give you the heebie-jeebies—and they give excellent guided tours (highly recommended). Heck, even the boat ride across the bay is worth the price, so don't miss this attraction. See p. 150.

- **A Walk across the Golden Gate Bridge:** Don your windbreaker and walking shoes and prepare for a wind-blasted, exhilarating journey across San Francisco's most famous landmark. It's simply one of those things you have to do at least once in your life. See p. 156.

- **A Stroll through Chinatown:** Chinatown is a trip. I've been through it at least 100 times, and it has never failed to entertain me. Skip the crummy camera and luggage stores and head straight for the markets, where a cornucopia of sights that you just don't see very often in America sits in boxes for you to scrutinize (one day we saw an armadillo for sale, and it wasn't meant to be a pet). Better yet, take one of Shirley Fong-Torres's Wok Wiz tours of Chinatown (p. 185). See "Walking Tour 1: Chinatown," beginning on p. 191, for our walking tour of Chinatown.

- **A Shopping Spree:** Up your credit card limit and bring an extra suitcase, because you're sure to find hundreds of must-haves in the department stores and boutiques surrounding San Francisco's retail epicenter, Union Square. Boutique hounds should head to North Beach's Grant Avenue, upper Fillmore, and Hayes Valley for the best selections of chic women's wear. See chapter 9 for more on San Francisco's shopping.

2 The Best Splurge Hotels

- **The Ritz-Carlton,** 600 Stockton St., Nob Hill (© **800/241-3333** or 415/296-7465; www.ritzcarlton.com), is the granddaddy of luxury, with all the traditional bells and whistles and every possible amenity. From afternoon tea to the city's best Sunday brunch to the best lobby restrooms to traditional abodes, your wish is their command. See p. 75.
- **Four Seasons Hotel San Francisco,** 757 Market St., SoMa (© **800/332-3442** or 415/633-3000; www.fourseasons.com), opened in 2001 after being built from the ground up. A perfect combination of opulence, hipness, and class, this is one of my favorite modern luxury hotels. It doesn't share the grandeur or sheer number of perks found at the Ritz, but it's pretty darned chic regardless and has a great bar and the very best gym. See p. 78.
- **The Mandarin Oriental,** 222 Sansome St., Financial District (© **800/622-0404** or 415/276-9888; www.mandarinoriental.com/sanfrancisco), doesn't have the common-area perks of the two mentioned above, but perched high above the Financial District it does have rooms with the best city views and fantastic contemporary Asian-inspired decor. The only problem: Once you check in, you won't want to leave your ultrachic nest. See p. 85.
- The new **St. Regis Hotel,** 125 Third St., SoMa (© **877/787-3447** or 415/284-4000; www.stregis.com/sanfrancisco) is giving the city's luxury contenders runs for their money with supersleek abodes blessed with a touch-screen control panel that orchestrates everything you could possibly want to do in the room—without ever leaving your bed. Add a destination restaurant, Ame, and a fabulous two-floor spa and you've got the city's newest VIP favorite. See p. 82.

3 The Best Moderately Priced Hotels

- **Laurel Inn,** 444 Presidio Ave., Pacific Heights (© **800/552-8735** or 415/567-8467; www.jdvhospitality.com), may be off the beaten track, but it's one of the best affordable, fashionable hotels in the city—and it has free parking. Just outside of the southern entrance to the Presidio in the midst of residential Presidio Heights, it's a chic motel with soothing, contemporary decor and equally calming prices. See p. 91.
- **White Swan Inn,** 845 Bush St., Union Square (© **800/999-9570** or 415/775-1755; www.jdvhospitality.com), is where to go if you prefer to be downtown and immersed in more classically San Francisco surroundings. Small, ridiculously charming rooms (complete with antiques) that

feel more like apartments combined with afternoon cookies make your stay here sweet and homey. See p. 63.

- **The Warwick Regis,** 490 Geary St., Union Square (✆ **800/827-3447** or 415/928-7900; www.warwicksf.com), is even closer to Union Square than the White Swan, and for travelers who prefer stately old-world style over floral fun, a better choice. Extremely well cared for and beautifully decorated, it's my favorite midrange pick. See p. 68.

- **Hotel Adagio,** 550 Geary St., Union Square (✆ **800/228-8830** or 415/775-5000; www.jdvhospitality.com), is far more chic and hip than its category counterparts. Part of its allure is due to its relative newness—the 1929 Spanish Revival building was renovated in 2003. The other part is that it was done very well—with sexy streamlined rooms swathed in rich shades of brown and a very chic restaurant and bar on the ground level. See p. 64.

4 The Most Unforgettable Dining Experiences

- **The Best of the City's Fine Dining:** Restaurant **Michael Mina,** 335 Powell St., Union Square (✆ **415/397-9222**), is the place to go if you want to have a totally different California-cuisine, fine-dining experience where dozens of fancifully presented small portions make up a long, lavish meal. And then there's **Restaurant Gary Danko,** 800 North Point St., Fisherman's Wharf (✆ **415/749-2060**), which is always a sure bet for a perfect contemporary French meal complete with polished service and flambéed finales. See p. 106 and 131 respectively.

- **The Best of Wine Country Dining:** If you're a foodie, you already know that one of the top restaurants in *the world,* **French Laundry,** 6640 Washington St. (✆ **707/944-2380**), is about 1½ hours north of the city in Wine Country's tiny town of Yountville. Only die-hard diners need apply: You'll need to fight for a reservation 2 months in advance, and dinner is more about the drama of the sights and tastes than it is about fun with friends around the table. See p. 297. A more relaxed, but absolutely outstanding alternative is Terra, 1345 Railroad Ave., St. Helena (✆ **707/963-8931**), where award-winning chef Hiro Sone shows his culinary creativity and mastery of French, Italian, and Japanese cuisine within a historic fieldstone split dining room. See p. 301.

- **Dungeness Crab and Sourdough Bread** are two of San Francisco's most famous edible delights. You'll be able to sample the Sourdough virtually everywhere—grocery stores, restaurants, and sandwich shops for the most part have exceptional bread. For a good selection, drop into any local grocer and browse the bread aisle and look for brands such as Acme and Grace. What makes it different from French bread is its notable tang or sourness. (The area's other breads tend to be some of the country's best as well.) Dungeness crab is a favorite seasonal delicacy. The season usually runs from November to April (with plenty of fluctuation over the years), and you can sample the fresh cracked crustaceans at most local restaurants that feature seasonal ingredients (practically every restaurant serving California cuisine or a seasonally changing menu), at stalls along Fisherman's Wharf, and, least expensive, at grocery stores—especially those along Stockton Street in Chinatown. Ask the seafood purveyor to crack it for you, grab some cocktail sauce or mayo or whatever you'd like to dip it in, load up on napkins, and you've got a heck of a San Francisco treat.

- **A Dim Sum Feast:** If you like Chinese food and the current small-plates craze, you'll love to "do dim sum." Whether you duck into one of the casual storefronts with steaming baskets in the window or head to the city's best dim sum house, **Ton Kiang,** 5821 Geary Blvd., the Richmond (© **415/387-8273**), you'll be delighted by the variety of dumplings and savory and sweet dishes that are offered for a few bucks each and meant to be shared. See p. 149.

5 The Best Things to Do for Free (or Almost)

- **Meander along the Marina's Golden Gate Promenade and Crissy Field:** Join the joggers, windsurfers, dog-walkers, and frolickers in one of the city's favorite pastimes—strolling the bayfront Marina in the Marina District. You won't find more fabulous views of the Golden Gate, Marin Headlands, beach, bay, and native flora and fauna anywhere else. See p. 178.
- **Stair Climb:** Forget the gym. Get great exercise and catch some of the coolest city and neighborhood views by hoofing it up (or down) the Filbert Street Steps on Telegraph Hill or Lyon Street Steps in Pacific Heights. See p. 187.
- **Explore the Neighborhoods:** The best way to experience San Francisco is to walk through it and its vibrant neighborhoods. Take one of the walking tours in this book (see chapter 8) or just chart your own path. Try the Mission around 16th Street and Valencia for a mix of Latin culture and hip shops and restaurants; North Beach for shopping, cafe culture, and Italian restaurants; and Pacific Heights for stunning mansions and bay views. See the "Neighborhoods Worth a Visit" section beginning on p. 166 for more information on these neighborhoods.
- **A Cocktail in the Clouds:** Some of the greatest ways to view the city are from top-floor lounges in fine hotels such as the Sir Francis Drake, Union Square (p. 62), the Grand Hyatt San Francisco (p. 58), and The Inter-Continental Mark Hopkins, Nob Hill (p. 75). Drinks aren't cheap, but it beats paying for a dinner. Besides, if you nurse your drink (or order something like tea or coffee), the combo of atmosphere, surroundings, and view are a bargain.

6 The Best Outdoor Activities

- **A Day in Golden Gate Park:** Golden Gate Park is a crucial—and relaxing—part of the San Francisco experience. Its arboreal paths stretch from the Haight all the way to Ocean Beach, offering dozens of fun things to do along the way. Top sights are the Conservatory of Flowers, Japanese Tea Garden, and the fabulous new de Young Museum (p. 161). The best time to go is Sunday, when portions of the park are closed to traffic (rent a bike for the full effect). Toward the end of the day, head west to the beach and watch the sunset. See p. 172.

The Best Activities for Families

For a list of San Francisco attractions that appeal to kids of all ages, see the "Especially for Kids" box on p. 182 of chapter 7.

- **A Walk along the Coastal Trail:** Stroll the forested Coastal Trail from Cliff House to the Golden Gate Bridge, and you'll see why San Franciscans put up with living on a fault line. Start at the parking lot just above Cliff House and head north. On a clear day, you'll have incredible views of the Marin Headlands, but even on foggy days, it's worth the trek to scamper over old bunkers and relish the crisp, cool air (dress warmly). See "The Presidio & Golden Gate National Recreation Area," beginning on p. 174, for more on this area.

- **A Wine Country Excursion:** It'll take you about an hour to get there, but once you arrive you'll want to hopscotch from one winery to the next, perhaps picnic in the vineyards, or have an alfresco lunch at someplace atmospheric like Tra Vigne. Besides, consider this: When the city is fogged in and cold, Napa and Sonoma are up to 20 degrees warmer. See chapter 12 for more information.

- **A Visit to Muir Woods, Stinson Beach, and Point Reyes:** If you have wheels, reserve a day for a trip across the Golden Gate Bridge. Take the Stinson Beach exit off Highway 101, and spend a few hours gawking at the monolithic redwoods at Muir Woods (this place is amazing). Next, head up the coast to the spectacular Point Reyes National Seashore. Rain or shine, it's a day trip you'll never forget. See "Muir Woods & Mount Tamalpais" and "Point Reyes National Seashore," beginning on p. 262 and 263, respectively.

7 Best Places to Hang with the Locals

- **Feasting at the Ferry Building:** During Farmers Market days, this bayfront alfresco market is packed with local shoppers vying for the freshest in local produce, breads, and flowers—or just mingling during their lunch breaks. But the building itself has become a mecca for food lovers who browse the outstanding artisan food shops and restaurants daily and then linger over glasses of wine at the festive wine bar. See p. 154.

- **Cafe-Hopping in North Beach:** Join residents by lingering at a cafe as the aroma of roasted coffee beans wafts down Columbus Avenue. Start the day with a cup of Viennese at Caffé Trieste (a haven for true San Francisco characters) and follow it with a walk in and around Washington Square. Continue with lunch at Mario's Bohemian Cigar Store (a la focaccia sandwiches), book browsing at City Lights, and dinner at L'Osteria del Forno or Moose's. Finish the day with a nightcap as Enrico Caruso plays on the jukebox at Tosca. See "Walking Tour 2: Getting to Know North Beach," beginning on p. 197, for a walking tour of the area.

8 The Best Offbeat Travel Experiences

- **A Soul-Stirring Sunday Morning Service at Glide Memorial United Methodist Church:** Senior Pastor Douglas Fitch turns churchgoing into a spiritual party here that leaves you feeling elated, hopeful, and unified with the world. All walks of life attend the service at this Tenderloin church just west of Union Square, which focuses not on any particular religion, but on what we have in common as people. It's great fun, with plenty of singing and hand clapping. See p. 179.

- **A Cruise through the Castro:** The most populated and festive street in the city is not just for gays and lesbians (although the best cruising in town *is* right here). While there are some great shops and cafes, it's the people-watching here that makes the trip a must. If you have time, catch a flick at the beautiful 1930s Spanish colonial movie palace, the Castro Theatre (p. 170). See "Neighborhoods Worth a Visit," beginning on p. 166, for more on the Castro.

- **A Date in the Haight:** It's not quite as groovy as it was during the Summer of Love, but the stretch of shops, restaurants, and bars along the strip between Masonic and Stanyan streets do make for good browsing, and the vibe underscores the city's counterculture, including a good deal of homeless folks, contemporary hippies, and funky-clad urban kids. See p. 170.

- **AsiaSF:** Rather than simply having dinner, this SoMa spot serves up great entertainment with gorgeous Asian transvestites serving baby back ribs and performing lip-synch ensembles throughout the evening. Trust me, it's pure fun. See p. 121.

2

Planning Your Trip to San Francisco

1 Visitor Information

The **San Francisco Convention and Visitors Bureau,** 900 Market St. (at Powell St.), Hallidie Plaza, Lower Level, San Francisco, CA 94102 (© **415/391-2000;** www.sfvisitor.org), is the best source of specialized information about the city. Even if you don't have a specific question, you might want to request the free *Visitors Planning Guide* and the *San Francisco Visitors* kit. The kit includes a 6-month calendar of events, a city history, shopping and dining information, and several good, clear maps, plus lodging information.

The bureau highlights only its members' establishments, so if it doesn't have what you're looking for, that doesn't mean it's nonexistent.

You can also get the latest on San Francisco at the following online addresses:

- The *Bay Guardian,* the city's free weekly paper: **www.sfbg.com**
- Hotel reservations: **www.hotelres. com**
- *SF Gate,* the city's *Chronicle* newspaper: **www.sfgate.com**
- CitySearch: **www.citysearch.com**

Destination San Francisco: Pre-Departure Checklist

- Have you packed a warm jacket or coat? When the fog's in and the wind picks up, San Francisco will feel like winter regardless of the time of year. And don't forget walking shoes.
- Have you made all critical restaurant reservations well in advance? (Ditto for theater or any other live performances.)
- If you're flying, are you carrying a current, government-issued ID, such as a driver's license or passport?
- Did you bring emergency drug prescriptions and extra glasses and/or contact lenses?
- If you have an e-ticket, do you have documentation?
- If you purchased traveler's checks, have you recorded the check numbers, and stored the documentation separately from the checks?
- Did you bring your ID cards that could entitle you to discounts, such as AAA and AARP cards, student IDs, and so forth?

2 Entry Requirements & Customs

ENTRY REQUIREMENTS
PASSPORTS

For an up-to-date, country-by-country listing of passport requirements around the world, go to the "Foreign Entry Requirement" Web page of the U.S. State Department at **http://travel.state.gov**. International visitors can obtain a visa application at the same website.

VISAS

The U.S. State Department has a **Visa Waiver Program** allowing citizens of the following countries (at press time) to enter the United States without a visa for stays of up to 90 days: Andorra, Australia, Austria, Belgium, Brunei, Denmark, Finland, France, Germany, Iceland, Ireland, Italy, Japan, Liechtenstein, Luxembourg, Monaco, the Netherlands, New Zealand, Norway, Portugal, San Marino, Singapore, Slovenia, Spain, Sweden, Switzerland, and the United Kingdom. Citizens of these nations need only a valid passport and a round-trip air or cruise ticket upon arrival. If they first enter the United States, they may also visit Mexico, Canada, Bermuda, and/or the Caribbean islands and return to the United States without a visa. Further information is available from any U.S. embassy or consulate. Canadian citizens may enter the United States without visas; they need only proof of residence.

Citizens of all other countries must have (1) a valid passport that expires at least 6 months later than the scheduled end of their visit to the United States, and (2) a tourist visa, which may be obtained without charge from any U.S. consulate.

MEDICAL REQUIREMENTS

Unless you're arriving from an area known to be suffering from an epidemic (particularly cholera or yellow fever), inoculations or vaccinations are not required for entry into the United States.

If you have a medical condition that requires **syringe-administered medications,** carry a valid signed prescription from your physician—the Federal Aviation Administration (FAA) no longer allows airline passengers to pack syringes in their carry-on baggage without documented proof of medical need. If you have a disease that requires treatment with **narcotics,** you should also carry documented proof with you—smuggling narcotics aboard a plane is a serious offense that carries severe penalties in the U.S.

For **HIV-positive visitors,** requirements for entering the United States are somewhat vague and change frequently. For up-to-the-minute information, contact **AIDSinfo** (© **800/448-0440** or 301/519-6616 outside the U.S.; www.aidsinfo.nih.gov) or the **Gay Men's Health Crisis** (© **212/367-1000;** www.gmhc.org).

CUSTOMS
WHAT YOU CAN BRING INTO SAN FRANCISCO

Every visitor more than 21 years of age may bring in, free of duty, the following: (1) 1 liter of wine or hard liquor; (2) 200 cigarettes, 100 cigars (but not from Cuba), or 3 pounds of smoking tobacco; and (3) $100 worth of gifts. These exemptions are offered to travelers who spend at least 72 hours in the United States and who have not claimed them within the preceding 6 months. It is altogether forbidden to bring into the country foodstuffs (particularly fruit, cooked meats, and canned goods) and plants (vegetables, seeds, tropical plants, and the like). Foreign tourists may carry in or out up to $10,000 in U.S. or foreign currency with no formalities; larger sums must be declared to U.S. Customs on entering or leaving, which includes filing form CM 4790. For details regarding U.S. Customs and Border Protection, consult your nearest U.S. embassy or consulate, or **U.S. Customs** (© 202/927-1770; www.customs.ustreas.gov).

WHAT YOU CAN TAKE HOME FROM SAN FRANCISCO
Canadian Citizens
For a clear summary of Canadian rules, write for the booklet *I Declare,* issued by the **Canada Border Services Agency** (© 800/461-9999 in Canada, or 204/983-3500; **www.cbsa-asfc.gc.ca**).

U.K. Citizens
For information, contact **HM Customs & Excise** at © 0845/010-9000 (from outside the U.K., 020/8929-0152), or consult their website at **www.hmce.gov.uk**.

Australian Citizens
A helpful brochure available from Australian consulates or Customs offices is *Know Before You Go.* For more information, call the **Australian Customs Service** at © 1300/363-263, or log on to **www.customs.gov.au**.

New Zealand Citizens
Most questions are answered in a free pamphlet available at New Zealand consulates and Customs offices: *New Zealand Customs Guide for Travellers, Notice no. 4.* For more information, contact **New Zealand Customs,** The Customhouse, 17–21 Whitmore St., Box 2218, Wellington (© 04/473-6099 or 0800/428-786; **www.customs.govt.nz**).

3 Money

ATMs
Nationwide, the easiest and best way to get cash away from home is from an ATM (automated teller machine), sometimes referred to as a "cash machine," or "cashpoint." The **Cirrus** (© 800/424-7787; www.mastercard.com) and **PLUS** (© 800/843-7587; www.visa.com) networks span the country; you can find them even in remote regions. Look at the back of your bank card to see which network you're on, then call or check online for ATM locations at your destination. Be sure you know your personal identification number (PIN) and daily withdrawal limit before you depart. *Note:* Remember that many banks impose a fee every time you use a card at another bank's ATM, and that fee can be higher for international transactions (up to $5 or more) than for domestic ones (where they're rarely more than $2). In addition, the bank from which you withdraw cash may charge its own fee. To compare banks' ATM fees within the U.S., use **www.bankrate.com**. For international withdrawal fees, ask your bank.

CREDIT CARDS & DEBIT CARDS
Credit cards are the most widely used form of payment in the United States: **Visa** (Barclaycard in Britain), **MasterCard** (EuroCard in Europe, Access in Britain, Chargex in Canada), **American Express, Diners Club,** and **Discover.** They also provide a convenient record of all your expenses, and they generally offer relatively good exchange rates. You can withdraw cash advances from your credit cards at banks or ATMs, provided you know your PIN.

Visitors from outside the U.S. should inquire whether their bank assesses a 1% to 3% fee on charges incurred abroad.

It's highly recommended that you travel with at least one major credit card. You must have one to rent a car, and hotels and airlines usually require a credit card imprint as a deposit against expenses.

ATM cards with major credit card backing, known as **"debit cards,"** are now a commonly acceptable form of payment in most stores and restaurants. Debit cards draw money directly from your checking account. Some stores enable you to receive "cash back" on your debit-card purchases as well. The same is true at most U.S. post offices.

TRAVELER'S CHECKS

Traveler's checks are widely accepted in the U.S., but foreign visitors should make sure that they're denominated in U.S. dollars; foreign-currency checks are often difficult to exchange.

You can buy traveler's checks at most banks. Most are offered in denominations of $20, $50, $100, $500, and sometimes $1,000. Generally, you'll pay a service charge ranging from 1% to 4%.

The most popular traveler's checks are offered by **American Express** (✆ **800/807-6233,** or 800/221-7282 for card holders—this number accepts collect calls, offers service in several foreign languages, and exempts Amex gold and platinum cardholders from the 1% fee); **Visa** (✆ **800/732-1322**)—AAA members can obtain Visa checks for a $9.95 fee (for checks up to $1,500) at most AAA offices or by calling ✆ **866/339-3378;** and **MasterCard** (✆ **800/223-9920**).

If you do choose to carry traveler's checks, keep a record of their serial numbers separate from your checks in the event that they are stolen or lost. You'll get a refund faster if you know the numbers.

4 When to Go

If you're dreaming of convertibles, Frisbee on the beach, and tank-topped evenings, change your reservations and head to Los Angeles. Contrary to California's sunshine-and-bikini image, San Francisco's weather is "mild" (to put it nicely) and can often be downright bone-chilling because of the wet, foggy air and cool winds—it's nothing like that of Southern California. Summer, the most popular time to visit, is often characterized by damp, foggy days; cold, windy nights; and crowded tourist destinations. A good bet is to visit in spring or, better yet, autumn. Every September, right about the time San Franciscans mourn being cheated (or fogged) out of another summer, something wonderful happens: The thermometer rises, the skies clear, and the locals call in sick to work and head for the beach. It's what residents call "Indian summer." The city is also delightful during winter, when the opera and ballet seasons are in full swing; there are fewer tourists, many hotel prices are lower, and downtown bustles with holiday cheer.

CLIMATE

San Francisco's temperate, marine climate usually means relatively mild weather year-round. In summer, chilling fog rolls in most mornings and evenings, and if temperatures top 70°F (21°C), the city is ready to throw a celebration. Even when autumn's heat occasionally stretches into the 80s (upper 20s Celsius) and 90s (lower 30s Celsius), you should still dress in layers, or by early evening you'll learn firsthand why sweatshirt sales are a great business at Fisherman's Wharf. In winter, the mercury seldom falls below freezing and snow is almost unheard of, but that doesn't mean you won't be whimpering if you forget your coat. Still, compared to

---

Tips **Travel Attire**

Even if it's sunny out, don't forget to bring a jacket; the weather can change almost instantly from sunny and warm to windy and cold in San Francisco.

most of the states' weather conditions, San Francisco's is consistently pleasant.

It's that beautifully fluffy, chilly, wet, heavy, sweeping fog that makes the city's weather so precarious. A rare combination of water, wind, and topography creates Northern California's summer fog bank. It lies off the coast, and rising air currents pull it in when the land heats up. Held back by coastal mountains along a 600-mile front, the low clouds seek out any passage they can find. The easiest access is the slot where the Pacific Ocean penetrates the continental wall—the Golden Gate.

San Francisco's Average Temperatures & Rainfall

	Jan	Feb	Mar	Apr	May	June	July	Aug	Sept	Oct	Nov	Dec
High °F	56	59	61	64	67	70	71	72	73	70	62	56
Low °F	43	46	47	48	51	53	55	56	55	52	48	43
High °C	13	15	16	18	19	21	22	22	23	21	17	13
Low °C	6	8	8	9	11	12	13	13	13	11	9	6
Rain (in.)	4.5	4.0	3.3	1.2	0.4	0.1	0.1	0.1	0.2	1.0	2.5	2.9
Rain (mm)	113.0	101.9	82.8	30.0	9.7	2.8	0.8	1.8	5.1	26.4	63.2	73.4

SAN FRANCISCO CALENDAR OF EVENTS

For more information, visit www.sfvisitor.org for an annual calendar of local events.

February

Chinese New Year, Chinatown. In 2007, public celebrations will again spill onto every street in Chinatown. Festivities begin with the "Miss Chinatown USA" pageant parade, and climax a week later with a celebratory parade of marching bands, rolling floats, barrages of fireworks, and a block-long dragon writhing in and out of the crowds. The revelry runs for several weeks and wraps up with a memorable parade through Chinatown that starts at Market and Second streets and ends at Kearny Street. Arrive early for a good viewing spot on Kearny Street. You can purchase bleacher seats online starting in December. Make your hotel reservations early. For dates and information, call © **415/982-3000** or visit www.chineseparade.com.

March

St. Patrick's Day Parade, Union Square and Civic Center. Everyone's an honorary Irish person at this festive affair, which starts at 11:30am at Market and Second streets and continues to City Hall. But the party doesn't stop there. Head down to the Civic Center for the post-party, or venture to The Embarcadero's Harrington's bar (245 Front St.) and celebrate with hundreds of the Irish-for-a-day yuppies as they gallivant around the closed-off streets and numerous pubs. For information, call © **415/675-9885;** www.sfstpatricksdayparade.com. Sunday before March 17.

April

Cherry Blossom Festival, Japantown. Meander through the arts-and-crafts and food booths lining the blocked-off streets around Japan Center and watch traditional drumming, flower arranging, origami making, or a parade celebrating the cherry blossom and Japanese culture. Call © **415/563-2313** for information. Mid- to late April.

San Francisco International Film Festival, around San Francisco with screenings at the AMC Kabuki 8 Cinemas (Fillmore and Post sts.), and at many other locations. Begun in 1957, this is America's oldest film festival. It features close to 200 films and videos from more than 50 countries. Tickets are relatively inexpensive, and screenings are accessible to the public. Entries include new films by beginning and established directors. For a schedule or information, call ✆ **415/561-5000** or visit www.sffs.org. Mid-April to early May.

May

Cinco de Mayo Festival, Mission District. This is when the Latino community celebrates the victory of the Mexicans over the French at Puebla in 1862; mariachi bands, dancers, food, and a parade fill the streets of the Mission. The parade starts at 10am at 24th and Bryant streets and ends at the Civic Center, though rumor has it that in 2007 the Festival will be held on 24th Street. Contact the Mission Neighborhood Center for more information at ✆ **415/206-0577.** The first Sunday in May.

Bay to Breakers Foot Race, The Embarcadero through Golden Gate Park to Ocean Beach. Even if you don't participate, you can't avoid this run from downtown to Ocean Beach, which stops morning traffic throughout the city. More than 75,000 entrants gather—many dressed in wacky, innovative, and sometimes X-rated costumes—for the approximately 7.5-mile run. If you don't want to run, join the throng of spectators who line the route. Sidewalk parties, bands, and cheerleaders of all ages provide a good dose of true San Francisco fun. For recorded information, call ✆ **415/359-2800,** or check their website www.baytobreakers.com. Third Sunday of May.

Carnaval Festival, Harrison Street between 16th and 23rd streets. The Mission District's largest annual event, held from 9:30am to 6pm, is a day of festivities that includes food, music, dance, arts and crafts, and a parade that's as sultry and energetic as the Latin American and Caribbean people behind it. For one of San Franciscans' favorite events, more than half a million spectators line the parade route, and samba musicians and dancers continue to entertain on 14th Street, near Harrison, at the end of the march where you'll find food and craft booths, music, and more revelry. Call the hot line at ✆ **415/920-0125** for information. Celebrations are held Saturday and Sunday of Memorial Day weekend, but the parade is on Sunday morning only. See www.carnavalsf.com for more information.

June

Union Street Art Festival, Pacific Heights, along Union Street from Steiner to Gough streets. This outdoor fair celebrates San Francisco with themes, gourmet food booths, music, entertainment, and a juried art show featuring works by more than 250 artists. It's a great time and a chance to see the city's young well-to-dos partying it up. Call the **Union Street Association** (✆ **415/441-7055**) for more information or see www.unionstreetfestival.com. First weekend of June.

Haight-Ashbury Street Fair, Haight-Ashbury. A far cry from the froufrou Union Street Fair, this grittier fair features alternative crafts, ethnic foods, rock bands, and a healthy number of hippies and street kids whooping it up and slamming beers in front of the blaring rock-'n'-roll stage. The fair usually extends along Haight between Stanyan and Ashbury streets. For details and the exact date, call ✆ **415/863-3489** or visit www.haightstreetfair.org.

North Beach Festival, Grant Avenue, North Beach. In 2006, this party celebrated its 52nd anniversary; organizers claim it's the oldest urban street fair in the country. Close to 100,000 city folk meander along Grant Avenue, between Vallejo and Union streets, to eat, drink, and browse the arts-and-crafts booths, poetry readings, swing-dancing venue, and *arte di gesso* (sidewalk chalk art). But the most enjoyable parts of the event are listening to music and people-watching. Call © **415/989-2220** or visit www.northbeachfestival.com for details. Usually Father's Day weekend, but call to confirm.

Stern Grove Music Festival, Sunset District. Pack a picnic and head out early to join the thousands who come here to lie in the grass and enjoy classical, jazz, and ethnic music and dance in the grove, at 19th Avenue and Sloat Boulevard. The Festival's 70th year will be marked in 2007. The free concerts take place every Sunday at 2pm between mid-June and August. Show up with a lawn chair or blanket. There are food booths if you forget snacks, but you'll be dying to leave if you don't bring warm clothes—the Sunset District can be one of the coldest parts of the city. Call © **415/252-6252** for listings; www.sterngrove.org. Sundays, mid-June through August.

San Francisco Lesbian, Gay, Bisexual, Transgender Pride Parade & Celebration, downtown's Market Street. This prideful event draws up to one million participants who celebrate all of the above—and then some. The parade proceeds west on Market Street until it gets to the Civic Center, where hundreds of food, art, and information booths are set up around several soundstages. Call © **415/864-3733** or visit www.sfpride.org for information. Usually the third or last weekend of June.

July

Fillmore Jazz Festival, Pacific Heights. July starts with a bang, when the upscale portion of Fillmore closes to traffic and the blocks between Jackson and Eddy are filled with arts and crafts, gourmet food, and live jazz from 10am to 6pm. Call © **510/970-3217** for more information; www.fillmorejazzfestival.com. First weekend in July.

Fourth of July Celebration & Fireworks, Fisherman's Wharf. This event can be something of a joke—more often than not, fog comes into the city, like everyone else, to join in the festivities. Sometimes it's almost impossible to view the million-dollar pyrotechnics from PIER 39 on the northern waterfront. Still, it's a party, and if the skies are clear, it's a darn good show. Visit www.4thofjulysf.com for more info.

San Francisco Marathon, San Francisco and beyond. This is one of the largest marathons in the world. It starts and ends at the Ferry Building at the base of Market Street, winds 26-plus miles through virtually every neighborhood in the City, and across the Golden Gate Bridge. For entry information, visit www.runsfm.com. Usually the last weekend in July.

September

Sausalito Art Festival, Sausalito. A juried exhibit of more than 20,000 original works of art, this festival includes music—provided by jazz, rock, and blues performers from the Bay Area and beyond—and international cuisine, enhanced by wines from some 50 Napa and Sonoma producers. Parking is impossible; take the **Blue & Gold Fleet ferry** (© **415/705-5555**) from Fisherman's Wharf to the festival site. For more information, call © **415/332-3555** or log on to www.sausalitoartfestival.org. Labor Day weekend.

Opera in the Park, usually in Sharon Meadow, Golden Gate Park. Each year the San Francisco Opera launches its season with a free concert featuring a selection of arias. Call © **415/861-4008** to confirm the location and date. Usually the Sunday after Labor Day.

San Francisco Blues Festival, on the grounds of Fort Mason, the Marina. The largest outdoor blues music event on the West Coast will be 35 years old in 2007 and continues to feature local and national musicians performing back-to-back during the 3-day extravaganza. You can charge tickets by phone at ℂ **415/421-8497** or online at www.ticketmaster.com. For information, call ℂ **415/979-5588** or visit www.sfblues.com. Usually in late September.

Folsom Street Fair, along Folsom Street between 7th and 12th streets, SoMa, from 11am to 6pm. This is a local favorite for its kinky, outrageous, leather-and-skin gay-centric blowout celebration. It's hard-core, so only open-minded and adventurous types need head into the leather-clad and partially dressed crowds. For info call ℂ **415/861-3247** or visit www.folsomstreetfair.org. Last Sunday of September.

October

Fleet Week, Marina and Fisherman's Wharf. Residents gather along the Marina Green, The Embarcadero, Fisherman's Wharf, and other vantage points to watch incredible (and loud!) aerial performances by the Blue Angels, flown in tribute to our nation's marines. Call ℂ **650/599-5057** or visit www.fleetweek.us/fleetweek for details and dates.

Artspan Open Studios, various San Francisco locations. Find an original piece of art to commemorate your trip, or just see what local artists are up to by grabbing a map to over 800 artists' studios that are open to the public during weekends in October. Call ℂ **415/861-9838** or visit www.artspan.org for more information.

Castro Street Fair, the Castro. Celebrate life in the city's most famous gay neighborhood. Call ℂ **415/841-1824** or visit www.castrostreetfair.org for information. First Sunday in October, from 11am to 6pm.

Italian Heritage Parade, North Beach and Fisherman's Wharf. The city's Italian community leads the festivities around Fisherman's Wharf, celebrating Columbus's landing in America. 2007 marks the festival's 139th year, and as usual includes a parade along Columbus Avenue. But for the most part, it's a great excuse to hang out in North Beach and people-watch. For information, call ℂ **415/587-8282** or visit www.sfcolumbusday.org. Observed the Sunday before Columbus Day.

Exotic Erotic Halloween Ball, The Cow Palace, on the southern outskirts of San Francisco. Thousands come here dressed in costume, lingerie, and sometimes even less than that. It's a wild fantasy affair with bands, dancing, and costume contests. ***Beware:*** It can be somewhat cheesy. Advance tickets range from $60 to $125 per person. For information, call ℂ **415/567-BALL** or visit www.exoticeroticball.com. One or two Friday or Saturday nights before Halloween.

Halloween, the Castro. This is a huge night in San Francisco, especially in the flamboyant gay community of the Castro. Drop by for music, costume contests, and all-around revelry with streets shut down and filled with a mixed crowd reveling in costumes of extraordinary imagination. For info visit www.halloweeninthecastro.com. October 31.

San Francisco Jazz Festival, various San Francisco locations. This festival presents eclectic programming in an array of fabulous jazz venues throughout the city. With close to 3 weeks of nightly entertainment and dozens of performers, the jazz festival is a hot ticket. Past events have featured Herbie Hancock, Dave Brubeck, the Modern Jazz Quartet, Wayne Shorter, and Bill Frisell. For information, call © **800/ 850-SFJF** or 415/788-7353; or visit www.sfjazz.org. Also check the website for other events throughout the year. Late October and early November.

December

The *Nutcracker,* War Memorial Opera House, Civic Center. The **San Francisco Ballet** (© **415/865-2000**) performs this holiday classic annually. Order tickets to this Tchaikovsky tradition well in advance. Visit www. sfballet.org for information.

5 Travel Insurance

The cost of travel insurance varies widely, depending on the cost and length of your trip, your age and health, and the type of trip you're taking, but expect to pay between 5% and 8% of the vacation itself. You can get estimates from various providers through **InsureMyTrip.com.** Enter your trip cost and dates, your age, and other information, for prices from more than a dozen companies.

TRIP-CANCELLATION INSURANCE

Trip-cancellation insurance will help retrieve your money if you have to back out of a trip or depart early, or if your travel supplier goes bankrupt. Permissible reasons for trip cancellation can range from sickness to natural disasters to the State Department declaring a destination unsafe for travel.

For more information, contact one of the following recommended insurers: **Access America** (© 866/807-3982; www.accessamerica.com); **Travel Guard**

International (© 800/826-4919; www. travelguard.com); **Travel Insured International** (© 800/243-3174; www.travel insured.com); and **Travelex Insurance Services** (© 888/457-4602; www.travelex-insurance.com).

MEDICAL INSURANCE

Although it's not required of travelers, health insurance is highly recommended. Most health insurance policies cover you if you get sick away from home—but verify that you're covered before you depart, particularly if you're insured by an HMO.

International visitors should note that unlike many European countries, the United States does not usually offer free or low-cost medical care to its citizens or visitors. Doctors and hospitals are expensive, and in most cases will require advance payment or proof of coverage before they render their services. Good policies will cover the costs of an accident, repatriation, or death. Packages such as **Europ Assistance's "Worldwide**

Travel in the Age of Bankruptcy

Airlines go bankrupt, so protect yourself by **buying your tickets with a credit card.** The Fair Credit Billing Act guarantees that you can get your money back from the credit card company if a travel supplier goes under (and if you request the refund within 60 days of the bankruptcy). **Travel insurance** can also help, but make sure it covers against "carrier default" for your specific travel provider. And be aware that if a U.S. airline goes bust mid-trip, a 2001 federal law requires other carriers to take you to your destination (albeit on a space-available basis) for a fee of no more than $25, provided you rebook within 60 days of the cancellation.

Healthcare Plan" are sold by European automobile clubs and travel agencies at attractive rates. **Worldwide Assistance Services, Inc.** (© 800/777-8710; www.worldwideassistance.com) is the agent for Europ Assistance in the United States.

Though lack of health insurance may prevent you from being admitted to a hospital in nonemergencies, don't worry about being left on a street corner to die: The American way is to fix you now and bill the living daylights out of you later.

INSURANCE FOR BRITISH TRAVELERS Most big travel agents offer their own insurance and will probably try to sell you their package when you book a holiday. Think before you sign. **Britain's Consumers' Association** recommends that you insist on seeing the policy and reading the fine print before buying travel insurance. **The Association of British Insurers** (© 020/7600-3333; www.abi.org.uk) gives advice by phone and publishes *Holiday Insurance,* a free guide to policy provisions and prices. You might also shop around for better deals: Try **Columbus Direct** (© 0870/033-9988; www.columbusdirect.net).

INSURANCE FOR CANADIAN TRAVELERS Canadians should check with their provincial health plan offices or call **Health Canada** (© 866/225-0709; www.hc-sc.gc.ca) to find out the extent of their coverage and what documentation and receipts they must take home in case they are treated in the United States.

LOST-LUGGAGE INSURANCE

On flights within the U.S., checked baggage is covered up to $2,500 per ticketed passenger. On flights outside the U.S. (and on U.S. portions of international trips), baggage coverage is limited to approximately $9.07 per pound, up to approximately $635 per checked bag. If you plan to check items more valuable than what's covered by the standard liability, see if your homeowner's policy covers your valuables, get baggage insurance as part of your comprehensive travel-insurance package, or buy Travel Guard's "BagTrak" product.

If your luggage is lost, immediately file a lost-luggage claim at the airport, detailing the luggage contents. Most airlines require that you report delayed, damaged, or lost baggage within 4 hours of arrival. The airlines are required to deliver luggage, once found, directly to your house or destination free of charge.

6 Health & Safety

STAYING HEALTHY

No worries about staying healthy in San Francisco. The water's A-OK to drink, food's fresh—and tasty—and we tend to be a fit bunch. That said, you can spend your vacation in your hotel room if you wear shoes impractical for hiking the city's hills, or if you catch a cold because you don't dress for winter, spring, and summer—which often occur all in 1 day. Also, consider bringing pants with expandable waistbands, because you'll probably overindulge in San Francisco's restaurants.

GENERAL AVAILABILITY OF HEALTHCARE

Contact the **International Association for Medical Assistance to Travelers (IAMAT)** (© 716/754-4883 or, in Canada, 416/652-0137; www.iamat.org) for tips on travel and health concerns in the countries you're visiting, and for lists of local, English-speaking doctors. The United States **Centers for Disease Control and Prevention** (© 800/311-3435; www.cdc.gov) provides up-to-date information on health hazards by region or country and offers tips on food safety.

The website **www.tripprep.com**, sponsored by a consortium of travel medicine practitioners, may also offer helpful advice on traveling abroad. You can find listings of reliable clinics overseas at the **International Society of Travel Medicine** (www.istm.org).

WHAT TO DO IF YOU GET SICK AWAY FROM HOME

We list **hospital** and **emergency numbers** under "Fast Facts: San Francisco," p. 49.

If you suffer from a chronic illness, consult your doctor before your departure. Pack **prescription medications** in your carry-on luggage, and carry them in their original containers, with pharmacy labels—otherwise they won't make it through airport security. Visitors from outside the U.S. should carry generic names of prescription drugs. For U.S. travelers, most reliable healthcare plans provide coverage if you get sick away from home. Foreign visitors may have to pay all medical costs upfront and be reimbursed later. See "Medical Insurance," under "Travel Insurance," above.

STAYING SAFE

San Francisco is as safe as any big city, and requires only that you use common sense (for example, don't leave your new video camera on the seat of your parked car). However, in neighborhoods such as Lower Haight, the Mission, the Tenderloin (a few blocks west of Union Square), and Fisherman's Wharf (at night especially), it's a good idea to pay attention to yourself and your surroundings.

ECO-TOURISM

You can find eco-friendly travel tips, statistics, and touring companies and associations—listed by destination under "Travel Choice"—at the TIES website, www.ecotourism.org. **Ecotravel.com** is part online magazine and part ecodirectory that lets you search for touring companies in several categories (water-based, land-based, spiritually oriented, and so on). Also check out **Conservation International** (www.conservation.org)—which, with *National Geographic Traveler,* annually presents **World Legacy Awards** (www.wlaward.org) to those travel tour operators, businesses, organizations, and places that have made a significant contribution to sustainable tourism.

7 Specialized Travel Resources

TRAVELERS WITH DISABILITIES

Most disabilities shouldn't stop anyone from traveling. There are more options and resources out there than ever before.

Most of San Francisco's major museums and tourist attractions have wheelchair ramps. Many hotels offer special accommodations and services for wheelchair users and other visitors with disabilities. As well as the ramps, they include extra large bathrooms and telecommunication devices for hearing-impaired travelers. The San Francisco Convention and Visitors Bureau (p. 10) should have the most up-to-date information.

Travelers in wheelchairs can request special ramped taxis by calling **Yellow Cab** (© **415/626-2345**), which charges regular rates for the service. Travelers with disabilities can also get a free copy of the *Muni Access Guide,* published by the San Francisco Municipal Railway, Accessible Services Program, One South Van Ness, third floor (© **415/923-6142**), which is staffed weekdays from 8am to 5pm. Many of the major car-rental companies offer hand-controlled cars for drivers with disabilities. **Alamo** (© **800/651-1223**), **Avis** (© **800/331-1212,** ext. 7305), and **Budget** (© **800/314-3932**) have special hot lines that help provide such a vehicle at any of their U.S. locations with 48 hours' advance notice; **Hertz** (🕾 **800/654-3131**) requires between 24 and 72 hours' advance notice at most locations.

Many travel agencies offer customized tours and itineraries for travelers with disabilities. **Flying Wheels Travel** (🕾 **507/451-5005;** www.flyingwheelstravel.com) offers escorted tours and cruises as well as private tours in minivans with lifts. **Access-Able Travel Source** (🕾 **303/232-2979;** www.access-able.com) offers extensive access information and advice for traveling around the world with disabilities. **Accessible Journeys** (🕾 **800/846-4537** or 610/521-0339; www.accessiblejourneys.com) caters specifically to slow walkers and wheelchair travelers and their families and friends.

Organizations that offer assistance to travelers with disabilities include **Moss-Rehab** (www.mossresourcenet.org), which provides a library of accessible-travel resources online; **SATH** (Society for Accessible Travel & Hospitality) (🕾 **212/447-7284;** www.sath.org; annual membership fees: $45 adults, $30 seniors and students), which offers a wealth of travel resources for people with all types of disabilities and informed recommendations on destinations, access guides, travel agents, tour operators, vehicle rentals, and companion services; and the **American Foundation for the Blind** (AFB; 🕾 **800/232-5463;** www.afb.org), a referral resource for the blind or visually impaired that includes information on traveling with Seeing Eye dogs.

For more information specifically targeted to travelers with disabilities, check out the quarterly magazine **Emerging Horizons** ($14.95 per year, $19.95 outside the U.S.; www.emerginghorizons.com).

GAY & LESBIAN TRAVELERS

If you head down to the Castro—an area surrounding Castro Street near Market Street—you'll understand why the city is a mecca for gay and lesbian travelers. Since the 1970s, this unique part of town has remained a colorfully festive neighborhood, teeming with "out" city folk who meander the streets shopping, eating, partying, or cruising. If anyone feels like an outsider in this part of town, it's heterosexuals, who, although warmly welcomed in the community, may feel uncomfortable or downright threatened if they harbor any homophobia or aversion to being checked out. For many San Franciscans, it's just a fun area (especially on Halloween) with some wonderful shops.

Gays and lesbians make up a good deal of San Francisco's population, so it's no surprise that clubs and bars all over town cater to them. Although lesbian interests are concentrated primarily in the East Bay (especially Oakland), a significant community resides in the Mission District, around 16th and Valencia streets.

Several local publications concentrate on in-depth coverage of news, information, and listings of goings-on around town for gays and lesbians. The *Bay Area Reporter* (www.ebar.com) has the most comprehensive listings, including a weekly calendar of events. Distributed free on Thursday, it can be found stacked at the corner of 18th and Castro streets and at Ninth and Harrison streets, as well as in bars, bookshops, and stores around town. It may also be available in gay and lesbian bookstores elsewhere in the country.

GUIDES & PUBLICATIONS   For a good book selection, contact **Giovanni's Room,** 345 S. 12th St., Philadelphia, PA 19107 (🕾 **215/923-2960;** www.giovannisroom.com), and **A Different Light Bookstore,** 489 Castro St., San Francisco, CA 94114 (🕾 **415/431-0891;** www.adlbooks.com). There's another Different Light location in Los Angeles (🕾 **310/854-6601**).

For other guides, try the *Spartacus International Gay Guide* (www.spartacus.de) and *Odysseus* (www.odyusa.com), both good, annual English-language guidebooks focused on gay men; and the *Damron* guides (www.damron.com), with separate, annual books for gay men and lesbians. You can also get lowdown on the best gay or gay-friendly hotels, restaurants, clubs, and other places in San Francisco or around the world by subscribing to Gay.com, which costs $10 for 1 month, $20 for additional months, or $89 for a year.

ORGANIZATIONS The **International Gay and Lesbian Travel Association** (**IGLTA**; © 800/448-8550 or 954/776-2626; www.iglta.org) is the trade association for the gay and lesbian travel industry, and offers an online directory of gay- and lesbian-friendly travel businesses; go to their website and click on "Members."

TRAVEL AGENCIES Many agencies offer tours and travel itineraries specifically for gay and lesbian travelers. **Now, Voyager** (© 800/255-6951; www.nowvoyager.com) is a well-known San Francisco–based gay-owned and operated travel service. You might also want to try **Skylink Women's Travel,** 1455 N. Dutton Ave., Suite A, Santa Rosa, CA 95401 (© 800/225-5759 or 707/546-1212).

SENIOR TRAVEL

Members of **AARP** (formerly known as the American Association of Retired Persons), 601 E St. NW, Washington, DC 20049 (© 888/687-2277; www.aarp.org), get discounts on hotels, airfares, and car rentals. AARP offers members a wide range of benefits, including *AARP: The Magazine* and a monthly newsletter. Anyone over 50 can join.

The **U.S. National Park Service** offers a **Golden Age Passport** that gives seniors 62 years or older lifetime entrance to all properties administered by the National Park Service—national parks, monuments, historic sites, recreation areas, and national wildlife refuges—for a one-time processing fee of $10, which must be purchased in person at any NPS facility that charges an entrance fee. Besides free entry, a Golden Age Passport also offers a 50% discount on federal-use fees charged for such facilities as camping, swimming, parking, boat launching, and tours. For more information, go to www.nps.gov/fees_passes.htm or call © **888/467-2757.**

Many reliable agencies and organizations target the 50-plus market. **Elderhostel** (© 877/426-8056; www.elderhostel.org) arranges study programs for those aged 55 and over. **ElderTreks** (© 800/741-7956; www.eldertreks.com) offers small-group tours to off-the-beaten-path or adventure-travel locations, restricted to travelers 50 and older. **INTRAV** (© 800/456-8100; www.intrav.com) is a high-end tour operator that caters to the mature, discerning traveler (not specifically seniors), with trips around the world that include guided safaris, polar expeditions, private-jet adventures, and small-boat cruises down jungle rivers.

Recommended publications offering travel resources and discounts for seniors include: the quarterly magazine *Travel 50 & Beyond* (www.travel50andbeyond.com); *Travel Unlimited: Uncommon Adventures for the Mature Traveler* (Avalon); *101 Tips for Mature Travelers,* available from Grand Circle Travel (© 800/221-2610 or 617/350-7500; www.gct.com); and *Unbelievably Good Deals and Great Adventures That You Absolutely Can't Get Unless You're Over 50* (McGraw-Hill), by Joann Rattner Heilman.

FAMILY TRAVEL

If you have enough trouble getting your kids out of the house in the morning, dragging them thousands of miles away may seem like an insurmountable challenge. But family travel can be immensely rewarding, giving you new ways of seeing the world through smaller pairs of eyes.

San Francisco is full of sightseeing opportunities and special activities geared toward children. See "Especially for Kids," in chapter 7, on p. 182 for information and ideas for families.

Recommended family travel websites include **Family Travel Forum** (www. familytravelforum.com), a comprehensive site that offers customized trip planning; **Family Travel Network** (www. familytravelnetwork.com), an award-winning site that offers travel features, deals, and tips; **Traveling Internationally with Your Kids** (www.travelwith yourkids.com), a comprehensive site offering sound advice for long-distance and international travel with children; and **Family Travel Files** (www.thefamily travelfiles.com), which offers an online magazine and a directory of off-the-beaten-path tours and tour operators for families.

PUBLICATIONS *Frommer's San Francisco with Kids* (Wiley Publishing, Inc.) is a good source of kid-specific information for your trip.

STUDENT TRAVEL

A valid student ID will often qualify students for discounts on airfare, accommodations, entry to museums, cultural events, movies, and more. If you're planning to travel outside the U.S., you'd be wise to arm yourself with an **International Student Identity Card (ISIC),** which offers substantial savings on rail passes, plane tickets, and entrance fees. It also provides you with basic health and life insurance and a 24-hour help line. The card is available from **STA Travel** (© **800/781-4040** in North America; www.sta.com or www.statravel.com), the biggest student travel agency in the world. If you're no longer a student but are still under 26, you can get an **International Youth Travel Card (IYTC)** from the same people, which entitles you to some discounts (but not on museum admissions). **Travel CUTS** (© **800/667-2887** or 416/614-2887; www.travelcuts. com) offers similar services for both Canadians and U.S. residents. Irish students may prefer to turn to **USIT** (© **01/602-1600;** www.usitnow.ie), an Ireland-based specialist in student, youth, and independent travel.

8 Getting There

BY PLANE

The northern Bay Area has two major airports: San Francisco International and Oakland International.

SAN FRANCISCO INTERNATIONAL AIRPORT Almost four dozen major scheduled carriers serve **San Francisco International Airport** (© **650/821-8211;** www.flysfo.com), 14 miles directly south of downtown on U.S. 101. Travel time to downtown during commuter rush hour is about 40 minutes; at other times, it's about 20 to 25 minutes.

The airport offers a **hot line** (© **415/817-1717**) for information on ground

transportation. It gives you a rundown of all your options for getting into the city from the airport (also see below for this information). Each of the three main terminals has a desk where you can get the same information.

You can also call **511** or visit www. 511.org for up-to-the-minute information about public transportation and traffic.

IMMIGRATION & CUSTOMS CLEARANCE Foreign visitors arriving by air, no matter what the port of entry, should cultivate patience and resignation before setting foot on U.S. soil. Clearing

(Tips) Prepare to Be Fingerprinted

As of January 2004, many international visitors traveling on visas to the United States are being photographed and fingerprinted at Customs in a new program created by the Department of Homeland Security called **US-VISIT.** Non-U.S. citizens arriving at airports and on cruise ships must undergo an instant background check as part of the government's efforts to deter terrorism by verifying the identity of incoming and outgoing visitors. Exempt from the extra scrutiny are visitors entering by land or those (mostly in Europe; see p. 11) that don't require a visa for short-term visits. For more information, go to the Homeland Security website at **www.dhs.gov/dhspublic.**

immigration control can take as long as 2 hours. This is especially true in the aftermath of the September 11, 2001, terrorist attacks, when U.S. airports considerably beefed up security clearances. People traveling by air from Canada, Bermuda, and certain Caribbean countries can sometimes clear Customs and Immigration at the point of departure, which is much faster.

GETTING INTO TOWN FROM SAN FRANCISCO INTERNATIONAL AIRPORT

Great news for the budget traveler! **BART** (Bay Area Rapid Transit; © 510/464-6000 or 415/989-2278; www.bart.gov) began running from SFO to numerous stops within downtown San Francisco in June 2003. This route, which takes about 35 minutes, avoids gnarly traffic on the way and costs a heck of a lot less than taxis or shuttles (around $5 each way, depending on exactly where you're going). Just jump on the airport's free shuttle bus to the International terminal, enter the BART station there, and you're on your way to San Francisco. Trains leave approximately every 15 minutes.

A **cab** from the airport to downtown costs $30 to $35, plus tip, and takes about 30 minutes, traffic permitting.

SuperShuttle (© 800/BLUE-VAN or 415/558-8500; www.supershuttle.com) is a private shuttle company that offers door-to-door airport service, in which you share a van with a few other passengers. They will take you anywhere in the city, charging $15 per person to a residence or business. On the return trip, add $8 to $15 for each additional person depending on whether you're traveling from a hotel or a residence. The shuttle stops at least every 20 minutes, sometimes sooner, and picks up passengers from the marked areas outside the terminals' upper levels. Reservations are required for the return trip to the airport only and should be made 1 day before departure. These shuttles often demand they pick you up 2 hours before your domestic flight and 3 hours before international flights and during holidays. Keep in mind that you could be the first one on and the last one off, so this trip could take a while; you might want to ask before getting in. For $65, you can either charter the entire van for up to seven people or an Execucar private sedan for up to four people. For more info on the Execucar, call © 800/410-4444.

The San Mateo County Transit system, **SamTrans** (© 800/660-4287 in Northern California, or 650/508-6200; www.samtrans.com), runs two buses between the San Francisco Airport and the Transbay Terminal at First and Mission streets. Bus no. 292 costs $1.50 and makes the trip in about 55 minutes. The KX bus costs $4 and takes just 35 minutes but permits only one carry-on bag. Both buses run daily. The no. 292 starts at 5:25am Monday through Friday and 5:30am on weekends; both run until 1am and run every half-hour until 7:30pm when it becomes hourly. The KX starts at 5:53am and ends at 10:37pm Monday through Friday. On weekends service runs from 7:19am to 9:30pm, runs every half-hour until 6:30pm, and then changes to an hourly schedule.

OAKLAND INTERNATIONAL AIR-PORT   About 5 miles south of downtown Oakland, at the Hegenberger Road exit of Calif. 17 (U.S. 880; if coming from south, take 98th Ave.). **Oakland International Airport** (© **510/563-3300** or 800/247-6255; www.oaklandairport.com) primarily serves passengers with East Bay destinations. Some San Franciscans prefer this less-crowded, accessible airport during busy periods—especially because by car it takes around half an hour to get there from downtown San Francisco (traffic permitting). The airport is also accessible by BART, which is not influenced by traffic because it travels on its own tracks (see below for more information).

GETTING INTO TOWN FROM OAKLAND INTERNATIONAL AIRPORT

Taxis from the Oakland Airport to downtown San Francisco are expensive—approximately $50, plus tip.

Bayporter Express (© **877/467-1800** in the Bay Area, or 415/467-1800 elsewhere; www.bayporter.com) is a shuttle service that charges $26 for the first person and $12 for each additional person for the ride from the Oakland Airport to downtown San Francisco. Children under 12 pay $7. The fare for outer areas of San Francisco is higher. The service accepts advance reservations. To the right of the Oakland Airport exit, there are usually shuttles that take you to San Francisco for around $20 per person. The

shuttles in this fleet are independently owned and prices vary.

The cheapest way to reach downtown San Francisco is to take the shuttle bus from the Oakland Airport to **BART** (Bay Area Rapid Transit; © **510/464-6000;** www.bart.gov). The AirBART shuttle bus runs about every 15 minutes Monday through Saturday from 5am to 12:05am and Sunday from 8am to 12:05am. It makes pickups in front of terminals 1 and 2 near the ground transportation signs. Tickets must be purchased at the Oakland Airport's vending machines prior to boarding. The cost is $2 for the 10-minute ride to BART's Coliseum station in Oakland. BART fares vary, depending on your destination; the trip to downtown San Francisco costs $3.15 and takes 15 minutes once you're on board. The entire excursion should take around 45 minutes.

AIRLINES

Dozens of carriers serve San Francisco International Airport and Oakland International Airport, including the following major domestic airlines: **Alaska Airlines** (© 800/252-7522; www.alaskaair.com), **American Airlines** (© 800/433-7300; www.aa.com), **Continental Airlines** (© 800/523-3273; www.continental.com), **Delta Air Lines** (© 800/221-1212; www.delta.com), **Hawaiian Airlines** (© 800/367-5320; www.hawaiianair.com), **JetBlue** (© 800/538-2583; www.jetblue.com), **Northwest Airlines** (© 800/225-2525; www.nwa.com); **Southwest Airlines** (© 800/I-FLY-SWA; www.southwest.com), **United Airlines** (© 800/864-8331; www.united.com), and **US Airways** (© 800/428-4322; www.usairways.com).

FLYING FOR LESS: TIPS FOR GETTING THE BEST AIRFARE

- Passengers who can book their ticket either **long in advance or at the last minute,** or who **fly midweek** or **at**

less-trafficked hours may pay a fraction of the full fare. If your schedule is flexible, say so, and ask if you can secure a cheaper fare by changing your flight plans.

- Search **the Internet** for cheap fares (see "Planning Your Trip Online," earlier in this chapter).
- Keep an eye on local newspapers for **promotional specials** or **fare wars,** when airlines lower prices on their most popular routes. You rarely see fare wars offered for peak travel times, but if you can travel in the off-months, you may snag a bargain.
- Try to book a ticket **in its country of origin.** If you're planning a one-way flight from Johannesburg to New York, a South Africa–based travel agent will probably have the lowest fares. For foreign travelers on multi-leg trips, book in the country of the first leg; for example, book New York–Chicago–Montreal–New York in the U.S.
- **Consolidators,** also known as bucket shops, are great sources for international tickets, although they usually can't beat Internet fares within North America. Start by looking in Sunday newspaper travel sections; U.S. travelers should focus on the *New York Times, Los Angeles Times,* and *Miami Herald.* U.K. travelers should search in the *Independent, The Guardian,* or *The Observer. Beware:* Bucket shop tickets are usually nonrefundable or rigged with stiff cancellation penalties, often as high as 50% to 75% of the ticket price, and some put you on charter airlines, which may leave at inconvenient times and experience delays. Several reliable consolidators are worldwide and available online. **STA Travel** has been the world's lead consolidator for students since purchasing Council Travel, but their fares are competitive for travelers of

all ages. **ELTExpress (Flights.com)** (*C* **800/TRAV-800;** www.eltexpress. com) has excellent fares worldwide, particularly to Europe. They also have "local" websites in 12 countries. **FlyCheap** (*C* **800/FLY-CHEAP;** www.1800flycheap.com) has especially good fares to sunny destinations. **Air Tickets Direct** (*C* **800/778-3447;** www.airticketsdirect.com) is based in Montreal and leverages the currently weak Canadian dollar for low fares; they also book trips to places that U.S. travel agents won't touch, such as Cuba.

- Join **frequent-flier clubs.** Frequent-flier membership doesn't cost a cent, but it does entitle you to better seats, faster response to phone inquiries, and prompter service if your luggage is stolen or your flight is canceled or delayed, or if you want to change your seat. And you don't have to fly to earn points; **frequent-flier credit cards** can earn you thousands of miles for doing your everyday shopping. With more than 70 mileage awards programs on the market, consumers have never had more options. Investigate the program details of your favorite airlines before you sink points into any one. Consider which airlines have hubs in the airport nearest you, and, of those carriers, which have the most advantageous alliances, given your most common routes. To play the frequent-flier game to your best advantage, consult Randy Petersen's **Inside Flyer** (www.inside flyer.com). Petersen and friends review all the programs in detail and post regular updates on changes in policies and trends.

LONG-HAUL FLIGHTS: HOW TO STAY COMFORTABLE

- Your choice of airline and airplane will definitely affect your leg room.

Find more details about U.S. airlines at **www.seatguru.com**. For international airlines, the research firm Skytrax has posted a list of average seat pitches at **www.airlinequality.com.**

- Emergency exit seats and bulkhead seats typically have the most legroom. Emergency exit seats are usually left unassigned until the day of a flight (to ensure that someone able-bodied fills the seats); it's worth getting to the ticket counter early to snag one of these spots for a long flight. Many passengers find that bulkhead seating (the row facing the wall at the front of the cabin) offers more legroom, but keep in mind that bulkheads are where airlines often put baby bassinets, so you may be sitting next to an infant.

- To have two seats for yourself in a three-seat row, try for an aisle seat in a center section toward the back of coach. If you're traveling with a companion, book an aisle and a window seat. Middle seats are usually booked last, so chances are good you'll end up with three seats to yourselves. And in the event that a third passenger is assigned the middle seat, he or she will probably be more than happy to trade for a window or an aisle.

- Ask about entertainment options. Many airlines offer seatback video systems where you get to choose your movies or play video games—but only on some of their planes. (Boeing 777s are your best bet.)

- To sleep, avoid the last row of any section or the row in front of an emergency exit, as these seats are the least likely to recline. Avoid seats near highly trafficked toilet areas. Avoid seats in the back of many jets—these can be narrower than those in the rest of coach. You also may want to reserve a window seat so you can rest your head and avoid being bumped in the aisle.

- Get up, walk around, and stretch every 60 to 90 minutes to keep your blood flowing. This helps avoid **deep vein thrombosis,** or "economy-class syndrome."

(*Tips* **Coping with Jet Lag**

Jet lag is a pitfall of traveling across time zones. If you're flying north–south and you feel sluggish when you touch down, your symptoms will be the result of dehydration and the general stress of air travel. When you travel east–west or vice versa, however, your body becomes thoroughly confused about what time it is, and everything from your digestive system to your brain is knocked for a loop. Traveling east, say from San Francisco to Boston, is more difficult on your internal clock than traveling west, say from Atlanta to Hawaii, because most peoples' bodies are more inclined to stay up late than fall asleep early.

Here are some tips for combating jet lag:

- **Reset your watch** to your destination time before you board the plane.
- **Drink lots of water** before, during, and after your flight. Avoid alcohol.
- **Exercise and sleep well** for a few days before your trip.
- If you have trouble sleeping on planes, **fly eastward on morning flights.**
- **Daylight** is the key to resetting your body clock. At the website for **Outside In** (www.bodyclock.com), you can get a customized plan of when to seek and avoid light.

Flying with Film

Never pack film—exposed or unexposed—in checked bags, because the new, more powerful scanners in U.S. airports can fog film. The film you carry with you can be damaged by scanners as well. X-ray damage is cumulative; the faster the film, and the more times you put it through a scanner, the more likely the damage. Film under 800 ASA is usually safe for up to five scans. If you're taking your film through additional scans, U.S. regulations permit you to demand hand inspections. In international airports, you're at the mercy of airport officials. On international flights, store your film in transparent baggies, so you can remove it easily before you go through scanners.

Most photo supply stores sell protective pouches designed to block damaging X-rays. The pouches fit both film and loaded cameras. They should protect your film in checked baggage, but they also may raise alarms and result in a hand inspection.

- Drink water before, during, and after your flight to combat the lack of humidity in airplane cabins. Avoid alcohol, which will dehydrate you.
- If you're flying with kids, don't forget to carry on toys, books, pacifiers, and chewing gum to help them relieve ear pressure buildup during ascent and descent.

BY CAR

San Francisco is easily accessible by major highways: **Interstate 5,** from the north, and **U.S. 101,** which cuts south–north through the peninsula from San Jose and across the Golden Gate Bridge to points north. If you drive from Los Angeles, you can take the longer coastal route (437 miles and 11 hr.) or the inland route (389 miles and 8 hr.). From Mendocino, it's 156 miles and 4 hours; from Sacramento, 88 miles and 1½ hours; from Yosemite, 210 miles and 4 hours.

If you are driving and aren't already a member, it's worth joining the **American Automobile Association** (AAA; © 800/922-8228; www.csaa.com). It charges

$49 to $79 per year (with an additional one-time joining fee), depending on where you join, and provides roadside and other services to motorists. **Amoco Motor Club** (© 800/334-3300; www.bpmotorclub.com) is another recommended choice.

For information about renting a car, see the "Car Rentals" section (beginning on p. 47) of chapter 4, "Getting to Know San Francisco."

BY TRAIN

Traveling by train takes a long time and usually costs as much as, or more than, flying. Still, if you want to take a leisurely ride across America, rail may be a good option.

San Francisco–bound **Amtrak** (© 800/872-7245 or 800/USA-RAIL; www.amtrak.com) trains leave from New York and cross the country via Chicago. The journey takes about 3½ days, and seats sell quickly. At this writing, the lowest round-trip fare costs $294 from New York and $270 from Chicago. Round-trip tickets from Los Angeles can cost as little as $108 or as much as $200.

Trains arrive in Emeryville, just north of Oakland, and connect with regularly scheduled buses to San Francisco's Ferry Building and the Caltrain station in downtown San Francisco.

Caltrain (© **800/660-4287** or 415/546-4461; www.caltrain.com) operates train service between San Francisco and the towns of the peninsula. The city depot is at 700 Fourth St., at Townsend Street.

9 Packages for the Independent Traveler

Package tours are simply a way to buy the airfare, accommodations, and other elements of your trip (such as car rentals, airport transfers, and sometimes even activities) at the same time and often at discounted prices.

One good source of package deals is the airlines themselves. Most major airlines offer air/land packages, including **American Airlines Vacations** (© **800/321-2121;** www.aavacations.com), **Delta Vacations** (© **800/221-6666;** www.deltavacations.com), **Continental Airlines Vacations** (© **800/301-3800;** www.covacations.com), and **United Vacations** (© **888/854-3899;** www.unitedvacations.com). Several big **online travel agencies**—Expedia, Travelocity, Orbitz, Site59, and Lastminute.com—also do a brisk business in packages.

Travel packages are also listed in the travel section of your local Sunday newspaper. Or check ads in the national travel magazines such as *Arthur Frommer's Budget Travel Magazine, Travel + Leisure, National Geographic Traveler,* and *Condé Nast Traveler.*

10 Special-Interest Trips

Just over an hour drive north of San Francisco are Napa Valley and Sonoma, the two world-famous counties that make up the heart of Northern California Wine Country. Whether you're interested in sipping and snacking on some of the best wine and food in the country or are just looking for a little of the good life (think spas, fresh air, rolling vine-trellised hillsides, and loads of cozy inns and B&Bs—plus a far better chance at T-shirt weather than San Francisco can offer), Wine Country is the place to do it. You'll need to drive, however, as public transportation is not ubiquitous enough to get you from site to site once you hit either of the valleys.

11 Tips on Accommodations

Whether you want a room with a view or just a room, San Francisco is more than accommodating to its 15.7 million annual guests. Most of the city's 200-plus hotels cluster near Union Square, but some smaller independent gems are scattered around town.

When reading over your options, keep in mind that prices listed are "rack" (published) rates. At big, upscale hotels, almost no one actually pays them—and with the dramatic travel downturn over the past few years, there are still deals to be had.

Therefore, you should always ask for special discounts or, even better, vacation packages. It's often possible to get the room you want for $100 less than what is quoted here, except when the hotels are packed (usually during summer and due to conventions) and bargaining is close to impossible. Use the rates listed here for the big hotels as guidelines for comparison only; prices for inexpensive choices and smaller B&Bs are closer to reality, though.

Hunting for hotels in San Francisco can be a tricky business, particularly if you're not a seasoned traveler. What you don't know—and the reservations agent may not tell you—could very well ruin your vacation, so keep the following pointers in mind when it comes time to book a room:

- Prices may not include state and city taxes, which total 14%. Other hidden extras include parking fees, which can be up to $45 per day (also subject to 14% tax!), and hefty surcharges—up to $1 per local call—for telephone use.
- San Francisco is Convention City, so if you want a room at a particular hotel during high season (summer, for example), book well in advance.
- Hotels usually hold reservations until 6pm. If you don't tell the staff you're arriving late, you might lose your room.
- Almost every hotel in San Francisco requires a credit card imprint for "incidentals" (and to prevent walkouts). If you don't have a credit card, be sure to make special arrangements with the management before you hang up the phone, and make a note of the name of the person you spoke with.
- When you check in, if your room isn't up to snuff, politely inform the front desk of your dissatisfaction and ask for another. If the hotel can accommodate you, they almost always will—and sometimes will even upgrade you!

SAVING ON YOUR HOTEL ROOM

The **rack rate** is the maximum rate that a hotel charges for a room. Hardly anybody pays this price, however, except in high season or on holidays. To lower the cost of your room:

- **Dial direct.** When booking a room in a chain hotel, you'll often get a better deal by calling the individual hotel's reservation desk rather than the chain's main number.
- **Book online.** Many hotels offer Internet-only discounts, or supply rooms to Priceline, Hotwire, or Expedia at rates much lower than the ones you can get through the hotel itself.
- **Look into group or long-stay discounts.** If you come as part of a large group, you should be able to negotiate a bargain rate. Likewise, if you're planning a long stay (at least 5 days), you might qualify for a discount. As a general rule, expect 1 night free after a 7-night stay.
- **Avoid excess charges and hidden costs.** When you book a room, ask whether the hotel charges for parking. Use your own cellphone, pay phones, or prepaid phone cards instead of dialing direct from hotel phones, which usually have exorbitant rates. And don't be tempted by the room's minibar offerings: Most hotels charge through the nose for water, soda, and snacks. Finally, ask about local taxes and service charges, which can increase the cost of a room by 15% or more.
- **Book an efficiency.** A room with a kitchenette allows you to shop for groceries and cook your own meals. This is a big money saver, especially for families on long stays.

LANDING THE BEST ROOM

Somebody has to get the best room in the house. It might as well be you. You can start by joining the hotel's frequent-guest program, which may make you eligible for upgrades. A hotel-branded credit card usually gives its owner "silver" or "gold" status in frequent-guest programs for free. Always ask about a corner room. They're often larger and quieter, with more windows and light, and they often cost the same as standard rooms. When you make your reservation, ask if the hotel is renovating; if it is, request a room away from the construction. Ask about nonsmoking rooms, rooms with views, rooms with twin-, queen-, or king-size beds. If you're a light sleeper, request a

House-Swapping

House-swapping is becoming a more popular and viable means of travel; you stay in their place, they stay in yours, and you both get an authentic and personal view of the area, the opposite of the escapist retreat that many hotels offer. Try **HomeLink International** (Homelink.org), the largest and oldest home-swapping organization, founded in 1952, with over 11,000 listings worldwide ($75 for a yearly membership). **HomeExchange.org** ($50 for 6,000 listings) and **InterVac.com** ($69 for over 10,000 listings) are also reliable.

quiet room away from vending machines, elevators, restaurants, bars, and discos. Ask for a room that has been most recently renovated or redecorated.

12 Tips on Dining

With Northern California's unparalleled abundance of organic produce, seafood, free-range meats, and wine, San Francisco's culinary world is more than every chef's oyster. It's ours, too. Especially now.

After a rather boring couple of years, during which the city's dining rooms played it safe, closed, or cut back while awaiting more freewheeling times, restaurants are again riding high with new additions, exciting menus, and bustling dining rooms.

While every spot tries to establish its own identity, today's dining trend remains firmly grounded in the "small plate" fad—menus that allow you to snack through a meal on smaller dishes. Unfortunately, smaller portions do not always correspond with more petite prices, so expect to pay to play.

That said, it's not just trendy new spots that satisfy cuisine-crazed San Franciscans. As one of the world's cultural crossroads, the city has long been blessed with a cornucopia of cuisines. Afghan, Cajun, Burmese, Jewish, Moroccan, Persian, Cambodian, vegan—whatever you're in the mood for, this town has it covered. So book your reservations and break out the credit cards, because half the fun of visiting San Francisco is the rare opportunity to sample most of the flavors of the world in one fell swoop.

As you join the locals in their most beloved pastime, there are a few things you should keep in mind:

- If you want a table at the restaurants with the best reputations, you probably need to book 6 to 8 weeks in advance for weekends, and a couple of weeks ahead for weekdays.
- If there's a long wait for a table, ask if you can order at the bar, which is often faster and more fun.
- Don't leave *anything* valuable in your car while dining, particularly in or near high-crime areas such as the Mission, downtown, or—believe it or not—Fisherman's Wharf (thieves know tourists with nice cameras and a trunk full of mementos are headed there). Also, it's best to give the parking valet only the key to your car, *not* your hotel room or house key.
- ***Remember:*** It is against the law to smoke in any restaurant in San Francisco, even if it has a separate bar or lounge area. You're welcome to smoke outside, however.
- This ain't New York: Plan on dining early. Most restaurants close their kitchens around 10pm.
- If you're driving to a restaurant, add extra time into your itinerary to find

parking, which can be an especially infuriating exercise in areas like the Mission, Downtown, the Marina, and most everywhere else for that matter. And expect to pay at least $10 for valet service, if the restaurant has it.

13 Recommended Books & Films

San Francisco was a popular setting for many early literary works, including Mark Twain's *San Francisco,* a collection of articles that glorified "the liveliest, heartiest community on our continent." It was also the birthplace of Jack London, who wrote several short stories of his younger days as an oyster pirate on the San Francisco Bay, as well as *Martin Eden,* his semiautobiographical account of life along the Oakland shores.

For all you mystery buffs, two must-reads are Frank Norris's *McTeague: A Story of San Francisco,* a violent tale of love and greed set at the turn of the 20th century; and Dashiell Hammett's *The Maltese Falcon,* a steamy detective novel that captures the seedier side of San Francisco in the 1920s (you can even take a walking tour of Hammett's famous haunts).

California has always been a hotbed of alternative—and, more often than not, controversial—literary styles. Joan Didion, in her novel *Slouching Toward Bethlehem,* and Hunter S. Thompson, in his columns for the *San Francisco Examiner* (brought together in the collection *Generation of Swine*), both used a "new journalistic" approach in their studies of San Francisco in the 1960s. Tom Wolfe's early work *The Electric Kool-Aid Acid Test* follows the Hell's Angels, the Grateful Dead, and Ken Kesey's Merry Pranksters as they ride through the hallucinogenic 1960s. Meanwhile, Beat writers Allen Ginsberg and Jack Kerouac were penning protests against political conservatism—and promoting their bohemian lifestyle—in the former's controversial poem "Howl" (daringly published by Lawrence Ferlinghetti, poet and owner of City Lights in San Francisco's North Beach District) and the latter's famous tale of American adventure, *On the Road.*

Among Wallace Stegner's many works of contemporary fiction and nonfiction about the West is his novel *All the Little Live Things,* which explores the conflicts faced by retired literary agent Joe Allston; the book is set in the San Francisco Bay Area of the 1960s. *The Spectator Bird* (winner of the 1976 National Book Award) revisits Allston's character as he reflects on his life and his memories of a search for his roots.

For a look at the dark side of The City by the Bay, pick up a copy of *San Francisco Noir,* edited by Peter Maravelis. A collection of some of the Bay Area's best contemporary fiction, it focuses on San Francisco's noir underbelly.

The City by the Bay has also been the setting of hundreds of films ranging from classics like *The Maltese Falcon, Dirty Harry, What's Up Doc?, Invasion of the Body Snatchers,* and a personal favorite, the Goldie Hawn and Chevy Chase comedy *Foul Play* to more recent blockbusters like *A View to A Kill, Mrs. Doubtfire,* and *The Joy Luck Club.*

You can get a sense of the city long before you come or after you've departed by revisiting these and more films. (See the San Francisco Film Commission's list at www.ci.sf.ca.us). But to get a flavor for Alcatraz, see *Birdman of Alcatraz* or Sean Connery and Nicolas Cage in *The Rock.* A movie that really captures the spirit of the city and its all-accepting culture is *The Wild Parrots of Telegraph Hill.* It will give you an idea of what the city used to be like, and how it still has room for eccentric people as well as compassion for newcomers of all walks of life who decide to call San Francisco home.

3

Suggested Itineraries

I imagine there are plenty of people who come to San Francisco and spend most or all of their time in Fisherman's Wharf or Union Square. And why not? The city's best-known tourist destinations are no-brainers: The wharf area, though unapologetically touristy and generally loathed by locals, is no doubt a scenic, extremely convenient place to explore, and also a lot of fun if you can enjoy the fact that it's a little tacky. For shoppers, such as myself, the key to an excellent vacation can easily be a few success-ful days of retail therapy—and Union Square's condensed blocks of department stores and boutiques provide more than ample opportunity. However, though these two des-tinations are fun, they do not remotely represent the heart of San Francisco, or, in my opinion, even close to the best of it. To make the most of your time in The City by the Bay, consider the following itineraries, which offer a brush with these attractions while en route to must-see famous landmarks and places or experiences that capture more of the city's nuances and soul. I've organized them as individual 1-day tours (and avoided ventures that require steep hill-hiking or require a car) in the order in which I would do them, so if you've got more than 1 day start with the first tour, and if you've got time, consider following up with the second and third itineraries.

1 The Best of San Francisco in 1 Day

If you've got only 1 day to explore the city, put on your walking shoes and start early. You've got a lot of ground to cover just to get to the must-sees, but luckily, condensed geography (and hopefully weather) is in your favor. The whirlwind tour starts with a scenic ride on a cable car and an Alcatraz tour or Bay cruise (with a requisite Fisher-man's Wharf embarkation; once you get there you'll know whether you're in the "hate it" or "love it" camp and can spend extra time there if you desire). Next you'll hoof it up to two of the city's most colorful neighborhoods, Chinatown and North Beach for lunch, shopping, browsing, and a coffee break. Finish with dinner in one of the city's outstanding restaurants and, if you're staying downtown, a nightcap amid the stars. *Start:* Buses: 2, 3, 4, 30, 45, or 76 to Union Square.

❶ Union Square

This square, which was named for a series of violent pro-union mass demonstra-tions staged here on the eve of the Civil War, isn't an attraction in itself, but it is the epicenter of the city's shopping dis-trict. Stop in its center to make mental notes of where you want to spend some money later—Macy's, Saks, Tiffany's, Neiman Marcus, and Victoria's Secret are all here, and are surrounded by blocks crammed with hundreds of other boutiques. Just 3 blocks down, at Powell and Market streets, is the cable car turnaround where you'll embark on a ride on one of the city's greatest landmarks. See p. 42.

❷ Cable Car, Powell-Hyde Line 👀👀👀

Don't be intimidated by the line of people waiting to board at the cable car turnaround at Market and Powell streets. Trust me. You'll see why it was worth the wait after you pay $5 per person, climb aboard, and get a fresh perspective on the city as the car drags itself uphill and slowly lunges down—all backed by ridiculously picturesque vistas. See p. 45.

Get off at the last stop, at Hyde and Beach streets, walk 1 block toward the water along Hyde, turn right on Jefferson Street, and follow it 5 blocks to arrive at Pier 41, where you can embark on the following adventure.

❸ Alcatraz Tour 👀👀👀

To tour "The Rock," the Bay Area's famous abandoned prison on its own island, you must first get there, and that is half the fun. The brief, but very beautiful, ferry ride offers captivating views of the Golden Gate Bridge, Marin Headlands, and perhaps most impressive, San Francisco itself. (The view's unparalleled from the island as well.) Once inside, an audio tour guides you through cellblocks and offers a colorful look at the prison's historic past as well as its most renowned inmates. Book in advance, because these tours consistently sell out. Bring snacks and beverages, too; the ferry's pickings are slim and expensive, and there's nothing available on the island. See p. 150.

Once you've had your fill of the wharf, cross The Embarcadero thoroughfare and follow Powell Street away from the water for 5 blocks to arrive in the heart of:

❹ North Beach 👀👀👀

One of the best ways to get the San Francisco vibe is to mingle with the locals, and one of the greatest places to do it is in this Italian neighborhood. Columbus Avenue is the epicenter of the North Beach action, where old Italian men who've gathered and lingered over espresso for decades at the strip's myriad cafes are joined by all other walks of life indulging in the cafe culture. Grant Avenue, which runs parallel to Columbus, is an excellent place to browse boutiques. See p. 167.

---

❺ MARIO'S BOHEMIAN CIGAR STORE

It's crowded, the menu's limited to beer, wine, coffee drinks, and a few sandwiches (like meatball—mmmmm), and it's touristy. But the convivial atmosphere and large windows perfect for people-watching make this tiny, crowded cafe (566 Columbus Ave.; ✆ 415/362-0536) a favorite even with locals. See p. 128. Afterward, follow Columbus Avenue 3 blocks south (away from the water) to Grant Avenue. Follow Grant for a block and you're instantly transported to:

---

❻ Chinatown 👀👀

One block from North Beach is a whole other world in San Francisco's epicenter for Chinese culture. Centered around Grant Avenue and its paralleling Stockton Street, the oldest part of the city is crammed with both cheesy knickknack shops for tourists and exotic herb and grocery stores, dim sum houses, restaurants, and bakeries catering to the city's most condensed Chinese population. It's worth a peek if only to see the Stockton Street markets hawking live frogs, fowl, and fish destined for tonight's dinner table. See p. 168.

The Best of San Francisco in 1 & 2 Days

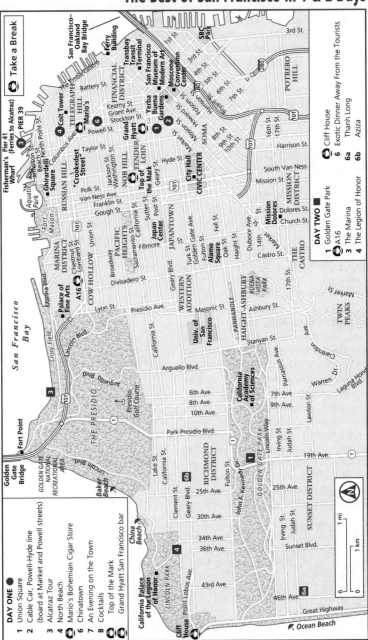

DAY ONE ●
1 Union Square
2 Cable Car, Powell-Hyde line
  (board at Market and Powell streets)
3 Alcatraz Tour
4 North Beach
5 Mario's Bohemian Cigar Store
6 Chinatown
7 An Evening on the Town
8 Cocktails
  Top of the Mark
  Grand Hyatt San Francisco bar

Take a Break

Exotic Dinner Away From the Tourists
6 Cliff House
6a Thanh Long
6b Aziza

DAY TWO ■
1 Golden Gate Park
  A16
3 The Marina
4 The Legion of Honor

❼ An Evening on the Town

There are so many exceptional restaurants in San Francisco that it's impossible to recommend just one or two—especially since you know best what your preferences are regarding ambience, food, and price. However, since you're here and the city is one of the best food destinations in the nation, it's worth carefully choosing where you'll dine, not to mention making an advance reservation. See chapter 6.

❽ Cocktails

Whether it's as a nightcap or as a pre-dinner cocktail, one of the most ambience-rich ways to unwind and take in San Francisco's regional beauty is from a bar with a great view. Good options include Nob Hill's the Top of the Mark (p. 237) and Union Square's Grand Hyatt Hotel bar (p. 58).

2 The Best of San Francisco in 2 Days

On your second day, get familiar with other alluring sections of the city—and its spectacular parks and nature areas. Start by exploring Golden Gate Park and its attractions. Next head to the city's northern edge for lunch (and shopping) along nearby Union or Chestnut streets before checking out the Marina area, including the Palace of Fine Arts and Crissy Fields. Then take a bus or taxi farther west to The Palace of the Legion of Honor. From here, taxi to the historic Cliff House (which was completely overhauled in 2004) at western water's edge for cocktails and head to a nearby restaurant for an exotic dinner. ***Start:*** *Buses: 7, 33, 66, 71, or 71L to Stanyan and Haight streets.*

❶ Golden Gate Park ✸✸✸

Stretching from the middle of the city to the Pacific Ocean and comprised of 1,017 acres, Golden Gate Park (p. 172) is one of the city's greatest attributes. Since its development in the late 1880s, it has afforded San Franciscans urban respite with dozens of well-tended gardens, museums, and great grassy expanses prime for picnicking, lounging, or tossing a Frisbee. Highlights include the Conservatory of Flowers, Stow Lake, and the stunning de Young Museum, which premiered in its new building in late 2005.

After enjoying the park, drive, take a taxi, or walk from the eastern end of the park 2 blocks to the corner of Haight and Cole streets. Catch the no. 43 bus, take it through the pretty Presidio, and disembark at Lombard and Divisadero streets. Walk 1 block north (toward the Golden Gate Bridge), turn right on Chestnut, and halfway down the block is:

⓶ A16 ✸✸

As one of the city's best, this slick but casual Italian restaurant (2355 Chestnut St.; ✆ 415/771-2216) is nearly impossible to get into at night. But lunch is a much easier and relaxed bet. Still, make a reservation and definitely ask the manager, Shelley, to direct you to some exciting Italian wines (by the glass) that you've probably never heard of. See p. 135. From here, take a right onto Chestnut when you leave the restaurant, turn left on Scott Street, and follow it 6 blocks to the bay. You'll be at:

❸ The Marina

The area that became famous for its destruction during the 1989 earthquake has long been one of the most picturesque and coveted patches of local real estate. Here, along the northern edge of the city, multimillion-dollar homes back up against the bayfront Marina (p. 43), where bobbing boats and Golden Gate Bridge views make for an exceptional backdrop for an afternoon stroll. This is also home to the beautiful Palace of Fine Arts building (p. 161), which houses The Exploratorium, built for the Panama-Pacific Exhibition of 1915 and Crissy Field (p. 178), where restored wetlands and a beachfront path lead to historic Fort Point or a path that will take you up to the foot of the Golden Gate Bridge, which you can cross on foot or bike.

After you've had your fill, drive or take a taxi to:

❹ The Palace of the Legion of Honor 🎡🎡

This well-hidden destination museum is as alluring for its breathtaking location on a grassy expanse overlooking the waters of the Golden Gate (though there is a bridge view, too, depending on where you stand) as it is for its art collection spanning 4,000 years, including an impressive collection of Rodin sculptures. Often overlooked by visitors, it's one of the city's finest museums, surpassing the MOMA by far. See p. 162.

Afterward, follow the footpath or road, both of which lead to Clement Street. Take a right on Clement and follow it 10 to 14 blocks (depending on whether you exit the museum's park via road or path), veer left as it becomes Point Lobos, and as you wind down toward Ocean Beach you'll arrive at:

🅢 CLIFF HOUSE

Originally designed in 1863 and rebuilt multiple times due to fire or age, this destination perched over the Pacific Ocean was, in its heyday, *the* place for San Franciscans to come, even though it was a long journey by rail or buggy from downtown. Today, it's pretty much a tourist trap of restaurants and knickknack shops. But what it does have going for it is natural scenery. Here you can view the ocean and the neighboring ruins of Sutro Baths (a giant oceanfront bathhouse destroyed by fire in 1966), see seals and surfers as they play in the water, and sip a cocktail while lounging in the completely renovated structure, which debuted in late 2004. See p. 178. Grab a cab to get to one of the two following destinations:

❻ Exotic Dinner away from the Tourists

Since you're already at the western edge of the city, why not have dinner in one of the great lesser-known destinations that underscore the area's exceptional ethnic food? Consider **Thanh Long** (4101 Judah St.; ✆ **415/665-1146**), an excellent, low-key Vietnamese restaurant that became so famous for its crab and garlic noodles that it opened more locations in Los Angeles and Vegas. See p. 140. Another alternative is **Aziza** (5800 Geary Blvd.; ✆ **415/752-2222**; p. 147), a Moroccan oasis with surroundings as delicious as the food.

3 The Best of San Francisco in 3 Days

It's hard to believe that the ultimate in rural luxury living is just an hour north of San Francisco, but one of the nation's hottest destinations, Napa Valley, is indeed a quick drive away, promising rewards of sunshine (except during winter), copious amounts of extraordinary wine, and truly outstanding culinary experiences. Head out early to begin hitting up a few wineries when they open at 10am, have a picnic lunch, do a little window-shopping, and then enjoy an exceptional dinner. The best way to get to Napa Valley is to rent a car and drive.

Take the scenic Highway 101 to 37 East to 12/121 to Highway 29 in Napa, which crosses the Golden Gate Bridge and offers the most rural landscape on the drive up. Turn left onto Highway 29 north, take the Trancas Exit east, follow it across town and take a left onto the Silverado Trail headed north. Look for the mailbox on the left marked 6154 Silverado Trail, turn right, and head up to:

❶ Shafer Vineyards 𝒢𝒢

Shafer Vineyards, an off-the-beaten-track winery, makes spectacular wines and offers a far more intimate and attentive tasting than most in the valley. It requires an advance reservation and $25 per person to pull up a chair within the bright, homey tasting room. But it's worth it—along with tasty sips of current releases you'll get a one-on-one education about the family-owned winery's eco-friendly practices, a tour, and personalized attention that you won't find at crowded tasting room bars. If you come on a weekend or major holiday, when Shafer is closed, consider heading to **Far Niente** on a Saturday for a $40 tour, which includes a wine tasting and views of their classic car collection and vast azalea gardens. See p. 273 and p. 274, respectively.

From Shafer, take a right onto the Silverado Trail heading north, turn left shortly afterward at Yountville Crossroad, turn left on Yount and right on Madison, and turn left (south) onto Highway 29. Take the ramp toward Yountville, turn right onto California and drive until you've arrived at:

❷ Domaine Chandon 𝒢𝒢

Founded in 1973 by French champagne house Moët et Chandon, this sparkling wine house is one of the valley's prettiest spots, complete with vast landscaped grounds, a tasting "salon" with outdoor shaded patio seating, and snacks to accompany the bubbly and still wines. Take the fun, comprehensive tour, which guides you through the sparkling wine-making process before settling you into a scenic seat with a glass of bubbly. See p. 273.

When departing the winery, turn left (north) onto Highway 29 and follow it for a few minutes until you see Oakville Crossroad, and on your right side the location of:

> ### ❸ OAKVILLE GROCERY
> Locally famous for its astounding array of gourmet to-go items and gifts, Oakville Grocery (7856 St., Helena Hwy., Oakville; ℂ 707/944-8802) is a must-visit. Whether you order a sandwich, the awesome Caesar salad, or one of the heated daily specials, savor it on a bench outside or at your next stop, Rubicon Estate. See p. 300. From here, again head north (right) on Highway 29. Follow it for a few minutes to get to the small town of Rutherford. On your left you will see signs and the entrance for:

❹ Rubicon Estate

Filmmaker Francis Ford Coppola knows how to set a scene, so it's not surprising that his restored historic winery, previously Niebaum-Coppola, is one of the valley's most picturesque and sprawling. Inside the 1880s stone winery, which was previously the home of Inglenook, guests can take a tour (make an appointment), taste a huge variety of wines, purchase from a vast collection of tabletop accessories, and peruse Coppola's movie memorabilia, including an antique Tucker car from the movie of the same name. See p. 276.

From here, turn left (north) onto Highway 29; a few minutes later you will be passing through the heart of:

❺ St. Helena's Main Street

A great way to work off what could easily turn into a wine stupor is to walk St. Helena's quaint historic downtown. The action centers along a 4-block stretch of Main Street, which is petitely packed with boutiques, candy shops, home stores, restaurants, and even a restored old movie theater showcasing new releases. See p. 283.

The Best of San Francisco in 3 Days

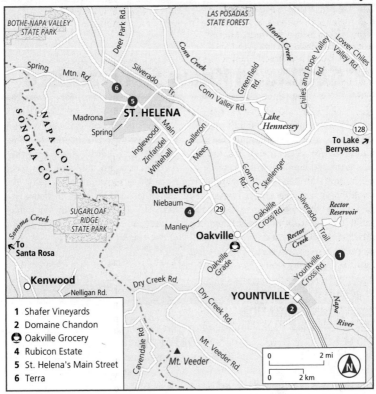

BOTHE-NAPA VALLEY
STATE PARK

LAS POSADAS
STATE FOREST

Deer Park Rd.

Moorel Creek

Chiles and Pope Valley Rd.

Lower Chiles Valley Rd.

Spring Mtn. Rd.

Silverado Tr.

Conn Creek

Greenfield Rd.

Conn Valley Rd.

6

5

Madrona

ST. HELENA

Lake Hennessey

128

To Lake ↗
Berryessa

Spring

Main

Galleron

Inglewood

Zinfandel

Whitehall

Mees

Conn Cr. Rd.

Skellenger

NAPA CO.

SONOMA CO.

Rutherford ○

Niebaum

4 29

Oakville Cross Rd.

Silverado Trail

Rector Reservoir

SUGARLOAF
RIDGE
STATE PARK

Sonoma Creek

Manley

Oakville ○

Rector Creek

1

↖ To
Santa Rosa

Oakville Grade

Yountville Cross Rd.

○ **Kenwood**

Dry Creek Rd.

Nelligan Rd.

Dry Creek Rd.

YOUNTVILLE ◇

2

Napa River

Cavendale Rd.

Mt. Veeder Rd.

▲
Mt. Veeder

0   2 mi

0   2 km

N

1 Shafer Vineyards
2 Domaine Chandon
◎ Oakville Grocery
4 Rubicon Estate
5 St. Helena's Main Street
6 Terra

You won't see the next attraction from the road, but when entering downtown St. Helena, if you take a right at the second light, Adams Street, take the next right at Railroad Avenue, and go 1½ blocks, you will arrive at:

❻ Terra ✫✫✫

Though this historic fieldstone building is incognito in its long-standing location behind St. Helena's Main Street, culinary connoisseurs know that one of the nation's greatest chefs, Hiro Sone, is behind the magical dinner menu served here. The choices change seasonally, but some items, such as the beloved sake-marinated cod with shiso broth and shrimp dumplings, are mainstays, as are the friendly, professional service and intimate and quiet surroundings. See p. 301.

Now that you're probably full and tired, just get on Highway 29. As the valley's main thoroughfare it will invariably lead toward wherever you've chosen to spend the night.

4

Getting to Know San Francisco

This chapter offers useful information on how to become better acquainted with San Francisco, even though half the fun of becoming familiar with this city is wandering around and haphazardly stumbling upon great shops, restaurants, and vistas that even locals might not know about. You'll find that although the city is metropolitan, San Francisco is still a small town—one where you won't feel like a stranger for long.

If you get disoriented, just remember that downtown is east and the Golden Gate Bridge is north—and even if you do get lost, you probably won't go too far, since water surrounds three sides of the city. The most difficult challenge you'll have, if you're traveling by car (which I suggest you avoid), is mastering the maze of one-way streets.

1 Orientation

VISITOR INFORMATION

The **San Francisco Visitor Information Center,** on the lower level of Hallidie Plaza, 900 Market St., at Powell Street (② **415/283-0177;** fax 415/362-7323; www.sfvisitor. org), has information, brochures, discount coupons, and advice on restaurants, sights, and events in the city. The on-site staff can provide answers in German, Japanese, French, Italian, and Spanish (as well as English, of course). To find the office, descend the escalator at the cable car turnaround. The office is open Monday through Friday from 8:30am to 5pm, Saturday and Sunday from 9am to 3pm from April through October. However, it is closed on Sundays during winter, January 1, Easter, Thanksgiving Day, and December 25.

Phones are answered in person Monday through Friday only. Otherwise, dial ② **415/283-0176** any time, day or night, for a recorded message about current cultural events, theater, music, sports, and other special happenings. This information is also available in German, French, Japanese, and Spanish. Keep in mind that this service recommends only businesses that are members of the Convention and Visitors Bureau and is very tourist oriented. While there is a ton of information available at this number, it's not representative of all that the city has to offer.

Pick up a copy of the *Bay Guardian* (www.sfbg.com) or the *S.F. Weekly* (www. sfweekly.com), the city's free alternative papers, to get listings of all city happenings. You'll find them in kiosks throughout the city and in most coffee shops.

For specialized information on Chinatown's shops and services, and on the city's Chinese community in general, contact the **Chinese Chamber of Commerce,** 730 Sacramento St. (② **415/982-3000**), open daily from 9am to 5pm.

CITY LAYOUT

San Francisco occupies the tip of a 32-mile peninsula between San Francisco Bay and the Pacific Ocean. Its land area measures about 46 square miles, although the city is often referred to as being 7 square miles. At more than 900 feet high, the towering Twin Peaks marks the geographic center of the city and is a killer place to take in a vista of San Francisco.

With lots of one-way streets and plenty of nooks and crannies, San Francisco might seem confusing at first, but it will quickly become easy to negotiate. The city's downtown streets are arranged in a simple grid pattern, with the exceptions of Market Street and Columbus Avenue, which cut across the grid at right angles to each other. Hills appear to distort this pattern, however, and can disorient you. As you learn your way around, the hills will become your landmarks and reference points. But even if you get lost, it's no big deal: San Francisco's a small town—so much so, in fact, that I've run from one end to the other (during the Bay to Breakers Foot Race) in an hour flat.

> (*Tips*
>
> For a full-color map of San Francisco and its public transportation, see the "San Francisco Neighborhoods" and "San Francisco Mass Transit" maps in the insert of this book.

MAIN ARTERIES & STREETS   **Market Street** is San Francisco's main thoroughfare. Most of the city's buses travel this route on their way to the Financial District from the outer neighborhoods to the west and south. The tall office buildings clustered downtown are at the northeast end of Market; 1 block beyond lies The Embarcadero and the bay.

The Embarcadero ✯—an excellent strolling, skating, and biking route (thanks to recent renovations)—curves along San Francisco Bay from south of the Bay Bridge to the northeast perimeter of the city. It terminates at Fisherman's Wharf, the famous tourist-oriented pier. Aquatic Park, Fort Mason, and the Golden Gate National Recreation Area are on the northernmost point of the peninsula.

From the eastern perimeter of Fort Mason, **Van Ness Avenue** runs due south, back to Market Street. The area just described forms a rough triangle, with Market Street as its southeastern boundary, the waterfront as its northern boundary, and Van Ness Avenue as its western boundary. Within this triangle lie most of the city's main tourist sights.

FINDING AN ADDRESS   Since most of the city's streets are laid out in a grid pattern, finding an address is easy when you know the nearest cross street. Numbers start with 1 at the beginning of the street and proceed at the rate of 100 per block. When asking for directions, find out the nearest cross street and the neighborhood where your destination is located, but be careful not to confuse numerical avenues with numerical streets. Numerical avenues (Third Ave. and so on) are in the Richmond and Sunset Districts in the western part of the city. Numerical streets (Third St. and so on) are south of Market Street in the east and south parts of town.

NEIGHBORHOODS IN BRIEF

For further discussion of some of the neighborhoods below, see the "Neighborhoods Worth a Visit" section of chapter 7, beginning on p. 166. For a color map of the city, see the "San Francisco Neighborhoods" map in the color insert of this book.

Union Square Union Square is the commercial hub of San Francisco. Most major hotels and department stores are crammed into the area surrounding the actual square, which was named for a series of violent pro-union mass demonstrations staged here on the eve of the Civil War. A plethora of upscale boutiques, restaurants, and galleries occupy the spaces tucked between the larger buildings. A few blocks west is the **Tenderloin** neighborhood, a patch of poverty and blight where you should keep your wits about you. The **Theater District** is 3 blocks west of Union Square.

The Financial District East of Union Square, this area, bordered by The Embarcadero and by Market, Third, Kearny, and Washington streets, is the city's business district and the stamping grounds for many major corporations. The pointy TransAmerica Pyramid, at Montgomery and Clay streets, is one of the district's most conspicuous architectural features. To its east sprawls The Embarcadero Center, an 8½-acre complex housing offices, shops, and restaurants. Farther east still is the old Ferry Building, the city's pre-bridge transportation hub. Ferries to Sausalito and Larkspur still leave from this point. However, in 2003, the building became an attraction in itself when it was completely renovated, jampacked with outstanding restaurant and gourmet food- and wine-related shops, and surrounded by a farmers market a few days a week, making it one of San Francisco's residents' favorite places to grace and gossip.

Nob Hill & Russian Hill Bounded by Bush, Larkin, Pacific, and Stockton streets, Nob Hill is a genteel, well-heeled district still occupied by the city's major power brokers and the neighborhood businesses they frequent.

Russian Hill extends from Pacific to Bay and from Polk to Mason. It contains steep streets, lush gardens, and high-rises occupied by both the moneyed and the more bohemian.

Chinatown A large red-and-green gate on Grant Avenue at Bush Street marks the official entrance to Chinatown. Beyond lies a 24-block labyrinth, bordered by Broadway, Bush, Kearny, and Stockton streets, filled with restaurants, markets, temples, shops, and, of course, a substantial percentage of San Francisco's Chinese residents. Chinatown is a great place for exploration all along Stockton and Grant streets, Portsmouth Square, and the alleys that lead off them, like Ross and Waverly. This area is jampacked, so don't even think about driving here.

North Beach This Italian neighborhood, which stretches from Montgomery and Jackson to Bay Street, is one of the best places in the city to grab a coffee, pull up a cafe chair, and do some serious people-watching. Nightlife is equally happening in North Beach; restaurants, bars, and clubs along Columbus and Grant avenues attract folks from all over the Bay Area, who fight for a parking place and romp through the festive neighborhood. Down Columbus toward the Financial District are the remains of the city's Beat Generation landmarks, including Ferlinghetti's City Lights Bookstore and Vesuvio's Bar. Broadway—a short strip of sex joints—cuts through the heart of the district. **Telegraph Hill** looms over the east side of North Beach, topped by Coit Tower, one of San Francisco's best vantage points.

Fisherman's Wharf North Beach runs into Fisherman's Wharf, which was once the busy heart of the city's great harbor and waterfront industries. Today, it is a kitschy but interesting tourist area with little, if any, authentic waterfront life, except for recreational boating and some friendly sea lions. What it does have going for it are activities for the whole family, with attractions, restaurants, trinket shops, and beautiful views and walkways everywhere you look.

The Marina District Created on landfill for the Pan Pacific Exposition of 1915, the Marina District boasts some of the best views of the Golden Gate, as well as plenty of grassy fields alongside San Francisco Bay. Elegant Mediterranean-style homes and apartments, inhabited by the city's well-to-do singles and wealthy families, line the streets. Here, too, are the Palace of Fine Arts, the Exploratorium, and Fort Mason Center. The main street is Chestnut, between Franklin and Lyon, which abounds with shops, cafes, and boutiques. Because of its landfill foundation, the Marina was one of the hardest-hit districts in the 1989 quake.

Cow Hollow Located west of Van Ness Avenue, between Russian Hill and the Presidio, this flat, grazable area supported 30 dairy farms in 1861. Today, Cow Hollow is largely residential and largely yuppie. Its two primary commercial thoroughfares are Lombard Street, known for its many relatively inexpensive motels, and Union Street, a flourishing shopping sector filled with restaurants, pubs, cafes, and shops.

Pacific Heights The ultra-elite, such as the Gettys and Danielle Steel—and those lucky enough to buy before the real-estate boom—reside in the mansions and homes in this neighborhood. When the rich meander out of their fortresses, they wander down to Union Street and join the yuppies and the young who frequent the street's long stretch of chic boutiques and lively neighborhood restaurants, cafes, and bars.

Japantown Bounded by Octavia, Fillmore, California, and Geary, Japantown shelters only a small percentage of the city's Japanese population, but exploring these few square blocks and the shops and restaurants within them is still a cultural experience.

Civic Center Although millions of dollars have gone toward brick sidewalks, ornate lampposts, and elaborate street plantings, the southwestern section of Market Street can still feel a little sketchy due to the large number of homeless who wander the area. The Civic Center at the "bottom" of Market Street, however, is a stunning beacon of culture and refinement. This large complex of buildings includes the domed and dapper City Hall, the Opera House, Davies Symphony Hall, and the Asian Art Museum. The landscaped plaza connecting the buildings is the staging area for San Francisco's frequent demonstrations for or against just about everything.

SoMa No part of San Francisco has been more affected by recent development than the area south of Market Street (dubbed "SoMa"), the area within the triangle of The Embarcadero, Highway 101, and Market Street. Until a decade ago it was a district of old warehouses and industrial spaces, with a few scattered underground nightclubs, restaurants, and shoddy residential areas. But when it became the hub of dot-commercialization and half-million-dollar-plus lofts, its fate changed forever. Today, though dot-coms don't occupy much of the commercial space, the area is jumping thanks to fancy loft residents, the baseball stadium, and surrounding businesses, restaurants, and nightclubs in addition to urban entertainment a la the Museum of Modern Art, Yerba Buena Gardens, Metreon, and a slew of big-bucks hotels that make tons of money from businesspeople. Though still gritty in some areas, it's growing more glittery by the year.

Mission District This is another area that was greatly affected by the city's new wealth. The Mexican and Latin American populations here, with their cuisine, traditions, and art, make the Mission District a vibrant area to visit. Some parts of the neighborhood are still poor and sprinkled with the homeless, gangs, and drug addicts, but young urbanites have also settled in the area, attracted by its "reasonably" (a relative term) priced rentals and endless oh-so-hot restaurants and bars that stretch from 16th and Valencia streets to 25th and Mission streets. Less adventurous tourists may just want to duck into Mission Dolores, cruise by a few of the 200-plus amazing murals, and head back downtown. But anyone who's interested in hanging with the hipsters and experiencing the hottest restaurant and bar nightlife should definitely beeline it here. Don't be afraid to visit this area, but do use caution at night.

The Castro One of the liveliest streets in town, the Castro is practically synonymous with San Francisco's gay community (even though it is technically a street in the Noe Valley District). Located at the very end of Market Street, between 17th and 18th streets, the Castro has dozens of shops, restaurants, and bars catering to the gay community. Open-minded straight people are welcome, too.

Haight-Ashbury Part trendy, part nostalgic, part funky, the Haight, as it's most commonly known, was the soul of the psychedelic, free-loving 1960s and the center of the counterculture movement. Today, the gritty neighborhood straddling upper Haight Street on the eastern border of Golden Gate Park is more gentrified, but the commercial area still harbors all walks of life. Leftover aging hippies mingle with grungy, begging street kids outside Ben & Jerry's Ice Cream Store (where they might still be talking about Jerry Garcia), nondescript marijuana dealers whisper "Buds" as shoppers pass, and many people walking down the street have Day-Glo hair. But you don't need to be a freak or wear tie-dye to enjoy the Haight—the ethnic food, trendy shops, and bars cover all tastes. From Haight Street, walk south on Cole Street for a more peaceful and quaint neighborhood experience.

Richmond & Sunset Districts San Francisco's suburbs of sorts, these are the city's largest and most populous neighborhoods, consisting mainly of small (but expensive) homes, shops, and neighborhood restaurants. Although they border Golden Gate Park and Ocean Beach, few tourists venture into "The Avenues," as these areas are referred to locally, unless they're on their way to the Cliff House, zoo, or the Palace of the Legion of Honor.

2 Getting Around

For a map of San Francisco's public transportation options, see the "San Francisco Mass Transit" color map in the insert of this book. You can also call 511 for current transportation and traffic information or check www.511.org.

BY PUBLIC TRANSPORTATION

The **San Francisco Municipal Railway,** 401 Van Ness Ave., better known as "Muni" (© **415/673-6864;** www.sfmuni.com), operates the city's cable cars, buses, and streetcars. Together, these three services crisscross the entire city. Fares for buses and streetcars are $1.50 for adults and 50¢ for seniors over 65, children 5 to 17, and riders with disabilities. Cable cars, which run from 6:30am to 12:50am, cost a whopping $5 for all people over 5 ($1 for seniors and riders with disabilities between 9pm–7am). Needless to say, they're packed primarily with tourists. Exact change is required on all vehicles except cable cars. Fares are subject to change. If you're standing waiting for Muni and have wireless Web access (or from any computer), check www.nextmuni. com to get up-to-the-minute information about when the next bus or streetcar is coming. Muni's NextBus uses satellite technology and advanced computer modeling to track vehicles on their routes. Each vehicle is fitted with a satellite tracking system so the information is constantly updated.

For detailed route information, phone Muni or consult the Muni map at the front of the San Francisco Yellow Pages. If you plan to use public transportation extensively, you might want to invest in a comprehensive transit and city map ($2), sold at the San Francisco Visitor Information Center (p. 40), Powell/Market cable car booth, and many downtown retail outlets. Also, see the "Muni Discounts" box for more information.

CABLE CAR   San Francisco's cable cars might not be the most practical means of transport, but the rolling historic landmarks are a fun ride. The three lines are concentrated in the downtown area. The most scenic, and exciting, is the **Powell-Hyde line,** which follows a zigzag route from the corner of Powell and Market streets, over both Nob Hill and Russian Hill, to a turntable at gaslit Victorian Square in front of Aquatic Park. The **Powell-Mason line** starts at the same intersection and climbs Nob Hill before descending to Bay Street, just 3 blocks from Fisherman's Wharf. The least scenic is the **California Street line,** which begins at the foot of Market Street and runs a straight course through Chinatown and over Nob Hill to Van Ness Avenue. All riders must exit at the last stop and wait in line for the return trip. The cable car system operates from approximately 6:30am to 12:50am, and each ride costs $5.

BUS   Buses reach almost every corner of San Francisco and beyond—they even travel over the bridges to Marin County and Oakland. Overhead electric cables power some buses; others use conventional gas engines. All are numbered and display their destinations on the front. Signs, curb markings, and yellow bands on adjacent utility poles designate stops, and most bus shelters exhibit Muni's transportation map and schedule. Many buses travel along Market Street or pass near Union Square and run from about 6am to midnight. After midnight, there is infrequent all-night "Owl" service. For safety, avoid taking buses late at night.

Popular tourist routes include bus nos. 5, 7, and 71, all of which run to Golden Gate Park; 41 and 45, which travel along Union Street; and 30, which runs between Union Square and Ghirardelli Square. A bus ride costs $1.50 for adults and 50¢ for seniors over 65, children 5 to 17, and riders with disabilities.

STREETCAR   Five of Muni's six streetcar lines, designated J, K, L, M, and N, run underground downtown and on the streets in the outer neighborhoods. The sleek rail cars make the same stops as BART (see below) along Market Street, including

(Value) Muni Discounts

Muni discount passes, called **Passports,** entitle holders to unlimited rides on buses, streetcars, and cable cars. A Passport costs $11 for 1 day, $18 for 3 days, and $24 for 7 consecutive days. Muni's **City Pass,** which costs $42 for adults and $34 for kids 5 to 17, entitles you to unlimited rides for 7 days, plus admission to the California Academy of Sciences, Palace of the Legion of Honor, Steinhart Aquarium, Museum of Modern Art, Exploratorium, Asian Art Museum, de Young Museum, and Blue & Gold Fleet Bay or Alcatraz cruises for 9 days. You can buy a Passport or City Pass online (www.sfmuni.com/passes), or at the San Francisco Visitor Information Center, Powell/Market cable car booth, Holiday Inn Civic Center, and TIX Bay Area booth at Union Square, among other outlets. But to include the Blue & Gold Fleet tour, you must purchase tickets through them by calling Blue & Gold Fleet at ℂ **415/705-5555.** A $2.25 fee applies when you get your tickets through this phone service.

Embarcadero Station (in the Financial District), Montgomery and Powell streets (both near Union Square), and the Civic Center (near City Hall). Past the Civic Center, the routes branch off: The J line takes you to Mission Dolores; the K, L, and M lines run to Castro Street; and the N line parallels Golden Gate Park and extends all the way to The Embarcadero and AT&T Park. Streetcars run about every 15 minutes, more frequently during rush hours. They operate Monday through Friday from 5am to 12:15am, Saturday from 6am to approximately 12:15am, and Sunday from approximately 8am to 12:20am. The L and N lines operate 24 hours a day, 7 days a week, but late at night, regular buses trace the L and N routes, which are normally underground, from atop the city streets. Because the operation is part of Muni, the fares are the same as for buses, and passes are accepted.

The most recent new line to this system is not a newcomer at all, but is, in fact, an encore performance of San Francisco's beloved rejuvenated 1930s streetcar. The beautiful, retro multicolored F-Market streetcar runs from 17th and Castro streets to Beach and Jones streets; every other streetcar continues to Jones and Beach streets in Fisherman's Wharf. This is a quick and charming way to get up- and downtown without any hassle.

BART BART, an acronym for **Bay Area Rapid Transit** (ℂ **415/989-2278;** www.bart.gov), is a futuristic-looking, high-speed rail network that connects San Francisco with the East Bay—Oakland, Richmond, Concord, and Fremont. Four stations are on Market Street (see "Streetcar," above). Fares range from $1.45 to $7.35, depending on how far you go. Machines in the stations dispense tickets that are magnetically encoded with a dollar amount. Computerized exits automatically deduct the correct fare. Children 4 and under ride free. Trains run every 15 to 20 minutes, Monday through Friday from 4am to midnight, Saturday from 6am to midnight, and Sunday from 8am to midnight. In keeping with its futuristic look, BART now offers online trip planners that you can download to your PDA, iPod, or phone.

The 33-mile BART extension, which extends all the way to San Francisco International Airport, opened in June 2003. See the "Getting There" section in chapter 2, beginning on p. 23, for information on getting into town from the airport.

BY TAXI

This isn't New York, so don't expect a taxi to appear whenever you need one—if at all. If you're downtown during rush hour or leaving a major hotel, it won't be hard to hail a cab; just look for the lighted sign on the roof that indicates the vehicle is free. Otherwise, it's a good idea to call one of the following companies to arrange a ride; even then, there's been more than one time when the cab never came for me. What to do? Call back if your cab is late and insist on attention, but don't expect prompt results on weekends, no matter how nicely you ask. The companies are: **Veteran's Cab** (© 415/ 552-1300), **Luxor Cabs** (© 415/282-4141), and **Yellow Cab** (© 415/626-2345). Rates are approximately $2.85 for the first mile and 45¢ each fifth of a mile thereafter.

BY CAR

You don't need a car to explore downtown San Francisco. In fact, with the city becoming more crowded by the minute, a car can be your worst nightmare—you're likely to end up stuck in traffic with lots of aggressive and frustrated drivers, pay upwards of $30 a day to park (plus a whopping new 14% parking lot tax), and spend a good portion of your vacation looking for a parking space. Don't bother. However, if you want to venture outside the city, driving is the best way to go.

Before heading outside the city, especially in winter, call © **800/427-7623** for California **road conditions.** You can also call 511 for current traffic information.

CAR RENTALS   All the major rental companies operate in the city and have desks at the airports. When we last checked, you could get a compact car for a week for anywhere from $165 to $315, including all taxes and other charges, but prices change dramatically on a daily basis and depend on which company you rent from.

Some of the national car-rental companies operating in San Francisco include **Alamo** (© 800/327-9633; www.alamo.com), **Avis** (© 800/331-1212; www. avis.com), **Budget** (© 800/527-0700; www.budget.com), **Dollar** (© 800/800-4000; www.dollar.com), **Enterprise** (© 800/325-8007; www.enterprise.com), **Hertz** (© 800/654-3131; www.hertz.com), **National** (© 800/227-7368; www.nationalcar. com), and **Thrifty** (© 800/367-2277; www.thrifty.com).

Car-rental rates vary even more than airline fares. Prices depend on the size of the car, where and when you pick it up and drop it off, the length of the rental period, where and how far you drive it, whether you buy insurance, and a host of other factors. A few key questions can save you hundreds of dollars, but you have to ask—reservations agents don't often volunteer money-saving information:

- Are weekend rates lower than weekday rates? Ask if the rate is the same for pickup Friday morning, for instance, as it is for Thursday night. Reservations agents won't volunteer this information, so don't be shy about asking.
- Does the agency assess a drop-off charge if you don't return the car to the same location where you picked it up?
- Are special promotional rates available? If you see an advertised price in your local newspaper, be sure to ask for that specific rate; otherwise, you could be charged the standard rate. Terms change constantly.
- Are discounts available for members of AARP, AAA, frequent-flier programs, or trade unions? If you belong to any of these organizations, you may be entitled to discounts of up to 30%.
- How much tax will be added to the rental bill? Will there be local tax and state tax?

• How much does the rental company charge to refill your gas tank if you return with the tank less than full? Most rental companies claim their prices are "competitive," but fuel is almost always cheaper in town, so you should try to allow enough time to refuel the car before returning it.

Some companies offer "refueling packages," in which you pay for an entire tank of gas upfront. The cost is usually fairly competitive with local prices, but you don't get credit for any gas remaining in the tank. If a stop at a gas station on the way to the airport will make you miss your plane, then by all means take advantage of the fuel purchase option. Otherwise, skip it.

Most agencies enforce a minimum-age requirement—usually 25. Some also have a maximum-age limit. If you're concerned that these limits might affect you, ask about rental requirements at the time of booking to avoid problems later.

Make sure you're insured. Hasty assumptions about your personal auto insurance or a rental agency's additional coverage could end up costing you tens of thousands of dollars, even if you are involved in an accident that is clearly the fault of another driver.

If you already have your own car insurance, you are most likely covered in the United States for loss of or damage to a rental car and liability in case of injury to any other party involved in an accident. Be sure to check your policy before you spend extra money (around $10 or more per day) on the **collision damage waiver (CDW),** offered by all agencies.

Most major credit cards (especially gold and platinum cards) provide some degree of coverage as well—if they were used to pay for the rental. Terms vary widely, however, so be sure to call your credit card company directly before you rent and rely on the card for coverage. If you are uninsured, your credit card may provide primary coverage as long as you decline the rental agency's insurance. If you already have insurance, your credit card may provide secondary coverage, which basically covers your deductible. However, note that *credit cards will not cover liability,* which is the cost of injury to an outside party and/or damage to an outside party's vehicle. If you do not hold an insurance policy, you should seriously consider buying additional liability insurance from your rental company, even if you decline the CDW.

Tips Safe Driving

Keep in mind the following handy driving tips:

• California law requires that both drivers and passengers wear seat belts.
• You can turn right at a red light (unless otherwise indicated), after yielding to traffic and pedestrians, and after coming to a complete stop.
• Cable cars always have the right of way, as do pedestrians at intersections and crosswalks.
• Pay attention to signs and arrows on the streets and roadways, or you might suddenly find yourself in a lane that requires exiting or turning when you want to go straight. What's more, San Francisco's many one-way streets can drive you in circles, but most road maps of the city indicate which way traffic flows.

PARKING   If you want to have a relaxing vacation, don't even attempt to find street parking on Nob Hill, in North Beach, in Chinatown, by Fisherman's Wharf, or on Telegraph Hill. Park in a garage or take a cab or a bus. If you do find street parking, pay attention to street signs that explain when you can park and for how long. Be especially careful not to park in zones that are tow areas during rush hours. And be forewarned, San Francisco has instituted a 14% parking tax, so don't be surprised by that garage fee!

Curb colors also indicate parking regulations. *Red* means no stopping or parking; *blue* is reserved for drivers with disabilities who have a California-issued disabled plate or placard; *white* means there's a 5-minute limit; *green* indicates a 10-minute limit; and *yellow* and *yellow-and-black* curbs are for commercial vehicles only. Also, don't park at a bus stop or in front of a fire hydrant, and watch out for street-cleaning signs. If you violate the law, you might get a hefty ticket or your car might be towed; to get your car back, you'll have to get a release from the nearest district police department and then go to the towing company to pick up the vehicle.

When parking on a hill, apply the hand brake, put the car in gear, and *curb your wheels*—toward the curb when facing downhill, away from the curb when facing uphill. Curbing your wheels not only prevents a possible "runaway" but also keeps you from getting a ticket—an expensive fine that is aggressively enforced.

BY FERRY

TO/FROM SAUSALITO, TIBURON, OR LARKSPUR   The **Golden Gate Ferry Service** fleet (⊘ **415/923-2000;** www.goldengateferry.com) shuttles passengers daily between the San Francisco Ferry Building, at the foot of Market Street, and downtown Sausalito and Larkspur. Service is frequent, departing at reasonable intervals every day of the year except January 1, Thanksgiving Day, and December 25. Phone or check the website for an exact schedule. The ride takes half an hour, and one-way fares are $6.45 for adults and $3.20 for seniors, passengers with disabilities, and youth 6 to 18. Children 5 and under travel free when accompanied by a full-fare paying adult (limit two children per adult). Family rates are available on weekends.

Ferries of the **Blue & Gold Fleet** (⊘ **415/773-1188** for recorded info, or 415/705-5555 for tickets; www.blueandgoldfleet.com) also provide round-trip service to downtown Sausalito and Tiburon, leaving from Fisherman's Wharf at Pier 41. The one-way cost is $8.50 for adults, $4.50 for kids 5 to 11. Boats run on a seasonal schedule; phone for departure information. Tickets can be purchased at Pier 41.

FAST FACTS: **San Francisco**

American Express For travel arrangements, traveler's checks, currency exchange, and other member services, an office is at 455 Market St., at First Street (⊘ **415/536-2600**), in the Financial District, open Monday through Friday from 9am to 5:30pm and Saturday from 10am to 2pm. To report lost or stolen traveler's checks, call ⊘ **800/221-7282.** For American Express Global Assist, call ⊘ **800/554-2639.**

Area Code The area code for San Francisco is **415;** for Oakland, Berkeley, and much of the East Bay, **510;** for the peninsula, generally **650.** Napa and Sonoma are **707.** Most phone numbers in this book are in San Francisco's 415 area code, but there's no need to dial it if you're within city limits.

Business Hours Most banks are open Monday through Friday from 9am to 5pm as well as Saturday mornings. Many banks also have ATMs for 24-hour banking (see the "Money" section, in chapter 2, beginning on p. 12).

Most stores are open Monday through Saturday from 10 or 11am to at least 6pm, with shorter hours on Sunday. But there are exceptions: Stores in China-town, Ghirardelli Square, and PIER 39 stay open much later during the tourist season, and large department stores, including Macy's and Nordstrom, keep late hours.

Most restaurants serve lunch from about 11:30am to 2:30pm and dinner from about 5:30 to 10pm. They sometimes serve later on weekends. Nightclubs and bars are usually open daily until 2am, when they are legally bound to stop serving alcohol.

Dentists In the event of a dental emergency, see your hotel concierge or con-tact the **San Francisco Dental Office,** 131 Steuart St., Suite 323 (② **415/777-5115),** between Mission and Howard streets, which offers emergency service and comprehensive dental care Monday, Tuesday, and Friday from 7:30am to 4:30pm, Wednesday and Thursday from 10:30am to 6:30pm.

Doctors **Saint Francis Memorial Hospital,** 900 Hyde St., between Bush and Pine streets on Nob Hill (② **415/353-6000),** provides emergency service 24 hours a day; no appointment is necessary. The hospital also operates a **physician-refer-ral service** (② **800/333-1355** or 415/353-6566).

Drugstores **Walgreens** pharmacies are all over town, including one at 135 Pow-ell St. (② **415/391-4433).** The store is open Monday through Friday from 7am to midnight and Saturday and Sunday from 8am to midnight; the pharmacy is open Monday through Friday from 8am to 9pm, Saturday from 9am to 5pm; it's closed on Sunday. The branch on Divisadero Street at Lombard (② **415/931-6415)** has a 24-hour pharmacy.

Earthquakes There will always be earthquakes in California, most of which you'll never notice. However, in case of a significant shaker, there are a few basic precautionary measures you should know. When you are inside a build-ing, seek cover; do not run outside. Stand under a doorway or against a wall, and stay away from windows. If you exit a building after a substantial quake, use stairwells, not elevators. If you are in your car, pull over to the side of the road and stop—but not until you are away from bridges, overpasses, telephone poles, and power lines. Stay in your car. If you're out walking, stay outside and away from trees, power lines, and the sides of buildings. If you're in an area with tall buildings, find a doorway in which to stand.

Emergencies Dial ② **911** for police, an ambulance, or the fire department; no coins are needed from a public phone.

Internet Access San Francisco is totally wired. You'll find that many cafes have wireless access, as do many hotels. Check www.wifi411.com for a huge list of

Wi-Fi hotspots—including every Starbucks coffee shop, Kinko's copy store, or McDonald's—or stop by one of the following locations around town where you can get online access, perhaps with a sandwich and a cup o' joe. You can do your laundry, listen to music, dine, and check your stocks online at SoMa's **Brainwash,** 1122 Folsom St., between Seventh and Eighth streets (✆ **415/861-FOOD;** www.brainwash.com). It's open Monday through Thursday from 7am to 11pm, Friday and Saturday from 7am to midnight, and Sunday from 8am to 11pm; rates are $3 for 20 minutes. You can't wash your clothes at **Quetzal,** 1234 Polk St., at Bush Street (✆ **415/673-4181**), but you can get a cup of coffee and a nosh while you're online for 16¢ a minute. They're open Monday through Saturday from 6:45am to 9pm and Sunday from 7:30am to 8pm. For access without the ambience, try **Copy Central,** 110 Sutter St., at Montgomery Street (✆ **415/392-6470;** www.copycentral.com), which provides access cards costing 20¢ per minute. It's open Monday through Thursday from 8am to 8pm and Friday from 8am to 7pm. Ditto **Kinko's,** 1967 Market St., near Gough Street (✆ **415/252-0864;** www.kinkos.com), which charges 25¢ per minute. Both of these companies have numerous locations around town. If you've got wireless access, you're in luck. Most major hotels have wireless access in their lobbies as well as their rooms, so if you stroll into a hotel lobby and pull up a sofa, you can almost always get instantly connected.

Laundry Most hotels offer laundry service. But if you want to save money you can easily tote your gear to a local laundromat or dry cleaner. Ask your hotel for the nearest location—they're all over town. Or for a scene with your suds, go to SoMa's **Brainwash,** 1122 Folsom St., between Seventh and Eighth streets (✆ **415/861-FOOD**). See above for hours.

Liquor Laws Liquor stores and grocery stores, as well as some drugstores, can sell packaged alcoholic beverages between 6am and 2am daily. Most restaurants, nightclubs, and bars are licensed to serve alcoholic beverages during the same hours. The legal age for purchase and consumption of alcohol is 21; proof of age is required.

Newspapers & Magazines The city's main daily is the *San Francisco Chronicle,* which is distributed throughout the city. Check out the *Chronicle*'s massive Sunday edition that includes a pink "Datebook" section—an excellent preview of the week's upcoming events. The free weekly *San Francisco Bay Guardian* (www.sfbg.com) and *San Francisco Weekly* (www.sfweekly.com), tabloids of news and listings, are indispensable for nightlife information; they're widely distributed through street-corner kiosks and at city cafes and restaurants.

Of the many free tourist-oriented publications, the most widely read are *San Francisco Guide* (www.sfguide.com), a handbook-size weekly containing maps and information on current events, and *Where San Francisco* (www.where magazine.com), a glossy regular format monthly magazine. You can find them in most hotels, shops, and restaurants in the major tourist areas.

Police For emergencies, dial ✆ **911** from any phone; no coins are needed. For other matters, call ✆ **415/553-0123.**

Post Office Dozens of post offices are located around the city. The closest to Union Square is inside the Macy's department store at 170 O'Farrell St. (✆ **800/ 275-8777** or 415/956-0131; www.usps.gov). You can pick up mail addressed to you and marked "General Delivery" (Poste Restante) at the **Civic Center Post Office Box Unit,** "General Delivery," San Francisco, CA 94142-9991 (✆ **800/275- 8777** or 415/563-7284). The street address is 101 Hyde St.

Safety San Francisco, like any other large city, has its fair share of crime, but most folks luckily don't have firsthand horror stories. In some areas, you need to exercise extra caution, particularly at night—notably the Tenderloin, the Western Addition (south of Japantown), the Mission District (especially around 16th and Mission sts.), the lower Fillmore area (also south of Japantown), around lower Haight Street, and around the Civic Center. In addition, there are a substantial number of homeless people throughout the city, with concentrations in and around Union Square, the Theater District (3 blocks west of Union Square), the Tenderloin, and Haight Street, so don't be alarmed if you're approached for spare change. Just use common sense.

For additional crime-prevention information, phone **San Francisco SAFE** (✆ **415/553-1984**).

Smoking If San Francisco is California's most European city in looks and style, the comparison stops when it comes to smoking in public. Each year, smoking laws in the city become stricter. Since 1998, smoking has been prohibited in restaurants and bars. Hotels are also offering more nonsmoking rooms, which often leaves those who like to puff out in the cold—sometimes literally.

Taxes An 8.5% sales tax is added at the register for all goods and services purchased in San Francisco. The city hotel and parking lot taxes are a whopping 14%. There is no airport tax.

Time Zone San Francisco is in the Pacific Standard Time zone, which is 8 hours behind Greenwich Mean Time and 3 hours behind Eastern Standard Time. To find out what time it is, call ✆ **415/767-8900.**

Transit Information The San Francisco Municipal Railway, better known as **Muni,** operates the city's cable cars, buses, and streetcars. For customer service, call ✆ **415/673-6864** weekdays from 6am to 8pm, weekends from 8am to 6pm. At other times, you can call this number to get recorded information. Also see the "Getting Around" section earlier in this chapter, beginning on p. 44 for information on all of San Francisco's transit options. You can also call 511 for transportation, traffic, ridesharing, and bicycling information.

Where to Stay

Whether you want a room with a view or just a room, San Francisco is more than accommodating to its 15.7 million annual guests. Most of the city's 200-plus hotels cluster near Union Square, but some smaller independent gems are scattered around town.

When reading over your options, keep in mind that prices listed are "rack" (published) rates. At big, upscale hotels, almost no one actually pays them—and with the dramatic travel downturn over the past few years, there are still deals to be had. Therefore, you should always ask for special discounts or, even better, vacation packages. It's often possible to get the room you want for $100 less than what is quoted here, except when the hotels are packed (usually during summer and due to conventions) and bargaining is close to impossible. Use the rates listed here for the big hotels as guidelines for comparison only; prices for inexpensive choices and smaller B&Bs are closer to reality, though.

Hunting for hotels in San Francisco can be a tricky business, particularly if you're not a seasoned traveler. What you don't know—and the reservations agent may not tell you—could very well ruin your vacation, so keep the following pointers in mind when it comes time to book a room:

- Prices listed below do not include state and city taxes, which total 14%. Other hidden extras include parking fees, which can be up to $45 per day (also subject to 14% tax!), and hefty surcharges—up to $1 per local call— for telephone use.
- San Francisco is Convention City, so if you want a room at a particular hotel during high season (summer, for example), book well in advance.
- Be sure to have a credit card in hand when making a reservation, and know that you may be asked to pay for at least 1 night in advance (this doesn't happen often, though).

Pricing Categories

The accommodations listed below are classified first by area, and then by price, using the following categories: **Very Expensive**, more than $250 per night; **Expensive**, $200 to $250 per night; **Moderate**, $150 to $200 per night; and **Inexpensive**, less than $150 per night. These categories reflect the rack rates for an average double room during the high season, which runs approximately from April to September.

- Hotels usually hold reservations until 6pm. If you don't tell the staff you're arriving late, you might lose your room.
- Almost every hotel in San Francisco requires a credit card imprint for "incidentals" (and to prevent walkouts). If you don't have a credit card, be sure to make special arrangements with the management before you hang up the phone, and make a note of the name of the person you spoke with.
- When you check in, if your room isn't up to snuff, politely inform the front desk of your dissatisfaction and ask for another. If the hotel can accommodate you, they almost always will—and sometimes will even upgrade you!

Read the following entries carefully: Many hotels also offer rooms at rates above and below the price category that applies to most of the units. If you like the sound of a place that's a bit over your budget, it never hurts to call and ask a few questions. Also note that we do not list single rates. Some hotels, particularly more affordable choices, do charge lower rates for singles, so inquire about them if you are traveling alone.

San Francisco is a wildly popular destination year-round so though there are bargains available, rooms here will still seem expensive compared to many other U.S. destinations. Still, you should always ask about weekend discounts, corporate rates, and family plans; most larger hotels, and many smaller ones, offer them, but many reservations agents don't mention them unless you ask about them specifically.

You'll find nonsmoking rooms available in all larger hotels and many smaller hotels; reviews indicate establishments that are entirely nonsmoking. Nowadays, the best advice for smokers is to confirm a smoking-permitted room in advance.

While you'll find that most accommodations have an abundance of amenities (including phones, unless otherwise noted), don't be alarmed by the lack of air-conditioned guest rooms. San Francisco weather is so mild, you'll never miss them.

Most larger hotels can accommodate guests who use wheelchairs and those who have other special needs. Ask when you make a reservation to ensure that your hotel can accommodate your needs, especially if you are interested in a bed-and-breakfast.

HELPING HANDS Having reservations about your reservations? Leave it up to the pros:

San Francisco Reservations, 360 22nd St., Suite 300, Oakland, CA 94612 (© **800/677-1500** or 510/628-4450; www.hotelres.com), arranges reservations for more than 150 of San Francisco's hotels and often offers discounted rates. Their nifty website allows Internet users to make reservations online.

Other good online sites with discounted rates include **www.hotels.com** and **www.placestostay.com**.

Value Dial Direct

When booking a room in a chain hotel, call the hotel's local line and the toll-free number and see where you get the best deal. A hotel makes nothing on a room that stays empty. The clerk who runs the place is more likely to know about vacancies than someone from the toll-free number and will often grant deep discounts in order to fill up rooms.

Tips **Get the Latest on Hotels**

Whenever I'm booking a room somewhere I haven't stayed before, I always check out www.TripAdvisor.com. Its unsolicited traveler reviews paint a full picture, provide a broad range of opinions, and give what I've found to be an excellent and trustworthy consensus.

---

1 The Best Hotel Bets

- **Best for Families:** Kids like the **Westin St. Francis,** 335 Powell St. (② 800/WESTIN-1 or 415/397-7000), because upon arrival, children under 12 get the travel-themed Westin Kids Club backpack filled with a make-your-own postcard kit, colored pencils, a travelogue, map of the world, and safari hat. Parents with babies get a rubber duck, night light, and an emergency kit. **The Fairmont Hotel & Tower,** 950 Mason St. (② 800/441-1414 or 415/772-5000), lets kids be a Doorman for a Day and wear a pint-size doorman's hat; they also get a miniwhistle and a camera to keep. At the nautically themed **Argonaut,** 495 Jefferson St. (② 866/415-0704 or 415/563-0800), kids get to pick a toy out of the "treasure chest" and parents will appreciate the free cribs and strollers. But the place kids will probably love the most is the **Hotel del Sol,** 3100 Webster St. (② 877/433-5765 or 415/921-5520), with its Kids are VIPs program that includes a lending library of books, toys, and videos; evening cookies and milk; and a plethora of toys to use by the heated outdoor pool. Parents will love the bonded babysitting services and the three babyproofed rooms, among many other perks for families. See p. 59, 74, 88, and 91, respectively.
- **Best for Romance:** Check out the whimsical and affordable **The Archbishop's Mansion,** 1000 Fulton St. (② 800/543-5820 or 415/563-7872); boutique spot **The Hotel Bohème,** 444 Columbus Ave. (② 415/433-9111); and old-world elegant **The Hotel Majestic,** 1500 Sutter St. (② 800/869-8966 or 415/441-1100). See p. 93, 89, and 95, respectively.
- **Best Public Space in a Historic Hotel: The Palace Hotel,** 2 New Montgomery St. (② 800/325-3589 or 415/512-1111), the extravagant creation of banker "Bonanza King" Will Ralston in 1875, has one of the grandest rooms in the city: the Garden Court. See p. 82. Running a close second is the magnificent lobby at Nob Hill's **The Fairmont Hotel & Tower,** 950 Mason St. (② 800/441-1414 or 415/772-5000). See p. 74.
- **Best Trendy Scene:** If you want to shack up with the tragically hip, head to **Clift Hotel,** 495 Geary St. (② 800/652-5438 or 415/775-4700), which promises upscale flirting at its bar, the Redwood Room. See p. 56. Less chichi and funkier in style and location is **The Phoenix Hotel,** 601 Eddy St. (② 800/248-9466 or 415/776-1380), where guests lounge poolside or hang at the too-cool Bambuddha Lounge. See p. 95.
- **Best Service and Amenities:** As usual, **The Ritz-Carlton,** 600 Stockton St. (② 800/241-3333 or 415/296-7465), corners the market in ultimate luxury, from its stunning ground-floor bathrooms to its fabulous restaurant to everything in between. Of course such pampering comes at a cost, but if you can afford it,

it's worth the splurge. See p. 75. While it doesn't have quite the number of perks that the Ritz has, the brand-new **St. Regis Hotel,** 125 Third St. (℡ **877/787-3447** or 415/284-4000), is one flat-out fabulous place to sleep. From its state-of-the-art rooms swathed in browns and creams to its huge spa, gym, hopping bar scene, and destination-restaurant Ame—not to mention its location next to the Museum of Modern Art—it's hot, hot, hot.

2 Union Square

VERY EXPENSIVE

Campton Place Hotel ✦✦   With a $15-million room renovation completed at the end of 2001, this already fabulous luxury boutique hotel offers some of the best accommodations in town—not to mention the most expensive. Rooms are compact but comfy, with limestone, pear wood, and Italian-modern decor. The two executive suites and one luxury suite push the haute envelope to even more luxurious heights. Discriminating returning guests will still find superlative service, California king-size beds, exquisite bathrooms, bathrobes, top-notch toiletries, slippers, and every other necessity and extra that's made Campton Place a favored temporary address. Alas, Campton Place Restaurant, which underwent a glamorous face-lift in 2002, lost its award-winning chef Daniel Humm in 2005, but the restaurant still offers a seasonal French/California menu. The jury's still out on whether it's a destination in its own right.

340 Stockton St. (between Post and Sutter sts.), San Francisco, CA 94108. ℡ **800/235-4300** or 415/781-5555. Fax 415/955-5536. www.camptonplace.com. 110 units. $340–$475 double; from $575–$2,000 suite. American breakfast $18. AE, DC, MC, V. Valet parking $38. Bus: 2, 3, 4, 30, 38, or 45. Cable car: Powell–Hyde or Powell–Mason lines (1 block west). BART and underground: Market St. **Amenities:** Restaurant; outdoor fitness terrace; concierge; secretarial services; room service; laundry service; same-day dry cleaning. *In room:* A/C, TV w/pay movies, dataport, minibar, hair dryer, iron, safe, T1 line.

Clift Hotel ✦   Ian Schrager, king of such ultrahip hotels as New York's Royalton and Paramount, L.A.'s Mondrian, and Miami's Delano, renovated this classic old luxury property in 2001 for trendy hipness. Young trendsetters flock here for overpriced monochrome lavender streamlined rooms with often-minuscule bathrooms, glamorous atmosphere, and a heavy dose of attitude. Its best attribute is the renovated historic Redwood Room, complete with sexy redwood walls (all made from one tree!) and deco lighting from 1933 and a luxurious and rather uncomfortable interior designed by Philippe Starck. The equally trendy, expensive, and mediocre Asia de Cuba restaurant adjoins the swank lounge. If you ask me, the only reason to pay the high prices here is if you're interested in being surrounded by the young and hip. Otherwise, there are far better rooms around town at a similar or lower price.

495 Geary St. (at Taylor St.), San Francisco, CA 94102. ℡ **800/652-5438** or 415/775-4700. Fax 415/441-4621. www.morganshotelgroup.com. 363 units. $325–$460 double; from $455 studio suite; from $950 deluxe suite. AE, DC, DISC, MC, V. Valet parking $45. Bus: 2, 3, 4, 30, 38, or 45. Cable car: Powell–Hyde or Powell–Mason lines (2 blocks east). **Amenities:** Restaurant; bar; exercise room; concierge; room service; same-day laundry service/dry cleaning. *In room:* TV/DVD, minibar, hair dryer, Wi-Fi ($10/day).

Fun Fact **Inflation at the Clift**

The Clift Hotel charged a mere $2 per night when it first opened in 1915. The price for a room now? More than $325.

Where to Stay near Union Square & Nob Hill

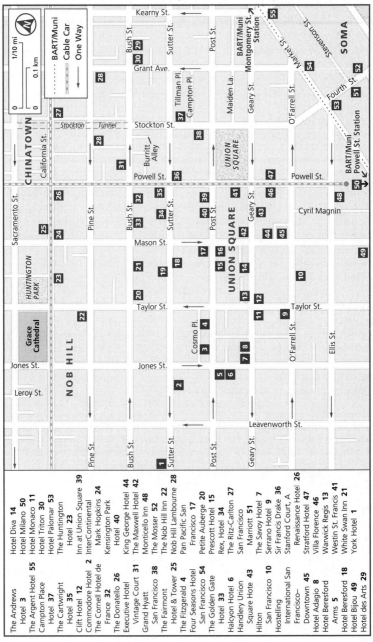

Legend:
- ░░░ BART/Muni
- ▦▦▦ Cable Car
- → One Way

Scale: 0 — 1/10 mi / 0 — 0.1 km

Map labels: Kearny St., Bush St., Sutter St., Post St., BART/Muni Montgomery St. Station, Market St., Stevenson St., SOMA, Grant Ave., Tillman Pl., Campton Pl., Maiden La., Geary St., O'Farrell St., Fourth St., CHINATOWN, Stockton Tunnel, Stockton St., Burritt Alley, UNION SQUARE, Powell St., BART/Muni Powell St. Station, California St., Sacramento St., Pine St., Bush St., Sutter St., Post St., Geary St., Cyril Magnin, HUNTINGTON PARK, Mason St., Grace Cathedral, NOB HILL, Taylor St., Cosmo Pl., Jones St., Leroy St., O'Farrell St., Ellis St., Leavenworth St.

The Andrews Hotel **3**
The Argent Hotel **55**
Campton Place Hotel **37**
The Cartwright Hotel **35**
Clift Hotel **12**
Commodore Hotel **2**
The Cornell Hotel de France **32**
The Donatello **26**
Executive Hotel Vintage Court **31**
Grand Hyatt San Francisco **38**
The Fairmont Hotel & Tower **25**
The Fitzgerald **4**
Four Seasons Hotel San Francisco **54**
The Golden Gate Hotel **33**
Halcyon Hotel **6**
Handlery Union Square Hote **43**
Hilton San Francisco **10**
Hostelling International San Francisco–Downtown **45**
Hotel Adagio **8**
Hotel Beresford **13**
Hotel Beresford Arms **5**
Hotel Bijou **49**
Hotel des Arts **29**
Hotel Diva **14**
Hotel Milano **50**
Hotel Monaco **11**
Hotel Triton **30**
Hotel Palomar **53**
The Huntington Hotel **23**
Inn at Union Square **39**
InterContinental Mark Hopkins **24**
Kensington Park Hotel **40**
King George Hotel **44**
The Maxwell Hotel **42**
Monticello Inn **48**
The Mosser **52**
The Nob Hill Inn **22**
Nob Hill Lambourne **28**
Pan Pacific San Francisco **17**
Petite Auberge **20**
Prescott Hotel **15**
Rex, Hotel **34**
The Ritz-Carlton San Francisco **27**
San Francisco Marriott **51**
The Savoy Hotel **7**
Serrano Hotel **9**
Sir Francis Drake **36**
Stanford Court, A Renaissance Hotel **26**
Stratford Hotel **47**
Villa Florence **46**
Warwick Regis **13**
Westin St. Francis **41**
White Swan Inn **21**
York Hotel **1**

The Donatello *Finds* *Value*   If you're not looking for trendy lodgings or an anonymous business hotel but want old-world elegance, book a room here. The Donatello is, in a word, dignified. The lobby is classy, with Italian marble and a serious staff. The airy, contemporary Art Nouveau rooms, which are some of the largest in the city (an average of 400 sq. ft.!), were overhauled in 2006 with new bedding, carpet, and furniture and feature original art, king-size mattresses, and textiles. Unfortunately, most of the extra large windows lack great views, but if it's fresh air you're after, the fifth floor has seven terrace rooms.

501 Post St. (at Mason St.), San Francisco, CA 94102. © 800/227-3184 or 415/441-7100. Fax 415/885-8842. 94 units. $139–$295 double. Children under 12 stay free in parent's room. AE, DC, DISC, MC, V. Valet parking $28. Bus: 2, 3, 4, 30, 38, or 45. Cable car: Powell–Hyde or Powell–Mason lines (1 block west). **Amenities:** Restaurant; bar; exercise room; concierge; limited room service; same-day laundry service/dry cleaning; 2 meeting spaces. *In room:* A/C, TV w/pay movies, dataport, fridge, microwave, toaster, coffeemaker, hair dryer, iron, free Wi-Fi, CD player.

Grand Hyatt San Francisco *Finds*   If the thought of a 10-second walk to Saks Fifth Avenue makes your pulse race, this high-rise luxury hotel is the place for you. The Grand Hyatt sits amid all the downtown shopping while also boasting some of the best views in the area. The lobby is indeed grand, with Chinese artifacts and enormous ceramic vases. Thankfully, the well-kept rooms were recently renovated; they're swankier than they used to be, and now feature the Hyatt's signature Grand Bed with pillow top mattresses, ultraplush pillows and down (or down alternative) duvets. Each room has a lounge chair as well as a small desk and sitting area. Views from most of the 36 floors are truly spectacular.

Rates for concierge-level Regency Club rooms ($50 extra) include access to the lounge, honor bar, continental breakfast, and evening hors d'oeuvres. Three floors hold business-plan guest rooms, which for $25 extra get you 24-hour access to a printer, a photocopier, and office supplies; free local calls and credit card phone access; and a daily newspaper.

345 Stockton St. (between Post and Sutter sts.), San Francisco, CA 94108. © 800/233-1234 or 415/398-1234. Fax 415/391-1780. www.sanfrancisco.grand.hyatt.com. 685 units. $159–$319 double; Regency Club $50 additional. AE, DC, DISC, MC, V. Valet parking $41. Bus: 2, 3, 4, 30, 38, or 45. Cable car: Powell–Hyde or Powell–Mason lines (2 blocks west). **Amenities:** Restaurant; bar; health club; concierge; business center; secretarial services; limited room service; laundry service; same-day dry cleaning; Wi-Fi in public areas. *In room:* A/C, TV w/pay movies, dataport, minibar, coffeemaker, hair dryer, iron, safe, high-speed Internet access ($9.95/day), 2 phone lines with speaker capability.

Hotel Monaco *Finds*   This remodeled 1910 Beaux Arts building has plenty of atmosphere thanks to a whimsically ethereal lobby with a two-story French inglenook fireplace. The guest rooms, which were upgraded in 2006, follow suit, with canopy beds, Asian-inspired armoires, bamboo writing desks, lively stripes, and vibrant color. Everything is bold but tasteful, and as playful as it is serious, with nifty extras like flatscreen TVs, complimentary high-speed wireless Internet access and Wi-Fi, and two-line cordless phones. The decor, combined with the truly grand neighboring Grand Café restaurant that's ideal for cocktails and mingling (but also serves breakfast and lunch), would put this place on my top-10 list if it weren't for rooms that tend to be way too small (especially for the price) and the lack of a sizable gym. That said, it's a fine Union Square option, which happens to include complimentary wine and cheese tasting accompanied by shoulder and neck massages.

501 Geary St. (at Taylor St.), San Francisco, CA 94102. © 800/214-4220 or 415/292-0100. Fax 415/292-0111. www.hotelmonaco-sf.com. 201 units. $209–$399 double; $269–$599 suite. Rates include evening wine and cheese tasting. Call for discounted rates. AE, DC, DISC, MC, V. Valet parking $39. Bus: 2, 3, 4, 27, or 38. Pets accepted.

Amenities: Restaurant; exercise room; spa; Jacuzzi; sauna; steam room; concierge; courtesy car; business center; room service; in-room massage; laundry service; dry cleaning. *In room:* A/C, TV, dataport, minibar, coffeemaker with Starbucks coffee, hair dryer, iron, safe, Wi-Fi, CD player.

Pan Pacific San Francisco 🏵🏵 The Pan Pacific—located conveniently close to Union Square—is artistically glitzy, enormous, and somehow romantic, all at the same time. Elegance starts in the gigantic (and a tiny bit convention-hotel-like) third-floor atrium lobby, which was spiffed up with all new furniture in 2006, and features views of the skylight ceiling another 18 floors up, a marble fountain with four dancing figures, a player piano, and a fireplace. Major room updating in 2004 means each rather large abode is now swathed in chic, contemporary, and tasteful decor and adorned with flatscreen TVs and Herman Miller chairs. The bathrooms remain regal and lavishly marble-clad with a mini-TV at the sink and cozy bathrobes. Other 2004 renovations included an improved fitness center and business center.

500 Post St. (at Mason St.), San Francisco, CA 94102. 📞 **800/533-6465** or 415/771-8600. Fax 415/398-0267. www.panpacific.com. 338 units. $289–$339 double; from $495 suite. AE, DC, DISC, MC, V. Valet parking $42. Bus: 2, 3, 4, 30, 38, or 45. Cable car: Powell–Hyde or Powell–Mason lines. **Amenities:** Restaurant; bar; fitness room; concierge; business center; room service; in-room massage; laundry service; same-day dry cleaning; butler service. *In room:* A/C, flatscreen TV, fax, dataport, minibar, hair dryer, iron, safe, high-speed Internet access and Wi-Fi for $9.95.

Prescott Hotel 🏵🏵 It may be small and lack common areas, but the boutique Prescott Hotel has some big things going for it. The staff treats you like royalty, rooms are attractively unfrilly and masculine (not to mention updated in 2004), the location (just a block from Union Square) is perfect, and limited room service is provided by Wolfgang Puck's restaurant Postrio. Ralph Lauren fabrics in dark tones of green, plum, and burgundy and crisp white Italian linens blend well with the cherrywood furnishings in each of the soundproof rooms; the view, alas, isn't so pleasant. The very small bathrooms contain terry robes and Aveda products, and the suites have Jacuzzi bathtubs. Concierge-level guests are pampered with a free continental breakfast and evening cocktails and hors d'oeuvres.

545 Post St. (between Mason and Taylor sts.), San Francisco, CA 94102. 📞 **866/271-3632** or 415/563-0303. Fax 415/563-6831. www.prescotthotel.com. 164 units. $235–$340 double; $270 concierge-level double (including breakfast and evening cocktail reception); from $365 suite. AE, DC, DISC, MC, V. Valet parking $40. Bus: 2, 3, 4, 30, 38, or 45. Cable car: Powell–Hyde or Powell–Mason lines (1 block east). **Amenities:** Restaurant; bar; small exercise room; concierge; limited courtesy car; limited room service. *In room:* TV w/pay movies, dataport, minibar, hair dryer, iron, safe, high-speed wireless Internet access, video games.

Westin St. Francis 🏵🏵 *Kids* At the turn of the 20th century, Charles T. Crocker and a few of his wealthy buddies decided that San Francisco needed a world-class hotel, and up went the St. Francis. Since then, hordes of VIPs have hung their hats and hosiery here, including Emperor Hirohito of Japan, Queen Elizabeth II of England, Mother Teresa, King Juan Carlos of Spain, the shah of Iran, and all the U.S. presidents from Taft through Clinton. In 1972, the hotel gained the 32-story Tower, doubling its capacity and adding banquet and conference centers. The older rooms of the main building vary in size and have more old-world charm than the newer rooms, but the Tower is remarkable for its great views of the city (including from the glass elevators) from above the 18th floor.

Although the St. Francis is too massive to offer the personal service you get at the smaller deluxe hotels on Nob Hill, few other hotels in San Francisco can match its majestic aura. Stroll through the vast, ornate lobby, and you can feel 100 years of history oozing from its hand-carved redwood paneling. The hotel has done massive renovations costing $185 million over the past decade, replacing the carpeting, furniture, and bedding in every main-building guest room; gussying up the lobby; restoring the facade; and adding the hottest downtown dining spot, the very expensive and fancy Michael Mina (p. 106).

The Westin makes kids feel right at home, too, with a goody bag upon check-in. The tower's Grandview Rooms evoke a contemporary design along the lines of the W Hotel. The historic main building accentuates its history with traditional, more elegant ambience, high ceilings, and crown molding. Alas, the venerable Compass Rose tearoom is no longer, so don't drop by for some Darjeeling and snacks.

(*Fun Fact* **Hotel Rendezvous**

For nearly a century, the most popular place for visitors to rendezvous in San Francisco has been under the magnificent hand-carved grandfather clock in the lobby of the Westin St. Francis hotel.

---

335 Powell St. (between Geary and Post sts.), San Francisco, CA 94102. (*©*) **800/WESTIN-1** or 415/397-7000. Fax 415/774-0124. www.westin.com. 1,195 units. Main building: $199–$499 double; Tower (Grand View): $219–$549 double; from $650 suite (in either building). Extra person $30. Continental breakfast $15–$18. AE, DC, DISC, MC, V. Valet parking $42. Bus: 2, 3, 4, 30, 38, 45, or 76. Cable car: Powell–Hyde or Powell–Mason lines (direct stop). Pets under 40 lb. accepted (dog beds available on request). **Amenities:** 2 restaurants; elaborate health club and spa; concierge; car-rental desk; business center; room service. *In room:* A/C, TV, dataport, minibar, fridge available upon request, hair dryer, iron, high-speed Internet access ($15), Wi-Fi ($9.95/day), cordless phones.

EXPENSIVE

Handlery Union Square Hotel *꒰* *Kids*   A mere half-block from Union Square, the Handlery was already a good deal frequented by European travelers before the 1908 building underwent a complete overhaul a few years ago. Now you'll find every amenity you could possibly need, plus lots of extras, in the extremely tasteful and modern (although sedate and a little dark) rooms. Rooms range from coral and gray in the historic building to taupe and tan in the newer club-level building. In between is a heated outdoor pool. Literally everything was replaced in the rooms: mattresses, alarm radios, refrigerators, light fixtures, paint, carpets, and furnishings. Perks include adjoining L.A.-based chain restaurant The Daily Grill (which is unfortunately not as tasty as its sister restaurants down south) and club-level options (all in the newer building) that include larger rooms, a complimentary morning newspaper, a bathroom scale, robes, two, two-line phones, and adjoining doors that make the units great choices for families. Downsides? Not a lot of direct light, no grand feeling in the lobby, and lots of trekking if you want to go to and from the adjoining buildings that make up the hotel. All in all, it's a good value for downtown, but, personally, this would be a choice second to the less expensive The Warwick Regis or Savoy.

351 Geary St. (between Mason and Powell sts.), San Francisco, CA 94102. (*©*) **800/843-4343** or 415/781-7800. Fax 415/781-0269. www.handlery.com. 377 units. $249–$269 double; Club section $249–$289 double; Owner's Suite $600. Extra person $10. AE, DC, DISC, MC, V. Parking $32. Bus: 2, 3, 4, 30, 38, or 45. Cable car: Powell–Hyde or Powell–Mason lines (direct stop). **Amenities:** Restaurant; heated outdoor swimming pool; access to nearby health club ($10/day); sauna; barbershop; room service; babysitting; same-day laundry. *In room:* Central air, TV w/Nintendo and pay movies, dataport, fridge, free coffee/tea-making facilities, hair dryer, iron, safe, Wi-Fi, voice mail.

Hilton San Francisco *꒰*   Complete with bustling conventioneers and a line to register that resembles airport check-in, the Hilton's lobby is so enormous and busy that it feels more like a convention hall than a hotel. The three connecting buildings (the original 19-story main structure, a 46-story tower topped by a panoramic restaurant, and a 23-story landmark with 386 luxurious rooms and suites) bring swarms of visitors. Even during quieter times, the sheer enormity of the place makes the Hilton somewhat overwhelming.

After you get past the sweeping grand lobby, jump on an elevator, and wind through endless corridors to your room, you're likely to find the mystique ends with clean but run-of-the-mill standard-size corporate accommodations. That said, some of the views from the floor-to-ceiling windows in the main tower's rooms are memorable. Eighty percent of the rooms were updated in 2006—complete with flatscreen TVs, updated bathrooms with walk-in showers (no tubs), and Hilton Serenity Bedding with a pillow top mattress, 200 thread count sheets, down (or down alternative) duvets, and a pillow menu that ensures you get a pillow that suits your firmness preference.

Still, the overall feel and decor of the hotel are impersonal and plain—perfect for conventioneers, but not for a romantic weekend. One bonus is the 13,000-square-foot health club and day spa. The Hilton has four restaurants: Cityscape, on the 46th floor, offers classic California cuisine and a breathtaking 360-degree view; Intermezzo serves Mediterranean-style food; The Café offers a buffet; and Kiku's of Japan offers—you guessed it—Japanese food. The Lobby Bar also offers bar snacks.

333 O'Farrell St. (between Mason and Taylor sts.), San Francisco, CA 94102. © 800/HILTONS or 415/771-1400. Fax 415/771-6807. www.sanfrancisco.hilton.com. 1,908 units. $195–$409 double; $315–$3,700 junior suite. Children stay free in parent's room. AE, DC, DISC, MC, V. Parking $36–$41 (some oversize vehicles cannot be accommodated, depending on height). Bus: 2, 3, 4, 7, 9, 21, 27, 30, 38, 45, or 71. Cable car: Powell–Hyde or Powell–Mason lines (1 block east). **Amenities:** 4 restaurants; bar; outdoor pool; outdoor whirlpool; health club; spa; sauna; concierge; tour desk; car-rental desk; business center; secretarial services; room service; laundry service; dry cleaning; wireless Internet access in public spaces. *In room:* A/C, 27-inch flatscreen TV, dataport, minibar, coffeemaker, hair dryer, iron, high-speed Internet access.

Hotel Milano ⚐ Neoclassical Italian design, elegantly streamlined rooms (with double-paned soundproof windows), moderate prices, and a central location next to the San Francisco Centre make Hotel Milano a popular choice for tourists and businesspeople alike. The hotel also has a film-production facility and private screening room to entice media types. Corporate travelers come for the spacious guest rooms, which feature everything an executive could want, from wireless Internet to Nintendo game systems to fax modems. Suites have spa tubs and bidets. Silky's Restaurant downstairs features Asian-fusion food.

55 Fifth St. (between Market and Mission sts.), San Francisco, CA 94103. © 800/398-7555 or 415/543-8555. Fax 415/543-5885. www.hotelmilanosf.com. 108 units. $119–$239 double. Extra person $20. AE, DC, DISC, MC, V. Valet parking $30 for midsize and $35 for SUVs. Bus: All Market St. buses. **Amenities:** Fitness room; spa; steam room and sauna; concierge; laundry; valet. *In room:* A/C, TV w/Nintendo, fax, dataport, fridge, hair dryer, iron, safe, Wi-Fi ($9.95/day).

Hotel Rex ⚐ Joie de Vivre, the most creative hotel group in the city, is the brilliance behind this restored historic building, which is near several fine galleries, theaters, and restaurants. The group kept some of the imported furnishings and the European boutique hotel ambience, but gave the lobby and rooms a $2-million face-lift at the end of 2003, adding the decorative flair that makes its hotels among the most popular in town. The clublike lobby lounge is modeled after a 1920s literary salon and is, like all the group's properties, cleverly stylish. The renovated rooms are above average in size.

If you have one of the rooms in the back, you'll look out over a shady, peaceful court-yard.

562 Sutter St. (between Powell and Mason sts.), San Francisco, CA 94102. © 800/433-4434 or 415/433-4434. Fax 415/433-3695. www.thehotelrex.com. 94 units. $249–$269 double; $400 suite. AE, DC, DISC, MC, V. Valet parking $34. Bus: 2, 3, 4, 30, 38, or 45. Cable car: Powell–Hyde or Powell–Mason lines (1 block east). **Amenities:** Access to nearby health club; concierge; business center; room service (7am–11pm); same-day laundry service/dry cleaning. In room: TV w/pay movies, dataport, minibar, hair dryer, iron, free high-speed Internet access and Wi-Fi throughout, CD player.

The Maxwell Hotel *Value Kids*   Its location, 1 block from Union Square, and chic-boutique surroundings make this 13-story 1908 hotel a favorite with business travelers, families, and die-hard shoppers. Alas, recently it's been looking a little shabby. Fortunately, a major renovation is planned for 2006 and 2007 to bring the hotel to a more upscale, boutique-hotel standard. Until then, expect the somewhat tired velvets, brocades, stripes, plaids, rich color, handcrafted artistic accents, uphol-stered chairs, hand-painted bedside lamps, writing desks, and vanities in rooms that show their age and tend to have small bathrooms. The hotel's roomy junior suites offer excellent value despite the slightly audible elevator noise, but best of all are the pair of one-bedroom suites on the 13th floor, both of which offer separate living rooms and exceptional views of the city (one has a private rooftop deck and kitchenette). Perks at The Maxwell include a foot masseuse on request for weary shoppers, discount coupons for the local department stores, and a "Kids are VIPs" program that lets par-ents rent an adjoining room for their kids at half the regular rate and tosses in some kid-friendly extras like a goody bag and crayons.

386 Geary St. (at Mason St.), San Francisco, CA 94102. © 888/734-6299 or 415/986-2000. Fax 415/986-2193. www.maxwellhotel.com. 153 units. $189–$225 double; $199–$649 suite. Extra person $15. Corporate discounts available. AE, DC, DISC, MC, V. Valet parking $30, self-parking $24. Bus: 2, 3, 4, 30, 38, or 45. Cable car: Powell–Hyde or Powell–Mason lines (1 block east). **Amenities:** Restaurant; concierge; meeting facilities; room service; dry clean-ing. In room: A/C, TV w/pay movies, hair dryer, iron, safe, wireless high-speed Internet access ($10 for 24 hr.; free for business rooms—top 4 floors), bathrobes, CD players in executive rooms and suites.

Sir Francis Drake   This venerable hotel shows signs of age despite the fact that the owners threw millions toward renovations in recent years. But the price of imperfec-tion certainly shows in the room rate: a good $100 less per night than its Nob Hill cousins. The hotel is perfect for people who are willing to trade a chipped bathroom tile, small rooms, and sometimes somewhat chilly rooms, or oddly matched furniture for the opportunity to vacation in pseudo-grand fashion right in Union Square. Allow Tom Sweeny, the ebullient (and legendary) Beefeater doorman, to handle your bags as you enter the elegant, captivating lobby and live like the king or queen of Union Square without all the pomp, circumstance, and credit card bills.

Fun Fact **A Living Legend**

Tom Sweeny, the head doorman at the Sir Francis Drake hotel, is a living San Francisco historical monument. Dressed in traditional Beefeater's attire (you can't miss those $1,400 duds), he's been the subject of countless snapshots—an average 200 per day for the past 25 years—and has shaken hands with every president since Jerry Ford.

Scala's Bistro (p. 109), one of the most festive restaurants downtown, serves good Italian cuisine in a stylish setting on the first floor; the Parisian-style Caffe Espresso does an equally commendable job serving coffees, pastries, and sandwiches daily in its spot adjacent to the hotel. The superchic Harry Denton's Starlight Room (p. 231), on the 21st floor, offers cocktails, entertainment, and dancing nightly with a panoramic view of the city.

450 Powell St. (at Sutter St.), San Francisco, CA 94102. ✆ **800/227-5480** or 415/392-7755. Fax 415/391-8719. www.sirfrancisdrake.com. 417 units. $219–$259 double; $500–$700 suite. AE, DC, DISC, MC, V. Valet parking $38. Bus: 2, 3, 4, 45, or 76. Cable car: Powell–Hyde or Powell–Mason lines (direct stop). **Amenities:** 2 restaurants; bar; exercise room; concierge; limited room service; same-day laundry service/dry cleaning; Wi-Fi. *In room:* A/C, TV w/Nintendo and pay movies, dataport, minibar, hair dryer, iron, Wi-Fi.

White Swan Inn ⭐⭐ *Value*   From the moment you're buzzed into this well-secured great-value inn, you'll know you're not in a generic bed-and-breakfast. If the nearly 50 teddy bears gracing the lobby don't cure homesickness, then the homemade cookies, tea, and coffee will. The romantically homey rooms are warm and cozy—the perfect place to snuggle up with a good book. They're also quite big, with hardwood entryways, rich dark-wood furniture, working fireplaces, and an assortment of books tucked in nooks. The decor is English elegance at its best, if not to excess, with floral prints almost everywhere. The luxury king suites are not much better than regular rooms, just a little bigger, and feature perks like chocolates, champagne, and a VCR and CD player. Each morning, a generous breakfast buffet is served in a common room just off a tiny garden. Afternoon reception, consisting of hors d'oeuvres, sherry, wine, and home-baked pastries, can be enjoyed in front of the fireplace while you browse through the books in the library or in the parlor.

The inn's location—2½ blocks from Union Square—makes this nonsmoking 1900s building a charming and serene choice, with service and style that will please even the most discriminating traveler.

845 Bush St. (between Taylor and Mason sts.), San Francisco, CA 94108. ✆ **800/999-9570** or 415/775-1755. Fax 415/775-5717. www.whiteswaninnsf.com. 26 units. $229–$319 double; $269 luxury king suite; $319 2-room suite. Extra person $20. Rates include breakfast and afternoon wine and hors d'oeuvres. AE, DC, DISC, MC, V. Valet parking (7:30am–10:30pm) $32, oversize vehicles for an additional $5. Bus: 1, 2, 3, 4, 27, or 45. Cable car: Powell St. line (1 block north). **Amenities:** Small exercise room; concierge; same-day laundry service; Internet station in conference room (20¢/min.). *In room:* Dataport, fridge with free beverages, coffeemaker, hair dryer, iron, Wi-Fi ($7.95/day).

MODERATE

A few worthy hotel companies operate many properties throughout the city. **Holiday Inn** (✆ **800/465-4329;** www.holiday-inn.com) has several strategic locations, including pretty properties in Fisherman's Wharf and along Van Ness Avenue. **Personality Hotels** (✆ **800/553-1900;** www.personalityhotels.com) spiffs up older buildings in central locales, and **Joie de Vivre** (✆ **800/SF-TRIPS;** www.jdvhospitality.com) has lots of festive options scattered around town.

The Commodore Hotel ⭐   San Francisco hotelier Chip Conley of Joie de Vivre Hospitality is behind this groovy, revamped, and now somewhat worn six-story Art Deco hotel frequented by an eclectic mix of 20-somethings and everyday folks in search of reasonably priced accommodations. Stealing the show is the Red Room, a small New York–slick bar and lounge that reflects no other color of the spectrum but ruby red (you've gotta see this one). The stylish lobby comes in a close second, followed by the adjoining Canteen, which was renovated in 2005 and features Franco

American Cuisine. The "Neo-Deco" rooms are simple but lively, with bright colors, whimsical furnishings, pretty artwork, and small bathrooms. If you choose to book, definitely splurge (about an extra $15 per night) for a "premium room." These rooms, on the fifth and sixth floors, were renovated in 2005 and have better amenities. Also, for the best night's sleep ask for a quiet room that gets less of the Sutter Street noise.

825 Sutter St. (at Jones St.), San Francisco, CA 94109. ℂ **800/338-6848** or 415/923-6800. Fax 415/923-6804. www.thecommodorehotel.com. 110 units. $89–$189 double. AE, DC, DISC, MC, V. Parking $28. Bus: 2, 3, 4, 19, 27, 47, or 49. **Amenities:** Restaurant; bar; access to nearby health club ($15/day); concierge; Internet access in lobby. *In room:* TV, dataport, minifridge, coffeemaker, hair dryer, iron, Wi-Fi.

Hotel Adagio 𝒦𝒦 🄥𝘢𝘭𝘶𝘦   Now under new management and after a $14-million renovation in 2003, this 1929 Spanish Revival hotel is revived again. This time it's in gorgeous modern style—often at half the price of other hotels in the area. Local hip hoteliers Joie de Vivre revamped its 171 large, bright guest rooms, which are real lookers with a walnut brown and mocha color palette, dark wood, firm mattresses, double-paned windows that open, quiet surroundings, all-around cleanliness, voice mail, lots and lots of elbowroom, and executive floors (7 through 16) with robes, upscale amenities, makeup mirrors, and stereos with iPod plugs. Bathrooms are old but clean, and have resurfaced tubs. Feel like splurging? Go for one of the two penthouse-level suites; one has lovely terraces with a New York vibe. Or simply step into the restaurant bar Cortez at night; it has funky glowing ball lamps, a youngish crowd, delicious "small plates," and a full bar. *Tip:* Rooms above the eighth floor have good, but not great, views of the city.

550 Geary St., San Francisco, CA 94102. ℂ **800/228-8830** or 415/775-5000. www.thehoteladagio.com. 171 units. $279 double. AE, DISC, MC, V. Valet parking $35. **Amenities:** Restaurant; bar; fitness center; concierge; business center w/free wireless Internet; room service; laundry service; dry cleaning; luggage storage room. *In room:* TV w/Nintendo and pay movies, dataport, minibar, fridge, hair dryer, iron, safe, free high-speed Internet access, CD player.

Hotel Diva 𝒦   A showbiz darling when it opened in 1985, the sleek, ultramodern Diva won "Best Hotel Design" from *Interiors* magazine. A profusion of curvaceous glass, marble, and steel marks the Euro-tech lobby; and the minimalist rooms are spotless and neat, with fashionable "Italian modern" furnishings of monochromatic colors, silver, and wood. Enormous headboards are made of polished stainless steel meant to evoke the bow of a ship. Personally, I find the hotel a little on the cold side (figuratively speaking). Also, rooms can be small and dark and, if you're on the street side, a little noisy. But toys and services abound, and fitness and business centers complete the package. *Insider tip:* Reserve one of the rooms ending in 09 because they have extra-large bathrooms with vanity mirrors and makeup tables. The downside is that these rooms have views that make you want to keep the chic curtains closed.

440 Geary St. (between Mason and Taylor sts.), San Francisco, CA 94102. ℂ **800/553-1900** or 415/885-0200. Fax 415/346-6613. www.hoteldiva.com. 115 units. $175 double; $215 junior suite; $450 suite. Extra person $10. AE, DC, DISC, MC, V. Valet parking $30. Bus: 38 or 38L. Cable car: Powell–Mason line. **Amenities:** Coffee/tea service from 6:30–10am; exercise room; concierge; laundry service; dry cleaning; free Wi-Fi (in rooms, too). *In room:* A/C, TV/DVD/CD, dataport, hair dryer, iron, safe.

Hotel Triton 𝒦   Described as vogue, chic, retrofuturistic, and even neo-baroque, this Kimpton Group property is whimsy at its boutique-hotel best. The completely renovated lobby features a 360-degree mural by emerging artist Kari Pei (yes, from *that* Pei family–she's I. M. Pei's daughter-in-law) that relates the history of San Francisco and Triton. The funky-fun (if not a wee bit too small) designer suites named after musicians and artists like Jerry Garcia, Wyland (the ocean artist), and Santana, along with all the other rooms are eco-friendly, featuring filtered water and air, all-natural linens, recycle trash cans, and water conservation fixtures. Even the cleaning products used in the hotel are all environmentally sensitive to please the tree-hugger in all of us. All the rooms were recently redone and include modern touches like the iPod IH5 docking station/player that doubles as a clock radio. Not to be outdone, the fitness center touts DirecTV in the cardio machines. One bummer: When I stayed in a south-facing suite, I could hear the garbage truck far too early in the morning. Ouch.

The hotel serves coffee and tea each morning, freshly baked cookies at 3pm and 8pm, and has wine, tarot readings, and chair massages available each evening (included in the room rate) in the lobby. The bustling and casual Café de la Presse has recently reopened after undergoing renovations. Now owned by the same folks behind the famed and fancy Aqua restaurant, it has its old French cafe vibe but the food is far better than it used to be.

342 Grant Ave. (at Bush St.), San Francisco, CA 94108. © 800/800-1299 or 415/394-0500. Fax 415/394-0555. www. hoteltriton.com. 140 units. $169–$229 double; $269–$369 suite. AE, DC, DISC, MC, V. Parking $37, oversize vehicles for an additional $2. Cable car: Powell–Hyde or Powell–Mason lines (2 blocks west). Pets stay free with conditional agreement. **Amenities:** Cafe; fitness center; business center (fee); room service; same-day laundry service/dry cleaning. *In room:* A/C, flatscreen TV, dataport, minibar, coffeemaker on request, hair dryer, iron, Web TV, free Wi-Fi.

Executive Hotel Vintage Court 🏨🏨 *Value*   Consistent personal service and great value attract a loyal clientele at this European-style hotel 2 blocks north of Union Square. The chocolate brown lobby, accented with comfy couches, is welcoming enough to actually spend a little time in, especially when California wines are being poured each evening from 5 to 6pm free of charge (each week a local vintner is on hand to do the pouring!).

But the varietals don't stop at ground level. Each tidy, quiet, and comfortable room is named after a winery and boasts a modern country look (think Pottery Barn meets Napa Valley), where greens and earth tones reign supreme, with cream duvets and lovely mahogany-slat blinds. Rubicon Estate (named after the winery owned by the movie maverick), the deluxe two-room penthouse suite, has an original 1912 stained-glass skylight, wood-burning fireplace, whirlpool tub, complete entertainment center, and panoramic views of the city. Smokers, book a room elsewhere, because puffing is prohibited in all rooms here. On the bright side, pets are welcome.

Masa's, one of the city's more upscale restaurants, serves very expensive contemporary French dinners here.

650 Bush St. (between Powell and Stockton sts.), San Francisco, CA 94108. © 800/654-1100 or 415/392-4666. Fax 415/433-4065. www.executivehotels.net/vintagecourt. 107 units. $139–$219 double; $325–$375 penthouse suite. Rates include continental breakfast and evening wine reception. AE, DC, DISC, MC, V. Valet parking $37; self-parking $27. Bus: 2, 3, 4, 30, 45, or 76. Cable car: Powell–Hyde or Powell–Mason lines (direct stop). **Amenities:** Restaurant; access to off-premises health club ($14/day); concierge; in-room massage; same-day laundry service/dry cleaning. *In room:* A/C, TV, dataport, minibar, coffeemaker, hair dryer, iron, video games, Wi-Fi.

The Inn at Union Square 🏨🏨   As narrow as an Amsterdam canal house, The Inn at Union Square is the antithesis of the big, impersonal hotels that surround Union Square. If you need plenty of elbowroom, skip this one. But if you're looking for an inn whose staff knows each guest's name, read on. One-half block west of the square, this six-story inn makes up for its small stature by spoiling guests with a pile of perks. Mornings start with a continental breakfast served in lounges stocked with daily newspapers, and evening emerges with appetizers of wine, cheese, fruits, and chocolates served in sweet little fireplace lounges at the end of each hall. The handsome rooms, which underwent a paint job and soft goods renovation in 2005, are individually decorated with Georgian reproductions and floral fabrics, and they are smaller than average but infinitely more appreciated than the cookie-cutter rooms of most larger hotels. Smoking is not allowed anywhere in the hotel.

440 Post St. (between Mason and Powell sts.), San Francisco, CA 94102. © 800/288-4346 or 415/397-3510. Fax 415/989-0529. www.unionsquare.com. 30 units. $159–$209 double; $350 suite (though prices may soon be increasing). Rates include continental breakfast; all-day tea and cider, afternoon wine and hors d'oeuvres; and evening cookies. AE, DC, DISC, MC, V. Valet parking $36. Bus: 2, 3, 4, 30, 38, or 45; all Market St. buses. Cable car: Powell–Hyde or Powell–Mason lines. **Amenities:** Access to nearby health club (for a nominal fee); concierge; secretarial services; laundry service; dry cleaning. *In room:* TV, dataport, hair dryer, iron, free Wi-Fi.

The Kensington Park Hotel 🍴🍴   The Kensington is a spiffed-up fairly old hotel with a cheery, eager-to-please (albeit sometimes short-handed) staff, tasteful accommodations, and extra efforts—like afternoon tea and sherry—that show the hotel cares about its guests. Large guest rooms on the 5th through 12th floors have handsome furnishings, and the bathrooms, though small, are sweetly appointed in brass and marble. As for the views, ask for an upper corner room, and you'll get far more than your money's worth with peeks at Nob Hill or Union Square. If you want the full treatment, book the Royal Suite, which contains a canopy bed, fireplace, Jacuzzi, and wet bar. The hotel adjoins popular fantasy—and fancy—seafood restaurant Farallon (p. 105).

450 Post St. (between Powell and Mason sts.), San Francisco, CA 94102. © 800/553-1900 or 415/788-6400. Fax 415/399-9484. www.kensingtonparkhotel.com. 92 units. $169–$205 double; $350 suite. Extra person $10. Rates include afternoon tea and sherry. AE, DC, DISC, MC, V. Valet parking $30; extra charge for oversize cars. Cable car: Powell–Hyde or Powell–Mason lines (½ block east). **Amenities:** Restaurant; coffee/tea service 7–10am; concierge; same-day dry cleaning. *In room:* TV w/pay movies, dataport, hair dryer, iron, free Wi-Fi.

The Monticello Inn 🍴   Federal-style decor, Chippendale furnishings, grandfather clocks, Revolutionary War paintings, two fireplaces, and other old stuff scattered around the lobby (renovated in 2002) attempt to create a Colonial milieu. Although it makes for a pleasant entrance, the period effect doesn't follow through to the comfortable, spacious rooms, which were updated in 2004 with new textiles, carpet, striped white and light blue wallpaper, and mattresses. Despite the homely air conditioners in the walls, you'll be quite content here, especially considering the extras— umbrellas, voice mail, a morning ride to the Financial District, complimentary coffee from 6:30 to 9am, and evening wine hour from 5 to 6pm. The service is wonderful and the downtown location is *primo.* The adjoining Puccini & Pinetti restaurant features modern Italian cuisine.

127 Ellis St. (at Powell St.), San Francisco, CA 94102. © 800/669-7777 or 415/392-8800. Fax 415/398-2650. www.monticelloinn.com. 91 units. $129–$219 double; $179–$229 suite. Extra person $20. Rates include coffee and tea in the lobby and evening wine; continental breakfast $6. AE, DC, DISC, MC, V. Valet parking $33. Bus: All Market St. buses. Streetcar: All Market St. streetcars. Cable car: Powell–Hyde or Powell–Mason lines (direct stop). Pets accepted. **Amenities:** Access to great nearby health club ($15/day); concierge; limited room service; laundry service; dry cleaning; Internet access. *In room:* A/C, TV w/Nintendo and pay movies, dataport, minibar, fridge, hair dryer, iron, free Wi-Fi.

Petite Auberge 🍴🍴   The Petite Auberge is so pathetically cute I can't stand it. I want to say it's overdone, that any hotel that's filled with teddy bears is absurd, but I can't. Bribed each year with fresh-baked cookies from the never-empty platter, I make rounds through the rooms and ruefully admit that I'm just going to have to use that word I loathe: adorable.

Nobody does French country like the Petite Auberge. The recently revamped rooms feature all new mattresses and duvets, new carpeting, and double-paned screened windows along with longtime standards of handcrafted armoires, delicate sheer curtains, cozy little fireplaces in most rooms, adorable (there's that word again) little antiques and knickknacks. Honeymooners should splurge on the petite suite, which has a private entrance, deck, and spa tub. The breakfast room, with its mural of a country market scene, terra-cotta tile floors, and gold-yellow tablecloths, opens onto a small garden. California wines, tea, and hors d'oeuvres (included in the room rates) are served each afternoon, and guests have free rein of the fridge stocked with soft drinks. Bathers take note: Eight rooms have showers only, while others have newly resurfaced tubs.

863 Bush St. (between Taylor and Mason sts.), San Francisco, CA 94102. (C) **800/365-3004** or 415/928-6000. Fax 415/673-7214. www.petiteaubergesf.com. 26 units. $199–$239 double; $269 petite suite. Rates include full breakfast and afternoon reception. AE, DC, DISC, MC, V. Parking $32. Bus: 2, 3, 4, 30, 38, or 45. Cable car: Powell–Hyde or Powell–Mason lines. **Amenities:** Access to small exercise room next door; concierge; babysitting; same-day laundry service/dry cleaning. *In room:* TV, dataport, hair dryer, robes; Wi-Fi ($7.95/day); high-speed Internet available at sister hotel next door, the **White Swan Inn,** see p. 63.

Serrano Hotel *⋒⋒*   Los Angeles designer Cheryl Rowley (who also designed the Hotel Monaco; p. 58) swathed this 17-story 1920s Kimpton Group property in her trademark vibrant color and added a playful dash of Moroccan flair while preserving the building's Spanish Revival integrity. Original architectural elements dot the colorful lobby, with its whimsically painted beams, high ceilings, large ornate fireplace, and dramatic colonnade. Equally vibrant guest rooms (sometimes small!) have oversize windows and high ceilings, cherrywood headboards, terry robes, and theater-themed artwork. The hotel is in the heart of the Theater District, right off Union Square, and is pet-friendly.

405 Taylor St. (at O'Farrell St.), San Francisco, CA 94102. (C) **877/294-9709** or 415/885-2500. Fax 415/474-4879. www.serranohotel.com. 236 units. From $179 double; from $299 suite. Rates include morning coffee and tea service and afternoon beverages. AE, DC, DISC, MC, V. Valet parking $39. Bus: 2, 3, 4, 27, or 38. Cable car: Powell or Market. Pets accepted. **Amenities:** Restaurant/bar; exercise room; sauna; concierge; courtesy car; business center with fax; limited room service; babysitting by referral; same-day laundry service/dry cleaning; Wi-Fi in meeting rooms and public spaces. *In room:* A/C, TV w/pay movies, dataport, minibar, hair dryer, iron, safe, free high-speed Internet access.

Villa Florence *⋒*   Located ½ block south of Union Square, fronting the Powell Street cable car line, the seven-story Villa Florence is in one of the liveliest sections of the city (no need to drive, 'cause you're already here). In 2004, a renovation brightened up the reasonably affordable rooms. In its newest reincarnation, Villa Florence provides guests a taste of contemporary Italian decor with cherrywood furniture and luxury perks such as 27-inch flatscreen TVs with DVD players and CD players. You'll like the large, comfortable beds draped in down comforters with Frette duvets, as well as such frivolities as Aveda bath products, Frette bathrobes, and umbrellas. Worth noting, however, is that the hotel itself is old and the structure looks it despite freshly applied lipstick and powder. It shouldn't worry you, though, since everything here is nice enough. The hotel's ground-floor restaurant helps make it a worthy contender among Union Square's medium-priced inns—as if the location alone weren't reason enough to book a room. Adjacent to the hotel is Kuleto's (p. 109), one of downtown's most bustling and stylish Italian restaurants.

225 Powell St. (between Geary and O'Farrell sts.), San Francisco, CA 94102. © **800/553-4411** or 415/397-7700. Fax 415/397-1006. www.villaflorence.com. 183 units. $199–$249 double; $249–$299 studio suites. Rates include evening wine. AE, DC, DISC, MC, V. Valet parking $35, plus an extra $10–$15 per day for oversize vehicles and SUVs. Bus: 2, 3, 4, 30, 38, or 45. Cable car: Powell–Hyde or Powell–Mason lines (direct stop). **Amenities:** Access to nearby health club ($15/day); concierge; courtesy car; business center; secretarial services; babysitting on request; same-day laundry service/dry cleaning. *In room:* A/C, ceiling fan, flatscreen TV w/pay movies, dataport, minibar, fridge, coffeemaker, hair dryer, iron, free Wi-Fi, CD player.

The Warwick Regis *Value* Louis XVI might have been a rotten monarch, but he certainly had taste. Fashioned in the style of pre-Revolutionary France, the Warwick is awash with pristine French and English antiques, Italian marble, chandeliers, four-poster beds, hand-carved headboards, and the like. The result is an expensive-looking hotel that, for all its pleasantries and perks, is surprisingly affordable when compared to its Union Square contemporaries—especially considering that all rooms underwent a renovation in 2002. Rooms can be on the small side; nonetheless, they're some of the city's most charming. Honeymooners should splurge on the fireplace rooms with four-poster beds—ooh la la! Adjoining the lobby is La Scene Restaurant and Bar, a beautiful place to start your day with a latte and end it with a nightcap.

490 Geary St. (between Mason and Taylor sts.), San Francisco, CA 94102. © **800/827-3447** or 415/928-7900. Fax 415/441-8788. www.warwicksf.com. 74 units. $199–$299 double; $299–$399 suite. AE, DC, DISC, MC, V. Parking $29. Bus: 2, 3, 4, 27, or 38. Cable car: Powell–Hyde or Powell–Mason lines. **Amenities:** Restaurant; access to nearby health club ($15/day); concierge; business center; secretarial services; 24-hr. room service; babysitting; laundry service; dry cleaning. *In room:* TV, dataport, minibar, hair dryer, iron, safe, Wi-Fi.

INEXPENSIVE

The Andrews Hotel For the location and price, the Andrews is a safe bet for an enjoyable stay. Two blocks west of Union Square, the Andrews was a Turkish bath before its conversion in 1981. As is typical in Euro-style hotels, the rooms are small but well maintained and comfortable, with nice touches like white lace curtains and fresh flowers. Continued upgrades, such as 2002's new mattresses and carpets, help keep things fresh. But large bathroom lovers beware: Though they were painted in 2003, the facilities are forever tiny. A bonus is the adjoining Fino Bar and Ristorante, which offers respectable Italian fare and free wine to hotel guests in the evening.

624 Post St. (between Jones and Taylor sts.), San Francisco, CA 94109. © **800/926-3739** or 415/563-6877. Fax 415/928-6919. www.andrewshotel.com. 48 units, some with shower only. $92–$142 double; $139–$179 superior rooms. Rates include continental breakfast, coffee in lobby, and evening wine. AE, DC, MC, V. Valet parking $25. Bus: 2, 3, 4, 30, 38, or 45. Cable car: Powell–Hyde or Powell–Mason lines (3 blocks east). **Amenities:** Restaurant; access to nearby health club; concierge; room service (5:30–10pm); babysitting; nearby self-service laundromat; laundry service; dry cleaning. *In room:* TV/VCR w/video library, dataport, fridge, hair dryer on request, iron, Wi-Fi ($10/day), CD player in suites only.

The Cartwright Hotel Diametrically opposed to the hip-hop, happenin' Hotel Triton down the street, The Cartwright Hotel is geared toward the more mature traveler. Management takes pride in its reputation for offering comfortable rooms at fair prices, which explains why most guests have been repeat customers for a long time. Remarkably quiet, despite its convenient location near one of the busiest downtown corners, the eight-story hotel looks not unlike it did when it opened some 80 years ago. Antiques collected during its decades of faithful service furnish the lobby and the individually decorated (and sometimes very small) rooms, all of which underwent a complete restoration in 2004 with new carpets, paint, mattresses, wallpaper, phones, and window treatments. A nice perk usually reserved for fancier hotels is the fully equipped bathrooms, all of which have tubs, rainfall shower heads, and Aveda products, terry robes (in deluxe rooms), and thick fluffy towels. Complimentary wine is served in the small library each night, and afternoon tea and fresh-baked cookies are a daily treat, as are the apples and hot beverages in the lobby 'round the clock. A breakfast room added in 2004 serves a complimentary expanded continental breakfast with a make-your-own-waffle station.

524 Sutter St. (at Powell St.), San Francisco, CA 94102. © **800/919-9779** or 415/421-2865. Fax 415/398-6345. www.cartwrighthotel.com. 114 units. $199–$259 double. Rates include 24-hr. tea, coffee, and apples in the lobby, continental breakfast, nightly wine hour, weekday newspapers, and afternoon cookies. AE, DC, DISC, MC, V. Valet parking $35; self-parking $25. Bus: 2, 3, 4, 30, or 45. Cable car: Powell–Hyde or Powell–Mason lines (direct stop). **Amenities:** Access to nearby health club for $15; concierge; free wireless Internet access. *In room:* TV, dataport, fridge upon request, hair dryer, iron, free Wi-Fi.

The Cornell Hotel de France

Its quirks make this old hotel more charming than many others in its price range. Resident pooch, Noel, greets you when you enter the small French-style hotel. Pass the office, where a few faces will glance in your direction and smile, and embark on a ride in the old-fashioned elevator (we're talking seriously old-school here) to get to your very basic room. Each floor is dedicated to a French painter and decorated with reproductions. Rooms are all plain and comfortable, with desks and chairs, and are individually and simply decorated. Smoking is not allowed. The full American breakfast included in the rate is served in the very cool cavernlike provincial basement restaurant, Jeanne d'Arc. Union Square is just a few blocks away.

715 Bush St. (between Powell and Mason sts.), San Francisco, CA 94108. © **800/232-9698** or 415/421-3154. Fax 415/399-1442. www.cornellhotel.com. 55 units. $85–$135 double. Rates include full American breakfast. Package including 7 breakfasts and 5 dinners: $1,085 double per week for deluxe room, or $1,015 for medium room. AE (for now), DC, DISC, MC, V. Parking across the street $17. Bus: 2, 3, 4, 30, or 45. Cable car: Powell–Hyde or Powell–Mason lines. **Amenities:** Restaurant; computer with Internet in lobby. *In room:* TV, dataport, hair dryer, Wi-Fi (for a fee).

The Fitzgerald

Some of the rooms may be outfitted with new half-canopy beds, fresh prints, and Victorian decor, but most of them are really small. (One that I saw had a dresser less than a foot from the bed.) Of course, at $80 per night, there's no room for complaining. But do ask for a larger room—and a quieter one. If you can live without a sizable closet, you'll find that the price, breakfast (home-baked breads, scones, muffins, juice, tea, and coffee), and cleanliness of this hotel make it a good value.

620 Post St. (between Jones and Taylor sts.), San Francisco, CA 94109. © **800/334-6835** or 415/775-8100. Fax 415/775-1278. www.fitzgeraldhotel.com. 47 units. $65–$125 double. Rates include continental breakfast. Lower rates in winter. DC, DISC, MC, V. Valet parking $33; self-parking $25. Bus: 2, 3, 4, or 27. Cable car: Powell–Hyde or Powell–Mason lines. **Amenities:** Access to a nearby exercise room (for a discounted fee); same-day dry cleaning; Internet access in lobby (for a fee). *In room:* TV, dataport, hair dryer.

The Golden Gate Hotel *Value*

San Francisco's stock of small hotels in historic turn-of-the-20th-century buildings includes some real gems, and The Golden Gate Hotel is one of them. It's 2 blocks north of Union Square and 2 blocks down (literally) from the crest of Nob Hill, with cable car stops at the corner for easy access to Fisherman's Wharf and Chinatown. The city's theaters and best restaurants are also within walking distance. But the best thing about the 1913 Edwardian hotel—which definitely has a B&B feel—is that it's family run: John and Renate Kenaston and daughter Gabriele are hospitable innkeepers who take obvious pleasure in making their guests comfortable. Each individually decorated room has recently been repainted and carpeted and has handsome antique furnishings (plenty of wicker) from the early 1900s, quilted bedspreads, and fresh flowers. Request a room with a claw-foot tub if you enjoy a good, hot soak. Afternoon tea is served daily from 4 to 7pm, and guests are welcome to use the house fax and computer with wireless DSL free of charge.

775 Bush St. (between Powell and Mason sts.), San Francisco, CA 94108. ℭ **800/835-1118** or 415/392-3702. Fax 415/392-6202. www.goldengatehotel.com. 25 units, 14 with bathroom. $95 double without bathroom; $130 double with bathroom. Rates include continental breakfast and afternoon tea. AE, DC, MC, V. Self-parking $18. Bus: 2, 4, 30, 38, or 45. Cable car: Powell–Hyde or Powell–Mason lines (1 block east). BART: Powell and Market. **Amenities:** Access to health club 1 block away; activities desk; laundry service/dry cleaning next door. *In room:* TV, dataport, hair dryer and iron upon request, free Wi-Fi.

Halcyon Hotel *€ Value* Inside this small, four-story brick building is a penny pincher's dream come true, the kind of place where you'll find everything you need yet won't have to pay through the nose to get it. The small but very clean studio guest rooms are equipped with microwave ovens, refrigerators, flatware and utensils, toasters, alarm clocks, coffeemakers and coffee, phones with free local calls, mail delivery, and voice mail—all the comforts of home in the heart of Union Square (you can even bring your pet!). A coin-operated washer and dryer are located in the basement, along with free laundry soap and irons. The managers are usually on hand to offer friendly, personal service, making this option all in all an unbeatable deal. Be sure to ask about special rates for weekly stays.

649 Jones St. (between Geary and Post sts.), San Francisco, CA 94102. ℭ **800/627-2396** or 415/929-8033. Fax 415/441-8033. www.halcyonsf.com. 25 units. $70–$90 double year-round; $350–$450 weekly. Minimum length of stay Oct–Apr is 7 days. AE, DC, DISC, MC, V. Parking garage nearby $14–$16 per day. Bus: 2, 3, 4, 9, 27, or 38. Pets accepted. **Amenities:** Access to nearby health club; concierge; tour desk; laundry facilities; free fax available in lobby. *In room:* TV, dataport, kitchen, fridge, coffeemaker, hair dryer, iron, voice mail.

Hostelling International San Francisco–Downtown For just around $25 per night (with a notarized ID), you can relive college-dorm life in an old San Francisco–style building right in the heart of Union Square. Occupying five sparsely decorated floors—each with its own pay phone—rooms here are simple and clean. Each has three or four bunk beds with linens, its own sink, a closet, and lockers (bring your own lock or buy one at the front desk). Although most private rooms share hallway bathrooms, a few have private facilities. Laminated posters adorn the hallways, and there are several common rooms, including a reading room and a large kitchen with lots of tables, chairs, and refrigerator space. There are laundry facilities in the building and a helpful information desk where you can book tours and sightseeing trips. The hostel is open 24 hours, and reservations are essential, especially during the summer. Persons under 18 must be accompanied by an adult or have a signed guardian release form, which is available from their website.

312 Mason St. (between Geary and O'Farrell sts.), San Francisco, CA 94102. ℭ **888/GOHIUSA** or 415/788-5604. Fax 415/788-3023. www.sfhostels.com. 37 private rooms, 193 dorm beds. Hostelling members $23–$26 per person in dorm; nonmembers $25–$29 per person in dorm; $70–$85 per private room. Children under 12 $12 when accompanied by a parent. Maximum stay 21 nights per month. AE, DC, MC, V. Bus: 7 or 38. Cable car: Powell–Mason line. BART: Powell St. **Amenities:** Tour desk; TV lounge; kitchen; Internet access at kiosks for small fee; laundry facilities. *In room:* Lockers, no phone.

Hotel Beresford *€* The small and friendly sister property of the Hotel Beresford Arms (see below), the seven-floor Hotel Beresford is another good, moderately priced choice near Union Square. Perks are the same: $5 movie rentals, clock radios, a mishmash of furniture, and stocked fridges. Everything's well kept and planned room upgrades underway as this book goes to press—paint, wallpaper, furniture, and the like—promise fresh-looking, modest surroundings. The on-site **White Horse Tavern,** an attractive and quaint replica of an old English pub, serves dinner Tuesday through Saturday and is a favorite for folks who like less trendy hullabaloo with their meal.

635 Sutter St. (near Mason St.), San Francisco, CA 94102. ✆ **800/533-6533** or 415/673-9900. Fax 415/474-0449. www.beresford.com. 114 units. $89–$165 double. Extra person $10. Rates include continental breakfast. Children under 12 stay free in parent's room. AE, DC, DISC, MC, V. Valet parking $20. Bus: 2, 3, 4, 30, 38, or 45. Cable car: Powell–Hyde line (1 block east). **Amenities:** Restaurant/pub; access to nearby health club ($10/day); laundry service; free high-speed Internet access in kiosk in lobby. In room: TV, dataport, minibar, hair dryer upon request, iron.

Hotel Beresford Arms 🏨🏨 _Value_   The bargain prices are the main reason I recommend this dependable, though slightly unfashionable, hotel. On the plus side, suites have bidets and Jacuzzi bathtubs and junior suites offer a wet bar or fully equipped kitchenette—an advantage for families—and pastries and coffee are included in the rock-bottom price of all rooms. All accommodations include plenty of in-room perks, including clock radios and $5 movie rentals, and there's a "Manager's Social Hour" (included in the room rates) with wine, tea, and snacks. The downsides are minimal: a few funky furnishings, small bathrooms, and the occasional old mattress. The location, between the Theater District and Union Square, in a quieter section of San Francisco, is ideal for visitors without cars, and the price for what you get is hard to beat. **_Tip:_** Rooms that face Post Street might be a bit noisier than others, but they're also larger and sunnier, and some have window seats.

701 Post St. (at Jones St.), San Francisco, CA 94109. ✆ **800/533-6533** or 415/673-2600. Fax 415/929-1535. www.beresford.com. 95 units. $99–$114 double; $144 Jacuzzi suite; $169 parlor suite. Extra person $10. Children under 12 stay free in parent's room. Rates include pastry, coffee, afternoon wine and tea. Senior and AAA discounts available. AE, DC, DISC, MC, V. Valet parking $20. Bus: 2, 3, 4, 27, or 38. Cable car: Powell–Hyde line (3 blocks east). **Amenities:** Access to nearby health club ($10/day); laundry service; free Internet access in lobby. In room: TV, dataport, minibar, hair dryer upon request, iron, free Wi-Fi.

Hotel Bijou 🏨 _Value_   Three words sum up this hotel: clean, colorful, and cheap. Although it's on the periphery of the gritty Tenderloin (just 3 blocks off Union Square), once inside this gussied-up 1911 hotel, all's cheery, bright, and perfect for budget travelers who want a little style with their savings. Joie de Vivre hotel group disguised the hotel's age with lively decor, a Deco theater theme, and a heck of a lot of vibrant paint. To the left of the small lobby is a "theater" where guests can watch San Francisco–based double features nightly (cute old-fashioned theater seating, though it's just a basic TV showing videos). Upstairs, rooms named after locally made films are small, clean, and colorful (think buttercup, burgundy, and purple), and have all the basics from clock radios, dressers, and small desks to tiny bathrooms (one of which is so small you have to close the door to access the toilet). Alas, a few mattresses could be firmer, and there's only one small and slow elevator. But considering the price, and perks like the continental breakfast and friendly service, you can't go wrong here.

111 Mason St., San Francisco, CA 94102. ✆ **800/771-1022** or 415/771-1200. Fax 415/346-3196. www.hotelbijou.com. 65 units. $95–$139 double. Rates include continental breakfast. AE, DC, DISC, MC, V. Valet parking $27. Bus: All Market St. buses. Streetcar: Powell St. station. **Amenities:** Concierge; limited room service; same-day laundry service/dry cleaning; DSL access in lobby ($4/20 min). In room: TV, dataport, hair dryer, iron, high-speed Internet, Wi-Fi ($7.95/day).

Hotel Carlton _Value_   If you're looking for wonderfully cheap, attractive, and clean accommodations and don't mind being in the middle of the city and simultaneously in the middle of nowhere, book a room here. The Joie de Vivre hotel group is behind this 163-room 1927 hotel revamped in May 2004 in "global vintage" decor. The interior is wonderful, with travel photographs from the American Himalayan Foundation, tribal figurines, Oriental rugs, a vibrant sarilike color scheme, and imported hand-painted Moroccan tables and cool Lucite-beaded table lamps in guest rooms. Outside the neighborhood is drab, but it's only a 7-block walk to Union Square, and with doubles starting at a mere $109, you can splurge for a taxi with the money saved. Or stick nearby and try **Saha,** their Arabian-fusion restaurant (think hummus, pizza, Yemenese meatballs, and seared scallops), which serves breakfast and dinner.

1075 Sutter St. (between Larkin and Hyde sts.), San Francisco, CA 94109. ℭ **800/922-7586** or 415/673-0242. Fax 415/673-4904. www.jdvhospitality.com. 163 units. $109–$199 double. Rates include evening wine reception. AE, MC, V. Valet parking $30; self parking $25. Bus: 2, 3, 4, 19, or 76. **Amenities:** Restaurant; concierge; laundry; dry cleaning. *In room:* TV, coffeemaker, hair dryer, iron, safe, free Wi-Fi.

Hotel des Arts *ℱℱ* *Value*   While this bargain find has the same floor plan as San Francisco's numerous other Euro-style hotels—small lobby, narrow hallways, cramped rooms—the owners of the des Arts have made an obvious effort to distance themselves from the competition by including a visually stimulating dose of artistic license throughout the hotel. The lobby, for example, hosts a rotating art gallery featuring contemporary works by emerging local artists and is outfitted with groovy furnishings, while the guest rooms are soothingly situated with quality furnishings and tasteful accouterments. There's one suite that can sleep up to four persons at no additional charge. You'll love the lively location as well: right across the street from the entrance to Chinatown and 2 blocks from Union Square. There's even a French brasserie right downstairs. Considering the price (rooms with a very clean shared bathroom start at $59), quality, and location, it's quite possibly the best budget hotel in the city. *Tip:* Log onto the hotel's website to check out the "Painted Rooms" designed by local artists, then call the hotel directly to book your favorite.

447 Bush St. (at Grant St.), San Francisco, CA 94108. ℭ **800/956-4322** or 415/956-3232. Fax 415/956-0399. www.sfhoteldesarts.com. 51 units, 26 with private bathroom. $79–$159 with bathroom; $59–$79 double without bathroom. Rates include continental breakfast. AE, DC, MC, V. Nearby parking $18. Cable car: Powell–Hyde and Powell–Mason lines. **Amenities:** 24-hr. concierge, fax, and copy services; laundry and valet service. *In room:* TV, 2-line direct-dial telephone with dataport and voice mail, minifridge and microwave in many rooms, hair dryer, iron and board.

King George Hotel *ℱ* *Value*   Built in 1914 for the Panama–Pacific Exhibition (when rooms went for $1 per night), the delightful boutique King George has fared well over the years with its mostly European clientele. The location—surrounded by cable car lines, the Theater District, Union Square, and dozens of restaurants—is superb, and the rooms, which recently received new pillow top beds, duvets and pillows, wallpaper and paint, are surprisingly quiet for such a busy spot (sadly, the interior noise is definitely audible through thin, old walls). Although rooms can be very, very small (in the smallest rooms it can be difficult for two people to maneuver at the same time), the hotel makes the most of the space; and truth be told, with affordable prices, spiffy updated bathrooms, desks, and a handsome studylike ambience, the smaller quarters come off pretty darned well. A big hit since it started a few years back is the hotel's English afternoon tea, served in the Windsor Tea Room Saturday, Sunday, and holidays from 1 to 4:30pm. Recent additions include a pub, 24-hour business center, and an upgraded "executive" level.

334 Mason St. (between Geary and O'Farrell sts.), San Francisco, CA 94102. ✆ **800/288-6005** or 415/781-5050. Fax 415/835-5991. www.kinggeorge.com. 153 units. $165 double; $185 suite. Breakfast $9.95–$13. Special-value packages available seasonally. AE, DC, DISC, MC, V. Valet parking $26; self-parking $23. Bus: 1, 2, 3, 4, 5, 7, 30, 38, 45, 70, or 71. Cable car: Powell–Hyde or Powell–Mason lines (1 block west). **Amenities:** Tearoom; evening lounge/bar; $12 access to health club ½ block away; concierge; 24-hr. business center; secretarial services; room service; same-day laundry service/dry cleaning; wireless Internet access in lobby. *In room:* TV w/Nintendo and pay movies, dataport, hair dryer, iron, safe, free Wi-Fi.

The Savoy Hotel ✸✸ *Value*   A European-style hotel through and through, the Savoy is one of my favorite moderately priced downtown hotels. (The Warwick Regis, see below, is my other top pick.) With a nice cozy apartment-like feel to each guest room, old well-cleaned bathrooms with original tiles, newly painted rooms as of 2005, classic furnishings, and 400 thread count sheets, it's easy to relax here. Not all rooms are alike—they can be small, but each has beautiful white wood shutters, large mirrors, new 37-inch LCD TVs, free Wi-Fi, and two-line telephones. They've also recently added a full service business center and fitness center. Guests also enjoy access to **Millennium** (p. 109), San Francisco's only gourmet vegan restaurant as well as a wine and cheese reception each afternoon from 4:30 to 6pm. The only downside: Even double-pane windows don't keep the street noise out.

580 Geary St. (between Taylor and Jones sts.), San Francisco, CA 94102. ✆ **800/227-4223** or 415/441-2700. Fax 415/441-0124. www.thesavoyhotel.com. 82 units. $119–$289 double; $129–$399 suite. Free wine and cheese 4–6pm daily. Ask about packages; full continental breakfast $7. AE, DC, DISC, MC, V. Valet parking $30. Bus: 2, 3, 4, 27, or 38. **Amenities:** Restaurant; fitness center; 24-hr. concierge; business center; laundry service; dry cleaning; free Wi-Fi. *In room:* LCD TV, dataport, hair dryer, iron, safe, free Wi-Fi.

Stratford Hotel ✸   Renovation fever has hit the ever-touristy downtown, and the Stratford is the latest to get the bug. Until recently, no one ever noticed that there were actually hotels along the noisiest, most densely tourist-populated section of Union Square. But the Stratford's colorful face-lift is drawing interested looks—and hotel reservations—to the southern corner of the area. The resurrection of this eight-story 1907 building includes the addition of colorfully painted hallways and brightly painted rooms done in a slightly tattered Euro-chic decor. Accommodations vary tremendously, so be sure to request what you want (and don't want); those that face Powell have more noise (clanging cable cars are far less cute when you're trying to sleep) but more sunlight and a great view; double-paned windows block much of the noise, however.

242 Powell St. (between Geary Blvd. and O'Farrell St.), San Francisco, CA 94102. ✆ **888/504-6835** or 415/397-7080. Fax 415/397-7087. www.hotelstratford.com. 100 units. $79–$139 double. Rates include continental breakfast. AE, MC, V. Garage parking nearby. BART: Powell. Cable car: Powell–Hyde line. Bus: 2, 3, 4, 27, 30, 38, 76, and all Market St. buses and Metros. **Amenities:** Babysitting; same-day laundry service/dry cleaning. *In room:* TV, dataport, hair dryer.

York Hotel ✸✸   Even as a local, I drop by the York frequently because it's home to the historic **Empire Plush Room** (p. 229), the city's best jazz and cabaret club. But for the visitor, the hotel, built in 1922 and boasting a role in Hitchcock's *Vertigo,* is a boon because it's a hell of a deal. Awarded three diamonds by AAA, the hotel has ridiculously helpful staff, a workout room, and promotional rates, which include a continental breakfast served in the Plush Room. Rooms swathed in terra cotta and green are abundantly cheery and come loaded with nice touches like dark-wood writing desks, newly upholstered and comfy chairs, alarm clocks, tub/showers, and walk-in closets. However, an upgrade is in the works for 2007, so anticipate more modern furniture, pillow top mattresses, new linens, and flatscreen TVs in all rooms.

940 Sutter St. (between Leavenworth and Hyde sts.), San Francisco, CA 94109. Ⓒ **800/808-9675** or 415/885-6800. Fax 415/885-2115. www.yorkhotel.com. 96 units. $134–$164 double. Rates include continental breakfast. AE, DISC, MC, V. Valet parking $35 (oversize vehicles extra); self parking $25. Bus: 2, 3, or 4. **Amenities:** Jazz club; bar; workout room. *In room:* TV w/pay movies, coffeemaker, hair dryer, iron, safe, Wi-Fi ($9.95/day; free in the Superior King rooms).

3 Nob Hill

VERY EXPENSIVE

The Fairmont Hotel & Tower 🏵🏵 (*Kids*)   The granddaddy of Nob Hill's elite cadre of ritzy hotels, the Fairmont wins high honors for an incredibly jaw-dropping lobby with vaulted ceilings, Corinthian columns, a spectacular spiral staircase, plus new paint and furniture. An $85-million renovation completed in 2001 carries the glamour to guest rooms where expected luxuries are accompanied by goose-down pillows, bathroom scales, and large walk-in closets. Spectacular views from the top floors remain the showstoppers, but nuances such as a 24-hour on-call dentist and doctor, high-speed Internet access, a notary public, and in-room access to PlayStations and dual phone lines enhance every guest's stay. Kids will enjoy the Fairmont's Doorman for a Day program where they're lent a pint-size doorman's hat, and a gift of a miniwhistle and camera to commemorate the adventure. Whatever you do, make a point of getting to the Tonga Room, a fantastically kitsch Disneyland-like tropical bar and restaurant where happy hour hops and "rain" falls every 30 minutes.

950 Mason St. (at California St.), San Francisco, CA 94108. Ⓒ **800/441-1414** or 415/772-5000. Fax 415/772-5086. www.fairmont.com. 591 units. Main building $229–$349 double; from $500 suite. Tower $289–$469 double; from $750 suite. Penthouse $12,500. Extra person $30. AE, DC, DISC, MC, V. Parking $43. Cable car: California St. line (direct stop). **Amenities:** 2 restaurants/bars; health club (free for Fairmont President's Club members; $15/day or $20/2 days, non-members); concierge; tour desk; car-rental desk; business center; shopping arcade; salon; room service; massage; babysitting; same-day laundry service/dry cleaning; wireless Internet in lobby. *In room:* A/C, TV w/pay movies and PlayStation and Nintendo available, dataport, kitchenette in some units, minibar, hair dryer, iron, safe, high-speed Internet access.

The Huntington Hotel 🏵🏵   One of the kings of Nob Hill, the stately Huntington Hotel has long been a favorite retreat for Hollywood stars and political VIPs who desire privacy and security. Family owned since 1924—an extreme rarity among large hotels—the Huntington eschews pomp and circumstance; absolute privacy and unobtrusive service are its mainstays. Although the lobby, decorated in grand 19th-century style, is rather petite, the guest rooms are like spacious apartments; they feature Brunschwig and Fils fabrics and bed coverings, antique French furnishings, and views of the city. Be warned, however, that they are also quirky and sprinkled with downscale items; one room where I recently stayed had motel-quality doorknobs, a tiny, plain bathroom, and a small, old TV that constantly flickered. Where they make up for the room deficiencies is in the celestial spa and genuinely gracious staff. The lavish suites, so opulent that they've been featured in *Architectural Digest,* are individually decorated with custom-made furnishings. Prices are steep, as you would expect, but special offers such as a Romance Package, which includes champagne, specialty teas, limousine service, and two 50-minute massages from their spa, make the Huntington worth considering for a special occasion.

The Big Four restaurant offers expensive contemporary American cuisine. Live piano music is played nightly in the lounge.

1075 California St. (between Mason and Taylor sts.), San Francisco, CA 94108. ℂ **800/227-4683** or 415/474-5400. Fax 415/474-6227. www.huntingtonhotel.com. 135 units. $350–$440 single or double; $540–$1,230 suite. Continental breakfast $14. Special packages available. AE, DC, DISC, MC, V. Valet parking $29. Bus: 1. Cable car: California St. line (direct stop). **Amenities:** Restaurant; lounge; indoor heated pool (ages 16 and up); health club; spa; steam room; sauna; yoga and pilates room; Jacuzzi; concierge; massage; babysitting; same-day laundry service/dry cleaning. *In room:* A/C, TV w/pay movies, dataport, kitchenettes in some units, minibar, fridges in some units, hair dryer, iron, safe, Wi-Fi ($9.95/day).

Inter-Continental Mark Hopkins 𝓇𝓇𝓇   Built in 1926 on the spot where railroad millionaire Mark Hopkins's turreted mansion once stood, the 19-story Mark Hopkins gained global fame during World War II when it was de rigueur for Pacific-bound servicemen to toast their goodbye to the States in the Top of the Mark cocktail lounge. Nowadays, this great hotel, which completed a $76-million hotel renovation in 2002, caters mostly to convention-bound corporate executives, since its prices often require corporate charge accounts. Each neoclassical room is exceedingly comfortable and comes with all the fancy amenities you'd expect from a world-class hotel, including custom furniture, plush fabrics, sumptuous bathrooms, Frette bathrobes, and extraordinary views of the city. The luxury suites are twice the size of most San Francisco apartments and cost close to a month's rent per night. A minor caveat: The hotel has only three guest elevators, making a quick trip to your room difficult during busy periods.

The Top of the Mark (p. 237), a fantastic bar/lounge (open daily), offers dancing to live jazz or swing, Sunday brunch, and cocktails in swank, old-fashioned style. (Romantics, this place is for you, but keep in mind that there's a $10 cover fee on Fri–Sat after 8:30pm for the live nightly entertainment.) The Nob Hill Restaurant offers California cuisine nightly and breakfast on Sunday.

1 Nob Hill (at California and Mason sts.), San Francisco, CA 94108. ℂ **800/327-0200** or 415/392-3434. Fax 415/421-3302. www.markhopkins.net. 380 units. $399–$599 double; from $650 suite; from $3,000 luxury suite. Breakfast $17 for juice, coffee, and pastry to $23 for full buffet. AE, DC, DISC, MC, V. Valet parking $44, some oversize vehicles prohibited. Bus: 1. Cable car: California St. or Powell lines (direct stop). **Amenities:** 2 restaurants; bar; exercise room; concierge; business center; secretarial services; room service; babysitting; laundry service/dry cleaning; concierge-level floors. *In room:* A/C, TV w/pay movies, VCR/DVD in suites only, dataport, minibar, coffeemaker, hair dryer, iron, safe, Wi-Fi in all rooms for nominal fee.

The Ritz-Carlton 𝓇𝓇𝓇   Ranked among the top hotels in the world, The Ritz-Carlton has been the benchmark for San Francisco's luxury hotels since it opened in 1991. A Nob Hill landmark, the former Metropolitan Insurance headquarters stood vacant for years until The Ritz-Carlton company acquired it and embarked on a $100-million, 4-year renovation. The interior was completely gutted and restored with fine furnishings, fabrics, and artwork, including a pair of Louis XVI blue marble urns with gilt mountings, and 19th-century Waterford candelabras. And just to make sure they stay on top, rooms are again undergoing upgrades—to the tune of $12.5 million and will include 32-inch LCD TVs, DVDs, and CD players, Wi-Fi, and two cordless phones. The Italian marble bathrooms offer every possible amenity: double sinks, telephone, name-brand toiletries, and plush terry robes. The more expensive rooms take advantage of the hotel's location—the south slope of Nob Hill—and have good views of the city. Clubrooms, on the top floors, have a dedicated concierge, separate elevator-key access, and complimentary minimeals throughout the day. No restaurant in town has more formal service than this hotel's **The Dining Room,** which is a fine place but is not included in this book's dining chapter, because, while excellent, others in its price range are more exciting. The less formal Terrace Restaurant offers contemporary Mediterranean cuisine and the city's best Sunday brunch. The lobby lounge serves classic afternoon tea and cocktails with low-key live entertainment daily, and sushi Wednesday through Saturday.

600 Stockton St. (between Pine and California sts.), San Francisco, CA 94108. © **800/241-3333** or 415/296-7465. Fax 415/986-1268. www.ritzcarlton.com. 336 units. $425–$460 double; $580–$830 club-level double; from $730–$830 executive suite. Buffet breakfast $32; Sun champagne brunch $65. Weekend discounts and packages available. AE, DC, DISC, MC, V. Parking $55. Cable car: California St. cable car line (direct stop). **Amenities:** 2 restaurants; 3 bars; indoor pool; outstanding fitness center; Jacuzzi; steam room; concierge; courtesy car; business center; secretarial services; room service; in-room massage and manicure; same-day laundry service/dry cleaning. *In room:* A/C, TV w/pay movies, dataport, minibar, hair dryer, iron, safe, high-speed Internet access and Wi-Fi ($13/day).

Stanford Court, A Renaissance Hotel ☆☆ The Stanford Court has maintained a long and discreet reputation as one of San Francisco's most exclusive hotels. Keeping company with the Ritz, Fairmont, Mark Hopkins, and Huntington hotels atop Nob Hill, it's frequented mostly by corporate execs. The foundation was originally the mansion of Leland Stanford, whose legacy lives on in the many portraits and biographies that adorn the rooms. At first, the guest rooms come across as austere and antiquated compared to those at most other top-dollar business hotels, but the quality and comfort of the furnishings are so superior that you're forced to admit there's little room for improvement. The Stanford Court also prides itself on its impeccable service. The lobby, furnished in 19th-century style with Baccarat chandeliers, French antiques, and a gorgeous stained-glass dome, makes for a grand entrance.

Many of the guest rooms have partially canopied beds; all have writing desks and feature the new signature Renaissance bedding with new linens and down duvets and oak armoires that conceal the television sets. Bathrooms contain robes, telephones, and heated towel racks. Deluxe rooms have Frette linens. A thoughtful perk: There is no charge for toll-free or credit card calls made from your room, and complimentary coffee and tea are available with a wake-up call request.

905 California St. (at Powell St.), San Francisco, CA 94108. © **800/MARRIOT** or 415/989-3500. Fax 415/391-0513. www.stanfordcourt.com. 393 units. $299 double; from $550 suite. Continental breakfast $17–$22; American breakfast $21–$26. AE, DC, DISC, MC, V. Valet parking $41. Bus: 1. Cable car: Powell–Hyde, Powell–Mason, or California–Van Ness lines (direct stop). **Amenities:** Restaurant; lounge; 24-hr. fitness center; concierge; free car to downtown destinations; business center; room service; same-day laundry service/dry cleaning. *In room:* A/C, TV w/pay movies and Web TV, dataport, hair dryer, iron, $9.95 high-speed Internet access and local call package.

MODERATE

The Nob Hill Inn ☆☆ *Value* Although most of the rooms at the luxurious Nob Hill Inn are well out of budget range, the three Gramercy rooms are among the most opulent you will find in the city for $100. Built in 1907 as a private home, the four-story inn has been masterfully refurbished with Victorian-style antiques, expensive fabrics, reproduction artwork, and a magnificent etched-glass European-style lift. Even the low-priced Gramercy rooms receive equal attention: with good-size bathrooms (with claw-foot tubs), antique furnishings, faux-antique phones, discreetly placed televisions, and comfortable full-size beds. Granted, the cheapest rooms are small. But they're so utterly charming that it's tough to complain, especially when you consider that rates include continental breakfast, afternoon tea and sherry, and the distinction of staying at one of the city's most prestigious hotels.

1000 Pine St. (at Taylor St.), San Francisco, CA 94109. © **415/673-6080.** Fax 415/673-6098. www.nobhillinn.com. 21 units. $100–$195 double; $245–$275 suite. Rates include continental breakfast, afternoon tea, and sherry. AE, DC, DISC, MC, V. Parking $25–$35 per day in nearby garages. Bus: 1. Cable car: California St. line. **Amenities:** Concierge. *In room:* TV, kitchenette in some, hair dryer, iron.

Nob Hill Lambourne ☆☆   One of San Francisco's top "business boutique" hotels, the Nob Hill Lambourne offers massages, aromatherapy, and yoga tapes to ease corporate-level stress. Even without this hook, the Lambourne deserves a top-of-the-class rating. Sporting one of San Francisco's most stylish interiors, the hotel flaunts the comfort and quality of its contemporary French design, made even better with its renovation in early 2003. Top-quality, hand-sewn mattresses and goose-down comforters complement a host of thoughtful in-room accouterments including kitchenettes, umbrellas, and CD player/stereos. Bathrooms have deep soaking tubs. One-bedroom suites include an additional sitting room. The wine hour starts at 6pm. Smokers should seek a room elsewhere: This place prohibits puffing.

725 Pine St. (between Powell and Stockton sts.), San Francisco, CA 94108. © **800/274-8466** or 415/433-2287. Fax 415/433-0975. www.nobhilllambourne.com. 20 units. From $219 double; $299 suite. Rates include continental breakfast and evening wine hour. AE, DC, DISC, MC, V. Valet parking $32. Cable car: Powell–Mason, Powell–Hyde, or California St. lines (1 block north). **Amenities:** Access to nearby health club for $15; Internet station near lobby (20¢/min.); spa treatments; concierge; in-room massage at guest request; laundry service; same-day dry cleaning. *In room:* TV/VCR, videos available for loan; dataport, kitchenette, minibar, coffeemaker, hair dryer, iron, free high-speed Internet access and Wi-Fi, CD player.

⟮Value⟯ Free Parking in The City by the Bay

With parking fees averaging $20 to $40 a night at most hotels, plus a 14% parking tax (talk about a monopoly), you might consider staying at one of the lodgings listed below if you're crazy enough to drive the sinister streets of San Francisco. (As one seasoned driver put it, "We separate pedestrians between the quick and the dead.") All offer free parking—some even offer free covered parking—and are moderate to low priced.

- **Beck's Motor Lodge,** 2222 Market St. (at 15th St.); © **800/227-4360** in the U.S., except CA, 800/955-2325 within CA, or 415/621-8212. See p. 96.
- **Cow Hollow Motor Inn & Suites,** 2190 Lombard St. (between Steiner and Fillmore sts.); © **415/921-5800.** See p. 92.
- **Hostelling International San Francisco—Fisherman's Wharf,** Building 240, Fort Mason; © **415/771-7277.** See p. 70.
- **Laurel Inn,** 444 Presidio Ave. (at California St.); © **800/552-8735** or 415/567-8467. See p. 91.
- **The Phoenix Hotel,** 601 Eddy St. (at Larkin St.); © **800/248-9466** or 415/776-1380. See p. 95.
- **The Wharf Inn,** 2601 Mason St. (at Beach St.); © **800/548-9918** or 415/673-7411. See p. 89.

4 SoMa

VERY EXPENSIVE

The Argent Hotel *✦✦*   The large number of rooms and fine location—just a block south of Market Street, and a block from the Moscone Convention Center—make the Argent attractive to both groups and business travelers. But the upcoming $30-million hotel renovation in the works will make it even more compelling, especially with a new fitness center and restaurant. But even now rooms, which are decorated with warm, modern, and surprisingly attractive furnishings and textiles (surprising considering what a corporate hotel it is), have floor-to-ceiling windows and are well outfitted with three telephones (with voice mail). Corner suites look across the Bay Bridge. But so long as you're on an upper story, you're bound to get good city views

50 Third St. (between Market and Mission sts.), San Francisco, CA 94103. ✆ **877/222-6699** or 415/974-6400. Fax 415/543-8268. www.argenthotel.com. 667 units. $199–$399 double; $599–$1,800 suite. AE, DC, DISC, MC, V. Valet parking $42. Bus: All Market St. buses. Streetcar: All Market St. streetcars. **Amenities:** Restaurant; bar; fitness center; concierge; business center; secretarial services; room service; in-room massage for fee; babysitting for fee; same-day laundry service/dry cleaning. *In room:* A/C, TV w/pay movies, dataport, minibar, coffeemaker, hair dryer, iron, safe, high-speed Internet access for a fee.

Four Seasons Hotel San Francisco *✦✦✦*   What makes this uberluxury hotel that opened in late 2001 one of my favorites in the city is its perfect combination of elegance, trendiness, and modern luxury. The entrance, either off Market or through a narrow alley off Third Street, is deceptively underwhelming, although it does tip you off to the hotel's overall discreetness. Take the elevators up to the lobby and you're instantly surrounded by calm, cool, and collected hotel perfection. If you're like me, you'll get confused by the elevators, since one set goes to residences and another goes to guest rooms, and quickly adopt the sexy cocktail lounge as your second home. After all, what's not to love about dark mood lighting, comfy leather chairs, bottomless bowls of olives and spicy wasabi-covered peanuts, a great wine and cocktail list, and a pianist playing jazz standards intermingled with No Doubt and Cold Play? Many of the oversize rooms (starting at 460 sq. ft. and including 46 suites) overlook Yerba Buena Gardens. Not too trendy, not too traditional, they're just right, with custom-made mattresses and pillows that guarantee the all-time best night's sleep, beautiful works of art, and huge luxury marble bathrooms with deep tubs and L'Occitane toiletries. Hues of taupe, beige, and green are almost as soothing as the impeccable service. Adding to the perks are free access to the building's huge Sports Club L.A. (the best hotel gym in the city by far!), round-the-clock business services, a 2-block walk to Union Square and the Moscone Convention Center, and a vibe that combines sophistication with a hipness far more refined than the W or the Clift. Its only contender in that department is the new St. Regis.

757 Market St. (between Third and Fourth sts.), San Francisco, CA 94103. ✆ **800/332-3442** or 415/633-3000. Fax 415/633-3001. www.fourseasons.com/sanfrancisco. 277 units. $415–$855 double; $825 executive suite. AE, DC, DISC, MC, V. Parking $39. Bus: All Market St. buses. Streetcar: F, and all underground streetcars. BART: All trains. **Amenities:** Restaurant; bar; huge fitness center; spa; concierge; high-tech business center; secretarial services; salon; room service; in-room massage; overnight laundry service/dry cleaning, wireless Internet access in lobby. *In room:* A/C, TV w/pay movies, fax, dataport, minibar, hair dryer, safe, high-speed Internet access ($13/day).

The Harbor Court *✦✦✦*   When The Embarcadero Freeway was torn down after the Big One in 1989, one of the major benefactors was the "wellness-themed" Harbor Court hotel: The 1926 landmark building's backyard view went from a wall of cement to a dazzling vista of the Bay Bridge (be sure to request a bay-view room, for an extra fee). Located just off The Embarcadero at the edge of the Financial District, this for-mer YMCA books a lot of corporate travelers, but anyone who seeks stylish, high-quality accommodations—half-canopy beds, large armoires, writing desks, soundproof windows, new beds, bedding, and carpet, and 27-inch LCD TVs in 2005—with a superb view and lively scene will be perfectly content here. A major bonus for health nuts is the free use of the adjoining fitness club, a top-quality facil-ity with a giant indoor swimming pool. And for the lounger in all of us, there's an evening wine reception and coffee, tea, and apples in the lobby at all times

165 Steuart St. (between Mission and Howard sts.), San Francisco, CA 94105. ℭ 800/346-0555 or 415/882-1300. Fax 415/882-1313. www.harborcourthotel.com. 131 units. $165–$399 double. Continental breakfast $10. AE, DC, DISC, MC, V. Parking $35. Bus: 14 or 80X. Streetcar: Embarcadero. Pets accepted. **Amenities:** Access to adjoining health club and large, heated indoor pool; courtesy car weekday mornings; room service (breakfast only); same-day laundry service/dry cleaning; safe. *In room:* A/C, TV, dataport, minibar, hair dryer, iron, free Wi-Fi.

The Hotel Griffon ✹✹   Among San Francisco's small hotels, this is a top con-tender. Ideally situated on the historic waterfront and steps from the heart of the Financial District, the Griffon is impeccably outfitted with a masculine design sensi-bility. It boasts contemporary features such as whitewashed brick walls, lofty ceilings, marble vanities, Aveda bath products, window seats, cherrywood furniture, and Art Deco–style lamps (really, this place is smooth). Be sure to request a bay-view room overlooking the Bay Bridge—the added perks and view make it well worth the extra cost. Smokers, book a room elsewhere—there's no puffing allowed here.

155 Steuart St. (between Mission and Howard sts.), San Francisco, CA 94105. ℭ 800/321-2201 or 415/495-2100. Fax 415/495-3522. www.hotelgriffon.com. 62 units. $189–$285 double; $375–$435 suite. Rates include extended continental breakfast and newspaper and free Mon–Fri morning town car service within the Financial District. AE, DC, DISC, MC, V. Parking $24. All Market St. buses and streetcars, BART, and ferries. **Amenities:** Restaurant; access to large health club and pool next door (for a fee); concierge; morning car service to downtown; secretarial services; lim-ited room service; in-room massage; laundry service; dry cleaning; free wireless Internet access in lobby and restau-rant. *In room:* TV, dataport, minibar, coffeemaker, hair dryer, iron, safe, free high-speed Internet access.

Hotel Palomar ✹✹   The Kimpton Boutique Hotels' most luxurious downtown property occupies the top five floors of a refurbished 1907 landmark office building. As the group's most refined boutique property, the Art Deco-inspired interior designed by Cheryl Rowley features rooms with an updated twist on 1930s modern design—artful, understated textural elements such as emerald-tone velvets, fine woods, and raffia. Tailored lines and rich textures throughout lend a sophisticated, fresh aspect to the overall air of elegance. Rooms, however, can range from very cozy (read: small) to ultracool and spacious (try for a corner room overlooking Market St.); they're also bound to be particularly fresh thanks to soft-goods upgrades in 2006 and 2007. There's not much in the way of public spaces, but the hotel makes up for it with its rooms' fab-factor, homey luxuries like DVD/CD players and flatscreen TVs, and its dining room, the **Fifth Floor Restaurant** (p. 119), which is one of the most expen-sive and upscale restaurants in town. That said, if you want the full-blown luxury hotel experience—with every hotel amenity under the sun—you're better off with one of the Nob Hill or Union Square big boys.

12 Fourth St. (at Market St.), San Francisco, CA 94103. ℭ 877/294-9711 or 415/348-1111. Fax 415/348-0302. www.hotelpalomar.com. 198 units. From $359 double; from $559 suite. Continental breakfast $22. AE, DC, DISC, MC, V. Parking $44. Streetcar: F, and all underground streetcars. BART: All trains. Pets welcome. **Amenities:** Restau-rant; fitness center; concierge; courtesy car; business center; secretarial services; room service; in-room massage; babysitting; same-day laundry service/dry cleaning. *In room:* A/C, TV, dataport, minibar, fridge, hair dryer, iron, safe, free high-speed Internet and Wi-Fi, CD player.

Where to Stay around Town

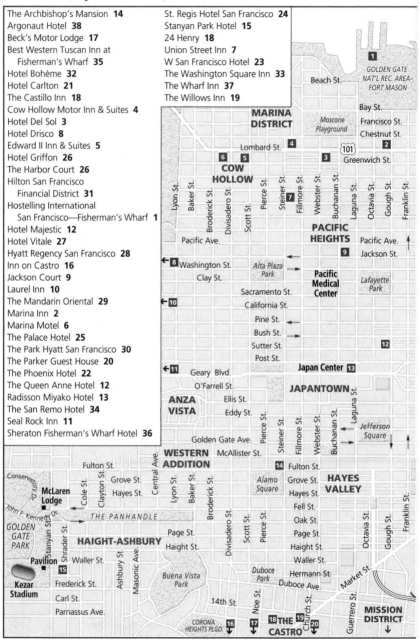

The Archbishop's Mansion **14**
Argonaut Hotel **38**
Beck's Motor Lodge **17**
Best Western Tuscan Inn at
  Fisherman's Wharf **35**
Hotel Bohème **32**
Hotel Carlton **21**
The Castillo Inn **18**
Cow Hollow Motor Inn & Suites **4**
Hotel Del Sol **3**
Hotel Drisco **8**
Edward II Inn & Suites **5**
Hotel Griffon **26**
The Harbor Court **26**
Hilton San Francisco
  Financial District **31**
Hostelling International
  San Francisco—Fisherman's Wharf **1**
Hotel Majestic **12**
Hotel Vitale **27**
Hyatt Regency San Francisco **28**
Inn on Castro **16**
Jackson Court **9**
Laurel Inn **10**
The Mandarin Oriental **29**
Marina Inn **2**
Marina Motel **6**
The Palace Hotel **25**
The Park Hyatt San Francisco **30**
The Parker Guest House **20**
The Phoenix Hotel **22**
The Queen Anne Hotel **12**
Radisson Miyako Hotel **13**
The San Remo Hotel **34**
Seal Rock Inn **11**
Sheraton Fisherman's Wharf Hotel **36**

St. Regis Hotel San Francisco **24**
Stanyan Park Hotel **15**
24 Henry **18**
Union Street Inn **7**
W San Francisco Hotel **23**
The Washington Square Inn **33**
The Wharf Inn **37**
The Willows Inn **19**

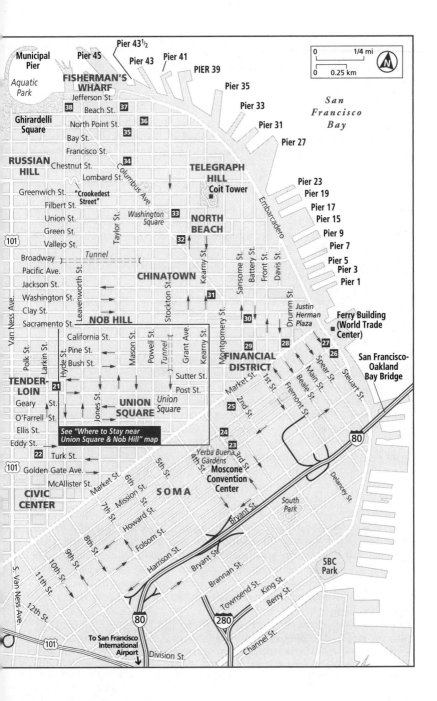

The Palace Hotel ☞ The original 1875 Palace was one of the world's largest and most luxurious hotels, and every time you walk through the doors here, you'll be reminded how incredibly majestic old luxury really is. Rebuilt after the 1906 quake, its most spectacular attributes remain the regal lobby and the Garden Court, a San Francisco landmark restaurant that was restored to its original 1909 grandeur. A double row of massive Italian-marble Ionic columns flank the court, and 10 huge chandeliers dangle above. The real heart-stopper, however, is the 80,000-pane stained-glass ceiling (good special effects made Mike Douglas look like he fell through it in the movie *The Game*). Regrettably, the rooms aren't *quite* as grand. But they're vastly improved and emulate yesteryear's refinement with mahogany beds, warm gold paint and upholstery, and tasteful artwork.

The Garden Court is famous for its $85 brunch on special holidays and a scaled-down version on regular weekends. Maxfield's Restaurant, a traditional San Francisco grill, serves lunch and dinner. Kyo-ya, an authentic Japanese restaurant, is highly regarded; and The Pied Piper Bar is named after the $2.5-million Maxfield Parrish mural that dominates the room.

2 New Montgomery St. (at Market St.), San Francisco, CA 94105. ☏ **800/325-3589** or 415/512-1111. Fax 415/543-0671. www.sfpalace.com. 552 units. $550–$650 double; from $775 suite. Extra person $40. Children under 18 sharing existing bedding stay free in parent's room. Weekend rates and packages available. AE, DC, DISC, MC, V. Parking $40. Bus: All Market St. buses. Streetcar: All Market St. streetcars. **Amenities:** 4 restaurants; bar; health club w/skylight-covered, heated lap pool; spa; Jacuzzi; sauna; concierge; 24-hr. business center; room service; laundry service; dry cleaning; wireless Internet in lobby, conference rooms w/wireless Internet access. *In room:* A/C, TV w/pay movies, dataport, minibar, hair dryer, iron, safe, high-speed Internet access ($16/day).

St. Regis Hotel ☞☞☞ The latest in full-blown high-tech luxury is yours at this new superchic 40-story SoMa tower, which debuted in late 2005. Strategically located near the Museum of Modern Art and Yerba Buena Gardens, this shrine to urban luxury living welcomes guests (and residents willing to pay upwards of $2 million for an apartment) with a 16-foot-long gas fireplace and streamlined lobby bar (frequented by socialites). A "personal butler" will take you to your room and show you how to use its coolest feature: a touch-screen control panel that works everything, from the phone to the drapes to the temperature to the lights. Decor is minimalist, with dark woods, cream, taupes, and sexy touches like Barcelona benches, 42-inch plasma TVs, and leather paneling (at least in the suites). Bathrooms beckon with deep soaking tubs, 13-inch LCD TVs, rainforest showerheads (and an alternative option for folks like me who don't care for them), and fancy toiletries. You may want to lounge on a chaise and can peek into the happenings of downtown bustle or the green patch of grass that marks Yerba Buena Gardens, but definitely leave your room for an afternoon at the super-posh two-floor Remède Spa where I had one of the best massages ever; the huge pool and fitness center; and restaurant Ame, where chef Hiro Sone, who also owns Terra in Napa Valley, presides over an Asian-influenced luxury menu that includes delicacies such as hamachi sashimi and decadences like foie gras and unagi (eel) over mushroom risotto.

125 Third St. (at Mission St.), San Francisco, CA 94103. ☏ **877/787-3447** or 415/284-4000. Fax 415/284-4100. www.stregis.com/sanfrancisco. 260 units. Double from $529–$679; suites from $1,050–$8,500. AE, DC, DISC, MC, V. Parking $45 per day. Bus: 15, 30, or 45. Streetcar: J, K, L, or M to Montgomery. **Amenities:** 2 restaurants; bar; health club with heated lap pool; giant spa; steam room; sauna; whirlpool; 24-hr. concierge; 24-hr. business center; room service; laundry service; dry cleaning; wireless Internet ($15/day), conference rooms. *In room:* A/C, 2 TVs w/pay movies, fax, dataport, minibar, hair dryer, iron upon request, safe, high-speed Internet access ($15/day), printer, scanner, copier.

W San Francisco Hotel ✿✿   Starwood Hotels & Resorts' 31-story property is as modern and hip as its fashionable clientele. Sophisticated, slick, and stylish, it suits its neighbors, which include the Museum of Modern Art, the Moscone Center, and the Metreon entertainment center. The striking gray granite facade, piped with polished black stone, complements the octagonal three-story glass entrance and lobby. The hip, urban style extends to the guest rooms, which have a residential feel. Each contains a feather bed with a goose-down comforter and pillows, Waterworks linens, an oversize dark-wood desk, an upholstered chaise longue, and louvered blinds that open to (usually) great city views. Each room also contains a compact media wall complete with a Sony CD/DVD player, an extensive CD library, and a 27-inch color TV with optional high-speed Internet service (and an infrared keyboard) at $15 per day. Bathrooms are supersleek and stocked with Bliss products. Furthering the supercool vibe is a bi-level bar and XYZ restaurant, which serves fresh Californian cuisine within a zippy white-on-white interior. In 2005, the W welcomed an outpost of NYC's Bliss spa to the premises. All in all, this is one of the top places to shack up in San Francisco.

181 Third St. (between Mission and Howard sts.), San Francisco, CA 94103. ☎ **877/WHOTELS** or 415/777-5300. Fax 415/817-7823. www.whotels.com/sanfrancisco. 410 units. From $359 double; $1,800–$2,500 suite. AE, DC, DISC, MC, V. Valet parking $40. Bus: 15, 30, or 45. Streetcar: J, K, L, or M to Montgomery. **Amenities:** Restaurant; 2 bars; heated atrium pool and Jacuzzi; fitness center; spa; concierge; business center; secretarial services; 24-hr. room service; same-day laundry service/dry cleaning; Wi-Fi in public spaces. *In room:* A/C, TV w/pay movies, fax (in some rooms), data-port, minibar, coffeemaker, hair dryer, iron, safe, high-speed Internet access, CD/DVD player.

EXPENSIVE

Hotel Vitale ✿✿   Perched at the foot of The Embarcadero with outstanding water-front and Bay Bridge views from east-facing rooms, this 199-unit hotel opened in early 2005 to instant popularity. In addition to its prime location across from the Ferry Building Marketplace (p. 154), Hotel Vitale looks pretty darned chic, from the clean-lined lobby, lounge, and decent but not destination-worthy restaurant (with a hopping after-work bar scene) to the modern and masculine rooms awash in earth tones and armed with contemporary perks like flatscreen TVs, CD players with groovy compilations, gourmet minibars and for-sale bath products, walk-in showers, and nature-themed pop art. It's the subtleties that separate Vitale from true luxury hotel status: For example, my flatscreen didn't face the bed or the couch and wasn't on hinges that allowed it to be adjusted, and the fitness room is flat-out lame with three cardio machines and a few weights. However, they're now offering access to the nearby YMCA health club, which has all the workout essentials. So, if you can live with a few quirks, it's a very attractive place to stay, especially if you book one of the suites with 270-degree San Francisco views.

8 Mission St. (at Embarcadero), San Francisco, CA 94105. ☎ **888/890-8868** or 415/278-3700. Fax 415/278-3750. www.hotelvitale.com. 199 units. $269–$399 double; from $699 suite. Rates include morning paper, free morning yoga, and free courtesy car to downtown locations on weekdays. AE, DC, DISC, MC, V. Valet parking $42. Bus: 2, 7, 14, 21, 71, or 71L. **Amenities:** Restaurant; exercise room; spa; concierge; business center; room service; laundry service; dry cleaning; free Internet salon; free Wi-Fi. *In room:* A/C, TV w/pay movies, dataport, minibar, hair dryer, iron, safe, high-speed Internet access, Wi-Fi, CD player.

San Francisco Marriott ✿✿   Some call it a masterpiece; others liken it to the world's biggest parking meter. In either case, the Marriott is one of the largest buildings in the city, making it a popular stop for convention-goers and those looking for a room with a view. Fortunately, the controversy does not extend to the rooms, which were renovated to the tune of $34 million in 2003 with suites getting an overhaul in

(Kids) The Best Family-Friendly Hotels

Argonaut Hotel (p. 88)   Not only is it near all the funky kid fun of Fisherman's Wharf and the National Maritime Museum, but this bayside hotel, a winner for the whole family, also has kid-friendly perks like the opportunity for each child to grab a gift from the hotel's "treasure chest."

Comfort Suites (p. 98)   Enough pay cable channels to keep you and your kids glued to the TV set for an entire day, and a pull-out sleeper sofa in addition to a king-size bed make this an attractive option for families.

Cow Hollow Motor Inn & Suites (p. 92)   Two-bedroom suites allow kids to shack up in style instead of camping on the pull-out couch.

Handlery Union Square Hotel (p. 60)   Never mind that it's been completely renovated. The real kid-friendly kickers here are the adjoining rooms in the "newer" addition; a heated, clean, outdoor pool; and the adjoining restaurant, The Daily Grill, which offers the gamut of American favorites.

Hotel Del Sol (p. 91)   It's colorful enough to represent a Crayola selection, but tots are more likely to be impressed by the "Kids are VIPs" program that includes a lending library, toys and videos, evening cookies and milk, and accouterments for the heated pool (think sunglasses, visors, beach balls). Parental perks include access to a bonded babysitting service and 3 babyproofed rooms and Family Suite (3 adjoining rooms).

The Maxwell Hotel (p. 62)   The colorful environs of this "theater Deco meets Victorian" style hotel are only half the reason kids will get a kick out of a stay here. Added bonuses are a VIP kids' program, which includes a second, adjoining room at half the regular price.

San Francisco Airport North Travelodge (p. 98)   It's nothing fancy, but if you've got an early flight out, want to stay near the airport, and don't want to rent an extra room to accommodate the little ones, this place (with pull-out couches in 20 out of the 199 rooms) is a good bet.

Stanyan Park Hotel (p. 97)   Plenty of elbowroom and a half-block walk to Golden Gate Park's Children's Playground make this a prime spot for crashing family style. But the biggest bonuses are the suites, which come with one or two bedrooms, a full kitchen, and a dining area.

Westin St. Francis (p. 59)   A classic San Francisco hotel down to its hospitality, the Westin welcomes the little ones with fun gifts and free drink refills at its restaurants.

2005; expect a pleasant, vibrant, and contemporary place to crash with large bathrooms and exceptional city vistas. *Tip:* Upon arrival, enter from Fourth Street, between Market and Mission, to avoid a long trek to the registration area.

55 Fourth St. (between Market and Mission sts.), San Francisco, CA 94103. (C) **800/228-9290** or 415/896-1600. Fax 415/486-8101. www.Marriott.com/sfodt. 1,500 units. $199–$349 double; $499–$3,250 suite. AE, DC, DISC, MC, V.

Parking $46. Bus: All Market St. buses. Streetcar: All Market St. streetcars. Cable car: Powell–Hyde or Powell–Mason lines (3 blocks west). **Amenities:** 2 restaurants; 2 bars; indoor pool; health club; tour desk; car rental; business center; dry cleaning; Wi-Fi in select areas. *In room:* A/C, TV w/pay movies, dataport, hair dryer, iron, high-speed Internet ($13/day).

MODERATE

The Mosser *Value* "Hip on the Cheap" might best sum up The Mosser, a highly atypical budget hotel that incorporates Victorian architecture with modern interior design. It originally opened in 1913 as a luxury hotel only to be dwarfed by the far more modern sky-rise hotels that surround it. But a major multimillion-dollar renovation a few years back transformed this aging charmer into a sophisticated, stylish, and surprisingly affordable SoMa lodging. Guest rooms, which recently underwent a soft goods upgrade, are replete with original Victorian flourishes—bay windows and hand-carved moldings—that juxtapose well with the contemporary custom-designed furnishings, granite showers, stainless steel fixtures, ceiling fans, Frette linens, and modern electronics. The least expensive rooms share a bathroom but are an incredible deal with rates starting at $69. The hotel's restaurant, Annabelle's Bar and Bistro, serves continental breakfast, lunch, and dinner, and The Mosser even houses Studio Paradiso, a state-of-the-art recording studio. The location is excellent as well—3 blocks from Union Square, 2 blocks from the MOMA and Moscone Convention Center, and half a block from the cable car turnaround. It also borders on a "sketchy" street, but then again, so do most hotels a few blocks west of Union Square.

54 Fourth St. (at Market St.), San Francisco, CA 94103. (C) **800/227-3804** or 415/986-4400. Fax 415/495-7653. www.themosser.com. 166 units, 112 with bathroom. $159–$249 double with bathroom; $69–$89 double without bathroom. Rates include safe-deposit boxes at front desk. AE, DC, DISC, MC, V. Parking $30, plus $10 for oversize vehicles. Streetcar: F, and all underground Muni and BART. **Amenities:** Restaurant; bar; 24-hr. concierge; same-day laundry service/dry cleaning. *In room:* Ceiling fan, TV, dataport, hair dryer, iron/ironing board, AM/FM stereo with CD player, voice mail, Wi-Fi ($9.95/day).

5 The Financial District

VERY EXPENSIVE

The Mandarin Oriental *Finds* No hotel boasts better ultraluxury digs with incredible views than this gem. The only reason to pause in the lobby or mezzanine is for the traditional tea service or cocktails. Otherwise, heaven begins after a rocketing ride on the elevators to the rooms, all of which are located between the 38th and 48th floors of a high-rise. Each of the spacious accommodations offers extraordinary panoramic views of the bay and city and were recently updated to include high definition TVs, new linens, and furnishings in gold tones. The opulent rooms also feature contemporary Asian-influenced decor, but the best details by far are the huge windows with superb city views. Not all rooms have tub-side views (incredible and standard with the signature rooms!), but every one does have a luxurious marble bathroom stocked with a natural loofah, a large selection of name-brand toiletries, terry and cotton cloth robes, a makeup mirror, and silk slippers. An added bonus: The restaurant, **Silks,** has a new kitchen crew working wonders with the Asian-influenced menu. If the dining room weren't so awkwardly empty, it'd be a recommended destination. That said, even without the whole package, it's an excellent place to dine.

222 Sansome St. (between Pine and California sts.), San Francisco, CA 94104. (C) **800/622-0404** or 415/276-9888. Fax 415/433-0289. www.mandarinoriental.com. 158 units. $355–$725 double; $635–$695 signature rooms; from $1,400 suite. Continental breakfast $21; American breakfast $32. AE, DC, DISC, MC, V. Valet parking $36. Bus: All

Market St. buses. Streetcar: J, K, L, or M to Montgomery. **Amenities:** Restaurant; bar; fitness center; concierge; car rental; business center; room service; in-room massage; laundry service; same-day dry cleaning; wireless Internet access. *In room:* A/C, TV w/pay movies, fax on request, dataport, minibar, hair dryer, iron, safe, Wi-Fi ($13/day), CD player.

The Park Hyatt San Francisco 🌶🌶   If you're looking for a small luxury business hotel in the heart of the Financial District—especially if you're billing it to the boss—stay at The Park Hyatt San Francisco. About half the size of Hyatt's typical mega-hotels, the 24-story Park Hyatt has a rather plain exterior, but it is a pleasure to behold from within. The lobby is lavishly appointed with Australian lace wood paneling, polished Italian granite, handmade custom carpets from China, and opalescent Spanish alabaster chandeliers. A magnificent spiral staircase leads to the upper-level restaurant, **The Park Grill.** Guest rooms, which underwent a complete soft-goods renovation in 2005 (including the signature Grand Bed with pillow top mattresses and Frette linens!) are more understated, with Italian wood furnishings, brand-new flatscreen TVs and CD players, large bathrooms, and exceedingly comfortable beds. They also have extraordinary views of the city, particularly from the corner suites on the upper floors, which also come with balconies or a Jacuzzi tub (a tough choice).

333 Battery St. (at Clay St.), San Francisco, CA 94111. ✆ **800/778-7477** or 415/392-1234. Fax 415/421-2433. www.parkhyattsanfrancisco.com. 360 units. $325–$585 double; $485–$4,400 suite. AE, DC, DISC, MC, V. Valet parking $43. Bus: 1, 12, 30, or 41. Cable car: California line. **Amenities:** Restaurant; 2 lounges; fitness center; concierge; courtesy car; business center; secretarial services; room service; in-room massage; babysitting; laundry service; same-day dry cleaning; free shoeshine. *In room:* A/C, TV w/pay movies, dataport, minibar, hair dryer, iron, safe, high-speed Internet access and Wi-Fi ($13/day), CD player.

EXPENSIVE

Hyatt Regency San Francisco 🌶   The Hyatt Regency, a convention favorite, rises from the edge of The Embarcadero Center at the foot of Market Street. The gray concrete structure, with a 1970s, bunkerlike facade, is shaped like a vertical triangle, serrated with long rows of jutting balconies. The 17-story atrium lobby, illuminated by museum-quality theater lighting, has a waterway flowing through it.

Rooms are furnished in "contemporary decor" a la corporate hotel fashion. Bonuses include ergonomic workstation chairs; textiles in shades of gold, charcoal gray, and celadon; and coffeemakers. Definitely not a standout choice for shacking up.

The Eclipse Café serves breakfast and lunch daily; during evenings it becomes A Cut Above steakhouse. Thirteen-Views Lounge serves cocktails and bar food for dinner. **The Equinox,** a revolving rooftop restaurant and bar that's open for cocktails and dinner, has 360-degree city views.

5 Embarcadero Center, San Francisco, CA 94111. ✆ **800/233-1234** or 415/788-1234. Fax 415/398-2567. www.sanfranciscoregency.hyatt.com. 802 units. $189–$349 double; extra $50 for executive suite. Continental breakfast $18. AE, DC, DISC, MC, V. Valet parking $41. Bus: All Market St. buses. Streetcar: All Market St. streetcars. **Amenities:** Restaurant; cafe; bar; fitness center; concierge; car rental; business center; dry cleaning. *In room:* A/C, TV w/pay movies, dataport, minibar, hair dryer, safe, high-speed wireless Internet access ($9.95/day).

Hilton San Francisco Financial District 🌶   Finally there's a good reason to stay in Chinatown! Newly reopened in March 2006 after a $40-million renovation, this upscale hotel geared toward the needs of the business traveler is a good choice for anyone seeking a convenient downtown location perfect for forays into Chinatown, North Beach, and beyond. All of the comfortably modern rooms feature either city or bay views, so you really can't go wrong. The panoramic bay views of Coit Tower, Telegraph Hill, and Alcatraz are wholly unobstructed as you look straight down the

(Finds) Sleeping Seaside

You would think that a city surrounded on three sides by water would have a slew of seaside hotels. Oddly enough, it has very few, one of which is the **Seal Rock Inn.** It's about as far from Union Square and Fisherman's Wharf as you can place a hotel in San Francisco, but that just makes it all the more unique. The motel fronts Sutro Heights Park, which faces Ocean Beach. Most rooms in the four-story structure have at least partial views of the ocean; at night, the sounds of the surf and distant foghorns lull guests to sleep. The rooms, although large and spotless, are old and basic, with rose and teal floral accents. Only some rooms have kitchenettes, but phones, TVs, fridges, covered parking, and use of the enclosed patio and pool area are standard. On the ground floor of the inn is a small old-fashioned restaurant serving breakfast and lunch—a place I've frequented since I was a little girl. Golden Gate Park and the Presidio are both nearby, and the Geary bus—which snails its way to Union Square and Market Street—stops right out front and takes at least a half-hour to get downtown.

The Seal Rock Inn (© **888/732-5762** or 415/752-8000; fax 415/752-6034; www.sealrockinn.com) is at 545 Point Lobos Ave. (at 48th Ave.), San Francisco, CA 94121. Double rooms range from $95 to $158.

Columbus Avenue thoroughfare to Ghirardelli Square. The in-room contemporary decor includes dark muted earth-tone carpets; warm honey-colored wood; and lush, pristine palette beds with crisp white linens and featherbeds swathed in masculine dusty blue, tan, and slate-gray pillows and accents. All units boast modern goodies such as MP3-compatible alarm clocks and flatscreen TVs. All signature-floor accommodations have balconies. The seven suites have bamboo floors, fireplaces, balconies, and large luxurious bathrooms, some with nice touches like sleek yours-and-mine sinks. For concierge-floor guests, a complimentary breakfast is served in a private lounge. A coffee bar in the lobby is perfect for getting your morning fix on the fly, and the renowned day spa, trū, offers world-class treatments, a variety of them in their one-of-a-kind rainforest room with walk-through waterfall. The restaurant, Seven Fifty, blends Mediterranean and Californian cuisine, while the high-backed Star Trek–esque chairs in the lounge make you feel like you are commander of the fleet.

750 Kearny St., at Washington St., San Francisco, CA 94108. © **800/HILTONS** or 415/433-6660. Fax 415/765-7891. www.sanfranciscofinancialdistrict.hilton.com. 549 units. $189–$419 double; $389–$1,200 suite. AE, DC, DISC, MC, V. Valet parking $42. Bus: 1, 9AX, 9BX, or 15. Cable car: California. **Amenities:** Restaurant; bar; coffee bar; spa; fitness room; concierge; 24-hr. business center; secretarial services; free car service to downtown; room service; laundry service; same-day dry cleaning; foreign currency exchange; notary public. *In room:* A/C, TV w/pay movies, dataport, minibar, hair dryer, iron, safe, Wi-Fi ($9.95).

6 North Beach/Fisherman's Wharf
EXPENSIVE
Best Western Tuscan Inn at Fisherman's Wharf ✦✦   Like an island of respectability in a sea of touristy schlock, this Best Western is one of the best midrange hotels at Fisherman's Wharf (probably because it's overseen by the Kimpton Group). It

continues to exude a level of style and comfort far beyond that of its neighboring competitors—even more so now thanks to room renovations in 2005 that included new carpeting, beds, and bedding. In 2006, the bathrooms will be upgraded as well. Splurge on hotel parking—which is actually cheaper than the wharf's outrageously priced garages—and then saunter toward the plush lobby, warmed by a grand fireplace. The rooms are a definite cut above competing Fisherman's Wharf hotels; all have writing desks and armchairs. The only caveat is the lack of scenic views—a small price to pay for a good hotel in a great location. This hotel also offers seven wheelchair-accessible rooms.

425 North Point St. (at Mason St.), San Francisco, CA 94133. © **800/648-4626** or 415/561-1100. Fax 415/561-1199. www.tuscaninn.com. 221 units. $189–$269 double; $229–$369 suite. Rates include coffee, tea, and evening fireside wine reception. AE, DC, DISC, MC, V. Parking $32. Bus: 10, 15, or 47. Cable car: Powell–Mason line. Pets welcome for $50 fee. **Amenities:** Access to nearby gym; concierge; courtesy car; secretarial services; limited room service; same-day laundry service/dry cleaning. *In room:* A/C, TV w/Nintendo and pay movies, dataport, minibar, coffeemaker, hair dryer, iron, free Wi-Fi.

Sheraton Fisherman's Wharf Hotel ♣   Built in the mid-1970s, this contemporary, four-story hotel offers the reliable comforts of a Sheraton in San Francisco's most popular tourist area. In other words, the clean, modern rooms are comfortable and well equipped but nothing unique to the city. On the bright side, they added their signature Sleeper Bed (read: upgraded bedding and pillows) in 2004. A corporate floor caters exclusively to business travelers.

2500 Mason St. (between Beach and North Point sts.), San Francisco, CA 94133. © **800/325-3535** or 415/362-5500. Fax 415/956-5275. www.sheratonatthewharf.com. 529 units. $199–$299 double; $550–$1,000 suite. Extra person $20. Continental breakfast $13. AE, DC, DISC, MC, V. Valet parking $36. Bus: 10 or 49. Streetcar: F. Cable car: Powell–Mason line (1 block east, 2 blocks south). **Amenities:** Restaurant; bar; outdoor heated pool; exercise room; concierge; car-rental desk; business center; limited room service; laundry; dry cleaning. *In room:* A/C, TV, fax (in suites only), dataport, coffeemaker, hair dryer, high-speed Internet ($9.95/day).

MODERATE
Argonaut Hotel ♣♣ *Kids*   The Kimpton Hotel Group is behind Fisherman's Wharf's best hotel, which opened in 2003 at the very cool San Francisco Maritime National Historical Park (p. 162). Half a block from the bay (though miraculously quiet), the four-story timber and brick landmark building, originally built in 1908 as a warehouse for the California Fruit Canners Association (and later used by William Randolph Hearst to store items that eventually ended up inside his Hearst Castle in San Simeon), is a true boutique gem. Its 239 rooms and 13 suites are whimsically decorated to emulate a luxury cruise ship in cheerful nautical colors of blue, white, red, and yellow (though evidence of its modest past appears in original brick walls, large timbers, and steel warehouse doors). Luxurious touches include flatscreen TVs, DVD and CD players, Aveda toiletries, and—get this—leopard-spotted bathrobes along with all the standard hotel amenities. All guests are welcome at nightly weekday wine receptions and can use the lobby's two popular (and free) Internet terminals. Suites have killer views and come fully loaded with telescopes and spa tubs. Get a "view" room, which peers onto the wharf or bay (some rooms offer fabulous views of Alcatraz and the Golden Gate Bridge). If you're bringing the kids, know that the Argonaut's friendly staff goes out of their way to make little ones feel at home and allows each pint-size guest to pick a new plaything from the hotel's "treasure chest." With so many offerings it's no surprise the hotel was awarded a Four Diamond rating from

AAA. *Tip:* The concierge seems to be able to work wonders when you need tickets to Alcatraz—even when the trips are officially sold out.

495 Jefferson St (at Hyde St.), San Francisco, CA 94109. © 866/415-0704 or 415/563-0800. Fax 415/563-2800. www.argonauthotel.com. 252 units. $179–$379 double; $479–$1,079 suite. Rates include evening wine in the lobby, daily newspaper, and kid-friendly perks like cribs and strollers. AE, DC, DISC, MC, V. Parking $39. Bus: 10, 30, or 47. Streetcar: F. Cable car: Powell–Hyde line. **Amenities:** Restaurant; bar; fitness center; concierge; laundry service; dry cleaning; yoga video and mats; Wi-Fi in public areas. *In room:* A/C, flatscreen TV w/Nintendo and pay movies, minibar, coffeemaker, hair dryer, iron, safe, free high-speed Internet access, DVD and CD players, Web TV.

The Hotel Bohème 🕷🕷 *Finds*   Romance awaits at the intimate Bohème. Although it's located on the busiest strip in the neighborhood, once you climb the staircase to this narrow second-floor boutique hotel, you'll discover a style and demeanor reminiscent of a home in upscale Nob Hill. Alas, there are no common areas other than a little booth for check-in and concierge, but rooms, updated in 2005 with new textiles and lining a skinny corridor, though small, are truly sweet, with gauze-draped canopies, stylish decor such as ornate parasols shading ceiling lights, and walls dramatically colored with lavender, sage green, black, and pumpkin. The staff is ultrahospitable, and bonuses include sherry in the lobby each afternoon. Some fabulous cafes, restaurants, bars, and shops are just a few steps away, and Chinatown and Union Square are within walking distance. *Note:* While the bathrooms are spiffy, they're also tiny and have showers only. *Tip:* Request a room off the street side; these rooms are quieter.

444 Columbus Ave. (between Vallejo and Green sts.), San Francisco, CA 94133. © 415/433-9111. Fax 415/362-6292. www.hotelboheme.com. 15 units. $159–$179 double. Rates include afternoon sherry. AE, DC, DISC, MC, V. Parking $12–$31 at nearby public garages. Bus: 12, 15, 30, 41, 45, or 83. Cable car: Powell–Mason line. **Amenities:** Concierge. *In room:* TV, dataport, hair dryer, iron, free Wi-Fi.

The Washington Square Inn 🕷   This small, comely bed-and-breakfast is ideal for older couples who prefer a quieter, more subdued environment than the commotion of downtown San Francisco. It's across from Washington Square in North Beach—a coffee-craver's haven—and within walking distance of Fisherman's Wharf and Chinatown. Some rooms boast fireplaces, and in 2005 and 2006, the hotel did some upgrading, and now most rooms have flatscreen TVs, new beds, and bedding.

1660 Stockton St. (between Filbert and Union sts.), San Francisco, CA 94133. © 800/388-0220 or 415/981-4220. Fax 415/397-7242. www.wsisf.com. 15 units. $149–$289 double. Rates include continental breakfast and afternoon tea, wine, and hors d'oeuvres. AE, DISC, MC, V. Valet parking $35; self parking $15. Bus: 15, 30, 41, or 45. **Amenities:** Limited room service. *In room:* Flatscreen TV, dataport, hair dryer, iron on request, free Wi-Fi, CD player.

The Wharf Inn 🕷🕷 *Value*   My top choice for good-value lodging at Fisherman's Wharf, The Wharf Inn offers above-average accommodations at one of the most popular tourist attractions in the world. Completely refurbished from 2002 through 2005, the well-stocked rooms are done in handsome tones of earth tones, muted greens, burnt orange, and sandy colors. But more important, they are well situated smack-dab in the middle of the wharf, 2 blocks from PIER 39 and the cable car turnaround, and they're within walking distance of The Embarcadero and North Beach. The inn is ideal for car-bound families because parking is free (that saves at least $25 a day right off the bat).

2601 Mason St. (at Beach St.), San Francisco, CA 94133. © 800/548-9918 or 415/673-7411. Fax 415/776-2181. www.wharfinn.com. 51 units. $99–$209 double; $299–$439 penthouse. AE, DC, DISC, MC, V. Free parking. Bus: 10, 15, 39, or 47. Streetcar: F. Cable car: Powell–Mason or Powell–Hyde lines. **Amenities:** Access to nearby health club ($10/day); concierge; tour desk; free coffee/tea, and newspapers. *In room:* TV, dataport, hair dryer on request, iron on request, free Wi-Fi.

INEXPENSIVE

The San Remo Hotel *✱✱* *(Value)* This small, European-style *pensione* is one of the best budget hotels in San Francisco. In a quiet North Beach neighborhood, within walking distance of Fisherman's Wharf, the Italianate Victorian structure originally served as a boardinghouse for dockworkers displaced by the great fire of 1906. As a result, the rooms are small and bathrooms are shared, but all is forgiven when it comes time to pay the bill. Rooms are decorated in cozy country style, with brass and iron beds; oak, maple, or pine armoires; and wicker furnishings. The immaculate shared bathrooms feature tubs and brass pull-chain toilets with oak tanks and brass fixtures. If the penthouse is available, book it: You won't find a more romantic place to stay in San Francisco for so little money. It has its own bathroom, TV, fridge, and patio.

2237 Mason St. (at Chestnut St.), San Francisco, CA 94133. ✆ **800/352-REMO** or 415/776-8688. Fax 415/776-2811. www.sanremohotel.com. 62 units, 61 with shared bathroom. $55–$95 double; $155–$175 penthouse suite. AE, DC, MC, V. Self-parking $13–$14. Bus: 10, 15, 30, or 47. Streetcar: F. Cable car: Powell–Mason line. **Amenities:** Access to nearby health club; 2 massage chairs; self-service laundry; TV room; Internet kiosk in lobby. *In room:* Ceiling fan.

7 The Marina/Pacific Heights/Cow Hollow

EXPENSIVE

Hotel Drisco *✱✱* *(Finds)* Located on one of the most sought-after blocks of residential property in all of San Francisco, the Drisco, built in 1903, is one of the city's best small hotels. Refinements by interior designer Glenn Texeira (who also did the Ritz-Carlton in Manila) are evident from the very small lobby and sitting areas to the calming atmosphere of the cream, yellow, and green guest rooms, which received a soft goods updating in early 2006. As in the neighboring mansions, traditional antique furnishings and thick, luxurious fabrics abound here. The hotel's comfy beds will make you want to loll late into the morning before primping in the large marble bathrooms, complete with robes and slippers. Each suite has a couch that unfolds into a bed (although you would never guess from the looks of it), an additional phone and TV, and superior views. A 24-hour coffee and tea service is available on the ground floor, in the same comfy rooms where breakfast is served. The only things here that prevent a top ranking are the lack of amenities, the fact that no parking options are offered, and the service, which is nowhere near the level of that at The Ritz-Carlton.

2901 Pacific Ave. (at Broderick St.), San Francisco, CA 94115. ✆ **800/634-7277** or 415/346-2880. Fax 415/567-5537. www.hoteldrisco.com. 48 units. $239 double; $359–$399 suite. Rates include buffet breakfast and evening wine hour. AE, DC, DISC, MC, V. No parking available. Bus: 3 or 24. **Amenities:** Exercise room and free pass to YMCA; concierge; business center; limited room service; same-day laundry service/dry cleaning. *In room:* TV/VCR, dataport, minibar, fridge, hair dryer, iron, safe, free high-speed Internet access, CD player.

Union Street Inn *✱✱* Who would have guessed that one of the most delightful B&Bs in California would be in San Francisco? This two-story 1903 Edwardian fronts perpetually busy (and trendy shopping and bar-hopping stop) Union Street, but is as quiet as a church on the inside. The individually decorated rooms are comfortably furnished with down comforters, fresh flowers, fruit baskets, and bay windows (beg for one with a view of the garden). A few even have Jacuzzi tubs for two. An extended full breakfast is served in the parlor, in your room, or on an outdoor terrace overlooking a lovely English garden. The ultimate honeymoon retreat is the private carriage house behind the inn, but any room at this warm, friendly inn is guaranteed to please.

2229 Union St. (between Fillmore and Steiner sts.), San Francisco, CA 94123. ✆ **415/346-0424.** Fax 415/922-8046. www.unionstreetinn.com. 5 units, 1 cottage. $189–$279 standard double; $299 cottage. Rates include breakfast, hors d'oeuvres, and evening beverages. AE, DISC, MC, V. Nearby parking $15. Bus: 22, 28, 41, or 45. *In room:* TV, free Wi-Fi, CD/DVD player.

MODERATE

Hotel Del Sol *Kids Value*   The cheeriest motel in town is located just 2 blocks off the Marina District's bustling section of Lombard. Three-level Hotel del Sol is all about festive flair and luxury touches. The sunshine theme extends from the Miami Beach–style use of vibrant color, as in the yellow, red, orange, and blue exterior, to the heated courtyard pool, which beckons the youngish clientele as they head for their cars parked (for free!) in cabana-like spaces. This is also one of the most family-friendly places to stay, with a "Kids are VIPs" program, including a family suite (three adjoining rooms with bunks and toys), a lending library of kids' books, toys and videos, childproofing kits, three rooms that have been professionally baby-proofed, bonded babysitting services, evening cookies and milk, and pool toys, and sunglasses and visors for the young ones. Fair-weather fun doesn't stop at the front door of the hotel, which boasts 57 spacious rooms (updated with all new bedding, paint, carpets, drapes, and sofas in 2006) with equally perky interior decor (read: loud and very colorful) as well as unexpected extras like CD players, Aveda products, and tips on the town's happenings and shopping meccas. Suites also include minifridges and DVD players. For those who are looking for a little camaraderie too, there's a complimentary barbecue every Friday from 4 to 7pm, Memorial Day through Labor Day. Sorry, smokers: You'll have to step outside to puff.

3100 Webster St. (at Greenwich St.), San Francisco, CA 94123. ✆ **877/433-5765** or 415/921-5520. Fax 415/931-4137. www.thehoteldelsol.com. 57 units. $129–$189 double; $169–$229 suite. Rates include continental breakfast and free newspapers in the lobby. AE, DC, DISC, MC, V. Free parking. Bus: 22, 28, 41, 43, 45, or 76. **Amenities:** Heated outdoor pool; same-day dry cleaning. *In room:* TV/VCR, dataport, kitchenettes in 3 units, fridge and DVD in suites only, iron, Wi-Fi ($7.95/day), CD player.

Jackson Court   The Jackson Court, a stately three-story brownstone Victorian mansion, is in one of San Francisco's most exclusive neighborhoods, Pacific Heights. Its only fault—that it's far from the action—is also its blessing: If you crave a blissfully quiet vacation in elegant surroundings, this is the place. The rooms, which were renovated in 2004, are individually furnished with superior-quality antique furnishings; two have wood-burning fireplaces (whose use is de rigueur in the winter) and two have gas fireplaces. The Blue Room features an inviting window seat; the Garden Suite has handcrafted wood paneling and a large picture window looking onto the private garden patio. After a continental breakfast of muffins, scones, croissants, oatmeal, juice, and fruit, spend the day browsing the shops along nearby Union and Fillmore streets and return in time for afternoon tea.

2198 Jackson St. (at Buchanan St.), San Francisco, CA 94115. ✆ **415/929-7670.** Fax 415/929-1405. www.jackson court.com. 10 units. $160–$225 double. Rates include continental breakfast and afternoon tea. AE, MC, V. Parking on street only. Bus: 1, 3, 12, or 22. **Amenities:** Concierge; dry cleaning; guests allowed to use high-speed Internet in office. *In room:* TV, dataport, hair dryer, iron available on request.

Laurel Inn *Value*   If you don't mind being out of the downtown area, this lovely hotel is one of the most tranquil, affordable places to rest your head. Tucked just beyond the southernmost tip of the Presidio and Pacific Heights, the outside is nothing impressive—just another motor inn. And that's what it was until the hotel group Joie de Vivre breathed new life into the place. Now decor is *très* chic and modern, with Zen-like influences (think W Hotel at half the price). The rooms, some of which have excellent city views, all got a soft-goods face-lift ending in 2006, including new carpet, bedding and lighting; all have spiffy bathrooms. The continental breakfast is fine, but why bother when you're across the street from **Ella's** (p. 135), which serves San Francisco's best breakfast? Other thoughtful touches: 24-hour coffee and tea service, pet-friendly rooms, and free parking! Add the great shopping 1 block away at Sacramento Street and the new and hip bar, **G,** which serves libations and a surprisingly active slice of glamorous young Pacific Heights–style revelry, and there are plenty of reasons to stay here, unless you're a smoker, as puffing isn't permitted.

444 Presidio Ave. (at California Ave.), San Francisco, CA 94115. (C) **800/552-8735** or 415/567-8467. Fax 415/928-1866. www.thelaurelinn.com. 49 units. $169–$209 double. Rates include continental breakfast and afternoon lemonade and cookies. AE, DC, DISC, MC, V. Free parking. Bus: 1, 3, 4, or 43. Pets accepted. **Amenities:** Adjoining bar; access to the mind-blowing JCC gym across the street at $10 per day; concierge; same-day laundry/dry cleaning. *In room:* TV/VCR, dataport, kitchenette in some units, hair dryer, iron, wired Internet access and Wi-Fi ($8/day), CD player.

INEXPENSIVE

Cow Hollow Motor Inn & Suites (*Kids*) If you're less interested in being downtown than in playing in and around the beautiful bayfront Marina, check out this modest brick hotel on busy Lombard Street. There's no fancy theme, but each room, completely renovated in 2004, has cable TV, free local phone calls, free covered parking, and a coffeemaker. Families will appreciate the one- and two-bedroom suites, which have full kitchens and dining areas as well as antique furnishings and surprisingly tasteful decor.

2190 Lombard St. (between Steiner and Fillmore sts.), San Francisco, CA 94123. (C) **415/921-5800.** Fax 415/922-8515. www.cowhollowmotorinn.com. 129 units. $86–$125 double; from $225 suite. Extra person $10. AE, DC, MC, V. Free parking. Bus: 28, 30, 43, or 76. **Amenities:** Laundry and dry cleaning within a block. *In room:* A/C, TV, dataport, full kitchens in suites only, coffeemaker, hair dryer, free high-speed internet access and Wi-Fi.

Edward II Inn & Suites This three-story "English country" inn has a room for almost anyone's budget, ranging from *pensione* units with shared bathrooms to luxuriously appointed suites and cottages with living rooms, kitchens, and whirlpool bathtubs. Originally built to house guests who attended the 1915 Pan-Pacific Exposition, it's still a good place to shack up in spotless and comfortably appointed rooms with cozy antique furnishings. They've recently added a small fitness center and the Café Maritime, a seafood restaurant open for dinner. Room prices even include a full continental breakfast. Nearby Chestnut and Union streets offer some of the best shopping and dining in the city. The adjoining pub serves drinks nightly. The only caveat is that the hotel's Lombard Street location is usually congested with traffic.

3155 Scott St. (at Lombard St.), San Francisco, CA 94123. (C) **800/473-2846** or 415/922-3000. Fax 415/931-5784. www.edwardii.com. 32 units, 21 with bathroom. $69–$99 double with shared bathroom; $95–$149 double with private bathroom; $169–$229 junior suite; $195–$249 apartment. Extra person $25. Rates include continental breakfast and evening sherry. AE, DISC, MC, V. Self-parking $12 1 block away. Bus: 28, 30, 43, or 76. **Amenities:** Pub; fitness center ($10/day); computer station (for nominal fee). *In room:* TV, hair dryer and iron available on request, free high-speed Internet access and Wi-Fi.

Hostelling International San Francisco—Fisherman's Wharf (*Finds*) Unbelievable but true—you can get front-row bay views for a mere $23 a night. This hostel, on national park property, provides dorm-style accommodations and offers easy access to the Marina's shops and restaurants. Rooms sleep 2 to 12 people and there are 10 private rooms available; communal space includes a fireplace, kitchen, dining room, coffee bar, pool table, and foosball. The breakfast alone practically makes it worth the price. Make reservations well in advance.

Fort Mason, Building 240, San Francisco, CA 94123. ℂ **800/909-4776** or 415/771-7277. Fax 415/771-1468. www.sfhostel.com. 150 beds. $23–$29 per person per night; kids $15–$17 per night. Rates include breakfast. MC, V. Free limited parking. Bus: 28, 30, 47, or 49. **Amenities:** Self-service laundry and kitchen; meeting room; baggage storage; secure lockers; free Wi-Fi; computer kiosks for small fee.

Marina Inn ℱ (Value   Marina Inn is one of the best low-priced hotels in San Francisco. How it offers so much for so little is mystifying. Each guest room in the 1924 four-story Victorian looks like something from a country furnishings catalog, complete with rustic pinewood furniture, a four-poster bed with silky-soft comforter, pretty wallpaper, and soothing tones of rose, hunter green, and pale yellow. You also get remote-control televisions discreetly hidden in pine cabinetry—all for as little as *$65 a night!* Combine that with continental breakfast, friendly service, a business center in the lobby with an Internet kiosk, free Wi-Fi, and an armada of shops and restaurants within easy walking distance, and there you have it: the top choice for best overall value. Don't be surprised if a few items need updating. This isn't the Ritz, after all. (***Note:*** Traffic can be a bit noisy here, so the hotel added double panes on windows facing the street.)

3110 Octavia St. (at Lombard St.), San Francisco, CA 94123. ℂ **800/274-1420** or 415/928-1000. Fax 415/928-5909. www.marinainn.com. 40 units. Nov–Feb $65–$105 double; Mar–May $75–$125 double; June–Oct $85–$135 double. Rates include continental breakfast. AE, DC, DISC, MC, V. Bus: 28, 30, 43, or 76. *In room:* TV, hair dryer and iron on request, free Wi-Fi.

Marina Motel ℱ   Established in 1939, the Marina Motel is one of San Francisco's first motels, built for the opening of the Golden Gate Bridge. The same family has owned this peach-colored, Spanish-style stucco building for three generations, and they've taken exquisite care of it. All rooms look out onto an inner courtyard, which is awash with beautiful flowering plants and wall paintings by local artists. Though the rooms show minor signs of wear and tear, they're all quite clean, bright, quiet, and pleasantly decorated with framed lithographs of old San Francisco—a thoughtful touch that adds to the motel's old-fashioned character and which makes these budget accommodations stand out from all the rest along busy Lombard Street. Two-bedroom suites with fully equipped kitchens are also available. Location-wise, the Presidio and Marina Green are mere blocks away, and you can easily catch a bus downtown. The only downside is the street noise, which is likely to burden light sleepers. ***Bonus:*** All rooms include a breakfast coupon valid for two entrees for the price of one at **Judy's Restaurant,** a short walk from the motel.

2576 Lombard St. (between Divisadero and Broderick sts.), San Francisco, CA 94123. ℂ **800/346-6118** or 415/921-9406. Fax 415/921-0364. www.marinamotel.com. 38 units. $89–$159 double; $199 suite. Lower rates in winter. Rates include 2-for-1 breakfast coupon at nearby cafe. AE, DISC, MC, V. Free covered parking. Bus: 28, 29, 30, 43, or 45. Dogs accepted with $10 nightly fee. *In room:* Dataport, fridge, coffeemaker, hair dryer, iron.

8 Japantown & Environs

EXPENSIVE

The Archbishop's Mansion ℱℱ (Finds   One thing is certain: The archbishop who built this 1904 Belle Epoque beauty was no Puritan. Though the hotel isn't world-class, it is drippingly romantic, tucked away in a very residential but central neighborhood, and likely to be the most opulently decorated B&B you could possibly imagine. Here, within the uniquely adorned rooms, it's all about whimsy and drama. The Don Giovanni suite—larger than many San Francisco houses—holds a huge, Italian four-poster bed with cherubs carved into it (a *real* antique, from 1639!), a grand fireplace, elaborate linens, and a shower with seven heads that you'll never want to leave. Slightly closer to earth is the Carmen suite, which has a deadly romantic combination of a claw-foot bathtub fronting a wood-burning fireplace. In the morning, breakfast is delivered to the guest rooms, and in the evening, wine is served in the elegant parlor. With a CD player in every room and a video and CD library accessible to every guest, this is one hotel that is enticing enough to make you linger in your room.

1000 Fulton St. (at Steiner St.), San Francisco, CA 94117. ⓒ **800/543-5820** or 415/563-7872. Fax 415/885-3193. www.thearchbishopsmansion.com. 15 units. $149–$499 double. Rates include continental breakfast and evening wine. AE, DC, MC, V. Limited free parking. Bus: 5, 22, or 24. **Amenities:** Access to nearby gym ($20/day); concierge; room service (snacks and alcohol only); same-day laundry service/dry cleaning. *In room:* TV/VCR, dataport, hair dryer, iron, Wi-Fi ($7.95/day), CD player.

Radisson Miyako Hotel ⚜   Japantown's Miyako is a tranquil alternative to staying downtown, which is only about 12 blocks away. The 16-story tower and five-story Garden Wing overlook the Japan Center, the city's largest complex of Japanese shops and restaurants (as well as a huge movie complex). The hotel, reportedly being sold in 2006 to a major hotel chain that will bring it up to a four-star property, manages to maintain a feeling of peace and quiet you'd expect somewhere much more remote. Rooms are Zen-like with East-meets-West decor. The Western-style (don't think cowboy) rooms are fine, but romantics and adventurers should opt for the traditional-style Japanese rooms in the Tower, with Japanese bathtubs, tatami mats and futons, a *tokonoma* (alcove for displaying art), and shoji screens that slide away to frame views of the city. A $30-upgrade will get you a room on the Club Floor of the Garden Wing, with bonuses like keyed entry, continental breakfast, and drinks and snacks throughout the day. All guests can take advantage of the nearby Cathedral Hill Athletic Club, a full service gym, for $10 a day, as well as the complimentary car service from 8 to 10am and from 5 to 7pm that encompasses a 2-mile radius (that'll get you to Union Square). Rumor has it that the hotel is also in negotiations with a hot chef to take over DOT Restaurant and Lounge, already a sleek, modern setting for breakfast and dinner. Stay tuned. *A bonus:* Fillmore Street's upscale boutiques are just a few blocks away.

1625 Post St. (at Laguna St.), San Francisco, CA 94115. ⓒ **800/533-4567** (within U.S. only) or 415/922-3200. Fax 415/921-0417. www.miyakohotel.com. 218 units. $149–$229 double; $300–$500 suite. Children under 18 stay free in parent's room. AE, DC, DISC, MC, V. Valet parking $22; self-parking $13. Bus: 2, 3, 4, or 38. **Amenities:** Limited exercise room; access to nearby Cathedral Hill Athletic Club ($10/day); business center; limited room service; in-room massage; same-day laundry service/dry cleaning; morning and evening free car service (2-mile radius). *In room:* TV w/pay movies, dataport, coffeemaker; hair dryer, iron; main tower building has Wi-Fi and smaller building has DSL.

MODERATE

The Queen Anne Hotel ⚜⚜ *Value*   This majestic 1890 Victorian building, once a grooming school for upper-class young women, is today a stunning hotel. Restored in 1980 and renovated in early 2006, the four-story building recalls San Francisco's golden days. Walk under rich red draperies to the lavish "grand salon" lobby, complete with English oak wainscoting and period antiques. Guest rooms also contain antiques—armoires, marble-top dressers, and other Victorian pieces. Some have corner turret bay windows that look out on tree-lined streets, as well as separate parlor areas and wet bars; others have cozy reading nooks and fireplaces. All rooms have a telephone and nice bath amenities in their marble-tiled bathroom. Guests can relax in the parlor, with two fireplaces, or in the hotel library. If you don't mind staying outside the downtown area, this hotel is highly recommended and very San Francisco.

1590 Sutter St. (between Gough and Octavia sts.), San Francisco, CA 94109. © 800/227-3970 or 415/441-2828. Fax 415/775-5212. www.queenanne.com. 48 units. $110–$199 double; $169–$350 suite. Extra person $10. Rates include continental breakfast on weekday mornings, local free limousine service (weekday mornings), afternoon tea and sherry, and morning newspaper. AE, DC, DISC, MC, V. Parking $14. Bus: 2, 3, or 4. **Amenities:** Access to nearby health club for $10; 24-hr. concierge; business center; same-day dry cleaning; front desk safe. *In room:* TV, dataport, hair dryer, iron, free wired Internet access in some rooms and Wi-Fi throughout.

INEXPENSIVE

The Hotel Majestic ☆☆ (Value)   Both tourists and business travelers adore the all-nonsmoking Majestic because it covers every professional need while retaining the ambience of a luxurious old-world hotel. It was built in 1902, and the lobby alone sweeps guests into another era, with an overabundance of tapestries, tasseled brocades, Corinthian columns, and intricate, lavish detail. Guest rooms are just as opulent, with French and English antiques; the centerpiece of many rooms is a large four-poster canopy bed. You'll also find custom-made, mirrored armoires and antique reproductions, and new paint, carpet, bedding, and upgraded bathrooms thanks to a renovation in 2005.

Perks go beyond the usual. As well as bathrobes, two phones (one of which is portable), and umbrellas, the hotel offers complimentary faxes sent and received by the office (a nice touch!), yummy treats with turndown service, and well-lit desks. All suites have fireplaces. Their intimate and very atmospheric Avalon cocktail lounge has a beautiful French mahogany bar topped with marble and a collection of African butterflies.

1500 Sutter St. (between Octavia and Gough sts.), San Francisco, CA 94109. © 800/869-8966 or 415/441-1100. Fax 415/673-7331. www.thehotelmajestic.com. 58 units. $115–$135 double; from $145–$220 suite. Rates include free continental breakfast in lobby 7–10am, and afternoon snacks 4–6pm. Group, government, corporate, and relocation rates available. AE, DC, DISC, MC, V. Valet parking $20. Bus: 2, 3, 4, 47, or 49. **Amenities:** Bar; access to nearby health club ($10/day); concierge; room service; in-room massage; babysitting; same-day laundry/dry-cleaning service; free laptop use. *In room:* TV, dataport, fridge in some rooms, hair dryer, iron, free Wi-Fi.

9 Civic Center

MODERATE

The Phoenix Hotel ☆☆   If you'd like to tell your friends back home that you stayed in the same hotel as Linda Ronstadt, David Bowie, Keanu Reeves, Moby, Franz Ferdinand, and Interpol, this is the place to go. On the fringes of San Francisco's less-than-pleasant Tenderloin District, which is rife with the homeless and crack addicts, this well-sheltered retro 1950s-style hotel is a gathering place for visiting rock musicians, writers, and filmmakers who crave a dose of Southern California—hence the palm trees and pastel colors. The focal point of the Palm Springs–style hotel is a small, heated outdoor pool adorned with a mural by artist Francis Forlenza and ensconced in a modern-sculpture garden.

The rooms, while more pop than plush, were updated in 2005 and are now equipped with bright island-inspired furnishings and original local art. But they are more standard motel-like than the hotel's air and guest list would lead you to believe. In addition to the usual amenities, the hotel offers VCRs and movies on request and a party vibe that's not part of the package at most city hotels. Some big bonuses: free parking and the hotel's restaurant and club, the groovy and very hip Bambuddha Lounge (© 415/885-5088), which serves Southeast Asian cuisine with cocktail-lounge flair. If you want luxury and quiet, stay elsewhere, but if you're looking for a great scene and fun vibe, head to The Phoenix.

601 Eddy St. (at Larkin St.), San Francisco, CA 94109. © **800/248-9466** or 415/776-1380. Fax 415/885-3109. www.thephoenixhotel.com. 44 units. $149–$169 double; $219–$399 suite. Rates include continental breakfast. AE, DC, MC, V. Free parking. Bus: 19, 31, 38, or 47. **Amenities:** Bar; heated outdoor pool; concierge; tour desk; in-room massage; same-day laundry service/dry cleaning. *In room:* TV, VCR on request, dataport, fridge and microwave in some rooms, hair dryer, iron, high-speed Internet and Wi-Fi ($7.95/day).

10 The Castro

Though most accommodations (usually converted homes) in the Castro cater to a gay and lesbian clientele, everyone is welcome. Unfortunately, there are few choices, and their amenities don't really compare to those at most of the better (and much larger) hotels throughout San Francisco.

MODERATE

The Parker Guest House *&&* This is the best B&B option in the Castro, and one of the best in the entire city. In fact, even some of the better hotels could learn a thing or two from this fashionable, gay-friendly, 5,000-square-foot, 1909 beautifully restored Edwardian home and adjacent annex a few blocks from the heart of the Castro's action. Within the bright, cheery urban compound, period antiques abound. But thankfully, the spacious guest rooms are wonderfully updated with smart patterned furnishings, voice mail, robes, and spotless private bathrooms (plus amenities) en suite or, in two cases, across the hall. A fire burns nightly in the cozy living room, and guests are also welcome to make themselves at home in the wood-paneled common library (with fireplace and piano), sunny breakfast room overlooking the garden, and spacious garden with fountains and a steam room. Animal lovers will appreciate the companionship of the house pugs Porter and Pasty.

520 Church St. (between 17th and 18th sts.), San Francisco, CA 94114. © **888/520-7275** or 415/621-3222. Fax 415/621-4139. www.parkerguesthouse.com. 21 units. $119–$219 double; $209 junior suite. Rates include extended continental breakfast and evening wine and cheese. AE, DISC, MC, V. Self-parking $17. Bus: 22 or 33. Streetcar: J Church. **Amenities:** Access to nearby health club; steam room; concierge. *In room:* TV, dataport, hair dryer, iron, free Wi-Fi.

INEXPENSIVE

Beck's Motor Lodge *&* In a town where DINK (double income, no kids) tourists happily spend fistfuls of money, you'd think someone would create a gay luxury hotel—or even a moderate hotel, for that matter. But absurdly, the most commercial and modern accommodations in the touristy Castro is this run-of-the-mill motel. Standard but contemporary, the ultratidy rooms include motel furnishings updated within the last year, a sun deck overlooking upper Market Street's action, and free parking. Unless you're into homey B&Bs, this is really your only choice in the area— fortunately, it's very well maintained. But be warned that this is a party spot; party people stay here, and the staff can be brusque.

2222 Market St. (at 15th St.), San Francisco, CA 94114. © **800/227-4360** in the U.S., except CA, 800/955-2325 within CA or 415/621-8212. Fax 415/241-0435. 58 units. $104–$145 double. AE, DC, DISC, MC, V. Free parking. Bus: 8 or 37. Streetcar: F. **Amenities:** Coin-operated washing machines. *In room:* TV, dataport, fridge, coffeemaker, free Wi-Fi.

The Castillo Inn *&* Just 2 minutes from the heart of the Castro, this charming little house provides a safe, quiet environment. Catering mostly to gay men (although anyone is welcome), the Castillo makes its clientele feel at home. Hardwood floors decorated with throw rugs aid in the warmth. Rooms are small yet cozy, and the front desk uses voice mail to collect phone messages. The Castillo also offers the shared use of a large refrigerator and microwave oven in the kitchen.

48 Henry St., San Francisco, CA 94114. ℂ 800/865-5112 or 415/864-5111. Fax 415/641-1321. E-mail: castilloinn@ yahoo.com. 4 units, none with bathroom. $80 double. Rates include continental breakfast. AE, MC, V. Bus: 8, 22, 24, or 37. Streetcar: F, J, K, L, or M. Internet access available.

Inn on Castro ℱ   One of the better choices in the Castro, half a block from all the action, is this Edwardian-style inn decorated with contemporary furnishings, original modern art, and fresh flowers throughout. It definitely feels more like a home than an inn, so if you like less commercial abodes, this place is for you. Most rooms share a small back patio, and the suite has a private entrance and outdoor sitting area. The inn also offers access to six individual nearby apartments ($85–$160, with discounts on stays of more than 4 nights) with complete kitchens.

321 Castro St. (at Market St.), San Francisco, CA 94114. ℂ 415/861-0321. Fax 415/861-0321. www.innoncastro. com. 8 units, 2 with bathroom across the hall; 6 apts. $85–$155 double; $145–$160 suite. Rates include full breakfast and evening brandy. AE, DC, MC, V. Streetcar: F, K, L, or M. **Amenities:** Hall fridges stocked with free sodas and water. *In room:* Flatscreen TV, dataport, hair dryer, free Wi-Fi, DVD/CD.

24 Henry   Its Castro location is not the only thing that makes 24 Henry a good choice for gay travelers. The building, an 1870s Victorian on a serene side street, is quite charming. The 10 guest rooms have high ceilings, period furniture, and voice mail. Guests tired of tromping around the neighborhood can watch TV or read in the double parlor (where breakfast is served). All rooms are nonsmoking.

24 Henry St. (near Sanchez St.), San Francisco, CA 94114. ℂ 800/900-5686 or 415/864-5686. Fax 415/864-0406. www.24henry.com. 10 units, 3 with bathroom. $55–$80 double with shared bathroom; $99–$119 double with private bathroom. 3-day minimum. Extra person $20. Rates include continental breakfast. AE, MC, V. Bus: 8, 22, 24, or 37. Streetcar: F, J, K, L, M, or N. **Amenities:** Wi-Fi throughout.

The Willows Inn ℱ   Right in the heart of the Castro, the all-nonsmoking Willows Inn employs a staff eager to greet and attend to visitors. The country and antique willow furnishings don't strictly suit a 1903 Edwardian home, but everything's quite comfortable—especially considering the extras, which include an expanded continental breakfast (fresh fruit, yogurt, baked goods, gourmet coffee, eggs, assorted teas, and orange juice), the morning paper, nightly cocktails, a sitting room (with a DVD player), and a pantry with limited kitchen facilities. The homey rooms vary in size from large (queen-size bed) to smaller (double bed) and are priced accordingly. Each room has a vanity sink, and all the rooms share eight water closets and shower rooms.

710 14th St. (near Church and Market sts.), San Francisco, CA 94114. ℂ 800/431-0277 or 415/431-4770. Fax 415/ 431-5295. www.willowssf.com. 12 units, none with bathroom. $99–$109 double; $139–$159 suite. Rates include continental breakfast. AE, DC, DISC, MC, V. Bus: 22 or 37. Streetcar: Church St. station (across the street) or F. *In room:* TV/VCR, fridge, free Wi-Fi.

11 Haight-Ashbury

MODERATE

Stanyan Park Hotel ℱℱ *Kids* *Value*   The only real hotel on the east end of Golden Gate Park and the west end of funky-chic Haight Street, this small inn offers classic San Francisco–style living at a very affordable price. The Victorian structure, which has operated as a hotel under a variety of names since the turn of the 20th century and is on the National Register of Historic Places, offers good-size rooms all done in period decor. Its three stories are decorated with antique furnishings; Victorian wallpaper;

and pastel quilts, curtains, and carpets. Families will appreciate the six one- and two-bedroom suites, each of which has a full kitchen and formal dining and living rooms and can sleep up to six comfortably. Tea is served each afternoon from 4 to 6pm. Continental breakfast is served in the dining room off the lobby from 6 to 10am. All rooms are nonsmoking.

750 Stanyan St. (at Waller St.), San Francisco, CA 94117. © **415/751-1000.** Fax 415/668-5454. www.stanyanpark. com. 36 units. $135–$189 double; $265–$315 suite. Rates include continental breakfast and afternoon and evening tea service. Rollaway $20; cribs free. AE, DISC, MC, V. Off-site parking $14. Bus: 7, 33, 43, 66, or 71. Streetcar: N. *In room:* TV, dataport, kitchen (in suites only), hair dryer, iron in suites or on request, free Wi-Fi.

12 Near San Francisco International Airport

MODERATE

Embassy Suites ⊛ If you've stayed at an Embassy Suites before, you know the drill. But this hotel is one of the best airport options, if only for the fact that every room is a suite. But there is more: The property has an indoor pool, whirlpool, courtyard with fountain, palm trees, and a bar/restaurant. Plus, each tastefully decorated two-room suite was updated in 2006 with all new linens and mattresses and has nice additions such as two TVs, and the all-new lobby debuted in early 2006. Additionally, a complimentary breakfast of your choice is available before you're whisked to the airport on the free shuttle—all that and the price is still right.

250 Gateway Blvd., South San Francisco, CA 94080. © **800/EMBASSY** or 650/589-3400. Fax 650/589-1183. www. embassysuites.com. 312 units. $129–$189 double. Rates include breakfast and free evening beverages. AE, DC, MC, V. **Amenities:** Restaurant; bar; indoor pool; Jacuzzi; airport shuttle. *In room:* A/C, TV, fridge, coffeemaker, hair dryer, iron, microwave, Wi-Fi ($9.95/day).

INEXPENSIVE

Comfort Suites (Kids Two miles north of the airport, well outside the heart of the city, Comfort Suites is a well-appointed option for travelers on the way into or out of town. Each studio-suite has a king-size bed, queen-size sleeper sofa (great for the kids), and all the basic amenities for weary travelers. There are also enough pay cable channels to keep you glued to your TV set for an entire day. Rooms are fine—and slated for an upgrade in 2007—but the freebies are the most attractive part of this hotel: a deluxe breakfast of waffles, eggs, sausage, and the like; an airport shuttle; and use of the outdoor hot tub.

121 E. Grand Ave., South San Francisco, CA 94080. © **800/293-1794** or 650/589-7100. Fax 650/589-7796. www. sfosuites.com. 168 units. $109 double. Rates include continental breakfast. AE, DC, DISC, MC, V. **Amenities:** Outdoor Jacuzzi; airport shuttle. *In room:* A/C, TV, fridge, coffeemaker, microwave, hair dryer, iron, free high-speed Internet access in some rooms and Wi-Fi in all rooms.

San Francisco Airport North Travelodge (Kids The Travelodge is a good choice for families, mainly because of the hotel's large heated pool. The rooms are as ordinary as you'd expect from a Travelodge. Still, they're comfortable and come with plenty of perks like Showtime and free toll-free and credit card calls. Each junior suite has a microwave and refrigerator. The clincher is the 24-hour complimentary shuttle, which makes the 2-mile trip to the airport in 5 minutes.

326 S. Airport Blvd. (off Hwy. 101), South San Francisco, CA 94080. © **800/578-7878** or 650/583-9600. Fax 650/873-9392. www.sfotravelodge.com. 199 units. $79–$129 double. AE, DC, DISC, MC, V. Free parking. **Amenities:** Restaurant; heated outdoor pool; courtesy shuttle to airport; dry cleaning; fax and copier services; high-speed Internet access at computer station (for fee). *In room:* A/C, TV w/pay movies, microwaves available, coffeemaker, hair dryer, iron, safe.

6

Where to Dine

With Northern California's unparalleled abundance of organic produce, seafood, free-range meats, and wine, San Francisco's culinary world is more than every chef's oyster. It's ours, too. Especially now.

After a rather boring couple of years, during which the city's dining rooms played it safe, closed, or cut back while awaiting more freewheeling times, restaurants are again riding high with new additions, exciting menus, and bustling dining rooms.

While every spot tries to establish its own identity, today's dining trend remains firmly grounded in the "small plate" fad—menus that allow you to snack through a meal on smaller dishes. Unfortunately, smaller portions do not always correspond with more petite prices, so expect to pay to play.

That said, it's not just trendy new spots that satisfy cuisine-crazed San Franciscans. As one of the world's cultural crossroads, the city has long been blessed with a cornucopia of cuisines. Afghan, Cajun, Burmese, Jewish, Moroccan, Persian, Cambodian, vegan—whatever you're in the mood for, this town has it covered. So book your reservations and break out the credit cards, because half the fun of visiting San Francisco is the rare opportunity to sample most of the flavors of the world in one fell swoop.

As you join the locals in their most beloved pastime, there are a few things you should keep in mind:

- If you want a table at the restaurants with the best reputations, you probably need to book 6 to 8 weeks in advance for weekends, and a couple of weeks ahead for weekdays.
- If there's a long wait for a table, ask if you can order at the bar, which is often faster and more fun.
- Don't leave *anything* valuable in your car while dining, particularly in or near high-crime areas such as the Mission, downtown, or—believe it or not—Fisherman's Wharf (thieves know tourists with nice cameras and a trunkful of mementos are headed there). Also, it's best to give the parking valet only the key to your car, *not* your hotel room or house key.
- *Remember:* It is against the law to smoke in any restaurant in San Francisco, even if it has a separate bar or lounge area. You're welcome to smoke outside, however.
- This ain't New York: Plan on dining early. Most restaurants close their kitchens around 10pm.
- If you're driving to a restaurant, add extra time into your itinerary to find parking, which can be an especially infuriating exercise in areas like the Mission, Downtown, the Marina, and most everywhere else for that matter. And expect to pay at least $10 for valet service, if the restaurant has it.

Pricing Categories

The restaurants listed below are classified first by area, then by price, using the following categories: **Very Expensive,** dinner from $75 per person; **Expensive,** dinner from $50 per person; **Moderate,** dinner from $35 per person; and **Inexpensive,** dinner less than $35 per person. These categories reflect prices for an appetizer, main course, dessert, and glass of wine.

1 The Best Dining Bets

- **Best Hotel Restaurant: Ame,** 689 Mission St. (© **415/284-4040**), located in the new and very swank St. Regis Hotel, means "rain" in Japanese. But the only drops you'll see coming down here are tears of joy from local foodies who no longer have to drive to St. Helena to enjoy a meal by Hiro Sone, James Beard Award winner and master of Japanese, French, and Italian cuisine. See p. 115. Melissa Perello whips up superb French fare at **Fifth Floor Restaurant** in the swank **Hotel Palomar,** 12 Fourth St. (© **415/348-1555**). See p. 119. **The Dining Room at the Ritz-Carlton,** 600 Stockton St. (© **800/241-3333** or 415/296-7465), serves up good and seriously formal French cuisine and surroundings. See p. 76.
- **Best for Impressing Clients:** Show your business associates you've got class—and deep pockets—by reserving a table at the Financial District's **Aqua,** 252 California St. (© **415/956-9662**). It pairs rather noisy power lunching with excellent seafood and wine. See p. 111.
- **Best Romantic Spot:** Anyone who loves classic French cooking will be seduced at **Fleur de Lys,** 777 Sutter St. (© **415/673-7779**), under the rich burgundy-tented canopy that swathes the elegant room in romance. There's lots of question-popping here, too. See p. 106.
- **Best for a Celebration:** Great food, a full bar, and a lively atmosphere are the key ingredients that make **Boulevard,** 1 Mission St. (© **415/543-6084**), the place to celebrate. See p. 118. Ditto **Hawthorne Lane,** 22 Hawthorne St. (© 415/777-9779). Care less about fancy food and more about an affordable bill, festive surroundings, and awesome grub? Head straight to the Haight's **Cha Cha Cha,** 1801 Haight St. (© **415/386-7670**). See p. 146.
- **Best Decor:** Celeb restaurant designer Pat Kuleto spent a week sketching sea life at the Monterey Bay Aquarium before applying his Midas touch to whimsical **Farallon,** 450 Post St. (© **415/956-6969**). The result is an orgy of oceanic artwork, from jellyfish lamps to sea urchin chandeliers. It's truly a spectacular achievement in restaurant design, although some argue that its underwater antics are over-the-top. See p. 105. Another fantastic design feat can be admired at **Grand Café,** 501 Geary St. (© **415/292-0101**), where the old-world European ballroom meets art Nouveau glamour surroundings are matched by equally noteworthy meals. See p. 106.
- **Best Wine List:** Thanks to renowned sommelier Raj Parr, **Michael Mina,** 335 Powell St. (© **415/397-9222**), is pouring to perfection, provided you can swallow the steep prices. See p. 106. Another sip-worthy spot is **bacar,** 448 Brannan St. (© **415/904-4100**), which offers 80 wines by the glass, taste, or carafe along with hundreds more by the bottle.

- **Best Pizza:** Gourmands and everyday diners squeeze into North Beach's **Tommaso's,** 1042 Kearny St. (© **415/398-9696**), for killer pizza and a no-frills Italian cafe atmosphere. See p. 130.
- **Best Desserts:** What a decision! Your sweet tooth can be satisfied in a number of spots around town, including my all-around favorite, **Piperade,** 1015 Battery St. (© **415/391-2555**), which woos with astoundingly tasty orange-essence beignets and chocolate cake with crème fraîche; and **Absinthe,** 398 Hayes St. (© **415/ 551-1590**), a glamorously casual and festive restaurant serving seasonal southern French cuisine and sensationally sweet finales by French pastry chef Murielle Roux. See p. 127 and 141, respectively.
- **Best Value:** No other place in town serves up heaping plates of fresh pasta at penny-pinching prices the way **Pasta Pomodoro,** 655 Union St. (© **415/399-0300**), does. See p. 129. It has other locations at 2304 Market St. (© **415/558-8123**), 3611 California St. (© **415/831-0900**), and 816 Irving St. (© **415/566-0900**). Want a little more atmosphere and sophisticated cooking with your value? Then head to the city's favorite Italian restaurant **Delfina,** 3621 18th St. (© **415/552-4055**). See p. 143.
- **Best Brunch:** The Sunday spread at the **Terrace Restaurant** in the **Ritz-Carlton,** 600 Stockton St. (© **415/773-6198**), is a full-blown feast with music to munch to. Strut around the lavish multitable buffet featuring sushi, caviar, freshly made blinis, traditional egg dishes, meats, and every other thing you can possibly think of, and then gulp it down to the sounds of live jazz. Book well in advance. Each weekend sells out. See p. 75. Want something more low key? Then head to **Ella's** (p. 135), 500 Presidio Ave. (© **415/441-5669**), for outstanding and revered breakfast food. But be prepared to wait. The line is fierce on weekends.
- **Best Dim Sum:** Downtown and Chinatown dim sum restaurants may be more centrally located, but that's all they've got on **Ton Kiang,** 5821 Geary Blvd. (© **415/ 387-8273**), where carts bring the freshest and most delicious Chinese dumplings and other dim sum delicacies to your table. See p. 149.
- **Best Vegetarian Food:** For excellent farm-fresh food and an equally stunning view of the Golden Gate, go to **Greens Restaurant,** Building A, Fort Mason Center (© **415/771-6222**). If you want to experience how rich and varied vegetables can taste, sample the extraordinary four-course menu, offered on Saturdays only. See p. 135. Also check out **Millennium,** 580 Geary St. (© **415/345-3900**).
- **Best Coffee Shop or Cafe:** With all the wonderful coffee shops throughout this cafe town, there can be no one winner. We do, however, love the authentic atmosphere at **Mario's Bohemian Cigar Store,** 566 Columbus Ave. (© **415/362-0536**), and **Caffé Trieste,** 601 Vallejo St. (© **415/392-6739**). See p. 128 and 201, respectively. If you see another cafe you like, pull up a chair and enjoy. Just do San Franciscans the favor of supporting our unique (and independent) coffee culture.

⟨Tips⟩ E-Reservations

Want to book your reservations online? Go to **www.opentable.com**, where you can save seats in San Francisco and the rest of the Bay Area in real time.

2 Restaurants by Cuisine

AMERICAN

Ame ☆☆, (SoMa, $$$$, p. 115)
Beach Chalet Brewery & Restaurant ☆ (Richmond District, $$, p. 147)
Bix ☆☆ (North Beach, $$$, p. 126)
Boudin at the Wharf (Fisherman's Wharf, $, p. 133)
Boulevard ☆☆ (SoMa, $$$$, p. 118)
Chow/Park Chow ☆☆ (The Castro/Sunset District, $, p. 145)
Dottie's True Blue Café ☆ (Union Square, $, p. 110)
Ella's ☆☆ (Pacific Heights, $$, p. 135)
Firewood Café ☆ (The Castro, $, p. 145)
Hard Rock Cafe (Fisherman's Wharf, $, p. 133)
Hawthorne Lane ☆☆ (SoMa, $$$$, p. 119)
Mecca (The Castro, $$$, p. 144)
Mel's Drive-In ☆ (The Marina/Civic Center/Richmond District/Cow Hollow/Mission District, $, p. 138)
Michael Mina ☆☆ (Union Square, $$$$, p. 106)
MoMo's (SoMa $$$, p. 119)
Moose's ☆ (North Beach, $$$, p. 126)
Mo's Gourmet Burgers ☆☆ (North Beach, $, p. 129)
The Ramp ☆ (China Basin, $, p. 140)
RNM ☆ (Haight-Ashbury, $$, p. 146)
San Francisco Art Institute Café ☆ (North Beach, $, p. 129)
Tablespoon ☆☆ (Russian Hill, $$$, p. 122)
Town Hall ☆ (SoMa, $$$, p. 120)

AMERICAN BRASSERIE

bacar ☆☆ (SoMa, $$$$, p. 118)

ARGENTINE

Il Pollaio ☆ (North Beach, $, p. 128)

ASIAN

AsiaSF ☆ (SoMa, $, p. 121)

BASQUE/BASQUE TAPAS

Bocadillos ☆☆ (Union Square, $$, p. 108)
Piperade ☆☆ (Telegraph Hill, $$, p. 127)

BELGIAN

Frjtz Fries ☆ (Civic Center, $, p. 142)

BREAKFAST

Dottie's True Blue Café ☆ (Union Square, $, p. 110)
Ella's ☆☆ (Pacific Heights, $$, p. 135)

BURMESE

Burma Superstar ☆☆ (Richmond District, $, p. 149)

CALIFORNIA

AsiaSF ☆ (SoMa, $, p. 121)
Bix ☆☆ (North Beach, $$$, p. 126)
Caffe Luna Piena ☆ (The Castro, $$, p. 145)
Cliff House ☆ (Richmond District, $$, p. 148)
Enrico's ☆ (North Beach, $$, p. 126)
Gordon Biersch Brewery Restaurant (SoMa, $$, p. 120)
Jardinière ☆☆ (Civic Center, $$$$, p. 139)
One Market ☆☆ (Financial District, $$$, p. 112)
PlumpJack Café ☆☆ (Cow Hollow, $$, p. 136)
Pluto's ☆ (The Marina/Sunset District, $, p. 139)
2223 Restaurant & Bar ☆ (The Castro, $$, p. 145)
The Waterfront Restaurant (Financial District, $$$, p. 114)

CALIFORNIA–ITALIAN

Quince ☆☆ (Pacific Heights, $$$, p. 134)

Tips Food Lover's Guide

Want more insider secrets on where to dine? Pick up Patricia Unterman's latest edition of *Patricia Unterman's San Francisco Food Lover's Guide,* fourth edition (Ten Speed Press, Feb 2005). Not only is Patty one of the best food writers in the States, she's also a chef and a local who noshes her way through the best-known and most obscure culinary must-visits, so you don't have to eat anything other than the best.

CARIBBEAN
Cha Cha Cha ☞☞ (Haight-Ashbury/Mission District, $, p. 146)

CAVIAR
Tsar Nicoulai Caviar Cafe ☞ (Financial District, $$, p. 115)

CHINESE
Brandy Ho's Hunan Food ☞ (Chinatown, $, p. 123)

Eliza's ☞☞ (Pacific Heights, $, p. 138)

House of Nanking ☞ (Chinatown, $, p. 123)

The Mandarin ☞ (Fisherman's Wharf, $$$, p. 132)

R&G Lounge ☞☞ (Chinatown, $, p. 123)

Tommy Toy's ☞ (Financial District, $$$, p. 113)

CHINESE/DIM SUM
Ton Kiang ☞☞ (Richmond District, $, p. 149)

Yank Sing ☞☞ (Financial District/SoMa, $$, p. 115)

CREPES
Ti Couz ☞ (Mission District, $, p. 144)

DELI
Boudin at the Wharf (Fisherman's Wharf, $, p. 133)

FRENCH
Absinthe ☞ (Civic Center, $$, p. 141)

Cafe Bastille (Financial District, $$, p. 113)

Café Claude ☞ (Union Square, $$, p. 108)

Chez Nous ☞☞ (Pacific Heights, $, p. 137)

Fifth Floor Restaurant ☞☞ (SoMa, $$$$, p. 119)

Fleur de Lys ☞☞ (Union Square, $$$$, p. 106)

Forbes Island ☞ (Fisherman's Wharf, $$$$, p. 131)

Grand Café (Union Square, $$$, p. 106)

Isa ☞☞ (The Marina, $$, p. 136)

Jardinière ☞☞ (Civic Center, $$$$, p. 139)

La Folie ☞☞☞ (Russian Hill, $$$$, p. 121)

PlumpJack Café ☞☞ (Cow Hollow, $$, p. 136)

Restaurant Gary Danko ☞☞☞ (Fisherman's Wharf, $$$$, p. 131)

Scala's Bistro ☞☞ (Union Square, $$, p. 109)

GREEK
Kokkari ☞ (Financial District, $$, p. 114)

ITALIAN
A16 ☞☞ (The Marina, $$, p. 135)

Cafe Pescatore ☞ (Fisherman's Wharf, $$, p. 133)

Cafe Tiramisu (Financial District, $$, p. 113)

Caffè Macaroni ☞☞ (North Beach, $, p. 127)

Capp's Corner ☞ (North Beach, $, p. 128)

Delfina ☞☞ (Mission District, $$, p. 143)

E'Angelo Restaurant ✦ (The Marina, $, p. 137)

Emporio Armani Cafe ✦ (Union Square, $, p. 110)

Firewood Café ✦ (The Castro, $, p. 145)

Il Pollaio ✦ (North Beach, $, p. 128)

Kuleto's ✦ (Union Square, $$, p. 109)

L'Osteria del Forno ✦✦ (North Beach, $, p. 128)

Mario's Bohemian Cigar Store ✦ (North Beach, $, p. 128)

Mocca ✦ (Union Square, $, p. 110)

Pane e Vino ✦ (Pacific Heights, $$, p. 136)

Pasta Pomodoro ✦✦ (North Beach/ Richmond District/The Castro/ Sunset District, $, p. 129)

Scala's Bistro ✦✦ (Union Square, $$, p. 109)

Steps of Rome Caffe ✦ (North Beach/Telegraph Hill, $$, p. 129)

The Stinking Rose (North Beach, $$, p. 127)

Tommaso's ✦✦ (North Beach, $, p. 130)

Zuppa ✦✦ (SoMa, $$, p. 120)

JAPANESE

Ace Wasabi's Rock 'n' Roll Sushi ✦ (The Marina, $$, p. 135)

Kabuto A&S ✦✦ (Richmond District, $$, p. 148)

Kyo-Ya ✦ (Financial District, $$$$, p. 112)

Sanraku Japanese Restaurant ✦ (Union Square, $, p. 111)

Takara ✦ (Japan Town, $$, p. 139)

MEDITERRANEAN

Caffe Luna Piena ✦ (The Castro, $$, p. 145)

Foreign Cinema ✦✦ (Mission District, $$, p. 143)

Kokkari ✦ (Financial District, $$, p. 114)

La Méditerranée ✦ (Pacific Heights/ Mission District, $, p. 138)

PlumpJack Café ✦✦ (Cow Hollow, $$, p. 136)

Zuni Café ✦✦ (Civic Center, $$, p. 142)

MEXICAN

Andalé Taqueria ✦✦ (The Marina, $, p. 137)

MIDDLE EASTERN

Maykadeh (North Beach, $$, p. 126)

MOROCCAN

Aziza ✦✦ (Richmond District, $$, p. 147)

PERSIAN

Maykadeh (North Beach, $$, p. 126)

PIZZA

Little Star Pizza ✦✦ (Western Addition, $, p. 141)

Pauline's ✦✦ (Mission District, $, p. 144)

SEAFOOD

A. Sabella's ✦✦ (Fisherman's Wharf, $$$$, p. 130)

Ame ✦✦ (SoMa, $$$, p. 115)

Alioto's (Fisherman's Wharf, $$$, p. 132)

Aqua ✦✦ (Financial District, $$$$, p. 111)

Tips **Multicourse Dining**

Ordering a "fixed-price," "prix-fixe," or "tasting" menu can be a good bargain as well as a great way to sample lots of dishes at one sitting. Many dining rooms in town offer these multicourse menus, which tend to cost around $75 for four courses, including dessert.

Cliff House ⋆ (Richmond District, $$, p. 148)

Farallon ⋆ (Union Square, $$$$, p. 105)

Hayes Street Grill ⋆ (Civic Center, $$, p. 142)

Plouf (Financial District, $$, p. 113)

Sam's Grill & Seafood Restaurant ⋆ (Financial District, $$, p. 114)

Scoma's ⋆ (Fisherman's Wharf, $$$$, p. 131)

Swan Oyster Depot ⋆⋆ (Russian Hill, $$, p. 122)

Tadich Grill ⋆⋆ (Financial District, $$, p. 114)

SINGAPOREAN

Straits Restaurant ⋆ (Union Square, $$, p. 110)

SPANISH

B44 (Financial District, $$, p. 113)

Bocadillos ⋆⋆ (Union Square, $$, p. 108)

STEAKHOUSE

Harris' ⋆⋆ (Pacific Heights, $$$$, p. 134)

House of Prime Rib ⋆⋆ (Russian Hill, $$$, p. 122)

SUSHI

Ace Wasabi's Rock 'n' Roll Sushi ⋆ (The Marina, $$, p. 135)

Kabuto A&S ⋆⋆ (Richmond District, $$, p. 148)

Kyo-Ya ⋆ (Financial District, $$$$, p. 112)

Sanraku Japanese Restaurant ⋆ (Union Square, $, p. 111)

Takara ⋆ (Japan Town, $$, p. 139)

THAI

Khan Toke Thai House ⋆⋆ (Richmond District, $$, p. 148)

Manora's ⋆ (SoMa, $, p. 121)

Thep Phanom ⋆ (Haight-Ashbury, $, p. 147)

VEGETARIAN

Greens Restaurant ⋆⋆ (The Marina, $$, p. 135)

Millennium ⋆⋆ (Union Square, $$, p. 109)

VIETNAMESE

Ana Mandara ⋆ (Fisherman's Wharf, $$$, p. 132)

Le Colonial ⋆⋆ (Union Square, $$$, p. 108)

Pho Hóa ⋆ (Union Square, $, p. 111)

The Slanted Door ⋆⋆ (Financial District, $$$, p. 112)

Thanh Long ⋆ (Sunset District, $$, p. 140)

3 Union Square

VERY EXPENSIVE

Farallon ⋆ SEAFOOD   While this seafood restaurant is hands-down the most whimsical in its stunning oceanic decor, the high price tag and fine, but not mind-blowing, food make it a better cocktail-and-appetizer stop than dinner choice. The multimillion-dollar attraction's outrageous decor follows the "coastal" cuisine theme; hand-blown jellyfish lamps, kelp bedlike backlit columns, glass clamshells, sea-urchin light fixtures, a sea-life mosaic floor, and a tentacle-encircled bar set the scene. (Thankfully, designer Pat Kuleto's impressive renovation of the 1924 building left the original Gothic arches intact.)

Executive chef Mark Franz, who opened the once-famous restaurant Stars with Jeremiah Tower, orchestrates the cuisine. He offers starters ranging from the expected (a variety of very expensive oysters) to the more ambitious (seared breast of squab with roasted foie gras, leg confit raviolo, and rhubarb chutney)—with a few meat and game items stuck in for good measure. The whimsy-meets-sophistication extends only as far as the food—the service and wine lists (more than 400 by the bottle; 30 by the glass) are seriously professional. Personally, I suggest stopping by for lunch or cocktails. The scene may be swank, but for seafood, Aqua (p. 111) is worlds better.

450 Post St. (between Mason and Powell sts., adjoining the Kensington Park Hotel). ⓒ **415/956-6969.** www.farallon restaurant.com. Reservations recommended. Pre-theater 3-course prix-fixe dinner menu $45; main courses $30–$39 dinner. AE, DC, DISC, MC, V. Tues–Sat 11:30am–2:30pm; Tues–Sat 2:30–5pm (bistro menu); Mon 5:30–10pm; Tues–Wed 5:30–10:30pm; Fri–Sat 5:30–11pm; Sun 5–10pm. Valet parking $12. Bus: 2, 3, 4, or 38.

Fleur de Lys ✿✿ FRENCH   Fleur de Lys is the city's most traditional and formal classic French affair. Draped in 900 yards of rich patterned fabric mood-lit with dim French candelabras, and accented with an extraordinary sculptural floral centerpiece, this restaurant is a romantic spot, so long as your way of wooing includes donning a dinner jacket, which is "appreciated" but not required. Equally formal is the cuisine of chef Hubert Keller (former President Clinton's first guest chef at the White House), who is usually in the kitchen preparing the menus and watching a closed-circuit TV of the dining room to ensure all goes smoothly. Diners in favor of grazing should start with the "Symphony" appetizer, a culinary medley with bite-size samplings of roasted beet and anchovies, pistachio crusted foie gras, Maine lobster tartare, and butternut squash vichyssoise. Other sure things include radicchio-wrapped salmon with cannellini beans and Banyuls vinegar and olive oil; and lamb loin with roasted potato stew, whole grain mustard, and honey and red-wine reduction. The selection of around 700 French, California, and Northwestern wines is also impressive.

777 Sutter St. (at Jones St.). ⓒ **415/673-7779.** www.fleurdelyssf.com. Reservations required. 3-course menu $70; 4-course $77; 5-course $88; vegetarian tasting menu $68. Vegan option available with advance notice. AE, DC, MC, V. Mon–Thurs 6–9:30pm; Fri 5:30–10:30pm; Sat 5–10:30pm. Valet parking $12. Bus: 2, 3, 4, 27, or 38.

Michael Mina ✿✿ AMERICAN   Chef Michael Mina, who became a celebrity chef while overseeing Aqua (p. 111), takes the small-plate dining concept to extremes at this sexy, swank spot. Previously the Compass Rose tearoom in the Westin St. Francis, the cream-on-cream room with deep leather lounge chairs and tables that are too wide for romance, sets the scene for this formal pre-fixed affair. But rather than three dishes, courses arrive as a trio of different renditions of the same theme (plus three sides to match!) on custom Mina-designed modular china. That's six different preparations per dish or a total of 18 different flavors over the course of an evening! It's a bit fussy for anyone who prefers to order a few things that sound good and eat lots of bites of them, but if the idea of sampling lots of styles and flavors appeals to you, this edible food-combination case study is likely to be a culinary wonder. Take diver scallops for example. One preparation is accented with lemon Osetra caviar while the other two pair them with yellow corn and summer truffles and smoked tomato and Maine lobster—not to mention three different "chilled salads" in tiny glasses. You might also find crispy pork loin done with risotto, as pulled pork with apple ravioli, and as barbecue with a corn fritter. Some dishes hit, some miss, but in all cases this is a swank affair with an incredible wine list by Raj Parr.

335 Powell St. (at Geary St.). ⓒ **415/397-9222.** Reservations recommended. 3-course tasting menu $88; seasonal classic tasting menu $135. AE, DC, DISC, MC, V. Dinner Mon–Sat 5:30–10pm; Sun 5:30–9:30pm. Valet parking $17. Bus: 2, 3, 4, 30, 38, 45, or 76.

EXPENSIVE

Grand Café FRENCH   If you aren't interested in exploring restaurants beyond those in Union Square and want a huge dose of atmosphere with your seared salmon,

Where to Dine in Union Square & the Financial District

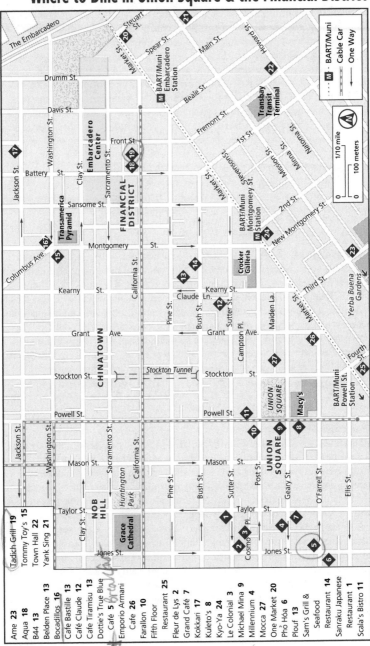

Ame **23**
Aqua **18**
B44 **13**
Belden Place **13**
Bocadillos **16**
Cafe Bastille **13**
Café Claude **12**
Cafe Tiramisu **13**
Dottie's True Blue
  Café **5**
Emporio Armani
  Cafe **26**
Farallon **10**
Fifth Floor
  Restaurant **25**
Fleur de Lys **2**
Grand Café **7**
Kokkari **17**
Kuleto's **8**
Kyo-Ya **24**
Le Colonial **3**
Michael Mina **9**
Millennium **4**
Mocca **27**
One Market **20**
Phô Hòa **6**
Plouf **13**
Sam's Grill &
  Seafood
  Restaurant **14**
Sanraku Japanese
  Restaurant **1**
Scala's Bistro **11**
Tadich Grill **19**
Tommy Toy's **15**
Town Hall **22**
Yank Sing **21**

M — BART/Muni
▬▬ Cable Car
→ One Way

107

Grand Café is your best bet. Its claims to fame? The most *grand* dining room in San Francisco, an enormous turn-of-the-20th-century grand-ballroom-like dining oasis that's a magnificent combination of old Europe and Art Nouveau; and a festive (read: crowded) cocktail area.

To match the surroundings, newly appointed chef Ron Boyd, a San Francisco native and Domaine Chandon alum, serves dressed-up French-inspired California dishes such as sautéed salmon with French lentils and house-cured bacon or salade niçoise. You can also drop by for a lighter meal in the more casual front room, the Petit Café, which offers a raw bar and similar dishes for about half the price. Sit at the cherrywood bar or at a cocktail table for food from $3 to $12 (including steak tartare; pizzas from the wood-burning oven; and a lyonnaise salad of frisee, bacon, poached egg, and a mustard vinaigrette). Libation lovers stop here for the great selection of small-batch American whiskeys and single-malt Scotches.

501 Geary St. (at Taylor St., adjacent to the Hotel Monaco). (415/292-0101. www.grandcafe-sf.com. Reservations recommended. Main courses $18–$28. AE, DC, DISC, MC, V. Mon–Fri 7–10:30am; Sat 8am–2:30pm; Sun 9am–2:30pm; Mon–Fri 11:30am–2:30pm; Sun–Thurs 5:30–10pm; Fri–Sat 5:30–11pm. Valet parking free at lunch, $15 for 3 hr. at dinner, $3 each additionalhalf-hour Bus: 2, 3, 4, 27, or 38.

Le Colonial *Finds* VIETNAMESE   Sexy environs and French Vietnamese food make this an excellent choice for folks who want to nosh at one of the sexiest bar lounges in town or amid slowly spinning ceiling fans and French Colonial decor. The upstairs lounge (which opens at 4:30pm) is where romance reigns, with cozy couches, seductive surroundings, a kicked-back cocktail crowd of swank professionals, and a yummy menu including coconut-crusted crab cakes and spring rolls. In the tiled downstairs dining room and along the stunning heated front patio guests savor the vibrant flavors of coconut curry with black tiger prawns, mangos, eggplant, and Asian basil and tender wok-seared beef tenderloin with watercress onion salad.

20 Cosmo Place (off Taylor St., between Post and Sutter sts.). (415/931-3600. www.lecolonialsf.com. Reservations recommended. Main courses $20–$38. AE, DC, MC, V. Sun–Wed 5:30–10pm; Thurs–Sat 5:30–11pm. Public valet parking $6 1st hr., $2 each additional half-hour. Bus: 2, 3, 4, or 27.

MODERATE

Bocadillos *Finds* SPANISH/BASQUE TAPAS   The sister to Piperade (p. 127) is flat-out fabulous if you're in the mood for tapas or Spanish-influenced small plates. Executive chef Gerald Hirigoyen celebrates his Basque roots with outstanding calamari with creamy tomato-and-garlic romesco sauce, scallops "mole cortado" with sherry and orange, sautéed hot peppers, tuna carpaccio, decadent foie gras sushi rolls, and astoundingly tasty warm chocolate cake with sautéed bananas. In fact, the menu has so many tasty snacks that you might find yourself returning to snack your way to heaven—especially since prices range from $3 to $12 per plate. You might also want to check out their breakfast, which includes baked eggs with chorizo and manchego cheese. But don't come anticipating a formal dining environment—or a strong cocktail. This small Financial District space is cafe-casual and beer-and-wine only.

710 Montgomery St. (at Washington St.). (415/982-2622. www.bocasf.com. Breakfast items $2–$6; lunch and dinner small items $3–$12. AE, DC, DISC, MC, V. Mon–Fri 7am–11pm; Sat 5–11pm. Closed Sun. Bus: 15, 30X, or 41.

Café Claude *Finds* FRENCH   Euro transplants love Café Claude, a crowded and lively restaurant tucked into a narrow (and very European feeling) side street near Union Square. Seemingly everything—every table, spoon, saltshaker, and waiter—is imported from France. With prices topping out at about $22 on the menu featuring classics like steak tartare; steamed mussels; duck confit; escargot; steak with spinach gratin and crisp potatoes; and quail stuffed with pine nuts, sausage, and wild rice, Café Claude offers an affordable slice of Paris without leaving the city. But beware: My last visit revealed the kind of service that would make snubbing Parisian waiters seem overly attentive. There is live jazz on Thursdays, Fridays, and Saturdays from 7:30 to 10:30pm, and atmospheric sidewalk seating for 30 diners is available when the weather permits.

7 Claude Lane (off Sutter St.). © 415/392-3515. www.cafeclaude.com. Reservations recommended. Main courses $8–$12 lunch, $14–$22 dinner. AE, DC, DISC, MC, V. Mon–Sat 11:30am–10:30pm; Sun 5:30–10:30pm. Bus: 30. Cable car: Powell–Mason.

Kuleto's ☞ ITALIAN   After systematic retrofitting and a face-lift in spring 2002, Kuleto's reclaimed its mark as one of downtown's Italian darlings. Muscle your way into a seat at the antipasto bar or at the chef's counter overlooking the kitchen, and fill up on Italian specialties and selections from the wine list featuring 30 by-the-glass options. Or partake in the likes of penne pasta drenched in tangy lamb-sausage marinara sauce, clam linguine (generously overloaded with fresh clams), or any of the grilled fresh-fish specials in the casually refined dining room. If you don't arrive by 6pm, expect to wait—this place fills up fast. Not to worry though, you can always cross the hotel lobby to the wine bar, which also serves the full menu and is open from 6 to 10pm daily. Don't have time to sit down? Try Cafe Kuleto's, which is located just outside and serves paninis, pastries, salads, and espresso to go, open daily from 7am to 8pm.

In the Villa Florence Hotel, 221 Powell St. (between Geary and O'Farrell sts.). © 415/397-7720. www.kuletos.com. Reservations recommended. Breakfast $5–$15; main courses $12–$25. AE, DC, DISC, MC, V. Mon–Fri 7–10:30am; Sat–Sun 8–10:30am; daily 11:30am–11pm. Bus: 2, 3, 4, or 38. Streetcar: All streetcars. Cable car: Powell–Mason or Powell–Hyde lines.

Millennium ☞☞ VEGAN   Banking on the trend toward lighter, healthier cooking, chef Eric Tucker and his band of merry waiters set out to prove that a meatless menu doesn't mean you have to sacrifice taste. In a narrow, handsome, Parisian-style dining room with checkered tile flooring, French windows, and sponge-painted walls, Millennium has had nothing but favorable reviews for its egg-, butter-, and dairy-free creations since the day it opened. Favorites include Balinese-style salt and pepper-crusted oyster mushrooms with blood orange chile jam, and main courses such as truffled potato Wellington stuffed with shiitake mushroom duxelles served with spring onion and lentil sugo, seared asparagus, blood orange, and capers, or *malasa dosai,* a lentil rice crepe with South Indian chickpea and red chard curry, sweet and spicy papaya chutney, and mint raita. No need to divert from PC dining with your wine choice— all the selections here are organic.

In the Savoy Hotel, 580 Geary St. (at Jones sts.). © 415/345-3900. www.millenniumrestaurant.com. Reservations recommended. Main courses $18–$22. AE, DC, DISC, MC, V. Sun–Thurs 5:30–9:30pm; Fri–Sat 5:30–10pm. Bus: 38. Streetcar: All Muni lines. BART: Powell Street.

Scala's Bistro ☞☞ FRENCH/ITALIAN   Firmly entrenched at the base of the refurbished Sir Francis Drake hotel, this downtown favorite blends Italian-bistro and old-world atmosphere with jovial and bustling results. With just the right balance of elegance and informality, this is a perfect place to have some fun (and apparently most people do).

Of the lovely array of Italian and French dishes, it's worth starting with the "Earth and Surf" calamari appetizer or grilled portobello mushrooms. Golden beet salad and garlic cream mussels are also good bets. Generous portions of moist, rich duck-leg confit will satisfy hungry appetites, but if you can order only one thing, make it Scala's signature dish: seared salmon. Resting on a bed of creamy buttermilk mashed potatoes and accented with a tomato, chive, and white-wine sauce, it's downright delicious. Finish with Bostini cream pie, a dreamy combo of vanilla custard and orange chiffon cake with a warm chocolate glaze.

In the Sir Francis Drake hotel, 432 Powell St. (at Sutter St.). ℂ 415/395-8555. www.scalasbistro.com. Reservations recommended. Breakfast $7–$10; main courses $12–$24 lunch and dinner. AE, DC, DISC, MC, V. Daily 8–10:30am and 11:30am–midnight. Bus: 2, 3, 4, 30, 45, or 76. Cable car: Powell–Hyde line.

Straits Restaurant ℱ SINGAPOREAN   As of October 2006 this exotic and cheery dining experience is relocating to downtown's newly expanded San Francisco Centre. As before, Straits remains an "adventure dining" experience showcasing chef Chris Yeo's spicy Malaysian-Indian-Chinese offerings, such as *murtabak* (stuffed Indian bread), chile crab, basil chicken, *nonya daging rendang* (beef simmered in lime leaves), *ikan pangang* (banana leaf-wrapped barbecued salmon with chile paste), and, hottest of all, his green curry (prawns, scallops, and mussels simmered in a jalapeño-based curry). What's different is the vibe. Once a casual cafe along bustling Geary Boulevard, it's slated to still be relaxed, but also offer more polished environs complete with a community table (where you sit with strangers and invariably make new friends), custom-built wine case, and cocktail lounge.

San Francisco Centre, 845 Market St., Suite 597. ℂ 415/668-1783. www.straitsrestaurants.com. Reservations recommended. Main courses $10–$27. AE, DC, MC, V. Daily 11–2am. Bus: 2, 3, 4, or 38.

INEXPENSIVE

Dottie's True Blue Café ℱ *Kids* AMERICAN/BREAKFAST   This family-owned breakfast restaurant is one of my favorite downtown diners. This is the kind of place you'd expect to see off Route 66, where most customers are on a first-name basis with the staff and everyone is welcomed with a hearty hello and steaming mug of coffee. Dottie's serves above-average American morning fare (big portions of French toast, pancakes, bacon and eggs, omelets, and the like), delivered to tables laminated with old movie star photos on rugged, diner-quality plates. Whatever you order arrives with delicious homemade bread, muffins, or scones, as well as homemade jelly. There are also daily specials and vegetarian dishes.

In the Pacific Bay Inn, 522 Jones St. (at O'Farrell St.). ℂ 415/885-2767. Reservations not accepted. Breakfast $5–$11. DISC, MC, V. Wed–Mon 7:30am–3pm (lunch served from 11:30–3pm). Bus: 2, 3, 4, 27, or 38. Cable car: Powell–Mason line.

Emporio Armani Cafe ℱ ITALIAN   All the hobnobbing of an elite luncheon comes at a moderate price at the Armani Cafe. It's nothing more than a circular counter in the middle of Armani's ever-fashionable (and expensive) clothing store, a few tables on a mezzanine, and some crowded sidewalk seats when the weather's right. But the fare and upscale casual atmosphere are enough to lure folks who have only lunch, not a new designer suit, on their minds. Local favorites include the homemade antipasto *misto,* panini, salads, and daily pizza specials. A nice variety of pricey lunch entrees, such as pasta specials, is on tap, and in case you need a stiff drink after swallowing the steep shopping prices, the bar stays open until 7pm.

1 Grant Ave. (at O'Farrell St., off Market St.). ℂ 415/677-9010. Reservations accepted. Main courses $9–$17. AE, DC, DISC, MC, V. Winter Mon–Sat 11am–4pm, Sun noon–4pm; summer Mon–Sat 11–4pm, Sun noon–4pm. Bus: All Union Square buses.

Mocca ℱ ITALIAN   If you're like me and can't be bothered with a long lunch when there's serious shopping to be done, head to this classic Italian deli on foot-traffic-only

Maiden Lane. Here it's counter service and cash only for sandwiches, caprese (Italian tomato and mozzarella salad), and big leafy salads. You can enjoy them at the few indoor tables or the umbrella-shaded tables on the pedestrian-only street-front, which look onto Union Square.

175 Maiden Lane (at Stockton St.). © 415/956-1188. Reservations not accepted. Main courses $7–$13. No credit cards. Pastry and coffee daily 10:30am–5:30pm; lunch daily 11am–5:30pm. Bus: All Union Square buses.

Pho Hóa ⟨ /Value VIETNAMESE   Although only a few blocks off of Union Square, the walk to this simple Vietnamese restaurant in the downtrodden Tenderloin District is quite an adventure, often characterized by crack-smoking loiterers (literally) and plenty of people down on their luck. Thing is, the folks along the way are usually friendly enough and the arrival promises huge, killer bowls of Vietnamese soup with all the classic fixings (basil, bean sprouts, and so on) at absurdly low prices. Any of the dozens of selections is a meal in itself, be it my favorite—the seafood soup with rice noodles—or those with beef, chicken, shrimp, or flank steak. There are also plenty of rice dishes—with beef, vegetables, deep-fried egg rolls, or barbecued pork, and intensely strong iced coffee. For a cheap, hearty, but light meal, this is my favorite downtown option, and could be yours, too, provided you can overlook the fact that they use MSG and that the atmosphere is nothing more than clean cafeteria-style.

431 Jones St. (between O'Farrell and Ellis sts.). © 415/673-3163. Reservations accepted. Soups and main courses $5–$8. No credit cards. Daily 8am–7pm. Bus: 27, 31, or 38.

Sanraku Japanese Restaurant ⟨ /Value JAPANESE/SUSHI   A perfect combination of great cooked dishes and sushi at bargain prices makes this straightforward, bright, and busy restaurant the best choice for folks hankering for Japanese food. The friendly, hardworking staff does its best to keep up with diners' demands, but the restaurant gets quite busy during lunch, when a special box lunch of the likes of a California roll, soup, salad, deep-fried salmon roll, and beef with noodles with steamed rice comes at a very digestible $8.75. The main menu, which is always available, features truly irresistible sesame chicken with teriyaki sauce and rice; tempura; a vast selection of *nigiri* (raw fish sushi) and rolls; and delicious combination plates of sushi, sashimi, and teriyaki. Dinner sees brisk business, too, but magically, there always seems to be an available table.

704 Sutter St. (at Taylor St.). © 415/771-0803. www.sanraku.com. Main courses $7.25–$13 lunch, $10–$26 dinner; 7-course fixed-price dinner $55. AE, DC, DISC, MC, V. Mon–Sat lunch 11am–4pm and dinner 4–10pm; Sun 4–10pm. Bus: 2, 3, 4, 27, or 38. Cable car: Powell–Mason line.

4 Financial District

VERY EXPENSIVE

Aqua ⟨⟨ SEAFOOD   At San Francisco's finest seafood restaurant heralded chef Laurent Manrique dazzles customers with a bewildering juxtaposition of earth and sea. Although I prefer the restaurant's original ahi tartare to his Moroccan-influenced take (thankfully both are offered!), everything else he's done to the menu since his arrival has been an improvement to an already excellent selection. Under his care, the artfully composed dishes are now more delicately decadent so that you can feast on gorgeous celery root soup with black truffle flan, frogs' legs, and rock shrimp; Alaskan black cod wrapped in smoked bacon and accompanied by tomato and date chutney and glazed carrots; and braised veal cheeks with smoked foie gras and beef consommé and still be able to easily button your pants afterward—even when the sommelier pairs wines to perfection. Desserts are not quite as dazzling, but they're still better than a lot served around town. Alas, the large dining room with high ceilings, three big floral arrangements, and otherwise stark decor can be loud, but that doesn't stop power-lunchers from powwowing by day and well-dressed gourmands from feasting in style at night. And it shouldn't stop you either. (The small bar scene is fun, too, if you're into flirting with suits.) Keep in mind that there's no valet or street parking at lunch, so you'll have to pull into one of The Embarcadero lots 2 blocks away.

252 California St. (near Battery). ✆ 415/956-9662. www.aqua-sf.com. Reservations recommended. Main courses $29–$39; 3-course menu $68; 6-course tasting menu $95; vegetarian tasting menu $65. AE, DC, DISC, MC, V. Mon–Fri 11:30am–2pm; Mon–Sat 5:30–10:30pm; Sun 5:30–9:30pm. Valet parking (dinner only) $8. Bus: All Market St. buses.

Kyo-Ya ⊛ JAPANESE/SUSHI   Anything but cheap, this restaurant offers an authentic Japanese experience, from the decor to the service to (most assuredly) the tasty sushi (skip the less impressive box lunch). Specialties include the freshest sushi, sashimi, and their elegant fixed-price menu. To start, try any of the appetizers, and move on to the grilled butterfish with miso sauce. Complete seven-course fixed-price dinners include *zensei* (tiny appetizer of chef's choice), sashimi, beef, fish, salad, chef's choice, and dessert courses. Kyo-Ya gets extra points for serving fresh wasabi, which puts the powdered stuff to shame. Many consider this—along with Kabuto (p. 148)—among the top five sushi restaurants in the city. (Unfortunately—and surprisingly—San Francisco is dreadfully lacking in truly great sushi spots.)

In the Palace Hotel, 2 New Montgomery St. (at Market St.). ✆ 415/546-5090. www.kyo-ya-restaurant.com. Reservations recommended. Sushi $5–$20; main courses $27–$50 lunch and dinner; 7-course fixed-price menu $80. AE, DC, DISC, MC, V. Mon–Fri 11am–2pm and 5–10pm. Bus: All Market St. buses. Streetcar: All Market St. streetcars.

EXPENSIVE

One Market ⊛⊛ CALIFORNIA   Some of the city's best food is coming out of this somewhat enormous but very attractive restaurant, which features an outstanding farm-fresh menu by Mark Dommen, previously at Julia's Kitchen in Napa. Amid the airy dining room of banquettes, mahogany, slate floors, seating for 220, and a bar that displays a prominent colorful painting of a market scene, a sea of diners feasts on delights from the ever-changing menu of fresh salads, fish, meat, and game, which manage to be fresh, far more inventive than most dishes around town, and outstanding in flavor. During my last visit, my table was wowed by the truly divine beet carpaccio, shellfish, and seafood sampler (seriously—try this; it's not your everyday platter!), and outrageously pristine crispy skin pork saddle with fava beans and chorizo broth. Arrive early to mingle with the corporate crowd that convenes from 4:30 to 7pm for happy hour. Or bring a gang with you—this is one restaurant that can easily accommodate large parties with some advance notice.

1 Market St. (at Stuart St., across from Justin Herman Plaza). ✆ 415/777-5577. www.onemarket.com. Reservations recommended. Lunch $16–$23; dinner $20–$33. AE, DC, DISC, MC, V. Mon–Fri 11:30am–2pm and 5:30–9pm; Sat 5:30–10pm. Valet parking $10. Bus: All Market St. buses, streetcar, and BART.

The Slanted Door ⊛⊛ *Finds* VIETNAMESE   This restaurant is so popular that Mick Jagger, Keith Richards, and Quentin Tarantino have eaten here. Why? The restaurant serves incredibly fresh and flavorful (albeit relatively expensive) Vietnamese food. Even after the April 2004 move to its beautiful bay-inspired custom-designed space in the Ferry Building Marketplace, The Slanted Door is still a city hot spot. Pull up a chair and order anything from clay-pot catfish or amazing green papaya salad to one of the lunch rice dishes topped with such options as grilled shrimp and stir-fried

Finds **The Sun on Your Face at Belden Place**

San Francisco has always been woefully lacking in the alfresco dining department. One exception is **Belden Place,** an adorable little brick alley in the heart of the Financial District that is open only to foot traffic. When the weather is agreeable, the restaurants that line the alley break out the big umbrellas, tables, and chairs, and *voilà*—a bit of Paris just off Pine Street.

A handful of adorable cafes line Belden Place and offer a variety of cuisines all at a moderate price. There's **Cafe Bastille,** 22 Belden Place (🕾 **415/ 986-5673**), a classic French bistro and fun speak-easy basement serving excellent crepes, mussels, and French onion soup; it schedules live jazz on Fridays. **Cafe Tiramisu,** 28 Belden Place (🕾 **415/421-7044**), is a stylish Italian hot spot serving addictive risottos and gnocchi. **Plouf,** 40 Belden Place (🕾 **415/986-6491**), specializes in big bowls of mussels slathered in your choice of seven sauces, as well as fresh seafood. **B44,** 44 Belden Place (🕾 **415/ 986-6287**), serves up a side order of Spain alongside its revered paella and other seriously zesty Spanish dishes.

Conversely, come at night for a Euro-speak-easy vibe with your dinner.

eggplant. If the crab and glass noodles are on the menu, trust me and order it. Dinner items, which change seasonally, might include beef with garlic and organic onions, grapefruit, and jicama salad. Whatever you order, it's bound to be wholesome, flavorful, and outstanding. An eclectic collection of teas comes by the pot for $4 to $7.

1 Ferry Plaza (at The Embarcadero and Market). 🕾 **415/861-8032.** www.slanteddoor.com. Reservations recommended. Lunch main courses $8.50–$17; most dinner dishes $15–$27; 7-item fixed-price dinner $45 (parties of 8 or more only). AE, MC, V. Mon–Sat 11am–2:30pm; Mon–Thurs 5:30–10pm; Fri–Sat 5:30–10:30pm. Bus: All Market Street buses. Streetcar: F, N-Judah line.

Tommy Toy's 𝕒 **Finds** CHINESE   If you want romantic, extravagant Chinese, come to Tommy's: Lavish, dark, unmistakably Asian, and perhaps the only Chinese restaurant where dressing up is apropos, here the dining room is glamorized with mood-lit candelabras and antique paintings. Most evenings, the restaurant is crowded with tourists, while some locals are more likely to come for the fixed-price lunches. Perhaps that's because not much changes on the expensive, French-influenced Chinese menu. But that's fine with the loyalists who return year after year for beautifully presented minced squab in leaves of lettuce; sautéed lobster with mushrooms, chives, and angel-hair crystal noodles; puff-pastry–topped creamy lobster bisque; Peking duck accompanied by lotus buns and sweet-and-tangy plum sauce; beef medallions; and a dessert of fluffy peach mousse. The a la carte menu flaunts vanilla prawns and other delicacies. During my visits, the food has varied from fine to very good, but the portions are always substantial and the environment is memorable. In any case, the many-course fixed-price "business" lunch is a steal at $23.

655 Montgomery St. (at Clay and Washington sts.). 🕾 **415/397-4888.** www.tommytoys.com. Reservations recommended. Main courses $17–$23; fixed-price lunch $23; fixed-price dinner $58–$65. AE, DC, DISC, MC, V. Mon–Fri 11:30am–2:30pm; daily 5:30–9:30pm. Valet parking (dinner only) $5. Bus: 9AX, 9BX, 12, 15, or 41.

The Waterfront Restaurant CALIFORNIA   Bay Bridge views, a sunny patio, a sleek industrial-chic dining room, and great food made The Waterfront an instant hit after its renovation and reopening in late 1997. Unfortunately, the parade of chefs in and out of the kitchen has made a sure thing more of an interesting gamble. Still, the atmosphere alone can induce idyllic San Francisco memories—especially when seated outdoors on a sunny day. Fortunately, the menu's now trying to stick with safe classics such as Dungeness crab cakes (yum); sautéed chicken breast with herbed polenta, spinach, and truffle rosemary pan sauce; and salads, pizzas, and wood-fired grill items. The wine list is fine and includes many selections starting at $27.

Pier 7 (on The Embarcadero near Broadway). © 415/391-2696. www.waterfrontsf.com. Reservations recommended. Main courses $18–$30. AE, DC, DISC, MC, V. Daily 11:30am–10pm. Valet parking $7. Streetcar: F.

MODERATE

Kokkari ★ (Finds) GREEK/MEDITERRANEAN   It figures that it would take a French chef to make Greek food fabulous, and executive chef Jean Alberti (the mastermind behind the moussaka) who departed in early 2004, did exactly that. Thankfully, he left his secret recipes behind, and Kokkari (Ko-*car*-ee) is still fashionable and flavorful under new executive chef, Erik Cosselmon, previously at Half Moon Bay's beloved Cetrella. The love affair starts with the setting: a beautifully rustic living-room-like dining area with a commanding fireplace and oversize furnishings. Past the tiny bar, the other main room is pure rustic revelry with exposed wood beams, pretty standing lamps, and a view of the glass-enclosed private dining room. Then there are the traditional Aegean dishes. Start with *pikilia* (a sampling of traditional Greek spreads served with dolmades and house-made pitas) or fabulous octopus salad. Try not to overindulge before the main courses, which include grilled whole petrale sole with lemon, olive oil, and braised greens; to-die-for moussaka (eggplant, lamb, potato, and béchamel); and lamb chops with oven-roasted lemon-oregano potatoes. Also keep an eye out for Cosselman's rotisserie specialties such as a rotisserie-roasted pork loin.

200 Jackson St. (at Front St.). © 415/981-0983. www.kokkari.com. Reservations recommended. Main courses $14–$23 lunch, $19–$35 dinner. AE, DC, DISC, MC, V. Lunch Mon–Fri 11:30am–2:30pm; bar menu 2:30–5:30pm; dinner Mon–Thurs 5:30–10pm, Fri 5:30–11pm, Sat 5–11pm. Valet parking (dinner only) $8. Bus: 12, 15, 41, or 83.

Sam's Grill & Seafood Restaurant ★ (Finds) SEAFOOD   Power-lunching at Sam's is a San Francisco tradition, and Sam's has done a brisk business with Financial District suits since—get this—1867. Even if you're not carrying a briefcase, this is the place to come for time-capsule dining at its most classically San Francisco. Pass the crowded entrance and small bar to get to the main dining room—packed with virtually all men—kick back, and watch yesteryear happen today. (Or conversely, slither into a curtained booth and see nothing but your dining companion.) Tuxedo-clad waiters race around, doling out big crusty cuts of sourdough bread and distributing salads overflowing with fresh crab and Roquefort vinaigrette, towering plates of seafood pasta with marinara, charbroiled fish, roasted chicken, and old-school standbys like calves' liver with bacon and onions or Salisbury steak. Don't worry—they didn't forget classic creamed spinach. The restaurant's mildly salty service and good old-fashioned character make everything on the menu taste that much better.

374 Bush St. (between Montgomery and Kearny sts.). © 415/421-0594. Reservations recommended for dinner and for 6 or more at lunch. Main courses $12–$24. AE, DC, DISC, MC, V. Mon–Fri 11am–9pm. Bus: 15, 45, or 76, all Market St. buses.

Tadich Grill ★★ (Finds) SEAFOOD   Not that the veteran restaurant needed more reason to be beloved, but the city's ongoing loss of local institutions makes 157-year-old

Tadich the last of a long-revered dying breed. This business began as a coffee stand during the 1849 gold rush and claims to be the very first to broil seafood over mesquite charcoal, in the early 1920s. An old-fashioned power-dining restaurant to the core, Tadich boasts its original mahogany bar, which extends the length of the restaurant, and seven booths for private powwows. Big plates of sourdough bread top the tables.

You won't find fancy California cuisine here. The novella-like menu features a slew of classic salads, such as sliced tomato with Dungeness crab or prawn Louis; daily specials; meats and fish from the charcoal broiler; grilled items; and casseroles. Hot dishes include seafood cioppino, baked avocado with shrimp Diablo; baked casserole of stuffed turbot with crab and shrimp a la Newburg; charcoal-broiled steaks; and petrale sole with butter sauce, a local favorite. Everything comes with a heaping side of fries, but if you crave something green, order the creamed spinach.

240 California St. (between Battery and Front sts.). © 415/391-1849. Reservations not accepted. Main courses $14–$20. MC, V. Mon–Fri 11am–9:30pm; Sat 11:30am–9:30pm. Bus: All Market St. buses. Streetcar: All Market St. streetcars. BART: Embarcadero.

Tsar Nicoulai Caviar Cafe CAVIAR   The name says it all, except perhaps that Tsar Nicoulai's casual ode to roe is a wonderful walk-up counter with a handful of bar seats serving all sorts of caviar, champagne by the glass, and roe-related snacks. Drop by without reservations for outstanding American and imported caviars by the taste or the ounce, blinis hot off the griddle, caviar samplers (5 grams of various selections for $48), and specials like seafood salads and truffled scrambled eggs. If you haven't yet done so elsewhere, try the fun, colorful varieties of whitefish roe, which come in flavors of beet and saffron, ginger, wasabi, and truffle.

Ferry Building Marketplace, 1 Ferry Building (at The Embarcadero and Market St.). © 415/288-8630. www.tsar nicoulai.com. Reservations not accepted. Caviar $10–$76 for samplers or 1-gram portions. Salads, etc. $10–$18. AE, MC, V. Tues–Fri 11am–6pm; Sat 9am–6pm; Sun 11am–5pm. Bus: All Market Street buses. Streetcar: F or N-Judah line.

Yank Sing CHINESE/DIM SUM   Cavernous Yank Sing is the best dim sum restaurant in the downtown area. Confident, experienced servers take the nervousness out of novices—they're good at guessing your gastric threshold as they wheel carts carrying small plates of exotic dishes past each table. Dim sum (which, translated, means "heart's delight") dishes include dumplings filled with tasty concoctions of pork, beef, fish, or vegetables, *congees* (porridges), spareribs, stuffed crab claws, scallion pancakes, shrimp balls, pork buns, and other palate-pleasers. While the food is delicious, the location makes this the most popular tourist spot and weekday lunch spot; at other times, residents generally head to Ton Kiang (p. 149), the undisputed top choice for these Chinese delicacies. A second location, open Monday through Friday from 11am to 3pm, is at 49 Stevenson St., off of First Street (© 415/541-4949) in SoMa, and has outdoor seating for fair weather dining.

101 Spear St. (at Mission St. at Rincon Center). © 415/957-9300. Dim sum $3.65–$9.30 for 2–6 pieces. AE, DC, MC, V. Mon–Fri 11am–3pm; Sat–Sun and holidays 10am–4pm. Validated parking in Rincon Center Garage. Bus: 1, 12, 14, or 41. Streetcar: F. Cable car: California St. line. BART: Embarcadero.

5 SoMa

For a map of restaurants in this section, see the "Where to Dine around town" map on p. 116.

VERY EXPENSIVE

Ame SEAFOOD   Hiro Sone and Lissa Doumani, the owners of my favorite Napa Valley special-occasion restaurant Terra, are behind the hottest opening in the

Where to Dine around Town

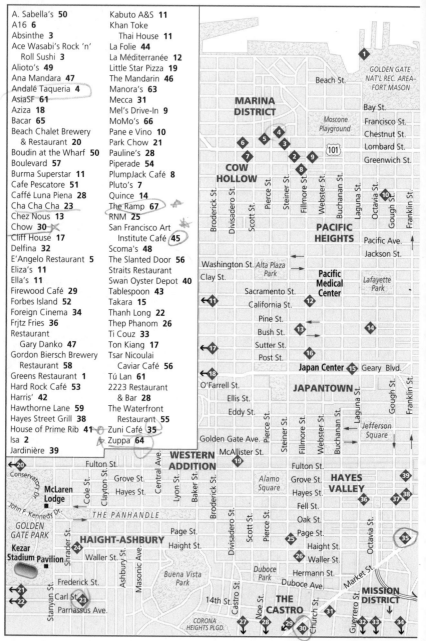

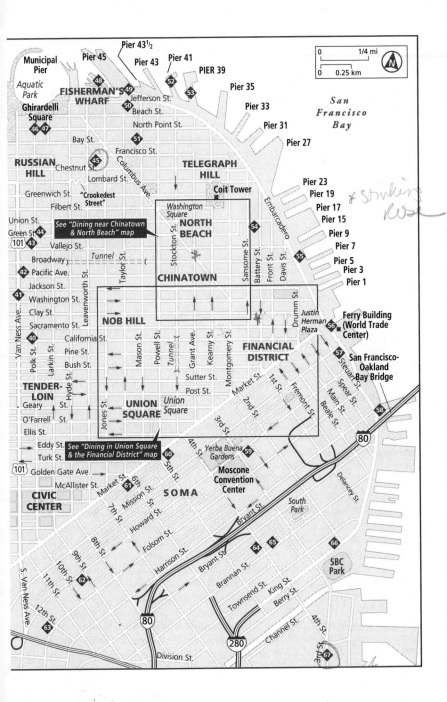

past year. Located on the ground level of the new and *très* chic St. Regis Hotel, Ame fits right in with dark woods, red accents, and long striped curtains hiding the street scene. But what makes it the new destination restaurant is the menu. Crafted by Sone, a master of Japanese, French, and Italian cuisine, it offers exotic selections ranging from pristine and creative sashimi from the sashimi bar to Japanese egg custard with lobster and urchin to wildly decadent mushroom risotto topped with foie gras and barbecued eel to lobster, scallops, and cuttlefish dressed in decidedly Italian lemon-garlic-parsley butter to Grilled "Wagyu" Beef with fried Miyagi oysters and rémoulade sauce. Afterward, hang out at the super-swank bar, where appetizers and cocktails are regularly downed by the city's elite.

689 Mission St. (at Third St.). ✆ 415/284-4040. www.amerestaurant.com. Reservations recommended. Main courses lunch $19–$25, dinner $22–$35. AE, DC, DISC, MC, V. Daily 11:30am–2pm and 6–10pm. Valet parking $12 for the 1st 3 hours. Bus: 15, 30, or 45. Streetcar: J, K, L, or M to Montgomery.

bacar ⟨F⟨F AMERICAN BRASSERIE   No other dining room makes wine as inte-gral to the meal as popular bacar. Up to 250 eclectic, fashionable diners pack into this warehouse-restaurant's three distinct areas—the casual (loud) downstairs salon; the bustling lounge, bar, and main dining room; or the more quiet upstairs mezzanine, which looks down on the lounge and bar's action—for chef and owner Arnold Eric Wong's "American Brasserie" (that is, French bistro with a California twist) cuisine. I'm a fan of the creamy salt-cod and crab *brandade* (purée) and zesty roasted mussels with a chile-and-garlic sauce that begs to be soaked up by the accompanying grilled bread. Ditto the grilled mesquite pork chop with mashed yams and pineapple-mango chutney. Just as much fun is the wine selection, which gives you 1,100 choices. Around 80 come by the glass, 2-ounce pour, or 250- or 500-milliliter decanter, and wine director Debbie Zachareas is often available to introduce you to new and excit-ing options. (She also offers monthly wine promotions featuring varying sections of the wine list.) If you want a festive night out, this is the place to come—especially when jazz is playing Monday through Saturday evenings. *Note:* bacar is open only 1 day per week (Fri) for lunch.

448 Brannan St. (at Third St.). ✆ 415/904-4100. www.bacarsf.com. Reservations recommended. Lunch 3-course fixed-price menu $22; main courses dinner $22–$38. AE, DC, DISC, MC, V. Sun 5:30–10pm; Mon–Thurs 5:30–11pm; Fri 11:30am–2:30pm and 5:30pm–midnight; Sat 5:30pm–midnight. Valet parking (Mon–Sat beginning at 6pm) $10. Bus: 15, 30, 45, 76, or 81.

Boulevard ⟨F⟨F *Finds* AMERICAN   Master restaurant designer Pat Kuleto and chef Nancy Oakes are behind one of San Francisco's most revered restaurants.Inside, the dramatically artistic Belle Epoque interior, with vaulted brick ceilings, floral ban-quettes, a mosaic floor, and tulip-shaped lamps, is the setting for Oakes's equally impressive sculptural and mouthwatering dishes. Starters alone could make a perfect meal, especially if you indulge in pan-seared day boat sea scallops with sautéed fresh hearts of palm, pomelo, basil, toasted shallots, and macadamia nuts; pan-seared foie gras with rhubarb syrup, whole grain toast, cara cara, tangelo, and blood orange salad; or Hawaiian ahi tuna tartare with habanero-chile tobiko, yellow tomato, tequila cream, guacamole and tortilla chips. The nine or so main courses are equally creative and might include grilled Pacific sea bass with fresh gulf prawns, grilled artichoke, spring asparagus, and green garlic purée; or fire roasted Angus filet with crispy Yukon gold potatoes, béarnaise sauce, sautéed spinach and crimini mushrooms, and red wine *jus.* Finish with warm chocolate cake with a chocolate caramel center, caramel corn, and butterscotch ice cream. Three levels of formality—bar, open kitchen, and main dining room—keep things from getting too snobby. Although steep prices prevent most from making Boulevard a regular gig, you'd be hard-pressed to find a better place for a special, fun-filled occasion.

1 Mission St. (between The Embarcadero and Stuart sts.). ⒸⒸ 415/543-6084. www.boulevardrestaurant.com. Reservations recommended. Main courses $14–$22 lunch, $28–$39 dinner. AE, DC, DISC, MC, V. Mon–Fri 11:30am–2:15pm; Sun–Thurs 5:30–9:30pm; Fri–Sat 5:30–10:30pm. Valet parking $12 lunch, $10 dinner. Bus: 12, 15, 30, 32, or 41. BART: Embarcadero.

Fifth Floor Restaurant ⒻⒻ FRENCH Fantastic, young executive chef and two-time James Beard nominee Melissa Perello, previously of Charles Nob Hill, sommelier Emily Wines (yes, that is her last name), and pastry chef Leena Hung are the all-female culinary dream team behind one of the city's finest restaurant experiences. The decor—rich colors and fabrics, burgundy velvet banquettes, Frette linens, zebra-striped carpeting, and a clublike atmosphere—is as luxurious as the perfectly executed and wonderfully fresh menu, which might include Alaskan halibut "en cocotte" with asparagus, spring onions, and lemon or veal rib-eye with wilted baby spinach, apricots, and chanterelle mushrooms. The wine program also reigns, with one of the most prestigious and expensive lists around and a professional team to serve it.

In the Hotel Palomar, 12 Fourth St. (at Market St.). ⒸⒸ 415/348-1555. www.fifthfloorrestaurant.com. Reservations recommended. Main courses $26–$45; tasting menu $75–$115. AE, DC, DISC, MC, V. Mon–Thurs 5:30–9:30pm; Fri–Sat 5:30–10:30pm. Valet parking $12 with validation. Bus: All Market St. buses.

Hawthorne Lane ⒻⒻCALIFORNIA Festive, elegant, relaxed, and comfortable all at the same time, this sleek hidden SoMa staple promises an excellent Asian-inspired "modern California" meal. The warm, colorful setting of an oval centerpiece bar surrounded by booths and larger back dining room with a corner view of the open kitchen is perfect for a first date or large group. Executive chef Bridget Batson gets the party started with melt-in-your-mouth tuna served three ways (sashimi, tartare, and grilled), tempura green beans (served during lunch—so good!), and killer roasted baby beet salad with warm goat cheese and candied walnuts. She brings it home with the likes of Chinese-style roasted duck with steamed green onion buns or candied ginger chutney and wild mushroom risotto. Snackers can rejoice here, too, as dinner entrees are available in half portions, and weekdays from 4 to 6pm a happy hour menu offers fantastic small plates for under $4 (think sliders, garlic fries, and tempura) plus great drink discounts. The free wi-fi is a nice bonus.

22 Hawthorne St., between Howard and Folsom sts. ⒸⒸ 415/777-9779. www.hawthornelane.com. Reservations recommended. Main courses lunch $11–$23, dinner $26–$36. AE, DC, DISC, MC, V. Mon–Thurs lunch 11:30am–1:30pm, bar menu 3–6pm, dinner 5:30–9pm; Fri lunch 11:30am–1:30pm, bar menu 3–6pm, dinner 5:30–10pm; Sat 5:30–10pm; Sun 5:30–9pm.

EXPENSIVE

MoMo's AMERICAN With an abundance of patio seating, a huge swank-yet-casual dining room, and proximity to AT&T Park baseball stadium, festive MoMo's hits a home run if you're headed to a Giants game, but is not a destination in itself. On the patio and in the bar, snack foods, like greasy-good thin-sliced onion rings, refreshing seared ahi salad, good old french fries, a-okay thin-crust pizza, and awesome burgers, as well as crowds of sports enthusiasts, make this place fun, if not a little claustrophobic. Come sundown, there are dozens of other restaurants where I'd prefer to spend my money. But singles appreciate the bar after work, and the dining room welcomes an eclectic mix of sports fans (midseason) and white-collar workers, many of whom are likely to start their lunch or dinner with a martini before indulging in slow-roasted sirloin tips or New York steak. Happy hour is hopping Monday through Friday in the baseball off season—especially during sunny weather. But if you're headed here on a game day, make a reservation or arrive early, because party people form a line around the block to get in, and it's no fun trying to eat standing at the bar or wrestling for one of the coveted patio tables.

760 Second St. (at King St.). ℂ 415/227-8660. www.sfmomos.com. Reservations recommended. Main courses $12–$39. AE, DC, DISC, MC, V. Sun–Wed 11:30am–9pm; Thurs–Sat 11:30am–10pm. Valet parking $8 lunch, $11 dinner, $20 game hours. Bus: 15, 30, 45, or 80x. Streetcar: F or N.

Town Hall ⋆ AMERICAN   Mitchell and Steven Rosenthal (Postrio) and front man Doug Washington (Vertigo, Jardiniere, and Postrio) are behind this SoMa warehouse hot spot, which opened at the end of 2003, featuring an attractive and rustically glitzy interior (exposed brick, windows, airy, a communal table) and huge portions of hearty American regional cuisine. The homey food's good, and might include the likes of fish and chips, duck confit enchiladas, and slow-braised lamb shank with summer beans, arugula, cherry tomatoes and natural *jus*. *Note:* A light menu is served between lunch and dinner.

342 Howard St. (at Fremont St.). ℂ 415/908-3900. www.townhallsf.com. Reservations recommended. Main courses $10–$17 lunch, $18–$26 dinner. AE, MC, V. Mon–Thurs 11:30am–10pm; Fri 11:30am–11pm; Sat 5:30–11pm; Sun 5:30–10pm. Bus: 10, 14, or 76.

MODERATE

Gordon Biersch Brewery Restaurant CALIFORNIA   Popular with the young Republican crowd (loose ties and tight skirts predominate), this modern, two-tiered brewery and restaurant eschews traditional brewpub fare—no cheesy nachos on this menu—in an attempt to attract a more upscale clientele. And it works. Goat cheese ravioli is a bestseller, followed by the pecan-crusted half-chicken with garlic mashed potatoes. Start with the delicate and crunchy fried calamari appetizer or, if you're a garlic hound, the tangy Caesar salad. Most dishes can be paired with one of the brewery's lagers. Couples bent on a quiet, romantic dinner can skip this place; when the lower-level bar fills up, you practically have to shout to be heard. Beer-lovers who want to pair their suds with decent grub, however, will be quite content.

2 Harrison St. (on The Embarcadero). ℂ 415/243-8246. www.gordonbiersch.com. Reservations recommended. Main courses $10–$23. AE, DC, DISC, MC, V. Mon–Thurs 11:30am–midnight; Fri–Sat 11:30am–1am; Sun 11:30am–10pm. Bus: 32.

Zuppa ⋆⋆ ITALIAN   If you're looking for a casual-chic dinner spot with good affordable food, lively ambience, and a somewhat hip crowd, Zuppa is it. Located among the warehouses of SoMa, this warmed industrial room awash with dark wood tables features a back-wall bar orchestrated by on-site owners Joseph and Mary (yes, really). Joe, whose career launched from Spago Hollywood more than 2 decades ago, oversees the menu executed by Rudy Mihal while Mary works the front of the house. With a menu of items that don't top $20, this is the way San Francisco dining used to be—where if you can't decide between the antipasti of lemon-cured tuna with veggies, pizza with clams and garlic, pasta (think the outstanding country pork ragu), or entree such as bone-in rib-eye, you can order all of them and not break the bank. A selection of cured meats, pizzas, and antipasti make it easy to snack through a meal, but don't. The pastas are fantastic and shouldn't be missed and the entrees are great as well—especially when washed down with an Italian wine. *Take note:* Parking in local lots around here costs more on game days (the ballpark is nearby)—expect to pay around $15. Otherwise, it's very affordable.

THE TRAVELOCITY GUARANTEE

...THAT SAYS EVERYTHING YOU BOOK WILL BE RIGHT, OR WE'LL WORK WITH OUR TRAVEL PARTNERS TO MAKE IT RIGHT, RIGHT AWAY.

To drive home the point,
we're going to use the word "right" in every single sentence.

Let's get right to it. Right to the meat! Only Travelocity guarantees everything about your booking will be right, or we'll work with our travel partners to make it right, right away. Right on!

Here's a picture taken smack dab right in the middle of Antigua, where the Guarantee also covers you.

The Guarantee covers all but one of the items pictured to the right.

For example, what if the ocean view you booked actually looks out at a downright ugly parking lot? You'd be right to call – we're there for you. And no one in their right mind would be pleased to learn the rental car place has closed and left them stranded. Call Travelocity and we'll help get you back on the right track.

Now, you may be thinking, "Yeah, right, I'm so sure." That's OK; you have the right to remain skeptical. That is until we mention help is always right around the corner. Call us right off the bat, knowing our customer service reps are there for you 24/7. Righting wrongs. Left and right.

Now if you're guessing there are some things we can't control, like the weather, well you're right. But we can help you with most things – to get all the details in righting,* visit travelocity.com/guarantee.

*Sorry, spelling things right is one of the few things not covered under the Guarantee.

I'd give my right arm for a guarantee like this, although I'm glad I don't have to.

travelocity
You'll never roam alone.

©2006 Travelocity.com LP. CST# 2056372-50.

Frommers.com

So many places, so little time?

TOKYO 7766 miles

LONDON 3818 miles

TORONTO 4682 miles

SYDNEY 5087 miles

NEW YORK 4947 miles

LOS ANGELES 2556 miles

HONG KONG 5638 miles

Frommers.com makes the going fast and easy.

Find a destination. ✓ Buy a guidebook. ✓ Book a trip. ✓ Get hot travel deals.
Enter to win vacations. ✓ Check out the latest travel news.
Share trip photos and memories. ✓ Download podcasts. ✓ And much more.

Frommers.com

Rated #1 Travel Web Site by *PC Magazine*®

564 Fourth St. (between Brannan and Bryant sts.) ✆ **415/777-5900**. www.zuppa-sf.com. Reservations recommended. Main courses $16–$19. AE, DC, DISC, MC, V. Tues–Sat 5:30–11pm; Sun–Mon 5:30–10:30pm. Street parking or pay at nearby lots. Bus: 9X, 12, 30, 45, 76.

INEXPENSIVE

AsiaSF ✎ ASIAN/CALIFORNIA   Part restaurant, part gender-illusionist musical revue, AsiaSF manages to be completely entertaining and extremely high quality. As you're entertained by mostly Asian men—dressed as women—who lip-sync show tunes, you can nibble on excellent grilled shrimp and herb salad; baby back pork ribs with honey tamarind glaze, pickled carrots, and sweet-potato crisps; or filet mignon with Korean dipping sauce, miso eggplant, and fried potato stars. The full bar, *Wine Spectator* award–winning wine list, and sake list add to the festivities. Fortunately, the food and the atmosphere are as colorful as the staff, which means a night here is more than a meal—it's a very happening event.

201 Ninth St. (at Howard St.). ✆ **415/255-2742**. www.asiasf.com. Reservations recommended. Main courses $9–$19; 3-course price-fixed menu Sun–Thurs $32, Fri–Sat $38. AE, DISC, MC, V (Mon–Wed $25 minimum). Sun–Thurs 6–10pm; Fri 6:45–10pm; Sat 5–10pm; cocktails and dancing until 2 on weekends. Bus: 9, 12, or 47. Streetcar: Civic Center on underground streetcar. BART: Civic Center.

Manora's ✎ THAI   Manora's cranks out some of the best Thai food in town and is well worth a jaunt to SoMa. But this is no relaxed affair: It's perpetually packed (unless you come early), and you'll be seated sardinelike at one of the cramped but well-appointed tables. During the dinner rush, the noise level can make conversation among larger parties almost impossible, but the food is so darned good, you'll probably prefer to turn toward your plate and stuff your face anyway. Start with a Thai iced tea or coffee and tangy soup or chicken satay, which comes with decadent peanut sauce. Follow these with any of the wonderful dinner dishes—which should be shared— and a side of rice. There are endless options, including a vast array of vegetarian plates. Every remarkably flavorful dish arrives seemingly seconds after you order it, which is great if you're hungry, a bummer if you were planning a long, leisurely dinner. *Tip:* Come before 7pm or after 9pm if you don't want a loud, rushed meal.

1600 Folsom St. (at 12th St.). ✆ **415/861-6224**. Reservations recommended for 4 or more. Main courses $7–$12. MC, V. Mon–Fri 11:30am–2:30pm; Mon–Sat 5:30–10:30pm; Sun 5–10pm. Bus: 9, 12, or 47.

6 Nob Hill/Russian Hill

For a map of restaurants in this section, see the "Where to Dine around town" map on p. 116.

VERY EXPENSIVE

La Folie ⭐⭐⭐ *Finds* FRENCH   My mother and I call this unintimidating, cozy, intimate French restaurant "the house of foie gras." Why? Because on our first visit, virtually every dish overflowed with the ultrarich delicacy. A recent visit after a complete interior remodel in 2005 proved that foie gras still reigns here, but more than that, it reconfirmed La Folie's long-standing reputation as one of the city's very best fine dining experiences—and without any stuffiness to boot. Chef/owner Roland Passot, who unlike many celebrity chefs is actually in the kitchen each night, offers melt-in-your-mouth starters such as seared foie gras with caramelized pineapple and star anise vanilla muscat broth. Generous main courses include rôti of quail and squab stuffed with wild mushrooms and wrapped in crispy potato strings; butter-poached lobster with glazed blood oranges and shisho, scallion, carrot, and toasted almond salad; and roast venison with vegetables, quince, and huckleberry sauce. The staff is extremely approachable and knowledgeable, and the new surroundings (think deep wood paneling, mirrors, long, rust-colored curtains, and gold-hued Venetian plaster) are now as elegant as the food. Best of all, the environment is relaxed, comfortable, and intimate. Finish with any of the delectable desserts. If you're not into the 3-, 4-, or 5-course tasting menu, don't be deterred; the restaurant tells me they'll happily price out individual items.

2316 Polk St. (between Green and Union sts.). © 415/776-5577. www.lafolie.com. Reservations recommended. 3-course tasting menu $65; 4-course tasting menu $75; 5-course chef's tasting menu $85; vegetarian tasting menu $65. AE, DC, DISC, MC, V. Mon–Sat 5:30–10:30pm. Bus: 19, 41, 45, 47, 49, or 76.

EXPENSIVE

House of Prime Rib 🌟🌟 STEAKHOUSE Anyone who loves a huge slab of meat and old-school–style dining will feel right at home at this shrine to prime (rib). It's a fun and ever-packed affair within the men's clublike dining rooms (fireplaces included), where drinks are stiff, waiters are loose, and all the beef is roasted in rock salt, sliced tableside, and served with salad dramatically tossed tableside followed by creamed spinach and either mashed potatoes or a baked potato and Yorkshire pudding, which accompany the entree. To placate the occasional non-meat eater, they offer a fish-of-the-day special. Another bonus: Kids' prime rib dinners are a paltry $9.45.

1906 Van Ness Ave. (near Washington St.). © 415/885-4605. Reservations recommended. Complete dinners $28–$33. AE, MC, V. Mon–Thurs 5:30–10pm; Fri–Sat 5–10pm; Sun 4–10pm. Valet parking $7. Bus: 47 or 49.

Tablespoon 🌟🌟 AMERICAN This crowded neighborhood restaurant ladles out such tasty and well-priced New American cuisine that no one seems to mind the narrow dining room, its rather loud acoustics, or the wait for a table—sometimes despite a reservation. The winning recipe is a savvy mix of casually sophisticated food and semiswank surroundings by co-owners chef Robert Riescher (previously of Central California's renowned Erna's Elderberry House) and frontman John Jasso who worked the crowds at destination restaurants Gary Danko and Fifth Floor. Like most hot spots these days, the menu highlights small plates (as well as entrees), but its selections are seasoned with uncommon panache, such as winter items like roasted Jerusalem artichoke soup with braised short rib ravioli, delicate ahi tuna carpaccio with fennel salad and Meyer lemon vinaigrette, and hearty oven-roasted pork tenderloin with roasted Brussels sprouts and root vegetables. If you're looking to taste your way through an affordable meal surrounded by locals, this is one of the best places to do it.

2209 Polk St. (between Vallejo and Green sts.). © 415/268-0140. www.tablespoonsf.com. Reservations recommended. Main courses $17–$23. AE, MC, V. Mon–Fri 5:30–10:30pm; Fri–Sat 5:30pm–midnight; Sun 5–10pm. Bus: 19, 36, 41, or 45.

MODERATE

Swan Oyster Depot 🌟🌟 *Finds* SEAFOOD Turning 94 years old in 2006, Swan Oyster Depot is a classic San Francisco dining experience you shouldn't miss. Opened in 1912, this tiny hole in the wall, run by the city's friendliest servers, is little more than a narrow fish market that decided to slap down some bar stools. There are only 20 or so seats here, jammed cheek-by-jowl along a long marble bar. Most patrons come for a quick cup of chowder or a plate of oysters on the half shell that arrive chilling on crushed ice. The menu is limited to fresh crab, shrimp, oyster, clam cocktails, a few types of smoked fish, Maine lobster, and Boston-style clam chowder, all of which are exceedingly fresh. *Note:* Don't let the lunchtime line dissuade you—it moves fast.

1517 Polk St. (between California and Sacramento sts.). © 415/673-1101. Reservations not accepted. Seafood cocktails $7–$15; clams and oysters on the half shell $7.95 per half-dozen. No credit cards. Mon–Sat 8am–5:30pm. Bus: 1, 19, 47, or 49.

7 Chinatown

For a map of restaurants in this section, see the "Where to Dine near Chinatown & North Beach" map on p. 125.

Brandy Ho's Hunan Food ★ *Kids* CHINESE   Fancy black-and-white granite table-tops and a large, open kitchen give you the first clue that the food at this casual and fun restaurant is a cut above the usual Hunan fare. Take my advice and start immediately with fried dumplings (in sweet-and-sour sauce) or cold chicken salad and then move on to fish-ball soup with spinach, bamboo shoots, noodles, and other goodies. The best main course is Three Delicacies, a combination of scallops, shrimp, and chicken with onion, bell pepper, and bamboo shoots, seasoned with ginger, garlic, and wine, and served with black-bean sauce. Most dishes are quite hot and spicy, but the kitchen will adjust the level to meet your specifications. A full bar includes Asian-food–friendly libations like plum wine and sake from 11:30am to 11pm.

217 Columbus Ave. (at Pacific Ave.). ✆ 415/788-7527. www.brandyhos.com. Reservations recommended. Main courses $8–$13. AE, DISC, MC, V. Sun–Thurs 11:30am–11pm; Fri–Sat 11:30am–midnight. Paid parking available at 170 Columbus Ave. Bus: 15 or 41.

House of Nanking ★ CHINESE   This place would be strictly a tourist joint if it weren't for the die-hard fans who happily wait—sometimes up to an hour—for a coveted seat at this inconspicuous little restaurant serving Shanghai-style cuisine. Order the requisite pot stickers, green-onion-and-shrimp pancakes with peanut sauce, or any number of pork, rice, beef, seafood, chicken, or vegetable dishes from the menu, but I suggest you trust the waiter when he recommends a special. Even with an expansion that doubled the available space, seating is tight, so prepare to be bumped around a bit and don't expect perky or attentive service—it's all part of the Nanking experience.

919 Kearny St. (at Columbus Ave.). ✆ 415/421-1429. Reservations accepted for groups of 8 or more. Main courses $6–$12. MC, V. Mon–Fri 11am–10pm; Sat–Sun noon–10pm. Bus: 9, 12, 15, or 30.

R&G Lounge ★★ CHINESE   It's tempting to take your chances and duck into any of the exotic restaurants in Chinatown, but if you want a sure thing, go directly to the three-story R&G Lounge. During lunch, all three floors are packed with hungry neighborhood workers who go straight for the $5.50 rice-plate specials. Even then, you can order from the dinner menu, which features legendary deep-fried salt-and-pepper crab (a little greasy for my taste); and delicious chicken with black-bean sauce. A personal favorite is melt-in-your-mouth R&G Special Beef, which explodes with the tangy flavor of the accompanying sauce. I was less excited by the tired chicken salad, house specialty noodles, and bland spring rolls. But that was just fine since I saved room for generous and savory seafood in a clay pot and delicious classic roast duck.

631 Kearny St. (at Clay St.). ✆ 415/982-7877. www.rnglounge.com. Reservations recommended. Main courses $9.50–$30. AE, DC, DISC, MC, V. Daily 11am–9:30pm. Parking validated across the street at Portsmouth Sq. garage 24 hr. or Holiday Inn after 5pm. Bus: 1, 9AX, 9BX, or 15. Cable Car: California.

8 North Beach/Telegraph Hill

For a map of restaurants in this section, see the "Where to Dine near Chinatown & North Beach" map on p. 125.

(Kids) The Best of San Francisco's Family-Friendly Restaurants

Andalé Taqueria (p. 137)   So casual, so inexpensive, and offering lots of options, you can feed the whole clan here—and fit them comfortably in the dining room or on the patio.

Beach Chalet Brewery & Restaurant (p. 147)   You can relax and enjoy house-made beers and snacks while the kids peer at the ocean through picture windows or check out the Beach Chalet historical displays downstairs. In the warmer months, the kids will love the outdoor barbecue and music scene on the lawn.

Brandy Ho's Hunan Food (p. 123)   So long as the kids like Chinese food, they're welcome in this bustling, casual dining room.

Cliff House (p. 148)   The folks at this oceanfront multiplex of restaurants are used to churning out fast meals for tourists with kids in tow.

Dottie's True Blue Café (p. 110)   This is a cramped, casual breakfast spot with lots of items to tempt the tots.

Eliza's (p. 138)   Serving some of the most flavorful and vibrant California-influenced Chinese food in town, Eliza's is fun for the whole family. Parents will love the quality of the cuisine and the casual surroundings that make it okay for the kids to really get into their meals. Kids will also get a kick out of the whimsical art-glass around the dining room.

Ella's (p. 135)   Provided your kids are patient enough to wait in the ever-growing line for the best breakfast in town, they'll be thrilled with the offerings in this bright, cheery, and bustling Pacific Heights restaurant—especially when they get their huge stack of yummy pancakes.

Hard Rock Cafe (p. 133)   You know the drill: loud music, pseudohip environs, and kid-friendly fare.

Mel's Drive-In (p. 138)   A 1950s-style diner with all the trappings (think shakes, burgers, fries, and 25¢ jukeboxes), this family-friendly spot gives tots crayons and coloring-book pages.

Mo's Gourmet Burgers (p. 129)   Perfect for everyone, it's got killer burgers and a very low-key atmosphere.

Pane e Vino (p. 136)   The accommodating staff at this neighborhood Italian restaurant makes it a good spot to take the kids. Plus the menu is classic Italian, which means there are plenty of inoffensive offerings for the tots in tow.

Pasta Pomodoro (p. 129)   Cheap, fast, and informal is the perfect recipe for a tasty Italian dining experience.

Tommaso's (p. 130)   You can satisfy the kids' (and your) pizza craving at this small North Beach joint, which is known to serve the best brick-oven baked pies in town in a very casual, cramped, and old-school authentic atmosphere.

Ton Kiang (p. 149)   Chinese families head here every weekend to gather around large round tables and indulge in dim sum small-plate feasts. Decor is minimal, which makes the folks feel that much better when the soy sauce hits the plate or a few bites of rice hit the floor.

Where to Dine near Chinatown & North Beach

Bix **16**
Bocadillos **17**
Brandy Ho's Hunan Food **13**
Caffè Macaroni **15**
Capp's Corner **5**
Enrico's **11**
House of Nanking **14**
Il Pollaio **4**
L'Osteria del Forno **6**

Mario's Bohemian Cigar Store **3**
Maykedeh **7**
Mo's Gourmet Burgers **8**
Moose's **1**
Pasta Pomodoro **2**
R & G Lounge **18**
Steps of Rome Coffee **10**
The Stinking Rose **9**
Tommaso's **12**

EXPENSIVE

Bix 𝒢𝒢 *Moments* AMERICAN/CALIFORNIA   The martini lifestyle may now be *en vogue*, but it was never out of style in this sexy and glamorous retro supper club. Bix is utterly stylish, with curving mahogany paneling, giant silver pillars, and dramatic lighting, all of which sets the stage for live music and plenty of hobnobbing. While the ultrasleek setting has overshadowed the food in the past, the legions of diners entranced by the Bix experience don't seem to care—and it seems as of late Bix is "on" again. Chicken hash has been a menu favorite for the past 18 years, but newer luxury comfort-food dishes—such as caviar service, marrowbones with toast and shallot confit, steak tartare, and pan-roasted seasonal fish dishes—are developing their own fan clubs. ***Bargain tip:*** At lunch there's a three-course prix-fixe menu for $22.

56 Gold St. (between Sansome and Montgomery sts.). 🕿 415/433-6300. Reservations recommended. Main courses $12–$15 lunch, $16–$32 dinner. AE, DC, DISC, MC, V. Mon–Thurs 4:30–11pm; Fri 11:30am–2pm and 5:30pm–midnight; Sat 5:30pm–midnight; Sun 5:30–10pm. Valet parking $10. Bus: 15, 30, 41, or 45.

Moose's 𝒢 *Value* AMERICAN   A big blue neon moose marks your arrival at North Beach's most schmoozy restaurant, where Nob Hill socialites and local politicians come to dine and be seen. But convivial Moose's is not just an image. On recent visits, the food—which highlights seasonal local small farm organic ingredients—has been quite good. Appetizers are innovative, fresh, and well balanced (thank goodness for a truly good Caesar salad and steamed Prince Edward Island mussels). Main courses (especially meats) tend to be lovingly prepared. Try the Massachusetts striped bass with broccoli, cauliflower, cipollini onions, and lemon; garlic pan-seared duck with shaved Brussels sprouts, black lentils, onions, and duck *jus;* or grilled Meyer Ranch rib-eye. Another reason to love Moose's: They make a darned good hamburger.

The bar, separated from the main dining room by a low, frosted-glass partition, remains busy long after the kitchen closes. There's excellent jazz piano nightly and during Sunday brunch.

1652 Stockton St. (between Filbert and Union sts.). 🕿 800/28-MOOSE or 415/989-7800. www.mooses.com. Reservations recommended. Main courses $11–$34. AE, DC, DISC, MC, V. Mon–Thurs 5:30–10:30pm; Fri–Sat 5:30–11pm; Sun 5–10pm; lunch Thurs–Fri 11:30am–2:30pm; brunch Sat–Sun 10am–2:30pm. 3-hr. valet parking $6 lunch, $9 dinner. Bus: 15, 30, 41, or 45.

MODERATE

Enrico's 𝒢 CALIFORNIA   Enrico's is the most fun sidewalk-restaurant/supperclub destination on North Beach's Broadway strip. Anyone with an appreciation for live jazz (featured nightly), late-night noshing, and people-watching from the patio will be quite content spending an alfresco evening under the heat lamps here. (However, the best view of the band is from inside.) I tend to drop by and snack on wine and addictive deep-fried olives or pizza Margherita and move on. But when I linger for dinner, entrees are usually satisfying and range from roasted chicken under a brick with mashed potatoes to flatiron steak or butternut-squash ravioli.

504 Broadway (at Kearny St.). 🕿 415/982-6223. www.enricossidewalkcafe.com. Reservations recommended. Main courses $7–$12 lunch, $11–$25 dinner. AE, MC, V. Sun–Thurs 11:30am–11pm; Fri–Sat 11:30am–midnight; bar daily 11:30am–1:30am or earlier depending on patronage. Valet parking (dinner only) $10. Bus: 9X, 12, or 15.

Maykadeh PERSIAN/MIDDLE EASTERN   If you're looking to add a little exotic adventure to your dinner plans, this is the place to go. Surrounded by a sea of Italian bistros, Maykadeh is one of San Francisco's best and most elegant Persian restaurants. The Middle East may no longer be the culinary capital of the world, but at Maykadeh you can still sample the exotic flavors that characterize Persian cuisine. Of the dozen or so appetizers, some of the best are eggplant with mint garlic sauce; stuffed grape leaves; and lamb tongue with lime juice, sour cream, and saffron (c'mon, live a little). About eight mesquite-grilled items are on the menu, including filet of lamb marinated in lime, homemade yogurt, saffron, and onions. House specialties include half a dozen vegetarian dishes, among them eggplant braised with saffron, fresh tomato, and dried lime.

470 Green St. (between Kearny St. and Grant Ave.). ℂ 415/362-8286. Reservations recommended. Main courses $13–$27. MC, V. Mon–Thurs 11:45am–10:30pm; Fri–Sat 11:45am–11pm; Sun 11:45am–10pm. Valet parking $7 lunch, $8 dinner. Bus: 15, 30, or 41.

Piperade 🎭🎭 BASQUE   Chef Gerald Hirigoyen takes diners on a Basque adventure in this charming, small restaurant. Surrounded by a low wood-beam-lined ceiling, oak floors, and soft sconce lighting, it's a casual affair where diners indulge in small and large plates of Hirigoyen's superbly flavorful West Coast Basque cuisine. Your edible odyssey starts with small plates—or plates to be shared—like my personal favorites: piquillo peppers stuffed with goat cheese; and a bright and simple salad of garbanzo beans with calamari, chorizo, and piquillo peppers. Share entrees, too. Indulge in New York steak with braised shallots and french fries or sop up every drop of the sweet and savory red-pepper sauce with the braised seafood and shellfish stew. Save room for orange blossom beignets: Light and airy with a delicate and moist web of dough within and a kiss of orange essence, the beignet is dessert at its finest. There's a communal table for drop-in diners and front patio seating during warmer weather.

1015 Battery St. (at Green St.). ℂ 415/391-2555. www.piperade.com. Reservations recommended. Main courses $17–$24. AE, DC, DISC, MC, V. Mon–Fri 11:30am–3pm and 5:30–10:30pm; Sat 5:30–10:30pm; closed Sun. Bus: 10, 12, 30, or 82x.

The Stinking Rose ITALIAN   Garlic is the "flower" from which this restaurant gets its name. From soup to ice cream, the supposedly healthful herb is a star ingredient in almost every dish. ("We season our garlic with food," exclaims the menu.) From a gourmet point of view, The Stinking Rose is unremarkable. Pizzas, pastas, and meats smothered in simple, overpowering sauces are tasty, but they're memorable only for their singular garlicky intensity. That said, this is a fun place; the restaurant's lively atmosphere and odoriferous aroma combine for good entertainment. The best dishes include iron-skillet–roasted mussels, shrimp and crab with garlic sauce; smoked mozzarella, garlic, and tomato pizza; salt-roasted tiger prawns with garlic parsley glaze; and 40-clove garlic chicken (served with garlic mashed potatoes, of course). *Note:* For those who are not garlic-inclined, they offer garlic-free "Vampire Faire."

325 Columbus Ave. (between Vallejo and Broadway). ℂ 415/781-7673. www.thestinkingrose.com. Reservations recommended. Main courses $13–$30. AE, DC, DISC, MC, V. Sun–Thurs 11am–11pm; Fri–Sat 11am–midnight. Bus: 15, 30, 41, or 45.

INEXPENSIVE

Caffè Macaroni 🎭🎭 ITALIAN   You wouldn't know it from the looks (or name) of it, but this tiny, funky restaurant on busy Columbus Avenue is one of the best southern Italian restaurants in the city. It looks as though it can hold only two customers at a time, and if you don't duck your head when entering the upstairs dining room, you might as well ask for one lump or two. Fortunately, the kitchen also packs a wallop, dishing out a large variety of antipasti and excellent pastas. The spinach-and-cheese ravioli with wild-mushroom sauce and the gnocchi are outstanding. The owners and staff are always vivacious and friendly, and young ladies in particular will enjoy the attentions of the charming Italian men manning the counter. If you're still pondering whether you should eat here, consider that most entrees are under $15.

124 Columbus Ave. (at Jackson St.). ℭ **415/956-9737**. www.caffemacaroni.com. Reservations accepted. Main courses $9–$15. AE, MC, V. Mon–Thurs 11am–10pm; Fri–Sat 11am–11pm; Sun noon–9pm. Closed last week of Dec to 1st week of Jan. Bus: 15 or 41.

Capp's Corner 𝄐 *Value* ITALIAN   Capp's is a place of givens: It's a given that high-spirited regulars are hunched over the bar and that you'll be served huge portions of straightforward Italian fare at low prices in a raucous atmosphere that prevails until closing. The waitresses are usually brusque and bossy, but always with a wink. Long tables are set up for family-style dining: bread, soup, salad, and choice of around 20 classic main dishes (herb-roasted leg of lamb, spaghetti with meatballs, *osso buco* with polenta, fettuccine with prawns and white-wine sauce)—all for $15 or $17 or so per person, around $10 for kids. You might have to wait awhile for a table, but if you want fun and authentic old-school dining without pomp or huge prices, you'll find the wait worthwhile.

1600 Powell St. (at Green St.). ℭ **415/989-2589**. www.cappscorner.com. Reservations accepted. Complete dinners $15–$17. AE, DC, MC, V. Daily 11:30am–2:30pm; Sun–Thurs 4:30–10:30pm; Fri–Sat 4:30–11pm. Bus: 15, 30, or 41.

Il Pollaio 𝄐 *Value* ITALIAN/ARGENTINE   Simple, affordable, and consistently delicious is a winning combination at superbasic Il Pollaio. Seat yourself in the tiny unfussy room, order, and wait for the fresh-from-the-grill chicken, which is so moist it practically falls off the bone. Each meal comes with a choice of salad or fries. If you're not in the mood for chicken, you can opt for rabbit, lamb, pork chop, or Italian sausage. On a sunny day, get your goods to-go and picnic across the street at Washington Square.

555 Columbus Ave. (between Green and Union sts.). ℭ **415/362-7727**. Reservations not accepted. Main courses $8–$15. DISC, MC, V. Mon–Sat 11:30am–9pm. Bus: 15, 30, 39, 41, or 45. Cable car: Powell–Mason line.

L'Osteria del Forno 𝄐𝄐 ITALIAN   L'Osteria del Forno might be only slightly larger than a walk-in closet, but it's one of the top three authentic Italian restaurants in North Beach. Peer in the window facing Columbus Avenue, and you'll probably see two Italian women with their hair up, sweating from the heat of the oven, which cranks out the best focaccia (and focaccia sandwiches) in the city. There's no pomp or circumstance here: Locals come strictly to eat. The menu features a variety of superb pizzas, salads, soups, and fresh pastas, plus a good selection of daily specials (pray for the roast pork braised in milk), which includes a roast of the day, pasta, and ravioli. Small baskets of warm focaccia keep you going until the arrival of the entrees, which should always be accompanied by a glass of Italian red. Good news for folks on the go: You can get pizza by the slice.

519 Columbus Ave. (between Green and Union sts.). ℭ **415/982-1124**. Reservations not accepted. Sandwiches $6–$7; pizzas $10–$18; main courses $6–$14. No credit cards. Sun–Mon and Wed–Thurs 11:30am–10pm; Fri–Sat 11:30am–10:30pm. Bus: 15, 30, 41, or 45.

Mario's Bohemian Cigar Store 𝄐 *Finds* ITALIAN   Across the street from Washington Square is one of North Beach's most popular neighborhood hangouts. The century-old bar—small, well worn, and perpetually busy—is best known for its focaccia sandwiches, including meatball and eggplant. Wash it down with an excellent cappuccino or a house Campari as you watch the tourists stroll by. And no, they do not sell cigars.

566 Columbus Ave. (at Union St.). ℭ **415/362-0536**. Sandwiches $7.75–$8.50. MC, V. Daily 10am–11pm. Closed Dec 24–25 and Jan 1. Bus: 15, 30, 41, or 45.

Mo's Gourmet Burgers *Kids* AMERICAN   This simple diner offers a straight-forward but winning combination: big, thick, grilled patties of fresh-ground, best-quality, center-cut chuck; fresh french fries; and choice of cabbage slaw, sautéed garlic mushrooms, or chili. *Voilà!* You've got the city's burger of choice (Zuni Café's is a con-tender, but at almost twice the price—p. 142). The other food—spicy chicken sand-wich; steak with veggies, garlic bread, and potatoes; and token veggie dishes—is also up to snuff, but that messy, memorable burger is what keeps the carnivores captivated (the sinisterly sweet shakes are fantastic, too). Bargain-diners will appreciate prices, with burgers ranging from $5.95 for a classic to $7.95 for an "Alpine" burger with Gruyere cheese and sautéed mushrooms. Entrees start at $9 for meatloaf with mashed potatoes, garlic bread, and a vegetable, and top out at $17 for New York steak. The classic breakfast menu is also a bargain. A second location at SoMa's Yerba Buena Gardens, 772 Folsom St., between Third and Fourth streets (© **415/957-3779**), is open Monday from 10am to 5pm, Tuesday through Friday from 10am to 8pm, Saturday from 9am to 8pm, and Sunday from 9am to 5pm. It features breakfast and burgers.

1322 Grant Ave. (between Vallejo and Green sts.). © **415/788-3779**. Main courses $5.95–$17. MC, V. Sun–Thurs 9am–10:30pm; Fri–Sat 9am–11:30pm; breakfast daily 9am–2pm. Bus: 9X, 15, 30, 39, 41, or 45.

Pasta Pomodoro *Kids* *Value* ITALIAN   If you're looking for a good, cheap meal in North Beach—or anywhere else in town, for that matter—this San Francisco chain can't be beat. There can be a short wait for a table, but after you're seated, you'll be surprised at how promptly you're served. Every dish is fresh and sizable and, best of all, costs a third of what you'd pay elsewhere. Winners include spaghetti *frutti di mare* made with calamari, mussels, scallops, tomato, garlic, and wine; and smoked rigatoni, with roast chicken, sun-dried tomatoes, cream, mushrooms, and Parmesan—both under $12. When I don't feel like cooking, I often stop here for angel-hair pasta with tomato and basil and a decadent spinach salad with peppered walnuts and bleu cheese. The tiramisu is huge, delicious, and cheap, too.

655 Union St. (at Columbus Ave.). © **415/399-0300**. www.pastapomodoro.com. Reservations not accepted. Main courses $6–$12. AE, MC, V. Sun–Thurs 11am–10:30pm; Fri–Sat 11am–11pm. Bus: 15, 30, 41, or 45. Cable car: Powell–Mason line. There are 7 other locations, including 2304 Market St., at 16th St. (© **415/558-8123**); 3611 California St., between Spruce St. and Parker Ave. (© **415/831-0900**); and 816 Irving St., between Ninth and 10th sts. (© **415/566-0900**).

San Francisco Art Institute Café *Finds* AMERICAN   Never in a million years would you stumble upon the Art Institute Café by accident. One of the best-kept secrets in San Francisco, this cafe offers fresh, affordable cafe standards for in-the-know residents and visitors as well as Art Institute students: a wide array of hearty breakfast dishes, fresh salads, sandwiches on homemade bread, daily ethnically inspired specials, and anything with caffeine in it—all priced at or under $6. The view, which extends from Alcatraz Island to Coit Tower and beyond, is so phenomenal that the exterior served as the outside of Sigourney Weaver's ridiculously chic apartment in the movie *Copycat*. The cafe itself boasts an open kitchen, sleek aluminum tables, and weekly rotating student art shows. A large courtyard with cement tables (and the same Hollywood view) is the perfect spot for an alfresco lunch high above the tourist fray.

800 Chestnut St. (between Jones and Leavenworth sts.). © **415/749-4567**. Main courses $4–$6. No credit cards. Fall–spring Mon–Thurs 8am–5pm, Fri 8am–4pm; summer Mon–Fri 9am–2pm. Closed Sat–Sun. Hours dependent on school schedule; please call to confirm. Bus: 30 or 49. Cable car: Powell–Hyde or Powell–Mason line.

Steps of Rome Caffe *Finds* ITALIAN   All the vibrancy and flavor of Italy can be found at this deliciously affordable and casual North Beach eatery. It's known as much as a meeting point for the young and social as it is for its heaping plates of fresh pasta, so if you head here, expect a lively time. Adding to the pleasure are prices—pastas top out at an unheard of $14. Start with tasty bruschetta, carpaccio, or Caesar or caprese salad, but save room for panini (sandwiches of pressed toasted bread with killer fillings like salmon, tomatoes, and citrus sauce or prosciutto and mozzarella), classic pastas—from alfredo to pomodoro to crab ravioli—pizzas, or entrees ranging from grilled chicken breast over salad to filet mignon (for $19.95!). Should you want the taste without the bustle, the more mild and formal Trattoria is next door. Also, keep this spot in mind for late-night hunger pangs; they serve until 2am weekdays, 3am weekends.

348 Columbus Ave. (between Broadway and Vallejo St.). © 415/397-0435. www.stepsofrome.com. Reservations recommended. Main courses $6.95–$20. No credit cards. Sun–Thurs 10–2am; Fri–Sat 10–3am. Bus: 15 or 41.

Tommaso's *Kids* ITALIAN   From the street, Tommaso's looks wholly unappealing—a drab, windowless brown facade sandwiched between sex shops. Then why are people always waiting in line to get in? Because everyone knows that Tommaso's, which opened in 1935, bakes one of San Francisco's best traditional-style pizzas. The center of attention in the downstairs dining room is the chef, who continuously tosses huge hunks of garlic and mozzarella onto pizzas before sliding them into the oak-burning brick oven. Nineteen different toppings make pizza the dish of choice, even though Italian classics such as veal Marsala, chicken cacciatore, superb lasagna, and wonderful calzones are also available. Tommaso's also offers half-bottles of house wines, homemade manicotti, and good Italian coffee. If you can overlook the seedy surroundings, this fun, boisterous restaurant is a great place to take the family.

1042 Kearny St. (at Broadway). © 415/398-9696. www.tommasosnorthbeach.com. Reservations not accepted. Pasta and pizza $14–$24; main courses $11–$18. AE, DC, DISC, MC, V. Tues–Sat 5–10:30pm; Sun 4–9:30pm. Closed Dec 15–Jan 15. Bus: 15 or 41.

9 Fisherman's Wharf

For a map of restaurants in this section, see the "Where to Dine around Town" map on p. 116.

VERY EXPENSIVE

A. Sabella's *Finds* SEAFOOD   One of the first families to open a restaurant at the wharf continues its old-fashioned hospitality with a genuine sense of place, honest dining, solid food, and a stellar staff all packaged in a pretty and spacious room overlooking the wharf. Accessed via an incognito elevator, this hidden restaurant offers something for everyone—classic renditions of steak, lamb, seafood, chicken, and pasta, all made from scratch with fresh local ingredients—but where A. Sabella's really shines is in the shellfish department. Its 1,000-gallon saltwater tank allows for fresh crab, abalone, and lobster year-round, which means no restaurant in the city can touch this spot when it comes to feasting on fresh Dungeness crab and abalone out of season. Of course, such luxuries are anything but cheap. But on the bright side, with the kids' menu, you can fill up tots' tummies for a mere $7.50. *Added bonuses:* This is and feels like a real family-owned deal, a merit that's practically extinct in this ever-evolving town. If Anton Sabella is in the house, ask him about the history of the area and his family. His gracious and chatty personality and knowledge brings extra flavor to an already tasty meal.

Fisherman's Wharf, 2766 Taylor St. (at Jefferson St.), 3rd floor. © 415/771-6775. www.asabellas.com. Reservations recommended. Most main courses $16–$28. AE, DC, DISC, MC, V. Daily 5–10pm. 2-hr. validated parking at the Wharf Garage, 350 Beach St. Streetcar: F. Cable car: Powell–Mason or Powell–Hyde lines.

Forbes Island *Moments* FRENCH   Been there and done that in every San Francisco dining room? Then it's time for Forbes Island, a wonderfully ridiculous floating restaurant disguised as an island (complete with lighthouse and real 40-ft. palm trees) and unknown to even most locals. The idea's kitschy, but the execution's actually quite wonderful. Here's how it works: Arrive at the dock next to PIER 39, call the restaurant via the courtesy phone, climb aboard its pontoon boat that takes you on a 4-minute journey to the "island" located 75 feet from the city's famed sea lions, and descend into the island's bowels to find a surprisingly classy, Tudor-like wood-paneled dining room. Warmed by a fireplace and amused by fish swimming past the portholes (yes, the dining room is a wee bit underwater), guests dine on surprisingly well-prepared classic French food such as decadent ragout of wild mushrooms, toasted brioche, and soft goat cheese or roasted half-rack of lamb with herbed flageolet beans, minted edamame, and natural lamb reduction *jus.* The added "Sea Lion" room boasts the closest view you'll ever get of the creatures. *But be warned:* The menu is very limited, the wine list features basic big-name producers without listing the vintage, and the "island" does gently rock (landlubbers need not apply or should take Dramamine a couple of hours beforehand). *One annoyance:* the mandatory $3 shuttle fee since the only other way to get there is to swim.

Water shuttle is just left of PIER 39. © 415/951-4900. www.forbesisland.com. Reservations recommended. Main courses $24–$34. AE, DC, MC, V. Wed–Sun arrive between 5–10pm. Validated parking at PIER 39 garage $8 for up to 6 hr.

Restaurant Gary Danko *Finds* FRENCH   James Beard Award–winning chef Gary Danko presides over my top pick for fine dining. Eschewing the white-glove formality of yesteryear's fine dining, Danko offers impeccable cuisine and perfectly orchestrated service in an unstuffy environment of wooden paneling and shutters and well-spaced tables (not to mention spa-style bathrooms). The three- to five-course fixed-price seasonal menu is freestyle, so whether you want a sampling of appetizers or a flight of meat courses, you need only ask. I am a devoted fan of his trademark buttery-smooth glazed oysters with lettuce cream, salsify, and Osetra caviar; seared foie gras, which may be accompanied by peaches, caramelized onions, and *verjus* (a classic French sauce); horseradish-crusted salmon medallions with dilled cucumbers; and adventurous Moroccan spiced squab with *chermoula* (a Moroccan sauce made with cilantro) and orange-cumin carrots. Truthfully, I've never had a dish here that wasn't precious. And wine? The list is stellar, albeit expensive. If after dinner you have the will to pass on the glorious cheese cart or flambéed dessert of the day, a plate of petit fours reminds you that Gary Danko is one sweet and memorable meal. *Tip:* If you can't get a reservation and are set on dining here, slip in and grab a seat at the 10-stool first-come, first-served bar where you can also order a la carte.

800 North Point St. (at Hyde St.). © 415/749-2060. www.garydanko.com. Reservations required except at walk-in bar. 3- to 5-course fixed-price menu $61–$89. AE, DC, DISC, MC, V. Daily 5:30–10pm; bar open 5pm. Valet parking $10. Bus: 10. Streetcar: F. Cable car: Hyde.

Scoma's *Good* SEAFOOD   A throwback to the dining of yesteryear, Scoma's eschews trendier trout preparations and fancy digs for good old-fashioned seafood served in huge portions amid a very casual windowed waterfront setting. Gourmands should skip this one. But if your idea of heaven is straightforward seafaring classics like fried calamari, raw oysters, pesto pasta with rock shrimp, crab cioppino, and lobster Thermidor with old-time hospitality to match, this is about as good as it gets. Unfortunately, a taste of tradition will cost you big time. Prices are as steep as those at some of the finest restaurants in town. Personally, I'd rather splurge at Gary Danko or A. Sabella's. But many of my out-of-town guests insist we meet at Scoma's, which is fine by me since it's a change of pace from today's chic spots, and the parking's free.

Pier 47 and Al Scoma Way (between Jefferson and Jones sts.). ℂ 800/644-5852 or 415/771-4383. www.scomas.com. Reservations not accepted. Most main courses $18–$35. AE, DC, DISC, MC, V. Mon–Thurs noon–10pm; Fri–Sat 11:30am–10:30pm; Sun 11:30am–10:30pm; bar opens 30 minutes prior to lunch daily; hours change seasonally so call to confirm. Free valet parking. Bus: 10 or 47. Streetcar: F.

EXPENSIVE

Alioto's SEAFOOD   One of San Francisco's oldest restaurants, run by one of the city's most prominent families, the Aliotos, this Fisherman's Wharf landmark has a long-standing reputation for great cioppino. The curbside crab stand, Café 8, the Steam Kettle Bar, and the newer Nonna Rose restaurant (all separate establishments in the same location) are great for quick, inexpensive doses of San Francisco's finest; for more formal and fancy selections, continue up the carpeted stairs to the multilevel, harbor-view dining room here. Don't mess around with the menu: If you're here, you're after Dungeness crab. Cracked, caked, stuffed, or stewed, it's impossible to get your fill, so bring plenty of money—particularly if you intend to order from Alioto's prodigious (and pricey) wine list. If you don't care for cracked crab (hard to imagine!), try the griddle-fried sand dabs or the rex sole served with tartar sauce.

Fisherman's Wharf (at Taylor St.). ℂ 415/673-0183. www.aliotos.com. Reservations recommended. Main courses $15–$30 lunch; most main courses $20–$35 dinner. AE, DC, DISC, MC, V. Daily 11am–11pm. Bus: 10, 15, 39, or 47. Streetcar: F. Cable car: Powell–Hyde line.

Ana Mandara ᴋ VIETNAMESE   Yes, Don Johnson is part owner. But more important, this Fisherman's Wharf favorite serves fine Vietnamese food in an outstandingly beautiful setting. Amid a shuttered room with mood lighting, palm trees, and Vietnamese-inspired decor, diners (mostly tourists) splurge on crispy rolls; lobster ravioli with mango and coconut sauce; and wok-charred tournedos of beef tenderloin with sweet onions and peppercress. There is no more expensive Vietnamese dining room in town, but, along with the enjoyable fare, diners pay for the atmosphere, which, if they're in the neighborhood and want something more exotic than the standby seafood dinner, is worth the price.

891 Beach St. (at Polk St.). ℂ 415/771-6800. www.anamandara.com. Reservations recommended. Main courses $19–$32. AE, DC, DISC, MC, V. Mon–Fri 11:30am–2pm; Sun–Thurs 5:30–9:30pm; Fri–Sat 5:30–10:30pm; bar until 1am. Valet parking Tues–Sun $9. Bus: 19, 30, or 45.

The Mandarin ᴋ CHINESE   Created by Madame Cecilia Chiang in 1968, The Mandarin is a fine choice if you don't want to stray from Fisherman's Wharf and want a Bay view. Meant to feel like a cultured northern Chinese home, elegant surroundings include fine furnishings, silk-covered walls, good-quality Asian art, and well-spaced tables. Three out of its four dining rooms offer matchless views of the bay.

True to its name, The Mandarin offers solid northern Chinese cuisine. Start with sesame prawns or Mandarin lettuce wrap. Follow with smoked tea duck (the house version of Beijing duck, but smoked over burning tea leaves until crispy) or—if you have a party of two or more and call a day in advance—you can order either Beggar's Chicken (encased in bread crust and slowly cooked to perfection) stuffed with ham, mushrooms, bamboo shoots, and water chestnuts or slow-roasted Peking Duck with homemade pao pin (pancakes), scallions, and plum sauce. A family style fixed-price four-course dinner costs $25 to $35 per person. If you have a large party (eight or more), you can order the 10-course fixed-price dinner for $28 to $64 per person. Yes, it's pricey for Chinese food, but if you want atmosphere with your pot stickers, this place is for you.

At Ghirardelli Sq., 900 North Point St. © 415/673-8812. www.themandarin.com. Reservations recommended. Main courses $16–$25. AE, DC, DISC, MC, V. Daily 11:30am–9:30pm. Parking in Ghirardelli Sq. lot (validation with purchase). Bus: 19, 30, 47, or 49. Cable car: Powell–Hyde line.

MODERATE

Cafe Pescatore ⚘ ITALIAN   This cozy trattoria is one of the better bets in Fisherman's Wharf. Two walls of sliding glass doors offer pseudo-sidewalk seating when the weather's warm, although heavy vehicular traffic can detract from the alfresco experience. All the classics are well represented here: crisp Caesar salad; fried calamari; bruschetta; cioppino; pastas; chicken Marsala; and veal saltimbocca (sautéed veal scaloppini) with whipped baby potatoes, spinach, prosciutto and lemon-caper butter sauce. The consensus is to order anything that's cooked in the open kitchen's wood-fired oven, such as pizza (margherita), roasts (sea bass with pine-nut crust, or Atlantic salmon), or panini (lunch only; grilled chicken or grilled veggies). By the way, they serve darned good breakfasts, too.

2455 Mason St. (at N. Point St., adjoining the Tuscan Inn). © 415/561-1111. www.cafepescatore.com. Reservations recommended. Main courses $6.50–$12 breakfast, $9–$22 lunch and dinner. AE, DC, DISC, MC, V. Sun–Thurs 7am–10pm; Fri–Sat 7am–11pm. Bus: 15, 39, or 42. Streetcar: F. Cable car: Powell–Mason line.

INEXPENSIVE

Boudin at the Wharf ⚘ DELI/AMERICAN   It's almost pointless to write about this shrine to the city's famous tangy French-style bread (pronounced "bo-*deen*" and created in 1849) because if you're in Fisherman's Wharf, it'll be impossible to miss it. But what you won't see from the industrial-chic all-windowed exterior is that along with two restaurants and to-go food, you'll find tours about the history of the bread and the city and a demonstration bakery. Drop in and you'll see bakers at work making 3,000 loaves daily. Take the tour and learn about the city and the bread's history (Boudin is the city's oldest continually operating business)—and see tools and baking equipment dating back to the days of the gold miners. If you desire you can also grab a good, strong coffee from Peet's Coffee (another Bay Area great) and browse Bakers Hall where you'll find picnic possibilities such as handcrafted cheeses, fruit spreads, chocolates, and a wall map highlighting the town's best places to spread a blanket and feast. Or grab sandwiches, soup in edible sourdough bread bowls, salads, and pastries at the self-serve cafe, which has indoor and outdoor tables. But for a serious feast, head to the more formal restaurant, Bistro Boudin, which offers Alcatraz views with its Dungeness crab Louis, pizza, crab cakes, and burgers on sourdough buns. Regardless, you'll probably do what millions of others have done—grab a loaf on your way out of town to bring home. You can't find sourdough like this anywhere else in the world.

160 Jefferson St., near Pier 43½ © 415/928-1849. www.boudinbakery.com. Reservations recommended. Main courses cafe $6–$10, bistro $11–$33. AE, DC, DISC, MC, V. Cafe daily 8am–10pm; bistro Sun–Thurs 4–10pm, Fri–Sat 4–10:30pm. Bus: 10, 15, or 47. Streetcar: F.

Hard Rock Cafe *(Kids* AMERICAN   I hate to plug chains, and this loud, rock-nostalgia-laden place would be no exception if: 1) I knew tourists were no longer interested in it; and 2) it didn't serve a fine burger and overall decent heaping plates of food at such moderate prices. For many, the real draw—more than 20 years past the time when it was hip to wear the restaurant's logo—is the merchandise shop, but a shopper's gotta eat. The friendly menu offers burgers, fajitas, baby back ribs, grilled fish, chicken, salads, and sandwiches, the munching of which tend to be muffled by blaring music. Although nothing unique to San Francisco, the Hard Rock is a fine place to bring the kids and grab a bite.

PIER 39. © **415/956-2013.** www.hardrock.com. Reservations accepted for groups of 25 or more. Main courses $8–$23. AE, DC, DISC, MC, V. Sun–Thurs 11am–11pm; Fri–Sat 11am–midnight. Validated parking for 1 hr. during lunch and 2 hr. after 6pm at PIER 39 lot. Bus: 10, 15, or 47. Streetcar: F.

10 The Marina/Pacific Heights/Cow Hollow

For a map of restaurants in this section, see the "Where to Dine around Town" map on p. 116.

VERY EXPENSIVE

Harris' *&&* STEAKHOUSE   Every big city has a great steak restaurant, and in San Francisco it's Harris'—a comfortably elegant establishment where the seriously handsome and atmospheric wood-paneled dining room has high-backed booths, banquettes, high ceilings, hunting murals, stately waiters, a convivial bar scene with live jazz Thursday through Saturday, and even a meat counter for the carnivore on the go. Here, the point, of course, is steak, which can be seen hanging in a glass-windowed aging room off Pacific Avenue. They are cut thick—New York–style or T-bone—and are served with a baked potato and seasonal vegetables. You'll also find classic French onion soup, spinach and Caesar salads, and sides of delicious creamed spinach, sautéed shiitake mushrooms, or caramelized onions. Harris' also offers lamb chops, fresh fish, lobster, and occasionally venison, buffalo, and other seasonal game. Desserts, such as a sculptural beehivelike baked Alaska, are surprisingly good. If you're debating between this place and House of Prime Rib, consider that aside from specializing in aged meats, this place is more "upscale," while HOPR features prime rib and a classic old-school vibe.

2100 Van Ness Ave. (at Pacific Ave.). © **415/673-1888.** www.harrisrestaurant.com. Reservations recommended. Most main courses $24–$42. AE, DC, DISC, MC, V. Mon–Thurs 5:30–9:30pm; Fri 5:30–10pm; Sat 5–10pm; Sun 5–9:30pm. Valet parking $7. Bus: 12, 47, or 49.

EXPENSIVE

Quince *&&* CALIFORNIA/ITALIAN   Its discreet location in a quiet residential neighborhood hasn't stopped this tiny and predominantly white-hued restaurant from becoming one of the city's hottest reservations since it opened in late 2003. With only 15 tables, diners are clamoring for a seat in order to savor the nightly changing Italian-inspired menu by Michael Tusk, who mastered the art of pasta while working at the East Bay's famed Chez Panisse and Oliveto restaurants. Regardless, it's worth the effort—especially if you love simple food that honors a few high-quality, organic ingredients. Dining divinity might start with a pillowy spring garlic soufflé or white asparagus with a lightly fried egg and brown butter, but it really hits heavenly notes with the pasta course, be it garganelli with English peas and prosciutto, tagliatelle with veal ragout and fava beans, or artichoke ravioli. Meat and fish selections don't fall short either, with delicately prepared mixed grill plates, tender Alaskan halibut with fava beans, and juicy lamb with fennel and olives. Desserts, though tasty, aren't as celestial, which is just fine since it may leave room for an extra pasta course.

1701 Octavia St. (at Bush St.). © **415/775-8500.** www.quincerestaurant.com. Reservations required. Main courses $16–$29. AE, MC, V. Sun–Thurs 5:30–10pm; Fri–Sat 5:30–10:30pm. Valet parking $8. Bus: 1, 31, or 38.

MODERATE

Ace Wasabi's Rock 'n' Roll Sushi ✿ JAPANESE/SUSHI   What differentiates this Marina hot spot from the usual sushi spots around town are the unique combinations, the varied menu, and the young, hip atmosphere. The innovative rolls are a nice change for those bored with traditional styles, but don't worry if someone in your party isn't a raw fish fan: There are also plenty of non-seafood and cooked items on the menu. Don't miss the rainbow "Three Amigos" roll, or the "Flying Kamikaze" with spicy albacore tuna wrapped around asparagus and topped with ponzu and scallions. The service, like the surroundings, is jovial.

3339 Steiner St. (at Chestnut St.). ✆ 415/567-4903. www.acewasabissushi.com. Reservations not accepted. Sushi $4–$14. AE, MC, V. Mon–Thurs 5:30–10:30pm; Fri–Sat 5:30–11pm; Sun 5–10pm. Bus: 30.

A16 ✿✿ ITALIAN   This sleek, casual, and wonderfully lively spot featuring Neapolitan-style pizza and cuisine from the region of Campania has been white-hot since its 2004 opening. Named after the motorway that traverses the region, the divided space boasts a wine and beer bar up front, a larger dining area and open kitchen in the back, and a wall of wines in between. But its secret weapon is the creative menu of outstanding appetizers, pizza, and entrees, which are orchestrated by new chef Nate Appleman with the same perfection as they were by opening chef Christophe Hille. Even if you must have the insanely good braised pork shoulder with white wine, chestnuts, garlic and herbs to yourself, start by sharing roasted asparagus with walnut cream and pecorino tartuffo or artichoke and tuna conserva with grilled bread and chiles. Add to that co-owner Shelley Lindgren, who guides diners through one of the city's most exciting wine lists featuring 40 wines by the half-glass, glass, and carafe, and you've got one of San Francisco's best and busiest restaurants–despite the fact that their desserts are definitely must-skips.

2355 Chestnut St. (between Divisadero and Scott sts.). ✆ 415/771-2216. www.a16sf.com. Reservations recommended. Main courses $8–$13 lunch, $14–$20 dinner. AE, DC, MC, V. Wed–Fri 11:30am–2:30pm; Sun–Thurs 5–10pm; Fri–Sat 5–11pm. Bus: 22, 30, or 30X.

Ella's ✿✿ *(Kids* AMERICAN/BREAKFAST   Well known throughout town as the undisputed king of breakfasts, this restaurant's acclaim means you're likely to wait to get in for up to an hour on weekends. But midweek and in the wee hours of morning, it's possible to slide onto a counter or table seat in the colorful split dining room and lose yourself in outstanding and obscenely generous servings of chicken hash, crisped to perfection and served with eggs any way you like them, with fluffy buttermilk biscuits. Pancakes, omelets, and the short list of other breakfast essentials are equally revered. Alas, service can be woefully slow, but at least the buspersons are quick to fill coffee cups. Come lunchtime, solid entrees like salads, chicken potpie, and grilled salmon with mashed potatoes remind you what's great about good old American cooking.

500 Presidio Ave. (at California St.). ✆ 415/441-5669. www.ellassanfrancisco.com. Reservations accepted for lunch. Main courses $5.50–$10 breakfast, $6–$12 lunch. AE, DISC, MC, V. Mon–Fri 7am–5pm; Sat–Sun 8:30am–2pm. Bus: 1, 3, or 43.

Greens Restaurant ✿✿ *(Finds* VEGETARIAN   In an old waterfront warehouse, with enormous windows overlooking the bridge, boats, and the bay, this vegetarian restaurant is a pioneer and a legend. Renowned vegetarian cook and executive chef Annie Somerville (author of *Fields of Greens*) cooks with the seasons, using produce from local organic farms. Within the quiet dining room, a weeknight dinner might feature such appetizers as mushroom soup with Asiago cheese and tarragon; or grilled portobello and endive salad. Entrees run the gamut from pizza with wilted escarole, red onions, lemon, Asiago, and Parmesan, to Vietnamese yellow curry or risotto with black trumpet mushrooms, leeks, savory spinach, white-truffle oil, Parmesan Reggiano, and thyme. Those interested in the whole shebang should make reservations for the $48 four-course dinner served on Saturday only. Lunch and brunch are equally fresh and tasty.

The adjacent Greens To Go sells sandwiches, soups, salads, and pastries.

Building A, Fort Mason Center (enter Fort Mason opposite the Safeway at Buchanan and Marina sts.). ⓒ 415/771-6222. www.greensrestaurant.com. Reservations recommended. Main courses $9.50–$14 lunch, $15–$20 dinner, fixed-price dinner $48; Sun brunch $8–$14. AE, DISC, MC, V. Tues–Sat noon–2:30pm; Sun 10:30am–2pm; Mon–Sat 5:30–9pm. Greens To Go Mon–Thurs 8am–8pm; Fri–Sat 8am–5pm; Sun 9am–4pm. Parking in hourly lot $4 for up to 2½ hours. Bus: 28 or 30.

Isa 🍴🍴 FRENCH   Luke Sung, who trained with some of the best French chefs in the city, has captured many locals' hearts by creating the kind of menu we foodies dream of: a smattering of small dishes, served a la carte family-style, that allow you to try numerous items in one sitting. It's a good thing the menu, considered "French tapas," offers small portions at reasonable prices. After all, it's asking a lot to make a diner choose between mushroom ragout with veal sweatbreads, seared foie gras with caramelized apples, potato-wrapped sea bass in brown butter, and rack of lamb. Here, a party of two can choose all of these plus one or two more and not be rolled out the door afterward. Adding to the allure is the warm boutique dining environment—70 seats scattered amid a small dining room in the front, and a large tented and heated patio out back that sets the mood with a warm yellow glow. Take a peek at the "kitchen," a shoebox of a cooking space, to appreciate Sung's accomplishments that much more. Cocktailers, take note: You'll only find beer, wine, and shoju cocktails (shoju is a smooth alcohol made from sweet potato that is used like vodka).

3324 Steiner St. (between Lombard and Chestnut sts.). ⓒ 415/567-9588. www.isarestaurant.com. Reservations recommended. Main courses $9–$16. MC, V. Mon–Thurs 5:30–10pm; Fri–Sat 5:30–10:30pm. Bus: 22, 28, 30, 30X, 43, or 76.

Pane e Vino 🍴 Kids ITALIAN   While the rest of the city tries to modernize their manicotti, this ultracasual Italian spot focuses on huge helpings of classics that are fine for the traditional diner, but not fabulous for the gourmand. That said, prices are reasonable, and the mostly Italian-accented staff is always smooth and efficient under pressure (you'll see). The menu offers a wide selection of appetizers, including a fine carpaccio, *vitello tonnato* (sliced roasted veal and capers in lemony tuna sauce), and the hugely popular chilled artichoke stuffed with bread and tomatoes and served with vinaigrette. The broad selection of pastas includes flavorful *penneputanesca* with tomatoes, capers, anchovies, garlic, and olives. Other specialties are grilled fish and meat dishes, including chicken breast marinated in lime juice and herbs. Top dessert picks are any of the Italian ice creams, panna cotta, and (but of course) creamy tiramisu.

1715 Union St. (between Gough and Octavia sts.). ⓒ 415/346-2111. www.paneevinotrattoria.com. Reservations highly recommended. Main courses $10–$24. AE, MC, V. Mon–Thurs 11:30am–2:30pm and 5–9pm; Fri–Sat 11:30am–10pm; Sun 5–9pm. No parking. Bus: 41 or 45.

PlumpJack Café 🍴🍴 CALIFORNIA/FRENCH/MEDITERRANEAN   Wildly popular among San Francisco's style-setters, this small, 55-seat Cow Hollow restaurant, with a hint of whimsical Shakespearean decor, is once again one of the neighborhood's most "in" places to dine. That's partly because the place is affiliated with the

Getty clan (as in J. Paul) and was founded by sweetheart Mayor Gavin Newsom, and partly because chef Jeff Smock has taken over the kitchen.

Smock comes by way of New York City's famed Union Square Café, which earned three stars from the *New York Times* during his tenure. Here he continues to rock the house and the palate with the like of minicones of ahi tartare enlivened with avocado, pink lady apples, ginger-coriander emulsion, yuzu crème fraîche, and wasabi tobiko, and the Liberty Farms duck trio—a sumptuous combo of roasted leg and confit of leg and thigh. The extraordinarily extensive California wine list—gleaned from the PlumpJack wine shop down the street—is sold at next to retail prices, with many wines available by the glass.

3127 Fillmore St. (between Filbert and Greenwich sts.). ✆ **415/563-4755**. www.plumpjack.com. Reservations recommended. Main courses $13–$16 lunch, $20–$34 dinner. AE, DC, DISC, MC, V. Mon–Fri 11:30am–2pm; daily 5:30–10pm. Valet parking $14 for 3 hr. after 6pm. Bus: 22, 41, or 45.

INEXPENSIVE

Andalé Taqueria *Kids* *Value* MEXICAN   Andalé (Spanish for "hurry up") offers incredible high-end fast food for the health-conscious and the just plain hungry. As the long menu explains, this small California chain prides itself on its fresh ingredients and low-cal options. Lard, preservatives, and canned items are eschewed; Andalé favors salad dressings made with double virgin olive oil, whole vegetarian beans (not refried), skinless chicken, salsas and *aguas frescas* made from fresh fruits and veggies, and mesquite-grilled meats. Add the location (on a sunny shopping stretch), sophisticated decor, full bar, and check-me-out patio seating (complete with corner fireplace), and it's no wonder the good-looking, fitness-fanatic Marina District residents consider this place home. Cafeteria-style service keeps prices low. *Bargain tips:* No one can complain about a quarter of a mesquite-roasted chicken with potatoes, salsa, and tortillas for $6.75. If you want to go traditional, stick with the giant burritos or the fantastic $2.95 tacos—a nibbler's dream.

2150 Chestnut St. (between Steiner and Pierce sts.). ✆ **415/749-0506**. Reservations not accepted. Most dishes $4.25–$11. MC, V. Daily 10am–10pm. Bus: 22, 28, 30, 30X, 43, 76, or 82X.

Chez Nous FRENCH   Diners get crammed into the 40-seat dining area of this bright, cheery, small, and bustling cafelike dining room, but the eclectic tapas are so delicious and affordable, no one seems to care. Indeed, this friendly and fast-paced neighborhood haunt has become a blueprint for other restaurants that understand the allure of small plates. But Chez Nous stands out as more than a petite-portion trendsetter. The clincher is that most of its Mediterranean dishes taste so clean and fresh you can't wait to come back and dine here again. Start with the soup, whatever it is; don't skip tasty french fries with *harissa* (Tunisian hot sauce) aioli; savor the lamb chops with lavender sea salt; and save room for their famed dessert, the minicustard-cakelike *canneles de Bordeaux*.

1911 Fillmore St. (between Pine and Bush sts.). ✆ **415/441-8044**. Reservations accepted, but walk-ins welcome. Main courses $5–$13. AE, MC, V. Daily 11:30am–3pm and 5:30–10pm (Fri–Sat until 11pm). Bus: 22, 41, or 45.

E'Angelo Restaurant ITALIAN   Back when I was barely making enough to cover my rent, I would often treat myself to a night out at E'Angelo. All the house specialties, pastas, and pizzas cost less than $19; the atmosphere is casual and fun; tables are cozy-cramped; and the Italian staff is friendly. For me, the combination made not only for a hearty meal, but for an opportunity to mingle with San Francisco: to live a little, eavesdrop on neighbors' conversations, and perhaps even run into local celebrities such as Robin Williams with his family. While years have passed, not much has changed at this traditional Italian hot spot: The place still won't take reservations or credit cards. It still serves decent portions of pastas, veal, lamb, chicken, and fish; a carafe of red or white wine for about 18 bucks (thrifty by-the-bottle prices, too); and one heck of a rich eggplant parmigiana. And unlike those at most of the neighboring restaurants, desserts are dirt-cheap.

2234 Chestnut St. (between Pierce and Scott sts.). ℂ 415/567-6164. Reservations not accepted. Main courses $13–$19. No credit cards. Tues–Sun 5–10pm. Bus: 22, 30, or 30X.

Eliza's 🍴🍴 *Value* *Kids* CHINESE   Despite the curiously colorful design of modern architecture, whimsy, and glass art, this perennially packed neighborhood haunt serves some of the freshest California-influenced Chinese food in town. Unlike comparable options, here the atmosphere (albeit unintentionally funky) and presentation parallel the food. The fantastically fresh soups, salads, seafood, pork, chicken, duck, and such specials as spicy eggplant are outstanding and are served on beautiful English and Japanese plates. (Get the sea bass with black-bean sauce and go straight to heaven!) I often come at midday and order the wonderful kung pao chicken lunch special (available weekdays only): a mixture of tender chicken, peanuts, chile peppers, subtly hot sauce, and perfectly crunchy vegetables. It's one of 32 main-course choices that come with rice and soup for around $6. The place is also jumping at night, so prepare to stand in line. A second location, in Potrero Hill at 1457 18th St. (ℂ 415/648-9999), is open Monday through Friday 11am to 3pm and daily 5 to 9pm.

2877 California St. (at Broderick St.). ℂ 415/621-4819. Reservations accepted for parties of 4 or more. Main courses $5.30–$6.15 lunch, $7.15–$15 dinner. MC, V. Mon–Thurs 11am–3pm and 5–9:30pm; Fri 11am–3pm and 5–10pm; Sat 4:30–10pm; Sun 4:30–9pm. Bus: 1 or 24.

La Méditerranée 🍴 *Value* MEDITERRANEAN   With an upscale-cafe ambience and quality food, La Méditerranée has long warranted its reputation as one of the quainter inexpensive restaurants on upper Fillmore. Here you'll find freshly prepared traditional Mediterranean food that's worlds apart from the Euro-eclectic fare many restaurants now call "Mediterranean." Baba ghanouj, tabbouleh, dolmas, and hummus start out the menu. More important, the menu offers one very tasty chicken Cilicia, a phyllo-dough dish that's hand-rolled and baked with cinnamony spices, almonds, chickpeas, and raisins; also good is zesty chicken pomegranate drumsticks on a bed of rice. Both come with green salad, potato salad, or soup for around $9.50. Ground lamb dishes, quiches, and Middle Eastern combo plates round out the affordable menu, and wine comes by the glass and in half- or full liters. A second location is at 288 Noe St., at Market Street (ℂ 415/431-7210).

2210 Fillmore St. (at Sacramento St.). ℂ 415/921-2956. www.cafelamed.com. Main courses $7–$10 lunch, $8–$12 dinner. AE, MC, V. Sun–Thurs 11am–10pm; Fri–Sat 11am–11pm. Bus: 1, 3, or 22.

Mel's Drive-In 🍴 *Kids* AMERICAN   Sure, it's contrived, touristy, and nowhere near healthy, but when you get that urge for a chocolate shake and banana cream pie at the stroke of midnight—or when you want to entertain the kids—no other place in the city comes through like Mel's Drive-In. Modeled after a classic 1950s diner, right down to the jukebox at each table, Mel's harkens back to the halcyon days when cholesterol and fried foods didn't jab your guilty conscience with every greasy, wonderful bite. Too bad the prices don't reflect the '50s; a burger with fries and a Coke costs about $9.50.

Another Mel's at 3355 Geary St., at Stanyan Street (© **415/387-2244**), is open from 6am to 1am Sunday through Thursday and 6am to 3am Friday and Saturday. Additional locations are: 1050 Van Ness (© **415/292-6357**), open Monday through Thursday 6am to 1am and Friday through Sunday 6am to 4am; and 801 Mission St (© **415/227-4477**), open Sunday through Thursday 6am to 1am and Friday and Saturday 24 hours.

2165 Lombard St. (at Fillmore St.). © **415/921-3039**. www.melsdrive-in.com. Main courses $6.50–$12 breakfast, $7–$10 lunch, $8–$15 dinner. MC, V. Sun–Wed 6am–2am; Thurs 6am–3am; Fri–Sat 24 hr. Bus: 22, 30, or 43.

Pluto's ⊛ ⦅Value⦆ CALIFORNIA   Catering to the Marina District's DINK (double income, no kids) crowd, Pluto's combines assembly-line efficiency with high quality. The result is cheap, fresh fare: huge salads with a dozen choices of toppings; oven-roasted poultry and grilled meats (the tri-tip is great); sandwiches; and a wide array of sides like crispy garlic potato rings, seasonal veggies, and barbecued chicken wings. Pluto's serves teas, sodas, bottled brews, and Napa wines as well as homemade desserts. The ordering system is bewildering to newcomers: Grab a checklist, and then hand it to the servers who check off your order and relay it to the cashier. Seating is limited during the rush, but the turnover is fairly fast. A second location is at 627 Irving St., at Eighth Avenue (© **415/753-8867**).

3258 Scott St. (at Chestnut St.). © **415/7-PLUTOS**. www.plutosfreshfood.com. Reservations not accepted. Main courses $3.50–$5.75. MC, V. Daily 11am–10pm. Bus: 28, 30, or 76.

Japan Town

MODERATE

Takara ⊛ JAPANESE/SUSHI   When I'm in the mood for sushi, I often head to this unassuming restaurant tucked at the eastern end of Japan Town. Not only is it large enough that you don't have to wait in a long line (unlike other local sushi spots), but the fish is extremely fresh and affordable and the other offerings are fantastic. Along with standard nigiri, I always go for the seaweed with fabulously tangy vinegar and a floating quail egg. But on the occasions that I can curb my sushi craving, I get more than my fill with their *yosenabe*. A meal for two that's under $20, it's a giant pot of soup brought to the table on a burner accompanied by a plate of fresh raw meat or seafood and vegetables. After you push the food into the liquid and briefly let it cook, you ladle it out and devour it. Even after serving two hungry people, there are still always leftovers. Other favorites are anything with shrimp—pulled live from the tank—and sukiyaki, another tableside cooking experience. Bargain hunters should come for a lunch plate.

22 Peace Plaza #202 (in Japan Center Miyako Mall). © **415/921-2000**. Reservations recommended. Main courses: $15–$23. MC, V. Daily lunch 11:30am–2:30pm; dinner 5:30–10pm.

Civic Center

For a map of restaurants in this section, see the "Where to Dine around Town" map on p. 116.

VERY EXPENSIVE

Jardinière ⊛⊛ CALIFORNIA/FRENCH   Jardinière is a pre- and postsymphony favorite, and it also happens to be the perfect setting for a cocktail. A culinary dream team runs the sexy dining room: owner-chef Traci Des Jardins and owner-designer Pat

(Finds) Hidden Treasures

They're on the way to nowhere, but because they're among the city's most unique, it would be a crime to leave out these destination restaurants. If you're not familiar with the streets of San Francisco, be sure to call first to get directions; otherwise, you'll spend more time driving than dining.

Thanh Long ⍟, 4101 Judah St. (at 46th Ave.; ℂ **415/665-1146;** www.an family.com; streetcar: N), is an out-of-the-way Sunset District Vietnamese standout that, long after my mom started taking me here as a tot for excellent roasted crab and addictive garlic noodles, has remained a San Francisco secret. Since the owners, the An family, have become rather famous for their aforementioned signature dishes now that they're served in sister restaurants Crustacean Beverly Hills and S.F., suffice it to say the crab's out of the bag. But this location is still far enough on the outskirts of the city to keep it from becoming overcrowded. The restaurant is more visually pleasing than most Southeast Asian outposts (white tablecloths, tastefully exotic decor), but the extra glitz is reflected in the prices of luxury dishes (main courses run from $14–$34) such as charbroiled tiger prawns with those famed garlic noodles and steamed sea bass with scallions and ginger sauce. On the plus side, unlike the cheaper options around town, there's a full bar here, too, serving fun cocktails such as the Pineapple and Litchi vodka infusion. Reservations are recommended. Thanh Long is open Sunday and Tuesday through Thursday from 4:30 to 9:30pm, open Friday and Saturday from 4:30 to 10:30pm, and is closed on Mondays

The Ramp ⍟, 855 China Basin (at the end of Mariposa St.; ℂ **415/621-2378;** bus: 22 or 48), is an out-of-the-way mecca for seaside snacks, dancing, and drinking that's at its best when the sun is shining. If you're lucky enough

Kuleto, who created the swank champagne-inspired decor. On most evenings, the two-story brick structure is abuzz with an older crowd (including ex-mayor Brown, a regular) who sip cocktails at the centerpiece mahogany bar or watch the scene discreetly from the circular balcony. The restaurant's champagne theme extends to twinkling lights and fun ice buckets built into the balcony railing, making the atmosphere conducive to throwing back a few in the best of style—especially when live jazz is playing (at 7:30pm nightly).

The daily changing menu is lovely; it might include seared scallops with truffled potatoes and truffle reduction, sautéed petrale sole with Alsatian cabbage and Riesling sauce, or venison with celery root, red wine, braised cabbage, and juniper sauce. But the atmosphere just doesn't have enough warmth for me. Still, anyone in search of a quality meal will not be disappointed. I also have to give kudos to the outstanding cheese selection, great wine list—many by the glass, and over 500 bottles—and Traci's commitment to leading the industry supporting sustainably farmed, wholesome ingredients and environmentally conscious business operations.

to be in San Francisco on one of those rare hot days, head to this bayside hangout. The fare is of the basic pub grub variety—burgers, sandwiches, salads, and soups from $8 to $13—but the rustic boatyard environment and patio seating make this a relaxing place to dine in the sun. In summer, the place really rocks when live bands perform (4:30–8:30pm Fri–Sun Apr–Oct) and tanned, cocktailing singles prowl the area. It's open for lunch Monday through Thursday from 11am to 3:30pm and Friday 11am to 4pm, and for brunch Saturday and Sunday from 8:30am to 4pm. The bar is open Monday through Friday from 11am to 8pm, Friday and Saturday from 8:30am to 8pm. From April to October, outdoor barbecue is offered Saturday and Sunday from 4 to 8pm; on non-barbecue days, appetizers are featured from 5:30 to 8pm, weather permitting.

Little Star Pizza ☆☆, 846 Divisadero St. (at McCallister St.; © **415/441-1118**; www.littlestarpizza.com; bus 5 or 24), may be on a dreary strip of busy Divisadero Street and feel like a bohemian speak-easy with its dark colored walls, low ceilings, and jukebox, but this joint is cranking out the best pizza in town. You're likely to have to wait for a seat at one of the well-spaced tables and you may have to strain to chat over the music and dining din, but there's little I wouldn't endure for one of Little Star's deep dish cornmeal-crust pizzas ($11–$22). Rather than inches of dough, these pies are thin and crisp with high sides that coddle fillings such as chicken, tomatoes, artichoke hearts, red bell peppers, sausage, and feta. These babies take about 25 minutes to bake, which is a great excuse to order chicken wings and a glass of wine for the wait. The place serves dinner Sunday through Thursday from 5 to 10pm, Friday and Saturday from 5 to 11pm, and offers happy hour drink specials from 5 to 6:30pm and 10 to 11:30pm.

300 Grove St. (at Franklin St.). © **415/861-5555**. www.jardiniere.com. Reservations recommended. Main courses $26–$38; 6-course tasting menu $79. AE, DC, DISC, MC, V. Sun–Wed 5–10:30pm; Thurs–Sat 5–11:30pm. Valet parking $10. Bus: 19 or 21.

MODERATE

Absinthe ☆ FRENCH   This Hayes Valley hot spot is sexy, fun, reasonably priced, and frequented by everyone from the theatergoing crowd to the young and chic. Decor is scrumptious brasserie, with French rattan cafe chairs, copper-topped tables, a pressed-tin ceiling, soft lighting, period art, and a rich use of color and fabric, including leather and mohair banquettes. The menu is hit-or-miss—from fun specialty cocktails (ever had a "Ginger Rogers," made with gin, mint, lemon juice, ginger ale, and a squeeze of lime?) and good wine list to the slew of bar snacks ranging from Caesar salad to chicken liver pâté to a respectable burger. In the divided dining room, main courses are equally satisfying, from coq au vin and steak frites to roasted whole Dungeness crab with poached leeks in mustard vinaigrette, salt roasted potatoes, and aioli. Interested in weekend brunch? Anticipate creamy polenta with mascarpone, maple syrup, bananas, and toasted walnuts; soft-boiled eggs with sage croutons; as well as the usual suspects.

398 Hayes St. (at Gough St.). ✆ 415/551-1590. www.absinthe.com. Reservations recommended. Brunch $8–$14, most main courses $12–$22 lunch, $18–$28 dinner. AE, DC, DISC, MC, V. Tues–Fri 11:30am–midnight (bar until 2am Fri); Sat 11am–midnight (bar until 2am); Sun 11am–10:30pm (bar until midnight). Valet parking (Tues–Sat after 5pm) $10. Bus: 21.

Hayes Street Grill ✦ SEAFOOD   For well over a decade, this small, no-nonsense seafood restaurant (owned and operated by revered food writer and chef Patricia Unterman) has maintained a solid reputation among San Francisco's picky epicureans for its impeccably fresh and straightforwardly prepared fish. The concise menu offers a dozen appetizers—most of which are fresh and lively salads—a half-dozen grilled fish selections cooked to perfection and matched with your sauce of choice (Szechuan peanut, tomatillo salsa, herb-shallot butter), and a side of signature fries. Fancier seafood specials, which change with the seasons and range from mahimahi (with Vietnamese dipping sauce, baby spinach, roasted peanuts, and basmati rice) to classic paella, are balanced by a few meat-driven dishes, which may include Niman Ranch (organic and wonderful) flatiron steak with mustard butter and balsamic onions. Finish your meal with the outstanding crème brûlée.

320 Hayes St. (near Franklin St.). ✆ 415/863-5545. www.hayesstreetgrill.com. Reservations recommended. Main courses $14–$20 lunch, $16–$23 dinner. AE, DC, DISC, MC, V. Mon–Fri 11:30am–2pm; Mon–Thurs 5–9pm; Fri 5–10:30pm; Sat 5:30–10:30pm; Sun 5–8:30pm. Bus: 19, 21, 31, or 38.

Zuni Café ✦✦ *Finds* MEDITERRANEAN   Zuni Café embodies the best of San Francisco dining: Its clientele spans young hipsters and gorgeous gays and lesbians, as well as the everyday foodie; its cuisine is consistently outstanding; and the atmosphere is electric. Its expanse of windows overlooking Market Street gives the place a sense of space despite the fact that it's always packed. For the full effect, stand at the bustling, copper-topped bar and order a glass of wine and a few oysters from the oyster menu (a dozen or so varieties are on hand at all times). Then, because *of course* you made advance reservations, take your seat in the stylish exposed-brick two-level maze of little dining rooms or on the outdoor patio. Then do what we all do: Splurge on chef Judy Rodgers's Mediterranean-influenced menu. Although the ever-changing menu always includes meat (such as hanger steak), fish (grilled or braised on the kitchen's wood grill), and pasta (tagliatelle with nettles, applewood-smoked bacon, butter, and Parmesan), it's almost sinful not to order her brick-oven roasted chicken for two with Tuscan-style bread salad. I rarely pass up the polenta with mascarpone and a proper Caesar salad. But then again, if you're there for lunch or after 10pm, the hamburger on grilled rosemary focaccia bread is a strong contender for the city's best. Whatever you decide, be sure to order a stack of shoestring potatoes.

1658 Market St. (at Franklin St.). ✆ 415/552-2522. Reservations recommended. Main courses $10–$19 lunch, $15–$29 dinner. AE, MC, V. Tues–Sat 11:30am–midnight; Sun 11am–11pm. Valet parking $10. Bus: 6, 7, or 71. Streetcar: All Market St. streetcars.

INEXPENSIVE

Frjtz Fries ✦ BELGIAN   This funky-artsy "Belgian fries, crepes, and DJ/Art teahouse" features killer, fat french fries with a barrage of exotic dipping sauces as well as fine sandwiches and salads. Grab a bag of the addictively crisp and thick fried potatoes—perhaps with chipotle rémoulade or balsamic mayo—or swerve toward less lardy options such as a sweet or savory crepe—ranging from Nutella, banana, and whipped cream to grilled rosemary chicken and Swiss cheese—a big, leafy salad, or a chunky focaccia sandwich packed with roasted peppers, red onions, pesto mayo, grilled eggplant, and melted Gorgonzola. Wash it down with Belgian ale.

579 Hayes St. (at Laguna St.). ℂ 415/864-7654. www.frjtzfries.com. Reservations not accepted. Fries $3–$4.50; crepes $5–$8; sandwiches $7–$8.25. AE, DC, DISC, MC, V. Mon–Thurs 9am–10pm; Fri 9am–midnight; Sat 10am–midnight; Sun 10am–9pm. Bus: 21.

13 Mission District

For a map of restaurants in this section, see the "Where to Dine around Town" map on p. 116.

MODERATE

Delfina 😀😀 *Value* ITALIAN   Unpretentious warehouse-chic atmosphere, reasonable prices, and chef/co-owner Craig Stoll's ultrafresh seasonal Italian cuisine have made this family-owned restaurant one of the city's most cherished. Stoll, who was one of *Food & Wine*'s Best New Chefs in 2001 and a 2005 James Beard Award nominee, changes the menu daily, while his wife Annie works the front of the house (when she's not being a mom). Standards include Niman Ranch flatiron steak with french fries, and roasted chicken with Yukon Gold mashed potatoes and royal trumpet mushrooms. The winter menu might include slow-roasted pork shoulder or gnocchi with squash and chestnuts, while spring indulgences can include sand dabs with frisée, fingerling potatoes, and lemon-caper butter, or lamb with polenta and sweet peas. Trust me—order the buttermilk *panna cotta* (custard) if it's available. *A plus:* A few tables and counter seating are reserved for walk-in diners. Delfina also has a heated and covered patio that's used mid-March through November. Cocktail alert: wine and beer only here.

3621 18th St. (between Dolores and Guererro sts.). ℂ 415/552-4055. www.delfinasf.com. Reservations recommended. Main courses $13–$22. MC, V. Sun–Thurs 5:30–10pm; Fri–Sat 5:30–11pm. Parking lot at 18th and Valencia sts. next to Sharin's Appliances, $8. Bus: 26 or 33. Streetcar: J.

Foreign Cinema 😀😀 MEDITERRANEAN   This place is so chic that it's hard to believe it's a San Francisco restaurant, and it's so well hidden on Mission Street that it eludes me every time I seek the valet. An indoor seat here is a lovely place to watch San Francisco's most fashionable. Outdoors (partially covered and heated, but still chilly), the enormous foreign (and occasionally American) film showing on the side of an adjoining building steals the show. (Although the primary purpose of dining here is not to watch the film, it's still a bummer for those facing away from it.) In 2001, husband-and-wife team John Clark and Gayle Pirie stepped into the kitchen and are now creating a fine Mediterranean-inspired menu using seasonal, sustainably farmed, organic ingredients when possible. Snackers like me find solace in the oyster bar, a devilish *brandade* (fish purée) gratin, and the cheese selections. Heartier eaters can opt for roasted half-chicken with golden chanterelle and mustard-green risotto; or grilled natural rib-eye with Tuscan-style beans and rosemary-fried peppercorn sauce. Truth be told, even if the food weren't good, I'd come here: It's just that cool. If you have to wait for your table, consider stepping into their adjoining bar, Laszlo's.

2534 Mission St. (between 21st and 22nd sts.). ℂ 415/648-7600. www.foreigncinema.com. Reservations recommended. Main courses $17–$26. AE, MC, V. Mon–Thurs 6–10pm; Fri–Sat 6–11pm; brunch Sat 11am–2:30pm and Sun 11am–3:30pm; cafe menu Sat–Sun 2:30–6pm. Valet parking $8. Bus: 14, 14L, or 49.

INEXPENSIVE

Pauline's 🐟🐟 PIZZA   Housed in a cheery yellow double-decker building that stands out like a beacon in a somewhat seedy neighborhood, Pauline's does only three things—pizzas, salads, and desserts—but it does them better than most restaurants in the city. Running the gauntlet of panhandlers for a slice of Louisiana Andouille pizza topped with Andouille sausage, bell peppers, and fontina cheese is completely worth it. Other gourmet toppings include house-made chicken sausage, French goat cheese, roasted eggplant, Danish fontina cheese, and *tasso* (spiced pork shoulder). The salads are equally amazing: certified organic, handpicked by California growers, and topped with fresh and dried herbs (including edible flowers) from Pauline's own gardens in Berkeley. Don't forget to leave room for the house-made ice cream and sorbets or chocolate mousse and butterscotch pudding. The wine list offers a smart selection of low-priced wines, where Star Canyon Vineyards, yet another of the owners' pursuits, is showcased. Yes, prices are a bit steep (small pizzas start at $12), but what a paltry price to pay for perfection.

260 Valencia St. (between 14th St. and Duboce Ave.). ✆ 415/552-2050. Reservations accepted for parties of 8 or more. Pizzas $12–$25. MC, V. Tues–Sat 5–10pm. Bus: 14, 26, or 49.

Ti Couz 🐟 CREPES   At Ti Couz (say "Tee Cooz"), one of the most architecturally stylish and popular restaurants in the Mission, the headliner is simple: the delicate, paper-thin crepe. More than 30 choices of fillings make for infinite expertly executed combinations. The menu advises you how to enjoy these wraps: Order a light crepe as an appetizer, a heftier one as a main course, and a drippingly sweet one for dessert. Recommended combinations are listed, but you can build your own from the 15 main-course selections (such as smoked salmon, mushrooms, sausage, ham, scallops, and onions) and over 15 dessert options (caramel, fruit, chocolate, Nutella, and more). Soups and salads are equally stellar; the seafood salad, for example, is a delicious and generous compilation of shrimp, scallops, and ahi tuna with veggies and five kinds of lettuce.

3108 16th St. (at Valencia St.). ✆ 415/252-7373. Reservations not accepted. Crepes $2–$12. MC, V. Mon and Fri 11am–11pm; Tues–Thurs 5–10pm; Sat–Sun 10am–11pm. Bus: 14, 22, 26, 33, 49, or 53. BART: 16th or Mission.

14 The Castro

Although you see gay and lesbian singles and couples at almost any restaurant in San Francisco, the following spots cater particularly to the gay community—but being gay is certainly not a requirement for enjoying them. For a map of restaurants in this section, see the "Where to Dine around Town" map on p. 116.

EXPENSIVE

Mecca *Finds* AMERICAN   In 1996, Mecca entered the San Francisco dining scene in a decadent swirl of chocolate-brown velvet, stainless steel, cement, and brown leather. It's an industrial-chic supper club that makes you want to order a martini just so you'll match the ambience. The eclectic city clientele (with a heavy dash of same-sex couples) mingles at the oval centerpiece bar. A night here promises a live DJ spinning hot grooves and a Latin-inspired American meal prepared by new chef Sergio Santiago and served at tables tucked into several nooks. On the menu are such classics as oysters on the half shell, seared ahi tuna, and wood-oven roasted pork tenderloin. Alas the food is no longer as vibrant as the only-in-San Francisco vibe, but when the place is jumping, few seem to care.

2029 Market St. (by 14th and Church sts.). ✆ 415/621-7000. www.sfmecca.com. Reservations recommended. Main courses $22–$34. AE, DC, MC, V. Tues–Thurs 5:45–10pm; Fri–Sat 5:45–11pm; Sun brunch 1–4pm; dinner

5:45–8:30pm. Bar Tues–Sat from 5pm; Sun from noon (stays open later than the restaurant every night). Valet parking $10. Bus: 8, 22, 24, or 37. Streetcar: F, K, L, or M.

MODERATE

Caffe Luna Piena ✦ CALIFORNIA/MEDITERRANEAN   This is one of the Castro's warmest dining environments. The room stretches back to the lush outdoor dining garden (yes, there are heat lamps and smoking is permitted). The fare is contemporary California during the day and Mediterranean, Italian, and French at night with daytime basics like soups, salads, and sandwiches. Dinner features such dishes as steak frites, New York steak, and penne pasta with house-made spicy sausage. If you come for Saturday or Sunday brunch, reserve in advance or be prepared to wait in a long line. The menu includes poached eggs and smoked salmon atop an English muffin smothered in hollandaise sauce, French toast with fruit compote and mascarpone cream, and other breakfast treats.

558 Castro St. (between 18th and 19th sts.). ✆ **415/621-2566.** Reservations recommended. Main courses $6–$15 brunch and lunch, $10–$20 dinner. AE, MC, V. Sun–Thurs 9am–9pm; Fri–Sat 9am–10pm. Bus: 24, 33, 35, or 37. Streetcar: K, L, or M.

2223 Restaurant & Bar ✦ CALIFORNIA   Surrounded by hardwood floors, candles, streamlined modern light fixtures, and loud music, a festive mixed crowd comes here for heavy-handed specialty drinks, grilled pork chops, the ever-popular roasted chicken with roasted potatoes, and sour cherry bread pudding. Along with Mecca (see above), this is one of the hottest dining and schmoozing spots in the area—and definitely one of the better Sunday brunch spots.

2223 Market St. (between Sanchez and Noe sts.). ✆ **415/431-0692.** www.2223restaurant.com. Reservations recommended. Main courses $4.75–$11 brunch, $9–$20 dinner. AE, DC, MC, V. Sun brunch 10am–2:30pm, dinner 5:30–10pm; Mon–Thurs 5:30–10pm; Fri–Sat 5:30–11pm. Bus: 8, 22, 24, or 37. Streetcar: F, K, L, or M.

INEXPENSIVE

Chow ✦✦ _Value_ AMERICAN   Chow claims to serve American cuisine, but the management must be thinking of today's America, because the menu is not exactly meatloaf and apple pie. And that's just fine for eclectic and cost-conscious diners. After all, what's not to like about starting with a Cobb salad before moving on to Thai-style noodles with steak, chicken, peanuts, and spicy lime-chile garlic broth, or cioppino? Better yet, everything except the fish of the day costs under $15, especially the budget-wise daily sandwich specials, which range from meatball with mozzarella (Sun) to grilled tuna with Asian-style slaw, pickled ginger, and a wasabi mayonnaise (Mon); both come with salad, soup, or fries. While the food and prices alone would be a good argument for coming here, beer on tap, a great inexpensive wine selection, and the fun, tavernlike environment clinch the deal. A second location, **Park Chow,** is at 1240 Ninth Ave. (✆ **415/665-9912**). You can't make reservations unless you've got a party of eight or more, but if you're headed their way, you can call ahead to place your name on the wait list (recommended).

215 Church St. (near Market St.). ✆ **415/552-2469.** Reservations not accepted. Main courses $7–$15. DISC, MC, V. Mon–Thurs 11am–11pm; Fri 11am–midnight; Sat 10am–midnight; Sun 10am–11pm; Brunch served Sat–Sun 10–2:30pm. Bus: 8, 22, or 37. Streetcar: F, J, K, L, or M.

Firewood Café ✦ _Value_ AMERICAN/ITALIAN   One of the sharpest rooms in the neighborhood, the colorful Firewood put its money in the essentials and eliminated extra overhead. There are no waiters or waitresses; everyone orders at the counter and then relaxes at the single family-style table, at one of the small tables facing the huge street-side windows, or in the cheery back dining room. Management didn't skimp on the cozy-chic atmosphere and inspired but limited menu: The fresh salads come with a choice of three "fixin's," ranging from caramelized onions to spiced walnuts, and three gourmet dressing options. Then there are the pastas—three tortellini selections, such as roasted chicken and mortadella—and gourmet pizzas. Or how about herb-roasted half or whole chicken ($8.25 or $15, respectively) with roasted new potatoes? Wines cost $4.95 to $5.95 by the glass and a reasonable $15 to $22 per bottle. Draft and bottled beers are also available, and desserts top off at $4. (Thank goodness someone realized that $7 for an after-dinner treat borders on ridiculous.)

4248 18th St. (at Diamond St.). **②** **415/252-0999.** www.firewoodcafe.com. Main courses $7–$15. MC, V. Mon–Thurs 11am–10:30pm; Fri–Sat 11am–11pm; Sun 11am–10pm. Bus: 8, 33, 35, or 37. Streetcar: F, K, L, or M.

15 Haight-Ashbury

For a map of restaurants in this section, see the "Where to Dine around Town" map on p. 116.

MODERATE

RNM *®* AMERICAN   Lower Haight is hardly known for glamour, and that's just what makes this ultraswank restaurant such a pleasant surprise. Beyond the full-length silver mesh curtain is a deliciously glitzy diversion that looks like it belongs in New York City rather than this funky 'hood. Warmly lit with dark-wood floors and tables, a cool full bar, and lounge mezzanine, this is the perfect setting for a decent Italian- and French-inspired American meal of tapas by chef Justine Miner who sharpened her culinary skills and knives at San Francisco's Postrio, Café Kati, and Globe. Anticipate appetizers such as ahi tuna tartare with waffle chips, quail egg, and microgreens; the charcuterie plate; and caramelized onion and wild-mushroom pizza with fontina cheese and truffle oil; and entrees such as porcini-crusted day boat scallops on a purée of artichokes with shiitake mushroom ragout and a salad of mâche greens and water-melon radishes with Meyer lemon vinaigrette; and pan roasted rib-eye steak with pancetta-wrapped red Irish potatoes, wild nettles, Oakville Ranch cabernet butter, and shaved black Himalayan truffles. It's not a destination, but if you're in the area or want to go off the beaten dining path, this is a good choice.

598 Haight St. (at Steiner St.). **②** **415/551-7900.** www.rnmrestaurant.com. Reservations recommended. Small plates and pizza $7–$14; main courses $12–$22. AE, MC, V. Tues–Thurs 5:30–10pm; Fri–Sat 5:30–11pm. Valet Thurs–Sat. Closed Sun–Mon. Bus: 7 or 22.

INEXPENSIVE

Cha Cha Cha *®®* *Value* CARIBBEAN   This is one of my all-time favorite places to get festive, but it's not for everybody. Dining at Cha Cha Cha is not about a meal, it's about an experience. Put your name on the list, crowd into the minuscule bar, and sip sangria while you wait. When you do get seated (it can take up to an hour), you'll dine in a loud—and I mean *loud*—dining room with Santería altars, banana trees, and plastic tropical tablecloths. The best thing to do is order from the tapas menu and share the dishes family-style. Fried calamari, fried new potatoes, Cajun shrimp, and mussels in saffron broth are all bursting with flavor and accompanied by rich, luscious sauces—whatever you choose, you can't go wrong. This is the kind of place where you take friends in a partying mood, let your hair down, and make an evening of it. If you want the flavor without the festivities, come during lunch. Their second, larger location, in the Mission District, at 2327 Mission St., between 19th and 20th streets (© **415/ 648-0504**), is open for dinner only and has a full bar specializing in mojitos.

1801 Haight St. (at Shrader St.). © **415/386-7670**. www.cha3.com. Reservations not accepted. Tapas $5–$9; main courses $12–$15. MC, V. Daily 11:30am–4pm; Sun–Thurs 5–11pm; Fri–Sat 5–11:30pm. Bus: 6, 7, or 71. Streetcar: N.

Thep Phanom ☆ THAI   It's the combination of fresh ingredients; the perfect lively balance of salty, sweet, hot, and sour flavors; and the attractive and atmospheric surroundings that usually fall short at other ethnic restaurants that make this place special. Those who like to play it safe will be more than happy with the likes of pad Thai and coconut-lemon-grass soup, but it's advisable to divert from the usual suspects for house specialties such as *Thaitanic Beef* (stir-fried beef and string beans in a spicy sauce), prawns with eggplant and crisped basil, and *ped sawan*—duck with a delicate honey sauce served over spinach. The Haight location usually attracts the young, but the restaurant's reputation does bring in a truly diverse San Francisco crowd. As for the neighborhood: Don't leave anything even remotely valuable in your car.

400 Waller St. (at Fillmore St.). © **415/431-2526**. www.thepphanom.com. Reservations recommended. Main courses $9–$13. AE, DC, DISC, MC, V. Daily 5:30–10:30pm. Bus: 6, 7, 22, 66, or 71.

16 Richmond/Sunset Districts

For a map of restaurants in this section, see the "Where to Dine around Town" map on p. 116.

MODERATE

Aziza ☆☆ MOROCCAN   If you're looking for something really different—or a festive spot for a large party—head deep into the Avenues for an exotic taste of Morocco. Chef-owner Mourad Lahlou creates an excellent dining experience through colorful and distinctly Moroccan surroundings and his modern but still authentic take on the food of his homeland. In any of the three opulently adorned dining rooms (the front room features private booths, the middle room is more formal, and the back has lower seating and a Moroccan lounge feel), you can indulge in the affordable five-course tasting menu ($39) or individual treats such as kumquat-enriched lamb shank, saffron guinea hen with preserved lemon and olives, or Paine Farm squab with Napa Valley's Wine Forest wild mushrooms, bitter greens, and a *ras el hanout* reduction (a traditional Moroccan blend of 40 or so spices). Consider finishing off with my favorite dessert (if you're lucky and it's in season): rhubarb *galette* with rose- and geranium-scented crème fraîche, vanilla aspic, and rhubarb consommé.

5800 Geary Blvd. (at 22nd Ave.). © **415/752-2222**. www.aziza-sf.com. Reservations recommended. Main courses $10–$22; 5-course menu $39. MC, V. Wed–Mon 5:30–10pm. Valet parking $8 weekdays, $10 weekends. Bus: 29 or 38.

Beach Chalet Brewery & Restaurant ☆ *Kids* AMERICAN   While Cliff House (see below) has historical character worth exploration, this is the most modern oceanside restaurant, with commanding views of the Pacific Ocean (fog permitting). The Chalet occupies the upper floor of a historic public lounge that originally opened in 1900, was renovated, closed, and was reopened in 1997. Today, the main floor's wonderful restored WPA frescoes and historical displays on the area are enough to lure tourists and locals, but there's nothing historic about the bright and cheery restaurant, which does the trick when you're in the 'hood, but is not a destination in itself. In fact, a great beer selection and live music have been the primary nighttime draws of late.

Dinner is pricey, and the view disappears with the sun, so come for breakfast or lunch when you can eat your hamburger, buttermilk fried calamari, or grilled Atlantic salmon with one of the best vistas around. After dinner, it's a more local thing, especially on Tuesday and Friday evenings when live bands accompany the cocktails and house-made house-brewed ales and root beer. *Note:* Be careful getting into the parking lot (accessible only from the northbound side of the highway)—it's a quick, sandy turn.

In early 2004, owners Lara and Greg Truppelli added the adjoining **Park Chalet** restaurant to the Beach Chalet. The 3,000-square-foot glass-enclosed extension behind the original landmark building offers more casual fare—with entrees ranging from $11 to $23—including rib-eye steak, fish and chips, roasted chicken, and pizza. Other reasons to come? Retractable glass walls reveal Golden Gate Park's landmark Dutch windmill, a fireplace warms the room on chillier evenings, and live music is performed Tuesday and Thursday through Sunday evenings. Weather permitting, you can eat out back on the lawn; there's even a weekend barbecue from 11am to dusk in the summer. The restaurant opens at 11am daily in the summer (noon in winter) and, like the Beach Chalet, has varying closing times, so call ahead.

1000 Great Hwy. (at west end of Golden Gate Park, near Fulton St.). ✆ **415/386-8439.** www.beachchalet.com. Main courses $8–$17 breakfast, $11–$27 lunch/dinner. AE, MC, V. Daily noon–9pm in winter and 11am–10pm in summer (however, hours may change based on business, so call ahead). Bus: 18, 31, or 38. Streetcar: N.

Cliff House ✦ (Kids) (Finds) CALIFORNIA/SEAFOOD

In the old days (we're talking way back), Cliff House was *the* place to go for a romantic night on the town. Nowadays, the newly revamped San Francisco landmark caters mostly to tourists who arrive to gander at the Sutro Baths remains next door or dine at the two remodeled restaurants. The more formal (read pricey) **Sutro's** has contemporary decor, truly spectacular panoramic views, and a fancy seafood-influenced American menu that showcases local ingredients. The food, while nothing revolutionary, is well prepared and features the likes of roasted organic beet salad; lobster and crab cakes with shaved fennel, romesco sauce, and caramelized Meyer lemon; and a mighty fine grilled lamb sirloin sandwich (at lunch). The same spectacular views in less dramatic but still beautiful surroundings can be found at the **Bistro,** which offers big salads, sandwiches, burgers, and other soul-satisfiers. For the most superb ocean views, come for sunset, so long as it looks like the fog will let up. Alternatively, overindulge to the tune of live harp music at the Sunday champagne buffet in the Terrace Room—a personal favorite of my family for years. (Reserve well in advance; it's a popular feast.)

1090 Point Lobos (at Merrie Way). ✆ **415/386-3330.** www.cliffhouse.com. Reservations accepted for Sutro's only. Bistro main courses $9–$26 breakfast/lunch, $13–$26 dinner; Sutro main courses $18–$25 lunch, $18–$30 dinner; 3-course prix-fixe $25 lunch and $35 dinner (Mon–Fri only). AE, DC, DISC, MC, V. Bistro: Mon–Fri 9am–9:30pm; Sat–Sun 9am–10pm. Sutro: daily 11:30am–3:30pm and 5–9:30pm; brunch Sun 11am–2pm. Bus: 18 or 38.

Kabuto A&S ✦✦ JAPANESE/SUSHI

In a town overflowing with seafood and pretentious taste buds, you'd think it would be easier to find great sushi. The truth is, finding an outstanding sushi restaurant in San Francisco is more challenging than spotting a parking space in Nob Hill. Chopsticking these fish-and-rice delicacies is one of the most joyous and adventurous ways to dine, and Kabuto is one of the best places to do it. Chef Sachio Kojima, who presides over the small, crowded sushi bar, constructs each dish with smooth, lightning-fast movements known only to master chefs. If you're big on wasabi, ask for the stronger stuff Kojima serves on request.

5121 Geary Blvd. (at 16th Ave.). ✆ **415/752-5652.** www.kabutosushi.com. Reservations not accepted. Sushi $2–$10; small plates $5–$12; main courses $15–$20. MC, V. Tues–Sat 5:30–10:30pm.

Khan Toke Thai House ★★ *Value* THAI   Khan Toke Thai is so traditional you're asked to remove your shoes before being seated. Popular for special occasions, this Richmond District fixture is easily the prettiest Thai restaurant in the city; lavishly carved teak interiors evoke the ambience of a Thai temple.

To start, I suggest ordering the *tom yam gong* soup of lemon grass, shrimp, mushroom, tomato, and cilantro. Follow with such well-flavored dishes as ground pork with fresh ginger, green onion, peanuts, and lemon juice; prawns with hot chiles, mint leaves, lime juice, lemon grass, and onions; or chicken with cashews, crispy chiles, and onions. For a real treat, have the deep-fried pompano topped with sautéed ginger, onions, peppers, pickled garlic, and yellow-bean sauce; or deep-fried red snapper with "three-flavors" sauce and basil leaves. A complete dinner, including appetizer, soup, salad, two main courses, dessert, and coffee, is a great value.

5937 Geary Blvd. (between 23rd and 24th aves.). (✆ 415/668-6654. Reservations recommended Fri–Sat for parties of 3 or more. Main courses $6–$13; fixed-price dinner $20. AE, MC, V. Daily 5–10pm. Bus: 38.

INEXPENSIVE

Burma Superstar ★★ *Value* BURMESE   Despite its gratuitous name, this basic dining room garners true superstar status by offering exceptional Burmese food at rock-bottom prices. Unfortunately, the allure of the tealeaf salad, Burmese style curry with potato, and sweet-tangy sesame beef is one of the city's worst-kept secrets. Add to that a no-reservations policy and you can count on waiting in line for up to an hour. (FYI, parties of two are seated more quickly than larger groups and it's less crowded at lunch.) On the bright side, you can pencil your cellphone number onto the waiting list and browse the Clement Street shops until you receive a call.

309 Clement St. (at Fourth Ave.). (✆ 415/387-2147. www.burmasuperstar.com. Reservations not accepted. Main courses $8–$16. MC, V. Mon–Thurs 11am–9:30pm; Fri–Sat 11am–10pm; Sun 11am–9:30pm. Bus: 2, 4, 38, or 44.

Ton Kiang ★★ *Kids* *Finds* CHINESE/DIM SUM   Ton Kiang is the number one place in the city to have dim sum (served daily), only partially due to the fact that they make all their sauces, pickles, and other delicacies in-house The experience goes like this: Wait in line (which is out the door from 11am–1:30pm on weekends), get a table on the first or second floor, and get ready to say yes to dozens of delicacies, which are brought to the table for your approval. From stuffed crab claws, roast Beijing duck, and a gazillion dumpling selections (including scallop and vegetable, shrimp, and beef) to the delicious and hard-to-find *doa miu* (snow pea sprouts flash-sautéed with garlic and peanut oil), shark-fin soup, and a mesmerizing mango pudding, every tray of morsels coming from the kitchen is an absolute delight. Though it's hard to get past the dim sum, which is served all day every day, the full menu of Hakka cuisine is worth investigation as well—fresh and flavorful soups; an array of seafood, beef, and chicken; and clay-pot specialties.

5821 Geary Blvd. (between 22nd and 23rd aves.). (✆ 415/387-8273. www.tonkiang.net. Reservations accepted for parties of 8 or more. Dim sum $2–$5.50; main courses $9–$25. AE, DC, DISC, MC, V. Mon–Thurs 10am–10pm; Fri 10am–10:30pm; Sat 9:30am–10:30pm; Sun 9am–10pm. Bus: 38.

Exploring San Francisco

San Francisco's parks, museums, tours, and landmarks are favorites for travelers the world over and offer an array of activities to suit every visitor. But no particular activity or place makes the city one of the most popular destinations in the world. It's San Francisco itself—its charm, its atmosphere, its perfect blend of big metropolis with small-town hospitality.

No matter what you do while you're here—whether you spend all your time in central areas like Union Square or North Beach, or explore the outer neighborhoods—you're bound to discover the reason classic crooner Tony Bennett—and millions of visitors—leave their hearts in The City by the Bay.

1 Famous San Francisco Sights

Alcatraz Island ✶✶✶ *Kids*   Visible from Fisherman's Wharf, Alcatraz Island (aka "The Rock") has seen a checkered history. Juan Manuel Ayala was the first European to discover it in 1775 and named it after the many pelicans that nested on the island. From the 1850s to 1933, when the army vacated the island, it served as a military post, protecting the bay's shoreline. In 1934, the government converted the buildings of the military outpost into a maximum-security prison. Given the sheer cliffs, treacherous tides and currents, and frigid water temperatures, it was believed to be a totally escape-proof prison. Among the famous gangsters who occupied cell blocks A through D were Al Capone, Robert Stroud, the so-called Birdman of Alcatraz (because he was an expert in ornithological diseases), Machine Gun Kelly, and Alvin Karpis. It cost a fortune to keep them imprisoned here because all supplies, including water, had to be shipped in. In 1963, after an apparent escape in which no bodies were recovered, the government closed the prison. In 1969, a group of Native Americans chartered a boat to the island to symbolically reclaim the island for the Indian people. They occupied the island until 1971, the longest occupation of a federal facility by Native Americans to this day, when they were forcibly removed by the U.S. government (see www.nps. gov/alcatraz/indian.html for more information on the Native American occupation of Alcatraz). The next year the island became part of the Golden Gate National Recreation Area. The wildlife that was driven away during the military and prison years has begun to return—the black-crested night heron and other seabirds are nesting here again—and a new trail passes through the island's nature areas. Tours, including an audio tour of the prison block and a slide show, are given by the park's rangers, who entertain guests with interesting anecdotes.

Allow about 2½ hours for the round-trip boat ride and the tour. Wear comfortable shoes (the National Park Service notes that there are a lot of hills to climb on the tour) and take a heavy sweater or windbreaker, because even when the sun's out, it's cold out there. You should also consider bringing snacks and drinks with you if you think you'll want them. While there is a beverage-and-snack bar on the ferry, the options are extremely limited and expensive, and once you get onto The Rock all you can buy is water. The excursion to Alcatraz is popular and space is limited, so purchase tickets as far in advance as possible. **Blue & Gold Fleet** (© **415/705-5555;** www.blueandgold fleet.com) operates the tour; they accept American Express, MasterCard, and Visa. You can also buy tickets in advance from the Blue & Gold ticket office on Pier 41 or on their website. Alcatraz night tours are also available and are a more intimate and wonderfully spooky experience.

For those who want to get a closer look at Alcatraz without going ashore, two boat-tour operators offer short circumnavigations of the island (see "Self-Guided & Organized Tours" on p. 183 for complete information).

Pier 41, near Fisherman's Wharf. © 415/773-1188 (info only). www.nps.gov/alcatraz. Admission (includes ferry trip and audio tour) $16 adults with headset, $12 without; $15 seniors 62 and older with headset, $9.75 without; $11 children 5–11 with headset, $8.25 without. Night tours cost $24 adults; $21 seniors 62 and older; $14 children 5–11. Fall, winter, and spring daily 9:30am–4:30pm; summer daily 9:30am–6:30pm. Ferries depart 15 and 45 min. after the hour. Arrive at least 20 min. before sailing time. Night tours leave Thurs–Sun at 4:20 and 5:10pm.

Cable Cars ★★★ *Moments* *Kids*   Although they may not be San Francisco's most practical means of transportation, cable cars are certainly the best loved and are a must-experience when visiting the city. Designated official historic landmarks by the National Park Service in 1964, they clank up and down the city's steep hills like mobile museum pieces, tirelessly hauling thousands of tourists each day to nowhere in particular.

London-born engineer Andrew Hallidie invented San Francisco's cable cars in 1869. He got the idea by serendipity. As the story goes, Hallidie was watching a team of overworked horses haul a heavily laden carriage up a steep San Francisco slope. As he watched, one horse slipped and the car rolled back, dragging the other tired beasts with it. At that moment, Hallidie resolved that he would invent a mechanical contraption to replace such horses, and just 4 years later, in 1873, the first cable car made its maiden run from the top of Clay Street. Promptly ridiculed as "Hallidie's Folly," the cars were slow to gain acceptance. One early onlooker voiced the general opinion by exclaiming, "I don't believe it—the damned thing works!"

Even today, many visitors have difficulty believing that these vehicles, which have no engines, actually work. The cars, each weighing about 6 tons, run along a steel cable, enclosed under the street in a center rail. You can't see the cable unless you peer straight down into the crack, but you'll hear its characteristic clickity-clanking sound whenever you're nearby. The cars move when the gripper (not the driver) pulls back a lever that closes a pincerlike "grip" on the cable. The speed of the car, therefore, is determined by the speed of the cable, which is a constant 9½ mph—never more, never less.

The two types of cable cars in use hold a maximum of 90 and 100 passengers, and the limits are rigidly enforced. The best views are from the outer running boards, where you have to hold on tightly when taking curves.

Hallidie's cable cars have been imitated and used throughout the world, but all have been replaced by more efficient means of transportation. San Francisco planned to do so, too, but the proposal met with so much opposition that the cable cars' perpetuation was actually written into the city charter in 1955. The mandate cannot be revoked without the approval of a majority of the city's voters—a distant and doubtful prospect.

San Francisco's three existing cable car lines form the world's only surviving system of cable cars, which you can experience for yourself should you choose to wait in the

Major San Francisco Attractions

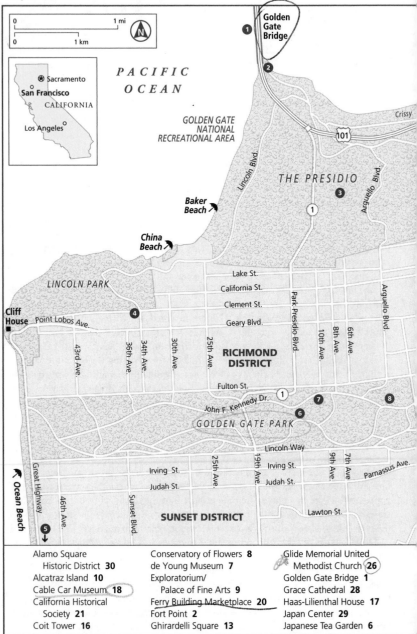

Golden Gate Bridge

1

2

PACIFIC OCEAN

GOLDEN GATE NATIONAL RECREATIONAL AREA

Crissy

THE PRESIDIO

3

1

Lincoln Blvd.

Arguello Blvd.

Baker Beach

China Beach

LINCOLN PARK

Lake St.

California St.

Clement St.

Geary Blvd.

Cliff House

Point Lobos Ave.

4

43rd Ave.

36th Ave.

34th Ave.

30th Ave.

25th Ave.

Park Presidio Blvd.

10th Ave.

8th Ave.

6th Ave.

Arguello Blvd.

RICHMOND DISTRICT

Fulton St.

1

7

8

John F. Kennedy Dr.

6

GOLDEN GATE PARK

Lincoln Way

Great Highway

46th Ave.

Sunset Blvd.

Irving St.

Judah St.

25th Ave.

19th Ave.

Irving St.

Judah St.

9th Ave.

7th Ave.

Parnassus Ave.

Lawton St.

SUNSET DISTRICT

Ocean Beach

5

Sacramento

San Francisco

CALIFORNIA

Los Angeles

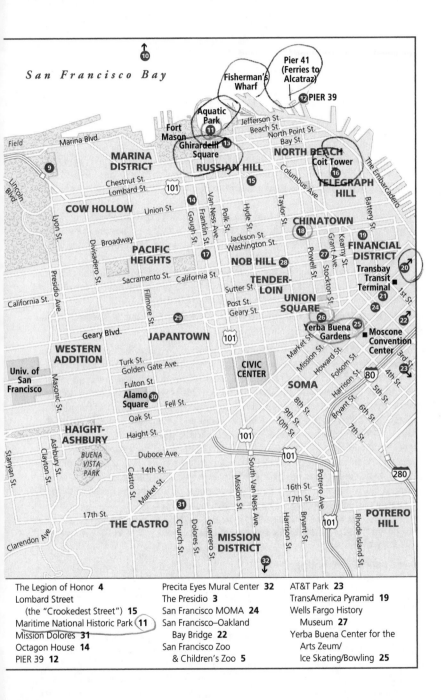

San Francisco Bay

↑
10

Fisherman's Wharf

Pier 41 (Ferries to Alcatraz)

12 PIER 39

Aquatic Park 11

Fort Mason

Ghirardelli Square 13

Jefferson St.
Beach St.
North Point St.
Bay St.

NORTH BEACH

Coit Tower 16

MARINA DISTRICT

Field

Marina Blvd.

9

RUSSIAN HILL

Columbus Ave.

TELEGRAPH HILL

The Embarcadero

Lincoln Blvd.

Chestnut St.
Lombard St.

COW HOLLOW

Union St.

101

14

Van Ness Ave.

Franklin St.

Polk St.

Hyde St.

Taylor St.

CHINATOWN

18

Kearny St.

Grant Ave.

19 FINANCIAL DISTRICT

Battery St.

20

Lyon St.

Divisadero St.

Broadway

PACIFIC HEIGHTS

Gough St.

Jackson St.
Washington St.

NOB HILL 28

Powell St.

Stockton St.

27

Transbay Transit Terminal

21

1st St.

Presidio Ave.

Sacramento St. California St.

TENDER-LOIN

UNION SQUARE

24

22

California St.

Fillmore St.

Sutter St.

Post St.
Geary St.

26 Yerba Buena Gardens 25

Moscone Convention Center

3rd St.

WESTERN ADDITION

Geary Blvd.

JAPANTOWN

101

Market St.

Mission St.

Howard St.

Folsom St.

Harrison St.

23

4th St.

5th St.

80

Univ. of San Francisco

Masonic Ave.

Turk St.
Golden Gate Ave.

CIVIC CENTER

SOMA

Fulton St.

Alamo Square 30

Fell St.

Oak St.

8th St.

9th St.

10th St.

Bryant St.

6th St.

7th St.

HAIGHT-ASHBURY

Ashbury St.

Clayton St.

Haight St.

BUENA VISTA PARK

Duboce Ave.

14th St.

Castro St.

Market St.

101

101

South Van Ness Ave.

Mission St.

16th St.

17th St.

Potrero Ave.

101

280

POTRERO HILL

Rhode Island St.

Stanyan St.

17th St.

THE CASTRO

Church St.

Dolores St.

Guerrero St.

31

MISSION DISTRICT

San Van Ness Ave.

Harrison St.

Bryant St.

Clarendon Ave.

32 ↓

endless boarding line (up to a 2-hr. wait in summer). For more information on riding them, see "Getting Around," in chapter 4, p. 44.

Powell–Hyde and Powell–Mason lines begin at the base of Powell and Market sts.; California St. line begins at the foot of Market St. $5 per ride.

Coit Tower ★★
In a city known for its great views and vantage points, Coit Tower is one of the best. Located atop Telegraph Hill, just east of North Beach, the round, stone tower offers panoramic views of the city and the bay.

Completed in 1933, the tower is the legacy of Lillie Hitchcock Coit, a wealthy eccentric who left San Francisco a $125,000 bequest "for the purpose of adding beauty to the city I have always loved" and as a memorial to its volunteer firemen. She had been saved from a fire as a child and held the city's firefighters in particularly high esteem.

Inside the base of the tower are impressive murals titled *Life in California* and *1934,* which were completed under the WPA during the New Deal. They are the work of more than 25 artists, many of whom had studied under Mexican muralist Diego Rivera.

The only bummer: The narrow street leading to the tower is often clogged with tourist traffic. If you can, find a parking spot in North Beach and hoof it. It's actually a beautiful walk—especially if you take the Filbert Street Steps (p. 187).

Telegraph Hill. ℂ **415/362-0808**. Admission is free to enter; to go to the top $3.75 adults, $2.50 seniors, $1.50 children 6–12. Daily 10am–6pm. Bus: 39 (Coit).

Farmers' Market ★★★ *(Finds*
If you're heading to the Ferry Building Marketplace or just happen to be in the area at the right time (especially a sunny Sat), make a point of visiting the Farmers' Market, which is held in the alfresco areas in front of and behind the marketplace several days per week. This is where San Francisco foodies, every type of citizen, and many of the best local chefs—including the famed Alice Waters of Chez Panisse—gather, hang out, and peruse alfresco stands hawking the finest Northern California fruits, vegetables, breads, dairy, flowers, and readymade snacks and complete meals by a few local restaurants. You'll be amazed at the variety and quality, and the crowded scene itself is something to behold. You can also pick up locally made vinegars and oils here—they make wonderful gifts. Drop by on Saturday from 10am to noon for a serious social fest along with stalls, interviews with local farmers, culinary demos and a chance to taste their recipes.

The Embarcadero, at Market St. ℂ **415/291-3276**. www.cuesa.org. Year-round Tues 10am–2pm, Sat 8am–2pm; May–Oct Tues 10am–2pm, Thurs 4–8pm, Sat 8am–2pm, Sun 10am–2pm. Bus: 2, 7, 12, 14, 21, 66, or 71. Streetcar: F. BART: Embarcadero.

Ferry Building Marketplace ★★ *(Finds*
There's no better way to enjoy a San Francisco morning than strolling this gourmet marketplace in the Ferry Building and snacking your way through breakfast or lunch. Tasty tenants, open daily, include many of the best of Northern California's gourmet bounty: Cowgirl Creamery's Artisan Cheese Shop, Recchiuti Confections (amazing!), Scharffen Berger Chocolate, Acme Breads, Wine Country's gourmet diner Taylor's Refresher, famed Vietnamese restaurant The Slanted Door, and myriad other restaurants, eateries, and wine bars. Check out the Imperial Tea Court where you'll be taught the traditional Chinese way to steep and sip your tea; buy cooking items at the Sur La Table shop; grab a bite and savor the bayfront views from in- and outdoor tables; or browse the Farmers' Market

when it's up and running (see above). Whatever you do, you'll be doing it with a swarm of San Franciscans who can't get enough of this place.

The Embarcadero, at Market St. ℂ **415/693-0996**. www.ferrybuildingmarketplace.com. Most stores daily 10am–6pm; restaurant hours vary. Bus: 2, 7, 12, 14, 21, 66, or 71. Streetcar: F. BART: Embarcadero.

Fisherman's Wharf *Overrated*   Few cities in America are as adept at wholesaling their historical sites as San Francisco, which has converted Fisherman's Wharf into one of the most popular tourist attractions in the world. Unless you come really early in the morning, however, other than a few Italian family restaurants founded in the 1920s you won't find any traces of the traditional waterfront life that once existed here—the only fishing going on at Fisherman's Wharf these days is for tourists' dollars.

Originally called Meigg's Wharf, this bustling strip of waterfront got its present moniker from generations of fishers who used to base their boats here. Today, the bay has become so polluted that bright yellow placards warn against eating fish from the waters. A small fleet of fewer than 30 fishing boats still sets out from here, but basically Fisherman's Wharf has been converted into one long shopping mall that stretches from Ghirardelli Square at the west end to PIER 39 at the east.

Accommodating a total of 300 boats, two marinas flank PIER 39 and house the Blue & Gold bay sightseeing fleet. In recent years, some 900 California sea lions have taken up residence on the adjacent floating docks. Until they abandon their new playground, which seems more and more unlikely, these playful, noisy creatures (some nights you can hear them all the way from Washington Sq.) are one of the best free attractions on the wharf. Weather permitting, the Marine Mammal Center (ℂ **415/ 289-SEAL**) offers an educational talk at PIER 39 on weekends from 11am to 5pm that teaches visitors about the range, habitat, and adaptability of the California sea lion.

Some people love Fisherman's Wharf; others can't get far enough away from it. Most agree that, for better or for worse, it has to be seen at least once in your lifetime. Personally, I've grown to like it. On a beautiful day, there are few better places to stroll, and while it's still got lots of tacky tourist shops and mediocre restaurants, it's definitely also got old-school San Francisco character—something that's quickly disappearing in these parts.

At Taylor St. and The Embarcadero. ℂ **415/674-7503**. www.fishermanswharf.org. Bus: 15, 30, 32, 39, 42, or 82X. Streetcar: F-line. Cable car: Powell–Mason to the last stop and walk to the wharf. If you're arriving by car, park on adjacent streets or on the wharf between Taylor and Jones sts. for $16 per day, $8 with validation from participating restaurants.

Ghirardelli Square   This National Historic Landmark property dates from 1864, when it served as a factory making Civil War uniforms, but it's best known as the former chocolate and spice factory of Domingo Ghirardelli (pronounced "*Gear*-a-deli"), who purchased it in 1893. The factory has since been converted into an unimpressive three-level mall containing 30-plus stores and five dining establishments. Scheduled street performers entertain regularly in the West Plaza and fountain area. Incidentally, the Ghirardelli Chocolate Company still makes chocolate, but its factory is in a lower-rent district in the East Bay. Still, if you have a sweet tooth, you won't be disappointed at the mall's fantastic (and expensive) old-fashioned soda fountain, which is open until midnight.

900 North Point St. (between Polk and Larkin sts.). ℂ **415/775-5500**. www.ghiradellisq.com. Stores generally open daily 10am–9pm in summer; Sun–Fri 10am–6pm, Sat 10am–9pm rest of year. Parking $2 per 20 minutes (1–1½ hr. free with purchase and validation, max. $16).

Golden Gate Bridge ⭑⭑⭑ *(Kids)*   The year 2007 marks the 70th birthday of possibly the most beautiful, and certainly the most photographed, bridge in the world. Often half-veiled by the city's trademark rolling fog, San Francisco's Golden Gate Bridge, named for the strait leading from the Pacific Ocean to the San Francisco Bay, spans tidal currents, ocean waves, and battering winds to connect The City by the Bay with the Redwood Empire to the north.

With its gracefully suspended single span, spidery bracing cables, and zooming twin towers, the bridge looks more like a work of abstract art than one of the 20th century's greatest practical engineering feats. Construction was completed in May 1937 at the then-colossal cost of $35 million (plus another $39 million in interest being financed entirely by bridge tolls).

The 1.7-mile bridge (including the approach), which reaches a height of 746 feet above the water, is awesome to cross. Although kept to a maximum of 45 miles an hour, traffic usually moves quickly, so crossing by car won't give you too much time to see the sights. If you drive from the city, take the last San Francisco exit, right before the toll plaza, park in the southeast parking lot and make the crossing by foot. Back in your car, continue to Marin's Vista Point, at the bridge's northern end. Look back, and you'll be rewarded with one of the greatest views of San Francisco.

Millions of people visit the bridge each year, gazing up at the tall orange towers, out at the vistas of San Francisco and Marin County, and down into the stacks of ocean-going liners. You can walk out onto the span from either end, but be prepared—it's usually windy and cold, and the bridge vibrates. Still, walking even a short distance is one of the best ways to experience the immense scale of the structure.

Hwy. 101 N. www.goldengatebridge.org. $5 cash toll collected when driving south. Bridge-bound Golden Gate Transit buses (ⓒ 511) depart hourly during the day for Marin County, starting from Mission and First sts. (across the street from the Transbay Terminal and stopping at Market and Seventh sts., at the Civic Center, along Van Ness Ave., at Lombard and Fillmore sts., and at Francisco and Richardson sts.

Lombard Street ⭑ *(Overrated)*   Known (erroneously) as the "crookedest street in the world," this whimsically winding block of Lombard Street draws thousands of visitors each year (much to the chagrin of neighborhood residents, most of whom would prefer to block off the street to tourists). The angle of the street is so steep that the road has to snake back and forth to make a descent possible. The brick-lined street zigzags around the residences' bright flower gardens, which explode with color during warmer months. This short stretch of Lombard Street is one-way, downhill, and fun to drive. Take the curves slowly and in low gear, and expect a wait during the weekend. Save your film for the bottom where, if you're lucky, you can find a parking space and take a few snapshots of the silly spectacle. You can also take staircases (without curves) up or down on either side of the street. In truth, most locals don't understand what the fuss is all about. I'm guessing the draw is the combination of a classic, unusually steep San Francisco street and a great photo op. *FYI:* Vermont Street, between 20th and 22nd streets in Potrero Hill, is even more crooked, but not nearly as picturesque. Between Hyde and Leavenworth sts.

PIER 39 *(Overrated)*   PIER 39 is a multilevel waterfront complex a few blocks east of Fisherman's Wharf. Constructed on an abandoned cargo pier, it is, ostensibly, a re-creation of a turn-of-the-20th-century street scene, but don't expect a slice of old-time maritime life here: Today, PIER 39 is a busy mall welcoming millions visitors per year. It has more than 110 stores, 13 bay-view restaurants, a two-tiered Venetian carousel,

Fisherman's Wharf & Vicinity

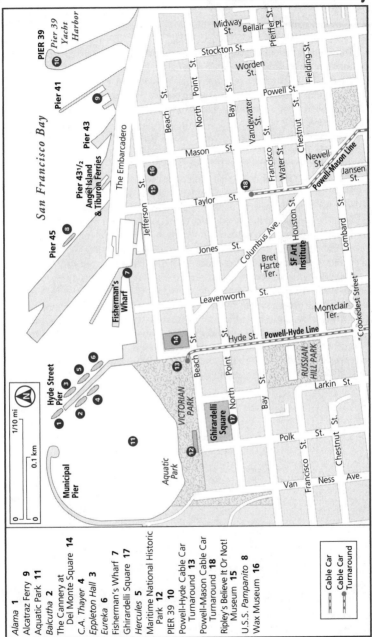

Alama **1**
Alcatraz Ferry **9**
Aquatic Park **11**
Balcutha **2**
The Cannery at
Del Monte Square **14**
C.A. Thayer **4**
Eppleton Hall **3**
Eureka **6**
Fisherman's Wharf **7**
Ghirardelli Square **17**
Hercules **5**
Maritime National Historic
Park **12**
PIER 39 **10**
Powell-Hyde Cable Car
Turnaround **13**
Powell-Mason Cable Car
Turnaround **18**
Ripley's Believe It Or Not!
Museum **15**
U.S.S. Pampanito **8**
Wax Museum **16**

Cable Car
Cable Car
Turnaround

(Kids) Funky Favorites at Fisherman's Wharf

The following sights clustered on or near Fisherman's Wharf are great fun for kids, adults, and kitsch-lovers of all ages. By bus, take no. 15, 30, 32, 39, 42, or 82X; by streetcar, take the F-line; to reach the area by cable car, take the Powell–Mason line to the last stop and walk to the wharf. If you're arriving by car, park on adjacent streets or on the wharf between Taylor and Jones streets.

The popular battle-scarred World War II fleet submarine **USS *Pampanito,*** Pier 45, Fisherman's Wharf (© **415/775-1943;** www.maritime.org), saw plenty of action in the Pacific. It has been completely restored, and visitors are free to crawl around inside. Admission, which includes an audio tour, is $9 for those 13 to 61, $5 for seniors 62 and older, $4 for children 6 to 12, and free for children under 6; the family pass (two adults, up to four kids) costs $20. The *Pampanito* is open Monday through Thursday from 9am to 8pm (to 6pm in winter), Friday through Sunday from 9am to 8pm.

Also on Pier 45, the Musée Mécanique (p. 178) is worth a look.

Ripley's Believe It or Not! Museum, 175 Jefferson St. (© **415/771-6188;** www.ripleysf.com), has drawn curious spectators through its doors for over 30 years. Inside, you'll experience a world of improbabilities: a ⅓-scale matchstick cable car, a shrunken human torso once owned by Ernest Hemingway, a dinosaur made from car bumpers, a walk through a kaleidoscope tunnel, and video displays and illusions. Robert LeRoy Ripley's infamous arsenal may lead you to ponder whether truth is, in fact, stranger than fiction. What it won't do is blow your mind or feel truly worth the money. That said, with the right attitude, it's easy to enjoy an hour here playing amid the

a Hard Rock Cafe, the Riptide Arcade, and the Aquarium of the Bay (below) for the kids. And everything here is slanted toward helping you part with your travel dollars. This is *the* place that locals love to hate. That said, it does have a few perks: absolutely beautiful natural surroundings and bay views, fresh sea air, and hundreds of sunbathing sea lions (about 900 in peak season) lounging along its neighboring docks (see p. 155 for info about the free weekend talks).

On the waterfront at The Embarcadero and Beach St. © **415/705-5500.** www.pier39.com. Shops daily 10am–8:30pm, with extended weekend hours during summer.

2 Museums

For information on museums in Golden Gate Park, see the "Golden Gate Park" section, beginning on p. 172.

Aquarium of the Bay *(Overrated)*   This $38-million, 1-million-gallon marine attraction filled with sharks, stingrays, and more transports visitors through clear acrylic goofy and interactive displays—something my husband and I did recently—with lots of laughs included in the admission price. Admission is $13 for adults, $11 for seniors over 60, $7.95 for children 5 to 12, and free for children 4 and under. The museum is open Sunday through Thursday from 10am to 10pm, until midnight on Friday and Saturday.

Conceived and executed in the Madame Tussaud mold, San Francisco's **Wax Museum,** 145 Jefferson St. (📞 **800/439-4305** or 415/202-0402; www.waxmuseum.com), has long been a kitschy harborside tourist trap. In 1998, with the closing of the adjoining Haunted Goldmine, the museum underwent a $20-million tear-down, renovation, and expansion. It reopened in June 2000 as a huge complex that includes the Rainforest Café, with walk-through aquariums. (Not any less of a tourist trap, mind you—only a newer, slicker one.) The overhaul spiffed up the museum's 270 lifelike figures, including Oprah Winfrey, Britney Spears, Marilyn Monroe, John Wayne, former President George Bush and current president George W. Bush, Giants baseball star Barry Bonds, rap artist Eminem, and "Feared Leaders" such as Fidel Castro. The Chamber of Horrors features Dracula, Frankenstein, and a werewolf, along with bloody victims hanging from meat hooks. New additions include pop icons such as Brad Pitt, Angelina Jolie, and Nicole Kidman. Admission is $13 for adults, $9.95 for juniors 12 to 17 and seniors 55 and older, $6.95 for children 6 to 11, and free for children under 5. Discount group rates are available and are arranged via telephone or the website, which also offers a $3 discount coupon for individual guests. The complex is open Monday through Friday from 10am to 9pm, Saturday and Sunday from 9am to 9pm.

tunnels via a moving footpath. Frankly, however, it's overrated and overpriced, and I recommend you skip it.

The Embarcadero at Beach St. 📞 **888/SEA-DIVE** or 415/623-5333. www.aquariumofthebay.com. Aquarium admission $14 adults, $7 seniors and children 3–11, free for children under 3. Family (2 adults, 2 children) package $34. Behind-the-scenes tour $25 per person, including admission to the aquarium. Mon–Thurs 10am–6pm; Fri–Sun 10am–7pm; summer hours 9am–8pm daily. Closed Dec 25.

Asian Art Museum 🎨   Previously in Golden Gate Park and reopened in what was once the Civic Center's Beaux Arts–style central library, San Francisco's Asian Art Museum is one of the Western world's largest museums devoted to Asian art. Its collection boasts more than 15,000 art objects, such as world-class sculptures, paintings, bronzes, ceramics, and jade items, spanning 6,000 years of history and regions of south Asia, west Asia, Southeast Asia, the Himalayas, China, Korea, and Japan. Inside you'll find 40,000 square feet of gallery space showcasing 2,500 objects at any given time. Add temporary exhibitions, live demonstrations, learning activities, Cafe Asia, and a store, and you've got one very good reason to head to the Civic Center.

200 Larkin St. (between Fulton and McAllister sts.). ℂ **415/581-3500.** www.asianart.org. Admission $10 adults, $7 seniors 65 and over, $6 youths 13–17 and college students with ID, free for children 12 and under, $5 flat rate for all (except children under 12 who are free) after 5pm Thurs. Free 1st Tues of the month. Tues–Wed and Fri–Sun 10am–5pm; Thurs 10am–9pm. Bus: All Market St. buses. Streetcar: Civic Center.

Cable Car Museum (Value) (Kids)   If you've ever wondered how cable cars work, this nifty museum explains (and demonstrates) it all. Yes, this is a museum, but the Cable Car Museum is no stuffed shirt. It's the living powerhouse, repair shop, and storage place of the cable car system and is in full operation. Built for the Ferries and Cliff House Railway in 1887, the building underwent an $18-million reconstruction to restore its original gaslight-era look, install an amazing spectators' gallery, and add a museum of San Francisco transit history.

The exposed machinery, which pulls the cables under San Francisco's streets, looks like a Rube Goldberg invention. Stand in the mezzanine gallery and become mesmerized by the massive groaning and vibrating winches as they thread the cable that hauls the cars through a huge figure-eight and back into the system using slack-absorbing tension wheels. For a better view, move to the lower-level viewing room, where you can see the massive pulleys and gears operating underground.

Also on display here is one of the first grip cars developed by Andrew S. Hallidie, operated for the first time on Clay Street on August 2, 1873. Other displays include an antique grip car and trailer that operated on Pacific Avenue until 1929, and dozens of exact-scale models of cars used on the various city lines. There's also a shop where you can buy a variety of cable car gifts. You can see the whole museum in about 45 minutes.

1201 Mason St. (at Washington St.). ℂ **415/474-1887.** www.cablecarmuseum.org. Free admission. Apr–Sept daily 10am–6pm; Oct–Mar daily 10am–5pm. Closed Thanksgiving, Christmas, and New Year's Day. Cable car: Both Powell St. lines.

California Academy of Sciences (Kids)   Originally clustered around the Music Concourse in Golden Gate Park (in multiple buildings) and intending to return there around 2008 after a complete rebuild, this duo of outstanding museums is poorly represented in its temporary home near Moscone West and the Yerba Buena Gardens and Center for the Arts. You'll find a small selection of **Steinhart Aquarium**'s sealife here, including sea horses, turtles, snakes, and poison dart frogs as well as a two-story 20,000-gallon living coral reef featuring Yellow Tangs, sea stars, and a giant clam. Kids love the "discovery tide pool" where they can get their mitts on live sea life and the African Penguin feeding show, which happens daily at 11am and 3:30pm.

A truncated version of the **Natural History Museum** has also been transplanted here with changing exhibits, such as the current Dinosaurs show (until February 4, 2007), and Snake Alley, where terrestrial snakes reside; and ScienceNOW, which presents a frequently changing display of Academy research, breaking science news, and expeditions around the globe. Kids 5 and under like the Nature Nest, a naturalist center with hands-on learning activities.

Families should look into the Academy's calendar of events, which includes fun kid-friendly festivities such as face painting, storytelling, art projects, and exhibit-related stories and demonstrations. All that said, I can't wait for these spectacular museums to reopen in their rightful spaces in the park: Their truncated versions don't offer nearly as much entertainment for the money as their complete collections did in their original locations.

875 Howard St. (between Fourth and Fifth sts.). ℂ **415/321-8000.** www.calacademy.org. Admission $7 adults; $4.50 seniors 65 and over, students with ID, and youth 12–17; $2 children 4–11; free for children under 3. Free on 1st Wed of the month. Daily 10am–5pm; 3rd Thurs until 9pm. Bus: 14, 15, 30, or 45. Streetcar: J, K, L, or M to Montgomery. BART: Powell St.

California Historical Society   As part of the plan to develop the Yerba Buena Gardens area as the city's cultural hub, the **California Historical Society** opened to house a research library, an ever-changing roster of exhibits that pertain to California's rich history, 2-hour walking tours of the Bay Area given by local eccentric, Gary L. Holloway, and a museum store. Call or check the website for current exhibit and walking tour information.

678 Mission St. (between Third and New Montgomery sts.). ℭ 415/357-1848. www.californiahistoricalsociety.org. North Baker Research Library Wed–Fri noon–4:30pm; Galleries Wed–Sat noon–4:30pm. Bus: 5, 9, 14, 15, 30, or 45. Streetcar: Powell or Montgomery.

M.H. de Young Museum 🎞🎞🎞   After closing for several years, San Francisco's oldest museum (founded in 1895) reopened in late 2005 in its new state-of-the-art Golden Gate Park facility. Its vast collections include American paintings, decorative arts and crafts, and arts from Africa, Oceania, and the Americas, as well as western and non-western textiles. Along with visit-worthy exhibitions, the de Young has long been beloved for its educational arts programs for both children and adults. But now it's equally enjoyed for its stunning surroundings. Besides beautiful exhibition areas, the structure boasts an all-copper exterior—intended to patinate with age. It's spectacular to behold and includes a tower from which you can get outstanding city views. Surrounding sculpture gardens and grassy expanses are perfect for kids to do some running or grown-ups to do some picnicking. Adding to the allure are surprisingly decent fare at the grab-and-go or order-and-wait cafe/restaurant and the underground parking, accessed at 10th Avenue and Fulton.

50 Hagiwara Tea Garden Drive (inside Golden Gate Park, 2 blocks from the park entrance at Eighth Ave. and Fulton). ℭ 415/863-3330. www.thinker.org. Adults $10, seniors $7, youths 13–17 and college students with ID $6, children 12 and under free. Free 1st Tues of the month. $2 discount for Muni riders with Fast Pass or transfer receipt. AE, MC, V. Tues–Sun 9:30am–5pm; Fri 9:30am–8:45pm. Closed Jan 1, Thanksgiving Day, and Dec 25. Bus: 5, 16AX, 16BX, 21, 44, or 71.

The Exploratorium 🎞🎞 *Kids*   *Scientific American* magazine rated The Exploratorium "the best science museum in the world"—pretty heady stuff for this exciting hands-on science fair. The Exploratorium is not a fancy place (it's more like a block-long warehouse), but it is substance, not style, that matters here. Inside you'll find hundreds of exhibits that explore everything from giant-bubble blowing to Einstein's theory of relativity. It's like a mad scientist's penny arcade, an educational fun house, and an experimental laboratory, all rolled into one. Touch a tornado, shape a glowing electrical current, finger-paint using a computer, or take a sensory journey in total darkness in the Tactile Dome ($3 extra, call to make advance reservations)—you could spend all day here and still not see everything. Every exhibit at The Exploratorium is designed to be interactive, educational, safe, and, most important, fun. And don't think it's just for kids; parents inevitably end up being the most reluctant to leave. On the way out, be sure to stop in the wonderful gift store, which is chock-full of affordable brain candy.

The museum is in the Marina District at the beautiful **Palace of Fine Arts** 🎞🎞, the only building left standing from the Panama-Pacific Exposition of 1915. The adjoining park and lagoon—the perfect place for an afternoon picnic—are home to ducks, swans, seagulls, and grouchy geese, so bring bread.

3601 Lyon St., in the Palace of Fine Arts (at Marina Blvd.). ℭ 415/563-7337, or 415/561-0360 (recorded information). www.exploratorium.edu. Admission $12 adults; $9.50 seniors, youth 13–17, visitors with disabilities, and college students with ID; $8 children 4–12; free for children under 4. Groups of 10 or more must make advance reservations. AE, MC, V. Tues–Sun 10am–5pm. Closed Mon except MLK, Jr., Day, Presidents' Day, Memorial Day, and Labor Day. Free parking. Bus: 28, 30, or Golden Gate Transit.

Haas–Lilienthal House   Of the city's many gingerbread Victorians, this handsome Queen Anne house is one of the most flamboyant. The 1886 structure features all the architectural frills of the period, including dormer windows, flying cupolas, ornate trim, and winsome turret. The elaborately styled house is now the only Victorian house museum in the city that has its rooms fully furnished with period pieces. The San Francisco Architectural Heritage maintains the house and offers docent-led 1-hour tours (the only way to see the house), which start every 20 to 30 minutes on Wednesdays, Saturdays, and Sundays.

2007 Franklin St. (at Washington St.). © 415/441-3004. www.sfheritage.org. 1-hr. guided tour $8 adults, $5 seniors and children 12 and under. Wed and Sat noon–3pm (**Note:** some Saturdays the house is closed for private functions, so call to confirm); Sun 11am–4pm. Bus: 1, 12, 19, 27, 47, or 49. Cable car: California St. line.

The Legion of Honor ★★   Designed as a memorial to California's World War I casualties, this neoclassical structure is an exact replica of The Legion of Honor Palace in Paris, right down to the inscription HONNEUR ET PATRIE above the portal.

The Legion of Honor reopened in late 1995, after a 2-year, $35-million renovation and seismic upgrading. The exterior's grassy expanses, cliff-side paths, and incredible view of the Golden Gate and downtown make this an absolute must-visit attraction before you even get in the door. The inside is equally impressive. The museum's permanent collection covers 4,000 years of art and includes paintings, sculpture, and decorative arts from Europe, as well as international tapestries, prints, and drawings. The chronological display of 4,000 years of ancient and European art includes one of the world's finest collections of Rodin sculptures. The sunlit Legion Café offers indoor and outdoor seating at moderate prices. Plan to spend 2 or 3 hours here.

In Lincoln Park (34th Ave. and Clement St.). © 415/750-3600, or 415/863-3330 (recorded information). www.thinker.org. Admission $10 adults, $7 seniors 65 and over, $6 youths 13–17 and college students with ID, free for children 12 and under. Fees may be higher for special exhibitions. Free 1st Tues of each month. Tues–Sun 9:30am–5pm. Bus: 18.

Octagon House   This unusual, eight-sided, cupola-topped house of interest to architecture buffs dates from 1861 and is maintained by the National Society of Colonial Dames of America. The architectural features are extraordinary, and from the second floor it is possible to look up into the cupola, which is illuminated at night. In the small museum, you'll find Early American furniture, portraits, silver, pewter, looking glasses, and English and Chinese ceramics. There are also some historic documents, including signatures of 54 of the 56 signers of the Declaration of Independence. Even if you're not able to visit the inside, this strange structure is worth a look from the outside.

2645 Gough St. (at Union St.). © 415/441-7512. Free admission; donation suggested. Feb–Dec 2nd Sun, and 2nd and 4th Thurs of each month noon–3pm. Tours by appointment only are the only way to see the house. Closed holidays. Bus: 41 or 45.

San Francisco Maritime National Historical Park ★ *Kids*   This park includes several marine-themed sites within a few blocks of each other. Although at press time, the park's signature Maritime Museum—on Beach Street at Polk Street, shaped like an Art Deco ship, and filled with sea-faring memorabilia—was entering its planned 2006–2007 renovations, it's worth walking by just to admire the building. Head 2 blocks east to the corner of Hyde and Jefferson and you'll find SFMNHP's new, state-of-the-art Visitor's Center, which offers a fun, interactive look at the City's maritime heritage. Housed in the historic Haslett Warehouse building, the Center tells the stories of voyage, discovery, and cultural diversity. Across the street, at the park's Hyde Street Pier, are several historic ships, which are moored and open to the public.

The *Balclutha,* one of the last surviving square-riggers and the handsomest vessel in San Francisco Bay, was built in Glasgow, Scotland, in 1886 and carried grain from California at a near-record speed of 300 miles a day. The ship is now completely restored.

The 1890 *Eureka* still carries a cargo of nostalgia for San Franciscans. It was the last of 50 paddle-wheel ferries that regularly plied the bay; it made its final trip in 1957. Restored to its original splendor at the height of the ferryboat era, the side-wheeler is loaded with deck cargo, including antique cars and trucks.

The black-hulled, three-masted *C. A. Thayer,* built in 1895 and recently restored, was crafted for the lumber trade and carried logs felled in the Pacific Northwest to the carpentry shops of California.

Other historic ships docked here include the tiny two-masted *Alma,* one of the last scow schooners to bring hay to the horses of San Francisco; the *Hercules,* a huge 1907 oceangoing steam tug; and the *Eppleton Hall,* a side-wheel tugboat built in England in 1914 to operate on London's River Thames.

At the pier's small-boat shop, visitors can follow the restoration progress of historic boats from the museum's collection. It's behind the maritime bookstore on your right as you approach the ships.

Visitor's Center: Hyde and Jefferson sts. (near Fisherman's Wharf). © 415/447-5000. www.nps.gov/safr. No fee for Visitor's Center. Tickets to board ships $5, free for children under 16. Visitor's Center Memorial Day–Oct 15 daily 9:30am–7pm; Oct 16–May 30 9:30am–5pm. Ships on Hyde St. Pier open Memorial Day to Oct 15 daily 9:30am–5:30pm; Oct 16 to May 30 daily 9:30am–5pm. Bus: 19, 30, or 47. Cable car: Powell–Hyde St. line to the last stop.

San Francisco Museum of Modern Art (SFMOMA) ☞ Swiss architect Mario Botta, in association with Hellmuth, Obata, and Kassabaum, designed this $65-million museum, which has made SoMa one of the more popular areas to visit, for tourists and residents alike. The museum's permanent collection houses the West Coast's most comprehensive collection of twentieth century art, including painting, sculpture, photography, architecture, design, and media arts. The collection features master works by Ansel Adams, Bruce Conner, Joseph Cornell, Salvador Dali, Richard Diebenkorn, Eva Hesse, Frida Kahlo, Ellsworth Kelly, Yves Klein, Sherrie Levine, Gordon Matta-Clark, Henri Matisse, Piet Mondrian, Pablo Picasso, Robert Rauschenberg, Diego Rivera, Cindy Sherman, Alfred Steiglitz, Clyfford Still, and Edward Weston, among many others, as well as an ever-changing program of special exhibits. Unfortunately, few works are on display at one time, and for the money the experience can be disappointing—especially compared to the finer museums of New York. However, this is about as good as it gets in our boutique city, so take it or leave it. Docent-led tours take place daily. Times are posted at the admission desk. Phone or check SFMOMA's website for current details of upcoming special events and exhibitions.

The **Caffé Museo,** to the right of the museum entrance, offers very good-quality fresh soups, sandwiches, and salads.

No matter what, don't miss the **MuseumStore,** which carries a wonderful array of modern and contemporary art books, innovative design objects and furniture, jewelry and apparel, educational children's books and toys, posters, and stationery: It's one of the best shops in town and always carries their famed "FogDome"—a snowglobe with a mini MOMA that when you shake it gets foggy rather than snowy.

151 Third St. (2 blocks south of Market St., across from Yerba Buena Gardens). © 415/357-4000. www.sfmoma.org. Admission $13 adults, $8 seniors, $7 students over 12 with ID, free for children 12 and under. Half-price for all Thurs 6–9pm; free to all 1st Tues of each month. Thurs 11am–8:45pm; Fri–Tues 11am–5:45pm. Closed Wed and major holidays. Bus: 15, 30, or 45. Streetcar: J, K, L, or M to Montgomery.

San Francisco Zoo (& Children's Zoo) *Kids*   Located between the Pacific Ocean and Lake Merced, in the southwest corner of the city, the San Francisco Zoo, which once had a reputation for being a bit shoddy and out-of-date, has come a long way in recent years. Though grown-ups who are into wildlife will enjoy their visit, it's an especially fun trip with kids, as they'll really get a kick out of the hands-on Children's Zoo, along with the many other animal attractions (the flock of shockingly pink flamingos near the entrance is especially appealing).

Founded at its present site adjacent to the ocean in 1929, the zoo is spread over 100 acres, and houses more than 930 animals including some 245 species of mammals, birds, reptiles, amphibians, and invertebrates. Exhibit highlights include the new Lipman Family Lemur Forest, a forest setting for five endangered species of lemurs from Madagascar that features interactive components for the visitor; Jones Family Gorilla World, a tranquil setting for a family group of western lowland gorillas; Koala Crossing, which connects to the Australian Walkabout exhibit with its kangaroos, wallaroos, and emu; Penguin Island, home to a large breeding colony of Magellanic Penguins (join them for lunch at 2:30pm daily); and the Primate Discovery Center, home to rare and endangered monkeys. In the South American Tropical Forest building, a large green anaconda can be found as well as other South American reptile and bird species. Puente al Sur (Bridge to the South) has a pair of giant anteaters and some capybaras. The Lion House is home to rare Sumatran and Siberian tigers and African lions. You can see the big cats fed every day at 2pm (except Mon when you are less likely to see them since when they're not eating they like to hang out in secluded areas). African Savanna, the latest exhibit (opened in mid-2004), is a 3-acre mixed-species habitat with giraffes, zebras, antelope, and birds.

The 6-acre Children's Zoo offers kids and their families opportunities for close-up encounters with domestic rare breeds of goats, sheep, ponies, and horses in the Family Farm. Touch and feel small mammals, reptiles, and amphibians along the Nature Trail and gaze at eagles and hawks stationed on Hawk Hill. Visitors can see the inner-workings of the Koret Animal Resource Center, a thriving facility that houses the animals used in the educational outreach programs, and visit the incredible Insect Zoo. One of the Children's Zoo's most popular exhibits is the Meerkat and Prairie Dog exhibit, where kids can crawl through tunnels and play in sand, just like these two amazing burrowing species.

Don't miss the Little Puffer miniature steam train, which takes passengers around a ⅓-mile track, and the historic Dentzel Carousel (both $2 per ride). There's a coffee cart by the entrance as well as two decent cafes inside, definitely good enough for a bite with the kids (though the lines can be long and slightly confusing if you're handling food and kid duty at the same time).

Great Highway between Sloat Blvd. and Skyline Blvd. ℂ 415/753-7080. www.sfzoo.org. Admission to main zoo and Children's Zoo $9 residents, $11 nonresidents for adults; $4.50 residents, $8 nonresidents for seniors 65 and over and youth 12–17; $2.50 for residents, $5 nonresident for children 3–11; free for children 2 and under accompanied by an adult; $1 discount with valid Muni transfer. Free to all 1st Wed of each month, except $2 fee for Children's Zoo. Carousel $2. Daily 10am–5pm, 365 days a year. Bus: 23 or 18. Streetcar: L from downtown Market St. to the end of the line.

Wells Fargo History Museum   Wells Fargo, one of California's largest banks, got its start in the Wild West. Its history museum, at the bank's head office, houses hundreds of genuine relics from the company's whip-and-six-shooter days, including pistols, photographs, early banking articles, posters, a stagecoach, and mining equipment.

420 Montgomery St. (at California St.). ℂ 415/396-2619. www.wellsfargohistory.com. Free admission. Mon–Fri 9am–5pm. Closed bank holidays. Bus: Any to Market St. Cable car: California St. line. BART: Montgomery St.

Yerba Buena Gardens & Environs

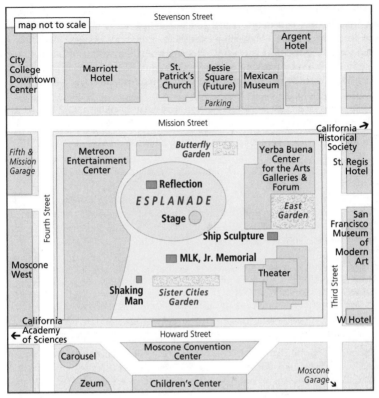

Yerba Buena Center for the Arts 𝕲 *Finds* *Kids* The **YBCA,** which opened in 1993, is part of the large outdoor complex that takes up a few city blocks across the street from SFMOMA, and sits atop the underground Moscone Convention Center. It's the city's cultural facility, similar to New York's Lincoln Center but far more fun on the outside. The Center's two buildings offer music, theater, dance, and visual arts programs and shows. James Stewart Polshek designed the 755-seat theater, and Fumihiko Maki designed the Galleries and Arts Forum, which features three galleries and a space designed especially for dance. Cutting-edge computer art, multimedia shows, contemporary exhibitions, and performances occupy the center's high-tech galleries.

701 Mission St. ℰ 415/978-ARTS (box office). www.ybca.org. Admission for gallery $6 adults, $3 seniors, teachers, and students. Free to all 1st Tues of each month. Free for seniors and students with ID every Thurs. Tues–Wed and Sun noon–5pm; Thurs–Sat noon–8pm. Contact YBCA for times and admission to theater. Bus: 5, 9, 14, 15, 30, or 45. Streetcar: Powell or Montgomery.

Yerba Buena Gardens 𝕲 Unless you're at Yerba Buena to catch a performance, you're more likely to visit the 5-acre gardens, a great place to relax in the grass on a sunny day and check out several artworks. The most dramatic outdoor piece is an emotional mixed-media memorial to Martin Luther King, Jr. Created by sculptor Houston Conwill, poet Estella Majozo, and architect Joseph de Pace, it features 12 panels, each inscribed with quotations from King, sheltered behind a 50-foot-high waterfall. There are also several actual garden areas here, including a Butterfly Garden, the Sister Cities Garden (highlighting flowers from the city's 13 sister cities), and The East Garden, blending Eastern and Western styles. May through October, Yerba Buena Arts & Events puts on a series of free outdoor festivals featuring dance, music, poetry, and more by the San Francisco Ballet, Opera, Symphony, and others.

Located on 2 square city blocks bounded by Mission, Folsom, Third, and Fourth sts. www.yerbabuenagardens.org. Daily 6am–10pm. No admission fee. Contact Yerba Buena Arts & Events: ✆ **415/543-1718** or www.ybgf.org for details about the free outdoor festivals. Bus: 5, 9, 14, 15, 30, or 45. Streetcar: Powell or Montgomery.

Zeum/The Yerba Buena Ice Skating and Bowling Center 🎠🎠 *Kids*   Also in Yerba Buena Gardens you'll find **Zeum,** an innovative, hands-on multimedia, arts and technology museum for kids of all ages. Zeum also features the fabulous 1906 carousel that once graced the city's bygone Oceanside amusement park, Playland-at-the-Beach; the Children's Garden; a cafe; and a fun store. Right behind Zeum, you'll find **The Yerba Buena Ice Skating and Bowling Center,** a great stopover if you're looking for fun, indoor activities with, you guessed it, a 12-lane bowling alley and an ice-skating rink with public sessions daily.

Zeum: 221 Fourth St. (at Howard St.) ✆ **415/820-3320.** www.zeum.com. Adults $8, seniors and students $7, youth 3–18 $6, free to children 2 and under. Summer Tues–Sun 11am–5pm; hours during the school year Wed–Sun 11am–5pm. Carousel $3 per person, each ticket good for 2 rides. Daily 11am–6pm. The Yerba Buena Ice Skating and Bowling Center: 750 Folsom St. ✆ **415/820-3521.** www.skatebowl.com. Bowling alley: $20–$30 per lane/per hour; Sun–Thurs 10am–10pm, Fri–Sat 10am–midnight. Skating rink: call for hours and admission. Bus: 5, 9, 14, 15, 30, or 45. Streetcar: Powell or Montgomery.

Metreon Entertainment Center *Kids*   This 350,000-square-foot hi-tech complex houses great movie theaters, an IMAX theater, the only Sony store in the country devoted to PlayStation, the one-of-a-kind Walk of Game (a la Hollywood's stars in the sidewalk, these steel stars honor the icons of the video game industry), a luxurious arcade (think big screens and a pub), a "Taste of San Francisco" food court with decent "international" fare, and lots more shops, many of which are gaming related. The whole place is wired for Wi-Fi, so if you're a true techie and want to hang out with other techies, grab some lunch, find a comfy spot, and log on.

101 Fourth St. (at the corner of Mission St.) ✆ **415/369-6000.** www.metreon.com. Building 10am–10pm daily; individual businesses may have different hours. Bus: 5, 9, 14, 15, 30, or 45. Streetcar: Powell or Montgomery.

3 Neighborhoods Worth a Visit

To really get to know San Francisco, break out of the downtown and Fisherman's Wharf areas to explore the ethnically and culturally diverse neighborhoods. Walk the streets, browse the shops, grab a bite at a local restaurant—you'll find that San Francisco's beauty and charm are around every corner, not just at the popular tourist destinations.

Note: For information on Fisherman's Wharf, see its entry under "Famous San Francisco Sights," on p. 150. For information on San Francisco neighborhoods and districts that aren't discussed here, see "Neighborhoods in Brief," in chapter 4, beginning on p. 41.

NOB HILL

When the cable car started operating in 1873, this hill became the city's exclusive residential area. Newly wealthy residents who had struck it rich in the gold rush (and were known by names such as the "Big Four" and the "Comstock Bonanza kings") built their mansions here, but they were almost all destroyed by the 1906 earthquake and fire. The only two surviving buildings are the Flood Mansion, which serves today as the **Pacific Union Club,** and **The Fairmont Hotel,** which was under construction when the earthquake struck and was damaged but not destroyed. Today, the burned-out sites of former mansions hold the city's luxury hotels—the Inter-Continental **Mark Hopkins,** the **Stanford Court, The Huntington Hotel,** and the spectacular **Grace Cathedral,** which stands on the Crocker mansion site. Nob Hill is worth a visit if only to stroll around **Huntington Park,** attend a Sunday service at the cathedral, or ooh and aah your way around the Fairmont's spectacular lobby.

SOUTH OF MARKET (SoMa)

From Market Street to Townsend Street and The Embarcadero to Division Street, SoMa has become the city's newest cultural and multimedia center. The process started when alternative clubs began opening in the old warehouses in the area nearly a decade ago. A wave of entrepreneurs followed, seeking to start new businesses in what was once an extremely low-rent area compared to the neighboring Financial District. Today, gentrification and high rents hold sway, spurred by a building boom that started with the **Moscone Convention Center** and continued with the **Yerba Buena Center for the Arts** and **Yerba Buena Gardens,** the **San Francisco Museum of Modern Art, Four Seasons Hotel, W Hotel, St. Regis Hotel,** and the **Metreon Entertainment Center.** Other institutions, businesses, and museums move into the area on an ongoing basis. A substantial portion of the city's nightlife takes place in warehouse spaces throughout the district.

NORTH BEACH ✦✦✦

In the late 1800s, an enormous influx of Italian immigrants to North Beach firmly established this aromatic area as San Francisco's "Little Italy." Dozens of Italian restaurants and coffeehouses continue to flourish in what is still the center of the city's Italian community. Walk down **Columbus Avenue** on any given morning, and you're bound to be bombarded by the wonderful aromas of roasting coffee and savory pasta sauces. Although there are some interesting shops and bookstores in the area, it's the dozens of eclectic little cafes, delis, bakeries, and coffee shops that give North Beach its Italian-bohemian character.

⟮Finds⟯ This City's for the Birds!

If you're walking around San Francisco—especially Telegraph Hill, Washington Park, Fort Mason, or The Embarcadero—and you suddenly hear lots of loud squawking overhead, look up. You're most likely witnessing a fly-by of the city's famous flock of wild parrots. These are a colony that started out as a few wayward house pets—mostly cherry-headed conures, which are indigenous to South America—who found each other, and bred. Years later they are hundreds strong, traveling in chatty packs through the city (with a few parakeets along for the ride), and stopping to rest on tree branches and delight residents who have come to consider them part of the family. To learn just how special these birds are to the city, check out the book *The Wild Parrots of Telegraph Hill* or see the heart-warming movie of the same name or visit www.pelican media.org/wildparrots.html.

For more perspective on this neighborhood, follow the detailed walking tour in chapter 8 (beginning on p. 197) or sign up for a guided Javawalk with coffee nut Elaine Sosa (see "Walking Tours," on p. 184 in this chapter).

CHINATOWN ★★

The first of the Chinese immigrants came to San Francisco in the early 1800s to work as servants. By 1851, 25,000 Chinese people were working in California, and most had settled in San Francisco's Chinatown. Fleeing famine and the Opium Wars, they had come seeking the good fortune promised by the "Gold Mountain" of California, and hoped to return with wealth to their families in China. For the majority, the reality of life in California did not live up to the promise. First employed as workers in the gold mines during the gold rush, they later built the railroads, working as little more than slaves and facing constant prejudice. Yet the community, segregated in the Chinatown ghetto, thrived. Growing prejudice led to the Chinese Exclusion Act of 1882, which halted all Chinese immigration for 10 years and severely limited it thereafter (the Chinese Exclusion Act was not repealed until 1943). Chinese people were also denied the opportunity to buy homes outside the Chinatown ghetto until the 1950s.

Today, San Francisco has one of the largest communities of Chinese people in the United States. More than 80,000 people live in Chinatown, but the majority of Chinese people have moved out into newer areas like the Richmond and Sunset districts. Although frequented by tourists, the area continues to cater to Chinese shoppers, who crowd the vegetable and herb markets, restaurants, and shops. Tradition runs deep here, and if you're lucky, through an open window you might hear women mixing mah-jongg tiles as they play the centuries-old game. (*Be warned:* You're likely to hear lots of spitting around here, too—it's part of local tradition.)

The gateway at Grant Avenue and Bush Street marks the entry to Chinatown. The heart of the neighborhood is Portsmouth Square, where you'll find locals playing board games (often gambling) or just sitting quietly.

On the newly beautified and renovated Waverly Place, a street where the Chinese celebratory colors of red, yellow, and green are much in evidence, you'll find three **Chinese temples:** Jeng Sen (Buddhist and Taoist) at no. 146, Tien Hou (Buddhist) at no. 125, and Norras (Buddhist) at no. 109. If you enter, do so quietly so that you do not disturb those in prayer.

A block west of Grant Avenue, **Stockton Street,** from 1000 to 1200, is the community's main shopping street, lined with grocers, fishmongers, tea sellers, herbalists, noodle parlors, and restaurants. Here, too, is the Buddhist Kong Chow Temple, at no. 855, above the Chinatown post office. Explore at your leisure. A Chinatown walking tour is outlined in chapter 8, beginning on p. 191. Visit www.sanfranciscochinatown. com for more info.

JAPANTOWN

More than 12,000 citizens of Japanese descent (1.4% of the city's population) live in San Francisco, or Soko, as the Japanese who first emigrated here often called it. Initially, they settled in Chinatown and south of Market along Stevenson and Jessie streets from Fourth to Seventh streets. After the earthquake in 1906, SoMa became a light industrial and warehouse area, and the largest Japanese concentration took root in the Western Addition between Van Ness Avenue and Fillmore Street, the site of today's Japantown, now 100 years old. By 1940, it covered 30 blocks.

Finds **Urban Renewal**

- **Kabuki Springs & Spa,** 1750 Geary Blvd. (© **415/922-6002;** www.kabukisprings. com), the Japan Center's most famous tenant, was once an authentic, traditional Japanese bathhouse. The Joie de Vivre hotel group bought and renovated it, however, and it's now more of a pan-Asian spa with a focus on wellness. The deep ceramic communal tubs—at a very affordable $20 to $25 per person—private baths, and shiatsu massages remain, and the joint is open from 10am to 10pm daily; joining them are an array of massages and ayurvedic treatments, body scrubs, wraps, and facials, which cost from $60 to $150.

- **Spa Radiance,** 3011 Fillmore St. (© **415/346-6281;** www.sparadiance.com), is an utterly San Francisco spa experience due to its unassuming Victorian surroundings and its wonderfully luxurious treatments such as facials, body treatments, massages, manicures, pedicures, Brazilian waxing, spray-tanning, and makeup application by in-house artists.

- A more posh and modern experience is yours at **International Orange,** 2044 Fillmore St., second floor (© **888/894-8811;** www.internationalorange.com). The self-described spa yoga lounge offers just what it says in a chic white-on-white space on the boutique-shopping stretch of Fillmore Street. They've also got a great selection of clothing and face and body products, including one of my personal favorites, locally made In Fiore body balms.

- Two new hotel spas up the city pampering ante. In the St. Regis, **Remède Spa,** 125 Third St. (© **415/284-4060;** www.remede.com) has two whole floors dedicated to melting away all your cares, worries, kinks, and knots—not to mention primping. Expect killer massage, facials, manis and pedis, waxes, and more. A few doors down in the W Hotel is the city's outpost of New York's **Bliss Spa,** 181 Third St., fourth floor (© **415/281-0990;** www.bliss world.com). The hip to St. Regis's chic, it offers a similar spa menu, including wedding specialties.

In 1913, the Alien Land Law was passed, depriving Japanese Americans of the right to buy land. From 1924 to 1952, the United States banned Japanese immigration. During World War II, the U.S. government froze Japanese bank accounts, interned community leaders, and removed 112,000 Japanese Americans—two-thirds of them citizens—to camps in California, Utah, and Idaho. Japantown was emptied of Japanese people, and war workers took their place. Upon their release in 1945, the Japanese found their old neighborhood occupied. Most of them resettled in the Richmond and Sunset districts; some returned to Japantown, but it had shrunk to a mere 6 or so blocks. Today, the community's notable sights include the **Buddhist Church of San Francisco,** 1881 Pine St. (at Octavia St.), www.bcsfweb.org; the **Konko Church of San Francisco,** 1909 Bush St. (at Laguna St.); the **Sokoji–Soto Zen Buddhist Temple,** 1691 Laguna St. (at Sutter St.); **Nihonmachi Mall,** 1700 block of Buchanan Street between Sutter and Post streets, which contains two steel fountains by Ruth Asawa; and the **Japan Center,** an Asian-oriented shopping mall occupying 3 square blocks bounded by Post, Geary, Laguna, and Fillmore streets. At its center stands the five-tiered **Peace Pagoda,** designed by world-famous Japanese architect Yoshiro Taniguchi "to convey the friendship and goodwill of the Japanese to the people of the

United States." Surrounding the pagoda, through a network of arcades, squares, and bridges, you can explore dozens of shops and showrooms featuring everything from TVs and tansu chests to pearls, bonsai (dwarf trees), and kimonos. **Kabuki Springs & Spa** (see the "Urban Renewal" box on p. 169) is the center's most famous tenant along with the Asian-inspired 14-story **Radisson Miyako Hotel** (p. 94). But locals also head to its numerous restaurants, teahouses, shops, and multiplex movie theater.

There is often live entertainment in this neighborhood on summer weekends, including Japanese music and dance performances, tea ceremonies, flower-arranging demonstrations, martial-arts presentations, and other cultural events. The Japan Center (© **415/922-6776**) is open daily from 10am to midnight, although most shops close much earlier. To get there, take bus no. 2, 3, or 4 (exit at Buchanan and Sutter sts.) or no. 22 or 38 (exit at the northeast corner of Geary Blvd. and Fillmore St.).

HAIGHT-ASHBURY

Few of San Francisco's neighborhoods are as varied—or as famous—as Haight-Ashbury. Walk along Haight Street, and you'll encounter everything from drug-dazed drifters begging for change to an armada of the city's funky-trendy shops, clubs, and cafes. Turn anywhere off Haight, and instantly you're among the clean-cut, young urban professionals who can afford the steep rents in this hip 'hood. The result is an interesting mix of well-to-do and well-screw-you aging flower children, former Deadheads, homeless people, and throngs of tourists who try not to stare as they wander through this most human of zoos. Some find it depressing, others find it fascinating, but everyone agrees that it ain't what it was in the free-lovin' psychedelic Summer of Love. Is it still worth a visit? Not if you are here for a day or two, but it's certainly worth an excursion on longer trips, if only to enjoy a cone of Cherry Garcia at the now-famous Ben & Jerry's Ice Cream Store on the corner of Haight and Ashbury streets, and then to wander and gawk at the area's intentional freaks.

THE CASTRO

Castro Street, between Market and 18th streets, is the center of the city's gay community as well as a lovely neighborhood teeming with shops, restaurants, bars, and other institutions that cater to the area's colorful residents. Among the landmarks are **Harvey Milk Plaza** and the **Castro Theatre** (www.castrotheatre.com), a 1930s movie palace with a Wurlitzer. The gay community began to move here in the late 1960s and early 1970s from a neighborhood called Polk Gulch, which still has a number of gay-oriented bars and stores. Castro is one of the liveliest streets in the city and the perfect place to shop for gifts and revel in free-spiritedness. Check www.castroonline.com for more info.

THE MISSION DISTRICT

Once inhabited almost entirely by Irish immigrants, The Mission District is now the center of the city's Latino community as well as a mecca for young, hip residents. It's an oblong area stretching roughly from 14th to 30th streets between Potrero Avenue on the east and Dolores on the west. In the outer areas, many of the city's finest Victorians still stand, although many seem strangely out of place in the mostly lower-income neighborhoods. The heart of the community lies along 24th Street between Van Ness and Potrero, where dozens of excellent ethnic restaurants, bakeries, bars, and specialty stores attract people from all over the city. The area surrounding 16th Street and Valencia is a hotbed for impressive—and often impressively cheap—restaurants

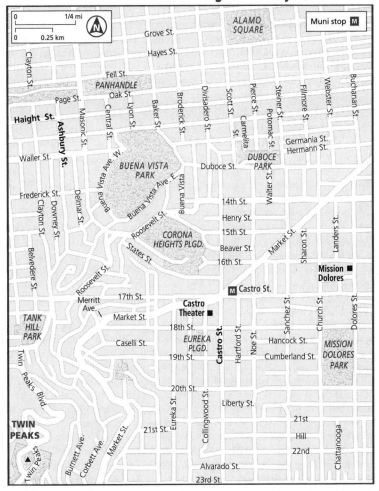

and bars catering to the city's hip crowd. The Mission District at night doesn't feel like the safest place (although in terms of creepiness, the Tenderloin, a few blocks off Union Square, beats The Mission by far), and walking around the area should be done with caution, but it's usually quite safe during the day and is highly recommended.

For an even better insight into the community, go to the **Precita Eyes Mural Arts Center,** 2981 24th St., between Harrison and Alabama streets (© **415/285-2287;** www.precitaeyes.org), and take one of the 1½- to 2-hour tours conducted on Saturdays and Sundays at 11am and 1:30pm, where you'll see 60 murals in an 8-block walk. Group tours are available during the week by appointment. The 11am tour costs $10 for adults, $8 for students with ID, $5 for seniors, and $2 for children under 18; the 1:30pm tour, which is half an hour longer and includes a slide show, costs $12 for adults, $8 for students with ID, and $5 for seniors and children under 18. All but the

Saturday-morning tour (which leaves from 3325 24th Street at the Café Venice) leave from the center's 24th Street location.

Other signs of cultural life in the neighborhood are progressive theaters such as Theatre Rhinoceros (www.therhino.org) and Theater Artaud (www.artaud.org). At 16th Street and Dolores is the Mission San Francisco de Asis, better known as **Mission Dolores** (p. 179). It's the city's oldest surviving building and the district's namesake.

4 Golden Gate Park ⚝⚝⚝

Everybody loves **Golden Gate Park**—people, dogs, birds, frogs, turtles, bison, trees, bushes, and flowers. Literally, everything feels unified here in San Francisco's enormous arboreal front yard. Conceived in the 1860s and 1870s, this great 1,017-acre landmark, which stretches inland from the Pacific coast, took shape in the 1880s and 1890s thanks to the skill and effort of John McLaren, a Scot who arrived in 1887 and began landscaping the park.

When he embarked on the project, sand dunes and wind presented enormous challenges. But McLaren had developed a new strain of grass called "sea bent," which he planted to hold the sandy soil along the Firth of Forth back home, and he used it to anchor the soil here, too. Every year the ocean eroded the western fringe of the park, and ultimately he solved this problem, too, though it took him 40 years to build a natural wall, putting out bundles of sticks that the tides covered with sand. He also built the two windmills that stand on the western edge of the park to pump water for irrigation. Under his brilliant eye, the park took shape.

Today's Golden Gate Park is a truly magical place. Spend 1 sunny day stretched out on the grass along JFK Drive, have a good read in the Shakespeare Garden, or stroll around Stow Lake, and you, too, will understand the allure. It's an interactive botanical symphony, and everyone is invited to play in the orchestra.

The park consists of hundreds of gardens and attractions connected by wooded paths and paved roads. While many worthy sites are clearly visible, there are infinite hidden treasures, so pick up information at **McLaren Lodge and Park Headquarters** (at Stanyan and Fell sts.; ℭ **415/831-2700**) if you want to find the more hidden spots. It's open daily and offers park maps for $3. Of the dozens of special gardens in the park, most recognized are **McLaren Memorial Rhododendron Dell, The Rose Garden, Strybing Arboretum,** and, at the western edge of the park, a springtime array of thousands of tulips and daffodils around the **Dutch windmill.**

In addition to the highlights described in this section, the park contains lots of recreational facilities: tennis courts; baseball, soccer, and polo fields; a golf course; riding stables; and fly-casting pools. The Strawberry Hill boathouse handles boat rentals. The park is also the home of two major museums: the **California Academy of Sciences** (currently relocated to SoMa during renovations; see listing on p. 160) and the **M. H. de Young Memorial Museum,** which recently relocated to its spectacular new home at 50 Tea Garden Drive (ℭ **415/750-3600** or 415/863-3330). For more information see p. 161.

For further information, call the San Francisco Visitor Information Center at ℭ **415/ 283-0177.** Enter the park at Kezar Drive, an extension of Fell Street; bus riders can take no. 5, 6, 7, 16AX, 16BX, 66, or 71.

MUSEUMS INSIDE THE PARK

In 2004, the California Academy of Sciences, which includes the Steinhart Aquarium, the Natural History Museum, and the Planetarium, moved from the park to a temporary location in downtown San Francisco to begin a 4-year renovation on its Golden Gate Park location. Limited aquarium and natural history exhibits are displayed in the temporary digs, but alas, the Planetarium did not relocate. See p. 160 for the temporary museums' details.

PARK HIGHLIGHTS

CONSERVATORY OF FLOWERS 🐸🐸   Opened to the public in 1879, this glorious Victorian glass structure is the oldest existing public conservatory in the Western Hemisphere. After a bad storm in 1995 and delayed renovations, the conservatory was closed and visitors were only able to imagine what wondrous displays existed within the striking glass assemblage. Thankfully, a $25-million renovation, including a $4-million exhibit upgrade, was completed a few years ago, and now the Conservatory is a cutting-edge horticultural destination with over 1,700 species of plants. Here you can check out the rare tropical flora of the Congo, Philippines, and beyond within the stunning structure. As one of only four public institutions in the U.S. to house a highland tropics exhibit, its five galleries also include the lowland tropics, aquatic plants, the largest Dracula orchid collection in the world, and special exhibits. It doesn't take long to visit, but make a point of staying a while; outside there are good sunny spots for people-watching as well as paths leading to impressive gardens begging to be explored. If you're around during summer and fall, don't miss the Dahlia Garden to the right of the entrance in the center of what was once a carriage roundabout—it's an explosion of colorful Dr. Seuss–like blooms. The conservatory is open Tuesday through Sunday from 9am to 5pm, closed Mondays. Admission is $5 for adults; $3 for youth 12 to 17 years of age, seniors, and students with ID; $1.50 for children 5 to 11, and free for children 4 and under and for all visitors the first Tuesday of the month. For more information, visit www.conservatoryofflowers.org or call ✆ **415/666-7001.**

JAPANESE TEA GARDEN   John McLaren, the man who began landscaping Golden Gate Park, hired Makoto Hagiwara, a wealthy Japanese landscape designer, to further develop this garden originally created for the 1894 Midwinter Exposition. It's a quiet place with cherry trees, shrubs, and bonsai crisscrossed by winding paths and high-arched bridges over pools of water. Focal points and places for contemplation include the massive bronze Buddha (cast in Japan in 1790 and donated by the Gump family), the Buddhist wooden pagoda, and the Drum Bridge, which, reflected in the water, looks as though it completes a circle. The garden is open daily November through February from 8:30am to 5pm (teahouse 10am–4:30pm), March through October from 8:30am to 6pm (teahouse 10am–5:30pm). For **information** on admission, call ✆ **415/752-4227.** For the **teahouse,** call ✆ **415/752-1171.** Also check www.frp.org/japanese_tea_garden.asp for more info.

STRAWBERRY HILL/STOW LAKE   Rent a paddle boat or rowboat and cruise around the circular Stow Lake as painters create still lifes, joggers pass along the grassy shoreline, ducks waddle around waiting to be fed, and turtles sunbathe on rocks and logs. Strawberry Hill, the 430-foot-high artificial island and highest point in the park that lies at the center of Stow Lake, is a perfect picnic spot; it boasts a bird's-eye view of San Francisco and the bay. It also has a waterfall and peace pagoda. For the **boathouse,** call ✆ **415/752-0347.** Boat rentals are available daily from 10am to 4pm, weather permitting; four-passenger rowboats go for $13 per hour, and four-person paddle boats run $17 per hour; fees are cash-only.

Golden Gate Park

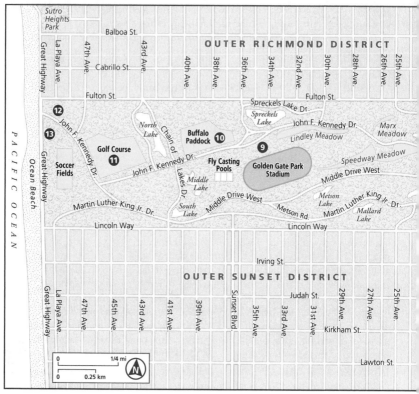

STRYBING ARBORETUM & BOTANICAL GARDENS   More than 7,000 plant species grow here, among them some ancient plants in a special "primitive garden," rare species, and a grove of California redwoods. Docent tours begin at 1:30pm daily, with an additional 10:20am tour on weekends. Strybing is open Monday through Friday from 8am to 4:30pm, and Saturday, Sunday, and holidays from 10am to 5pm. Admission is free. For more information, call ☎ **415/661-1316** or visit www. strybing.org.

5 The Presidio & Golden Gate National Recreation Area

THE PRESIDIO

In October 1994, the Presidio passed from the U.S. Army to the National Park Service and became one of a handful of urban national parks that combines historical, architectural, and natural elements in one giant arboreal expanse. (It also contains a previously private golf course and a home for George Lucas's production company.) The 1,491-acre area incorporates a variety of terrain—coastal scrub, dunes, and prairie grasslands—that shelter many rare plants and more than 200 species of birds, some of which nest here.

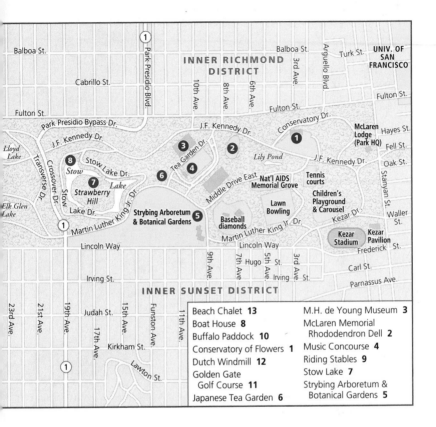

Beach Chalet **13**	M.H. de Young Museum **3**
Boat House **8**	McLaren Memorial
Buffalo Paddock **10**	Rhododendron Dell **2**
Conservatory of Flowers **1**	Music Concourse **4**
Dutch Windmill **12**	Riding Stables **9**
Golden Gate	Stow Lake **7**
Golf Course **11**	Strybing Arboretum &
Japanese Tea Garden **6**	Botanical Gardens **5**

This military outpost has a 220-year history, from its founding in September 1776 by the Spanish under José Joaquin Moraga to its closure in 1994. From 1822 to 1846, the property was in Mexican hands.

During the war with Mexico, U.S. forces occupied the fort, and in 1848, when California became part of the Union, it was formally transferred to the United States. When San Francisco suddenly became an important urban area during the gold rush, the U.S. government installed battalions of soldiers and built Fort Point to protect the entry to the harbor. It expanded the post during the Civil War and during the Indian Wars of the 1870s and 1880s. By the 1890s, the Presidio was no longer a frontier post but a major base for U.S. expansion into the Pacific. During the war with Spain in 1898, thousands of troops camped here in tent cities awaiting shipment to the Philippines, and the Army General Hospital treated the sick and wounded. By 1905, 12 coastal defense batteries were built along the headlands. In 1914, troops under the command of Gen. John Pershing left here to pursue Pancho Villa and his men. The Presidio expanded during the 1920s, when Crissy Army Airfield (the first airfield on the West Coast) was established, but the major action was seen during World War II, after the attack on Pearl Harbor. Soldiers dug foxholes along nearby beaches, and the Presidio became the headquarters for the Western Defense Command. Some 1.75

Golden Gate National Recreation Area

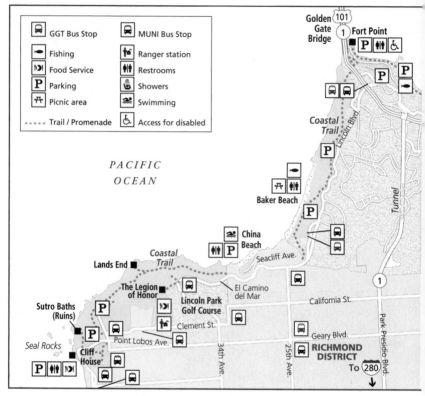

million men were shipped out from nearby Fort Mason to fight in the Pacific; many returned to the Presidio's hospital, whose capacity peaked one year at 72,000 patients. In the 1950s, the Presidio served as the headquarters for the Sixth U.S. Army and a missile defense post, but its role slowly shrank. In 1972, it was included in new legislation establishing the Golden Gate National Recreation Area; in 1989, the Pentagon decided to close the post and transfer it to the National Park Service.

Today, the area encompasses more than 470 historic buildings, a scenic golf course, a national cemetery, 22 hiking trails (to be doubled over the next decade), and a variety of terrain and natural habitats. The National Park Service offers walking and biking tours around the Presidio (reservations are suggested) as well as a free shuttle "PresidioGo." For more information, call the **Presidio Visitors Center** at ✆ **415/ 561-4323;** www.nps.gov/prsf or www.presidio.gov. Take bus no. 28, 45, 76, or 82X to get there.

GOLDEN GATE NATIONAL RECREATION AREA

The largest urban park in the world, GGNRA makes New York's Central Park look like a putting green, covering three counties along 28 miles of stunning, condo-free shoreline. Run by the National Park Service, the Recreation Area wraps around the northern and western edges of the city, and just about all of it is open to the public

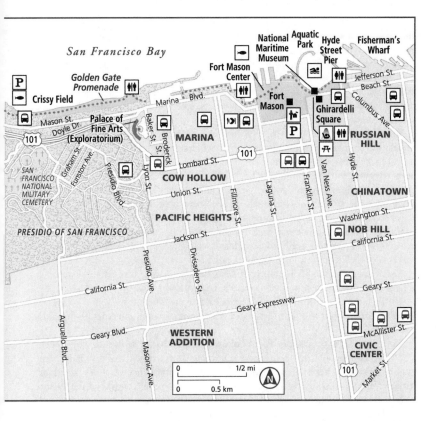

with no access fees. The Muni bus system provides transportation to the more popular sites, including Aquatic Park, Cliff House, Fort Mason, and Ocean Beach. For more information, contact the **National Park Service** (© **415/561-4700;** www.nps.gov/goga). For more detailed information on particular sites, see the "Getting Outside" section, later in this chapter.

Here is a brief rundown of the salient features of the park's peninsula section, starting at the northern section and moving westward around the coastline:

Aquatic Park, adjacent to the Hyde Street Pier, has a small swimming beach, although it's not that appealing (and darned cold). Far more entertaining is a visit to the San Francisco Maritime National Historical Park's Visitor's Center a few blocks away (see p. 162 for more information).

Fort Mason Center, from Bay Street to the shoreline, consists of several buildings and piers used during World War II. Today they hold a variety of museums, theaters, shops, and organizations, and Greens vegetarian restaurant (p. 135), which affords views of the Golden Gate Bridge. For information about Fort Mason events, call © **415/441-3400;** www.fortmason.org. The park headquarters is also at Fort Mason.

Farther west along the bay at the northern end of Laguna Street is **Marina Green,** a favorite local spot for kite-flying, jogging, and walking along the Promenade. The St. Francis Yacht Club is also here.

Next comes the 3½-mile paved **Golden Gate Promenade** ⚘, San Francisco's best and most scenic biking, jogging, and walking path. It runs along the shore past **Crissy Field** (www.crissyfield.org) and ends at Fort Point under the Golden Gate Bridge (be sure to stop and watch the gonzo windsurfers and kite surfers, who catch major wind here, and admire the newly restored marshlands). The Crissy Field Café and Bookstore is open from 9am to 5pm Wednesday through Sunday and offers yummy, organic soups, salads, sandwiches, coffee drinks, and a decent selection of outdoor-themed books and cards.

Fort Point ⚘ (ⓒ **415/556-1693;** www.nps.gov/fopo) was built in 1853 to 1861 to protect the narrow entrance to the harbor. It was designed to house 500 soldiers manning 126 muzzle-loading cannons. By 1900, the fort's soldiers and obsolete guns had been removed, but the formidable brick edifice remains. Fort Point is open Friday through Sunday only from 10am to 5pm, and guided tours and cannon demonstrations are given at the site once or twice a day on open days, depending on the time of year.

Lincoln Boulevard sweeps around the western edge of the bay to **Baker Beach,** where the waves roll ashore—a fine spot for sunbathing, walking, or fishing. Hikers can follow the **Coastal Trail** (www.californiacoastaltrail.org) from Fort Point along this part of the coastline all the way to Lands End.

A short distance from Baker Beach, **China Beach** is a small cove where swimming is permitted. Changing rooms, showers, a sun deck, and restrooms are available.

A little farther around the coast is **Lands End** ⚘, looking out to Pyramid Rock. A lower and an upper trail offer hiking amid windswept cypresses and pines on the cliffs above the Pacific.

Still farther along the coast lie **Point Lobos,** the **Sutro Baths** (www.sutrobaths.com), and **Cliff House** ⚘. Cliff House (www.cliffhouse.com), which recently underwent major renovations, has been serving refreshments to visitors since 1863. It's famed for its views of Seal Rocks (a colony of sea lions and many marine birds) and the Pacific Ocean. Immediately northeast of Cliff House you'll find traces of the once-grand Sutro Baths, a swimming facility that was a major summer attraction accommodating up to 24,000 people until it burned down in 1966. (Alas, my favorite Cliff House attraction, the **Musée Mécanique** ⚘⚘, an arcade featuring antique games, moved to digs at Pier 45; for more information, call ⓒ **415/346-2000** or visit www.musee mecanique.org.

A little farther inland at the western end of California Street is **Lincoln Park,** which contains a golf course and the spectacular Legion of Honor museum (p. 162).

At the southern end of Ocean Beach, 4 miles down the coast, is another area of the park around Fort Funston (ⓒ **415/561-4700;** www.nps.gov/goga/fofu), where there's an easy loop trail across the cliffs. Here you can watch hang gliders take advantage of the high cliffs and strong winds.

Farther south along Route 280, **Sweeney Ridge** (www.nps.gov/goga/clho/swri) affords sweeping views of the coastline from the many trails that crisscross its 1,000 acres. From here the expedition led by Don Gaspar de Portolá first saw San Francisco Bay in 1769. It's in Pacifica; take Sneath Lane off Route 35 (Skyline Blvd.) in San Bruno.

The GGNRA extends into Marin County, where it encompasses the Marin Headlands, Muir Woods National Monument, and the Olema Valley behind the Point Reyes National Seashore. See chapter 11 for information on those areas' highlights.

6 Religious Buildings Worth Checking Out

Glide Memorial United Methodist Church ☆☆ *Moments*   There would be nothing special about this Tenderloin-area church if it weren't for its exhilarating lively sermons and accompanying gospel choir. Reverend Cecil Williams's enthusiastic and uplifting preaching and singing with homeless and poor people of the neighborhood attracted nationwide fame over the past 30-plus years. In 1994, during the pastor's 30th-anniversary celebration, singers Angela Bofill and Bobby McFerrin joined comedian Robin Williams, author Maya Angelou, and talk-show queen Oprah Winfrey to honor him publicly. Cecil Williams now shares pastor duties with Douglas Fitch and alternates presiding over the nondogmatic, fun Sunday services in front of a diverse audience that crosses all socioeconomic boundaries. Go for an uplifting experience and some hand-clapping gospel choir music.

330 Ellis St. (west of Union Square). © **415/674-6000**. www.glide.org. Services Sun at 9 and 11am. Bus: 27. Streetcar: Powell. BART: Powell.

Grace Cathedral   Although this Nob Hill cathedral, designed by architect Lewis P. Hobart, appears to be made of stone, it is in fact constructed of reinforced concrete beaten to achieve a stonelike effect. Construction began on the site of the Crocker mansion in 1928 but was not completed until 1964. Among the more interesting features of the building are its stained-glass windows, particularly those by the French Loire studios and Charles Counick, depicting such modern figures as Thurgood Marshall, Robert Frost, and Albert Einstein; the replicas of Ghiberti's bronze *Doors of Paradise* at the east end; the series of religious murals completed in the 1940s by Polish artist John de Rosen; and the 44-bell carillon. Along with its magical ambience, Grace lifts spirits with services, musical performances (including organ recitals on many Sundays), and its weekly Forum (Sun 9:30–10:30am except during summer and major holidays), where guests lead discussions about spirituality in modern times and have community dialogues on social issues.

1100 California St. (between Taylor and Jones sts.). © **415/749-6300**. www.gracecathedral.org.

Mission Dolores   San Francisco's oldest standing structure, the Mission San Francisco de Asis (aka Mission Dolores), has withstood the test of time, as well as two major earthquakes, relatively intact. In 1776, at the behest of Franciscan missionary Junípero Serra, Father Francisco Palou came to the Bay Area to found the sixth in a series of missions that dotted the California coastline. From these humble beginnings grew what was to become the city of San Francisco. The mission's small, simple chapel, built solidly by Native Americans who were converted to Christianity, is a curious mixture of native construction methods and Spanish-colonial style. A statue of Father Serra stands in the mission garden, although the portrait looks somewhat more contemplative, and less energetic, than he must have been in real life. A 45-minute self-guided tour costs $5; otherwise, admission is $3 for adults and $2 for children.

16th St. (at Dolores St.). © **415/621-8203**. www.missiondolores.org. Admission $3 adults, $2 children. Daily 9am–5pm summer; 9am–4pm winter; 9am–4:30pm spring; 9am–noon Good Friday. Closed Thanksgiving, Easter, and Dec 25. Bus: 14, 26, or 33 to Church and 16th sts. Streetcar: J.

7 Architectural Highlights

MUST-SEES FOR ARCHITECTURE BUFFS

ALAMO SQUARE HISTORIC DISTRICT   San Francisco's collection of Victorian houses, known as **Painted Ladies,** is one of the city's most famous assets. Most of the 14,000 extant structures date from the second half of the 19th century and are private residences. Spread throughout the city, many have been beautifully restored and ornately painted. The small area bordered by Divisadero Street on the west, Golden Gate Avenue on the north, Webster Street on the east, and Fell Street on the south—about 10 blocks west of the Civic Center—has one of the city's greatest concentrations of Painted Ladies. One of the most famous views of San Francisco—seen on postcards and posters all around the city—depicts sharp-edged Financial District skyscrapers behind a row of Victorians. This fantastic juxtaposition can be seen from Alamo Square, in the center of the historic district, at Fulton and Steiner streets.

CITY HALL & CIVIC CENTER   Built between 1913 and 1915, City Hall, located in the Civic Center District, is part of this "City Beautiful" complex done in the Beaux Arts style. The dome rises to a height of 306 feet on the exterior and is ornamented with oculi and topped by a lantern. The interior rotunda soars 112 feet and is finished in oak, marble, and limestone, with a monumental marble staircase leading to the second floor. With a major renovation completed in the late 1990s, the building was returned to its former splendor. No doubt you saw it on TV during early 2004, when much of the hoopla surrounding the short-lived and controversial gay marriage proceedings was depicted on the front steps. (Remember Rosie O'Donnell emerging from this very building after getting married to her girlfriend?) Public tours are given Monday through Friday at 10am, noon, and 2pm. Call © **415/554-4933** for details.

OTHER ARCHITECTURAL HIGHLIGHTS

San Francisco is a center of many architecturally striking sights. This section concentrates on a few highlights.

The Union Square and Financial District areas have a number of buildings worth checking out. One is the former **Circle Gallery,** 140 Maiden Lane. Now a gallery housing Folk Art International, Xanadu Tribal Arts, and Boretti Amber & Design, it's the only building in the city designed by Frank Lloyd Wright (in 1948). The gallery was the prototype for the Guggenheim's seashell-shaped circular gallery space, even though it was meant to serve as a retail space for V. C. Morris, a purveyor of glass and crystal. Note the arresting exterior, a solid wall with a circular entryway to the left. Maiden Lane is just off Union Square between Geary and Post streets.

The **Hallidie Building,** 130–150 Sutter St., designed by Willis Polk in 1917, is an ideal example of a glass-curtain building. The vast glass facade is miraculously suspended between the two cast-iron cornices. The fire escapes that course down each side of the building complete the proscenium-like theatrical effect.

Two prominent pieces of San Francisco's skyline are in the Financial District. The **TransAmerica Pyramid,** 600 Montgomery St., between Clay and Washington streets, is one of the tallest structures in San Francisco. This corporate headquarters was completed in 1972, stands 48 stories tall, and is capped by a 212-foot spire. The former **Bank of America World Headquarters,** 555 California St., was designed by Wurster, Bernardi, and Emmons with Skidmore, Owings, and Merrill. This carnelian-marble-covered building dates from 1969. Its 52 stories are topped by a panoramic restaurant and bar, the Carnelian Room (p. 236). The focal point of the building's formal plaza

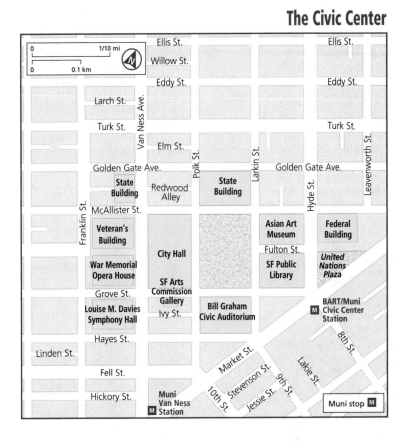

is an abstract black granite sculpture, known locally as the "Banker's Heart," designed by Japanese architect Masayuki Nagare.

The **Medical Dental Building,** 450 Sutter St., is a steel-frame structure beautifully clad in terra cotta. It was designed by Miller and Pflueger in 1929. The entrance and the window frames are elaborately ornamented with Mayan relief work; the lobby ceiling is similarly decorated with gilding. Note the ornate elevators.

At the foot of Market Street you will find the **Ferry Building.** Built between 1895 and 1903, it served as the city's major transportation hub before the Golden Gate and Bay bridges were built; some 170 ferries docked here daily unloading Bay Area commuters until the 1930s. The tower that soars above the building was inspired by the Campanile of Venice and the Cathedral Tower in Seville. In 2003, a 4-year renovation was completed and the building is now a spectacular mixed-use landmark building featuring a 660-foot-long, skylit nave, which had been partially filled in and destroyed in the 1950s. If you stop by the Ferry Building, you might also want to go to **Rincon Center,** 99 Mission St., to see the WPA murals painted by the Russian artist Refregier in the post office.

Several important buildings are on or near Nob Hill. The **Flood Mansion,** 1000 California St., at Mason Street, was built between 1885 and 1886 for James Clair Flood. Thanks to the Comstock Lode, Flood rose from being a bartender to one of the city's wealthiest men. He established the Nevada bank that later merged with Wells Fargo. The house cost $1.5 million to build at the time; the fence alone cost $30,000. It was designed by Augustus Laver and modified by Willis Polk after the 1906 earthquake to accommodate the Pacific Union Club. Unfortunately, you can't go inside: The building is now a private school.

Built by George Applegarth in 1913 for sugar magnate Adolph Spreckels, the **Spreckels Mansion,** 2080 Washington St., is currently home to romance novelist Danielle Steel (don't even try to get in to see her!). The extraordinary building has rounded-arch French doors on the first and second floors and curved balconies on the second floor. Inside, the original house featured an indoor pool in the basement, Adamesque fireplaces, and a circular Pompeian room with a fountain.

Finally, one of San Francisco's most ingenious architectural accomplishments is the **San Francisco–Oakland Bay Bridge.** Although it's visually less appealing than the

---

Kids **Especially for Kids**

The following San Francisco attractions appeal to kids of all ages:

- Alcatraz Island (p. 150)
- Cable Car Museum (p. 160)
- Cable cars (p. 151)
- California Academy of Sciences, including Steinhart Aquarium (p. 160)
- The Exploratorium (p. 161)
- Golden Gate Bridge (p. 156)
- Golden Gate Park, including the Children's Playground, Bison Paddock, and Japanese Tea Garden (p. 172)
- Maritime Museum (San Francisco Maritime National Historical Park) and the historic ships anchored at Hyde Pier (p. 162)
- The Metreon Entertainment Center (p. 166)
- The San Francisco Zoo (p. 164)

In addition to the sights listed above, a number of playgrounds are of particular interest to kids. One of the most enormous, fun playgrounds for kids is in **Golden Gate Park,** where you'll find a fantastic kids' playground just west of the Stanyan Street entrance. But other playful perks include Stow Lake's boats and peeks at the bison in the bison paddock. Apartment buildings surround the **Cow Hollow Playground,** Baker Street between Greenwich and Filbert streets, on three of four sides. The landscaped playground features a bi-level play area fitted with well-conceived, colorful play structures, including a tunnel, slides, swings, and a miniature cable car. **Huntington Park,** Taylor Street between Sacramento and California streets, sits atop Nob Hill. This tiny play area contains several small structures particularly well suited to children under 5. **Julius Kahn Playground,** West Pacific Avenue at Spruce Street, is a popular playground inside San Francisco's great Presidio Park. Larger play structures and forested surroundings make this area attractive to children and adults alike. Go to www.parks.sfgov.org and click on "Recreation Programs" for more info.

nearby Golden Gate Bridge (except at night when it's lit up), the Bay Bridge is in many ways more spectacular. The silvery giant that links San Francisco with Oakland is one of the world's longest steel bridges (8¼ miles). It opened in 1936, 6 months before the Golden Gate. Each of its two decks contains five automobile lanes. The Bay Bridge is not a single bridge at all, but a superbly dovetailed series of spans joined mid-bay, at Yerba Buena Island, by one of the world's largest (in diameter) tunnels. To the west of Yerba Buena, the bridge is actually two separate suspension bridges, joined at a central anchorage. East of the island is a 1,400-foot cantilever span, followed by a succession of truss bridges. This east span of the bridge is finally being replaced after being damaged in the 1989 Loma Prieta earthquake and a years-long fight between city residents, planners, and designers. And it looks even more complex than it sounds. You can drive across the bridge (the toll is $3, paid westbound), or you can catch a bus at the Transbay Terminal (Mission at First St.) and ride to downtown Oakland.

8 Self-Guided & Organized Tours

THE 49-MILE SCENIC DRIVE 🐦🐦

The self-guided, 49-mile drive is one easy way to orient yourself and to grasp the beauty of San Francisco and its extraordinary location. It's also a flat-out stunning and very worthy excursion. Beginning in the city, it follows a rough circle around the bay and passes virtually all the best-known sights, from Chinatown to the Golden Gate Bridge, Ocean Beach, Seal Rocks, Golden Gate Park, and Twin Peaks. Originally designed for the benefit of visitors to San Francisco's 1939 and 1940 Golden Gate International Exposition, the route is marked by blue-and-white seagull signs. Although it makes an excellent half-day tour, this miniexcursion can easily take longer if you decide, for example, to stop to walk across the Golden Gate Bridge or to have tea in Golden Gate Park's Japanese Tea Garden.

The San Francisco **Visitor Information Center,** at Powell and Market streets (p. 40), distributes free route maps, which are handy since a few of the Scenic Drive marker signs are missing. Try to avoid the downtown area during the weekday rush hours from 7 to 9am and 4 to 6pm.

A BART TOUR

One of the world's best commuter systems, **Bay Area Rapid Transit (BART)** runs along 104 miles of rail, linking 43 stations between San Francisco, Millbrae, and the East Bay. Under the bay, BART runs through one of the longest underwater transit tubes in the world. This link opened in September 1972, 2 years behind schedule and 6 months after the general manager resigned under fire. The train cars are 70 feet long and were designed to represent the latest word in public transport luxury. More than 3 decades later, they no longer seem futuristic, but they're still attractively modern, with carpeted floors, tinted picture windows, air-conditioning, and recessed lighting. The trains can hit a top speed of 80 mph; a computerized control system monitors and adjusts their speed.

The people who run BART think so highly of their trains and stations that they sell a $4.65 **"Excursion Ticket,"** which allows you, in effect, to "sightsee" the BART system, or basically ride it. "Tour" the entire system as much as you like for up to 3 hours; you must exit at the station where you entered (if you get out anywhere else along the line, the gate instantly computes the normal fare). For more information, call ⓒ **415/989-BART** or visit www.bart.gov, where you can also download trip plans directly to your iPod, PDA, or wireless.

BOAT TOURS

One of the best ways to look at San Francisco is from a boat bobbing on the bay. There are several cruises to choose from, and many of them start from Fisherman's Wharf.

Blue & Gold Fleet, PIER 39, Fisherman's Wharf (© **415/773-1188;** www.blue andgoldfleet.com), tours the bay year-round in a sleek, 350-passenger sightseeing boat, complete with food and beverage facilities. The fully narrated, 1-hour cruise passes beneath the Golden Gate Bridge and comes within yards of Alcatraz Island. Don a jacket, bring the camera, and make sure it's a clear day for the best bay cruise. Frequent daily departures from PIER 39's West Marina begin at 10:45am daily during winter and 10am daily during summer. Tickets cost $20 for adults, $16 for seniors over 62 and juniors 12 to 18, and $12 for children 5 to 11; children under 5 are admitted free. There's a $2.25 charge for ordering tickets by phone; discounts are available on their website.

The **Red & White Fleet,** Pier 43½ (© **415/447-0597;** www.redandwhite.com), offers daily "Bay Cruises" tours that leave from Pier 43½. The tour boats cruise along the city waterfront, beneath the Golden Gate Bridge, past Angel Island, and around Alcatraz and are narrated in eight languages. Prices are $21 for adults, $17 for seniors and teens 12 to 17, and $13 for children 5 to 11. Discounts are available through online purchase.

BUS TOURS

Gray Line (© **800/826-0202** or 415/434-8687; www.sanfranciscosightseeing.com) is San Francisco's largest bus-tour operator. It offers several itineraries daily. Free pickup and return are available between centrally located hotels and departure locations. Reservations are required for most tours, and keep in mind that those available in French, German, Spanish, Italian, Japanese, Mandarin, and Korean depart at 9am only.

WALKING TOURS

Javawalk is a 2-hour walking tour by self-described "coffeehouse lizard" Elaine Sosa. As the name suggests, it's loosely a coffee walking tour through North Beach, but there's a lot more going on than drinking cups of brew. Javawalk also serves up a good share of historical and architectural trivia, offering something for everyone. The best part of the tour may be the camaraderie that develops among the participants. Sosa keeps the excursion interactive and fun, and it's obvious she knows a profusion of tales and trivia about the history of coffee and its North Beach roots. It's a guaranteed good time, particularly if you're addicted to caffeine. Javawalk is offered Saturday at 10am and Sunday through Friday for private parties of 6 or more by appointment only (on hiatus Jan–Mar). The price is $20 per person, $10 for kids under 12. For information and reservations, call © **415/673-WALK;** or visit www.javawalk.com.

Cruisin' the Castro (© **415/255-1821;** www.cruisinthecastro.com) is an informative historical tour of San Francisco's most famous gay quarter, which will give you new insight into the contribution of the gay community to the city's political maturity, growth, and beauty. Cathy Amandola leads this fun and easy walking tour for all ages, highlighting gay and lesbian history from 1849 to present. Stops include America's only Pink Triangle Park and Memorial, the original site of the AIDS Quilt Name Project, Harvey Milk's residence and photo shop, the Castro Theatre, the Human Rights Campaign and Action Center. Lunch at the Firewood Café (p. 145) is included. Tours run Tuesday through Saturday from 10am to 1pm, and meet at the

Rainbow Flag at the Harvey Milk Plaza on the corner of Castro and Market streets above the Castro Muni station. Reservations are required. The tour, with lunch, costs $45 per adult, $35 for children 3 to 12. On the **Haight-Ashbury Flower Power Walking Tour** (© 415/863-1621), you explore hippie haunts with Pam and Bruce Brennan ("the Hippy Gourmet"—see www.hippygourmet.com). You'll revisit the Grateful Dead's crash pad, Janis Joplin's house, and other reminders of the Summer of Love in 2½ short hours. Tours begin at 9:30am on Tuesdays and Saturdays. The cost is $15 per person (cash only). Reservations are required, and the tour starts at the corner of Stanyan and Waller streets.

San Francisco's Chinatown is always fascinating, but for many visitors with limited time it's hard to know where to search out the "nontouristy" shops, restaurants, and historical spots in this microcosm of Chinese culture. **Wok Wiz Chinatown Walking Tours & Cooking Center,** 250 King St., Suite 268 (© 650/355-9657; www.wokwiz.com), founded over 2 decades ago by author and cooking instructor Shirley Fong-Torres, is the answer. The Wok Wiz tours take you into Chinatown's nooks and crannies. Guides are Chinatown natives, speak fluent Cantonese, and are intimately acquainted with the neighborhood's alleys and small enterprises, as well as Chinatown's history, folklore, culture, and food. Tours are conducted daily from 10am to 1pm and include a 7-course dim sum lunch (a Chinese meal made up of many small plates of food). There's also a less expensive tour that does not include lunch. The walk is easy, as well as fun and fascinating. Groups are generally held to a maximum of 15, and reservations are essential. Prices (including lunch) are $40 for adults and $35 for children under 11; without lunch, prices are $28 and $23, respectively.

The gregarious and entertaining tour owner Shirley Fong-Torres also operates an **I Can't Believe I Ate My Way Through Chinatown** tour. It starts with breakfast, moves to a wok shop, and stops for nibbles at a vegetarian restaurant and dim sum, and at a marketplace before taking a break for a sumptuous authentic Cantonese luncheon. It's offered on most Saturdays and costs $75 per person, food included. The **Walk & Wok** tour includes shopping for food in Chinatown, and then cooking (and eating) it together at Shirley's Cooking Center (by appointment; $100 per person). Shirley also offers a by-appointment nighttime tour, which includes dinner and starts at $75 per person; the price goes up depending on what you want to eat.

Jay Gifford, founder of the **Victorian Homes Historical Walking Tour** (© 415/252-9485; www.victorianwalk.com) and a San Francisco resident for 2 decades, communicates his enthusiasm and love of San Francisco throughout this highly entertaining walking tour. The 2½-hour daily tour, at a leisurely pace, starts in the lobby of the Westin St. Francis hotel and incorporates a wealth of knowledge about San Francisco's Victorian architecture and the city's history—particularly the periods before and after the great earthquake and fire of 1906. You'll stroll through Japantown, Pacific Heights, and Cow Hollow. In the process, you'll see more than 200 meticulously restored Victorians, including the sites where *Mrs. Doubtfire* and *Party of Five* were filmed. Jay's guests often find that they are the only ones on the quiet neighborhood streets, where tour buses are forbidden. The tour ends in Cow Hollow where you can have lunch on your own, or return to Union Square, passing through North Beach and Chinatown. Tours, which start at Union Square at 11am, are offered daily April through December and Thursday through Monday from January through March and cost $20 per person (cash only).

9 Getting Outside

Half the fun in San Francisco takes place outdoors. If you're not in the mood to trek it, there are other things to do that allow you to enjoy the surroundings.

BALLOONING Although you must drive an hour to get to the tour site, hot-air ballooning is an ethereal and silent flight over the Wine Country. **Adventures Aloft,** P.O. Box 2500, Vintage 1870, Yountville, CA 94599 (© **800/944-4408** or 707/944-4408; www.nvaloft.com), is Napa Valley's oldest hot-air balloon company, staffed with full-time professional pilots. Groups are small, and each flight lasts about an hour. The cost of $205 per person ($170 ages 6–17) includes a postadventure champagne brunch and a framed "first-flight" certificate. Flights launch daily at sunrise (weather permitting).

BEACHES For beach information, call the San Francisco Visitor Information Center at © **415/283-0177.** Most days it's too chilly to hang out at the beach, but when the fog evaporates and the wind dies down, one of the best ways to spend the day is ocean side in the city. On any truly hot day, thousands flock to the beach to worship the sun, build sandcastles, and throw the ball around. Without a wet suit, swimming is a fiercely cold endeavor and is not recommended. In any case, dip at your own risk—there are no lifeguards on duty and San Francisco's waters are cold and have strong undertows. On the South Bay, **Baker Beach** is ideal for picnicking, sunning, walking, or fishing against the backdrop of the Golden Gate (though pollution makes your catch not necessarily worthy of eating).

Ocean Beach, at the end of Golden Gate Park, on the westernmost side of the city, is San Francisco's largest beach—4 miles long. Just offshore, at the northern end of the beach, in front of Cliff House, are the jagged Seal Rocks, inhabited by various shorebirds and a large colony of barking sea lions (bring binoculars for a close-up view). To the left, Kelly's Cove is one of the more challenging surf spots in town. Ocean Beach is ideal for strolling or sunning, but don't swim here—tides are tricky, and each year bathers drown in the rough surf.

Stop by Ocean Beach bus terminal at the corner of Cabrillo and La Playa to learn about San Francisco's playful history in local artist Ray Beldner's whimsically historical sculpture garden. Then hike up the hill to explore Cliff House and the ruins of the Sutro Baths. These baths, once able to accommodate 24,000 bathers, were lost to fire in 1966.

BIKING The San Francisco Parks and Recreation Department maintains two city-designated bike routes. One winds 7.5 miles through Golden Gate Park to Lake Merced; the other traverses the city, starting in the south, and continues over the Golden Gate Bridge. These routes are not dedicated to bicyclists, who must exercise caution to avoid crashing into pedestrians. Helmets are recommended for adults and required by law for kids under 18. A bike map is available from the San Francisco Visitor Information Center, at Powell and Mason streets for $3 (see "Visitor Information," in chapter 4), and from bicycle shops all around town.

Ocean Beach has a public walk- and bikeway that stretches along 5 waterfront blocks of the Great Highway between Noriega and Santiago streets. It's an easy ride from Cliff House or Golden Gate Park.

Avenue Cyclery, 756 Stanyan St., at Waller Street, in the Haight (© **415/387-3155**), rents bikes for $7 per hour or $28 per day. It's open daily, April through September from 10am to 7pm and October through March from 10am to 6pm.

BOATING   At the **Golden Gate Park Boat House** (© 415/752-0347) on Stow Lake, the park's largest body of water, you can rent a rowboat or pedal boat by the hour and steer over to Strawberry Hill, a large, round island in the middle of the lake, for lunch. There's usually a line on weekends. The boathouse is open daily from 10am to 4pm, weather permitting.

Cass' Marina, 1702 Bridgeway, Sausalito; P.O. Box 643; Sausalito, CA 94966 (© 800/472-4595 or 415/332-6789; www.cassmarina.com), is a certified sailing school that rents sailboats measuring 22 to 38 feet. Sail to the Golden Gate Bridge on your own or with a licensed skipper. In addition, large sailing yachts leave from Sausalito on a regularly scheduled basis. Call or check the website for schedules, prices, and availability of sailboats. The marina is open Wednesday through Monday from 9am to sunset.

CITY STAIR CLIMBING 👟👟   Many health clubs have stair-climbing machines and step classes, but in San Francisco, you need only go outside. The following city stair climbs will give you not only a good workout, but seriously stunning neighborhood, city, and bay views as well. Check www.sisterbetty.org/stairways for more ideas.

Filbert Street Steps, between Sansome Street and Telegraph Hill, are a particular challenge. Scaling the sheer eastern face of Telegraph Hill, this 377-step climb winds through verdant flower gardens and charming 19th-century cottages. Napier Lane, a narrow, wooden plank walkway, leads to Montgomery Street. Turn right and follow the path to the end of the cul-de-sac, where another stairway continues to Telegraph's panoramic summit.

The **Lyon Street Steps,** between Green Street and Broadway, were built in 1916. This historic stairway street contains four steep sets of stairs totaling 288 steps. Begin at Green Street and climb all the way up, past manicured hedges and flower gardens, to an iron gate that opens into the Presidio. A block east, on Baker Street, another set of 369 steps descends to Green Street.

FISHING   **Berkeley Marina Sports Center,** 225 University Ave., Berkeley (© 510/849-2727; www.berkeleysportfishing.com), makes daily trips for ling cod, rock fish, and many other types of game fish year-round, and it makes trips for salmon runs April through October. Fishing equipment is available; the cost, including boat ride and bait, is $80 per person. Reservations are required, as are licenses for adults. One-day licenses can be purchased for $11 before departure. Find out the latest on the season by contacting their hot line at © 510/486-8300. Excursions run daily from 6am to 4pm. Fish are cleaned, filleted, and bagged on the return trip for a small fee (free for salmon fishing).

GOLF   San Francisco has a few beautiful golf courses. One of the most lavish is the **Presidio Golf Course** (© 415/561-4664; www.presidiogolf.com). Greens fees are $60 until 12:30pm for residents Monday through Thursday and $96 for nonresidents; rates drop to $50 until 2pm, then $35 for the rest of the day for residents and nonresidents. Friday though Sunday rates are $96 for residents and $108 for nonresidents from 8 to 11am; from 11am to 12:30pm, the cost is $60 for residents, and after that it's $50 for everyone until 2pm and for the rest of the day $35. Carts are included. There are also two decent municipal courses in town.

The 9-hole **Golden Gate Park Course,** 47th Avenue and Fulton Street (© 415/751-8987; www.goldengateparkgolf.com), charges greens fees of $14 per person Monday through Thursday, $18 Friday through Sunday. The 1,357-yard course is par

27. All holes are par 3, and this course is appropriate for all levels. The course is a little weathered in spots, but it's casual, fun, and inexpensive. It's open daily from sunup to sundown.

The 18-hole **Lincoln Park Golf Course,** 34th Avenue and Clement Street (© **415/ 221-9911;** www.parks.sfgov.org), charges greens fees of $31 per person Monday through Thursday, $36 Friday through Sunday, with rates decreasing after 4pm in summer, 2pm in winter. It's San Francisco's prettiest municipal course, with terrific views and fairways lined with Monterey cypress and pine trees. The 5,181-yard layout plays to par 68, and the 17th hole has a glistening ocean view. This is the oldest course in the city and one of the oldest in the West. It's open daily at daybreak.

HANDBALL   The city's best handball courts are in Golden Gate Park, opposite Seventh Avenue, south of Middle Drive East. Courts are available free, on a first-come, first-served basis.

PARKS   In addition to **Golden Gate Park** and the **Golden Gate National Recreation Area** (p. 172 and 176, respectively), San Francisco boasts more than 2,000 acres of parkland, most of which is perfect for picnicking or throwing around a Frisbee.

Smaller city parks include **Buena Vista Park** (Haight St. between Baker and Central sts.), which affords fine views of the Golden Gate Bridge and the area around it and is also a favored lounging ground for gay lovers; **Ina Coolbrith Park** (Taylor St. between Vallejo and Green sts.), offering views of the Bay Bridge and Alcatraz; and **Sigmund Stern Grove** (19th Ave. and Sloat Blvd.) in the Sunset District, which is the site of a famous free summer music festival.

One of my personal favorites is **Lincoln Park,** a 270-acre green on the northwestern side of the city at Clement Street and 34th Avenue. The Legion of Honor is here (p. 162), as is a scenic 18-hole municipal golf course (see "Golf," above). But the best things about this park are the 200-foot cliffs that overlook the Golden Gate Bridge and San Francisco Bay. To get to the park, take bus no. 38 from Union Square to 33rd and Geary streets, then walk a few blocks.

RUNNING   The **ING Bay to Breakers Foot Race** ☀ (© **415/359-2800;** www.ing baytobreakers.com) is an annual 7.5-mile run from downtown to Ocean Beach. About 80,000 entrants take part in it, one of San Francisco's trademark events. Costumed participants and hordes of spectators add to the fun. The event is held on the third Sunday of May.

The San Francisco **Marathon** takes place annually in the middle of July. For more information, visit www.runsfm.com (no phone contact).

Great **jogging paths** include the entire expanse of Golden Gate Park, the shoreline along the Marina, and The Embarcadero.

TENNIS   The **San Francisco Parks and Recreation Department** (© **415/753-7001**) maintains more than 132 free courts throughout the city. Almost all are available free, on a first-come, first-served basis. An additional 21 courts are available in **Golden Gate Park,** which cost $5 for 90 minutes during weekdays and $10 on weekends. Check the website for details on rules for reserving courts (www.parks.sfgov.org).

WALKING & HIKING   The **Golden Gate National Recreation Area** offers plenty of opportunities. One incredible walk (or bike ride) is along the Golden Gate Promenade, from Aquatic Park to the Golden Gate Bridge. The 3.5-mile paved trail heads along the northern edge of the Presidio out to Fort Point, passing the marina, Crissy Field's new restored wetlands, a small beach, and plenty of athletic locals. You can also hike the Coastal Trail all the way from the Fort Point area to Cliff House. The park service maintains several other trails in the city. For more information or to pick up a map of the Golden Gate National Recreation Area, stop by the park service headquarters at Fort Mason; enter on Franklin Street (© **415/561-4700**).

Although most people drive to this spectacular vantage point, a more rejuvenating way to experience **Twin Peaks** is to walk up from the back roads of U.C. Medical Center (off Parnassus) or from either of the two roads that lead to the top (off Woodside or Clarendon aves.). The best time to trek is early morning, when the city is quiet, the air is crisp, and sightseers haven't crowded the parking lot. Keep an eye out for cars, however, because there's no real hiking trail, and be sure to walk beyond the lot and up to the highest vantage point.

10 Spectator Sports

The Bay Area's sports scene includes several major professional franchises. Check the local newspapers' sports sections for daily listings of local events.

MAJOR LEAGUE BASEBALL
The **San Francisco Giants** ℛ play at the absolutely stunning **AT&T Park,** Third and King streets (© **415/972-2000;** www.sfgiants.com), in the China Basin section of SoMa. From April to October, 41,503 fans fill the seats here to root for the National League Giants. The unobstructed bay vistas take in bobbing boats beyond the outfield at this recently completed ballpark. Tickets are hard to come by, but you can try to track them down through **Tickets.com** (© **800/225-2277;** www.tickets.com).

The American League's **Oakland Athletics** play across the bay at McAfee Coliseum, at the Hegenberger Road exit from I-880, Oakland (© **510/430-8020;** www. athletics.mlb.com). The stadium holds over 50,000 spectators and is accessible through BART's Coliseum station. Tickets are available from the Coliseum Box Office or by phone through **Tickets.com** (© **800/225-2277;** www.tickets.com).

PRO BASKETBALL
The **Golden State Warriors** of the NBA play at the Arena in Oakland, a 19,200-seat facility at 7000 Coliseum Way in Oakland (© **510/986-2200;** www.nba.com/ warriors). The season runs November through April, and most games start at 7:30pm. Tickets are available at the arena, online, and by phone through **Tickets.com** (© **800/ 225-2277;** www.tickets.com).

PRO FOOTBALL
The **San Francisco 49ers** (www.sf49ers.com) play at Monster Park, Giants Drive and Gilman Avenue, on Sundays August through December; kickoff is usually at 1pm. Tickets sell out early in the season but are available at higher prices through ticket agents beforehand and from "scalpers" (illegal ticket-sellers who are usually at the gates). Ask your hotel concierge for the best way to track down tickets.

The 49ers' archenemies, the **Oakland Raiders** (www.raiders.com), play at McAfee Coliseum, off the I-880 freeway (Nimitz). Call © **800/RAIDERS** for ticket information.

COLLEGE FOOTBALL
The **University of California Golden Bears** play at Haas Pavilion, University of California, Berkeley (© **800/GO-BEARS** or 510/642-3277; www.calbears.com), on the

university campus across the bay. Tickets are usually available at game time. Phone for schedules and information.

HORSE RACING

Ten miles northeast of San Francisco is scenic **Golden Gate Fields,** Gilman Street off I-80, Albany (© **510/559-7300;** www.goldengatefields.com). The racing schedule changes yearly; please call or check the website for current schedule and admission prices. The track is on the seashore.

Bay Meadows, 2600 S. Delaware St., off U.S. 101, San Mateo (© **650/574-7223;** www.baymeadows.com), is a thoroughbred track on the peninsula about 20 miles south of downtown San Francisco. Call for admission prices and post times.

City Strolls

Despite a handful of killer hills, San Francisco is best explored on foot. In this chapter, I provide suggestions for introductory walks in two of the city's many great neighborhoods. For more extensive city walks, check out *Frommer's Memorable Walks in San Francisco* (Wiley Publishing, Inc.).

WALKING TOUR 1	CHINATOWN: HISTORY, CULTURE, DIM SUM & THEN SOME

Start:	Corner of Grant Avenue and Bush Street.
Public Transportation:	Bus no. 2, 3, 4, 9X, 15, 30, 38, 45, or 76.
Finish:	Commercial Street between Montgomery and Kearny streets.
Time:	2 hours, not including museum or shopping stops.
Best Times:	Daylight hours, when the streets are most active.
Worst Times:	Early or late in the day, because shops are closed and no one is milling around.
Hills That Could Kill:	None.

This tiny section of San Francisco, bounded loosely by Broadway and by Stockton, Kearny, and Bush streets, is said to harbor one of the largest Chinese populations outside Asia. Daily proof is the crowds of Chinese residents who flock to the herbal stores, vegetable markets, restaurants, and businesses. Chinatown also marks the spot where the city began its development in the mid-1800s. On this walk, you'll learn why Chinatown remains intriguing to all who wind through its narrow, crowded streets, and how its origins are responsible for the city as we know it.

To begin the tour, make your way to the corner of Bush Street and Grant Avenue, 4 blocks from Union Square and all the downtown buses, where you can't miss the Chinatown Gateway Arch.

❶ Chinatown Gateway Arch

Traditional Chinese villages have ceremonial gates like this one. A lot less formal than those in China, this gate was built more for the benefit of the tourist industry than anything else.

Once you cross the threshold, you'll be at the beginning of Chinatown's portion of Grant Avenue.

❷ Grant Avenue

This is a mecca for tourists who wander in and out of gift shops that offer a variety of unnecessary junk interspersed with quality imports. You'll also find decent restaurants and grocery stores frequented by Chinese residents, ranging from children to the oldest living people you've ever seen.

Tear yourself away from the shops and turn right at the corner of Pine Street. Cross to the other side of Pine, and on your left you'll come to St. Mary's Square.

❸ St. Mary's Square

Here you'll find a huge metal-and-granite statue of Dr. Sun Yat-sen, the founder of the Republic of China. A native of Guangdong (Canton) Province, Sun Yat-sen led the rebellion that ended the reign of the Qing Dynasty.

Note also the second monument in the square, which honors Chinese-American victims of both World Wars.

Walk to the other end of the square, toward California Street, turn left, cross California Street at Grant Street, and you'll be standing in front of Old St. Mary's Cathedral.

❹ Old St. Mary's Cathedral

The first Catholic cathedral in San Francisco and the site of the Chinese community's first English-language school, St. Mary's was built primarily by Chinese laborers and dedicated on Christmas Day 1854.

Step inside to find a written history of the church and turn-of-the-20th-century photos of San Francisco.

Upon leaving the church, take a right and walk to the corner of Grant Avenue and California Street, and then go right on Grant. Here you'll find a shop called Canton Bazaar.

❺ Canton Bazaar

Of the knickknack and import shops lining Grant Avenue, this is one of the most popular; it's located at 616 Grant Ave.

Continue in the same direction on Grant Avenue, and cross Sacramento Street to the northwest corner of Sacramento and Grant. You'll be at the doorstep of the Bank of America.

❻ Bank of America

This bank is an example of traditional Chinese architectural style. Notice the dragons subtly portrayed on many parts of the building.

Head in the same direction (north) on Grant, and a few doors down is the Chinatown Kite Shop.

❼ Chinatown Kite Shop

This store, located at 717 Grant Ave., has an assortment of flying objects, including attractive fish kites, nylon or cotton windsock kites, hand-painted Chinese paper kites, wood-and-paper biplanes, and pentagonal kites.

Cross Grant, and you'll arrive at The Wok Shop.

❽ The Wok Shop

Here's where you can purchase just about any cleaver, wok, cookbook, or vessel you might need for Chinese-style cooking in your own kitchen. It's located at 718 Grant Ave.

When you come out of The Wok Shop, go right. Walk past Commercial Street, and you'll arrive at the corner of Grant Avenue and Clay Street; cross Clay, and you'll be standing on the original street of "American" California.

❾ Original Street of "American" California

Here an English seaman named William Richardson set up the first tent in 1835, making it the first place that an Anglo set up base in California.

Continue north on Grant to Washington Street. Turn right, and at 743 Washington St. you will be standing in front of the former Bank of Canton, now known as the United Commercial Bank.

❿ United Commercial Bank

This building boasts the oldest (from 1909) Asian-style edifice in Chinatown. The three-tiered temple-style building once housed the China Telephone Exchange, known as "China-5" until 1945.

You're probably thirsty by now, so follow Washington Street a few doors down (east); on your right-hand side you will come upon Washington Bakery & Restaurant.

TAKE A BREAK
Washington Bakery & Restaurant is at 733 Washington St. No need to have a full meal here—the service can be abrupt. Do stop in, however, for a little potable adventure: snow red beans with ice cream. The sugary-sweet drink mixed with whole beans and ice cream is not something you're likely to have tried elsewhere, and it happens to be quite tasty. Whatever you do, don't fill up— a few blocks away, some wonderfully fresh dim sum awaits you.

Walking Tour 1: Chinatown

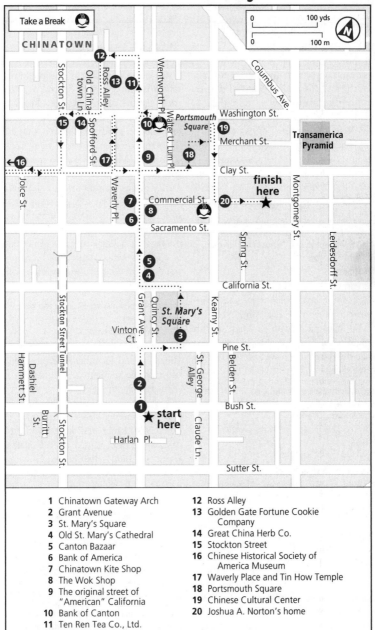

1 Chinatown Gateway Arch
2 Grant Avenue
3 St. Mary's Square
4 Old St. Mary's Cathedral
5 Canton Bazaar
6 Bank of America
7 Chinatown Kite Shop
8 The Wok Shop
9 The original street of "American" California
10 Bank of Canton
11 Ten Ren Tea Co., Ltd.
12 Ross Alley
13 Golden Gate Fortune Cookie Company
14 Great China Herb Co.
15 Stockton Street
16 Chinese Historical Society of America Museum
17 Waverly Place and Tin How Temple
18 Portsmouth Square
19 Chinese Cultural Center
20 Joshua A. Norton's home

Head back to Grant Avenue, cross Washington Street, cross Grant, and follow the west side of Grant 1 block to Ten Ren Tea Co., Ltd.

⑪ Ten Ren Tea Co., Ltd.

In this amazing shop at 949 Grant Ave., you can sample a freshly brewed tea variety and check out the dozens of drawers and canisters labeled with more than 40 kinds of tea. Like Washington Bakery, Ten Ren offers unusual drinks worth trying: delightful hot or iced milk teas containing giant blobs of jelly or tapioca. Try black tea or green tea and enjoy the outstanding flavors and the giant balls of tapioca slipping around in your mouth.

Leave Ten Ren, make a left, and when you reach Jackson Street, make another left. Follow Jackson Street until you reach Ross Alley, and turn left into the alley.

⑫ Ross Alley

As you walk along this narrow street, just one of the many alleyways that crisscrossed Chinatown to accommodate the many immigrants who jammed into the neighborhood, it's not difficult to believe that this block once was rife with gambling dens.

As you follow the alley south, on the left side of the street you'll encounter the Golden Gate Fortune Cookie Company.

⑬ Golden Gate Fortune Cookie Company

Located at 56 Ross Alley, this store is little more than a tiny place where three women sit at a conveyer belt, folding messages into warm cookies as the manager invariably calls out to tourists, beckoning them to buy a big bag of the fortunetelling treats.

You can purchase regular fortunes, unfolded flat cookies without fortunes, or, if you bring your own fortunes, make custom cookies (I often do this when I'm having dinner parties) at around $6 for 50 cookies—a very cheap way to impress your friends! Or, of course, you can just take a peek and move on.

As you exit the alley, cross Washington Street, take a right heading west on Washington, and you're in front of the Great China Herb Co.

⑭ Great China Herb Co.

For centuries, the Chinese have come to shops like this one, at 857 Washington St., which are full of exotic herbs, roots, and other natural substances. They buy what they believe will cure all types of ailments and ensure good health and long life. Thankfully, unlike owners in many similar area shops, Mr. and Mrs. Ho speak English, so you will not be met with a blank stare when you inquire what exactly is in each box, bag, or jar arranged along dozens of shelves. It is important to note that you should not use Chinese herbs without the guidance of a knowledgeable source such as an herb doctor. They may be natural, but they also can be quite powerful and are potentially harmful if misused.

Take a left upon leaving the store and walk to Stockton Street.

⑮ Stockton Street

The section of Stockton Street between Broadway and Sacramento Street is where most of the residents of Chinatown do their daily shopping.

One noteworthy part of this area's history is **Cameron House** (actually up the hill at 920 Sacramento St., near Stockton St.), which was named after Donaldina Cameron (1869–1968). Called Lo Mo, or "the Mother," by the Chinese, she spent her life trying to free Chinese women who came to America in hopes of marrying well but who found themselves forced into prostitution and slavery. Today, the house still helps women free themselves from domestic violence.

A good stop if you're in the market for some jewelry is **Jade Galore** (1000 Stockton St., at Washington St.). Though the employees aren't exactly warm and fuzzy, they've got the goods. In addition to purveying jade jewelry, the store does a fair trade in diamonds.

After browsing at Jade Galore, you might want to wander up Stockton Street to absorb the atmosphere and street life of this less-tourist-oriented Chinese community before doubling back to Washington Street. At 1068 Stockton St. you'll find **AA Bakery & Café,** an extremely colorful bakery with Golden Gate Bridge–shaped cakes, bright green and pink snacks, moon cakes, and a flow of Chinese diners catching up over pastries. Another fun place at which to peek is **Gourmet Delight B.B.Q.,** at 1045 Stockton St., where barbecued duck and pork are supplemented by steamed pigs' feet and chicken feet. Everything's to go here, so if you grab a snack, don't forget napkins. Head farther north along the street and you'll see live fish and fowl awaiting their fate as the day's dinner.

Meander south on Stockton Street to Clay Street and turn west (right) onto Clay. Continue to 965 Clay St. Make sure you arrive Tuesday through Friday between noon and 5pm or Saturday or Sunday between noon and 4pm. You've arrived at 965 Clay St., the:

⑯ Chinese Historical Society of America Museum

Founded in 1963, this museum (© **415/ 391-1188**) has a small but fascinating collection that illuminates the role of Chinese immigrants in American history, particularly in San Francisco and the rest of California.

The interesting artifacts on display include a shrimp-cleaning machine; 19th-century clothing and slippers of the Chinese pioneers; Chinese herbs and scales; historic hand-carved and painted shop signs; and a series of photographs that document the development of Chinese culture in America.

The goal of this organization is not only to "study, record, acquire, and preserve all suitable artifacts and such cultural items as manuscripts, books, and works of art . . . which have a bearing on the history of the Chinese living in the United States of America," but also to "promote the contributions that Chinese Americans living in this country have made to the United States of America." It's an admirable and much-needed effort, considering what little recognition and appreciation the Chinese have received throughout American history.

The museum is open Tuesday through Friday from noon to 5pm and Saturday and Sunday from noon to 4pm. Admission is $3 for adults, $2 for college students with ID and seniors, and $1 for kids 6 to 17.

Retrace your steps, heading east on Clay Street back toward Grant Avenue. Turn left onto Waverly Place.

⑰ Waverly Place

Also known as "The Street of Painted Balconies," Waverly Place is probably Chinatown's most popular side street or alleyway because of its painted balconies and colorful architectural details—a sort of Chinese-style New Orleans street. And though you can admire the architecture only from the ground, because most of the buildings are private family associations or temples, with a recent beautification and renovation by the City, it's definitely worth checking out.

One temple you can visit (but make sure it's open before you climb the long, narrow stairway) is the **Tin How Temple,** at 125 Waverly Place. Accessible via the stairway three floors up, this incense-laden sanctuary, decorated in traditional black, red, and gold lacquered wood, is a house of worship for Chinese Buddhists, who come here to pray, meditate, and send offerings to their ancestors and to Tin How, the Queen of the Heavens and Goddess of the Seven Seas. There are no scheduled services, but you are welcome to visit. Just remember to quietly respect those who are here to pray, and try to be as unobtrusive as possible. It is customary to give a donation or buy a bundle of incense during your visit.

Once you've finished exploring Waverly Place, walk east on Clay Street, past Grant Avenue, and continue until you come upon the block-wide urban playground that is also the most important site in San Francisco's history:

⑱ Portsmouth Square

This very spot was the center of the region's first township, which was called Yerba Buena before it was renamed San Francisco in 1847. Around 1846, before any semblance of a city had taken shape, this plaza lay at the foot of the bay's eastern shoreline. There were fewer than 50 non–Native American residents in the settlement, there were no substantial buildings to speak of, and the few boats that pulled into the cove did so less than a block from where you're sitting.

In 1846, when California was claimed as a U.S. territory, the marines who landed here named the square after their ship, the USS *Portsmouth*. (Today, a bronze plaque marks the spot where they raised the U.S. flag.)

Yerba Buena remained a modest township until the gold rush of 1849 when, over the next 2 years, the population grew from under 1,000 to over 19,000, as gold seekers from around the world made their way here.

When the square became too crowded, long wharves were constructed to support new buildings above the bay. Eventually, the entire area became landfill. That was almost 150 years ago, but today the square still serves as an important meeting place for neighborhood Chinese—a sort of communal outdoor living room.

Throughout the day, the square is heavily trafficked by children and—in large part—by elderly men, who gamble over Chinese cards. If you arrive early in the morning, you might come across people practicing tai chi.

It is said that Robert Louis Stevenson used to love to sit on a bench here and watch life go by. (At the northeast corner of the square, you'll find a monument to his memory, consisting of a model of the *Hispañola*, the ship in Stevenson's novel *Treasure Island*, and an excerpt from his "Christmas Sermon.")

Once you've had your fill of the square, exit to the east at Kearny Street. Directly across the street, at 750 Kearny, is the Holiday Inn. Cross the street, enter the hotel, and take the elevator to the third floor, where you'll find the Chinese Culture Center.

⑲ Chinese Culture Center

This center is oriented toward both the community and tourists, offering interesting display cases of Chinese art and a gallery with rotating exhibits of Asian art and writings. The center is open Tuesday through Saturday from 10am to 4pm.

When you leave the Holiday Inn, take a left on Kearny and go 3 short blocks to Commercial Street. Take a left onto Commercial and note that you are standing on the street once known as the site of:

⑳ Joshua A. Norton's Home

Norton, the self-proclaimed "Emperor of the United States and Protector of Mexico," used to walk around the streets in an old brass-buttoned military uniform, sporting a hat with a "dusty plume." He lived in a fantasy world, and San Franciscans humored him at every turn.

Norton was born around 1815 in the British Isles and sailed as a young man to South Africa, where he served as a colonial rifleman. He came to San Francisco in 1849 with $40,000 and proceeded to double and triple his fortune in real estate. Unfortunately for him, he next chose to go into the rice business. While Norton was busy cornering the market and forcing prices up, several ships loaded with rice arrived unexpectedly in San Francisco's harbor. The rice market was suddenly flooded, and Norton was forced into bankruptcy. He left San Francisco for about 3 years and must have experienced a breakdown (or revelation) of some sort, for upon his return, Norton thought he was an emperor.

Finds **Do-It-Yourself Excursions**

The Convention & Visitors Bureau distributes a brochure detailing self-guided walking tours of North Beach, Union Square, Fisherman's Wharf, Chinatown, and Pacific Heights. Send a request plus a self-addressed business-size envelope to the San Francisco Convention & Visitors Bureau, 201 Third Street, Suite 900, San Francisco, CA 94103. You can also get the information online at **www.sf visitor.org/visitorinfo/html/walkpdfs.html**.

Instead of ostracizing him, however, San Franciscans embraced him as their own homegrown lunatic and gave him free meals.

When Emperor Norton died in 1880 (while sleeping at the corner of California St. and Grant Ave.), approximately 10,000 people passed by his coffin, which was bought with money raised at the Pacific Union Club, and more than 30,000 people participated in the funeral procession. Today you won't see a trace of his character, but it's fun to imagine him cruising the street.

From here, if you've still got an appetite, you should go directly to 631 Kearny (at Clay St.), home of the R&G Lounge.

TAKE A BREAK
The **R&G Lounge** is a sure thing for tasty $5 rice-plate specials, chicken with black-bean sauce, and gorgeously tender and tangy R&G Special Beef.

Otherwise, you might want to backtrack on Commercial Street to Grant Avenue, take a left, and follow Grant back to Bush Street, the entrance to Chinatown. You'll be at the beginning of the Union Square area, where you can catch any number of buses (especially on Market St.) or cable cars or do a little shopping. Or you might backtrack to Grant, take a right (north), and follow Grant to the end. You'll be at Broadway and Columbus, the beginning of North Beach, where you can venture onward for our North Beach tour (see below).

WALKING TOUR 2   GETTING TO KNOW NORTH BEACH

Start:	Intersection of Montgomery Street, Columbus Avenue, and Washington Street.
Public Transportation:	Bus no. 10, 12, 15, 30X, or 41.
Finish:	Washington Square.
Time:	3 hours, including a stop for lunch.
Best Times:	Monday through Saturday between 11am and 4pm.
Worst Times:	Sunday, when shops are closed.
Hills That Could Kill:	The Montgomery Street hill from Broadway to Vallejo Street; otherwise, this is an easy walk.

Along with Chinatown, North Beach is one of the city's oldest neighborhoods. Originally the Latin Quarter, it became the city's Italian district when Italian immigrants moved "uphill" in the early 1870s, crossing Broadway from the Jackson Square area and settling in. They quickly established restaurants, cafes, bakeries, and other businesses familiar to them from their homeland. The "Beat Generation" helped put North Beach on the map, with the likes of Jack Kerouac and Allen Ginsberg holding court in the area's cafes during the 1950s. Although most of the original Beat poets are gone, their spirit lives on in North Beach, which is still a haven for bohemian artists and writers. The neighborhood, thankfully, retains its Italian village feel; it's a place where residents from all walks of life enjoy taking time for conversation over pastries and frothy cappuccinos.

If there's one landmark you can't miss, it's the familiar building on the corner of Montgomery Street and Columbus Avenue, the TransAmerica Pyramid (take bus 15, 30X, or 41 to get there).

❶ TransAmerica Pyramid

Noted for its spire (which rises 212 ft. above the top floor) and its "wings" (which begin at the 29th floor and stop at the spire), this pyramid is San Francisco's tallest building and a hallmark of the skyline. You might want to take a peek at one of the rotating art exhibits in the lobby or go around to the right and into ½-acre Redwood Park, which is part of the TransAmerica Center.

The TransAmerica Pyramid occupies part of the 600 block of Montgomery Street, which once held a historic building called the Montgomery Block.

❷ The Montgomery Block

Originally four stories high, the Montgomery Block was the tallest building in the West when it was built in 1853. San Franciscans called it "Halleck's Folly" because it was built on a raft of redwood logs that had been bolted together and floated at the edge of the ocean (which was right at Montgomery St. at that time). The building was demolished in 1959 but is fondly remembered for its historical importance as the power center of the city. Its tenants included artists and writers of all kinds, among them Jack London, George Sterling, Ambrose Bierce, Bret Harte, and Mark Twain. This is a picturesque area, but there's no particular spot to direct you to. It's worth looking around, however, if only for the block's historical importance.

From the southeast corner of Montgomery and Washington streets, look across Washington to the corner of Columbus Avenue, and you'll see the original TransAmerica Building, located at 4 Columbus Ave.

❸ Original TransAmerica Building

The original TransAmerica Building is a Beaux Arts flatiron-shaped building covered in terra cotta; it was also the home of Sanwa Bank and Fugazi Bank. Built for the Banco Populare Italiano Operaia Fugazi in 1909, it was originally a two-story building and gained a third floor in 1916. In 1928, Fugazi merged his bank with the Bank of America, which was started by A. P. Giannini, who also created the TransAmerica Corporation. The building now houses a Church of Scientology.

Cross Washington Street and continue north on Montgomery Street to no. 730, the Golden Era Building.

❹ Golden Era Building

Erected around 1852, this San Francisco historic landmark building is named after the literary magazine, *The Golden Era,* which was published here. Some of the young writers who worked on the magazine were known as "The Bohemians"; they included Samuel Clemens (aka Mark Twain) and Bret Harte (who began as a typesetter here). Backtrack a few dozen feet and stop for a minute to admire the exterior of the annex, at no. 722, which, after years of neglect and lawsuits, has finally been stabilized and is going to be developed. The Belli Annex, as it is currently known, is registered as a historic landmark.

Continue north on Washington Street, and take the first right onto Jackson Street. Continue until you hit the 400 block of Jackson Square.

❺ 400 Block of Jackson Square

Here's where you'll find some of the only commercial buildings to survive the 1906 earthquake and fire. The building at no. 415 Jackson (ca. 1853) served as headquarters for the Ghirardelli Chocolate

Walking Tour 2: North Beach

0 ——— 1/10 mile
0 ——— 100 meters

Take a Break
Cable Car

finish here
★ ⑳ Washington Square

Greenwich St.

Filbert St.

Telegraph Hill Park

Union St.

Columbus Ave.

⑲
⑱
⑰

Grant Ave.

Greene St.

NORTH BEACH

Varennes St.
Sonoma St.
Kearny St.

⑮
⑭
⑯

Vallejo St.

Margrave Pl.

Omolo Pl.

Fresno St.

Montgomery St.

Bartol St.

⑧

Broadway

⑩ ⑨

⑪

⑫ ⑬

JACKSON

Osgood Pl.

Sansome St.

Powell St.
Stockton St.

Jack Kerouac St.

Pacific Ave.

SQUARE

HISTORIC

⑦

Grant Ave.
Beckett St.
Wentworth Pl.
Kearny St.

DISTRICT

Gold St.

Jackson St.

⑥

Columbus Ave.

CHINATOWN

Ross Alley

Washington St.

Spofford St.
Waverly Pl.

Portsmouth Square

Merchant St.

③
④
⑤

start here ★

① ②

Transamerica Pyramid

Clay St.

1 Transamerica Pyramid
2 The Montgomery Block
3 Original Transamerica Building
4 Golden Era Building
5 400 block of Jackson Square
6 Columbus Tower
7 140 Columbus Avenue
8 1010 Montgomery Street
9 hungry i
10 Former site of the Condor Club
11 City Lights Bookstore
12 Vesuvio
13 Specs' Adler Museum Café
and Tosca Café
14 Caffè Trieste
15 Biordi Art Imports
16 Molinari Delicatessen
17 North Beach Museum
18 Club Fugazi
19 Mario's Bohemian Cigar Store
20 Washington Square

Company from 1855 to 1894. The Hotaling Building (no. 451) was built in 1866 and features pediments and quoins of cast iron applied over the brick walls. At no. 441 is another of the buildings that survived the disaster of 1906. Constructed between 1850 and 1852 with ship masts for interior supporting columns, it served as the French Consulate from 1865 to 1876.

Cross the street, and backtrack on Jackson Street. Continue toward the intersection of Columbus Avenue and Jackson Street. Turn right on Columbus and look across the street for the small triangular building at the junction of Kearny Street and Columbus Avenue, Columbus Tower (aka the Sentinel Building).

❻ Columbus Tower

If you walk a little farther, and then turn around and look back down Columbus, you'll be able to get a better look at Columbus Tower. The flatiron beauty, a building shaped to a triangular site, went up between 1905 and 1907. Movie director and producer Francis Ford Coppola bought and restored it in the mid-1970s; it is now home to his film production company, American Zoetrope Studios. The building's cafe showcases all things Rubicon (Coppola's winery)—including olive oil, Parmesan cheese, and wine. It's a great place to stop for a glass of wine, an espresso, or a thin-crusted pizza snack. This is one of the few pre–1906 earthquake buildings left in the city center.

Across the street from Columbus Tower on Columbus Avenue is 140 Columbus Ave.

❼ 140 Columbus Ave.

Although it was closed for a few years, the **Purple Onion** (© **415/956-1653**), famous for its many renowned headliners, who played here often before they were famous, is now hosting an eclectic mix of music and comedy again. Let's hope the next Phyllis Diller, who's now so big that she's famous for something as simple as her laugh—and who was still struggling when she played a 2-week

engagement here in the late 1950s—will catch her big break here, too.

Continue north on Columbus, and then turn right on Pacific Avenue. After you cross Montgomery Street, you'll find brick-lined Osgood Place on the left. A registered historic landmark, it is one of the few quiet—and car-free—little alleyways left in the city. Stroll up Osgood and go left on Broadway to 1010 Montgomery St. (at Broadway).

❽ 1010 Montgomery St.

This is where Allen Ginsberg lived when he wrote his legendary poem, "Howl," first performed on October 13, 1955, in a converted auto-repair shop at the corner of Fillmore and Union streets. By the time Ginsberg finished reading, he was crying and the audience was going wild. Jack Kerouac proclaimed, "Ginsberg, this poem will make you famous in San Francisco."

Continue along Broadway toward Columbus Avenue. This stretch of Broadway is San Francisco's answer to New York's Times Square, complete with strip clubs and peep shows that are being pushed aside by restaurants, clubs, and an endless crowd of visitors. It's among the most sought-after locations in the city as more and more profitable restaurants and clubs spring up. Keep walking west on Broadway, and on the right side of the street, you'll come to Black Oak Books, 540 Broadway. It sells new and used discount books and is worth a quick trip inside for a good, cheap read. A few dozen yards farther up Broadway is the current location of the hungry i.

❾ hungry i

Now a seedy strip club (at 546 Broadway), the original hungry i (at 599 Jackson St., which is under construction for senior housing) was owned and operated by the vociferous "Big Daddy" Nordstrom. If you had been here while Enrico Banducci (also of Enrico's restaurant) was in charge, you would have found only a plain room with an exposed brick wall and director's chairs around small tables. A who's who of nightclub entertainers fortified their careers at the original hungry i, including Lenny Bruce, Billie Holiday (who first sang "Strange Fruit" there), Bill Cosby, Richard Pryor, Woody Allen, and Barbra Streisand.

At the corner of Broadway and Columbus Avenue, you will see the former site of the Condor Club.

❿ Former Site of the Condor Club

The Condor Club was located at 300 Columbus Ave.; this is where Carol Doda scandalously bared her breasts and danced topless for the first time in 1964. Note the bronze plaque claiming the Condor Club as BIRTHPLACE OF THE WORLD'S FIRST TOPLESS & BOTTOMLESS ENTERTAINMENT. Go inside what is now the Condor Sports Bar and have a look at the framed newspaper clippings that hang around the dining room. From the elevated back room, you can see Doda's old dressing room and, on the floor below, an outline of the piano that would descend from the second floor with her atop it.

When you leave the Condor Sports Bar, cross to the south side of Broadway. Note the mural of jazz musicians painted on the entire side of the building directly across Columbus Avenue. Diagonally across the intersection from the Condor Sports Bar is the City Lights bookstore.

⓫ City Lights Booksellers & Publishers

Founded in 1953 and owned by one of the first Beat poets to arrive in San Francisco, Lawrence Ferlinghetti, City Lights is now a city landmark and literary mecca. Located at 261 Columbus Ave., it's one of the last of the Beat-era hangouts in operation. An active participant in the Beat movement, Ferlinghetti established his shop as a meeting place where writers and bibliophiles could (and still do) attend poetry readings and other events. A vibrant part of the literary scene, the well-stocked bookshop prides itself on its collection of art, poetry, and political paperbacks.

Upon exiting City Lights bookstore, turn right, cross aptly named Jack Kerouac Street, and stop by Vesuvio, the bar on your right.

⓬ Vesuvio

Because of its proximity to City Lights bookstore, Vesuvio became a favorite hangout of the Beats. Dylan Thomas used to drink here, as did Jack Kerouac, Ferlinghetti, and Ginsberg. Even today, Vesuvio, which opened in 1949, maintains its original bohemian atmosphere. The bar is located at 255 Columbus Ave. (at Jack Kerouac St.) and dates from 1913. It is an excellent example of pressed-tin architecture.

Facing Vesuvio across Columbus Avenue is another favorite spot of the Beat Generation:

⓭ Spec's Adler Museum Café

Located at 12 Saroyan Place, this is one of the city's funkiest bars, a small, dimly lit watering hole with ceiling-hung maritime flags and exposed brick walls crammed with memorabilia. Within the bar is a mini-museum that consists of a few glass cases filled with mementos brought by seamen who frequented the pub from the '40s and onward.

From here, walk back up Columbus across Broadway to Grant Avenue. Turn right on Grant, and continue until you come to Vallejo Street. At 601 Vallejo St. (at Grant Ave.) is Caffè Trieste.

⓮ Caffè Trieste

Yet another favorite spot of the Beats and founded by Gianni Giotta in 1956, Caffè Trieste is still run by family members. The quintessential San Francisco coffeehouse, Trieste features opera on the jukebox, and the real thing, performed by the Giottas, on Saturday afternoons. Any day of the week is a good one to stop in for a cappuccino or espresso—the beans are roasted right next door.

Go left out of Caffè Trieste onto Vallejo Street, turn right on Columbus Avenue, and bump into the loveliest shop in all of North Beach, Biordi Art Imports, located at 412 Columbus Ave.

⓯ Biordi Art Imports

This store has carried imported hand-painted majolica pottery from the hill towns of central Italy for more than 50 years. Some of the colorful patterns date from the 14th century. Biordi handpicks its artisans, and its catalog includes biographies of those who are currently represented.

Across Columbus Avenue, at the corner of Vallejo Street, is the Molinari Delicatessen.

⑯ Molinari Delicatessen

This deli, located at 373 Columbus Ave., has been selling its pungent, air-dried salamis since 1896. Ravioli and tortellini are made in the back of the shop, but it's the mouthwatering selection of cold salads, cheeses, and marinades up front that captures the attention of most folks. Each Italian sub is big enough for two hearty appetites.

Walk north to the lively intersection of Columbus, Green, and Stockton streets, and look for the U.S. Bank at 1435 Stockton St. On the second floor of the bank, you'll find the North Beach Museum.

⑰ North Beach Museum

The North Beach Museum displays historical artifacts that tell the story of North Beach, Chinatown, and Fisherman's Wharf. Just before you enter the museum, you'll find a framed, handwritten poem by Lawrence Ferlinghetti that captures his impressions of this primarily Italian neighborhood. After passing through the glass doors, visitors see many photographs of some of the first Chinese and Italian immigrants, as well as pictures of San Francisco after the 1906 earthquake. You can visit the museum any time the bank is open (unfortunately, it's closed on weekends), and admission is free.

Now backtrack toward Columbus Avenue and go left on Green Street to Club Fugazi, at 678 Green St.

⑱ Club Fugazi

It doesn't look like much from the outside, but Fugazi Hall was donated to the city (and more important, the North Beach area) by John Fugazi, the founder of the Italian bank that was taken over by A. P. Giannini and turned into the original TransAmerica Corporation. For many years, Fugazi Hall has been staging the zany and whimsical musical revue *Beach Blanket Babylon.* The show evolved from Steve Silver's Rent-a-Freak service, which consisted of a group of partygoers who would attend parties dressed as any number of characters in outrageous costumes. The fun caught on and soon became *Beach Blanket Babylon.*

If you love comedy, you'll love this show. We don't want to spoil it for you by telling you what it's about, but if you get tickets and they're in an unreserved-seat section, you should arrive fairly early because you'll be seated around small cocktail tables on a first-come, first-served basis. (Two sections have reserved seating, four don't, and all of them frequently sell out weeks in advance; however, sometimes it is possible to get tickets at the last minute on weekdays.) You'll want to be as close to the stage as possible. This supercharged show (see p. 226 for more information) is definitely worth the price of admission.

> ☕ **TAKE A BREAK**
> Head back the way you came on Green Street. Before you get to Columbus Avenue, you'll see **O'Reilly's Irish Pub** (622 Green St.), a homey watering hole that dishes out good, hearty Irish food and a fine selection of beers (including Guinness, of course) that are best enjoyed at one of the sidewalk tables. Always a conversation piece is the mural of Irish authors peering from the back wall. (How many can you name?)

As you come out of O'Reilly's, turn left, cross Columbus Avenue, and then take a left onto Columbus. Proceed 1 block northwest to Mario's Bohemian Cigar Store.

⑲ Mario's Bohemian Cigar Store

Located at 566 Columbus Ave., across the street from Washington Square, this is one of North Beach's most popular neighborhood hangouts. No, it does not sell cigars, but the cramped and casual space overlooking Washington Square does sell killer focaccia sandwiches, coffee drinks, beer, and wine.

Our next stop, directly across Union Street, is Washington Square.

⑳ Washington Square

This is one of the oldest parks in the city. The land was designated a public park in 1847 and has undergone many changes since then. Its current landscaping dates from 1955. You'll notice **Saints Peter and Paul Church** (the religious center for the neighborhood's Italian community) on the northwest end. Take a few moments to go inside and check out the

traditional Italian interior. Note that this is the church in which baseball great Joe DiMaggio married his first wife, Dorothy Arnold. He wasn't allowed to marry Marilyn Monroe here because he had been divorced. He married Monroe at City Hall and came here for publicity photos.

Today the park is a pleasant place in which to soak up the sun, read a book, or chat with a retired Italian octogenarian who has seen the city grow and change.

From here, you can see the famous Coit Tower at the top of Telegraph Hill to the northwest. If you'd like to get back to your starting point at Columbus and Montgomery streets, walk south (away from the water) on Columbus.

9

Shopping

Like its population, San Francisco's shopping is both worldly and intimate. Every persuasion, style, era, and fetish is represented, not in big, tacky shopping malls, but in hundreds of quaint, dramatically different boutiques scattered throughout the city. Whether you're looking for Chanel or Chinese herbal medicine, San Francisco's got it. Just pick a neighborhood and break out your credit cards—you're sure to end up with at least a few take-home treasures.

1 The Shopping Scene

MAJOR SHOPPING AREAS

San Francisco has many shopping areas, but the following places are where you'll find most of the action.

UNION SQUARE & ENVIRONS   San Francisco's most congested and popular shopping mecca is centered on Union Square and bordered by Bush, Taylor, Market, and Montgomery streets. Most of the big department stores and many high-end specialty shops are here. Be sure to venture to Grant Avenue, Post and Sutter streets, and Maiden Lane. This area is a hub for public transportation; all Market Street and several other buses run here, as do the Powell–Hyde and Powell–Mason cable car lines. You can also take the Muni streetcar to the Powell Street station.

CHINATOWN   When you pass through the gate to Chinatown on Grant Avenue, say goodbye to the world of fashion and hello to a swarm of cheap tourist shops selling everything from linen and jade to plastic toys and $2 slippers. But that's not all Chinatown has to offer. The real gems are tucked away on side streets or are small, one-person shops selling Chinese herbs, original art, and jewelry. Grant Avenue is the area's main thoroughfare, and the side streets between Bush Street and Columbus Avenue are full of restaurants, markets, and eclectic shops. Stockton Street is best for grocery shopping (including live fowl and fish). Walking is the way to get around, because traffic through this area is slow and parking is next to impossible. Most stores in Chinatown are open daily from 10am to 10pm. Take bus no. 1, 9X, 15, 30, 41, or 45.

UNION STREET   Union Street, from Fillmore Street to Van Ness Avenue, caters to the upper-middle-class crowd. It's a great place to stroll, window-shop the plethora of boutiques, try the cafes and restaurants, and watch the beautiful people parade by. Take bus no. 22, 41, 45, 47, 49, or 76.

CHESTNUT STREET   Parallel and a few blocks north, Chestnut is a younger version of Union Street. It holds endless shopping and dining choices, and an ever-tanned, superfit population of postgraduate singles who hang around cafes and scope each other out. Take bus no. 22, 28, 30, 43, or 76.

> **_Tips_ Just the Facts: Hours, Taxes & Shipping**
>
> **Store hours** are generally Monday through Saturday from 10am to 6pm and Sunday from noon to 5pm. Most department stores stay open later, as do shops around Fisherman's Wharf, the most heavily visited area (by tourists).
>
> **Sales tax** in San Francisco is 8.5%, which is added on at the register for all goods and services purchased. If you live out of state and buy an expensive item, you might want to have the store ship it home for you. You'll have to pay for shipping, but you'll escape paying the sales tax.
>
> Most of the city's shops can wrap your purchase and **ship** it anywhere in the world. If they can't, you can send it yourself, either through **UPS** (© 800/742-5877), **FedEx** (© 800/463-3339), or the U.S. Postal Service (see "Fast Facts: San Francisco," in chapter 4).

FILLMORE STREET   Some of the best shopping in town is packed into 5 blocks of Fillmore Street in Pacific Heights. From Jackson to Sutter streets, Fillmore is the perfect place to grab a bite and peruse the high-priced boutiques, crafts shops, and incredible housewares stores. (Don't miss Zinc Details; p. 216.) Take bus no. 1, 2, 3, 4, 12, 22, or 24.

HAIGHT STREET   Green hair, spiked hair, no hair, or mohair—even the hippies look conservative next to Haight Street's dramatic fashion freaks. The shopping in the 6 blocks of upper Haight Street between Central Avenue and Stanyan Street reflects its clientele. It offers everything from incense and European and American street styles to furniture and antique clothing. Bus nos. 6, 7, 66, and 71 run the length of Haight Street, and nos. 33 and 43 run through upper Haight Street. The Muni streetcar N line stops at Waller Street and Cole Street.

SOMA   Although this area isn't suitable for strolling, you'll find almost all the discount shopping in warehouse spaces south of Market. You can pick up a discount-shopping guide at most major hotels. Many bus lines pass through this area.

HAYES VALLEY   It's not the prettiest area in town, with some of the shadier housing projects a few blocks away. But while most neighborhoods cater to more conservative or trendy shoppers, lower Hayes Street, between Octavia and Gough streets, celebrates anything vintage, chic, artistic, or downright funky. With new shops opening frequently, it's definitely the most interesting new shopping area in town, with furniture and glass stores, thrift shops, trendy shoe stores, and men's and women's clothiers. You can find lots of great antiques shops south on Octavia and on nearby Market Street. Take bus no. 16AX, 16BX, or 21.

FISHERMAN'S WHARF & ENVIRONS _(Overrated)_   The tourist-oriented malls along Jefferson Street include hundreds of shops, restaurants, and attractions. Among them are Ghirardelli Square, PIER 39, The Cannery, and The Anchorage (see "Shopping Centers & Complexes," on p. 219).

2 Shopping A to Z

ANTIQUES

Jackson Square, a historic district just north of the Financial District's Embarcadero Center, is the place to go for the top names in fine furniture and fine art. More than

San Francisco Shopping

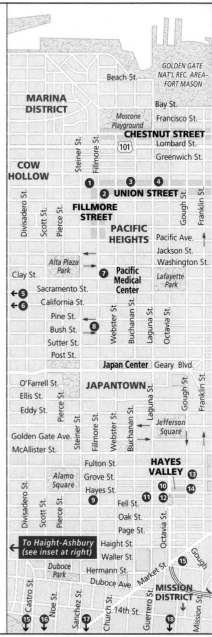

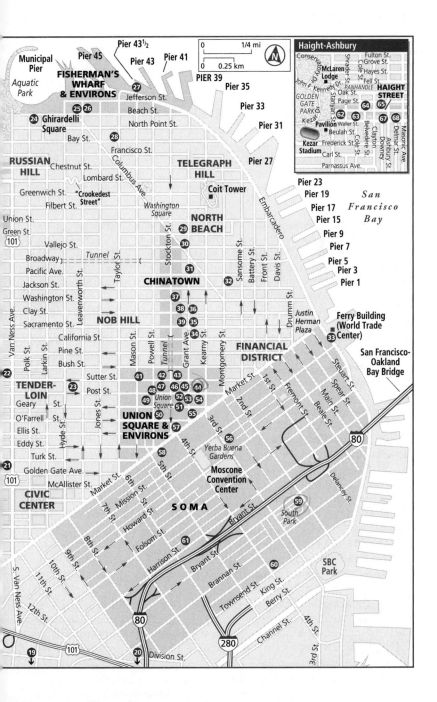

Municipal
Pier

Aquatic
Park

Pier 45
Pier 43½
Pier 43 **Pier 41**

FISHERMAN'S
WHARF
& ENVIRONS

27

Jefferson St.

PIER 39
Pier 35
Pier 33
Pier 31

0   1/4 mi
0   0.25 km

Haight-Ashbury

Conservatory Dr.   Fulton St.
                    Grove St.
    McLaren   Hayes St.
    Lodge   Fell St.
John F. Kennedy Dr. PANHANDLE **HAIGHT**
    Oak St.   **STREET**
GOLDEN Page St.
GATE   **64** **65**
PARK   **62** **63** **67** **68**
Kezar   **Pavilion** Waller St.
        Beulah St.
Kezar   Frederick St. Cole St.
Stadium Carl St.
        Parnassus Ave.

25 **26**

24 Ghirardelli
Square

Beach St.

North Point St.

Bay St.   **28**

Francisco St.

RUSSIAN Chestnut St.
HILL

Lombard St.

Greenwich St. **"Crookedest**
Filbert St.   **Street"**

Union St.

Green St.
101

Vallejo St.

Broadway _Tunnel_

Pacific Ave.

Jackson St.

Washington St.

Clay St.

Sacramento St.

California St.

Pine St.

Bush St.

22

TENDER-
LOIN   **23**

Sutter St.

Post St.

Geary St.

O'Farrell St.

Ellis St.

Eddy St.

Turk St.

21   Golden Gate Ave.
101
        McAllister St.

CIVIC
CENTER

Columbus Ave.

TELEGRAPH
HILL

Coit Tower

Washington
Square

NORTH
BEACH

29

30

31

CHINATOWN

32

37

38 36

39 35

34

NOB HILL

Tunnel

FINANCIAL
DISTRICT

41 42 43

48 47 46 45 44
49 52 53 54
    Union **51**
50 **Square** **55**
        57

UNION
SQUARE &
ENVIRONS

58

56

Yerba Buena
Gardens

Moscone
Convention
Center

S O M A

Pier 27
Pier 23
Pier 19   _San_
Pier 17   _Francisco_
Pier 15   _Bay_
Pier 9
Pier 7
Pier 5
Pier 3
Pier 1

Embarcadero

Sansome St.
Battery St.
Front St.
Davis St.

Drumm St.

Justin
Herman
Plaza   **33**

Ferry Building
(World Trade
Center)

San Francisco-
Oakland
Bay Bridge

Steuart St.
Spear St.
Main St.
Beale St.

80

59

South
Park

Delancey St.

SBC
Park

61

60

Bryant St.

Brannan St.

Townsend St.

King St.

Berry St.

Market St.

Mission St.

Howard St.

Folsom St.

Harrison St.

80

280

Channel St.

3rd St.

4th St.

19   **101**

20   Division St.

a dozen dealers on the 2 blocks between Columbus and Sansome streets specialize in European furnishings from the 17th to the 19th centuries. Most shops here are open Monday through Friday from 9am to 5pm and Saturday from 11am to 4pm.

Bonhams & Butterfield   This renowned auction house holds preview weekends for upcoming auctions of furnishings, silver, antiques, art, and jewelry. Call for auction schedules. 220 San Bruno Ave. (at 16th St.). (C) **800/223-2854** or 415/861-7500. www.bonhams.com/us.

Therien & Co.   For the best in Scandinavian, French, and eastern European antiques, head beyond SoMa's design center to this boutique, where you can find the real thing or antique replicas, as well as made-to-order furniture from their neighboring custom furniture shop. 411 Vermont St. (at 17th St.). (C) **415/956-8850**. www.therien.com.

ART

The San Francisco Bay Area Gallery Guide, a comprehensive, bimonthly publication listing the city's current shows, is available free by mail. Send a self-addressed, stamped envelope to San Francisco Bay Area Gallery Guide, 1369 Fulton St., San Francisco, CA 94117 ((C) **415/921-1600**); or pick one up at the San Francisco Visitor Information Center at 900 Market St. Most of the city's major art galleries are clustered downtown in the Union Square area.

Catharine Clark Gallery *Value*   Catharine Clark's is a different kind of gallery experience. While many galleries focus on established artists and out-of-this-world prices, Catharine's exhibits works by up-and-coming contemporary as well as established artists (mainly from California). It nurtures beginning collectors by offering a purchasing plan that's almost unheard of in the art business. You can buy a piece on layaway and take up to a year to pay for it—interest free! Prices here make art a realistic purchase for almost everyone for a change, but serious collectors also frequent the shows because Clark has such a keen eye for talent. Shows change every 6 weeks. Open Tuesday through Friday 10:30am to 5:30pm and Saturday 11am to 5:30pm. Closed Sunday and Monday. 49 Geary St. (between Kearny and Grant sts.), 2nd floor. (C) **415/399-1439**. www.cclarkgallery.com.

Fraenkel Gallery   This photography gallery features works by contemporary American and European artists. Excellent shows change every 2 months. Open Tuesday through Friday 10:30am to 5:30pm and Saturday 11am to 5pm. Closed Sunday and Monday. 49 Geary St. (between Grant Ave. and Kearny St.), 4th floor. (C) **415/981-2661**. www.fraenkelgallery.com.

Hang *Value*   Check out this amazingly affordable gallery for attractive pieces by yet-to-be-discovered Bay Area artists. The staff is friendly and helpful, and the gallery is designed to cater to new and seasoned collectors who appreciate original art at down-to-earth prices. 556 Sutter St. (C) **415/434-4264**. www.hangart.com.

Images of the North   The highlight here is one of the most extensive collections of Canadian and Alaskan Inuit art in the United States. There's also a small collection of Native American masks and jewelry. Open Tuesday through Saturday 11am to 5:30pm and by appointment. 2036 Union St. (at Buchanan St.). (C) **415/673-1273**. www.imagesnorth.com.

Meyerovich Gallery   Paintings, sculptures, and works on paper here are by modern and contemporary masters, including Chagall, Matisse, Miró, and Picasso. Meyerovich's new Contemporary Gallery, across the hall, features works by Lichtenstein, Stella, Frankenthaler, Dine, and Hockney. Open Monday through Friday 10am to 6pm and

Saturday 10am to 5pm. Closed Sunday. 251 Post St. (at Stockton St.), 4th floor. ℂ **415/421-7171.**
www.meyerovich.com.

BODY PRODUCTS

Showroom by In Fiore *Finds*   I'm totally addicted to In Fiore—a high-end line of
body balms, oils, perfumes, and facial serums—so I was especially thrilled when San
Francisco–based founder Julie Elliott opened her by-appointment-only shop in what
she calls the "Tender-Nob" (on the border of Nob Hill and the Tenderloin near Union
Square). Come here to check out her whole line, as well as limited-edition balms, and
see why celebrities like Julia Roberts and Meg Ryan are fans. Open Tuesday through
Saturday and by appointment only. 868 Post St. (between Leavenworth and Hyde sts.). ℂ **415/**
928-5661. www.infiore.net.

BOOKS

In addition to the listings below, there's a **Barnes & Noble** superstore at 2550 Taylor
St., between Bay and North Point streets, near Fisherman's Wharf (ℂ **415/292-6762**)
and a four-storied **Borders** at 400 Post St., at Union Square (ℂ **415/399-1633**).

Book Passage   If you're moseying through the Ferry Building Marketplace, drop
into this cozy independent that emphasizes (for tourists and locals alike) local travel,
boating on the Bay, food, cooking, sustainable agriculture and ecology, fiction, culinary and regional history and literature, and photo and gift books about the Bay Area.
The store also hosts lots of author events: Check their website for details. Ferry Building
Marketplace (at The Embarcadero and Market St.). ℂ **415/835-1020.** www.bookpassage.com.

The Booksmith   Haight Street's best selection of new books is in this large, well-
maintained shop. It carries all the top titles, along with works from smaller presses,
and more than 1,000 different magazines. 1644 Haight St. (between Clayton and Cole sts.).
ℂ **800/493-7323** or 415/863-8688.

City Lights Booksellers & Publishers *Finds*   Brooding literary types browse this
famous bookstore owned by Lawrence Ferlinghetti, the renowned Beat Generation
poet. The three-level bookshop prides itself on a comprehensive collection of art,
poetry, and political paperbacks, as well as more mainstream books. Open daily until
midnight. 261 Columbus Ave. (at Broadway). ℂ **415/362-8193.** www.citylights.com.

A Clean, Well-Lighted Place for Books *Finds*   This independent store has good
new fiction and nonfiction sections, and specializes in music, art, mystery, and cookbooks. The store is well known for its author readings and events. For a calendar of
events, call or check the website. 601 Van Ness Ave. (between Turk St. and Golden Gate Ave.).
ℂ **415/441-6670.** www.bookstore.com.

Green Apple Books *Finds*   The local favorite for used books, Green Apple is
crammed with titles—more than 60,000 new and 100,000 used books and DVDs. Its
extended sections in psychology, cooking, art, and history; collection of modern first
editions; and rare graphic comics are superseded only by the staff's superlative service.
506 Clement St. (at Sixth Ave.). ℂ **415/387-2272.** www.greenapplebooks.com.

William Stout Architectural Books *Finds*   Step inside this shrine to all things
architectural, and even if you think you're not interested in exquisite bathrooms,
Southern California's modern homes, or great gardens, you can't help but bury yourself in the thousands of design books. Their recent expansion into a second level

means that if they don't have what you're looking for, it probably doesn't exist. 804 Montgomery St. (at Jackson St.). © 415/391-6757. www.stoutbooks.com.

CHINA, SILVER & GLASS

Gump's *Finds*   Founded over a century ago, Gump's offers gifts and treasures ranging from Asian antiquities to contemporary art glass and exquisite jade and pearl jewelry. Many items are made specifically for the store. Gump's also has one of the city's most revered holiday window displays and is a huge wedding registry destination, though the staff can act very affected. 135 Post St. (between Kearny St. and Grant Ave.). © 800/766-7628 or 415/982-1616. www.gumps.com.

CRAFTS

The Canton Bazaar   Amid a wide variety of handicrafts, here you'll find an excellent selection of rosewood and carved furniture, cloisonné enamelware, porcelain, carved jade, embroideries, jewelry, and antiques from mainland China. Open daily until 10pm. 616 Grant Ave. (between Sacramento and California sts.). © 415/362-5750. www. cantonbazaar.com.

The New Unique Company   Primarily a calligraphy- and watercolor-supplies store, this shop also has a good assortment of books on these topics. In addition, there's a wide selection of carved stones for use as seals on letters and documents. Should you want a special design or group of initials, the store will carve seals to order. 838 Grant Ave. (between Clay and Washington sts.). © 415/981-2036.

DEPARTMENT STORES (DOWNTOWN)

Macy's   The seven-story Macy's West features contemporary fashions for women, juniors, and children, plus jewelry, fragrances, cosmetics, and accessories. The sixth floor offers a "hospitality suite" where visitors can leave their coats and packages, grab a cup of coffee, or find out more about the city from the concierge. The top floors contain home furnishings, and the Cellar sells kitchenware and gourmet foods. You'll even find a Boudin Cafe (though the food is not as good compared to their food at other locations) and a Wolfgang Puck Cafe on the premises. Across the street, Macy's East has five floors of men's fashions. Stockton and O'Farrell sts., Union Square. © 415/397-3333.

Neiman Marcus   Some call this Texas-based chain "Needless Mark-ups." But those who can afford the best of everything can't deny that the men's and women's clothes, precious gems, and conservative formalwear are some of the most glamorous in town. The Rotunda Restaurant, located on the fourth floor, is a beautiful place for lunch and afternoon tea that was recently renovated along with the rest of the store. 150 Stockton St. (between Geary and O'Farrell sts.), Union Square. © 415/362-3900.

Nordstrom   Renowned for its personalized service, this is the largest branch of the Seattle-based fashion department-store chain. Nordstrom occupies the top five floors of the San Francisco Shopping Centre (see "Shopping Centers & Complexes," on p. 219) and is the mall's primary anchor. Equally devoted to women's and men's fashions, the store has one of the best shoe selections in the city and thousands of suits in stock. The Bistro, on the fourth floor, has a panoramic view and is ideal for an inexpensive lunch or light snack. Nordstrom Spa, on the fifth floor, is the perfect place to relax after a hectic day of bargain hunting. In the San Francisco Shopping Centre, 865 Market St. (between Fourth and Fifth sts.). © 415/243-8500.

DISCOUNT SHOPPING

Jeremys *Value*   This boutique is a serious mecca for fashion hounds thanks to the wide array of top designer fashions, from shoes to suits, at rock-bottom prices. There are no cheap knockoffs here, just good men's and women's clothes and accessories that the owner scoops up from major retailers who are either updating merchandise or discarding returns. 2 S. Park (between Bryant and Brannan sts. at Second St.). (C) **415/882-4929. www.jeremys.com.**

FABRICS

Britex Fabrics   A San Francisco institution since 1952 and newly renovated, Britex offers an absurd number and variety of fabrics, not to mention a selection of more than 30,000 buttons. Closed Sundays. 146 Geary St. (between Stockton and Grant sts.). (C) **415/392-2910. www.britexfabrics.com.**

FASHION

See also "Vintage Clothing," later in this section.

CHILDREN'S FASHIONS

Minis   Christine Pajunen, who used to design for Banana Republic, opened this children's clothing store to sell her own creations. Every piece, from shirts to pants and dresses, is made from natural fibers. Every outfit perfectly coordinates with everything else in the store. In 2004, Pajunen expanded the store so that it now includes baby gear, including functional and versatile strollers and cribs. Minis also offers educational and creative toys and books with matching dolls as well as maternity wear. 2278 Union St. (between Steiner and Fillmore sts.). (C) **415/567-9537. www.minis-sf.com.**

MEN'S FASHIONS

All American Boy   Long known for setting the mainstream style for gay men, All American Boy is the quintessential Castro clothing shop. 463 Castro St. (between Market and 18th sts.). (C) **415/861-0444.**

Brooks Brothers   In San Francisco, this bulwark of tradition is 1 block east of Union Square. Brooks Brothers introduced the button-down collar and single-handedly changed the standard of the well-dressed businessman. The multilevel shop also sells traditional casual wear, including sportswear, sweaters, and shirts. 150 Post St. (at Grant Ave.). (C) **415/397-4500. www.brooksbrothers.com.**

Cable Car Clothiers   Dapper men head to this fashion institution for traditional attire, such as three-button suits with natural shoulders, Aquascutum coats, McGeorge sweaters, and Atkinson ties. Closed Sundays. 200 Bush St. (at Sansome St.). (C) **415/397-4740. www.cablecarclothiers.com.**

Citizen Clothing   The Castro has some of America's best men's casual clothing stores, and this is one of them. Stylish (but not faddish) pants, tops, and accessories are in stock here. Its sister store, Body, located at 450 Castro St. (between 17th and 18th sts.), carries men's sportswear. 536 Castro St. (between 18th and 19th sts.). (C) **415/575-3560.**

UNISEX

A B fits   Now in Union Square as well as North Beach, this is the place to pop in for jeans to fit all shapes, styles, and sizes as well as smart and sassy contemporary wear for gals and guys on the go. The snugly fitting stock with over 100 styles of jeans and pants ranges from Chip & Pepper, Earnest Sewn, Edwin, Notify, and Rogan, to chic wear from the likes of Twelfth Street by Cynthia Vincent, Ya-Ya, and Twinkle by Wenlan. There's another location in North Beach at 1519 Grant Ave. (at Union and Filbert sts.) with the same phone number. 40 Grant Ave. (between O'Farrell and Geary sts.). © 415/982-5726. www.abfits.com.

American Rag Cie *(Finds)*   Fashionistas flock to this find, on an unlikely stretch of busy Van Ness, for vintage and new duds sure to make you look street-swank. Check it out for everything from Juicy Couture to Paul & Joe and European vintage to modern masters such as Diesel. 1305 Van Ness Ave. (at Sutter St.). © 415/474-5214.

Gucci America   Donning Gucci's golden Gs is not a cheap endeavor. But if you've got the cash, you'll find all the latest lines of shoes, leather goods, scarves, and pricey accessories here, such as a $9,000 handmade crocodile bag. 200 Stockton St. (between Geary and Post sts.). © 415/392-2808. www.gucci.com.

H & M   This ever trendy and cheap Swedish clothing chain opened in Union Square at the end of 2004, and had lines out the door all through the holiday season—and not just for their collection by Stella McCartney. Drop in anytime for trendy cuts and styles sure to satisfy the hip him and her along on the trip. 150 Powell St. (between Ellis and O'Farrell sts.) © 415/986-4215.

MAC *(Finds)*   No, we're not talking cosmetics. The more-modern-than-corporate stock at this hip and hidden shop (Modern Apparel Clothing) just combined its men's and women's fashion meccas in a new space next door to pastry pit stop Citizen Cake. Drop in for men's imported tailored suits and women's separates in new and intriguing fabrics as well as gorgeous ties, vibrant sweaters, and a few choice home accouterments. Lines include Belgium's Dries Van Noten and Martin Margiela, New York's John Bartlett, and local sweater sweetheart Laurie B. The best part? Prices are more reasonable than at many of the trendy clothing stores in the area. 387 Grove St. (at Gough St.). © 415/863-3011.

Niketown   Here it's not "I can," but "I can spend." At least that's what the kings of sportswear were banking on when they opened this megastore in 1997. As you'd expect, inside the doors shoppers find themselves in a Nike world offering everything the merchandising team could create. 278 Post St. (at Stockton St.). © 415/392-6453.

Three Bags Full   Snuggling up in a cozy sweater can be a fashionable event if you do your shopping at this pricey boutique, which carries the gamut in handmade, playful and extravagant knitwear. Other city locations, which are also closed on Sunday, are 500 Sutter St., © 415/398-7987 and 3314 Sacramento St. (also closed Mon), © 415/923-1454. 2181 Union St. (at Fillmore St.). © 415/567-5753. www.threebagsfull.com.

Wilkes Bashford *(Finds)*   Wilkes Bashford is one of the most expensive and best-known clothing stores in the city. In its 3-plus decades in business, the boutique has garnered a reputation for stocking only the finest clothes in the world (which can often be seen on ex-Mayor Willie Brown and current Mayor Gavin Newsom, who do their suit shopping here). Most fashions come from Italy and France; they include women's designer sportswear and couture and men's Kiton and Brioni suits (at $2,500 and up, they're considered the most expensive suits in the world). Closed Sundays. 375 Sutter St. (at Stockton St.). © 415/986-4380. www.wilkesbashford.com.

WOMEN'S FASHIONS

The Chanel Boutique   Ever fashionable and expensive, Chanel is appropriately located on Maiden Lane, the quaint downtown side street where the most exclusive stores and spas cluster. You'll find here what you'd expect from Chanel: clothing, accessories, scents, cosmetics, and jewelry. 155 Maiden Lane (between Stockton St. and Grant Ave.). © 415/981-1550. www.chanel.com.

emily lee   More mature fashionistas head to the quaint shopping street of Laurel Village, a block-long strip mall of shops that includes emily lee, for everything from elegant to artsy-designer garb that tends to be stylish, sensible, and loose-fitting. Designers include the likes of Blanque, Eileen Fisher, Flax, Ivan Grundahl, and Three Dots. 3509 California St. (at Locust St.). © 415/751-3443.

Métier *(Finds*   Discerning and well-funded shoppers consider this the best women's clothing shop in town. Within its walls you'll find classic, sophisticated, and expensive creations, which include European ready-to-wear lines and designers; fashions by Italian designers Anna Molinari, Hache, and Blumarine and by French designer Martine Sitbone. You will also find a distinguished collection of antique-style, high-end jewelry from L.A.'s Cathy Waterman as well as ultra popular custom-designed poetry jewelry by Jeanine Payer. Closed Sunday. 355 Sutter St. (between Stockton and Grant sts.). © 415/989-5395. www.metiersf.com.

RAG *(Finds*   If you want to add some truly unique San Francisco designs to your closet, head to RAG, or Residents Apparel Gallery, a co-op shop where around 55 local emerging designers showcase their latest creations. Prices are great, fashions are forward, young, and hip, and if you grab a few pieces, no one at home's going to be able to copy your look. 541 Octavia St. (at Hayes St.). © 415/621-7718. www.ragsf.com.

FOOD

Boulangerie *(Finds*   A bit of Paris on Pine Street, this true-blue bakery sells authentically French creations, from delicious and slightly sour French country wheat bread to rustic-style desserts, including the locally famous *cannele de Bordeaux,* custard baked in a copper mold. And if you're looking for a place to eat Boulangerie bread and pastries, visit their cafes—**Boulange de Polk,** at 2310 Polk St. near Green St. (© 415/345-1107), or **Boulange de Cole,** at 1000 Cole St. at Parnassas St. (© 415/242-2442). Closed Mondays. 2325 Pine St. (at Fillmore St.). © 415/440-0356, ext. 204. www.baybread.com.

Ferry Building Marketplace *(Finds*   A one-stop shop for some of the city's finest edibles, the renovated historic Ferry Building is home to Cowgirl Creamery Artisan Cheese Shop—a coo for cheese lovers—the revered Acme Bread Company, Scharffen Berger Chocolate, the Imperial Tea Court, Peet's Coffee, Recchiuti Confections, and more. There's no better place to load up on the Bay Area's outstanding bounty.

Ferry Building Plaza (at the foot of Market St. at The Embarcadero). © 415/693-0996. www.ferrybuildingmarketplace.com.

Golden Gate Fortune Cookies Co.   This tiny, touristy factory sells fortune cookies hot off the press. You can purchase them in small bags or in bulk, and you can even bring your own messages and watch them fold them into fresh cookies before your eyes. Even if you're not buying, stop in to see how these sugary treats are made (although the staff can get pushy for you to buy). Open daily until 8:30pm. 56 Ross Alley (between Washington and Jackson sts.). © 415/781-3956.

Joseph Schmidt Confections *(Finds*   Here, chocolate takes the shape of exquisite sculptural masterpieces—such as long-stemmed tulips and heart-shaped boxes—that are so beautiful, you'll be hesitant to bite the head off your adorable panda bear. Once you do, however, you'll know why this is the most popular—and reasonably priced—chocolatier in town. 3489 16th St. (at Sanchez St.). ☎ **800/861-8682** or 415/861-8682. www.josephschmidtconfections.com.

Ten Ren Tea Co., Ltd. *(Finds)*   At the Ten Ren Tea Co. shop, you will be offered a steaming cup of tea when you walk in the door. In addition to a selection of almost 50 traditional and herbal teas, the company stocks a collection of cold tea drinks and tea-related paraphernalia, such as pots, cups, and infusers. If you can't make up your mind, take home a mail-order form. The shop is open daily from 9am to 9pm. 949 Grant Ave. (between Washington and Jackson sts.). ☎ **415/362-0656.** www.tentea.com.

GIFTS

Art of China   Amid a wide variety of collectibles, this shop features exquisite, hand-carved Chinese figurines. You'll also find a lovely assortment of ivory beads, bracelets, necklaces, and earrings. Pink-quartz dogs, jade figurines, porcelain vases, cache pots, and blue-and-white barrels suitable for use as table bases are just some of the many items stocked here. 839–843 Grant Ave. (between Clay and Washington sts.). ☎ **415/981-1602.** www.artsofchinasf.com.

Babushka   Located near Fisherman's Wharf, adjacent to The Anchorage mall, Babushka sells only Russian products, most of which are wooden nesting dolls. 333 Jefferson St. (at Leavenworth St.). ☎ **415/673-6740.**

Cost Plus World Market   At the Fisherman's Wharf cable car turntable, Cost Plus is a vast warehouse crammed to the rafters with Chinese baskets, Indian camel bells, Malaysian batik scarves, and innumerable other items from Algeria to Zanzibar. More than 20,000 items from 50 nations, imported directly from their countries of origin, pack this warehouse. There's also a decent wine shop here. It's open Monday through Saturday from 9am to 9pm and Sunday from 10am to 8pm. 2552 Taylor St. (between N. Point and Bay sts.). ☎ **415/928-6200.**

Dandelion *(Finds)*   Tucked in an out-of-the-way location in SoMa is the most wonderful collection of gifts, collectibles, and furnishings. There's something for every taste and budget here, from an excellent collection of teapots, decorative dishes, and gourmet foods to silver, books, cards, and picture frames. Don't miss the Zen-like second floor, with its peaceful furnishings in Indian, Japanese, and Western styles. The store is closed Sunday and Monday except during November and December, when it's open daily. Hours are 10am to 6pm. 55 Potrero Ave. (at Alameda St.). ☎ **415/436-9500.** www.tampopo.com.

Distractions   This is the best of the Haight Street shops selling underground-rave wear, street fashion, and electronica CDs. You'll find pipes, toys, and stickers liberally mixed with lots of cool stuff to look at. 1552 Haight St. (between Ashbury and Clayton sts.). ☎ **415/252-8751.**

Flax   If you go into an art store for a special pencil and come out $300 later, don't go near this shop. Flax has everything you can think of in art and design supplies, an amazing collection of blank bound books, children's art supplies, frames, calendars—you name it. There's a gift for every type of person here, especially you. 1699 Market St. (at Valencia and Gough sts.). ☎ **415/552-2355.** www.flaxart.com.

Good Vibrations   A laypersons' sex-toy, book, and video emporium, Good Vibrations is a women-owned, worker-owned cooperative. Unlike most sex shops, it's not a back-alley business, but a straightforward shop with healthy, open attitudes about human sexuality. It also has a vibrator museum. 603 Valencia St. (at 17th St.). (€) **415/522-5460** or 800/BUY-VIBE (for mail order). www.goodvibes.com. A 2nd location is at 1620 Polk St. (at Sacramento St.; (€) **415/345-0400**), and a 3rd is at 2504 San Pablo Ave., Berkeley ((€) **510/841-8987**).

Kati Koos   Need a little humor in your life? Previously called Smile, this store specializes in whimsical art, furniture, clothing, jewelry, and American crafts guaranteed to make you grin. Closed Sundays. 500 Sutter St. (between Powell and Mason sts.). (€) **415/362-3437**. www.katikoos.com.

SFMOMA MuseumStore *(Finds)*   With an array of artistic cards, books, jewelry, housewares, furniture, knickknacks, and creative tokens of San Francisco, it's virtually impossible not to find something here you'll consider a must-have. (Check out the FogDome!) Aside from being one of the locals' favorite shops, it offers far more tasteful mementos than most Fisherman's Wharf options. Open late (until 9:30pm) on Thursday nights. 151 Third St. (2 blocks south of Market St., across from Yerba Buena Gardens). (€) **415/357-4035**. www.sfmoma.org.

HOUSEWARES/FURNISHINGS

Alabaster *(Finds)*   Any interior designer who knows Biedermeier from Bauhaus knows that this Hayes Valley shop sets local home accessories trends with its collection of high-end must-haves. Their selection includes everything from lighting—antique and modern Alabaster fixtures, Fortuny silk shades, Venetian glass chandeliers—to other home accessories, like one-of-a-kind antiques, body products from Florence, and more. 597 Hayes St. (at Laguna St.). (€) **415/558-0482**. www.alabastersf.com.

Alessi   Italian designer Alberto Alessi, who's known for his whimsical and colorful kitchen-utensil designs, such as his ever-popular spiderlike lemon squeezer, opened a flagship store here. Drop by for everything from gorgeous stainless-steel double boilers to corkscrews shaped like maidens. 424 Sutter St. (at Stockton St.). (€) **415/434-0403**. www.alessi.com.

Big Pagoda Company   When I need to buy a stylish friend a gift, I head to this downtown Asian-influenced design shop for cool, unique, and contemporary finds. Within the bi-level boutique, East meets West and old meets new in the form of anything from an antique Chinese scholar's chair to a new wave table that hints at Ming or Mondrian. Its furniture and glass art is hardly cheap (an antique Tibetan dragonhead goes for $30,000), but you can get fabulous designer martini glasses at $15 a pop. Open Monday through Saturday 10am to 6pm. 310 Sutter St. (at Grant St.). (€) **415/296-8881**. www.bigpagoda.com.

Biordi Art Imports *(Finds)*   Whether you want to decorate your dinner table, color your kitchen, or liven up the living room, Biordi's Italian majolica pottery is the most exquisite and unusual way to do it. The owner has been importing these hand-painted collectibles for 60 years, and every piece is a showstopper. Call for a catalog. They'll ship anywhere. Closed Sundays. 412 Columbus Ave. (at Vallejo St.). (€) **415/392-8096**. www.biordi.com.

Diptyque   If the idea of spending $40 on a candle makes you laugh, this isn't the place for you. But if you're the type willing to throw down good money to scentualize your living space, don't skip this French shop offering dozens of spectacular flaming fragrances. I'm such a fan that every time I went to Paris I'd weigh down my luggage with these 50-hour burners. (Before the horrible exchange rate, that is.) But now I can scoop them up in my own backyard. They also make great gifts. 171 Maiden Lane (near Stockton St.). © **415/402-0600. www.diptyqueusa.com.**

Limn For the latest in Europe's trendsetting and ultramodern furniture and lighting, go straight to SoMa celebrity Limn, which also showcases artworks in its adjoining gallery. 290 Townsend St. (at Fourth St.). © **415/543-5466. www.limn.com.**

Nest *(Finds)* Don't come into Fillmore's cutest French interiors store without your credit cards. Nest carries adorable throws, handmade quilts, must-have slippers and sleepwear, and a number of other things you never knew you needed until now. 2300 Fillmore St. (at Clay St.). © **415/292-6199.**

Propeller *(Finds)* This airy skylight-lit shop is a must-stop for lovers of the latest in ubermodern furniture and home accessories. Owner/designer Lorn Dittfeld hand-picks pieces done by emerging designers from as far away as Sweden, Italy, and Canada as well as a plethora of national newbies. Drop in to lounge on the hippest sofas; grab pretty and practical gifts like ultracool magnetic spice racks; or adorn your home with Bev Hisey's throws and graphic pillows, diamond-cut wood tables by William Earle, or hand-tufted graphic rugs by Angela Adams. 555 Hayes St. (between Laguna and Octavia sts.). © **415/701-7767. www.propeller-sf.com.**

Sue Fisher King *(Finds)* For the ultimate in everything on the traditional side for the tabletop, bedroom, and beyond, head to this exclusive neighborhood boutique known by the society set as the only place to shop. It's filled with items like exquisite table linens, cashmere blankets, towels, china, silver flatware, and more. Closed Sundays. 3067 Sacramento St. (at Baker St.). © **415/922-7276. www.suefisherking.com.**

Sur La Table Cooks should beeline it to this Union Square shop specializing in all things culinary. Its two floors are packed to the rafters with pricey but stylish high-quality pots and pans, utensils, tabletop items, books, and more coupled with an extremely helpful and knowledgeable staff. A second location is at the Ferry Building Marketplace, stall #37 (© **415/262-9970**). 77 Maiden Lane (at Grant St.). © **415/732-7900. www.surlatable.com.**

The Wok Shop This shop has every conceivable implement for Chinese cooking, including woks, brushes, cleavers, circular chopping blocks, dishes, oyster knives, bamboo steamers, and strainers. It also sells a wide range of kitchen utensils, baskets, handmade linens from China, and aprons. 718 Grant Ave. (at Clay St.). © **415/989-3797** or 888/780-7171 for mail order. www.wokshop.com.

Zinc Details *(Finds)* This contemporary furniture and knickknack shop has received accolades everywhere from *Elle Decor Japan* to *Metropolitan Home* to *InStyle* for its amazing collection of glass vases, pendant lights, ceramics from all over the world, and furniture from local craftsmen. A portion of these true works of art is made specifically for the store. While you're in the 'hood, check out their new sister store around the corner at 2410 California St. (© **415/776-9002**), which showcases contemporary designer furniture. 1905 Fillmore St. (between Bush and Pine sts.). © **415/776-2100. www.zinc details.com.**

JEWELRY
De Vera Galleries *(Finds)* Don't come here unless you've got money to spend. Designer Federico de Vera's unique rough-stone jewelry collection, art glass, and vintage knick-knacks are too beautiful to pass up and too expensive to be a painless purchase. Still, if

you're looking for a keepsake, you'll find it here. Closed Sundays and Mondays. 29 Maiden Lane (at Kearny St.). ✆ **415/788-0828.** www.deveraobjects.com.

Dianne's Old & New Estates Many local girls, myself included, get engagement rings from this fantastic little shop featuring top-of-the-line antique jewelry—pendants, diamond rings, necklaces, bracelets, and pearls. For a special gift, check out the collection of platinum wedding and engagement rings and vintage watches. Don't worry if you can't afford it now—the shop offers 1-year interest-free layaway. And, if you buy a ring, they'll send you off with a thank-you bottle of celebration bubbly. 2181A Union St. (at Fillmore St.). ✆ **888/346-7525** or 415/346-7525.www.diannesestatejewelry.com.

Jeanine Payer If you want to buy a trinket that is truly San Franciscan, stop by this boutique hidden on the street level of the beautifully ornate Phelan Building where designer Jeanine Payer showcases gorgeous, handmade contemporary jewelry that she crafts in sterling silver and 18-karat gold five stories above in her studio. All of her pieces, including fabulous baby gifts, sport engraved poetry—and can even be custom done. Sound familiar? Not surprising. Celebrities such as Sheryl Crow, Debra Messing, and Ellen DeGeneres are fans. 760 Market St., Suite 533 (at O'Farrell St.). ✆ **415/788-2414.** www.jeaninepayer.com.

Pearl & Jade Empire The Pearl & Jade Empire has been importing jewelry from all over the world since 1957. It specializes in unusual pearls and jade and offers restringing on the premises as well as boasting a collection of amber from the Baltic Sea. 427 Post St. (between Powell and Mason sts.). ✆ **415/362-0606.** www.pearlempire.com.

Tiffany & Co. Even if you don't have lots of cash with which to buy an exquisite bauble that comes in Tiffany's famous light-blue box, enjoy this renowned store a la Audrey Hepburn in *Breakfast at Tiffany's.* The designer collection features Paloma Picasso, Jean Schlumberger, and Elsa Peretti in both silver and 18-karat gold, and there's an extensive gift collection in sterling, china, and crystal. 350 Post St. (at Powell St.). ✆ **415/781-7000.** www.tiffany.com.

Union Street Goldsmith A showcase for Bay Area goldsmiths, this exquisite shop sells a contemporary collection of fine custom-designed jewelry in platinum and all karats of gold. Many pieces emphasize colored stones. 1909 Union St. (at Laguna St.). ✆ **415/776-8048.** www.unionstreetgoldsmith.com.

MUSIC

Ameoba Records Don't be scared off by the tattooed, pierced, and fierce-looking employees (and other shoppers!) in this beloved new and used record store highlighting indie labels. They're actually more than happy to recommend some great music to you. If you're looking for the latest from Britney, this might not be the store for you (though they *do* have everything), but if you're into interesting music that's not necessarily on every station all the time, check this place out. You can buy, sell and trade in this cavernous, loud Haight Street hot spot. 1855 Haight St. (between Shrader and Stanyan sts.). ✆ **415/831-1200.**

Recycled Records *Finds* Easily one of the best used-record stores in the city, this loud shop in the Haight has cases of used "classic" rock LPs, sheet music, and tour programs. It's open from 10am to 8pm daily. 1377 Haight St. (between Central and Masonic sts.). ✆ **415/626-4075.** www.recycled-records.com.

Streetlight Records   Overstuffed with used music in all three formats, this place is best known for its records and excellent CD collection. It also carries new and used DVDs and computer games. Rock music is cheap, and the money-back guarantee guards against defects. 3979 24th St. (between Noe and Sanchez sts.). ✆ 415/282-3550. www. streetlightrecords.com. A 2nd location is at 2350 Market St., between Castro and Noe sts, ((✆ 415/282-8000).

Virgin Megastore   With thousands of CDs, including an impressive collection of imports, videos, DVDs, a multimedia department, a cafe, and related books, this enormous Union Square store can make any music-lover blow his or her entire vacation fund. It's open Sunday through Thursday from 10am to 11pm and Friday and Saturday from 10am to midnight. 2 Stockton St. (at Market St.). ✆ 415/397-4525.

SAKE
True Sake   Amid woven sea grass flooring, colorful backlit displays, and a so-hip Hayes Valley location are more than 140 varieties of Japanese-produced sake ranging from an $8 300ml bottle of Ohyama to an $180 720ml bottle of Kotsuziami Rojohanaari—which, incidentally, owner Beau Timken (who is on hand to describe each wine), says is available at no other retail store in the U.S. 560 Hayes St. (between Laguna and Octavia sts.). ✆ 415/355.9555. www.truesake.com.

SHOES
Bulo   If you have a fetish for foot fashions, you must check out Bulo, which carries nothing but imported Italian shoes. The selection is small but styles run the gamut, from casual to dressy, reserved to wildly funky. New shipments come in every 3 to 4 weeks, so the selection is ever-changing, eternally hip, and, unfortunately, ever-expensive, with many pairs going for close to $200. Men's and women's store: 437A Hayes St. (at Gough St.). ✆ 415/864-3244. Women's store: across the street, at 418 Hayes St. (✆ 415/255-4939). www.buloshoes.com.

Gimme Shoes   The staff is funky-fashion snobby, the prices are steep, and the European shoes and accessories are utterly chic. 2358 Fillmore St. (at Washington St.). ✆ 415/441-3040. Additional locations are 416 Hayes St. (✆ 415/864-0691) and 50 Grant Ave. (✆ 415/434-9242). www.gimmeshoes.com.

Kenneth Cole   This trendy shop carries high-fashion footwear for men and women. There is also an innovative collection of handbags and small leather goods and accessories. 865 Market St. (in the San Francisco Shopping Centre). ✆ 415/227-4536. www.kennethcole.com. Other shops are at 2078 Union St., at Webster St. (✆ 415/346-2161) and 166 Grant St., at Post St. (✆ 415/981-2653).

Paolo Shoes   This Italian import store is run by owner Paolo Iantorno, who actually designs the shoes for his hipster shops. If gorgeous, handcrafted, colorful shoes are what you're looking for, this is the shop for you. You can get your low-heeled slip-ons here—this store features men's and women's footwear and bags—but they might be in silver python. Check out the men's perforated orange slip-ons—not for the faint of heart or fashion-modest. You might not even mind that many shoes are upwards of 200 bucks when you realize that Paolo's women's shoes are so sexy and comfortable, you won't want to take them off. 524 Hayes St. ✆ 415/552-4580. A 2nd location is at 2000 Fillmore St. (✆ 415/771-1944). www.paoloshoes.com.

SHOPPING CENTERS & COMPLEXES

The Anchorage   This touristy waterfront mall has close to 35 stores that offer everything from music boxes to home furnishings; street performers entertain during open hours. This is not a stop for staples, but more for tourist trinkets. 2800 Leavenworth St. (between Beach and Jefferson sts. on Fisherman's Wharf). ℂ 415/775-6000.

The Cannery at Del Monte Square   This attractive complex was built in 1907 as a Del Monte fruit-canning plant and converted to a mall in the 1960s. It contains 30 plus unimpressive shops, a ceramic studio and gallery, and several restaurants including **Jack's Cannery Bar** (ℂ 415/931-6400). I'd recommend skipping The Cannery completely, except it's now got something great going for it: Famed wine country gourmet grocer and deli **The Oakville Grocery** (ℂ 415/614-1600) has opened here, and this is now the spot to grab an awesome picnic lunch (think sandwiches, cheeses, charcuterie, and brick oven pizzas) as well as excellent edible gifts. 2801 Leavenworth St. (between Beach and Jefferson sts.). ℂ 415/771-3112. www.delmontesquare.com.

Crocker Galleria   Modeled after Milan's Galleria Vittorio Emanuele, this glass-domed, three-level pavilion, about 3 blocks east of Union Square, features around 40 high-end shops with expensive and classic designer creations. Fashions include Aricie lingerie, Gianni Versace, and Polo/Ralph Lauren. Closed Sundays. 50 Post St. (at Kearny St.). ℂ 415/393-1505. www.shopatgalleria.com.

Ghirardelli Square   This former chocolate factory is one of the city's quaintest shopping malls and most popular landmarks. It dates from 1864, when it served as a factory making Civil War uniforms, but it's best known as the former chocolate and spice factory of Domingo Ghirardelli (say "Gear-a-deli"). A clock tower, an exact replica of the one at France's Château de Blois, crowns the complex. Inside the tower, on the mall's plaza level, is the fun Ghirardelli soda fountain. It still makes and sells small amounts of chocolate, but the big draw is the old-fashioned ice-cream parlor. If you're coming to shop, think again: It's pretty lame in that department, but you can dine decently at Ana Mandara (p. 132). Main plaza shops' and restaurants' hours are 10am to 6pm Sunday through Thursday and 10am to 9pm Friday and Saturday, with extended hours during the summer. 900 North Point St. (at Polk St.). ℂ 415/775-5500. www. ghirardellisq.com.

PIER 39 *Overrated*   This bayside tourist trap also happens to have stunning views. To residents, that pretty much wraps up PIER 39—an expensive spot where out-of-towners go to waste money on worthless souvenirs and greasy fast food. For vacationers, though, PIER 39 does have some redeeming qualities—fresh crab (in season), playful sea lions, phenomenal views, and plenty of fun for the kids. If you want to get to know the real San Francisco, skip the cheesy T-shirt shops and limit your time here to 1 afternoon, if at all. Located at Beach St. and The Embarcadero.

Westfield San Francisco Centre   Opened in 1988, this $140-million complex is one of the few vertical malls (multilevel rather than sprawling) in the United States. Its most attractive features are the four-story spiral escalators that circle up to Nord-strom (p. 210) and the nine-story atrium covered by a retractable skylight. More than 135 specialty shops include Abercrombie & Fitch, Ann Taylor, bebe, Benetton, Foot-locker, J.Crew, and Victoria's Secret. In 2006, the center will expand to include a Bloomingdale's department store and a Century movie theater. 865 Market St. (at Fifth St.). ℂ 415/495-5656. www.westfield.com.

TOYS

The Chinatown Kite Shop   This shop's playful assortment of flying objects includes attractive fish kites, windsocks, hand-painted Chinese paper kites, wood-and-paper biplanes, pentagonal kites, and do-it-yourself kite kits, all of which make great souvenirs or decorations. Computer-designed stunt kites have two or four control lines to manipulate loops and dives. Open daily from 10am to 8pm. 717 Grant Ave. (between Clay and Sacramento sts.). ℂ 415/391-8217. www.chinatownkite.com.

TRAVEL GOODS

Flight 001   Jetsetters zoom into this space-shuttle-like showroom for hip travel accessories. Check out the sleek luggage, "security friendly" manicure sets, and other mid-air must-haves. 525 Hayes St. (between Laguna and Octavia sts.). ℂ 415/487-1001. www. flight001.com.

VINTAGE CLOTHING

Aardvark's   One of San Francisco's largest secondhand clothing dealers, Aardvark's has seemingly endless racks of shirts, pants, dresses, skirts, and hats from the past 30 years. It's open daily from 11am to 7pm. 1501 Haight St. (at Ashbury St.). ℂ 415/621-3141.

Buffalo Exchange   This large and newly expanded storefront on upper Haight Street is crammed with racks of antique and new fashions from the 1960s, 1970s, and 1980s. It stocks everything from suits and dresses to neckties, hats, handbags, and jewelry. Buffalo Exchange anticipates some of the hottest new street fashions. A second shop is at 1210 Valencia St., at 24th St. (ℂ 415/647-8332). 1555 Haight St. (between Clayton and Ashbury sts.). ℂ 415/431-7733. www.buffaloexchange.com.

Good Byes *(Finds*   One the best new- and used-clothes stores in San Francisco, Good Byes carries only high-quality clothing and accessories, including an exceptional selection of men's fashions at unbelievably low prices (for example, $350 pre-owned shoes for $35). Women's wear is in a separate boutique across the street. 3464 Sacramento St. and 3483 Sacramento St. (between Laurel and Walnut sts.). ℂ 415/346-6388. www.goodbyessf.com.

La Rosa   On a street packed with vintage-clothing shops, this is one of the more upscale options. Since 1978, it has featured a selection of high-quality, dry-cleaned secondhand goods. Formal suits and dresses are its specialty, but you'll also find sport coats, slacks, and shoes. The more moderately priced sister store, **Held Over,** is located at 1543 Haight St., near Ashbury (ℂ 415/864-0818), and their discount store, **Clothes Contact,** is located at 473 Valencia St., at 16th St. (ℂ 415/621-3212). 1711 Haight St. (at Cole St.). ℂ 415/668-3744.

WINE

Wine Club San Francisco *(Value*   The Wine Club is a discount warehouse that offers bargains on more than 1,200 domestic and foreign wines. Bottles cost between $4 and $1,100. 953 Harrison St. (between Fifth and Sixth sts.). ℂ 415/512-9086.

10

San Francisco After Dark

For a city with fewer than a million inhabitants, San Francisco boasts an impressive after-dark scene. Dozens of piano bars and top-notch lounges augment a lively dance-club culture, and skyscraper lounges offer dazzling city views. The city's arts scene is also extraordinary: The opera is justifiably world renowned, the ballet is on its toes, the Asian Art Museum has settled into its new Civic Center digs, and theaters are high in both quantity and quality. In short, there's always something going on, so get out there.

For up-to-date nightlife information, turn to the *San Francisco Weekly* (www.sfweekly.com) and the *San Francisco Bay Guardian* (www.sfbg.com), both of which run comprehensive listings. They are available free at bars and restaurants and from street-corner boxes all around the city. *Where* (www.wheresf.com), a free tourist-oriented monthly, also lists programs and performance times; it's available in most of the city's finer hotels. The Sunday edition of the *San Francisco Chronicle* features a "Datebook" section, printed on pink paper, with information on and listings of the week's events. If you have Internet access, it's a good idea to check out www.citysearch.com or www.sfstation.com for the latest in bars, clubs, and events. And if you want to secure seats at a hot-ticket event, either buy well in advance or contact the concierge of your hotel and see if they can swing something for you.

Tix Bay Area (aka **TIX**; ⓒ 415/433-7827; www.tixbayarea.org) sells half-price tickets on the day of performance and full-price tickets in advance to select Bay Area cultural and sporting events. TIX is also a Ticketmaster outlet and sells Gray Line tours and transportation passes. Tickets are primarily sold in person with some half-price tickets available on their website. To find out which shows they are selling half-price tickets for, call their info line or check out their website. A service charge, ranging from $1.75 to $6, is levied on each ticket depending on its full price. You can pay with cash, traveler's checks, Visa, MasterCard, American Express, or Discover Card with photo ID. TIX, located on Powell Street between Geary and Post streets, is open Tuesday through Thursday from 11am to 6pm, Friday from 11am to 7pm, Saturday from 10am to 7pm, and Sunday from 10am to 3pm. *Note:* Half-price tickets go on sale at 11am.

You can also get tickets to most theater and dance events through **City Box Office,** 180 Redwood St., Suite 100, between Golden Gate and McAllister streets off Van Ness Avenue (ⓒ 415/392-4400; www.cityboxoffice.com). MasterCard and Visa are accepted.

Tickets.com (ⓒ 800/225-2277; www.tickets.com) sells computer-generated tickets (with a hefty service charge of $3–$19 per ticket!) to concerts, sporting events, plays, and special events. **Ticketmaster** (ⓒ 415/421-TIXS; www.ticketmaster.com) also offers advance ticket purchases (also with a service charge).

For information on local theater, check out www.bayareatheatre.org.

For information on major league baseball, pro basketball, pro and college football, and horse racing, see the "Spectator Sports" section of chapter 7, beginning on p. 189.

And don't forget that this isn't New York: Bars close at 2am, so get an early start if you want a full night on the town in San Francisco.

1 The Performing Arts

Special concerts and performances take place in San Francisco year-round. **San Francisco Performances,** 500 Sutter St., Suite 710 (© **415/398-6449;** www.performances. org), has brought acclaimed artists to the Bay Area for 27 years. Shows run the gamut from chamber music to dance to jazz. Performances are in several venues, including the Herbst Theater and the Yerba Buena Center for the Arts. The season runs from late September to June. Tickets cost from $12 to $50 and are available through **City Box Office** (© **415/392-2545**) or through the San Francisco Performances website.

CLASSICAL MUSIC

Philharmonia Baroque Orchestra   This orchestra of baroque, classical, and "early Romantic" music performs in San Francisco and all around the Bay Area. The season lasts September through April. Performing in Herbst Theater, 401 Van Ness Ave. © **415/392-4400** (box office) or 415/252-1288 (administrative offices). www.philharmonia.org. Tickets $29–$67.

San Francisco Symphony   Founded in 1911, the internationally respected San Francisco Symphony has long been an important part of the city's cultural life under such legendary conductors as Pierre Monteux and Seiji Ozawa. In 1995, Michael Tilson Thomas took over from Herbert Blomstedt; he has led the orchestra to new heights and crafted an exciting repertoire of classical and modern music. The season runs September through June. Summer symphony activities include a Summer Festival and a Summer in the City series. Tickets are very hard to come by, but if you're desperate, you can usually pick up a few outside the hall the night of the concert. Also, the box office occasionally has a few last minute tickets. Performing at Davies Symphony Hall, 201 Van Ness Ave. (at Grove St.). © **415/864-6000** (box office). www.sfsymphony.org. Tickets $12–$107.

OPERA

In addition to San Francisco's major opera company, you might check out the amusing **Pocket Opera,** 469 Bryant St. (© **415/972-8930;** www.pocketopera.org). From early March to mid-July, the comic company stages farcical performances of well-known operas in English. The staging is intimate and informal, without lavish costumes and sets. The cast ranges from 3 to 16 players, supported by a chamber orchestra. The rich repertoire includes such works as *Don Giovanni, The Barber of Seville,* and over 80 other operas. Performances are Fridays at 7:30pm, throughout the day on Saturdays, and Sundays at 2pm. Call the box office for complete information, location (which varies), and showtimes. Tickets cost from $18 (students) to $35.

San Francisco Opera   The San Francisco Opera was the second municipal opera in the United States and is one of the city's cultural icons. Brilliantly balanced casts may feature celebrated stars like Frederica Von Stade and Plácido Domingo along with promising newcomers and regular members in productions that range from traditional to avant-garde. All productions have English supertitles. The season starts in September, lasts 14 weeks, takes a break for a few months, and then picks up again in

June and July. During the interim winter period, future opera stars are featured in showcases and recitals. Performances are held most evenings, except Monday, with matinees on Sunday. Tickets go on sale as early as June for subscribers and August for the general public, and the best seats sell out quickly. Unless Domingo is in town, some less coveted seats are usually available until curtain time. War Memorial Opera House, 301 Van Ness Ave. (at Grove St.). ☏ 415/864-3330 (box office). www.sfopera.com. Tickets $24–$235; standing room $10 cash only; student rush $15 cash only.

THEATER

American Conservatory Theater (A.C.T.) *Finds*   The Tony Award–winning American Conservatory Theater made its debut in 1967 and quickly established itself as the city's premier resident theater group and one of the nation's best. The A.C.T. season runs September through July and features both classic and experimental works. Its home is the fabulous **Geary Theater,** a national historic landmark that is regarded as one of America's finest performance spaces. The 2006–2007 season marks A.C.T.'s 40th anniversary; they haven't been resting on their laurels. In their 4-decade history, they've reached a combined audience of seven million people. Performing at the Geary Theater, 415 Geary St. (at Mason St.). ☏ 415/749-2ACT. www.act-sf.org. Tickets $11–$75.

Eureka Theatre Company   Eureka houses contemporary performances throughout the year, usually Wednesday through Sunday. Check their website or call the theater for information on upcoming shows and how to purchase tickets (but be aware: Since they don't produce the shows themselves, they won't take reservations for any shows at the theater or sell them online). 215 Jackson St. (between Battery and Front sts.). ☏ 415/788-7469. www.eurekatheatre.org. Ticket prices vary by company but are generally $17–$30.

Lorraine Hansberry Theatre   San Francisco's top African-American theater group performs in a 300-seat state-of-the-art theater. It mounts special adaptations from literature along with contemporary dramas, classics, and music. The year 2006 marks the theater's 25th anniversary and with it will likely come some special performances. Phone for dates and programs. Performing at 620 Sutter St. (at Mason St.). ☏ 415/474-8800. www.lhtsf.org. Tickets $25–$32.

The Magic Theatre   The highly acclaimed Magic Theatre, celebrating its 40th season in 2006, is a major West Coast company dedicated to presenting the works of new plays; over the years it has nurtured the talents of such luminaries as Sam Shepard and David Mamet. Shepard's Pulitzer Prize–winning play *Buried Child* had its premiere here, as did Mamet's *Dr. Faustus.* The season usually runs from October through June; performances are held Tuesday through Sunday. A perk for anyone who's been in previous years: In 2005 and 2006 they redecorated the lobby and added new seats in one of the theaters. Performing at Building D, Fort Mason Center, Marina Blvd. (at Buchanan St.). ☏ 415/441-8822. www.magictheatre.org. Tickets $20–$40; discounts for students, educators, and seniors.

Theatre Rhinoceros   Founded in 1977, this was America's first (and remains its foremost) theater ensemble devoted solely to works addressing gay, lesbian, bisexual, and transgender issues. The company presents main-stage shows and studio productions of new and classic works each year. The theater is 1 block east of the 16th Street/Mission BART station. 2926 16th St. ☏ 415/861-5079. www.therhino.org. Tickets $15–$35.

DANCE

In addition to the local companies, top traveling troupes like the Joffrey Ballet and the American Ballet Theatre make regular appearances in San Francisco. Primary modern

San Francisco After Dark

American Conservatory
  Theater (A.C.T.) **55**
Bambuddha Lounge **20**
BATS Improv **1**
Beach Blanket Babylon **34**
Bimbo's 365 Club **29**
Biscuits and Blues **56**
The Bliss Bar **8**
The Boom Boom Room **5**
Bottom of the Hill **73**
The Bubble Lounge **44**
Buena Vista Café **26**
The Café **9**
Cafe du Nord **11**
Caffè Greco **35**
Caffè Trieste **36**
Carnelian Room **46**
Castro Theatre **9**
Center for the Performing
  Arts at Yerba Buena
  Center **64**
The Cinch Saloon **24**
Cityscape **53**
Cobb's Comedy Club **30**
Cowell Theater **1**
Davies Symphony Hall **17**
The Eagle Tavern **70**
Edinburgh Castle **22**
Empire Plush Room **50**
The Endup **65**
Eos **74**
Equinox **50**
Eureka Theatre **41**
The Factory **62**
The Fillmore **6**
First Crush **54**
Fort Mason Center **1**
Geary Theater **55**
Gold Dust Lounge **58**
Gordon Biersch Brewery
  Restaurant **61**
Grant & Green Saloon **33**
Great American
  Music Hall **21**
Greens Sports Bar **25**
Harry Denton's
  Starlight Room **59**
Herbst Theater **19**
Holy Cow **69**
Jazz at Pearl's **37**
Kimo's **23**
Levende Lounge **14**

Li Po Cocktail Lounge **40**
London Wine Bar **45**
Lone Star Saloon **67**
Lorraine Hansberry
  Theatre **49**
Lou's Pier 47 Club **28**
The Magic Theatre **1**
Matrix Fillmore **3**
Metro **10**
The Mint
  Karaoke Lounge **15**
The Monkey Club **72**
Nectar Wine Lounge **2**
ODC Theatre **13**
Perry's **4**
Philharmonia Baroque
  Orchestra **19**
Pied Piper Bar **60**
Pier 23 **32**
Pocket Opera **16**
Punch Line
  Comedy Club **42**
Rasselas **6**
The Red Room **51**
Red Vic **75**
The Redwood Room **52**
Roxie **12**
Ruby Skye **57**
The Saloon **36**
San Francisco Ballet **18**
San Francisco
  Brewing Company **39**
San Francisco Opera **18**
San Francisco
  Symphony **17**
Slim's **68**
Spec's **38**
The Stud **66**
Teatro ZinZanni **31**
Theatre Rhinoceros **71**
ThirstyBear
  Brewing Company **63**
The Tonga Room
  & Hurricane Bar **47**
Top of the Mark **48**
Toronado **7**
Tosca **39**
Twin Peaks Tavern **9**
Vesuvio **37**
Wish Bar **69**
Zeitgeist **71**

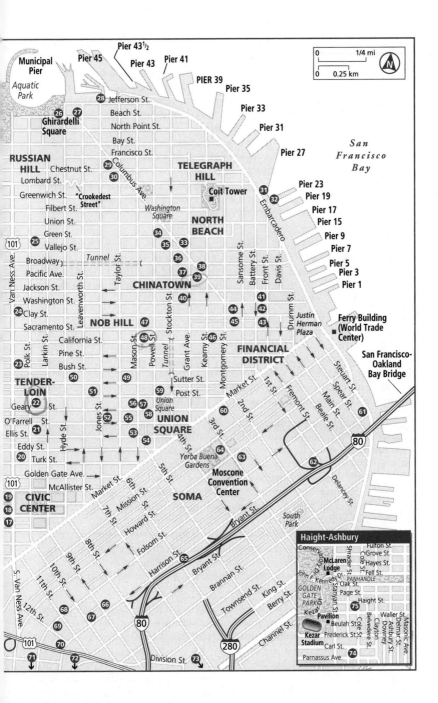

Municipal Pier

Aquatic Park

Pier 45 Pier 43½ Pier 43 Pier 41

PIER 39 Pier 35

Pier 33

Pier 31

Pier 27

San Francisco Bay

㉘ Jefferson St.

Beach St.

North Point St.

㉖ ㉗ **Ghirardelli Square**

Bay St.

Francisco St.

Pier 23 Pier 19

Pier 17

Pier 15

Pier 9

Pier 7

Pier 5 Pier 3

Pier 1

RUSSIAN HILL Chestnut St.

TELEGRAPH HILL

Lombard St.

Greenwich St. **"Crookedest Street"**

Filbert St.

Union St.

㉙ ㉚ Columbus Ave.

Coit Tower

NORTH BEACH

Washington Square

㉛ ㉜ Embarcadero

Green St.

㉕ Vallejo St.

Broadway *Tunnel* Taylor St.

Pacific Ave.

Jackson St.

㉞ ㉟ ㉝

㊱

㊲ ㊳

㊳

CHINATOWN

Sansome St. Battery St. Front St. Davis St.

㉑㉑ Van Ness Ave.

101

Washington St.

㉔ Clay St.

Sacramento St.

NOB HILL ㊼

㊸

Stockton St.

㊵

Ferry Building (World Trade Center)

Justin Herman Plaza

㊱ ㊲ ㊴

㊹

㊺

㊷

Leavenworth St.

California St.

Pine St.

㉓ Bush St.

Polk St. Larkin St.

㊿

㊾

Mason St. Powell St. *Tunnel* Grant Ave.

Kearny St. Montgomery St.

㊻

FINANCIAL DISTRICT

Drumm St.

San Francisco–Oakland Bay Bridge

TENDER-LOIN

㉒ Geary St.

O'Farrell St.

㉑ Ellis St.

Eddy St.

㉒

Hyde St.

㊾

Sutter St.

㊾

Post St.

Union Square

㊾ ㊼ ㊽

㊾

㊸

UNION SQUARE

Jones St.

Market St. 1st St. 2nd St.

Fremont St. Beale St. Main St.

Steuart St. Spear St.

㊱

㊱ ㉚ San Francisco

80

㉞ Turk St.

Golden Gate Ave.

101

McAllister St.

㉚

㉙ **CIVIC CENTER**

㉘

㉗

㉚ ㊵ ㊷

㊳

4th St. 3rd St. 5th St.

Yerba Buena Gardens

㊽

㊸

Moscone Convention Center

SOMA

Market St. 6th St. Mission St. 7th St. Howard St. Folsom St. 8th St.

Bryant St.

South Park

Delancey St.

80

9th St. 10th St. 11th St. 12th St.

S. Van Ness Ave.

Harrison St.

Bryant St.

Brannan St.

Townsend St. King St. Berry St.

㊽ ㊻

㊼

㊸

80

101

㊱

㊲

Division St.

㊴

280

Channel St.

Haight-Ashbury

Conservatory Fulton St.

McLaren Lodge

Grove St.

Hayes St.

Shrader St. Cole St.

John F. Kennedy Dr. **PANHANDLE** Oak St.

GOLDEN GATE PARK Stanyan St.

Page St.

Haight St.

㊵

Kezar

Pavilion

Beulah St.

Kezar Stadium Frederick St.

Cole St. Belvedere St. Clayton St. Ashbury St. Downey St.

Waller St. Delmar St.

Masonic Ave.

Carl St.

㊴

Parnassus Ave.

225

(*Tips*) **Dinner Party**

Hungry for dinner and a damned good time? It ain't cheap, but Teatro ZinZanni is a delightfully rollicking ride of food, whimsy, drama, and song within a stunningly elegant 1926 spiegelten tent on The Embarcadero. Part musical theater and part comedy show, the 3-hour dinner theater includes a surprisingly decent five-course meal served by dozens of performers who weave both the audience and astounding physical acts (think Cirque du Soleil) into their wacky and playful world. Anyone in need of a night of giggles should definitely book a table here. Shows are held Wednesday through Sunday and tickets are $110 to $135 including dinner. The tent is located at Pier 29 on The Embarcadero at Battery Street. Call (✆ **415/438-2668** or see www.zinzanni.org for more details.

dance spaces include the **Cowell Theater,** at Fort Mason Center, Marina Boulevard at Buchanan Street (✆ **415/345-7575;** www.fortmason.org/performingarts), and the **ODC Theatre,** 3153 17th St., at Shotwell Street in the Mission District (✆ **415/863-9834;** www.odcdance.org). Check the local papers for schedules or contact the theater box offices for more information.

San Francisco Ballet   Founded in 1933, the San Francisco Ballet is the oldest professional ballet company in the United States and is regarded as one of the country's finest. It performs an eclectic repertoire of full-length, neoclassical and contemporary ballets. The Repertory Season generally runs February through May; the company performs the *Nutcracker* in December. The San Francisco Ballet Orchestra accompanies most performances. War Memorial Opera House, 301 Van Ness Ave. (at Grove St.). (✆ **415/865-2000** for tickets and information. www.sfballet.org. Tickets $8–$199.

2 Comedy & Cabaret

BATS Improv ✷ (*Finds*)   Combining improvisation with competition, BATS performs hilarious improvisational tournaments in which teams of actors compete against each other in scenes, songs, and games, based on suggestions from the audience. There are also long-form shows throughout the year with improvisations of movies, musicals, and even Shakespeare; audience members supply suggestions for titles and plot points, and characters and dialogue are then made up and performed immediately onstage. Main Company shows are Fridays and Saturdays at 8pm; student performance ensemble shows on Sundays at 7pm. Reservations and discount tickets available through their website. Remaining tickets are sold at the box office the night of the show. Performing at Bayfront Theatre at the Fort Mason Center, Building B #350, 3rd floor. (✆ **415/474-8935.** www.improv.org. Tickets $5–$15.

Beach Blanket Babylon ✷✷ (*Moments*)   A San Francisco tradition, *Beach Blanket Babylon* evolved from Steve Silver's Rent-a-Freak service—a group of "party guests" extraordinaire who hired themselves out as a "cast of characters" complete with fabulous costumes and sets, props, and gags. After their act caught on, it moved into the Savoy-Tivoli, a North Beach bar. By 1974, the audience had grown too large for the facility, and *Beach Blanket* has been at the 400-seat Club Fugazi ever since. The show is a comedic musical send-up that is best known for outrageous costumes and oversize headdresses. It's been playing for over 30 years, and almost every performance sells out. The show is updated often enough that locals still attend. Those under 21 are welcome at both Sunday matinees (2 and 5pm), when no alcohol is served; photo ID is required for evening performances. Write for weekend tickets at least 3 weeks in advance, or get them through their website or by calling their box office. *Note:* Only a handful of tickets per show are assigned seating; all other tickets are within specific sections depending on price, but seating is first-come, first-seated within that section. Performances are Wednesday and Thursday at 8pm, Friday and Saturday at 7 and 10pm, and Sunday at 2 and 5pm. At Club Fugazi, Beach Blanket Babylon Blvd., 678 Green St. (between Powell St. and Columbus Ave.). *C* **415/421-4222**. www.beachblanketbabylon.com. Tickets $25–$77.

Cobb's Comedy Club   Cobb's features such national headliners as Joe Rogan, Brian Regan, and Jake Johannsen. Comedy reigns Wednesday through Sunday, including a 15-comedian All-Pro Wednesday showcase (a 3-hr. marathon). Cobb's is open to those 18 and over, and occasionally to kids 16 and 17 when accompanied by a parent or legal guardian (call ahead). Shows are held Wednesday, Thursday, and Sunday at 8pm, Friday and Saturday at 8 and 10:15pm. 915 Columbus Ave. (at Lombard St.). *C* **415/928-4320**. www.cobbscomedy.com. Cover $15–$30. 2-beverage minimum.

Punch Line Comedy Club   Adjacent to The Embarcadero One office building, this is the largest comedy nightclub in the city. Three-person shows with top national and local talent are featured here Tuesday through Saturday. Showcase night is Sunday, when 15 comics take the mic. There's an all-star showcase or a special event on Monday. Shows are Sunday through Thursday at 8pm, Friday and Saturday at 8 and 10pm (18 and over; 2-drink minimum). They serve a full menu Thursday through Saturday (think wings, chicken sandwiches, and curiously, ravioli) and pizzas, appetizers and salads Sunday through Wednesday. 444 Battery St. (between Washington and Clay sts.), plaza level. *C* **415/397-4337** or 415/397-7573 for recorded information. www.punchlinecomedyclub.com. Cover Mon $5; Tues–Sat $5–$30; Sun $7.50.

3 The Club & Music Scene

The greatest legacy from the 1960s is the city's continued tradition of live entertainment and music, which explains the great variety of clubs and music enjoyed by San Francisco. The hippest dance places are South of Market Street (SoMa), in former warehouses; the artsy bohemian scene centers are in the Mission; and the most popular cafe culture is still in North Beach.

Note: The club and music scene is always changing, often outdating recommendations before the ink can dry on a page. Most of the venues below are promoted as different clubs on various nights of the week, each with its own look, sound, and style. Discount passes and club announcements are often available at clothing stores and other shops along upper Haight Street.

Tips Club-Hopping Tour

If you prefer to let someone else take the lead (and the driver's seat) for a night out, contact **3 Babes and a Bus** (*C* **800/414-0158**; www.threebabes.com). The nightclub tour company (the head babe is a stockbroker by day) will take you and a gaggle of 20- to 40-something partyers (mostly single women) out on the town, skipping lines and cover charges, for $35 per person.

Tips **Scope-a-Scene**

The local newspapers won't direct you to the city's underground club scene, nor will they advise you which of the dozens of clubs are truly hot. To get dialed in, check out reviews from the ravers themselves at www.sfstation.com. The far more commercial **Club Line** (© **415/339-8686;** www.sfclubs.com) offers up-to-date schedules for the city's larger dance venues.

Drink prices at most bars, clubs, and cafes range from about $3.50 to $9, unless otherwise noted.

ROCK & BLUES CLUBS

In addition to the following listings, see "Dance Clubs," below, for (usually) live, danceable rock.

Bimbo's 365 Club 🦋🦋   Originally located on Market Street when it opened in 1931, this North Beach live destination is a fabulous spot to catch outstanding live rock and jazz (think Chris Isaak and the Brian Setzer Orchestra) and dance amid glamorous surroundings. Grab tickets in advance at the box office, which is open Monday through Friday, 10am to 4pm. 1025 Columbus Ave. (at Chestnut St.). © **415/474-0365.** www.bimbos365club.com.

Biscuits and Blues   With a crisp, blow-your-eardrums-out sound system, New Orleans–speak-easy (albeit commercial) appeal, and a nightly lineup of live, national acts, there's no better place to muse the blues than this basement-cum-nightclub. From 7pm on, they serve drink specials, along with their signature fried chicken, namesake moist, flaky biscuits, some new small-plate entrees dubbed "Southern tapas," and a newly expanded wine list. Menu items range from $7.95 to $17. 401 Mason (at Geary St.). © **415/292-2583.** www.biscuitsandblues.com. Cover (during performances) $10–$20.

The Boom Boom Room *Finds*   The late John Lee Hooker and his partner Alex Andreas bought this Western Addition club several years back and used Hooker's star power to pull in some of the best blues bands in the country (even the Stones showed up for an unannounced jam session). Though it changed focus and is now a roots music oriented club, it's still a fun, dark, small, cramped, and steamy joint where you can hear good live tunes—ranging from New Orleans funk, soul, and new wave, to trance jazz, live drum 'n' bass, electronica, house, and more—7 nights a week until 2am. If you're going to The Fillmore (see below) to see a band, stop by here first for a drink and come back after your show for more great music. The neighborhood's a bit rough, so be sure to park in the underground lot across the street. 1601 Fillmore St. (at Geary Blvd.). © **415/673-8000.** www.boomboomblues.com. Cover varies from free to $15.

Bottom of the Hill *Value*   Voted one of the best places to hear live rock in the city by the *San Francisco Bay Guardian,* this popular neighborhood club attracts a diverse crowd ranging from rockers to real-estate salespeople; it also offers tons of all-ages shows. The main attraction is an eclectic range of live music almost every night (focusing on indie punk with the occasional country band thrown in), but the club also offers pretty good burgers, a bar menu, and outdoor seating on the back patio Wednesday through Friday from 4pm to 2am, Saturday through Tuesday 8:30pm to 2am. Happy hour runs Wednesday to Friday from 4 to 7pm. 1233 17th St. (at Missouri St.). © **415/621-4455.** www.bottomofthehill.com. Cover $6–$12.

Empire Plush Room *(Finds* San Francisco is woefully short on cabaret and jazz venues, but thanks to the Plush Room, there's still one swank little boutique establishment that lures national talent on stage. Check out their schedule and perhaps you'll get to catch acts such as Paula West, Dixie Carter, Maude Magart, Jane Oliver or others doing their classic and under-celebrated thing. Come thirsty: There's a two-drink minimum. In the York Hotel, 940 Sutter St. (between Hyde and Leavenworth sts.). ℭ **415/885-2800.** www.empireplushroom.com. Tickets $20–$55. 2 drink minimum.

The Fillmore *(Finds* Made famous by promoter Bill Graham in the 1960s, The Fillmore showcases big names in a moderately sized standing room only space. Check listings in papers, call the theater, or visit their website for information on upcoming events. And if you make it to a show, check out the fabulous collection of vintage concert posters chronicling the hall's history. 1805 Geary Blvd. (at Fillmore St.). ℭ **415/346-6000.** www.thefillmore.com. Tickets $17–$45.

Grant & Green Saloon The atmosphere at this historic North Beach dive bar is not that special, but Mondays feature jazz, Tuesdays are DJ and karaoke, and the local bands on Thursday through Saturday are decent. All in all, the space is an all-around great place to let your hair down. 1371 Grant Ave. (at Green St.). ℭ **415/693-9565.** www.grant andgreen.com.

Great American Music Hall *⋘* Built in 1907 as a restaurant/bordello, the Great American Music Hall is likely one of the most gorgeous rock venues you'll encounter. With ornately carved balconies, frescoed ceilings, marble columns, and huge, hanging light fixtures, you won't know whether to marvel at the structure or watch the acts, which have ranged from Duke Ellington and Sarah Vaughan to Arctic Monkeys, The Radiators, and She Wants Revenge. All shows are all ages (6 and up) so you can bring your family, too. You can buy a ticket for just the show and order bar snacks (such as nachos, black bean and cheese flautas, burgers, and sandwiches) or one that includes a complete dinner (an extra $19.95), which changes nightly but always includes a salad and choice of meat, fish, or veggie entree. Alas, you can't buy your ticket via telephone, but you can download a form from their website and fax it to **415/885-5075** with your Visa or MasterCard info; there is a service charge of $2 per ticket. You can also stop by the box office to purchase tickets directly ($1 service charge), or buy them at virtuous.com or Tickets.com (ℭ **800/225-2277**). Valet parking is available for selects shows; check website for additional parking information. 859 O'Farrell (between Polk and Larkin sts.). ℭ **415/885-0750;** www.musichallsf.com. Ticket prices and starting times vary; call or check website for individual show information.

Lou's Pier 47 Club You won't find many locals in the place, but Lou's happens to be good, old-fashioned fun. It's a casual spot where you can relax with Cajun seafood (downstairs) and live blues bands (upstairs) nightly. A vacation attitude makes the place one of the more, um, jovial spots near the wharf. There's a $3 to $5 cover for bands that play between 4 and 8pm and a $3 to $10 cover for bands that play between 8 or 9pm and midnight or 1am. 300 Jefferson St. (at Jones St.). ℭ **415/771-5687.** www.lous pier47.com. Cover $5–$10.

Pier 23 If there's one good-time destination that's an anchor for San Francisco's party people, it's The Embarcadero's Pier 23. Part ramshackle patio spot and part dance floor with a heavy dash of dive bar, here it's all about fun for a startlingly diverse clientele (including a one-time visit by Bill Clinton!). The well-worn box of a restaurant with tented patio is a prime sunny-day social spot for white collars, but on weekends, it's a straight-up people zoo where every age and persuasion coexist more peacefully than the cast in a McDonald's commercial. Expect to boogie down shoulder-to-shoulder to 1980s hits and leave with a contagious feel-good vibe. Pier 23, at The Embarcadero (at Battery St.). ℂ 415/362-5125. www.pier23cafe.com. Cover $5–$10 during performances.

The Saloon   An authentic gold rush survivor, this North Beach dive is the oldest bar in the city. Popular with both bikers and daytime pinstripers, it schedules live blues nightly and afternoons Friday through Sunday. 1232 Grant Ave. (at Columbus St.). ℂ 415/989-7666. Cover $5–$10 Fri–Sat.

Slim's   Co-owned by musician Boz Scaggs, this glitzy restaurant and bar serves California cuisine and seats 200, but its usually standing room only during almost nightly shows ranging from performers of homegrown rock, jazz, blues, and alternative music. An added bonus for the musically inclined family: All ages are always welcome. Call or check their website for a schedule; hot bands sell out in advance. 333 11th St. (at Folsom St.). ℂ 415/522-0333. www.slims-sf.com. Cover free to $30.

JAZZ & LATIN CLUBS

Cafe du Nord *Finds*   Although it's been around since 1907, this basement supper club is rightfully self-proclaimed as the place for a "slightly lurid indie pop scene set in a beautiful old speakeasy." It's also where you'll find an eclectic (and usually younger) crowd that flocks here to linger at the front room's 40-foot mahogany bar or dine on the likes of phyllo-wrapped prawns with romesco sauce or sip cocktails at the back room tables—while listening to national indie rock bands like Gomez and Arab Strap, and old school acts like Frank Black and the Pixies. 2170 Market St. (at Sanchez St.). ℂ 415/861-5016. www.cafedunord.com. Cover $5–$25. Food $8–$15.

Rasselas   Large, casual, and comfortable with couches and small tables, this is a favorite spot for local jazz, blues, soul, and R&B combos. The adjacent restaurant serves Ethiopian cuisine in a Bedouin tent. Menu items range from $4 to $14. 1534 Fillmore St. (at Geary Blvd.). ℂ 415/567-5010. www.rasselasjazzclub.com. Cover $7 Fri–Sat. 2-drink minimum.

DANCE CLUBS

Although a lot of clubs allow dancing, the following are the places to go if all you want to do is shake your groove thang.

⟨Tips⟩ Local Talent

Want to see the best of local jazz, cabaret, or blues performers? Check the *San Francisco Chronicle*'s Sunday "Datebook" to see if the following artists are in the house. Better yet, buy their CDs and take San Francisco's music scene home with you:

- **Faith Winthrop,** a veteran cabaret diva with a velvet voice and heartfelt delivery.
- **Ledisi,** a young local blues singer with a penchant for scatting and smoky, deep, soulful, self-written tunes.
- **Jacqui Naylor,** a seductive young talent with a love for standards and reinventing a phrase with her own modern twist.
- **Lavay Smith & Her Red Hot Skillet Lickers,** a sizzling and toe-tapping swing-style crooner, proves that swing hasn't swung this hard since it was invented.

The Endup   This unique party space with a huge, heated outdoor deck (with waterfall and fountain), indoor fireplace, and eclectic clientele has always thrown some of the most kickin' parties in town. There's a different theme every night: Thursday's Wind Up offers up a variety of house DJs; Fag Friday is just what it sounds like, plus lots of throw-down dancing; and The Endup is ever-popular with the sleepless dance-all-day crowd that comes here after the other clubs close (it's open Sat morning from 6am–noon and then nonstop from Sat night around 10pm until Sun night/Mon morning at 4am). Call to confirm nights—offerings change from time to time. 401 Sixth St. (at Harrison St.). (C) 415/357-0827. www.theendup.com. Cover $5–$15.

The Factory   The maze of rooms and nonstop barrage of house, funk, lounge vibes, salsa, and club classics attract swarms of young urbanites (read: 21- to 25-year-olds) here looking to rave it up. Management tries to eliminate the riffraff by enforcing a dress code (collared shirts and shoes for men and no sports caps). Open Saturday only 9:30pm to 3:30am. 525 Harrison St. (at First St.). (C) 415/339-8686. Cover $20.

Ruby Skye   Downtown's most glamorous and gigantic nightspot is all aglitter thanks to a dramatic renovation and the addition of killer light and sound systems within the 1890s Victorian playhouse previously known as The Stage Door. Inside, hundreds of partyers boogie on the ballroom floor to house music, mingle on the mezzanine and around the three bars, and puff freely in the smoking room while DJs or live music bring down the dancing house Thursday through Saturday. Big spenders should book the VIP lounge, which offers a glitzy place to "kick it" and bird's-eye views of the whole club scene. 420 Mason St. (between Geary and Post sts.). (C) 415/693-0777. www.rubyskye.com. Cover $10–$25.

SUPPER CLUBS

If you can eat dinner, listen to live music, and dance (or at least wiggle in your chair) in the same room, it's a supper club—those are our criteria here.

Harry Denton's Starlight Room *(Moments*   Come to this celestial high-rise cocktail lounge and nightclub, where tourists and locals watch the sunset at dusk and boogie down to live '70s, '80s, Motown covers, and jazz and funk Friday through Tuesday nights; '80s vogue DJ on Thursday nights; or the DJs' hip-hop and Top-40 tunes after dark on Wednesdays. The room is classic 1930s San Francisco, with red-velvet banquettes, chandeliers, and fabulous views. But what really attracts flocks of all ages is a night of Harry Denton–style fun, which usually includes plenty of drinking and unrestrained dancing. The full bar stocks a decent collection of single-malt Scotches and champagnes, and you can snack from the pricey Starlight appetizer menu (make a reservation to guarantee a table and you'll also have a place to rest your weary dancing-dogs). Early evening is more relaxed, but come the weekend, this place gets loose. *Tip:* Come dressed for success (no casual jeans, open-toed shoes for men, or sneakers), or you'll be turned away at the door. Atop the Sir Francis Drake Hotel, 450 Powell St., 21st floor. (C) 415/395-8595. www.harrydenton.com. Cover $10 Wed after 7pm; $10 Thurs–Fri after 8pm; $15 Sat after 8pm.

Jazz at Pearl's   A change of ownership in 2003 converted one of the best jazz venues in the city into one of the best supper clubs. Voted Top 30 Club Worldwide by *Condé Nast Traveler* and Best Live Jazz Venue by *San Francisco Magazine,* Jazz at Pearl's combines a 1930s vibe, Spanish tapas, and great live music. With a variety of acts throughout the week (big band on Mon to national acts Thurs–Sat), there's something for everyone at this all-ages club. However, with only 25 tables, advance tickets are recommended if you want to sit; general admission tickets are available as well, but don't guarantee seating. Shows start at 8 and 10pm nightly; doors open at 7pm. Tickets range from $10 to $185 (for VIP seating which includes preferred seating, champagne, and meet and greet with artist), and there's a 2-drink minimum. Cash only. 256 Columbus Ave. (at Broadway). © 415/291-8255. www.jazzatpearls.com.

DESTINATION BARS WITH DJ GROOVES

Bambuddha Lounge *(Finds)* A hot place for the young and the trendy to feast, flirt, or just be fabulous is this restaurant/bar adjoining the funky-cool Phoenix Hotel. With a 20-foot reclining Buddha on the roof, ultramodern San Francisco–meets–Southeast Asia decor (including waterfalls in the dining room and outdoor poolside cocktail lounge and *salas,* Balinese-style lounge areas by an outdoor pool), very affordable and above-average Southeast Asian cuisine served late into the evening and topping out at $22, and a state-of-the-art sound system streaming ambient, down-tempo, soul, funk, and house music, this is the "it" joint of the moment. 601 Eddy St. (at Larkin St.). © 415/885-5088. www.bambuddhalounge.com. Cover $5–$10 Thurs–Sat.

The Bliss Bar Surprisingly trendy for sleepy family-oriented Noe Valley, this small, stylish, and friendly bar is a great place to stop for a varied mix of locals, colorful cocktail concoctions, and a DJ spinning at the front window from 9pm to 2am every night except Sunday and Monday. If it's open, take your cocktail into the too-cool back Blue Room. And if you're on a budget, stop by from 4:00 to 7pm when martinis, lemon drops, cosmos, watermelon cosmos, and apple martinis are $4. 4026 24th St. (between Noe and Castro sts.). © 415/826-6200. www.blissbarsf.com.

Levende Lounge A fusion of fine dining and cocktails, Levende Lounge is one of the Mission's hottest spots and has been noted as the best bar in the city for singles, romance, bar food, and a slew of other accolades. Drop in early for happy hour Monday through Friday from 5 to 7pm or sit down for a meal of "world-fusion" small plates (think French, Asian, and Nuevo Latino) in a more standard dinner setting amid exposed brick walls and cozy lighting. Later, tables are traded for lounge furnishings for some late-night noshing and grooving. *Tip:* Some nights have cover charges, but you can avoid the fee with a dinner reservation, and food is served until 11pm. 1710 Mission St. (at Duboce St.). © 415/864-5585. www.levendesf.com.

The Monkey Club Casual and tucked away in a quiet section of the Mission, this hip locals bar (think 20s through 30s) is an ever fun and rather red spot to kick it on plush and comfy couches backed by giant picture windows; nibble on decent and inexpensive appetizers; and down stiff drinks while a DJ spins grooving house, jazz, and world music. Tuesday 6pm to 2am (with all-night happy hour), Wednesday through Friday 5pm to 2am (with happy hour until 8pm), and Saturday 8pm to 2am. 2730 21st St. (at Bryant St.). © 415/647-6546.

Wish Bar Flirtation, fun, and a very attractive staff await at this somewhat mellow, narrow bar in the popular night crawler area around 11th and Folsom streets. Swathed in burgundy and black with exposed cinder-block walls and cement floors, all's aglow a la candlelight and red-shaded sconces. With a bar in the front, DJ spinning upbeat lounge music in the back, and seating—including cushy leather couches—in between, it's often packed with a surprisingly diverse (albeit youthful) crowd and ever filled with eye candy. 1539 Folsom St. (between 11th and 12th sts.). © 415/278-9474. www.wishsf.com.

4 The Bar Scene

Finding your idea of a comfortable bar has a lot to do with picking a neighborhood filled with your kind of people and investigating that area further. There are hundreds of bars throughout San Francisco, and although many are obscurely located and can't be classified by their neighborhood, the following is a general description of what you'll find, and where:

- **Chestnut and Union Street** bars attract a postcollegiate crowd.
- Young alternatives frequent **Mission District** haunts.
- **Upper Haight** caters to eclectic neighborhood cocktailers.
- **Lower Haight** is skate- and snowboarder grungy.
- Tourists mix with theatergoers and thirsty businesspeople in **downtown** pubs.
- **North Beach** serves all types.
- **The Castro** caters to gay locals and tourists.
- **SoMa** offers an eclectic mix.

The following is a list of a few of San Francisco's most interesting bars. Unless otherwise noted, these bars do not have cover charges.

Buena Vista Café *(Moments* "Did you have an Irish coffee at the Buena Vista?" The myth is that the Irish coffee was invented at the Buena Vista, but the real story is that this popular wharf cafe was the first bar in the country to serve Irish coffee after a local journalist came back from a trip and described the drink to the bartender. Since then, the bar has poured more of these pick-me-up drinks than any other bar in the world, and ordering one has become a San Francisco must-do. Fact is, it's entertaining just to watch the venerable tenders pour up to 10 whiskey-laden coffees at a time (a rather messy event). The cafe is in a prime tourist spot along the wharf, so plan on waiting for a stool or table to free up. And don't worry if you need a little snack to soak up the booze—they serve food here, too. 2765 Hyde St. (at Beach St.). © 415/474-5044. www.thebuenavista.com.

Edinburgh Castle Since 1958, this legendary Scottish pub has been known for unusual British ales on tap and the best selection of single-malt Scotches in the city. The huge pub is decorated with horse brasses, steel helmets, and an authentic Ballantine caber (a long wooden pole) used in the annual Scottish games. Fish and chips and other traditional foods are available until 11pm. The Edinburgh also features author readings and performances and has hosted such noteworthy writers as Po Bronson, Beth Lisick, and Anthony Swofford. Open 5pm to 2am daily. 950 Geary St. (between Polk and Larkin sts.). © 415/885-4074. www.castlenews.com.

Gold Dust Lounge *(Finds* If you're staying downtown and want to head to a friendly, festive bar loaded with old-fashioned style and revelry, you needn't wander far off of Union Square. This classically cheesy watering hole is all that. The red banquettes, gilded walls, dramatic chandeliers, pro bartenders, and "regulars" are the old-school real deal. Add live music and cheap drinks and you're in for a good ol' time. *Tip:* It's cash only, so come with some greenbacks. 247 Powell St. (at Geary St.). © 415/397-1695.

Holy Cow Its motto, "Never a cover, always a party" has been the case since 1987 when this industrial SoMa bar opened. A top choice when I used to hit the bars in my early 20s and still a prime pick a heck of a long time later, this is the spot to come if you really want to do some drinking in a casual environment with DJ music ranging from club classics from the '70s to the '90s to top 40s. Nightly drink specials—from $1 well drinks and Buds from 9 to 10pm and half-price drinks from 9 to 11:30pm on

---

Tips Smoke Signals

California forbids smoking in bars, restaurants, hotel lobbies, and public areas of any kind. Some bars break the rules. Others ask their guests to step outside. Either way, don't count on lighting up inside any public place. Establishment owners are quick to enforce the rule because they can be fined if patrons disobey.

Thursdays to $3 drinks from 9 to 10pm on Fridays—make sure no one leaves sober, so plan your transportation accordingly. The bar's only open Thursday through Saturday, 9pm to 2am. 1535 Folsom St. (between 11th and 12th sts.). ℂ 415/621-6087.

Li Po Cocktail Lounge *Finds*   A dim, divey, slightly spooky Chinese bar that was once an opium den, Li Po's alluring character stems from its mishmash clutter of dusty Asian furnishings and mementos, including an unbelievably huge ancient rice-paper lantern hanging from the ceiling and a glittery golden shrine to Buddha behind the bar. The bartenders love to creep out patrons with tales of opium junkies haunting the joint. 916 Grant Ave. (between Washington and Jackson sts.). ℂ 415/982-0072.

Matrix Fillmore   Despite its previous life as the Pierce Street Annex, Matrix Fillmore remains one of the young and yuppies' hottest singles scenes. Those already spoken for can still appreciate the slick lounge atmosphere of candlelight, dyed concrete floors, flatscreen TVs, and free-standing centerpiece fireplace with its "Zen minimalist" mantel. Though it hosts a martini and mojito crowd, the bar also offers 10 wines by the glass and a large by-the-bottle selection including cult classics like Dalla Valle. Drinks range from $7 to $10. Valet parking available at the nearby Balboa Café (Fillmore and Greenwich sts.). 3138 Fillmore St. (between Greenwich and Filbert sts.). ℂ 415/563-4180. www.plumpjack.com.

Perry's   If you read *Tales of the City,* you already know that this bar and restaurant has a colorful history as a pickup place for Pacific Heights and Marina singles. Although the times are not as wild today, locals still come to casually check out the happenings at the dark mahogany bar. A separate dining room offers breakfast, lunch, dinner, and weekend brunch. It's a good place for hamburgers, simple fish dishes, and pasta. Menu items range from $6 to $22. 1944 Union St. (at Laguna St.). ℂ 415/922-9022.

Pied Piper Bar   The huge Pied Piper mural by Edwardian illustrator Maxfield Parrish steals the show at this historic mahogany bar, where high stakes were once won and lost on the roll of the dice. Happy hour Thursday and Friday from 5 to 7pm features a complimentary buffet and 75¢ oysters on Fridays. In the Palace Hotel, 2 New Montgomery (at Market St.). ℂ 415/512-1111.

The Red Room   Ultramodern, small, and deliciously dim, this lounge reflects no other color but ruby red. It's a sexy place to sip the latest cocktail. In the Commodore Hotel, 827 Sutter St. (at Jones St.). ℂ 415/346-7666.

The Redwood Room   When hotelier Ian Schrager and designer Philippe Starck updated the furniture in this historic Art Deco room, they retained its gorgeous redwood paneling, legendarily made from a single 2,000-year-old tree. With its plush yet modern feel, illuminated by beautiful original Deco sconces, the vibe is definitely updated to attract swinging singles, the tragically hip, and posers who mix, mingle, and seem to have a pretty fab and glamorous time here despite steep drink prices ($9–$25). In the Clift Hotel, 495 Geary St. © **415/775-4700.**

Spec's *Finds* The location of Spec's—Saroyan Place, a tiny alley at 250 Columbus Ave.—makes it less of a walk-in bar and more of a lively local hangout. Its funky decor—maritime flags hang from the ceiling; posters, photos, and oddities line the exposed-brick walls—gives it a character that intrigues every visitor. A "museum," displayed under glass, contains memorabilia and items brought back by seamen who drop in between voyages. The clientele is funky enough to keep you preoccupied while you drink a beer. 12 Saroyan Place (at 250 Columbus Ave.). © **415/421-4112.**

The Tonga Room & Hurricane Bar *Finds* It's kitschy as all get-out, but there's no denying the goofy Polynesian pleasures of the Fairmont Hotel's tropical oasis. Drop in and join the crowds for an umbrella drink, a simulated thunderstorm and downpour, and a heavy dose of whimsy that escapes most San Francisco establishments. If you're on a budget, you'll definitely want to stop by for the weekday happy hour from 5 to 7pm, when you can stuff your face at the all-you-can-eat bar-grub buffet (baby back ribs, chow mein, pot stickers) for $7 and the cost of one drink. Settle in and you'll catch live Top-40 music after 8pm Wednesday through Sunday, when there's a $3 to $5 cover. In the Fairmont Hotel, 950 Mason St. (at California St.). © **415/772-5278.** www.tongaroom.com.

Toronado Gritty Lower Haight isn't exactly a charming street, but there's plenty of nightlife here, catering to an artistic/grungy/skateboarding 20-something crowd. While Toronado definitely draws in the young'uns, its 50-plus microbrews on tap and 100 bottled beers also entice a more eclectic clientele in search of beer heaven. The brooding atmosphere matches the surroundings: an aluminum bar, a few tall tables, minimal lighting, and a back room packed with tables and chairs. Happy hour runs 11:30am to 6pm everyday with $2.50 pints. 547 Haight St. (at Fillmore St.). © **415/863-2276.** www.toronado.com.

Tosca Cafe *Finds* Open Tuesday through Saturday from 5pm to 2am, Sunday 7pm to 2am, Tosca is a low-key and large popular watering hole for local politicos, writers, media types, incognito celebrities such as Johnny Depp or Nicholas Cage, and similar cognoscenti of unassuming classic characters. Equipped with dim lights, red leather booths, and high ceilings, it's everything you'd expect an old North Beach legend to be. No credit cards. 242 Columbus Ave. (between Broadway and Pacific Ave.). © **415/986-9651.**

Vesuvio Situated along Jack Kerouac Alley, across from the famed City Lights bookstore, this renowned literary beatnik hangout is packed to the second-floor rafters with neighborhood writers, artists, songsters, wannabes, and everyone else ranging from longshoremen and cabdrivers to businesspeople, all of whom come for the laid-back atmosphere. The convivial space consists of two stories of cocktail tables, complemented by changing exhibitions of local art. In addition to drinks, Vesuvio features an espresso machine. 255 Columbus Ave. (at Broadway). © **415/362-3370.** www.vesuvio.com.

Zeitgeist The front door is black, the back door is adorned with a skeleton Playboy bunny, and inside is packed to the rafters with tattooed, pierced, and hard-core-looking partyers. But forge on. Zeitgeist is such a friendly and fun punk-rock-cum-biker-bar beer garden that even the occasional yuppie can be spotted mingling around the slammin' juke box featuring tons of local bands and huge back patio filled with picnic tables. (There tend to be cute girls here, too.) Along with fantastic dive-bar environs, you'll find 30 beers on draft, a pool table, and pinball machines. The regular crowd, mostly locals, including a hunky motorcycle enthusiast set and bike messengers, come here to kick back with a pitcher, and welcome anyone else interested in the same pursuit. And if your night turns out, um, better than expected . . . there's a hotel upstairs. Cash only. 199 Valencia St. (at Duboce). (✆ 415/255-7505.

BREWPUBS

Gordon Biersch Brewery Restaurant   Gordon Biersch Brewery is San Francisco's largest brew restaurant, serving decent food and tasty beer to an attractive crowd of mingling professionals. There are always several house-made beers to choose from, ranging from light to dark. Menu items run $9.50 to $20. (See p. 120 for more information.) 2 Harrison St. (on The Embarcadero). (✆ 415/243-8246. www.gordonbiersch.com.

San Francisco Brewing Company   Surprisingly low key for an alehouse, this cozy brewpub serves its creations with burgers, fries, grilled chicken breast, and the like. The bar is one of the city's few remaining old saloons (ca. 1907), aglow with stained-glass windows, tile floors, skylit ceiling, beveled glass, and a mahogany bar. A massive overhead fan runs the full length of the bar—a bizarre contraption crafted from brass and palm fronds. The handmade copper brew kettle is visible from the street. Most evenings the place is packed with everyday folks enjoying music, darts, chess, backgammon, cards, dice, and, of course, beer. Menu items range from $4.15—curiously, for edamame (soybeans)—to $21 for a full rack of baby back ribs with all the fixings. The happy-hour special, an $8^{1}/_{2}$-ounce microbrew beer for $1.50 (or a pint for $2.50), is offered daily from 4 to 6pm and midnight to 1am. 155 Columbus Ave. (at Pacific St.). (✆ 415/434-3344. www.sfbrewing.com.

ThirstyBear Brewing Company   Nine superb, handcrafted varieties of brew are always on tap at this stylish high-ceilinged brick edifice. Good Spanish food is served here, too. Pool tables and dartboards are upstairs, and live flamenco can be heard on Sunday nights. 661 Howard St. (1 block east of the Moscone Center). (✆ 415/974-0905. www.thirsty bear.com.

COCKTAILS WITH A VIEW

See "Supper Clubs," earlier, for a full review of **Harry Denton's Starlight Room.** Unless otherwise noted, these establishments have no cover charge.

Carnelian Room   On the 52nd floor of the Bank of America Building, the Carnelian Room offers uninterrupted views of the city. From a window-front table you feel as though you can reach out, pluck up the TransAmerica Pyramid, and stir your martini with it. In addition to cocktails, the restaurant serves a three-course meal ($45 per person) as well as a la carte items ($22–$50 for main entrees). Jackets are required and ties are optional for men, but encouraged. **Note:** The restaurant has one of the most extensive wine lists in the city—1,600 selections, to be exact. 555 California St., in the Bank of America Building (between Kearny and Montgomery sts.). (✆ 415/433-7500. www.carnelian room.com.

Cityscape   When you sit under the glass roof and sip a drink here, it's as though you're sitting out under the stars and enjoying views of the bay. Dinner, focusing on California cuisine, is available (though not destination worthy), and there's dancing to a DJ's picks nightly from 10:30pm. The mirrored columns and floor-to-ceiling windows help create an elegant and romantic ambience here. **FYI:** They also offer a live jazz champagne brunch on Sundays from 10am to 2pm. Hilton San Francisco, Tower One, 333 O'Farrell St. (at Mason St.), 46th floor. © **415/923-5002.** Cover $10 Fri–Sat nights.

Equinox   Though locals don't frequent this Fi-Di (Financial District) place, it's very popular with tourists. The hook? The 17-story Hyatt's rooftop restaurant has a revolving floor that gives each table a 360-degree panoramic view of the city every 45 minutes. Equinox serves cocktails Wednesday through Sunday from 5 to 11pm (until 1am on Fri–Sat); dinner is served from 6 to 10pm. In the Hyatt Regency Hotel, 5 Embarcadero Center. © **415/788-1234.**

Top of the Mark *Moments*   This is one of the most famous cocktail lounges in the world, and for good reason—the spectacular glass-walled room features an unparalleled 19th-floor view. During World War II, Pacific-bound servicemen toasted their goodbyes to the States here. While less dramatic today than they were back then, evenings spent here are still sentimental, thanks to the romantic atmosphere. Live bands play throughout the week; a jazz pianist on Tuesdays starts at 7pm; salsa on Wednesdays begins with dance lessons at 8pm and the band starts up at 9pm; on Thursdays Stompy Jones brings a swing vibe from 7:30pm, and a dance band playing everything from '50s hits through contemporary music keeps the joint hopping Fridays and Saturdays starting at 9pm. Drinks range from $8 to $10. A $59 three-course fixed-price sunset dinner is served Friday and Saturday at 7:30pm. Sunday brunch, served from 10am to 2pm, costs $59 for adults and includes a glass of champagne; for children 4 to 12, the brunch is $30. In the Mark Hopkins Inter-Continental, 1 Nob Hill (California and Mason sts.). © **415/616-6916.** www.topofthemark.citysearch.com. Cover $5–$10.

Finds **Midnight (or Midday) Mochas**

If you happen to be wandering around North Beach past your bedtime and need your caffeine fix, seek out these two cafes. They offer not only excellent espresso, but also a glimpse back at the days of the beatniks, when nothing was as crucial as a strong cup of coffee, a good smoke, and a stimulating environment.

Doing the North Beach thing is little more than hanging out in a sophisticated but relaxed atmosphere over a well-made cappuccino. You can do it at **Caffè Greco,** 423 Columbus Ave., between Green and Vallejo streets (© **415/397-6261**), and grab a bite, too—until midnight. The affordable cafe fare includes beer and wine as well as a good selection of coffees, focaccia sandwiches, and desserts (try the gelato or homemade tiramisu).

Caffè Trieste, 601 Vallejo St., at Grant Avenue (© **415/392-6739;** www.caffetrieste.com), is one of San Francisco's most beloved cafes—very down-home Italian, with espresso drinks, wine, pizza, and pastries at indoor and outdoor seating. Opera is always on the jukebox, unless it's Saturday afternoon, when the family and their friends break out in arias during an operatic performance from 2 to 5pm every other Saturday. Another perk: They offer access to free Wi-Fi with purchase, but you'll have to bring your own laptop. Check 'em out until 10pm Sunday through Thursday and midnight on Friday and Saturday.

A SPORTS BAR

Greens Sports Bar   If you think San Francisco sports fans aren't as enthusiastic as those on the East Coast, try to get a seat at Green's during a 49ers game. It's a classic old sports bar, with lots of polished dark wood and windows that open onto Polk Street, but it's loaded with modern appliances (including two large-screen televisions and 25 smaller ones) and modern partyers (read: the mid-20s and -30s set). With 18 beers on tap, a pool table, and a happy hour Monday through Friday from 4 to 7pm, there are reasons to cheer here even when the home team's got a day off. 2239 Polk St. (at Green St.). ✆ 415/775-4287. www.greenssportsbar.citysearch.com.

WINE & CHAMPAGNE BARS

The Bubble Lounge   Toasting the town is a nightly event at this two-level champagne bar. With 300 champagnes and sparkling wines, about 30 by the glass, brick walls, couches, and velvet curtains, there's plenty of pop in this fizzy lounge. 714 Montgomery St. (between Washington and Jackson sts.). ✆ 415/434-4204. www.bubblelounge.com.

Eos   If you're in the Financial District, head for the London Wine Bar (see below). For anything west of there, your top choice should be Eos, a highly successful restaurant in Cole Valley (near the Haight), with an adjoining wine bar where you can sip from the huge by-the-glass selection or choose a bottle from some 200 vintages from around the world. 901 Cole St. (at Carl St.). ✆ 415/566-3063. www.eossf.com.

First Crush   If you're staying downtown and want to sip through regional specialties, stop by this winecentric restaurant and bar. Amid a sleek and stylish interior, an eclectic clientele noshes on reasonably priced "progressive American cuisine" paired, if desired, with an outstanding selection of California wines. But plenty of people drop in simply to sample wine—especially since there are around three dozen excellent choices for filling your glass, and the joint serves until 11pm (until midnight Thurs–Sat). 101 Cyril Magnin St. (aka Fifth St., just north of Market St., at Ellis St.). ✆ 415/982-7874. www.firstcrush.com.

London Wine Bar   This British-style wine bar and store is a popular after-work hangout for Financial District suits. It's more of a place to drink and chat, however, than one in which to admire fine wines. Usually 60 wines, mostly from California, are open at any given time and 800 are available by the bottle. It's a great venue for sampling local Napa Valley wines before you buy. 415 Sansome St. (between Sacramento and Clay sts.). ✆ 415/788-4811. www.londonwinebarsf.com.

Nectar Wine Lounge   Catering to the Marina's young and beautiful, this ultrahip place to sip—and snack—pours an exciting and well-edited wine selection (plus 900 choices by the bottle) along with creative small plates (pairings optional). Industrial-slick decor includes cube chairs, a long bar, and lounge areas that are often packed with 20- through 40-somethings. 3330 Steiner St. (at Chestnut St.). ✆ 415/345-1377. www.nectarwinelounge.com.

5 Gay & Lesbian Bars & Clubs

Just like straight establishments, gay and lesbian bars and clubs target varied clienteles. Whether you're into leather or Lycra, business or bondage, San Francisco has something just for you.

Check the free weeklies, the *San Francisco Bay Guardian* and *San Francisco Weekly,* for listings of events and happenings around town. The *Bay Area Reporter* is a gay paper with comprehensive listings, including a weekly community calendar. All these papers are free and distributed weekly on Wednesday or Thursday. They can be found stacked at the corners of 18th and Castro streets and Ninth and Harrison streets, as well as in bars, bookshops, and other stores around town. There are also a number of gay and lesbian guides to San Francisco. See "Gay & Lesbian Travelers," in chapter 2, beginning on p. 21, for further details and helpful information. Also check out the rather homely, but very informative site titled "Queer Things to Do in the San Francisco Bay Area" at www.io.com/~larrybob/sanfran.html or www.leatherandbears.com for a plethora of gay happenings.

Listed below are some of the city's most established mainstream gay hangouts.

The Café *Finds*   When this place first got jumping, it was the only predominantly lesbian dance club on Saturday nights in the city. Once the guys found out how much fun the girls were having, however, they joined the party. Today, it's a happening mixed gay and lesbian scene with three bars, two pool tables, a steamy, free-spirited dance floor, and a small, heated patio and balcony where smoking and schmoozing is allowed. A perk: They open at 4pm weekdays and 3pm weekends. 2367 Market St. (at Castro St.). ℭ 415/861-3846. www.cafesf.com.

The Cinch Saloon   Part cruisy neighborhood bar, part modern-day penny arcade, The Cinch Saloon features free Wi-Fi, two pool tables, five TVs, video games, an Internet juke box, pinball, and an outdoor smoking patio. They even have their own softball team, The Renegades! With happy hour Monday through Friday 4 to 8pm (all night on Mon), progressive music by DJs after 9pm (except for Mon–Tues), and a host of other fun theme nights (like Hot Fudge Sundays, billed as "cocktails, food, fun, and fabulosity"), the bar attracts a mixed crowd of gays, lesbians, and gay-friendly straights. 1723 Polk St. (near Washington St.). ℭ 415/776-4162. www.thecinch.com.

The Eagle Tavern   One of the city's most traditional Levi's 'n' leather bars, The Eagle boasts a heated outdoor patio (where smoking is permitted), a happy hour (Mon–Fri 4–8pm), live bands every Thursday at 9pm, and a popular Sunday afternoon beer fest from 3 to 6pm. 398 12th St. (at Harrison St.). ℭ 415/626-0880. www.sfeagle.com.

The Endup   It's a different nightclub every night of the week, but regardless of who's throwing the party, the place is always jumping to the tunes blasted by DJs. There are two pool tables, a fireplace, an outdoor patio and, on the dance floor, a mob of gyrating souls. Some nights are straight, so call ahead. (See p. 231 for more information.) 401 Sixth St. (at Harrison St.). ℭ 415/357-0827. www.theendup.com. Cover $5–$15.

Kimo's   This gay-owned and -operated neighborhood bar in the seedier gay section of town is a friendly oasis, decorated with plastic plants and random pictures on the walls. The bar provides a relaxing venue for chatting, drinking, and quiet cruising and livens up with indie, punk rock and jazz bands nightly at Kimo's Penthouse upstairs. 1351 Polk St. (at Pine St.). ℭ 415/885-4535. Cover $5–$10 for live music.

Lone Star Saloon   Expect lesbians and a heavier, furrier motorcycle crowd (both men and women) here most every night. The Thursday night and Saturday and Sunday afternoon beer busts on the patio are especially popular and cost $7 to $9 per person. 1354 Harrison St. (between 9th and 10th sts.). ℭ 415/863-9999. www.lonestarsaloon.com.

Metro   This bar provides the gay community with high-energy music and the best view of the Castro District from its large balcony. The bar seems to attract people of all ages who enjoy the friendliness of the bartenders and the highly charged, cruising atmosphere. There's a Spanish restaurant on the premises if you get hungry. 3600 16th St. (at Market St.). ☎ **415/703-9751.**

The Mint Karaoke Lounge   This is a gay and lesbian karaoke bar—sprinkled with a heavy dash of straight folks on weekends—where you can get up and sing your heart out every night. Along with song, you'll encounter a mixed 20- to 40-something crowd that combines cocktails with do-it-yourself cabaret. Want to eat and listen at the same time? Feel free to bring in the Japanese food from the attached restaurant. Sashimi goes for about $7, main entrees $8, and sushi combo plates are about $11. 1942 Market St. (at Laguna St.). ☎ **415/626-4726.** www.themint.net. 2-drink minimum.

The Stud   The Stud, which has been around for almost 40 years, is one of the most successful gay establishments in town. The interior has an antiques-shop look. Music is a balanced mix of old and new, and nights vary from cabaret to oldies to discopunk. Check their website in advance for the evening's offerings. Drink prices range from $3 to $8. Happy hour runs Monday through Saturday 5 to 9pm with $1 off well drinks. 399 Ninth St. (at Harrison St.). ☎ **415/863-6623** or 415/252-STUD for event info. www.studsf.com. Cover free–$9.

Twin Peaks Tavern   Right at the intersection of Castro, 17th, and Market streets is one of the Castro's most famous (at 35 years old) gay hangouts. It caters to an older crowd but often has a mixture of patrons and claims to be the first gay bar in America. Because of its relatively small size and desirable location, the place becomes fairly crowded and convivial by 8pm, earlier than many neighboring bars. 401 Castro St. (at 17th and Market sts.). ☎ **415/864-9470.**

6 Film

Celebrating its 50th anniversary in 2006, the **San Francisco International Film Festival** (☎ **415/561-5000;** www.sffs.org), held at the end of April, is one of America's longest-running film festivals. Entries include new films by new and established directors. Call or surf ahead for a schedule or information, and check out their website for more information on purchasing tickets, which are relatively inexpensive.

If you're not here in time for the festival, don't despair. The classic, independent, and mainstream cinemas in San Francisco are every bit as good as the city's other cultural offerings.

REPERTORY CINEMAS

Castro Theatre *(Finds)*   Built in 1922 by renowned Bay Area architect Timothy Pflueger, and listed as a City of San Francisco registered landmark, the beautiful Castro Theatre is known for its screenings of classics and for its Wurlitzer organ, which is played before each evening show. There's a different feature almost nightly, and more often than not it's a double feature. They also play host to a number of festivals throughout the year. Bargain matinees are usually offered on Wednesday, Saturday, Sunday, and holidays. Phone or visit their website for schedules, prices, and showtimes. 429 Castro St. (near Market St.). ☎ **415/621-6120.** www.castrotheatre.com.

Red Vic   The worker-owned Red Vic movie collective originated in the neighboring Victorian building that gave it its name. The theater specializes in independent releases and premieres and contemporary cult hits, and situates its patrons among an array of couches. Prices are $8 for adults ($6 for matinees) and $4 for seniors and kids

12 and under. Tickets go on sale 20 minutes before each show. Phone for schedules and showtimes or look around the city for printouts. 1727 Haight St. (between Cole and Shrader sts.). (C) **415/668-3994**. www.redvicmoviehouse.com.

The Roxie Film Center   Founded in 1909, The Roxie is the oldest continually running theater in San Francisco, and so when it almost went under in 2005, a private donor saved it with a huge donation and a great idea; the theater merged with the New College of California and is now a nonprofit film center serving both students and the general public. Management has promised that the programming will stay the same and that they will continue to screen the best new alternative films anywhere, as well as host filmmakers like Akira Kurosawa and Werner Herzog. The low-budget contemporary features are largely devoid of Hollywood candy coating; many are West Coast premieres. Films change weekly and sometimes more often. Phone for schedules, prices, and showtimes. Admission is $8 adults, $4 seniors 65 plus and children under 12; $5 matinee is first show on weekends. 3117 16th St. (at Valencia St.). (C) **415/863-1087**. www.roxie.com.

11

Side Trips from San Francisco

The City by the Bay is, without question, captivating, but don't let it ensnare you to the point of ignoring its environs. The surrounding areas contain a multitude of natural spectacles such as Mount Tamalpais and Muir Woods; scenic communities like Tiburon and Sausalito; and great cities such as up-and-coming Oakland and its youth-oriented next-door neighbor, Berkeley.

From San Francisco, you can reach any of these points in an hour or less by car.

Public transportation options are also listed throughout the chapter. Another option is to hitch a ride with **San Francisco Sightseeing** (© **415/434-8687** or 800/826-0202; www.sanfranciscosightseeing.com), which runs regularly scheduled bus tours to neighboring towns and the countryside. Half-day trips to Muir Woods and Sausalito, and full-day trips to Napa and Sonoma are available, as are excursions to Yosemite and the Monterey Peninsula. Phone for prices and schedules.

1 Berkeley

10 miles NE of San Francisco

Berkeley is famous as the home of the University of California at Berkeley, which is world-renowned for its academic standards, 18 Nobel prize winners (seven are active staff), and protests that led to the most famous student riots in U.S. history. Today, there's still hippie idealism in the air, but the radicals have aged; the 1960s are present only in tie-dye and paraphernalia shops. The biggest change the town is facing is yuppification; as San Francisco's rent and property prices soar out of the range of the average person's budget, everyone with less than a small fortune is seeking shelter elsewhere, and Berkeley is one of the top picks (although Oakland is quickly becoming a favorite, too). Berkeley is a charming town teeming with all types of people, a beautiful campus, vast parks, great shopping, and some incredible restaurants.

ESSENTIALS

The Berkeley **Bay Area Rapid Transit (BART)** station is 2 blocks from the university. The fare from San Francisco is less than $4. Call © **511** or visit www.bart.gov for trip info, fares, or to download trip planners to your iPod, mobile phone, or PDA.

If you are coming **by car** from San Francisco, take the Bay Bridge (go during the evening commute, and you'll think Los Angeles traffic is a breeze). Follow I-80 east to the University Avenue exit, and follow University until you hit the campus. Parking is tight, so either leave your car at the Sather Gate parking lot at Telegraph Avenue and Durant Street, or expect to fight for a spot.

WHAT TO SEE & DO

Hanging out is the preferred Berkeley pastime, and the best place to do it is **Telegraph Avenue,** the street that leads to the campus's southern entrance. Most of the action lies

The Bay Area

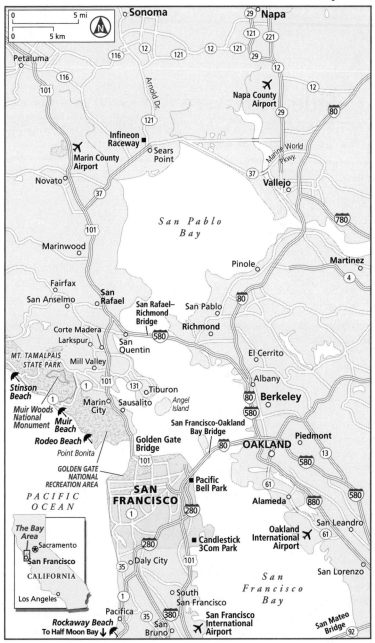

Pricing Categories

Note: In this chapter, hotels are organized by location, then by price range, as follows: **Very Expensive,** more than $250 per night; **Expensive,** $200 to $250 per night; **Moderate,** $150 to $200 per night; and **Inexpensive,** less than $150 per night.

Restaurants are organized by location, then by price range for a complete dinner (appetizer, entree, dessert, and glass of wine) as follows: **Expensive,** dinner from $50 per person; **Moderate,** dinner from $35 per person; and **Inexpensive,** less than $35 per person for dinner. (*Note:* The "Very Expensive" category—dinner from $75 per person—has been omitted since no restaurants in this chapter fall under its umbrella.)

between Bancroft Way and Dwight Way, where coffeehouses, restaurants, shops, great book and record stores, and crafts booths (with vendors selling everything from T-shirts and jewelry to I Ching and tarot-card readings) swarm with life. Pretend you're a local: Plant yourself at a cafe, sip a latte, and ponder something intellectual, or survey the town's unique residents.

Bibliophiles must stop at **Cody's Books,** 2454 Telegraph Ave. (© 510/845-7852; www.codysbooks.com), to peruse its gargantuan selection of titles, independent-press books, and magazines. If used and antiquarian books are your thing, stop by **Moe's Books,** 2476 Telegraph Ave. (© 510/849-2087; www.moesbooks.com). After exploring four floors of new, used, and out-of-print books, you're unlikely to leave empty-handed.

UC BERKELEY CAMPUS

The University of California at Berkeley (www.berkeley.edu) campus is worth a stroll. It's a beautiful old place with plenty of woodsy paths, architecturally noteworthy buildings and, of course, 33,000 students, many of them scurrying to and from classes. Among the architectural highlights of the campus are a number of buildings by Bernard Maybeck, Bakewell and Brown, and John Galen Howard.

Contact the **Visitor Information Center,** 101 University Hall, 2200 University Ave., at Oxford Street (© 510/642-5215; www.berkeley.edu/visitors), to join a free 90-minute campus tour. Reservations are required; see website for details. Tours are available year-round Monday through Saturday at 10am and Sunday at 1pm. Weekday tours depart from the Visitor's Center and weekend tours start from Sather Bell Tower in the middle of campus. Electric cart tours are available year-round for travelers with disabilities for $40; 2 weeks advance reservations required; no tours are given the week between Christmas and New Year's Day. Or stop by the office and pick up a self-guided walking-tour brochure or a free Berkeley map. *Note:* The information center is closed on weekends, but you can find the latest information on their website.

The university's southern, main entrance is at the northern end of Telegraph Avenue, at Bancroft Way. Walk through the entrance into Sproul Plaza, and when school is in session, you'll encounter the gamut of Berkeley's inhabitants: colorful street people, rambling political zealots, and ambitious students. You might be lucky enough to stumble upon some impromptu musicians or a heated, and possibly absurd, debate. There's always something going on here, so stretch out on the grass for a few minutes and take in the Berkeley vibe. You'll also find the student union, complete

Berkeley

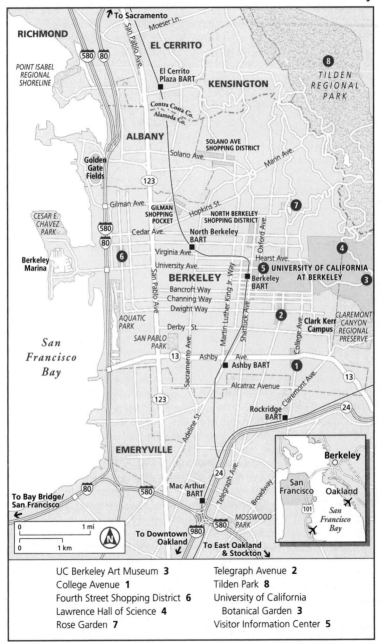

UC Berkeley Art Museum **3**
College Avenue **1**
Fourth Street Shopping District **6**
Lawrence Hall of Science **4**
Rose Garden **7**

Telegraph Avenue **2**
Tilden Park **8**
University of California
  Botanical Garden **3**
Visitor Information Center **5**

with a bookstore, cafes, and an information desk on the second floor where you can pick up the student newspaper (also found in dispensers throughout campus).

For viewing more traditional art forms, there are some noteworthy museums, too. The **Lawrence Hall of Science** ✦ (east of campus on Centennial Dr., just above the Botanical Gardens; ✆ **510/642-5132;** www.lawrencehallofscience.org) offers hands-on science exploration, is open daily from 10am to 5pm, and is a wonderful place to watch the sunset. Also included in the admission price is a new outdoor science park called Forces That Shape the Bay, which lets visitors explore ongoing geologic forces. The site includes activity stations such as earthquake simulators, a geologic uplift bench, a water feature, telescopes, BayLab programs and demonstrations, an audio tour and picnic sites. Admission is $9.50 for adults; $7.50 for seniors 62 and over, students, and children 5 to 18; $5.50 for children 3 or 4; and free for kids under 3. The **UC Berkeley Art Museum** ✦ (2626 Bancroft Way, between College and Telegraph aves.; ✆ **510/642-0808;** www.bampfa.berkeley.edu) is open Wednesday through Sunday from 11am to 5pm. Admission is $8 for adults; $5 for seniors, non-UCB students, visitors with disabilities, and children 17 and under; and $4 for UCB students. This museum contains a substantial collection of Hans Hofmann paintings, a sculpture garden, and the Pacific Film Archive.

People's Park/People's Power

In late 1968, the university demolished an entire block of buildings north of Telegraph Avenue. The destruction, which forced hippies and other "undesirables" from the slum housing that stood there, was done under the guise of university expansion and urban renewal—good liberal causes. But after the lot lay vacant for months, a group of Berkeley radicals, whose names read like a who's who of 1960s leftists, including Jerry Rubin, Bobby Seale, and Tom Hayden, decided to take the land for "the people."

On April 20, 1969, hundreds of activists invaded the vacant lot with gardening tools and tamed the muddy ground into a park. One month later, Berkeley's Republican mayor sent 250 police officers into the park, and 6,000 demonstrators materialized to challenge them. A riot ensued, and the police fired buckshot at the crowd. One rioter was killed and another blinded. Gov. Ronald Reagan sent in the National Guard, and for the next 17 days, the guardsmen repeatedly gassed innocent students, faculty, and passersby. Berkeley was a war zone, and People's Park became the decade's most important symbol of "people power."

The park again sparked controversy in 1992, when university officials decided to build volleyball courts there. In August, a park activist broke into the campus home of the university's chancellor. When a police officer arrived, the activist lunged at him with a machete and was shot dead. On the victim's body was a note with the message: "We are willing to die for this land. Are you?" On news of the contemporary radical's death, more than 150 of her supporters rioted.

Postscript: The volleyball courts didn't get much use, and now basketball courts have taken their place. Visit www.peoplespark.org for more information.

PARKS

Unbeknownst to many travelers, Berkeley has some of the most extensive and beautiful parks around. If you want to wear the kids out or enjoy hiking, swimming, sniffing roses, or just getting a breath of California air, jump in your car and make your way to **Tilden Park** *. On the way, stop at the colorful terraced **Rose Garden** * (© 510/981-5151) in north Berkeley on Euclid Avenue between Bay View and Eunice Street. Then head high into the Berkeley hills to Tilden, where you'll find plenty of flora and fauna, hiking trails, an old steam train and merry-go-round, a farm and nature area for kids, and a chilly tree-encircled lake. The East Bay's public transit system, AC Transit (© 511; www.actransit.org), runs the air-conditioned no. 67 bus line around the edge of the park on weekdays and all the way to the Tilden Visitors Center on Saturdays and Sundays. Call © 510/562-PARK or see www.ebparks.org for further information.

Another worthy nature excursion is **The University of California Botanical Garden** (© 510/643-2755; www.botanicalgarden.berkeley.edu), which features a vast collection of herbage ranging from cacti to redwoods. It's on campus in Strawberry Canyon on Centennial Drive. Unfortunately no public bus can take you directly there, so driving is the way to go. Call for directions. Open daily from 9am to 5pm; closed the first Tuesday of every month; docent-led tours on Thursdays, Saturdays and Sundays at 1:30pm. Admission is $5 adults, $3 seniors 65 and over, $1 youth 3 to 17, and free for children under 3 and UC students.

SHOPPING

If you're itching to exercise your credit cards, head to one of two places. **College Avenue** from Dwight Way to the Oakland border overflows with eclectic boutiques, antiques shops, and restaurants. The other option is **Fourth Street,** in west Berkeley, 2 blocks north of the University Avenue exit. This shopping strip is the perfect place to go on a sunny morning. Grab a cup of java, read the paper at a patio table, then hit the **Crate & Barrel Outlet,** 1785 Fourth St., between Hearst and Virginia (© 510/528-5500). Prices are 30% to 70% off retail. It's open daily from 10am to 6pm. This area also boasts small, wonderful stores crammed with imported and locally made housewares. Nearby is **REI,** the Bay Area's favorite outdoors outfitter, 1338 San Pablo Ave., near Gilman Street (© 510/527-4140). It's open Monday through Friday from 10am to 9pm, Saturday from 10am to 8pm, and Sunday from 10am to 7pm.

WHERE TO STAY

Unfortunately, a little research will prove that Berkeley is not even remotely close to a good hotel town. Most accommodations are extremely basic motels and funky B&Bs. The one exception (though it's overpriced) is **The Claremont Resort & Spa,** 41 Tunnel Rd., Berkeley (© 800/551-7266 or 510/843-3000; www.claremontresort.com), a grand Victorian hotel, also on the border of Oakland, with a fancy spa and gym, three restaurants, a hip bar, and grandiose surroundings. Though it's the most luxurious thing going, it's overpriced and rooms aren't nearly as charming as the exterior. Rates range from $290 to $450 for doubles and $460 to $1,050 for suites. Or you can contact the **Berkeley & Oakland Bed and Breakfast Network** (© 510/547-6380; www.bbonline.com/ca/berkeley-oakland), which books visitors into private homes and apartments in the East Bay area.

Finds **Sweet Sensations at Berkeley's Chocolate Factory**

If you haven't had chocolate nibs, you haven't lived—at least that's what chocoholics are likely to discover upon visiting **Scharffen Berger Chocolate Maker,** California's runaway-success chocolatier that opened its factory and retail-shop doors in Berkeley in mid-2001. Within the brick building, visitors can not only taste the nibs (crunchy roasted and shelled cocoa beans), but also see how the famous chocolate company uses vintage European equipment during regularly scheduled free tours (call or visit their website to reserve a spot as spaces are limited). And let's not forget that plenty of tasty products, from candy bars to cocoa powder to chocolate sauce, are available in the retail shop (© **510/ 981-4066**). You can also have coffee, pastries, lunch, or brunch at their restaurant, **Café Cacao,** which is open Monday through Friday 8am to 5pm (serving lunch 11am–3pm) and Saturday and Sunday 9am to 3pm. The factory is located at 914 Heinz Ave., Berkeley (© **510/981-4050;** www.scharffenberger.com). From I-80 East take the Ashby Avenue exit, turn left on Seventh Street, and turn right on Heinz.

MODERATE

Rose Garden Inn   Like a Merchant-Ivory movie, the accommodations at this 40-room five-building compound with two landmark mansions, range from English Country to Victorian, making it a favorite for visiting grandparents and vacationing retirees. Despite your age or design sense, the stunning and expansive garden exploding with rose bushes, hydrangeas, and an abundance of flora and fauna is sure to delight as well as erase all memories that you're on a characterless stretch of Telegraph Avenue a few blocks south of the student action. Rooms, many of which have fireplaces, cable TVs, and all the basic amenities, show some wear and tend to be a little dark, but they are spacious, updated, and very clean despite the obvious age of some bathroom nooks and crannies.

2740 Telegraph Ave. (at Stuart St.), Berkeley, CA 94705. www.rosegardeninn.com. © 800/992-9005 or 510/549-2145. Fax 510/549-1085. 40 units. $115–$265 double. Breakfast included. AE, DC, DISC, MC, V. Free parking on a space-available basis. **Amenities:** Wi-Fi in lobby; coffee and afternoon cookies. *In room:* TV, hair dryer, iron upon request, high-speed Internet access in deluxe rooms.

WHERE TO DINE

East Bay dining is a relaxed alternative to San Francisco's gourmet scene. There are plenty of ambitious Berkeley restaurants and, unlike in San Francisco, plenty of parking, provided you're not near the campus.

If you want to dine student-style, eat on campus Monday through Friday. Buy something at a sidewalk stand or in the building directly behind the Student Union. There's also the **Bear's Lair Pub and Coffee House,** the **Terrace,** and the **Golden Bear Restaurant.** All the university eateries have both indoor and outdoor seating.

Telegraph Avenue has an array of small, ethnic restaurants, cafes, and sandwich shops. Follow the students: If the place is crowded, it's good, supercheap, or both.

EXPENSIVE

Chez Panisse ✷✷✷ CALIFORNIA   California cuisine is so much a product of Alice Waters's genius that all other restaurants following in her wake should be dated

A.A.W. (After Alice Waters). Read the menus posted outside, and you'll understand why. Most of the produce and meat comes from local farms and is organically produced, and after all these years, Alice still tends her restaurant with great integrity and innovation. Chez Panisse is a delightful redwood and stucco cottage with a brick terrace filled with flowering potted plants. The two dining areas, the cafe and the restaurant, both serve Mediterranean-inspired cuisine.

In the upstairs cafe are displays of pastries and fruit and an oak bar adorned with large bouquets of fresh flowers. At lunch or dinner, the menu might feature delicately smoked gravlax or roasted eggplant soup with pesto, followed by lamb ragout garnished with apricots, onions, and spices and served with couscous.

The cozy downstairs restaurant, strewn with blossoming floral bouquets, is an appropriately warm environment in which to indulge in the $65 fixed-price four-course gourmet dinner, which is served Tuesday through Thursday. Friday and Saturday, it's $85 for four courses; and Monday is bargain night, with a three-course dinner for $50.

The restaurant posts the following week's menu, which changes daily, every Saturday. There's also an excellent wine list, with bottles ranging from $28 to $300.

1517 Shattuck Ave. (between Cedar and Vine). ⓒ **510/548-5525**, or 510/548-5049 cafe reservations. Fax 510/548-0140. www.chezpanisse.com. Reservations required for the dining room and taken 1 month prior to calendar date requested. Reservations are recommended for the cafe, but walk-ins are welcomed. Restaurant fixed-price menu $50–$85; cafe main courses $15–$25. AE, DC, DISC, MC, V. Restaurant seatings Mon–Sat 6–6:30pm and 8:30–9:15pm most times of the year (in slower months, like Jan–Mar, times vary; please call to confirm). Cafe Mon–Thurs 11:30am–3pm and 5–10:30pm; Fri–Sat 11:30am–3:30pm and 5–11:30pm. BART: Downtown Berkeley. From I-80 north, take the University Ave. exit and turn left onto Shattuck Ave.

MODERATE

Cafe Rouge ⊛ MEDITERRANEAN   After cooking at San Francisco's renowned Zuni Cafe for 10 years, chef-owner Marsha McBride launched her own restaurant, a sort of Zuni East. She brought former staff members and some of the restaurant's flavor with her, and now her sparse, loftlike dining room serves salads, rotisserie chicken with oil and thyme, grilled lamb chops, steaks, and homemade sausages. East Bay carnivores are especially happy with the burger; like Zuni's, it's top-notch. During warm days, outdoor dining overlooking the shopping square is ideal.

1782 Fourth St. (between Delaware and Hearst). ⓒ **510/525-1440**. www.caferouge.net. Reservations recommended. Main courses $14–$32. MC, V. Daily 11:30am–3pm; Tues–Thurs 5:30–9:30pm; Fri–Sat 5:30–10:30pm; Sun 5–9:30pm; interim bar menu available daily.

Rivoli ⊛⊛ (Finds) CALIFORNIA   One of the favored dinner destinations in the East Bay, Rivoli offers top-notch food at amazingly reasonable prices. In an otherwise uninteresting space, the owners have created a warm, intimate dining room, which overlooks a sweet little garden with visiting raccoons and possums and a wine bar near the entrance. Aside from a few house favorites, the menu changes entirely every 3 weeks to feature whatever's freshest and in season; the wine list follows suit with around 10 by-the-glass options handpicked to match the food. While many love it, I'm not a fan of the portobello-mushroom fritter, a gourmet variation of the fried zucchini stick. However, plenty of dishes shine, including chicken cooked with prosciutto di Parma, wild mushroom chard and ricotta cannelloni, Marsala *jus*, snap peas, and baby carrots; and braised lamb shank with green garlic risotto, sautéed spinach, and oven-dried tomatoes. Finish the evening with an assortment of cheeses or a warm chocolate truffle torte with hazelnut ice cream, orange crème anglaise, and chocolate sauce.

1539 Solano Ave. ⓒ 866/496-2489 or 510/526-2542. www.rivolirestaurant.com. Reservations recommended. Main courses $16–$22. AE, DC, DISC, MC, V. Mon–Thurs 5:30–9:30pm; Fri 5:30–10pm; Sat 5–10pm; Sun 5–9pm.

INEXPENSIVE

O Chamé 𝒢𝒢 JAPANESE   Spare and plain in its decor, with ocher-colored walls etched with patterns, this spot has a meditative air to complement the traditional, experimental, and very fresh and clean Japanese-inspired cuisine. The menu, which changes daily, offers meal-in-a-bowl dishes ($9–$13) that allow a choice of soba or udon noodles in a clear soup with a variety of toppings—from shrimp and wakame seaweed to beef with burdock root and carrot. Appetizers include a flavorful melding of grilled shiitake mushrooms, as well as portobello mushrooms and green-onion pancakes. Their main entree selection always includes delicious roasted salmon, but you can also easily fill up on a bowl of soba or udon noodles with fresh, wholesome fixings (think roasted oysters, sea bass, and tofu skins).

1830 Fourth St. (near Hearst). ⓒ 510/841-8783. www.themenupage.com/ochame.html. Reservations recommended Fri–Sat dinner. Main courses lunch $9–$19, dinner $18–$24. AE, MC, V. Mon–Sat 11:30am–3pm; Mon–Thurs 5:30–9pm; Fri–Sat 5:30–9:30pm.

2 Oakland

10 miles E of San Francisco

Although it's less than a dozen miles from San Francisco, Oakland is worlds apart from its sister city across the bay. Originally little more than a cluster of ranches and farms, Oakland exploded in size and stature practically overnight, when the last mile of transcontinental railroad track was laid down. Major shipping ports soon followed and, to this day, Oakland remains one of the busiest industrial ports on the West Coast.

The price for economic success, however, is Oakland's lowbrow reputation as a predominantly working-class city; it is forever in the shadow of chic San Francisco. However, as The City by the Bay has become crowded and expensive in the past few years, Oakland has experienced a rush of new residents and businesses. As a result, Oaktown is in a renaissance, and its future continues to look brighter and brighter.

Rent a sailboat on Lake Merritt, stroll along the waterfront, explore the fantastic Oakland Museum: They're all great reasons to hop the bay and spend a fog-free day exploring one of California's largest and most ethnically diverse cities.

ESSENTIALS

BART connects San Francisco and Oakland through one of the longest underwater transit tunnels in the world. Fares range from $2 to $4, depending on your station of origin; children under 5 ride free. BART trains operate Monday through Friday from 4am to midnight, Saturday from 6am to midnight, and Sunday from 8am to midnight. Exit at the 12th Street station for downtown Oakland. Call ⓒ **511** or visit www.bart.gov for more info.

By car from San Francisco, take I-80 across the San Francisco–Oakland Bay Bridge and follow signs to downtown Oakland. Exit at Grand Avenue South for the Lake Merritt area.

For a calendar of events in Oakland, contact the **Oakland Convention and Visitors Bureau,** 463 11th St., Oakland, CA 94607 (ⓒ **510/839-9000;** www.oakland cvb.com). The city also sponsors eight free guided tours, including African-American Heritage and downtown tours held Wednesdays and Saturdays May through October; call ⓒ **510/238-3234** or visit www.oaklandnet.com/walkingtours for details.

Oakland

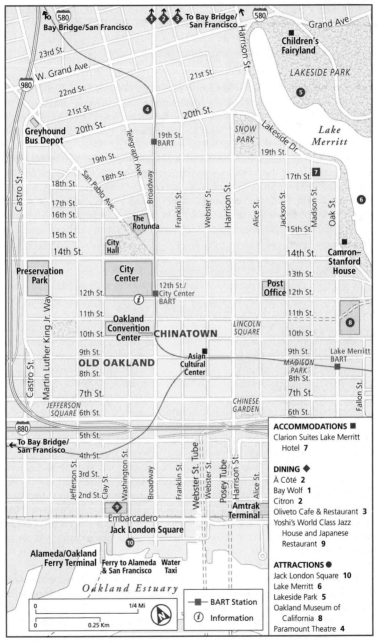

ACCOMMODATIONS ■
Clarion Suites Lake Merritt
  Hotel **7**

DINING ◆
À Côté **2**
Bay Wolf **1**
Citron **2**
Oliveto Cafe & Restaurant **3**
Yoshi's World Class Jazz
  House and Japanese
  Restaurant **9**

ATTRACTIONS ●
Jack London Square **10**
Lake Merritt **6**
Lakeside Park **5**
Oakland Museum of
  California **8**
Paramount Theatre **4**

Downtown Oakland lies between Grand Avenue on the north, I-980 on the west, Inner Harbor on the south, and Lake Merritt on the east. Between these landmarks are three BART stations (12th St., 19th St., and Lake Merritt), City Hall, the Oakland Museum, Jack London Square, and several other sights.

WHAT TO SEE & DO

Lake Merritt is Oakland's primary tourist attraction, along with Jack London Square (see below). Three and a half miles in circumference, the tidal lagoon was bridged and dammed in the 1860s and is now a wildlife refuge that is home to flocks of migrating ducks, herons, and geese. The 122-acre **Lakeside Park,** a popular place to picnic, feed the ducks, and escape the fog, surrounds the lake on three sides. Visit www.oakland net.com/parks for more info. At the **Municipal Boathouse** ✛ (℃ **510/238-2196**), in Lakeside Park along the north shore, you can rent sailboats, rowboats, pedal boats, canoes, or kayaks for $8 to $15 per hour (cash only). Or you can take an hour-long gondola ride with **Gondola Servizio** (℃ **888/737-8494**; www.gondolaservizio.com). Experienced gondoliers will serenade you, June through October, as you glide across the lake; the cost ranges from $45 to $225 for two depending on the time and gondola style.

Another site worth visiting is Oakland's **Paramount Theatre** ✛, 2025 Broadway (℃ **510/893-2300**; www.paramounttheatre.com), an outstanding National Historic Landmark and example of Art Deco architecture and decor. Built in 1931 and authentically restored in 1973, it's the city's main performing-arts center, hosting big-name performers like Smokey Robinson and Alicia Keys. Guided tours of the 3,000-seat theater are given the first and third Saturday morning of each month, excluding holidays. No reservations are necessary; just show up at 10am at the box office entrance on 21st Street at Broadway. The tour lasts 2 hours, cameras are allowed, and admission is $1.

If you take pleasure in strolling sailboat-filled wharves or are a die-hard fan of Jack London, you might enjoy a visit to **Jack London Square** ✛ (℃ **866/295-9853**; www.jacklondonsquare.com). It's bound to get even more interesting in the coming years as it is currently undergoing a $300-million renovation and expansion.

Oakland's only patently tourist area remains a relatively low-key version of San Francisco's Fisherman's Wharf, which shamelessly plays up the fact that Jack London spent most of his youth along the waterfront. The square fronts the harbor, housing a tourist-tacky complex of boutiques and eateries that are about as far from the "call of the wild" as you can get, as well as a more locals-friendly farmers market year-round on Sundays from 10am to 2pm. Most shops are open daily from 11am to 6pm (some restaurants stay open later). One of the best options is live jazz at **Yoshi's World Class Jazz House & Japanese Restaurant** ✛, 510 Embarcadero W. (℃ **510/238-9200**; www.yoshis.com), which serves some fine sushi in its adjoining restaurant. In the center of the square is a small, reconstructed Yukon cabin in which Jack London lived while prospecting in the Klondike during the gold rush of 1897.

In the middle of Jack London Square you'll find a more authentic memorial, **Heinold's First and Last Chance Saloon** (℃ **510/839-6761**), a funky, friendly little bar and historic landmark that's worth a visit. This is where London did some of his writing and most of his drinking; the corner table he used has remained exactly as it was nearly a century ago.

Jack London Square is at Broadway and Embarcadero. Take I-880 to Broadway, turn south, and drive to the end. Or you can ride BART to 12th Street station and then walk south along Broadway (about half a mile). Or take bus no. 72R or 72M to the foot of Broadway.

Oakland Museum of California ⊛   Two blocks south of Lake Merritt, the Oakland Museum of California incorporates just about everything you'd want to know about the state and its people, history, culture, geology, art, environment, and ecology. Inside a low, modern building set among sweeping gardens and terraces, it's actually three museums in one: exhibitions of works by California artists from Bierstadt to Diebenkorn; collections of historic artifacts, from Pomo Indian basketry to Country Joe McDonald's guitar; and re-creations of California habitats from the coast to the Sierra Mountains. The museum holds major shows of California artists as well as exhibitions dedicated to California's rich nature and history. Recent exhibits included *Aftershock: Personal Stories from the '06 Quake and Fire* and *Baseball as America,* which showcased artifacts and photos of the nation's favorite sport. The museum also frequently shows photography from its huge collections.

   Forty-five-minute guided tours leave from the gallery information desks on request or by appointment. There's a fine cafe, a **Collector's Gallery** (✆ **510/834-2296**) that sells works by California artists, and a museum shop. The cafe is open Wednesday through Saturday from 10:30am to 4pm, Sunday from 1:30 to 4pm.

1000 Oak St. (at 10th St.). ✆ **888/625-6873,** or 510/238-2200 for recorded information. www.museumca.org. Admission $8 adults, $5 students and seniors, free for children under 6. 2nd Sun of the month is free (special exhibitions excepted). Wed–Sat 10am–5pm; Sun noon–5pm; open until 9pm 1st Fri of the month. Closed Jan 1, July 4, Thanksgiving, and Dec 25. BART: Lake Merritt station; follow the signs posted in the station. From I-880 north, take the Oak St. exit; the museum is 5 blocks east. Or take I-580 to I-980 and exit at the Jackson St. ramp.

WHERE TO STAY

Two fine midrange hotel options in Oakland are the **Waterfront Plaza Hotel,** 10 Washington St., Jack London Square (✆ **800/729-3638** or 510/836-3800; www. waterfrontplaza.com), and the **Oakland Marriott City Center,** 1001 Broadway (✆ **800/228-9290** or 510/451-4000; fax 510/835-3466; www.marriott.com). Most major motel chains also have locations (and budget prices) around town and near the airport. If you want to stay near the fabulous shopping and dining neighborhood of Oakland's Rockridge and pamper yourself with a killer gym, outdoor pools, and lit tennis courts, your best hotel bet (though it's undoubtedly overpriced) is **The Claremont Resort & Spa,** 41 Tunnel Rd., Berkeley (✆ **800/551-7266** or 510/843-3000; www. claremontresort.com), a grand Victorian hotel (with modern rooms) that borders both Berkeley and Oakland. It ain't downtown, but it's just a quick drive to all the action, and it is one of the area's prettiest options (see p. 247 for more information).

WHERE TO DINE
EXPENSIVE
Citron ⊛ FRENCH/CALIFORNIA   This petite, adorable French bistro was an instant smash when it opened in 1992, and it continues to earn raves for its small yet enticingly eclectic menu. Chef and owner Chris Rossi draws the flavors of France, Italy, and Spain together with fresh California produce for results you aren't likely to have tasted elsewhere. The menu changes every few weeks; dishes range from succulent roasted Sonoma leg of lamb, served with gigande beans, cardoons, and fennel to spicy bayou seafood stew brimming with fried oysters, shrimp, snapper, bell pepper, and tomato sauce to fresh chèvre lasagna with braising greens and truffled crimini mushrooms. They've also added a lunch and brunch menu. *A word of advice:* If

you're into classic foods you can identify by name, head elsewhere. It's all about creative cooking here.

5484 College Ave. (north of Broadway between Taft and Lawton sts.). ⓒ 510/653-5484. www.citronrestaurant.biz. Reservations recommended. Lunch and brunch main courses $8–$15; 3-course fixed-price menu $15; dinner main courses $20–$26; 3- to 5-course fixed-price menu $32–$48. AE, DC, DISC, MC, V. Tues–Fri 11:30am–4:30pm; Sat–Sun 10am–3pm; Mon–Tues 5:30–9pm; Wed–Thurs 5:30–9:30pm; Fri 5:30–10pm; Sat 5–10pm; Sun 5–9pm.

Oliveto Cafe & Restaurant 🐹🐹🐹 ITALIAN   Opened 20 years ago by Bob and Maggie Klein and, now under the helm of executive chef Paul Canales (who has been with the Kleins for 11 years, working his way up through the ranks in the kitchen), Oliveto is one of the top Italian restaurants in the Bay Area (and certainly the best in Oakland). Local workers pile in at lunchtime for wood-fired pizzas, simple salads, and sandwiches served in the lower-level cafe. The upstairs restaurant—with suave neo-Florentine decor and a partially open kitchen—is more elegant and packed nightly with fans of the mind-blowing house-made pastas, sausages, and prosciutto. Oliveto has a wood-burning oven, flame-broiled rotisserie, and a full bar which sports a high-end liquor cabinet. An assortment of pricey grills, braises, and roasts anchor the daily changing menu, but the heavenly pastas, pizzetas, and awesome salads offer the most tang for your buck. Still, the Arista (classic Italian pork with garlic and rosemary and pork *jus*) is insanely good; and no one does fried calamari, onion rings, and lemon slices better than Oliveto. *Tip:* Free parking is available in the lot at the rear of the Market Hall building.

Rockridge Market Hall, 5655 College Ave. (off the northeast end of Broadway at Shafter/Keith St., across from the Rockridge BART station). ⓒ 510/547-5356. www.oliveto.com. Reservations recommended for restaurant. Main courses cafe $2.50–$12 breakfast, $4–$8 lunch, $12–$15 dinner; restaurant $11–$15 lunch, $16–$30 dinner. AE, DC, MC, V. Cafe Mon 7am–9pm; Tues–Fri 7am–10pm; Sat 8am–10pm; Sun 8am–9pm. Restaurant Mon–Fri 11:30am–2pm; Tues–Wed 5:30–9:30pm; Thurs–Sat 5:30–10pm; Sun 5–9pm, Mon 5:30–9pm.

MODERATE

À Côté 🐹🐹 FRENCH TAPAS   Jack and Daphne Knowles look to chef Matthew Colgan to serve up killer rustic Mediterranean-inspired small plates at this loud, festive, and warmly lit joint. A "limited reservations" policy means there's usually a long wait during prime dining hours, but once seated you can join locals in a nosh fest featuring the likes of croque-monsieur; *pommes frites* with aioli; wood-oven cooked mussels in Pernod; grilled pork tenderloin with creamy polenta, traviso cheese, and pancetta; and cheese plates—and wash it down with Belgian ales, perky cocktails, or excellent by-the-glass or -bottle selections from the great wine list. *Note:* The heated and covered outdoor seating area tends to be quieter.

5478 College Ave. (at Taft Ave.). ⓒ 510/655-6469. www.acoterestaurant.com. Limited reservations accepted. Small plates $5–$14. MC, V. Sun–Tues 5:30–10pm; Wed–Thurs 5:30–11pm; Fri–Sat 5:30pm–midnight.

Bay Wolf 🐹 CALIFORNIA   The lifespan of most Bay Area restaurants is about a year; Bay Wolf, one of Oakland's most revered restaurants has, fittingly, been going strong for over 3 decades. The converted brown Victorian is a comfortably familiar sight for most East Bay diners, who have come here for years to let executive chef-owner Michael Wilds and his chef de cuisine Louis Le Gassic do the cooking. Bay Wolf enjoys a reputation for simple yet sagacious preparations using only fresh ingredients. Main courses include Liberty Ranch duck three ways (grilled breast, braised leg, and crepinette) with turnips, curly endive, apples, and Calvados; flavorful seafood stew seasoned with saffron; and tender braised *osso buco* with creamy polenta and gremolata.

Informal service means you can leave the tie at home. The front deck has heat lamps and a radiant heat floor, allowing for open-air evening dining year-round—a treat that San Franciscans rarely experience.

3853 Piedmont Ave. (off Broadway between 40th St. and MacArthur Blvd.). ⓒ 510/655-6004. www.baywolf.com. Reservations recommended. Main courses $8.50–$18 lunch, $17–$24 dinner. AE, MC, V. Mon–Fri 11:30am–1:45pm; Mon–Thurs 5:30–9pm; Fri–Sat 5:30-10pm; Sun 5:30–9:30pm. Paid parking at Piedmont Ave. and Yosemite St.

3 Angel Island & Tiburon

8 miles N of San Francisco

A California State Park, Angel Island is the largest of San Francisco Bay's three islets (the others are Alcatraz and Yerba Buena). The island has been, at various times, a prison, a quarantine station for immigrants, a missile base, and even a favorite site for duels. Nowadays, most visitors are content with picnicking on the large green lawn that fronts the docking area; loaded with the appropriate recreational supplies, they claim a barbecue pit, plop their fannies down on the lush green grass, and while away an afternoon free of phones, televisions, and traffic. Hiking, mountain biking, and guided tram tours are other popular activities here.

Tiburon, situated on a peninsula of the same name, looks like a cross between a fishing village and a Hollywood Western set—imagine San Francisco reduced to toy dimensions. The seacoast town rambles over a series of green hills and ends up at a spindly, multicolored pier on the waterfront, like a Fisherman's Wharf in miniature. In reality, it's an extremely plush patch of yacht-club suburbia, as you'll see by the marine craft and the homes of their owners. Ramshackle, color-splashed old frame houses line Main Street, sheltering chic boutiques, souvenir stores, antiques shops, and art galleries. Other roads are narrow, winding, and hilly and lead up to dramatically situated homes. The view from here of San Francisco's skyline and the islands in the bay is a good enough reason to pay the precious price to live here.

Although there is a hotel in Tiburon, I wouldn't recommend staying there: It's a 1-block town, and the hotel is very expensive. There are no hotels on Angel Island. Both destinations are better as day trips.

ESSENTIALS

Ferries of the **Blue & Gold Fleet** (ⓒ 415/705-5555; www.blueandgoldfleet.com) from Pier 41 (Fisherman's Wharf) travel to both Angel Island and Tiburon. Boats run on a seasonal schedule; phone or look online for departure information. The round-trip fare is $15 to Angel Island, $8.50 for kids 6 to 11, and free for kids 5 and under. The fare includes state park fees. Tickets to Tiburon are $8.50 each way for adults, $4.50 for kids 6 to 11, and free for kids 5 and under. Tickets are available at Pier 41, online, or over the phone.

By car from San Francisco, take U.S. 101 to the Tiburon/Highway 131 exit, then follow Tiburon Boulevard all the way downtown, a 40-minute drive from San Francisco. Catch the **Tiburon–Angel Island Ferry** (ⓒ 415/435-2131; www.angelisland ferry.com) to Angel Island from the dock at Tiburon Boulevard and Main Street. The 15-minute round-trip costs $10 for adults, $8 for children 5 to 11, and $1 for bikes. One child under 5 is admitted free of charge with each paying adult (after that it's $8 each). Boats run on a seasonal schedule, but usually depart hourly from 10am to 5pm on weekends, with a more limited schedule on weekdays. Call ahead or look online for departure information. Tickets can only be purchased when boarding, and include state park fees. No credit cards.

WHAT TO SEE & DO ON ANGEL ISLAND

Passengers disembark from the ferry at **Ayala Cove,** a small marina abutting a huge lawn area equipped with tables, benches, barbecue pits, and restrooms. During the summer season, there's also a small store, gift shop, cafe (with surprisingly good grub), and an overpriced mountain-bike rental shop at Ayala Cove. Call ℂ **415/435-5390** or 415/435-1915 (recorded info only) to confirm what's open.

Angel Island's 12 miles of hiking and mountain-bike trails include the **Perimeter Road,** a paved path that circles the island. It winds past disused troop barracks, former gun emplacements, and other military buildings; several turnoffs lead to the top of Mount Livermore, 776 feet above the bay. Sometimes referred to as the "Ellis Island of the West," Angel Island was used as a holding area for detained Chinese immigrants awaiting admission papers from 1910 to 1940. You can still see faded Chinese characters on the walls of the barracks where the immigrants were held. (*Note:* The Immigration Station Barracks are currently closed for renovations and are rumored to reopen late in 2007.) For more information about the island, call **Angel Island** at ℂ **415/435-5390** or 415/435-1915 (recorded info only) or visit www.angelisland.org.

During the warmer months you can camp at a limited number of reserved sites; call **Reserve America** at ℂ **800/444-7275** or visit www.reserveamerica.com to find out about environmental campgrounds at Angel Island. Reservations are taken 2 days to 7 months in advance.

Guided **sea-kayak tours** ℛ are also available. The all-day trips, which include a catered lunch, combine the thrill of paddling stable, two- or three-person kayaks with an informative, naturalist-led tour around the island (conditions permitting). All equipment is provided, kids are welcome, and no experience is necessary. Rates run about $110 per person. A shorter trip takes 2½ hours and costs $75 per person. For more information, contact the Sausalito-based **Sea Trek** at ℂ **415/332-8494;** www.sea trekkayak.com. *Note:* Tours depart from Sausalito, not Angel Island.

The 1-hour **Angel Island Tram Tour** (ℂ **415/897-0715;** www.angelisland.com) costs $13 for adults, $11 for seniors, $7.50 for children 6 to 12, and is free for children 5 and under; schedules vary depending on the time of year, though they generally do not run during winter. It's the lazy man's (or woman's) way to check out the island's flora and fauna, though the reason most come here is to trek around—on foot.

WHAT TO SEE & DO IN TIBURON

The main thing to do in touristy, but pretty, and very tiny Tiburon is stroll along the waterfront, pop into the stores, and spend an easy $50 on drinks and appetizers before heading back to the city. For a taste of the Wine Country, stop at **Windsor Vineyards,** 72 Main St. (ℂ **800/214-9463** or 415/435-3113; www.windsorvineyards.com)—its Victorian tasting room dates from 1888. Twenty or more choices are available for a free tasting. Wine accessories and gifts—glasses, cork pullers, carry packs (which hold six bottles), gourmet sauces, posters, and maps—are also available. Ask about personalized labels for your selections. The shop is open Sunday through Thursday from 10am to 6pm, Friday and Saturday from 10am to 7pm.

WHERE TO DINE IN TIBURON

Guaymas MEXICAN   Guaymas offers authentic Mexican regional cuisine and a spectacular panoramic view of San Francisco and the bay. In good weather, the two

Marin County

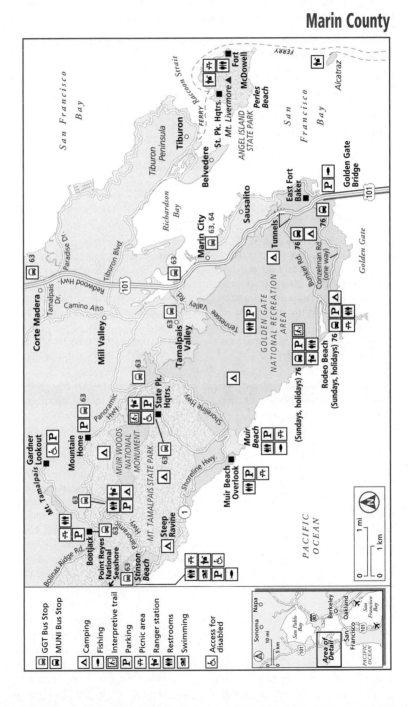

heated outdoor patios are almost always packed with diners soaking in the sun and scene. Inside the very large dining room, colorful Mexican artwork and tons of colored paper cutouts strewn overhead on string brighten the beige walls. Should you feel chilled, to the rear of the dining room is a beehive-shaped adobe fireplace.

Guaymas is named after a fishing village on Mexico's Sea of Cortez, and both the town and the restaurant are famous for their *camarones* (giant shrimp). The restaurant also features seviche, handmade tamales, and charcoal-grilled beef, seafood, and fowl. It's not fancy, nor is it gourmet. But it is a good place to come with large parties or family. In addition to a small selection of California and Central American wines, the restaurant offers an exceptional variety of tequilas and Mexican beers.

5 Main St. © **415/435-6300.** www.guaymas.com. Reservations recommended. Main courses $13–$23. AE, DC, DISC, MC, V. Mon–Thurs 11:30am–10pm; Fri–Sat 11:30am–11pm; Sun 10:30am–10pm. Ferry: Walk about 10 paces from the landing. From U.S. 101, exit at Tiburon/Hwy. 131; follow Tiburon Blvd. 5 miles and turn right onto Main St. Restaurant is behind the bakery.

Sam's Anchor Café ✦ *Finds* SEAFOOD Summer Sundays are liveliest in Tiburon, when weekend boaters tie up at the docks of waterside restaurants like this one, and good-time cyclists pedal from the city to kick it here. Sam's is the kind of place where you and your cronies can take off your shoes and have a fun, relaxing time eating burgers and drinking margaritas outside on the pier. The fare is typical—sandwiches, salads, and such—but the quality and selection are inconsequential: Beers, burgers, and a designated driver are all you really need.

27 Main St. © **415/435-4527.** www.samscafe.com. Main courses $9–$17 brunch, $11–$24 lunch, $15–$24 dinner. AE, DC, DISC, MC, V. Mon–Fri 11am–10pm; Sat–Sun 9:30am–10pm. Ferry: Walk from the landing. From U.S. 101, exit at Tiburon/Hwy. 131; follow Tiburon Blvd. 4 miles and turn right onto Main St.

4 Sausalito

5 miles N of San Francisco

Just off the northern end of the Golden Gate Bridge is the eclectic little town of Sausalito, a slightly bohemian, nonchalant, studiedly quaint adjunct to San Francisco. With fewer than 8,000 residents, Sausalito feels rather like St. Tropez on the French Riviera—minus the starlets and the social rat race. It has its quota of paper millionaires, but they rub their permanently suntanned elbows with a good number of hardup artists, struggling authors, shipyard workers, and fishers. Next to the swank restaurants, plush bars, and antiques shops and galleries, you'll see hamburger joints, beer parlors, and secondhand bookstores. Sausalito's main strip is Bridgeway, which runs along the water. Those in the know make a quick detour to Caledonia Street, 1 block inland; not only is it less congested, but it also has a far better selection of cafes and shops. Since the town is all along the waterfront and only stretches a few blocks, it is easy to find your way around.

ESSENTIALS

The **Golden Gate Ferry Service** fleet, Ferry Building (© **415/923-2000;** www.golden gate.org), operates between the San Francisco Ferry Building, at the foot of Market Street, and downtown Sausalito. Service is frequent, running at reasonable intervals every day of the year except January 1, Thanksgiving, and December 25. Phone for an exact schedule. The ride takes a half-hour, and one-way fares are $6.45 for adults; $3.20 for youth 6–18, seniors 65 plus, and passengers with disabilities (50% off full fare); children 5 and under ride free (limit to two children per full-fare adult). Family rates are available on weekends.

Ferries of the **Blue & Gold Fleet** (© **415/705-5555;** www.blueandgoldfleet.com) leave from Pier 41 (Fisherman's Wharf); the one-way cost is $8.50 for adults, $4.50 for kids 5 to 11. Boats run on a seasonal schedule; phone for departure information.

By car from San Francisco, take U.S. 101 north, then take the first right after the Golden Gate Bridge (Alexander exit). Alexander becomes Bridgeway in Sausalito.

WHAT TO SEE & DO

Above all else, Sausalito has scenery and sunshine, for once you cross the Golden Gate Bridge, you're out of the San Francisco fog patch and under blue California sky (we hope). Houses cover the town's steep hills, overlooking a forest of masts on the waters below. Most of the tourist action, which is almost singularly limited to window-shopping and eating, takes place at sea level on Bridgeway.

Sausalito is a mecca for shoppers seeking handmade, original, and offbeat clothes and footwear, as well as arts and crafts. Many of the town's shops are in the alleys, malls, and second-floor boutiques reached by steep, narrow staircases on and off Bridgeway. Caledonia Street, which runs parallel to Bridgeway 1 block inland, is home to more shops.

Bay Area Discovery Museum *Kids*   If you just can't stand the thought of one more trip to PIER 39 or Fisherman's Wharf and are looking for something else to do with your kids (infants to 8 years old), check out this museum. Located on 7½ acres in the Golden Gate National Recreation Area at Fort Baker, the museum offers spectacular (jaw-dropping even!) views of the city and Golden Gate Bridge (you're literally at the northern base of the bridge) and is also the ultimate indoor-outdoor interactive kids' adventure. Tot Spot is tops for crawlers and toddlers (up to 42 in.); Lookout Cove is a 2-½-acre outdoor area with a scaled-down model of the GGB that kids can add rivets to, a shipwreck to explore, tidal pools, and lovely site-specific art; Art Studios splits kids into age groups 5 and under and 6 and older, and the Wave Workshop re-creates the habitat under the GGB. There's even a small cafe that serves yummy, organic food that's far better than typical family-friendly fare. Remi Hayashi, a California Culinary Academy grad, is at the helm here, serving up Niman Ranch hot dogs, fresh sandwiches, paninis, and pizzas plus a host of snacks (think Stonyfield yogurt and Horizon milk) that you'll feel good about. *One thing to note:* If you're here alone with two kids of different ages, it can be difficult to navigate, as they do keep the little ones separate from the older ones in the Tot Spot. If you explain your situation, they'll give your older one (12 and up) a "Tot Spot Helper" sticker, and let them in, but they won't be allowed to play, they'll have to stick by you. But if it's a nice day, you could spend the whole time in Lookout Cove with both kids, have lunch outside, and still feel like you got your money's worth.

East Fort Baker, 557 McReynolds Rd. © 415/339-3900. www.baykidsmuseum.org. Admission $8.50 adults, $7.50 children, free for children under 1 and members. Discounts available to AAA members and members of reciprocal museum organizations (see website). Tues–Fri 9am–4pm; Sat–Sun 10am–5pm. Closed Mon and all major holidays. By car: Cross the Golden Gate Bridge and take the Alexander Ave. exit. Follow signs to East Fort Baker and the Bay Area Discovery Museum.

Bay Model Visitors Center *Kids*   The U.S. Army Corps of Engineers once used this high-tech, 1½-acre model of San Francisco's bay and delta to resolve problems and observe the impact of changes in water flow. Today the model is strictly for educational purposes and reproduces (in scale) the rise and fall of tides and the flows and currents of water. There's a 10-minute film, self-guided and audio tours ($3 donation requested), and a 1-hour tour (free; book a reservation), but the most interesting time to visit is when the model is in operation, so call ahead.

2100 Bridgeway. ℭ 415/332-3871. www.spn.usace.army.mil/bmvc. Free admission. Labor Day to Memorial Day (winter hours) Tues–Sat 9am–4pm; Memorial Day to Labor Day (summer hours) Tues–Fri 9am–4pm, Sat–Sun and holidays 10am–5pm.

WHERE TO STAY

Sausalito is such a desirable enclave that it offers little in the way of affordable lodging. On the bright side, it's so close to San Francisco that it takes only about 15 minutes to get here, traffic permitting. While the hotels listed below are great destinations in themselves, Sausalito itself is more of a day trip, not a destination.

VERY EXPENSIVE

The Inn Above Tide 𝒜𝒜   Perched directly over the bay atop well-grounded pilings, this former luxury-apartment complex underwent a $4-million transformation in 2004 into one of Sausalito's—if not the Bay Area's—finest accommodations. The view clinches it: Every room affords an unparalleled panorama of the San Francisco Bay, including a postcard-quality vista of the city glimmering in the distance. Should you manage to tear yourself away from your private deck, you'll find that 23 of the sumptuously appointed rooms sport romantic little fireplaces. Some have vast oversize tubs with spa jets, remote-control air-conditioning, and wondrously comfortable queen- or king-size beds. Soothing warm earth tones highlight the decor, which blends in well with the bayscape outside. Be sure to request that your breakfast and newspaper be delivered to your deck, and then cancel your early appointments—on sunny mornings, nobody checks out early.

30 El Portal (next to the Sausalito Ferry Landing), Sausalito, CA 94965. ℭ 800/893-8433 or 415/332-9535. Fax 415/332-6714. www.innabovetide.com. 29 units. $295–$925 double. Rates include continental breakfast and evening wine and cheese. AE, DC, MC, V. Valet parking $12. **Amenities:** Concierge; in-room massage; same-day laundry service/dry cleaning; free shoeshine. *In room:* A/C, TV/DVD, dataport, minibar, fridge, hair dryer, free Wi-Fi access, CD player.

EXPENSIVE

Casa Madrona 𝒜𝒜   Sooner or later most visitors to Sausalito look up and wonder at the ornate mansion on the hill. It's part of Casa Madrona, a hideaway by the bay built in 1885 by a wealthy lumber baron. The epitome of luxury in its day, the mansion had slipped into decay when John Gallagher purchased it in 1910 and converted it into a hotel. By 1976 it was damaged and facing the threat of demolition when John Mays acquired the property and revitalized the hotel. Successive renovations and extensions have added a rambling, New England–style building to the hillside below the main house. Now listed on the National Register of Historic Places, the hotel offers whimsically decorated rooms, suites, and cottages, which are accessed by steep, gorgeously landscaped pathways. The 16 free-standing units, seven cottages, and the rooms in the mansion have individual themes such as Lilac and Lace, Renoir, or the Artist's Loft. Some have claw-foot tubs and others have fireplaces. Rooms in the newer adjoining building are seriously swank, with very streamlined-chic contemporary decor, four-poster beds, marble bathrooms, and great marina views from some rooms. The classy Italian Poggio restaurant (see below) has been Sausalito's hottest since its late-2003 opening.

801 Bridgeway, Sausalito, CA 94965. ℭ 415/332-0502. Fax 415/332-2537. www.casamadrona.com. 63 units. $295–$450 double; $550 suite. AE, DC, DISC, MC, V. Valet parking $20. Ferry: Walk across the street from the landing. From U.S. 101 north, take the 1st right after the Golden Gate Bridge (Alexander exit); Alexander becomes Bridgeway.

Amenities: Restaurant; concierge; room service; babysitting upon request; laundry service; dry cleaning. *In room:* TV, VCR upon availability, minibar, coffeemaker, hair dryer, robes.

WHERE TO DINE
MODERATE

Hamburgers BURGERS   Like the name says, the specialty at this tiny, narrow cafe is juicy flame-broiled hamburgers, arguably Marin County's best. Look for the rotating grill in the window off Bridgeway, and then stand in line and salivate with the rest. Chicken burgers are a slightly healthier option. Order a side of fries, grab a bunch of napkins, and head to the park across the street.

737 Bridgeway. ℭ 415/332-9471. Sandwiches $5.50–$6.50. No credit cards. Daily 11am–5pm. From U.S. 101 north, take the 1st right after the Golden Gate Bridge (Alexander exit); Alexander becomes Bridgeway in Sausalito.

Poggio ⊛⊛ ITALIAN   Sausalito has long been low on upscale dining options, but all that changed with the late-2003 opening of elegant "Poggio," which is a loose Italian translation for "special hillside place." Adjoining the Casa Madrona hotel and across the street from the marina, everything *is* special here, from the floor-to-ceiling doors opening to the sidewalk to its interior with arches and earthen colors, mahogany accents, well-directed light, and centerpiece wood-oven manned by a cadre of chefs to the wine cellar, terra-cotta-tiled floors, comfy mohair banquettes, and white linen-draped tables. Executive chef and partner Christopher Fernandez ensures the food is equally elegant with his daily changing menu featuring things like the superb salad of endive, Gorgonzola, walnuts, figs, and honey; pizzas; addictively excellent pastas (try the spinach ricotta gnocchi with beef ragout); and tasty entrees. (Think whole local petrale sole deboned and served tableside, or grilled lamb chops with roasted fennel and gremolata.) With a full bar, great, well-priced wine list, and yummy desserts, this is Sausalito's premier dining destination—excluding the more casual and decidedly Asian restaurant Sushi Ran (see below).

777 Bridgeway (at Bay St.). ℭ 415/332-7771. www.poggiotrattoria.com. Italian-style breakfast a la carte $2.50–$5.50; main courses lunch $8–$18, dinner $13–$25. AE, DC, DISC, MC, V. Continental breakfast daily 6:30–11am; lunch 11:30am–5:30pm; dinner Sun–Thurs 5:30–10pm, Fri–Sat 5:30–11pm. Free valet parking.

Sushi Ran ⊛⊛ SUSHI/JAPANESE   San Francisco isn't exactly stellar in its Japanese-food selection, but right across from the Golden Gate Bridge is a compact, but fashionable, destination for seriously delicious sushi and cooked dishes. All walks of sushi-loving life cram into the bar, window seats, and more roomy back dining area for Master Sushi Chef Haruo Komatsu's nigiri sushi and standard and specialty rolls. You'll also find a slew of creative dishes by Executive Chef Scott Whitman, such as generously sized and unbelievably moist and buttery miso-glazed black cod (a must-have), oysters on the half shell with ponzu sauce and *tobiko* (fish eggs), and a Hawaiian-style ahi *poke* (Hawaiian-style minced raw fish) salad with seaweed dressing that's authentic enough to make you want to hula. Pay the extra $2.50 or so for fresh wasabi, select from the fine sake and wine list, and don't miss dessert, because here they are more creative and delicious than those served at most Japanese restaurants.

107 Caledonia St. ℭ 415/332-3620. www.sushiran.com. Reservations recommended. Sushi $5–$14; main courses $8.50–$16. AE, MC, V. Mon–Fri 11:45am–2:30pm; Mon–Sat 5:30–11pm; Sun 5–10:30pm. From U.S. 101 north, take the 1st right after the Golden Gate Bridge (Alexander exit); Alexander becomes Bridgeway in Sausalito. At Johnson St. turn left, then right onto Caledonia.

5 Muir Woods & Mount Tamalpais

12 miles N of the Golden Gate Bridge

While the rest of Marin County's redwood forests were being devoured to feed San Francisco's turn-of-the-20th-century building spree, Muir Woods, in a remote ravine on the flanks of Mount Tamalpais, escaped destruction in favor of easier pickings.

MUIR WOODS

Although the magnificent California redwoods have been successfully transplanted to five continents, their homeland is a 500-mile strip along the mountainous coast of southwestern Oregon and Northern California. The coast redwood, or *Sequoia sempervirens,* is the tallest living thing known to man (!); the largest known specimen in the Redwood National Forest towers 368 feet. It has an even larger relative, the *Sequoiadendron giganteum* of the California Sierra Nevada, but the coastal variety is stunning enough. Soaring toward the sky like a wooden cathedral, Muir Woods is unlike any other forest in the world and an experience you won't soon forget.

Granted, Muir Woods is tiny compared to the Redwood National Forest farther north, but you can still get a pretty good idea of what it must have been like when these giants dominated the entire coastal region. What is truly amazing is that they exist a mere 6 miles (as the crow flies) from San Francisco—close enough, unfortunately, that tour buses arrive in droves on the weekends. You can avoid the masses by hiking up the **Ocean View Trail,** turning left on **Lost Trail,** and returning on the **Fern Creek Trail.** The moderately challenging hike shows off the woods' best sides and leaves the lazy-butts behind.

To reach Muir Woods from San Francisco, cross the Golden Gate Bridge heading north on Highway 101, take the Stinson Beach/Highway 1 exit heading west, and follow the signs (and the traffic). The park is open daily from 8am to sunset, and the admission fee is $5 per person over 16. There's also a small gift shop, educational displays, and ranger talks. For more information, call the **National Parks Service at Muir Woods** (© 415/388-2596) or visit www.nps.gov.

If you don't have a car, you can book a bus trip with **San Francisco Sightseeing/ Gray Line** (© 415/434-8687, 888/428-6937 or 800/826-0202; www.sanfrancisco sightseeing.com), which takes you straight to Muir Woods and makes a short stop in Sausalito on the way back. The 3½-hour tour runs twice daily at 9:15am and 2:15pm and costs $47 for adults, $45 for seniors, $22 for children 5 through 11, and is free for kids under 5. Pickup and return from select San Francisco hotels. Call for information and departure times.

MOUNT TAMALPAIS

The birthplace of mountain biking, Mount Tam—as the locals call it—is the Bay Area's favorite outdoor playground and the most dominant mountain in the region. Most every local has his or her secret trail and scenic overlook, as well as an opinion on the raging debate between mountain bikers and hikers (a touchy subject). The main trails—mostly fire roads—see a lot of foot and bicycle traffic on weekends, particularly on clear, sunny days when you can see a hundred miles in all directions, from the foothills of the Sierra to the western horizon. It's a great place to escape from the city for a leisurely hike and to soak in breathtaking views of the bay.

To get to Mount Tamalpais **by car,** cross the Golden Gate Bridge heading north on Highway 101, and take the Stinson Beach/Highway 1 exit. Follow the signs up the shoreline highway for about 2½ miles, turn onto Pantoll Road, and continue for about a mile to Ridgecrest Boulevard. Ridgecrest winds to a parking lot below East Peak. From there, it's a 15-minute hike up to the top. You'll find a visitor center with a small museum, video, fun diorama, and store, as well as enthusiastic and informative "Mount Tam Hosts" who are more than happy to help you plan a hike, identify plants, and generally share their love of the mountain. Visitor center admission is free; open Saturday and Sunday from 11am to 4pm (standard time) and Saturday and Sunday 10am to 5:30pm (daylight saving time). Park hours are 7am to 6pm daily in winter; 7am to 9pm for about 1 month during the height of summer. Two-hour, 2-mile moonlight hikes, among many others, are offered (© 415/388-2070; www.mttam.net).

6 Point Reyes National Seashore

35 miles N of San Francisco

The National Seashore system was created to protect rural and undeveloped stretches of the coast from the pressures brought by soaring real-estate values and increasing population. Nowhere is the success of the system more evident than at Point Reyes. Residents of the surrounding towns—Inverness, Point Reyes Station, and Olema—have steadfastly resisted runaway development. You won't find any strip malls or fast-food joints here, just laid-back coastal towns with cafes, country inns, and vast expanses of open, undeveloped space in between, where gentle living prevails.

Although the peninsula's people and wildlife live in harmony above the ground, the situation beneath the soil is much more volatile. The infamous San Andreas Fault separates Point Reyes—the northernmost landmass on the Pacific Plate—from the rest of California, which rests on the North American Plate. Point Reyes is making its way toward Alaska at a rate of about 2 inches per year, but at times it has moved much faster. In 1906, Point Reyes jumped north almost 20 feet in an instant, leveling San Francisco and jolting the rest of the state. The half-mile Earthquake Trail, near the Bear Valley Visitor Center, illustrates this geological drama with a loop through an area torn by the slipping fault. Shattered fences, rifts in the ground, and a barn knocked off its foundation by the quake illustrate how alive the earth is. If that doesn't convince you, a seismograph in the visitor center will.

ESSENTIALS

Point Reyes is only 30 miles northwest of San Francisco, but it takes at least 90 minutes to reach **by car** (it's all the small towns, not the topography, that slow you down). The easiest route is Sir Francis Drake Boulevard from Highway 101 south of San Rafael; it takes its time getting to Point Reyes, but it does so without any detours. For a much longer but more scenic route, take the Stinson Beach/Highway 1 exit off Highway 101 just south of Sausalito and follow Highway 1 north.

As soon as you arrive at Point Reyes, stop at the **Bear Valley Visitor Center** (© 415/464-5100; www.nps.gov/pore) on Bear Valley Road (look for the small sign just north of Olema on Hwy. 1) and pick up a free Point Reyes trail map. The rangers are extremely friendly and helpful and can answer any questions about the National Seashore. Be sure to check out the great natural history and cultural displays while you're there. The center is open weekdays from 9am to 5pm, weekends and holidays from 8am to 5pm.

Entrance to the park is free. **Camping** is $15 per site per night for up to 6 people, and permits are required. All the sites range from a 1.4- to 5.5-mile hike in from the

Tips **Whale Sightings**

Rangers suggest that during the whales' southern migration (Jan), you should go to the lighthouse for the best view. During their northern migration (Mar), you can see 'em from any of the area's beaches.

---

nearest trail head. Reservations can be made up to 3 months in advance by calling © **415/663-8054** Monday through Friday from 9am to 2pm.

WHAT TO SEE & DO

When headed to any part of the Point Reyes coast, expect to spend the day surrounded by nature at its finest; however, bear in mind that as beautiful as the wilderness can be, it's also untamable. The bone-chilling waters in these areas are not only home to a vast array of sea life, including sharks, but are unpredictable and dangerous. There are no lifeguards on duty, and swimming is strongly discouraged because of the waves and rip tides. Pets are not permitted on any of the area's trails. However, if you are looking for a place to swim, consider heading toward Tomales Bay during the summer months.

By far the most popular—and crowded—attraction at Point Reyes National Seashore is the venerable **Point Reyes Lighthouse** ⭐ (© **415/669-1534**), at the westernmost tip of Point Reyes. Even if you plan to forgo the 308 steps to the lighthouse itself (sorry—no strollers or wheelchairs), the area is still worth a visit. The dramatic scenery includes thousands of common murres and prides of sea lions that bask on the rocks far below (binoculars come in handy). It's open Thursday through Monday from 10am to 4:30pm and admission is free. There is a parking area designated for travelers with disabilities, at the visitor center. Call © **415/464-5100** to make arrangements.

The lighthouse is also the top spot on the California coast from which to observe **gray whales** as they make their southward and northward migrations along the coast January through April. The annual round-trip is 10,000 miles—one of the longest mammal migrations known. The whales head south in January and return north in March. There's never a guarantee that you will see a whale, but it's best to come during clear, calm weather. *Note:* If you plan to drive to the lighthouse to whale-watch, arrive early because parking is limited. If possible, come on a weekday. On a weekend or holiday January through the beginning of April, you have to park at the Drake's Beach Visitor Center and take the shuttle bus (weather permitting) to the lighthouse and on to Chimney Rock to watch elephant seals; the shuttle bus runs from around New Year's Day to the beginning of April and costs $5 for adults and is free for children under 16. Dress warmly when you come here—it's often quite cold and windy—and bring binoculars. And expect to spend about 2½ hours.

Whale-watching is far from the only activity at the Point Reyes National Seashore. On weekend afternoons or daily during the summer months, many different tours are offered: You can walk along the Bear Valley Trail, spotting the wildlife at the ocean's edge; see the waterfowl at Alamere Falls; explore tide pools; view some of North America's most beautiful ducks in the wetlands of Limantour; hike to the promontory overlooking Chimney Rock to see the sea lions, harbor seals, elephant seals, and seabirds; or take a guided walk along the San Andreas Fault to observe the epicenter of the 1906 earthquake and learn about the regional geology. And this is just a sampling. Tours vary seasonally; for the most up-to-date details, call the **Bear Valley Visitor Center** (✆ 415/464-5100) or visit the National Park Service's website (www.nps.gov/pore) where you can also get a lay of the land and more details, including area maps, in the "Plan Your Visit" section of the site. *Note:* Many tours are suitable for travelers with disabilities.

Some of the park's best—and least crowded—highlights can be approached only on foot. They include **Alamere Falls,** a freshwater stream that cascades down a 40-foot bluff onto Wildcat Beach, and **Tomales Point Trail,** which passes through the Tule Elk Reserve, a protected haven for roaming herds of tule elk that once numbered in the thousands. Hiking most of the trails usually ends up being an all-day outing, however, so it's best to split a 2-day trip into a "by car" day and a "by foot" day.

If you're into bird-watching, you'll definitely want to visit the **Point Reyes Bird Observatory** (✆ 415/868-1221), one of the few full-time ornithological research stations in the United States. It's at the southeast end of the park on Mesa Road. This is where ornithologists keep an eye on more than 400 feathered species. Admission to the visitor center and nature trail is free, and visitors are welcome to observe the tricky process of catching and banding the birds. The observatory is open daily from 15 minutes after sunrise to sunset. Banding hours vary; contact them at (✆ **415/868-0655; www.prbo.org**) for exact times.

One of my favorite things to do in Point Reyes is paddle through placid Tomales Bay, a haven for migrating birds and marine mammals. **Blue Waters Kayaking** ✦ (✆ 415/663-1743; www.bwkayak.com) organizes nature tours and hiking and kayak trips, including 3-hour morning or sunset outings, oyster tours, day trips, and longer excursions. Instruction, private groups and classes, clinics, and boat rental are available, and all ages and levels are welcome. Prices for tours start at $68. Rentals begin at $30 per person. Don't worry—the kayaks are very stable, and there aren't any waves to contend with. There are two launching points: One is on Highway 1 at the Marshall

---

Finds   Johnson Drake's Oyster Farm

If you want to escape the crowds and enjoy some man-made entertainment, head to **Johnson Drake's Oyster Farm.** Located on the edge of Drakes Estero (a large saltwater lagoon on the Point Reyes peninsula that produces nearly 20% of California's commercial oyster yield), **Johnson Drake's Oyster Farm** doesn't look like much—a cluster of trailer homes, shacks, and oyster tanks surrounded by huge piles of oyster shells. A change of ownership promises some general clean-up, but don't expect much more than the opportunity to tour, buy delicious fresh-out-of-the-water oysters along with Johnson's special sauce, and use a bathroom that makes you want to wear gloves. That said, they've added barbecues (supplies available) and are working on getting some picnic tables so you can enjoy your recently purchased bivalves right then and there. Johnson Drake's (✆ **415/669-1149**) is off Sir Francis Drake Boulevard, about 6 miles west(ish) of Inverness. It's open daily 8am to 4:30pm.

Boatworks in Marshall, 8 miles north of Point Reyes Station and the other is on Sir Francis Drake Boulevard, in Inverness, 5 miles west of Point Reyes Station. The Inverness site is open daily from 9am to 5pm; the Marshall site is open, weather permitting, on weekends and by appointment. Call or visit their website to confirm.

WHERE TO STAY

Inns of Marin, P.O. Box 547, Point Reyes Station, CA 94956 (© **800/887-2880** or 415/663-2000; www.innsofmarin.com), is a free service that can help you find accommodations ranging from one-room cottages to inns to complete vacation homes. Many places have a 2-night minimum, but at slow times they might make an exception. The service can also refer you to restaurants, hiking trails, and area attractions.

EXPENSIVE

Manka's Inverness Lodge & Restaurant *(★★★ (finds)*   If there was ever a reason to pack your bags and leave San Francisco for a day or two, this is it. A former hunting and fishing lodge, Manka's looks like something out of a Hans Christian Andersen fairy tale, right down to the tree-limb bedstands. It's all terribly romantic in a Jack London-ish sort of way, and tastefully done. The lodge consists of a superb restaurant on the first floor, four rooms upstairs (room nos. 1 and 2 have large private decks), and four rooms in the Redwood Annex. Two spacious one-bedroom cabins, behind the lodge and on the water, have living rooms and bathrooms with vintage 6-foot double-ended tubs and private outdoor showers opening up to the sky. For the ultimate romantic splurge, inquire about the three secluded guesthouses: Boat House, Perch, and Cabin 125. The lodge's reputation was built on its rustic and romantic restaurant, which dominates the bottom floor and continues to make visitors swoon with house specialties of game and fish. The menu is price-fixed, ranging from $58 to $88 (on Sat), and features limited selections that might include pheasant with Madeira *jus,* mashed potatoes, and wild-huckleberry jam; black-buck antelope chops with sweet-corn salsa; or, everybody's favorite, pan-seared elk tenderloin. The restaurant is open for dinner Thursday through Sunday for a single seating (7pm to 7:30 Thurs–Sat; 4 to 4:30pm Sun) except for the first 6 weeks of the year, when it's closed.

30 Calendar Way (at Argyle St., off Sir Francis Drake Blvd., ¼ mile north of downtown Inverness), P.O. Box 1110, Inverness, CA 94937. © **415/669-1034.** Fax 415/669-1598. www.mankas.com. 14 units, including 4 cabins. $215–$385 double; $365–$565 cabin. AE, MC, V. **Amenities:** Restaurant; room service; in-room massage; movies on request; personal music library; free Wi-Fi access. *In room:* MP3 player with CD library, phones in guesthouses, redwood soaking tubs in some rooms, massage.

INEXPENSIVE

Motel Inverness *(Kids)*   Homey, well-maintained and fronting Tomales Bay, this is the perfect pick for the spendthrift or the outdoor adventurer who plans to spend as little time indoors as possible. (Those seeking romance should dig a little deeper into their pockets and opt for Manka's; see above.) All of the guest rooms except one twin-bed option have queen-size beds and skylights. Attached to the hotel is a giant great room, complete with fireplace and pool table to distract the kids; parents can relax and children can play on the back lawn overlooking the bay, bird sanctuary, and rolling green hills beyond. There are two 2-bedroom suites, one with wheelchair access and a deck to take in the views that sleeps 4; the other is billed as the "luxury" suite and has a king-size bed, Jacuzzi, and a kitchenette. Both are ideal for families, as is the Dacha cottage, located a few miles away, which is on the water and boasts three bedrooms, a living/dining room, large sitting room, and deck with Tomales Bay views. *Note:* The motel is nonsmoking.

12718 Sir Francis Drake Blvd., Inverness, CA 94937. © **888/669-6909** or 415/669-1081. www.motelinverness.com. 8 units. $99–$160 double; $285–$400 suites; Dacha Cottage $500. MC, V. *In room:* TV, coffeemaker.

WHERE TO DINE

See "Where to Stay," above, for details on the highly recommended **Manka's Inverness Lodge & Restaurant.**

MODERATE

Station House Café ⚔ AMERICAN   For more than 2 decades, the Station House Café has been a favorite pit stop for Bay Area residents headed to and from Point Reyes. It's a friendly, low-key place with an open kitchen, an outdoor garden dining area (key on sunny days), and live music on weekend nights. Breakfast dishes include a Hangtown omelet with local oysters and bacon, and eggs with creamed spinach and mashed-potato pancakes. Lunch and dinner specials might be fettuccine with fresh local mussels steamed in white wine and butter sauce, two-cheese polenta served with fresh spinach sauté and grilled garlic-buttered tomato, or a daily fresh salmon special—all made from local produce, seafood, and organically raised Niman Ranch beef. The cafe has an extensive list of fine California wines and local microbrew beers.

11180 Hwy. 1, Main St., Point Reyes Station. © **415/663-1515.** www.stationhousecafe.com. Reservations recommended. Breakfast $5.25–$9.25; main courses $7.50–$18 lunch, $9–$25 dinner. AE, DISC, MC, V. Sun–Tues and Thurs 8am–9pm; Fri–Sat 8am–10pm (bar until 11pm).

INEXPENSIVE

Rosie's Cowboy Cookhouse ⚔ MEXICAN/AMERICAN   Fresh, good, fast, and cheap: What more could you ask for in a restaurant? Taqueria La Quinta, which was a favorite lunch stop in downtown Point Reyes for years and years, is now known as Rosie's Cowboy Cookhouse. At press time, they were promising to keep the huge selection of Mexican-American standards on the menu, adding some new, more Southwestern fare such as rib-eye steak and chiles rellenos. Watch out for the salsa—that sucker's hot.

11285 Hwy. 1 (at Third and Main sts.), Point Reyes Station. © **415/663-8868.** No credit cards. Wed–Mon 11am–9pm.

12

The Wine Country

Even if you're having the time of your life in downtown San Francisco, I highly recommend at least a quick jaunt to the Wine Country, an hour or so north by car. Amid the mountains dipping into grapevine-trellised valleys, you'll experience an entirely different Northern California: fresh country air, mustard-flower-draped hillsides in spring, hot weather during summer, some of the world's finest wineries, incredible restaurants, cow-studded pastures, and virtually nothing to do but overindulge. With eating, drinking, and lounging the encouraged attractions, there's virtually no better definition of a vacation than a few days here. Spend even 24 hours and you'll understand why this native San Franciscan chooses to call Wine Country home.

To decide which of the Wine Country's two distinct valleys (Napa and Sonoma) you prefer to visit, you need to consider their differences: The most obvious is size—Napa Valley dwarfs Sonoma Valley in population, number of wineries, and sheer volume of tourism (and traffic). Napa is definitely the more commercial of the two, with many more wineries and spas to choose from, and a superior selection of restaurants, hotels, and quintessential Wine Country activities, like hot-air ballooning. Furthermore, if your goal is to really learn about the world of winemaking, Napa Valley should be your choice. World-class wineries such as Sterling and Robert Mondavi offer the most interesting and edifying wine tours in North America, if not the world (although Sonoma's Benziger Winery does give them a run for their money).

Meanwhile, Sonoma Valley is the answer for those who are in the less-is-more camp. Napa Valley's neighbor has fewer wineries (about 35), fewer big hotels and restaurants, and a less commercial feel. As a result, there are fewer crowds on the low-key country roads; more down-home charm in the country communities, B&Bs, and little family-run restaurants; and, in general, more opportunities for intimate pastoral experiences. For more on Sonoma Valley's offerings (as spectacular as Napa Valley's but more low-key), see the "Sonoma Valley" section.

If you're planning a more extensive trip to the area, consult *Frommer's Portable California Wine Country* (Wiley Publishing, Inc.).

1 Napa Valley

Just 55 miles north of San Francisco, the city of Napa and its neighboring towns have an overall tourist and big-business feel. You'll see plenty of rolling hills, flora and fauna, and vast stretches of vineyards, but they come hand-in-hand with upscale restaurants, designer discount outlets, rows of hotels and, in summer, traffic clustered more tightly than the grapes hanging heavy on the vine. Even with hordes of visitors year-round, Napa is still pretty sleepy, focusing on daytime attractions (wine, outdoor

The Wine Country

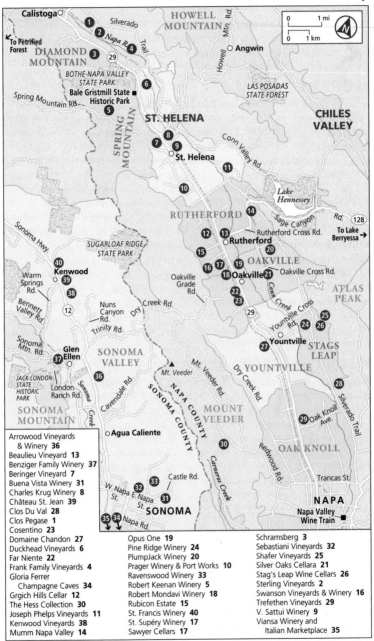

Calistoga
To Petrified Forest
DIAMOND MOUNTAIN
HOWELL MOUNTAIN
Silverado
Napa Rd.
Angwin
BOTHE-NAPA VALLEY STATE PARK
Bale Gristmill State Historic Park
Spring Mountain Rd.
SPRING MOUNTAIN
ST. HELENA
St. Helena
Conn Valley Rd.
LAS POSADAS STATE-FOREST
CHILES VALLEY
RUTHERFORD
Rutherford Cross Rd.
Rutherford
Lake Hennessey
Sage Canyon Rd.
To Lake Berryessa
SUGARLOAF RIDGE STATE PARK
Sonoma Hwy.
Kenwood
Warm Springs Rd.
Bennett Valley Rd.
OAKVILLE
Oakville Grade Rd.
Oakville
Oakville Cross Rd.
ATLAS PEAK
Nuns Canyon Rd.
Dry Creek Rd.
Trinity Rd.
Conn Creek Rd.
Youtville Cross
STAGS LEAP
Yountville
Sonoma Mtn. Rd.
Glen Ellen
JACK LONDON STATE HISTORIC PARK
London Ranch Rd.
SONOMA VALLEY
Mt. Veeder
Mt. Veeder Rd.
YOUNTVILLE
Dry Creek Rd.
Silverado Trail
SONOMA MOUNTAIN
Cavendale Rd.
SONOMA COUNTY
NAPA COUNTY
MOUNT VEEDER
Oak Knoll Ave.
OAK KNOLL
Agua Caliente
Carneros Creek
Redwood Rd.
Trancas St.
Castle Rd.
W. Napa St.
E. Napa St.
SONOMA
Napa Rd.
NAPA
Napa Valley Wine Train

Arrowood Vineyards & Winery **36**
Beaulieu Vineyard **13**
Benziger Family Winery **37**
Beringer Vineyard **7**
Buena Vista Winery **31**
Charles Krug Winery **8**
Château St. Jean **39**
Clos Du Val **28**
Clos Pegase **1**
Cosentino **23**
Domaine Chandon **27**
Duckhead Vineyards **6**
Far Niente **22**
Frank Family Vineyards **4**
Gloria Ferrer Champagne Caves **34**
Grgich Hills Cellar **12**
The Hess Collection **30**
Joseph Phelps Vineyards **11**
Kenwood Vineyards **38**
Mumm Napa Valley **14**

Opus One **19**
Pine Ridge Winery **24**
PlumpJack Winery **20**
Prager Winery & Port Works **10**
Ravenswood Winery **33**
Robert Keenan Winery **5**
Robert Mondavi Winery **18**
Rubicon Estate **15**
St. Francis Winery **40**
St. Supéry Winery **17**
Sawyer Cellars **17**

Schramsberg **3**
Sebastiani Vineyards **32**
Shafer Vineyards **25**
Silver Oaks Cellara **21**
Stag's Leap Wine Cellars **26**
Sterling Vineyards **2**
Swanson Vineyards & Winery **16**
Trefethen Vineyards **29**
V. Sattui Winery **9**
Viansa Winery and Italian Marketplace **35**

activities, and spas) and, of course, food. Nightlife is very limited, but after indulging all day, most visitors are ready to turn in early anyway.

Although the name "Napa Valley" seems sprawling, the actual area is relatively condensed and only 35 miles long. You can venture from the town of Napa all the way to Calistoga in half an hour (traffic permitting).

ESSENTIALS

GETTING THERE From San Francisco, cross the Golden Gate Bridge and continue north on U.S. 101. Turn east on California Highway 37, turn left onto the 12/121 turnoff and follow it through the Carneros District to Highway 29, the main road through the Wine Country. Head north on 29. Downtown Napa is a few minutes ahead, while Yountville, Oakville, Rutherford, St. Helena, and Calistoga are further along.

Highway 29 (the St. Helena Hwy.) runs the length of Napa Valley. You really can't get lost—there's just one north-south road, on which most of the wineries, hotels, shops, and restaurants are located. The other main thoroughfare, which parallels Highway 29, is the Silverado Trail. You'll find lots of great wineries here, too.

VISITOR INFORMATION Once you're in Napa Valley, you can stop at the **Napa Valley Conference & Visitors Bureau,** 1310 Napa Town Center, Napa, CA 94559 (✆ **707/226-7459,** ext. 106; www.napavalley.com). You can call or write in for the *Napa Valley Guidebook,* which includes information on lodging, restaurants, wineries, and other things to do, along with a winery map; the Bureau charges a $5 postage fee. If you don't want to pay for the official publication, point your browser to www.napavalley.org, the NVCVB's official site, which has lots of the same information for free.

TOURING THE NAPA VALLEY & WINERIES

Napa Valley claims more than 37,000 acres of vineyards, making it the most densely planted winegrowing region in the United States. The venture from one end to the other is easy; you can drive it in around half an hour (but expect it to take closer to 50 min. during high season, Apr–Nov). With more than 300 wineries tucked into the nooks and crannies surrounding Highway 29 and the Silverado Trail—almost all of which offer tastings and sales—it's worthwhile to research which wineries you'd like to visit before you hit the wine trails. If you'd like a map outlining the details around all of the region's wineries, you can grab one from the visitor center or see *Frommer's Portable California Wine Country.*

Conveniently, most of the large wineries—as well as most of the hotels, shops, and restaurants—are along a single road, Highway 29. It starts at the mouth of the Napa River, near the north end of San Francisco Bay, and continues north to Calistoga and

Tips Reservations at Wineries

Plenty of wineries' doors are open to everyone between 10am and 4:30pm. Most wineries that require reservations for visits do so because of local permit laws. It's always best to call ahead if you have your heart set on visiting a certain winery. A few wineries limit the number of guests to create a more intimate experience. In many cases, however, they'll be just as happy to see you if you arrive unannounced.

> ### ⓘ Tips Napa Valley Traffic
>
> Travel the Silverado Trail as often as possible to avoid California Highway 29's traffic. It runs parallel to and about 2 miles east of Highway 29. You get there from the city of Napa or by taking any of the "crossroads" from Highway 29. Crossroads are not well signposted, but they're clearly defined on most maps. If you take the Trail, keep us locals happy by driving at least the speed limit. Slow-rubberneckers are no fun to follow when you're trying to get from one end of the valley to the other. Also, avoid passing through Main Street in St. Helena (on Hwy. 29) during high season. While a wintertime ride from Napa to Calistoga can take 30 minutes, in summer you can expect the trek to take closer to 50 minutes.

the northern limits of the grape-growing region. When planning your tour, keep in mind that most wineries are closed on major holidays.

Each of the Napa Valley establishments in this chapter—every town, winery, hotel, and restaurant—is organized below from south to north, beginning in the city of Napa, and can be reached from the main thoroughfare of Highway 29.

NAPA
55 miles N of San Francisco

The city of Napa serves as the commercial center of the Wine Country and the gateway to Napa Valley—hence the high-speed freeway that whips you right past it and on to the "tourist" towns of St. Helena and Calistoga. However, if you veer off the highway, you'll be surprised to discover a small but burgeoning community of nearly 75,000 residents with the most cosmopolitan (if you can call it that) atmosphere in the county—and some of the most affordable accommodations in the valley. It is in the process of gentrification, thanks to (relatively) affordable housing, a charming old-fashioned downtown, and ongoing additions of new restaurants. Heading north on either Highway 29 or the Silverado Trail leads you to Napa's wineries and the more quintessential Wine Country atmosphere of vineyards and wide-open country views.

The Hess Collection ⋆⋆ *Finds*   Tucked into the hillside of rural Mount Veeder, one of the region's sexiest wineries brings art and wine together like no other destination in the valley. Swiss art collector Donald Hess is behind the 1978 transformation of the Christian Brothers' 1903 property into a winery-art gallery exhibiting huge, colorful works by the likes of Frank Stella, Francis Bacon, Anselm Kiefer and the latest addition, an Andy Goldsworthy multimedia sculptural piece. A free self-guided tour leads through the collection and offers glimpses through tiny windows into the winemaking facilities. Equally alluring is the picturesque courtyard and exceptionally tasteful gift shop. *The only downside:* Staff can be cold and stuffy. For $10, you can sample the current cabernet and chardonnay and one other featured wine; $20 gets you a reserve tasting. For bottles, current-release prices start at $18 and top off at around $115.

4411 Redwood Rd., Napa. ⓒ 707/255-1144. www.hesscollection.com. Daily 10am–4pm, except some holidays. From Hwy. 29 north, exit at Redwood Rd. west, and follow Redwood Rd. for 6½ miles.

Trefethen Vineyards   Listed on the National Register of Historic Places, the vineyard's main building was built in 1886 and is Napa's last example of 19th-century wooden, gravity-flow wineries. Although Trefethen is one of the valley's oldest wineries, it didn't produce its first chardonnay until 1973—but thank goodness it did. The award-winning whites and reds are a pleasure to the palate. Tastings are $10 for four estate wines, but if you want to sample a reserve, it'll cost you $20. A thirty-minute tour is available by appointment only.

1160 Oak Knoll Ave. (east of Hwy. 29), Napa. ✆ 707/255-7700. www.trefethen.com. Daily 10am–4:30pm. From Hwy. 29 north, take a right onto Oak Knoll Ave. Tours by appointment.

Clos Du Val   Outside French and American flags mark the entrance to the ivy-covered building and well-manicured rose garden. Inside, you'll experience a friendly, small-business atmosphere along with a matter-of-fact tasting room pouring California wines made in subtler French style.

Cabernet makes up 70% of the winery's production, but other varietals include chardonnay, pinot noir, and merlot. There's a $5 tasting charge (refunded with purchase) for about four wines, and a $20 reserve tasting which includes a logo glass and a library selection or two.

Lovely picnic facilities and free access to the lawn game *petanque* are available in grassy nooks along the grounds.

5330 Silverado Trail (north of Oak Knoll Ave.), Napa. ✆ 707/259-2200. www.closduval.com. Daily 10am–5pm. Tours by appointment only.

Stag's Leap Wine Cellars   Founded in 1972, Stag's Leap shocked the oenological world in 1976 when its 1973 cabernet won first place over French wines in a Parisian blind tasting. Visit the charmingly landscaped, unfussy winery and its very cramped "tasting room" where, for $10 per person, you can judge the four to six current releases; or you can fork over up to $30 for estate and library selections. A 1-hour tour and tasting runs through everything from the vineyard and production facilities to the ultraswank (by appointment only) wine caves (used to store and age wine).

5766 Silverado Trail, Napa. ✆ 707/944-2020. www.cask23.com. Daily 10am–4:30pm. Tours by appointment only. From Hwy. 29, go east on Trancas St. or Oak Knoll Ave., then north to the cellars.

Pine Ridge Winery   More for the serious wine taster than the casual winery hopper, Pine Ridge welcomes guests with a pretty hillside location, less tourist traffic than most, and good wines. Outside, vineyards surround the well-landscaped property. Across the parking lot is a demonstration vineyard, which is somewhat educational if

---

Tips Paying to Taste

It used to be out of the norm to pay for wine tasting, and when the tides first started to change, I wasn't really for it. But over the past decade, sipping through the region has become such a pastime that in the more popular—and cheap or free—tasting spots you'll often find yourself competing for room at the bar, never mind a refill or a little wine chatter with your host. As a result, I've changed my view on paying a premium to taste. With the flash of a 10- or 20-spot per person you not only avoid crowding in with the hundreds of tipsy souls who come merely for the fun and the buzz, but you also usually get a more intimate experience, complete with attention from staff and usually far more exclusive (and sometimes even seated) surroundings.

you know something about grape growing and even more helpful if you take their $20 tour (by appointment), which also covers the cellar and barrel tastings. Otherwise, tastings, which are held inside a modest room, start at $10 for current releases. Their appointment-only Cab and reserve barrel-to-bottle tastings are $20 and $30, respectively, and are held at 11am, 1pm, and 3pm. They also offer a $40 Sunday Cooking Seminar at 11am during which you'll learn about food and wine pairings; in the winter it's held indoors, but during great summer weather it's done alfresco. (Unfortunately, it's canceled if the weather's not great.) If you're visiting in summer and want to know about food and wine pairing, call to learn whether they're holding their tasty weekend seminars.

5901 Silverado Trail, Napa. © 800/575-9777 or 707/253-7500. www.pineridgewinery.com. Daily 10:30am–4:30pm. Tours by appointment at 10am, noon, and 2pm.

Shafer Vineyards 🎯🎯 *Finds*   For an intimate, off-the-beaten-track wine experience, make an appointment to tour and taste at this Stag's Leap destination. Unlike many Napa wineries, this one is family owned—by John and Doug Shafer. After 23 years in publishing, John bought 209 Wine Country hillside acres and planted vines on 50 of them. Today, he and his son Doug, joined by winemaker Elias Fernandez, use sustainable farming and solar energy to make exceptional chardonnay, merlot, cabernet sauvignon, and syrah. Though they produce only 34,000 cases per year, their wines are well known and highly regarded. But more importantly, they share it and their winemaking philosophy with you during a really enjoyable and relaxed $25-per-person 1½-hour tour and tasting, which includes sipping at one long wooden table within a bright, homey room with a fireplace, pitched ceiling, and windows overlooking vineyards from every angle, and perhaps patting their yellow lab, Tucker. Most wines go for $37 to $60, but their Hillside Select cabernet will cost you $150.

6154 Silverado Trail, Napa. © 707/944-2877. www.shafervineyards.com. By appointment only Mon–Fri 10:30am and 2pm.

YOUNTVILLE
70 miles N of San Francisco

Yountville (pop. 2,916) was founded by the first white American to settle in the valley, George Calvert Yount. While it lacks the small-town charm of neighboring St. Helena and Calistoga—primarily because its main street, though filling up with hotels, restaurants, and shops, doesn't feel like a center—it's still a great starting point for valley exploration. It's home to a handful of excellent wineries and inns and a small stretch of fab restaurants, including the world-renowned French Laundry.

Domaine Chandon 🎯🎯 *Finds*   Founded in 1973 by French champagne house Moët et Chandon, the valley's most renowned sparkling winemaker rises to the grand occasion with truly elegant grounds and atmosphere. Here manicured gardens showcase locally made sculpture, and guests linger—their glasses fizzing with bubbly—under the patio's umbrella shade. In the restaurant, diners indulge in a somewhat formal French-inspired meal (there's a more casual menu at lunchtime). If you can pull yourself away from the Salon's bubbly (sold in tastings for $9–$14), the comprehensive tour of the facilities is interesting, very informative, and friendly. There's also a new $25 Epicurean Experience Tour that includes stops along the way to taste wine paired with foods prepared by Chandon's chef. The Shop at Domaine Chandon carries some varietal wines not sold elsewhere, along with some liqueurs, spa items, and requisite logo mementos. *Note:* The restaurant, which is closed on Tuesday and Wednesday and has even more restricted winter hours, usually requires reservations.

1 California Dr. (at Hwy. 29), Yountville. ✆ **707/944-2280**. www.chandon.com. Daily 10am–6pm; hours vary by season, so call to confirm. Call for free tour schedules.

Cosentino Known for its friendly, laid-back atmosphere and vast selection of wines, Cosentino's tasting room is a great stop for anyone interested in covering a lot of wine-tasting ground under one roof. Pay $5 to taste ($10 for reserve wines) and you'll get to keep the glass, plus sample an array of wines from their portfolio, which includes the brands Cosentino, CE2V, and Crystal Valley Cellars, and nearly 40 different wines on sale ($12–$100). There's lots of entertainment value at the long copper-top bar. Join the wine club for free tastings and 25% off purchases.

7415 St. Helena Hwy. (Hwy. 29), Yountville. ✆ **707/944-1220**. www.cosentinowinery.com. Daily 10am–6pm.

OAKVILLE
68 miles N of San Francisco

Driving farther north on Highway 29 brings you to Oakville, most easily recognized by Oakville Cross Road.

Far Niente ᴄ̠ This storybook stone winery is a serious treat for wine, garden, and classic car lovers. Founded in 1885, it was abandoned for 60 years around prohibition, purchased in 1979 by Gil Nickel (also of nearby Nickel & Nickel winery), and opened to the public for the first time in spring 2004. The tour includes a walk around the beautiful historic stone property, caves, private car collection (truly stunning!), and azalea garden. It finishes with a sampling of five delicious wines (including a delicious chardonnay, cabernet sauvignon, and "Dolce"—their spectacular semillon and sauvignon blanc dessert blend sure to make converts of even sweet wine naysayers). Tastings are $50 and by appointment only. Wines aren't cheap either—from around $52 for the chardonnay to $115 for their estate cabernet sauvignon.

1350 Acacia Dr., Oakville. ✆ **800-FN-DOLCE** or 707/944-2861. www.farniente.com. Tours and tastings by appointment only daily 10am–4pm.

Silver Oak Cellars Colorado oilman Ray Duncan and former Christian Brothers monk Justin Meyer formed a partnership and a mission to create the finest cabernet sauvignon in the world. The answer was this winery, which produces one of the valley's cabernet kings.

A narrow, tree-lined road leads to the handsome Mediterranean-style winery, where roughly 25,000 cases of Napa Valley Cabernet Sauvignon are produced annually (an additional 50,000 cases are produced annually at their Alexander Valley winery in Geyserville). The elegant tasting room is refreshingly quiet and soothing, adorned with redwood panels stripped from old wine tanks and warmed by a wood fire. Tastings, which include a keepsake bordeaux glass, are $10. No picnic facilities are available. *Note:* Due to a fire, Silver Oak will be rebuilding at the end of 2006, but they promise that it will not affect their tours.

915 Oakville Cross Rd. (at Money Rd.), Oakville. ✆ **800/273-8809** or 707/944-8808. www.silveroak.com. Tasting room Mon–Sat 9am–4pm. Tours Mon–Fri at 1:30pm, by appointment only.

PlumpJack Winery If most wineries are like a Brooks Brothers suit, PlumpJack stands out as the Todd Oldham of wine tasting: chic, colorful, a little wild, and popular with a young, hip crowd as well as a growing number of aficionados. Like the franchise's PlumpJack San Francisco restaurants and wine shop, and Lake Tahoe resort, this playfully medieval winery is a welcome diversion from the same old same old. With Getty bucks behind what was once Villa Mt. Eden winery, the budget covers far more than just atmosphere: There's some serious winemaking going on here, too. For $5 you can sample current releases. Alas, there are no tours or picnic spots.

620 Oakville Cross Rd. (just west of the Silverado Trail), Oakville. ⓒ 707/945-1220. www.plumpjack.com. Daily 10am–4pm.

Robert Mondavi Winery 𝒦 *Finds*

At mission-style Mondavi, computers control almost every variable in the winemaking process—it's fascinating to watch, especially since Mondavi gives the most comprehensive tours in the valley. Basic jaunts, which cost $25 and last about an hour and 15 minutes, take you through the vineyards—complete with examples of varietals—and through their newest winemaking facilities. Ask the guides anything; they know a heck of a lot. After the tour, you taste the results of all this attention to detail in selected current wines. If you're really into learning more about wine, ask about their myriad in-depth tours, such as the $60 "essence tasting," which explores the flavor profiles of wine by sniff-comparing varietals alongside the scents of fresh fruits, spices, and nuts, or their $110 "Celebrating California Wine and Food" tour, which includes a presentation on the history of wine, a tour of the winery, and a three-course luncheon with wine pairing. In summer, the winery also schedules some great outdoor concerts; previous performers included Buena Vista Social Club, Aimee Mann, and Chaka Kahn. Call about upcoming events.

7801 St. Helena Hwy. (Hwy. 29), Oakville. ⓒ 888/766-6328, ext. 2000 or 707/226-1395. www.robertmondaviwinery. com. Daily 10am–5pm. Reservations recommended for guided tour; book 1 week ahead, especially for weekend tours.

Opus One

A visit to Opus One is a serious and stately affair that was developed in a partnership between Robert Mondavi and Baron Phillipe de Rothschild. Today, the state-of-the-art collaboration continues between Baron Phillipe de Rothschild and Constellation Brands, which bought out much of Mondavi's winery empire. Architecture buffs in particular will appreciate the tour, which takes in both the impressive Greco-Roman-meets-20th-century building and the no-holds-barred ultra-high-tech production and aging facilities.

This entire facility caters to one ultrapremium wine, which is offered here for a whopping $25 per 4-ounce taste (and a painful $165 per bottle). But wine lovers should happily fork over the cash: It's a memorable red. Grab your glass and head to the redwood rooftop deck to enjoy the view.

7900 St. Helena Hwy. (Hwy. 29), Oakville. ⓒ 707/944-9442. www.opusonewinery.com. Daily 10am–4pm. Tours daily by appointment only; in high season, book a month in advance.

RUTHERFORD
3 miles N of Oakville

If you so much as blink after Oakville, you're likely to overlook Rutherford, the next small town that borders on St. Helena. Each town in Napa Valley has its share of spectacular wineries, but you won't see most of them while driving along Highway 29.

Swanson Vineyards & Winery 𝒦 *Finds*

The valley's most posh and unique wine tasting is yours with a reservation and a $25–$55 fee at Swanson. Here the shtick is to treat a tasting more like a private party, which they call a "SA-lon." You and up to seven other guests sit at a centerpiece round table in a vibrant coral parlor adorned with huge paintings, seashells, and a fireplace, and take in the uncommonly refined yet whimsical atmosphere. The table's set more for a dinner party than for a tasting, with Reidel stemware, caviar on potato crisps, slivers of a fine cheese or two, crackers, and one Alexis ganache-filled bonbon, the likes of which you will be glad to know can be purchased on the premises. Over the course of the hour-or-more snack-and-sip event, a winery host will pour four to seven wines, perhaps a bright pinot grigio, merlot, and hearty Alexis, their signature cab-syrah blend, and you're bound to befriend those at the table with you. Definitely a must-do for those who don't mind spending the money.

1271 Manley Lane, Rutherford. © **707/967-3500.** www.swansonvineyards.com. Appointments available Wed–Sun 11am, 1:30pm, and 4pm.

Sawyer Cellars *(Finds* The most attractive thing about Sawyer, aside from its clean and tasty wines, is its dedication to extremely high quality while it maintains a humble, accommodating attitude. Step into the simple restored 1920s barn to see what I mean. Whatever you ask, the tasting-room host will answer. Whatever your request, they do their best to accommodate it. Want to picnic on the back patio overlooking the vineyards? Be their guest. Like to participate in a crush? Come on over and get your hands dirty. Fancy reserving their charming wine library for a private luncheon? Pay a minimal fee and make yourself at home. Here you can tour the property on a little tram or learn more about winemaker Brad Warner, who spent 30 years at Mondavi before embarking on this exclusive endeavor. Plunk down $7.50 to taste delicious estate-made wines: sauvignon blanc, merlot, cabernet sauvignon, and Meritage ($18–$46 for current releases), which some argue are worth twice the price. With a total production of only 4,200 cases and a friendly attitude, this winery is a rare treat.

8350 St. Helena Hwy. (Hwy. 29), Rutherford. © **707/963-1980.** www.sawyercellars.com. Tasting by appointment. Tours by appointment. 10am–5pm daily.

St. Supéry Winery *(Kids* The outside looks like a modern corporate office building, but inside you'll find a functional, welcoming winery that encourages first-time tasters to learn more about oenology. On the self-guided tour, you can wander through the demonstration vineyard, where you'll learn about growing techniques. Inside, kids gravitate toward coloring books and "SmellaVision," an interactive display that teaches you how to identify different wine ingredients. Adjoining it is the Atkinson House, which chronicles more than 100 years of winemaking history during public tours at 1 and 3pm. For $10, you'll get lifetime tasting privileges and a tour, which includes samples of four wines, which hopefully includes their excellent and very well-priced sauvignon blanc; there's a limited edition reserve tasting for $15. Even the prices make visitors feel at home: Bottles start at $19, although the tag on their high-end bordeaux red blend is $60.

8440 St. Helena Hwy. (Hwy. 29), Rutherford. © **800/942-0809** or 707/963-4507. www.stsupery.com. Daily 10am–5pm (until 5:30pm during summer). $10 tour at 1 and 3pm daily.

Rubicon Estate Hollywood meets Napa Valley at Francis Ford Coppola's historic Inglenook Vineyards, previously known as Niebaum-Coppola (*Nee*-bom *Coh*-pa-la) and now named after their most prestigious wine. You'll have to fork over $25 to visit the estate, but that includes a tasting of five wines, tour of various historic properties, and valet parking. Outside the spectacular 1880s ivy-draped stone winery and grounds are historic

grandeur. Inside, downstairs is one giant wine bar and retail center. Upstairs displays his film memorabilia, from Academy Awards to trinkets from *The Godfather* and *Bram Stoker's Dracula*. Wine, food, and gift items dominate the cavernous tasting area, where wines such as an estate-grown blend, cabernet franc, merlot, and zinfandel made from organically grown grapes are sampled. Bottles range from around $19 to more than $100. Along with the basic tour, you can pay extra for more exclusive, specialized tours as well.

1991 St. Helena Hwy. (Hwy. 29), Rutherford. ℰ **800/RUBICON** or 707/968-1100. www.rubiconestate.com. 10am–5pm daily. Tours daily.

Beaulieu Vineyard Bordeaux native Georges de Latour founded the third-oldest continuously operating winery in Napa Valley in 1900. With the help of legendary oenologist André Tchelistcheff, he produced world-class, award-winning wines that have been served by every president of the United States since Franklin D. Roosevelt. The brick-and-redwood tasting room isn't much to look at, but with Beaulieu's (*Bowl*-you) stellar reputation, it has no need to visually impress. Appellation tastings cost $10, and a variety of bottles sell for under $20. The recently remodeled Reserve Tasting Room offers a "flight" of five reserve wines to taste for $25, but if you want to take a bottle to go, it may cost upwards of $100.

1960 St. Helena Hwy. (Hwy. 29), Rutherford. ℰ 707/967-5233. www.bvwines.com. Daily 10am–5pm.

Grgich Hills Cellar Croatian émigré Miljenko (Mike) Grgich (*Grr*-gitch) made his presence known to the world when his 1973 Château Montelena chardonnay bested the top French white burgundies at the famous 1976 Paris tasting. Since then, the master vintner teamed up with Austin Hills (of the Hills Brothers coffee fortune) and started this extremely successful and respected winery featuring estate grown wines from organically and biodynamically farmed vineyards.

The ivy-covered stucco building isn't much to behold, and the tasting room is even less appealing, but people don't come here for the scenery: As you might expect, Grgich's chardonnays are legendary—and priced accordingly. The smart buys are the outstanding zinfandel and cabernet sauvignon, which cost around $28 and $65, respectively. The winery also produces a fantastic fumé blanc for around $24 a bottle. Before you leave, be sure to poke your head into the barrel-aging room and inhale the divine aroma. Tastings cost $10 (which includes the glass). No picnic facilities are available.

1829 St. Helena Hwy. (Hwy. 29), north of Rutherford Cross Rd., Rutherford. ℰ 707/963-2784. www.grgich.com. Daily 9:30am–4:30pm. $15 tours by appointment only, daily 11am and 2pm.

Mumm Napa Valley At first glance, Mumm, housed in a big redwood barn, looks almost humble. Once you're through the front door, however, you'll know that they mean business—big business. Just beyond the extensive gift shop (filled with all sorts of namesake mementos) is the tasting room, where you can purchase sparkling wine by the glass ($5–$8), three-wine flights ($8–$20), or the bottle ($16–$70), and appreciate breathtaking vineyard and mountain views on the open patio. You can also take a 45-minute free educational tour (with your dog—this joint's pooch friendly!) and stroll the impressive photography gallery, which features a permanent Ansel Adams collection and ever-changing photography exhibits. Sorry, there's no food or picnicking here.

8445 Silverado Trail (just south of Rutherford Cross Rd.), Rutherford. ℰ **800/686-6272** or 707/967-7730. www.mummnapa.com. Daily 10am–5pm. Tours offered every hour daily 10am–3pm.

ST. HELENA
73 miles N of San Francisco

Located 17 miles north of Napa on Highway 29, this former Seventh-day Adventist village maintains a pseudo–Old West feel while catering to upscale shoppers with deep pockets—hence Vanderbilt and Company, purveyor of fine housewares, at 1429 Main St. (© **707/963-1010;** www.vanderbiltandcompany.com). St. Helena is a quiet, attractive little town, where you'll find a slew of beautiful old homes and first-rate restaurants and accommodations.

V. Sattui Winery ⊛ (Kids) (Finds)
So what if it's touristy and crowded? This enormous winery is also a fun picnic-party stop thanks to a huge gourmet deli and grassy expanse. It's especially great for families since you can fill up on wine, pâté, and cheese samples without ever reaching for your pocketbook, while the kids romp around the grounds. The gourmet store stocks more than 200 cheeses, sandwich meats, pâtés, breads, exotic salads, and desserts such as white-chocolate cheesecake. (It would be an easy place to graze were it not for the continuous mob scene at the counter.) Meanwhile, the extensive wine offerings flow at the long wine bar in the back. Wines aren't distributed, so if you taste something you simply must have, buy it. (A case purchase will get you membership into their private cellar and its less crowded, private tasting room.) Wine prices start at around $9, with many in the $16 neighborhood; reserves top out at around $75. *Note:* To use the picnic area, you must buy food and wine here.

1111 White Lane (at Hwy. 29), St. Helena. © **707/963-7774.** www.vsattui.com. Daily 9am–6pm; winter daily 9am–5pm.

Prager Winery & Port Works (Finds)
If you want a real down-home, off-the-beaten-track experience, Prager's can't be beat. Turn the corner from Sutter Home winery and roll into the small gravel parking lot; you're on the right track, but when you pull open the creaky old wooden door to this shack of a wine-tasting room, you'll begin to wonder. Don't turn back! Pass the oak barrels, and you'll quickly come upon the clapboard tasting room, made homey with a big Oriental rug and a Prager family host. Fork over $10 (includes a complimentary glass), and they'll pour you samples of late-harvest Johannesburg Riesling and 3 to 4 ports (which cost $35–$75 per bottle). Also available is "Prager Chocolate Drizzle," a chocolate liqueur that tops ice creams and other desserts. If you're looking for a special gift, consider their bottles, which can be custom etched in the design of your choice on request.

1281 Lewelling Lane (just west of Hwy. 29, behind Sutter Home), St. Helena. © **800/969-PORT** or 707/963-7678. www.pragerport.com. Daily 10:30am–4:30pm.

Joseph Phelps Vineyards ⊛
Visitors interested in intimate, comprehensive tours and a knockout tasting should schedule a tour at this winery. A quick turn off the Silverado Trail in Spring Valley (there's no sign—watch for Taplin Rd., or you'll blast right by), Joseph Phelps was founded in 1973 and is a major player in both the regional and the worldwide wine market. Phelps himself accomplished a long list of valley firsts, including launching the syrah varietal in the valley and extending the 1970s Berkeley food revolution (led by Alice Waters) to the Wine Country by founding the Oakville Grocery Co. (p. 300).

A favorite stop for serious wine lovers, this modern, state-of-the-art winery and big-city vibe are proof that Phelps's annual 80,000 cases prove fruitful in more ways than one. When you pass the wisteria-covered trellis to the entrance of the redwood building, you'll encounter an air of seriousness that hangs heavier than harvest grapes. Fortunately, the mood lightens during the informal tasting for $20 or any of the "seminars" like the Blending Seminar, Le Nez Seminar, or the Wine Appreciation Seminar (all $30) that include tastings of five or six wines, mostly reds with a few whites. There's also a short film on the history of the winery. Seminars are 1½ hours on weekdays and 1 hour on weekends. Unfortunately, some wines are so popular that they sell out quickly; come late in the season, and you may not be able to taste or buy them. The three excellently located picnic tables, on the terrace overlooking the valley, are available on a first-come, first-served basis, with preference given to Phelps wine club members (join and get wine shipped a certain number of times per year) who are also able to make a reservation.

200 Taplin Rd. (off the Silverado Trail), P.O. Box 1031, St. Helena. ℭ 800/707-5789 or 707/963-4831. www.jpvwines.com. Mon–Sat 9am–5pm; Sun 10am–4pm. $300 seminars and tastings by appointment only; weekends at 10am, 11:30am, 1pm, and 2:30pm; weekdays at 11am and 2:30pm. $10 per person for 2-oz. pour of Insignia.

Robert Keenan Winery (Finds)

It's a winding, uphill drive to reach secluded Robert Keenan, but this far off the tourist track you're guaranteed more elbowroom at the tasting bar and a quieter, less commercial experience. When you drive in, you'll pass a few modest homes and wonder whether one of the buildings is the family winery. It's not. Keep driving (slowly—kids and dogs at play) until you get to the main building and its redwood tasting room.

The 10,000 cases produced here per year are the result of yet another fast-paced professional who left his business behind and headed for the hills. In this case, it's native San Franciscan Robert Keenan, who ran his own insurance agency for 20 years. When his company merged with another firm and was bought out in 1981, he had already purchased his "retirement property," the winery's 176 acres (48 of which are now planted with grapes), and he soon turned his fascination with winemaking into a second career. The renovated stone building has a much older history, dating back to the old Conradi Winery, which was founded in 1890.

Today, Robert Keenan Winery is known for its big, full-bodied reds, such as the Mountain cab and merlot. Chardonnay, cabernet franc, and zin sold exclusively at the winery range from $22 to $40 per bottle. Older vintages, which you won't find elsewhere, are for sale here as well. Take the tour to learn about the vineyards, production facilities, and winemaking in general. Those looking for a pastoral picnic spot should consider spreading their blankets out here. The three tables, situated right outside the winery and surrounded by vineyards, offer stunning views.

3660 Spring Mountain Rd. (off Hwy. 29), St. Helena. ℭ 707/963-9177. www.keenanwinery.com. Weekends 11am–4pm. Free tours and tastings daily 11am–4pm, by appointment.

Beringer Vineyards ⚘ (Finds)

You won't find a personal experience at this tourist-heavy stop. But you will find a regal 1876 estate founded by brothers Jacob and Frederick and hand-dug tunnels in the hillside. The oldest continuously operating winery in Napa Valley, Beringer managed to stay open even during Prohibition by making "sacramental" wines. White zinfandel is the winery's most popular seller, but plenty of other varietals are available to enjoy. Tastings of current vintages for $5 are conducted in new facilities, where there's also a large selection of bottles for less than $20. Reserve wines are available for tasting in the remarkable Rhine House for $25 (applied toward purchase), and tours range from the $10 standard or $20 historical to the $35 1½-hour vintage legacy tour. There are several other tours in the $15 to $30 range; check the website for details.

2000 Main St. (Hwy. 29), St. Helena. ℭ 707/963-7115. www.beringer.com. May 30–October 23 daily 10am–6pm; October 24–May 29 10am–5pm.

Tips **The Ins & Outs of Shipping Wine Home**

Perhaps the only things more complex than that $800 case of cabernet you just purchased are the rules and regulations about shipping it home. Because of absurd and forever fluctuating laws—which supposedly protect the business of the country's wine distributors—wine shipping is limited by regulations that vary in each of the 50 states. Shipping rules also vary from winery to winery.

Every single time I write this book, the rules change. This go-round the government is said to be phasing out reciprocity laws and requiring that each state be approved to ship or receive wine. Individual wineries must buy permits for each state they want to ship to, making it difficult for smaller wineries to ship to many states (so most will probably opt only for the states that brandish the most visitors or mail-order demands). There are currently 20 states with permits and 13 with the old reciprocal agreement (that will probably change soon, too) and as this book goes to press, several more are pending. Technically, only wineries with permits are allowed to ship wine; shipping stores are not supposed to ship any wine or liquor. That said, they do it anyway, so don't fret if you want to send wine.

If you do get stuck shipping illegally (not that we're recommending you do that, but believe me, it's done all the time and most shipping companies are well aware of it), you might want to package your wine in an unassuming box and head to a post office, UPS, or other shipping company outside the Wine Country area. It's less obvious that you're shipping wine from Vallejo or San Francisco than from Napa Valley.

Charles Krug Winery   Founded in 1861, Krug was the first winery built in the valley. The family of Peter Mondavi, Sr. (yes, Robert is his brother) owns it today (and at 91 he still comes to work 5 days a week—the story being that he drinks a glass of red wine a day, of course). It's worth paying your respects here by dropping $10 and $15 on a weekend to sip current releases and reserves, respectively, and $12 on weekdays for a combo. On the grounds are picnic facilities with umbrella-shaded tables overlooking vineyards or the wine cellar.

2800 Main St. (St. Helena Hwy.; just north of the tunnel of trees at the northern end of St. Helena), St. Helena. © 707/963-5057. www.charleskrug.com. Daily 10:30am–5pm. No tours available.

CALISTOGA

81 miles N of San Francisco

Calistoga, the last tourist town in Napa Valley, got its name from Sam Brannan, entrepreneur extraordinaire and California's first millionaire. After making a bundle supplying miners during the gold rush, he went on to take advantage of the natural geothermal springs at the north end of the valley by building a hotel and spa here in 1859. Flubbing up a speech, in which he compared this natural California wonder to New York State's Saratoga Springs resort town, he serendipitously coined the name "Calistoga," and it stuck. Today, this small, simple resort town, with 5,225 residents and an old-time main street (no building along the 6-block stretch is more than two

However, you can try these companies. They are likely to help you out.

Napa Valley Shipping Companies

The UPS Store, at 3212 Jefferson St. in the Grape Yard Shopping Center (© 707/259-1398), claims to pack and ship anything anywhere. Rates for a case of wine were quoted at approximately $25 for ground shipping to Los Angeles and $70 to New York.

  St. Helena Mailing Center, 1241 Adams St., at Highway 29, St. Helena (© 707/963-2686), says they will pack and ship to certain states within the U.S. Rates for pre-wrapped shipments are around $23 per case for ground delivery to Los Angeles.

Sonoma Valley Shipping Companies

The UPS Store, 19229 Sonoma Hwy., in Maxwell Village, Sonoma (© 707/935-3438), has a lot of experience with shipping wine. It claims it will ship your wine to any state. Prices vary from $28 to Los Angeles to as much as $79 to the East Coast and $150 to Hawaii and Alaska.

  The **Wine Exchange of Sonoma,** 452 First St. E., between East Napa and East Spain streets, Sonoma (© 707/938-1794), will ship your wine, but there's a catch: You must buy an equal amount of any wine at the store (which they assured me would be in stock, and probably at a better rate). Shipping rates range from $20 to Los Angeles to $50 to the East Coast.

stories high), is popular with city folk who come here to unwind. Calistoga is a great place to relax and indulge in mineral waters, mud baths, Jacuzzis, massages and, of course, wine. The vibe is more casual—and a little groovier—than you find in neighboring towns to the south.

Frank Family Vineyards ⭐ (Finds)   "Wine dudes" Dennis, Tim, Jeff, Rick, and Pat will do practically anything to maintain their rightfully self-proclaimed reputation as the "friendliest winery in the valley." In recent years the name may have changed from Kornell Champagne Cellars to Frank-Rombauer to Frank Family, but the vibe's remained constant; it's all about down-home, friendly fun. No muss, no fuss, no intimidation factor. At Frank Family, you're part of their family—no joke. They'll greet you like a long-lost relative and serve you all the bubbly you want (three to four varieties: blanc de blanc, blanc de noir, reserve, and rouge, at $20–$70 a bottle). Still-wine lovers can slip into the equally casual back room to sample chardonnay and a very well-received cabernet sauvignon. Behind the tasting room is a choice picnic area, situated under the oaks and overlooking the vineyards.

1091 Larkmead Lane (just off the Silverado Trail), Calistoga. © 707/942-0859. Daily 10am–5pm. No tours; tastings free.

Schramsberg ⭐⭐ (Finds)   This 217-acre sparkling wine estate, a landmark once frequented by Robert Louis Stevenson and the second-oldest property in Napa Valley, has a wonderful old-world feel and is one of the valley's all-time best places to explore.

Schramsberg is the label that presidents serve when toasting dignitaries from around the globe, and there's plenty of historical memorabilia in the front room to prove it. But the real mystique begins when you enter the sparkling wine caves, which wind 2 miles (reputedly the longest in North America) and were partly hand-carved by Chinese laborers in the 1800s. The caves have an authentic Tom Sawyer ambience, complete with dangling cobwebs and seemingly endless passageways; you can't help but feel you're on an adventure. The comprehensive, unintimidating tour ends in a charming, cozy tasting room, where you'll sample four surprisingly varied selections of their high-end bubbly. Tastings are a bit dear ($25 per person), but it's money well spent. Note that tastings are offered only to those who take the free tour, and you must make reservations in advance.

1400 Schramsberg Rd. (off Hwy. 29), Calistoga. ℂ 707/942-2414. www.schramsberg.com. Daily 10am–4pm. Tours and tastings by appointment only.

Sterling Vineyards 🎔 *Kids* *Finds*   No, you don't need climbing shoes to reach this dazzling white Mediterranean-style winery, perched 300 feet up on a rocky knoll. Just fork over $15 ($20 weekends and holidays from Apr 1–Nov 1 and $10 for kids at all times—including a goodie bag) and take the aerial tram, which offers stunning bucolic views along the way. Once you're back on land, follow the self-guided tour (one of the most comprehensive in the Wine Country) of the winemaking process. Wine tastings of five varietals in the panoramic tasting room are included in the tram fare, but more sophisticated sips—limited releases or reserve flights—will set you back anywhere from $3 to $15, respectively. They also offer a guided reserve tasting and tour, limited to 8 people at 11am daily; it's $45 and reservations are highly recommended. Expect to pay anywhere from $14 to $75 for a souvenir bottle.

1111 Dunaweal Lane (off Hwy. 29, just south of downtown Calistoga), Calistoga. ℂ 707/942-3344. www.sterling vineyards.com. Daily 10:30am–4:30pm.

Clos Pegase 🎔 *Finds*   Renowned architect Michael Graves designed this incredible oasis, which integrates art, 20,000 square feet of aging caves, and a luxurious hilltop private home. Viewing the art is as much the point as tasting the wines—which, by the way, don't come cheap: Prices range from $15 for the 2000 Vin Gris merlot to as much as $75 for the 2001 Hommage Artist Series Reserve, an extremely limited edition of the winery's finest lots of cabernet sauvignon. Current release tastings cost $10. The grounds at Clos Pegase (Cloh Pey-*goss*) feature an impressive sculpture garden as well as scenic picnic spots.

1060 Dunaweal Lane (off Hwy. 29 or the Silverado Trail), Calistoga. ℂ 707/942-4981. www.clospegase.com. Daily 10:30am–5pm. Tours daily at 11am and 2pm.

Duckhorn Vineyards   With quintessential pastoral surroundings and a unique wine-tasting program, Duckhorn Vineyards has much to offer for visitors interested in spending a little money and time to relax and taste. Here the airy Victorian farmhouse is very welcoming, not only because you can stand on the veranda and look out on the surrounding meadow, but also because the interior affords equally bucolic views. If you're going to taste wine in their surprisingly modern tasting room, complete with cafe tables and a centerpiece bar, you'll pay $10 for a tasting of three wines, $15 for a flight of five limited-release wines, or $25 for a semi-private estate-wine tasting, the latter of which you can book in advance. The fee may sound steep, but this is not your run-of-the-mill drink and dash. You'll get plenty of attention and information on their current releases of sauvignon blanc, merlot, and cabernet sauvignon.

1000 Lodi Lane (at the Silverado Trail), St. Helena. ℂ 707/963-7108. www.duckhorn.com. Daily 10am–4pm. Estate wine tastings by appointment only.

BEYOND THE WINERIES: WHAT TO SEE & DO IN NAPA VALLEY
NAPA/ST. HELENA

If you have plenty of time and a penchant for Victorian architecture, seek out the **Napa Valley Conference & Visitors Bureau,** 1310 Napa Town Center, off First Street (© **707/226-7459,** ext. 106; www.napavalley.com), which offers $2 self-guided walking tours of the town's historic buildings.

A MUSEUM   COPIA: The American Center for Wine Food & the Arts, at 500 First St. (© **707/259-1600;** www.copia.org), opened at the end of 2001 with a mission to explore and celebrate how wine and food influence our culture. This $50-million multifaceted facility, which was spearheaded by Robert Mondavi, tackles the topic in a myriad of ways, including visual arts a la rotating exhibitions, vast organic vegetable and demonstration gardens, superfun culinary programs, basic and advanced wine classes, concerts, films, and opportunities to dine and drink on the premises. There's not a ton to look at, but youngsters will get a kick out of the Kids' Garden with rabbits and chickens, while connoisseurs might pay extra to slip into seasonal cooking demos by famous chefs. Drop by the cafe for gourmet picnic items or neighboring gift shop for accessories and food-related finds, but skip the so-so adjoining restaurant. Also, drop by Tuesday or Saturday mornings April through November for the outdoor farmers market and check out their Thursday Outdoor Summer Concert Series for great affordable alfresco entertainment.

Copia admission is $5 for adults, $4 for seniors and students and free for children 12 and under. Wednesday admissions are half-price for Napa and Sonoma residents. The center is open Wednesday through Monday from 10am to 5pm. The restaurant stays open until 9:30pm Thursday through Sunday.

BIKING   The quieter northern end of the valley is an ideal place to rent a bicycle and ride the Silverado Trail. **St. Helena Cyclery,** 1156 Main St. (© **707/963-7736;** www.sthelenacyclery.com), rents bikes for $10 per hour or $30 a day, including rear rack, helmet, lock, and bag in which you can pack a picnic.

SHOPPING   Shopaholics should make a beeline to the **Napa Premium Outlets** (© **707/226-9876;** www.premiumoutlets.com), where Barneys New York can inspire even a jaded local to take the First Street exit off Highway 29 and brave the crowds. Unfortunately, Barneys now carries only cheap outlet-store stuff, but, you'll find multiple places to part with your money, including TSE (killer cashmere at basement prices), Banana Republic, Calvin Klein, Nine West, Benetton, Jones New York, BCBG, more fashion shops, a few kitchenware shops, a food court, and a decent (but expensive) sushi restaurant. Shops are open Monday through Saturday from 10am to 8pm and Sunday from 10am to 6pm. Call for seasonal hours.

In Yountville, it's worth peeking into Elizabeth Roth's store, **Mosswood Collection,** with its selection of home accessories, cookbooks, furniture, local art, jewelery, antique corkscrews, garden art, tabletop items, children's toys, and a great selection of ribbons. Open daily 10am to 5pm. (6550 Washington St.; © **707/944-8151**).

St. Helena's Main Street ⚓ is the best place to go if you're suffering from serious retail withdrawal. Here you'll find trendy fashions at **Pearl** (1428 Main St.; © 707-963-3236), Jimmy Choo shoes at **Footcandy** (1239 Main St.; © 707/963-2040), chic pet gifts at **Fideaux** (1312 Main St.; © 707/967-9935), custom-embroidered French linens at **Jan de Luz** (1219 Main St.; © 707/963-1550), estate jewelry at **Patina** (1342 Main St.; © 707/963-5445), and European home accessories, sample

---

(*Finds*) **Enjoying Art & Nature**

Anyone with an appreciation for art absolutely must visit the **di Rosa Preserve.** Rene and Veronica di Rosa collected contemporary American art for more than 40 years and then converted their 215 acres of prime property into a monument to Northern California's regional art and nature. Veronica has passed on, but Rene still carries the torch through his world-renowned collection featuring 2,000 works in all media, by more than 900 Greater Bay Area artists. You're not likely to meet him, as the day-to-day operations are now run by a nonprofit staff, but you will be privy to his treasures, which are on display practically everywhere—along the shores of the property's 35-acre lake and in each nook and cranny of their 125-year-old winery-turned-residence, adjoining building, two newer galleries, and gardens. With hundreds of surrounding acres of rolling hills (protected under the Napa County Land Trust), this place is a must-see for both art and nature lovers. It's at 5200 Carneros Hwy. (Hwy. 121/12); look for the gate. Drop-ins are welcome at the Gatehouse Tuesday through Friday from 9:30am to 5pm; $3 suggested donation. One-hour docent tours run nearly hourly and cost $10. Two-hour, docent-led tours are given at 12:30 and cost $15. On Saturday, you can catch the extended 2-hour tour by appointment only, also $15.

Reservations recommended. Call ⓒ **707/226-5991** to make reservations. www.dirosapreserve.org. Hours may change seasonally; call or check website to confirm.

---

holiday table settings, and free gift-wrapping at **Vanderbilt and Company** (1429 Main St.; ⓒ 707/963-1010).

Most stores are open 10am to 5pm daily; the mall is on Main Street, between Pope and Pine streets, St. Helena.

Shopaholics should also take the sharp turn off Highway 29 two miles north of downtown St. Helena to the **St. Helena Premier Outlets** (ⓒ 707/963-7282; www.st helenapremieroutlets.com). Featured designers include Escada, Coach, Tumi, and Movado. The stores are open daily from 10am to 6pm.

One last favorite stop: **Napa Valley Olive Oil Manufacturing Company,** 835 Charter Oak Ave., at the end of the road behind Tra Vigne restaurant (ⓒ 707/963-4173). The tiny market presses and bottles its own oils and sells them at a fraction of the price you'll pay elsewhere. In addition, it has an extensive selection of Italian cooking ingredients, imported snacks, great deals on dried mushrooms, and a picnic table in the parking lot. You'll love the age-old method for totaling the bill, which you simply must find out for yourself.

SPA-ING IT If the Wine Country's slow pace and tranquil vistas aren't soothing enough for you, the region's diverse selection of spas can massage, bathe, wrap, and steam you into an overly pampered pulp. Should you choose to indulge, do so toward the end of your stay—when you've wined and dined to the point where you have only enough energy left to make it to and from the spa.

Compared to the cosmopolitan-chic day spas of the Fairmount Sonoma Mission Inn (Sonoma; see "The Super Spa" box on p. 312) and Health Spa Napa Valley (St. Helena), which isn't much more than a gym and a spa, **White Sulphur Springs Retreat & Spa** ⚘, 3100 White Sulphur Springs Rd. (© **707/963-8588;** www.white sulphursprings.com), offers a more spiritual day of cleansing and pampering. Yes, you will encounter the namesake soaking pool with natural sulfur water, massages, aromatherapy treatments, seaweed or mineral mud wraps, and a pool and Jacuzzi for guests' use. But the most blissful benefits at this funky-chic spot come from the surrounding acres of redwoods, streams, grassy fields, and wooded groves. Massages ($80 for 50 min.; $50 for 25 min.) are given in the homey spa building or outside.

CALISTOGA

BIKING   Cycling enthusiasts can rent bikes from **Getaway Adventures/Wine Country Adventures** (© **800/499-BIKE** or 707/568-3040; www.getawayadventures.com). Full-day group tours cost $125 per person, including lunch and a visit to four or five wineries, $105 per person for private groups of six or more. Bike rental without a tour costs $30 per day plus a $20 delivery fee. You can also inquire about the company's kayaking and hiking tours.

MUD BATHS   The one thing you should do while you're in Calistoga is what people have been doing here for the past 150 years: Take a mud bath. The natural baths contain local volcanic ash, imported peat, and naturally boiling mineral hot-springs water, mulled together to produce a thick mud that simmers at a temperature of about 104°F (40°C).

Indulge yourself at any of these Calistoga spas: **Dr. Wilkinson's Hot Springs,** 1507 Lincoln Ave. (© 707/942-4102); **Golden Haven Hot Springs Spa,** 1713 Lake St. (© 707/942-6793); **Calistoga Spa Hot Springs,** 1006 Washington St. (© 707/942-6269); **Calistoga Village Inn & Spa,** 1880 Lincoln Ave. (© 707/942-0991); **Indian Springs Resort,** 1712 Lincoln Ave. (© 707/942-4913); or **Roman Spa Motel,** 1300 Washington St. (© 707/942-4441).

NATURAL WONDERS   Old Faithful Geyser of California, 1299 Tubbs Lane (© **707/942-6463;** www.oldfaithfulgeyser.com), is one of only three "old faithful" geysers in the world. It's been blowing off steam at regular intervals for as long as anyone can remember. On average, the 350°F (176°C) water spews at a height of about 40–60 feet every 40 minutes, day and night, and the performance lasts about 3 minutes (*Note:* height and length of time are weather-dependent).You can bring a picnic

---

(*Tips* **SIP TIP**

You can cheaply sip your way through downtown Napa without ever getting behind the wheel with the new "Taste Napa Downtown" wine card. For a mere $20, you get 10-cent tasting privileges at 10 local winecentric watering holes and tasting rooms, all of which are within walking distance of each other. Plus you'll get 10% discounts at tasting rooms and half-off admission to Copia. Available at the **Napa Valley Conference & Visitors Bureau** (1310 Napa Town Center, off First St.; © **707/226-7459,** ext. 106) and Copia (see above). Learn more at **www.napadowntown.com**.

Pricing Categories

The listings below are arranged first by area, then by price, using the following categories: **Very Expensive,** more than $250 per night; **Expensive,** $200 to $250 per night; **Moderate,** $150 to $200 per night; and **Inexpensive,** less than $150 per night.

---

lunch to munch on between spews. An exhibit hall, gift shop, and snack bar are open every day. Admission is $8 for adults, $7 for seniors, $3 for children 6 to 12, and free for children under 6. Check the website for discount coupons. The geyser is open daily from 9am to 6pm (to 5pm in winter). To get there, follow the signs from downtown Calistoga; it's between Highway 29 and Calif. 128.

You won't see thousands of trees turned into stone, but you'll still find many interesting petrified specimens at the **Petrified Forest,** 4100 Petrified Forest Rd. (© **707/ 942-6667;** www.petrifiedforest.org). Volcanic ash blanketed this area after an eruption near Mount St. Helena 3 million years ago. You'll find redwoods that have turned to rock through the slow infiltration of silicas and other minerals, a .5-mile walking trail, museum, discovery shop, and picnic grounds. Admission is $6 for adults, $5 for seniors over 60 and juniors 12 to 17, $3 for children 6 to 11, and free for children under 6; look on their website for discount coupons. The forest is open daily from 9am to 7pm (to 5pm in winter). Heading north from Calistoga on Calif. 128, turn left onto Petrified Forest Road, just past Lincoln Street.

WHERE TO STAY IN NAPA VALLEY

Accommodations in Napa Valley run the gamut—from motels and B&Bs to world-class luxury retreats—and all are easily accessible from the main highway. While I recommend staying in the more romantically pastoral areas such as St. Helena, there's no question you're going to find better deals in the towns of Napa or laid-back Calistoga.

When planning your trip, keep in mind that during the high season—April to November—most hotels charge peak rates and sell out completely on weekends; many also have a 2-night minimum. If you need help organizing your Wine Country vacation, contact an agency. **Bed & Breakfast Inns of Napa Valley** (© **707/944-4444;** www.bbinv.com), an association of B&Bs, provides descriptions and lets you know who's got availability. **Napa Valley Reservations Unlimited** (© **800/251-NAPA** or 707/252-1985; www.napavalleyreservations.com) is also a source for booking everything from hot-air balloon rides to wine-tasting tours by limousine.

NAPA

Wherever tourist dollars are to be had, you're sure to find big hotels with familiar names, catering to independent vacationers, business travelers, and groups. **Embassy Suites,** 1075 California Blvd., Napa, CA 94559 (© **800/362-2779** or 707/253-9540; www.embassynapa.com), offers 205 of its usual two-room suites. Each includes a "galley kitchen" complete with coffeemaker, fridge, microwave, and wet bar; they also have a dataport and two TVs and access to indoor and outdoor pools and a restaurant. Rates range from $169 to $289 and include cooked-to-order breakfast, 2-hour beverage reception from 5:30 to 7:30pm, complimentary passes to a nearby health club, and free parking. The 272-room **Napa Valley Marriott,** 3425 Solano Ave., Napa, CA 94558 (© **800/228-9290** or 707/253-8600; www.marriott.com), has an exercise room, a heated outdoor pool and spa, and two restaurants; rates range from $129 to $329 for rooms, $350 to $500 for suites.

Very Expensive

Milliken Creek Inn ☆☆   This riverfront retreat, just north of downtown Napa, combines upscale boutique hotel accommodations with country living. Right off the Silverado Trail and surrounded by tranquil gardens, oaks, and redwoods, the 12 spacious and luxuriously appointed rooms are located in three neighboring buildings (including the restored 1857 Coach House). Soothing shades of brown and beige, greens, and yellows become even warmer and more welcoming when the fireplace is in action. King-size beds are firm and draped in Frette linens, tubs are the whirlpool variety, and fluffy robes await you. Delicious perks include a picnic breakfast delivered to your door, a wine-and-cheese tasting nightly in the equally sophisticated parlor, and the new spa rooms for facials and massages. Live jazz piano accompanies the affair on Fridays and Saturdays. No doubt this hotel is one of Napa's finest choices.

1815 Silverado Trail, Napa, CA 94558. ✆ **888/622-5775** or 707/255-1197. Fax 707/255-3112. www.milliken creekinn.com. 12 units. $395–$695 double. AE, DC, DISC, MC, V. **Amenities:** Yoga gazebo; spa rooms. *In room:* A/C, plasma-screen TVs with TiVo, dataport, minibar, hair dryer, iron, Wi-Fi throughout entire property, CD player.

Moderate

Cedar Gables Inn ☆☆ *Finds*   This grand, romantic B&B in Old Town Napa is in a stunning Shakespearean/Renaissance style building, built in 1892. Rooms reflect that era, with rich tapestries and stunning gilded antiques. Four have fireplaces, five have whirlpool tubs, and all feature queen-size brass, wood, or iron beds. Guests meet each evening in front of the roaring fireplace in the lower "tavern" parlor for wine and cheese. At other times, the family room is a perfect place to cuddle up and watch the large-screen TV. Bonuses include a gourmet breakfast each morning, port in every room, and VIP treatment at many local wineries.

486 Coombs St. (at Oak St.), Napa, CA 94559. ✆ **800/309-7969** or 707/224-7969. Fax 707/224-4838. www.cedar gablesinn.com. 9 units. $199–$319 double. Rates include full breakfast, evening wine and cheese, and port. AE, DISC, MC, V. From Hwy. 29 north, exit onto First St. and follow signs to downtown; turn right onto Jefferson, and left on Oak; house is on the corner. **Amenities:** Dataport (in the shared living room). *In room:* A/C, hair dryer, iron, ironing board, deluxe bathrobes, free Wi-Fi.

Napa River Inn ☆☆   Downtown Napa's most luxurious hotel manages an old-world boutique feel throughout most of its three buildings. The main building, part of the renovated Historic Napa Mill and Hatt Market Building, is an 1884 historic landmark. Each of its fantastically appointed rooms is exceedingly romantic, with burgundy-colored walls, original brick, wood furnishings, plush fabrics, seats in front of the gas fireplace, and claw-foot tubs in the bathrooms. A newer and more modern themed addition overlooking the river and a patio boasts bright and airy accommodations. Yet another building houses the less luxurious, but equally well appointed mustard-and-brown rooms that also overlook the riverfront, but have a nautical theme and less daylight. Perks abound and include instant access to downtown dining, complimentary vouchers to breakfast at adorable Sweetie Pie's bakery, and wine at the nearby swank wine bar, The Bounty Hunter. A small but excellent spa is located in the hotel's parking lot.

500 Main St., Napa, CA 94559. ✆ **877/251-8500** or 707/251-8500. Fax 707/251-8504. www.napariverinn.com. 66 units. $179–$499 double. Rates include vouchers to a full breakfast and evening cocktails at one of the adjoining restaurants. AE, DC, DISC, MC, V. Pets $25 per night. **Amenities:** 2 restaurants; concierge; business services; same-day laundry service/dry cleaning. *In room:* A/C, TV, dataport, fridge, coffeemaker, hair dryer, iron, free Wi-Fi, CD clock radio.

Inexpensive

Chablis Inn 🔆   There's no way around it: If you want to sleep cheaply in a town where the *average* room rate tops $200 per night in high season, you're destined for a motel. Look on the bright side: Because your room is likely to be little more than a crash pad after a day of eating and drinking, a clean bed and a remote control are all you'll really need anyway. And Chablis offers much more than that. All of the motel-style rooms are superclean, and some even boast kitchenettes or whirlpool tubs. Guests have access to a heated outdoor pool and hot tub.

3360 Solano Ave., Napa, CA 94558. ☎ **800/443-3490** or 707/257-1944. Fax 707/226-6862. www.chablisinn.com. 34 units. May to mid-Nov $99–$165 double; mid-Nov to Apr $79–$150 double. AE, DC, DISC, MC, V. **Amenities:** Heated outdoor pool; Jacuzzi. *In room:* A/C, satellite TV, dataport in some rooms, kitchenette in some rooms, fridge, coffeemaker, hair dryer.

Wine Valley Lodge 🔆 *Value*   Dollar for dollar, the Wine Valley Lodge offers a great deal. At the south end of town in a quiet residential neighborhood, the mission-style motel is extremely well kept and accessible, just a short drive from Highway 29 and the wineries to the north. The reasonably priced two-bedroom deluxe units are great for families. The Lodge is nonsmoking.

200 S. Coombs St. (between First and Imola sts.), Napa, CA 94559. ☎ **800/696-7911** or 707/224-7911. www.wine valleylodge.com. 54 units. $89–$124 double; $150–$165 deluxe. Rates include continental breakfast. AE, DC, DISC, MC, V. **Amenities:** Heated outdoor pool (closed during the winter). *In room:* A/C, TV.

YOUNTVILLE
Very Expensive

Napa Valley Lodge 🔆 *Finds*   Just off Highway 29, beyond a wall that does a good job of disguising the road, the lodge's guest rooms are large, ultraclean, and better appointed than many in the area. Many have vaulted ceilings, and 39 have fireplaces. Each comes with a king-size or 2 queen-size beds, wicker furnishings, robes, and a private balcony or a patio. Ground level units are smaller and get less sunlight than those on the second floor. Suites boast king-size beds and Jacuzzi tubs. Extras are a concierge, afternoon tea and cookies in the lobby, Friday-evening wine tasting in the library, and a full champagne breakfast—with all this, it's no wonder AAA gave the Napa Valley Lodge the four-diamond award for excellence. Ask about winery tour packages and winter discounts, the latter of which can be as high as 30%.

2230 Madison St., Yountville, CA 94599. ☎ **800/368-2468** or 707/944-2468. Fax 707/944-9362. www.napavalley lodge.com. 55 units. $252–$475 double. Rates include champagne breakfast buffet, afternoon tea and cookies, and Fri-evening wine tasting. AE, DC, DISC, MC, V. **Amenities:** Heated outdoor pool; small exercise room; Jacuzzi spa; redwood sauna; concierge; in-room massage; free wireless in lobby and conference rooms. *In room:* A/C, ceiling fan, TV w/pay movies, minibar, coffeemaker, hair dryer, iron, Wi-Fi access.

Vintage Inn 🔆🔆   This contemporary, French-country complex situated on an old 23-acre winery estate in the heart of Yountville feels far more corporate than "inn" would suggest. But big business does have its perks, like a very professional staff, bright cozy rooms, each of which comes equipped with a fireplace and private veranda, oversize bed, Jacuzzi tub, plush bathrobes, and welcoming bottle of wine. If you're looking for a workout, you may rent a bike, reserve one of the two tennis courts, or take a dip in the 60-foot swimming pool or outdoor whirlpool, both heated year-round. A champagne breakfast buffet and afternoon tea are served daily in the lobby. If they're booked, ask about their sister property, the spa-centric Villagio Inn & Spa, a Tuscan-style hotel complex just down the road.

6541 Washington St. (between Humboldt St. and Webber Ave.), Yountville, CA 94599. ⓒ 800/351-1133 or 707/
944-1112. Fax 707/944-1617. www.vintageinn.com. 80 units. $230–$545 double; $345–$585 minisuites and villas.
Rates include champagne breakfast buffet, free wine upon arrival, and afternoon tea. AE, DC, MC, V. Free parking.
From Hwy. 29 north, take the Yountville exit and turn left onto Washington St. Pets $30. **Amenities:** Concierge; busi-
ness center; secretarial services; room service; in-room massage; laundry service; dry cleaning. *In room:* A/C, TV/VCR
w/movie library, fridge, coffeemaker, hair dryer, iron, free Wi-Fi access.

Inexpensive

Maison Fleurie 🏵🏵   It's impossible not to enjoy your stay at Maison Fleurie. One
of the prettiest garden-set B&Bs in the Wine Country, it's comprised of a trio of beautiful 1873 brick-and-fieldstone buildings overlaid with ivy. The main house—a
charming Provençal replica with thick brick walls, terra-cotta tile, and paned windows—holds seven rooms; the rest are in the old bakery building and the carriage
house. Some feature private balconies, patios, sitting areas, Jacuzzi tubs, and fireplaces.
An above-par breakfast is served in the quaint little dining room; afterward, you're
welcome to wander the landscaped grounds or hit the wine-tasting trail, returning in
time for afternoon hors d'oeuvres and wine.

6529 Yount St. (between Washington St. and Yountville Cross Rd.), Yountville, CA 94599. ⓒ 800/788-0369 or 707/
944-2056. Fax 707/944-9342. www.maisonfleurienapa.com. 13 units. $130–$285 double. Rates include full breakfast
and afternoon hors d'oeuvres. AE, DC, DISC, MC, V. **Amenities:** Heated outdoor pool; Jacuzzi; free use of bikes. *In
room:* A/C, TV, dataport, hair dryer, iron, Wi-Fi.

Napa Valley Railway Inn 🏵   This is a favorite place to stay in the Wine Country.
Why? Because it's inexpensive and it's cute as all get-out. Looking hokey as heck from
the outside, the Railway Inn consists of two rows of sun-bleached cabooses and rail
cars sitting on a stretch of Yountville's original track and connected by a covered
wooden walkway. Things get considerably better when you enter your private caboose
or car, especially since they've all been recently redecorated and updated with
flatscreen TVs, new furniture, armoires with fridges, and Wi-Fi. Each is sumptuously
appointed, with comfy love seat, king- or queen-size black iron bed, and tiled bathroom. The coups de grâce are the bay windows and skylights, which let in plenty of
California sunshine. Guests enjoy complimentary passes to the nearby Yountville Fitness Center. Adjacent to the inn is Yountville's main shopping complex.

6523 Washington St., Yountville, CA 94599. ⓒ 707/944-2000. 9 units. $90–$210 double. AE, MC, V. Free parking.
In room: A/C, TV, coffeemaker, hair dryer upon request, heater, iron, Wi-Fi.

OAKVILLE & RUTHERFORD
Very Expensive

Auberge du Soleil 🏵🏵🏵 *Moments*   This spectacular Relais & Châteaux member is the
kind of place you'd imagine movie stars frequenting for clandestine affairs or weekend
retreats. Set high above Napa Valley in a 33-acre olive grove, it's quiet, indulgent, and luxuriously romantic. The contemporary California bungalow-like rooms, which were completely overhauled in 2005, are large enough to get lost in, and you might want to once
you discover all the amenities. The bathtub alone—an enormous soaking tub with a skylight overhead—will entice you to grab your complimentary bottle of California wine
and settle in for a while. In the private living room, oversize, cushy furniture surrounds a
wood-burning fireplace—the ideal place to relax and listen to CDs (the stereo comes with
a few selections) or watch one of the room's two flatscreen TVs. Fresh flowers, original art,
wood floors, cozy new persimmon-color couches, and a wet bar complete with complimentary sodas and snacks are the best of luxury home-away-from-home. Each sun-
washed private deck has views of the valley that are nothing less than spectacular. Those

with money to burn should opt for one of the $2,800–$3,500-per-night private cottages which were updated in 2006; one has two fireplaces, two full bathrooms, a den, a patio Jacuzzi and a private fitness studio. Now, that's living. Both have kitchens outfitted with espresso makers and wine fridges. All guests have access to a celestial swimming pool, exercise room, and the Wine Country's most fabulous spa, which opened in 2001. Only guests can use the spa, but if you want to get all the romantic grandeur of Auberge without staying overnight, have lunch on the terrace at the restaurant overlooking the valley (see p. 299 for more information). Overall, this is one of my favorite Wine Country places. *Parents take note:* This is not the kind of place you take the kids.

180 Rutherford Hill Rd., Rutherford, CA 94573. (C) **800/348-5406** or 707/963-1211. Fax 707/963-8764. www.auberge dusoleil.com. 50 units. $500–$925 double; $950–$1,750 suite; $2,800–$3,500 private cottage. AE, DC, DISC, MC, V. From Hwy. 29 in Rutherford, turn right on Calif. 128 and go 3 miles to the Silverado Trail; turn left and head north about 600 ft. to Rutherford Hill Rd.; turn right. **Amenities:** Restaurant; 3 outdoor pools ranging from hot to cold; tennis court; health club and full-service spa; outdoor Jacuzzi; sauna; steam room; bikes; concierge; secretarial services; room service; massage; same-day laundry service/dry cleaning; free wired or wireless Internet access; art gallery. *In room:* A/C, TV/DVD w/pay movies, dataport, kitchenette, minibar, fridge, coffeemaker, hair dryer, iron, Wi-Fi, stereo, MP3 docking stations.

Moderate

Rancho Caymus Inn 𝒜   This cozy Spanish-style hacienda, with two floors opening onto wisteria-covered balconies, was the creation of sculptor Mary Tilden Morton (whose dad was a forestry baron; Berkeley's Tilden Park is named for him). Morton wanted each room in the hacienda to be a work of art, so she employed the most skilled craftspeople she could find. As a result you'll find Morton-designed adobe fireplaces in 22 of 26 rooms, and artifacts she gathered in Mexico and South America.

Decent-size guest rooms surround a whimsical garden courtyard with an enormous outdoor fireplace. The mix-and-match decor is on the funky side, with braided rugs and overly varnished imported carved wood furnishings. But it's hard to balk when they include wet bars, sitting areas with sofa beds, small private patios and new beds and fresh paint added in 2005. Most of the suites have fireplaces, one has a kitchenette, and five have whirlpool tubs. Breakfast, which includes fresh fruit, granola, orange juice, and pastries, is served in the inn's dining room. The fancy, formal, and French-influenced La Toque restaurant (see p. 300 for complete details) is on-site and is where breakfast is served.

1140 Rutherford Rd., P.O. Box 78, Rutherford, CA 94573. (C) **800/845-1777** or 707/963-1777. Fax 707/963-5387. www.ranchocaymus.com. 26 suites. $155–$320 double; $215–$410 master suite; $275–$450 2-bedroom suite. Rates include continental breakfast. AE, MC, V. From Hwy. 29 north, turn right onto Rutherford Rd./Calif. 128 east; the hotel is on your left. **Amenities:** Restaurant. *In room:* A/C, TV, dataport, kitchenette in 1 room, minibar, fridge, microwaves in master suites, coffeemaker, hair dryer, iron in some rooms, Wi-Fi.

ST. HELENA
Very Expensive

The Inn at Southbridge 𝒜   It's absurdly expensive for what it is, but if you want to be in St. Helena and prefer upscale Pottery Barn decor to lace and latticework, this is a good place to shack up. Along with modern digs you'll find terry robes, fireplaces, bathroom skylights, down comforters, private balconies, and a host of other luxuries. One notable bummer: The inn is along the highway, so it lacks that reclusive feel offered by many other upscale hotels. Additionally, this isn't the ideal stop for families, but the adjoining casual and cheap Italian restaurant Pizzeria Tra Vigne does lure the little ones with games, TV, and pizzas.

1020 Main St., St. Helena, CA 94574. © **800/520-6800** or 707/967-9400. www.innatsouthbridge.com. Fax 707/967-9486. 21 units. $255–$625 double. AE, DC, MC, V. **Amenities:** Restaurant; large heated outdoor pool; excellent health club and full-service spa; Jacuzzi; concierge; room service; massage; same-day dry cleaning; Wi-Fi in lobby. *In room:* A/C, TV, dataport, minibar, coffeemaker, hair dryer, iron, high-speed Internet.

Meadowood Napa Valley *Finds*   Originally a private country club for Napa's well-to-do families, Cape Cod–like Meadowood is one of California's top-ranked privately owned resorts. On 250 secluded acres of pristine mountainside dotted with madrones and oaks, it's a favorite retreat for celebrities and CEOs. Units, which vary in size tremendously depending on the price, are furnished with American country classics and have beamed ceilings, private patios, stone fireplaces, and views of the forest. Many are individual suite-lodges so far removed from the common areas that you must drive to get to them. Lazier folks can opt for more centrally located rooms.

The resort offers a wealth of activities: golf on a challenging 9-hole course, tennis on seven championship courts, and croquet (yes, croquet) on two international regulation lawns. There are private hiking trails, a health spa, two heated pools, and two whirlpools.

900 Meadowood Lane, St. Helena, CA 94574. © **800/458-8080** or 707/963-3646. Fax 707/963-3532. www.meadowood.com. 85 units. Double $475–$825; 1-bedroom suite from $775–$1,250; 2-bedroom from $1,275–$2,075; 3-bedroom from $1,775–$2,900; 4-bedroom from $2,275–$3,725. Ask about promotional offers and off-season rates. 2-night minimum stay on weekends. AE, DC, DISC, MC, V. **Amenities:** 2 restaurants; 2 large heated outdoor pools; golf course; 7 tennis courts; health club and full-service spa; Jacuzzi; sauna; concierge; secretarial services; business center; room service; same-day laundry service/dry cleaning weekdays only; 2 croquet lawns. *In room:* A/C, TV, dataport, kitchenette in some rooms, minibar, coffeemaker, hair dryer, iron, free high-speed Internet access and Wi-Fi.

Moderate

Deer Run Inn   If romantic solitude is a big part of your vacation plan, Deer Run should be on your itinerary. Situated 4½ miles (10 min. by car) from downtown St. Helena along a winding mountain road, this four-room B&B is a heavenly hideaway. All of the wood-paneled rooms look onto owners Tom and Carol Wilson's 4 acres of forest, and each features gorgeous antiques, a feather bed, a private entrance, a deck, a decanter of brandy, a fridge, coffee and tea, robes, fireplaces, and access to hiking trails. One unit adjoins the cedar-shingled main house and boasts a king-size bed, Ralph Lauren textiles, a wood-burning fireplace, and an open-beam ceiling. The Carriage House Suite coddles guests with an antique queen-size bed, Spanish tile floors, a gas stove, and a huge bathroom. The Studio Bungalow is fashioned after Ralph Lauren, with Spanish tiles, a gas fireplace, a cathedral ceiling, and whitewashed cedar walls. The highly romantic Cottage, a honeymooner fave, is the most secluded and includes a gas fireplace and breakfast delivered to your door. Outside, you'll find a small pool and perhaps the owner's chocolate Labrador, Cocoa.

3995 Spring Mountain Rd., P.O. Box 311, St. Helena, CA 94574. © **877/333-7786** or 707/963-3794. Fax 707/963-9026. 4 units, all with bathroom (shower only). $160–$195 double. Rates include full breakfast. AE, MC, V. **Amenities:** Heated outdoor pool. *In room:* A/C, TV, fridge, coffeemaker, hair dryer, robes, fireplace.

Wine Country Inn   Just off the highway behind Freemark Abbey vineyard is one of Wine Country's most personable choices. The attractive wood-and-stone inn, complete with a French-style mansard roof and turret, overlooks a pastoral landscape of vineyards. The individually decorated rooms contain antique furnishings and handmade quilts; most have fireplaces and private terraces overlooking the valley, and others have private hot tubs. The five luxury cottages include king-size beds, a single bed (perfect for the tot in tow), sitting areas, fireplaces, private patios, and three-headed walk-in showers. One of the inn's best features (besides the absence of TVs) is the heated outdoor pool, which is attractively landscaped into the hillside. Another favorite feature is the selection of suites, which come with two-person jetted tubs, stereos, plenty of space, and lots of privacy. The family that runs this place puts personal touches everywhere and makes every guest feel welcome. They serve wine and plenty of appetizers nightly, along with a big dash of hotel-staff hospitality in the inviting living room. A full buffet breakfast is served there, too.

1152 Lodi Lane, St. Helena, CA 94574. ℂ **888/465-4608** or 707/963-7077. Fax 707/963-9018. www.winecountry inn.com. 29 units, 12 with shower only. $195–$410 double; $270–$485 suites; $505–$590 cottages. Rates include breakfast and appetizers. MC, V. **Amenities:** Heated outdoor pool; Jacuzzi; concierge; free Internet access at a computer station; big-screen TV in common room. *In room:* A/C, hair dryer, iron.

Inexpensive

El Bonita Motel ℱ *(Kids) (Value)*   This 1940s Art Deco motel is a bit too close to Highway 29 for comfort, but the 2½ acres of beautifully landscaped gardens behind the building (away from the road) help even the score. The rooms, while small and nothing fancy (think motel basic), are spotlessly clean and decorated with newer furnishings and kitchenettes; some have a whirlpool bathtub. It ain't heaven, but it is cheap for St. Helena.

195 Main St. (at El Bonita Ave.), St. Helena, CA 94574. ℂ **800/541-3284** or 707/963-3216. Fax 707/963-8838. www.elbonita.com. 41 units. $89–$259 double. Rates include continental breakfast. AE, DC, DISC, MC, V. **Amenities:** Heated outdoor pool; spa; Jacuzzi; free high-speed Internet access in lobby. *In room:* A/C, TV, fridge, microwave, coffeemaker, hair dryer, iron, free Wi-Fi.

White Sulphur Springs Retreat & Spa ℱ   If your idea of the ultimate vacation is a cozy cabin on 45 acres, paradise is a short, winding drive away from downtown St. Helena. Established in 1852, Sulphur Springs claims to be the oldest resort in California. The property holds a creek, a waterfall, a naturally heated sulfur hot spring, and redwood, madrone, and fir trees. Guests stay in different-size creek-side cabins, the inn, or the Carriage House. The cabins are decorated with simple but homey furnishings; cabin no. 9 has two queen-size beds and a kitchenette. From here you can take a dip in the natural hot sulfur spring; lounge by the large unheated outdoor pool; sit under a tree and watch for deer, fox, raccoon, spotted owl, or woodpecker; or schedule a day of massage (they're fantastic!), aromatherapy, and other spa treatments in their spa, which was completed in early 2001. *Note:* No RVs are allowed. All rooms are nonsmoking. Call well in advance; the resort is often rented by large groups.

3100 White Sulphur Springs Rd., St. Helena, CA 94574. ℂ **800/593-8873** in California, or 707/963-8588. Fax 707/ 963-2890. www.whitesulphursprings.com. 37 units, 14 with shared bathroom; 9 cabins. Carriage House (shared bathroom) $95–$120; small creek-side cabins $170–$190; large cabins $185–$200; cabin no. 9 $190–$210. Rates include continental breakfast. 2-night minimum stay on weekends Apr–Oct and all holidays. AE, DC, DISC, MC, V. **Amenities:** Outdoor pool; soaking pool; full-service spa; Jacuzzi; free Internet hook-up in hospitality room. *In room:* A/C in some rooms, fridge, hair dryer, iron in large cottage.

CALISTOGA
Very Expensive

Calistoga Ranch ℱℱℱ   Napa Valley's hottest new luxury resort is my absolute favorite. Tucked into the eastern mountainside on 157 pristine hidden-canyon acres, each of the 46 rural-chic free-standing luxury cottages may cost more than $525 per night. But it combines the best of sister property Auberge du Soleil and rival Meadowood, is beautifully decorated, and is packed with every conceivable amenity (including fireplaces, patios along a wooded area, and cushy outdoor furnishings).

Reasons not to leave include a giant swimming pool, a reasonably large gym, incredibly designed indoor-outdoor spa with a natural thermal pool, and individual pavilions with private-garden soaking tubs, as well as a breathtakingly beautiful restaurant with stunning views of the property's Lake Lommel. Add the startlingly good food (that can be experienced only by guests) to the resort architecture that intentionally tries to blend with the natural surroundings and you've got a romantically rustic slice of Wine Country heaven.

580 Lommel Rd., Calistoga, CA 94515. ℭ 707/254-2800. Fax 707/942-4706. www.calistogaranch.com. 46 cottages. $475–$3,000 double. AE, DC, DISC, MC, V. **Amenities:** Restaurant; large heated outdoor pool; gym; spa; Jacuzzi; steam room; concierge; room service; massage; laundry service; dry cleaning (next-day); Wi-Fi in lobby. *In room:* A/C, TV/DVD w/DVDs, fax upon request, dataport, 1 lodge with full kitchen, minibar, fridge, coffeemaker, hair dryer, iron, safe, free high-speed Internet.

Expensive

Cottage Grove Inn 🏵🏵   Standing in two parallel rows at the end of the main strip in Calistoga is the perfect retreat—adorable cottages that, though on a residential street (with a paved road running between two rows of accommodations), seem removed from the action once you've stepped across the threshold. Each compact guesthouse has a wood-burning fireplace, homey furnishings, king-size bed with down comforter, and an enormous bathroom with a skylight and a deep, two-person Jacuzzi tub. Guests enjoy such niceties as gourmet coffee, a stereo with CD player, a DVD (the inn has a complimentary DVD library), and a wet bar. Several major spas are within walking distance. This is a top pick if you want to do the Calistoga spa scene in comfort and style. Smoking is allowed only in the gazebos. Bicycles are provided for cruises around town, and guests can recoup a few bucks by using the complimentary tasting passes to more than a dozen nearby wineries.

1711 Lincoln Ave., Calistoga, CA 94515. ℭ 800/799-2284 or 707/942-8400. Fax 707/942-2653. www.cottagegrove. com. 16 cottages. $250–$325 double. Rates include continental breakfast and evening wine and cheese. AE, DC, DISC, MC, V. *In room:* A/C, TV/DVD, dataport, fridge, coffeemaker, hair dryer, iron, safe, robes, wet bar, 40 digital music channels.

Moderate

Christopher's Inn 🏵 *(Kids)*   A cluster of seven buildings makes up one of Calistoga's more attractive accommodations options. Ten years of renovations and expansions by architect-owner Christopher Layton have turned sweet old homes at the entrance to downtown into hotel rooms with a little pizazz. Options range from somewhat simple but tasteful rooms with colorful and impressive antiques and small bathrooms to huge lavish abodes with four-poster beds, rich fabrics and brocades, and sunken Jacuzzi tubs facing a fireplace. Room no. 3 impresses you with its commanding 9-foot-tall black-wood carved Asian panels. Two of the rooms have recently been renovated into "luxury suites" and overlook the fountain courtyard. Most rooms have fireplaces, and some have flatscreen TVs and DVDs (with cable). Outstanding bouquets (during the seasons when flowers abound) attest that the management goes the distance on the details. Those who prefer homey accommodations will feel comfortable here, since the property doesn't have corporate polish or big-business blandness. The lobby features a 6-foot high fireplace and cappuccino machine, making it a great place for an afternoon pick-me-up pit stop. The two rather plain but very functional two-bedroom units are ideal for families, provided you're not expecting the Ritz. An extended continental breakfast is delivered to your room daily.

1010 Foothill Blvd., Calistoga, CA 94515. ℭ 866/876-5755 or 707/942-5755. Fax 707/942-6895. www.christophers inn.com. 24 units. $150–$475 double; $330–$350 house sleeping 5–6. Rates include continental breakfast. AE, MC, V. **Amenities:** Massage studio. *In room:* TV, dataport, Wi-Fi wireless, free computer hookups.

Euro Spa & Inn 🐾🐾 In a quiet residential section of Calistoga, this small inn and spa provides a level of solitude and privacy that few other spas can match. The horseshoe-shaped inn consists of 13 stucco bungalows, a spa center, and an outdoor patio, where a light breakfast and snacks are served. The rooms, although small, are pleasantly decorated in Pottery Barn decor, whirlpool tubs, decks, gas wood stoves, and kitchenettes. Spa treatments range from clay baths and foot reflexology to minifacials.

1202 Pine St. (at Myrtle), Calistoga, CA 94515. © 707/942-6829. www.eurospa.com. Fax 707/942-1138. 13 units. $89–$239 double. Rates include deluxe continental breakfast. Seven package discounts available. AE, DC, DISC, MC, V. **Amenities:** Outdoor heated pool; Jacuzzi. *In room:* A/C, TV, kitchenette, hair dryer, iron, robes, free Wi-Fi.

Silver Rose Inn & Spa 🐾 If you'd like a big, ranch-style spread complete with a large wine bottle–shaped heated pool, a smaller unheated pool, two hot tubs, dual tennis courts, and even a chipping and putting green, then you'll love the Silver Rose Inn & Spa. Situated on a small oak-covered knoll overlooking the upper Napa Valley, the inn, which is known for its polished hospitality, offers so many amenities that you'll have a tough time searching for reasons to leave (other than to eat dinner). Each of the spacious guest rooms, which surround a centerpiece two-story atrium living room, is individually—and whimsically—decorated in sometimes over-the-top themes ranging from the peach-colored Peach Delight to the Oriental room, complete with shoji screens and Oriental rugs, to the Mardi Gras room adorned with colorful masks. Several rooms come with fireplaces, whirlpool baths, and private balconies or terraces. Guests can partake of the exclusive full-service spa as well as an afternoon "hospitality hour" of wine, cheese, and crackers. Also, the winery is open and offers free samples ($5 for outside guests) as well as daily 11am barrel tastings ($10 for outsiders).

351 Rosedale Rd. (off the Silverado Trail), Calistoga, CA 94515. © 800/995-9381 or 707/942-9581. www.silverrose. com. 20 units. $165–$265 double weekdays; $195–$310 double weekends. Rates include continental breakfast. AE, DISC, MC, V. **Amenities:** 2 pools; spa; 2 Jacuzzis; tennis courts; chipping and putting green. *In room:* A/C, dataport, hair dryer, iron upon request.

Inexpensive

Calistoga Spa Hot Springs 🐾 *Kids* *Value* Very few hotels in the Wine Country cater specifically to families with children, which is why I recommend Calistoga Spa Hot Springs if you're bringing the little ones: They classify themselves as a family resort and are very accommodating to visitors of all ages. In any case, it's a great bargain, offering unpretentious yet comfortable rooms, as well as a plethora of spa facilities. All of Calistoga's best shops and restaurants are within easy walking distance, and you can even whip up your own grub at the barbecue grills near the large pool and patio area.

1006 Washington St. (at Gerrard St.), Calistoga, CA 94515. © 866/822-5772 or 707/942-6269. www.calistogaspa. com. 57 units. Winter $109–$169 double; summer $129–$189 double. MC, V. **Amenities:** 3 heated outdoor pools; kids' wading pool; exercise room; spa. *In room:* A/C, TV, kitchenette, fridge, coffeemaker, hair dryer, iron.

Dr. Wilkinson's Hot Springs Resort 🐾 This spa/"resort," located in the heart of Calistoga, is one of the best deals in Napa Valley. The rooms range from attractive Victorian-style accommodations to modern, cozy, recently renovated guest rooms in the main 1960s-style motel. All rooms are spiffier than most in the area's other hotels, with surprisingly tasteful textiles and basic motel-style accouterments. Larger rooms have refrigerators and/or kitchens. Facilities include three mineral-water pools (two outdoor and one indoor), a Jacuzzi, a steam room, and mud baths. All kinds of body treatments are available in the spa, including famed mud baths, steams, and massage—all of which

Pricing Categories

The restaurants listed below are classified first by town, then by price, using the following categories: **Expensive,** dinner from $50 per person; **Moderate,** dinner from $35 per person; and **Inexpensive,** less than $35 per person for dinner. (*Note:* The "Very Expensive" category—dinner from $75 per person—has been omitted since no restaurants in this chapter fall under its umbrella.) These categories reflect prices for an appetizer, a main course, a dessert, and a glass of wine.

I highly recommend. Be sure to inquire about their excellent packages, their new, fantastic facial held in the facial cottage, and hot stone massage therapy.

1507 Lincoln Ave. (Calif. 29, between Fairway and Stevenson aves.), Calistoga, CA 94515. © 707/942-4102. www. drwilkinson.com. 42 units. $119–$229 double. Weekly discounts and packages available. AE, MC, V. **Amenities:** 3 pools; Jacuzzi; spa; steam room; mud baths; Internet access in lobby. *In room:* A/C, TV, dataport, coffeemaker, hair dryer, iron, voice mail.

WHERE TO DINE IN NAPA VALLEY

Napa Valley's restaurants draw as much attention to the valley as its award-winning wineries. Nowhere else in the state are kitchens as deft at mixing fresh seasonal, local, organic produce into edible magic, which means that menus change constantly to reflect the best available ingredients. Add that to a great bottle of wine and stunning views, and you have one heck of an eating experience. To best enjoy Napa's restaurant scene, keep one thing in mind: Reserve in advance—especially for a seat in a famous room.

NAPA
Moderate

Angèle 🏵🏵 COUNTRY FRENCH   I love this riverside spot for two reasons: The food is great, and the surroundings are some of the best in the valley. Its cozy combo of raw wood beams, taupe-tinted concrete-block, concrete slab floors, bright yellow leather bar stools, candlelight, and a heated, shaded patio (weather permitting) has always been great for intimate dining. But chef Tripp Mauldin, previously at Michael Mina and the Ritz-Carlton in San Francisco, who arrived in mid-2005, has upped the culinary ante in a big way, offering fabulous crispy roast chicken with summer corn, chanterelles, lardons, baby potatoes, and *jus;* outstanding burgers; and tasty seafood such as King salmon with arugula salad, heirloom tomatoes, olives, basil, and Parmesan. During winter eves, opt for the rustic-chic indoors; for summer, settle into one of the outdoor seats. And whatever you do, if they're offering it, get the chocolate soup for dessert. It sounds weird, but trust me, it's shamelessly delicious.

540 Main St. (in the Hatt Building). © 707-252-8115. Reservations recommended. Main courses $16–$26. AE, MC, V. Daily 11:30am–10pm.

Bistro Don Giovanni 🏵🏵🏵 (Value) REGIONAL ITALIAN   Donna and Giovanni Scala—who launched Scala's Bistro in San Francisco (but, sadly, are no longer involved with that venture)—own this bright, bustling, and cheery Italian restaurant, which also happens to be one of my favorite restaurants in Napa Valley. Fare prepared by chef/partner Scott Warner highlights quality ingredients and California flair and never disappoints, especially when it comes to the thin-crusted pizzas and house-made pastas. Every time I grab a menu, I can't get past the salad of beets and *haricots verts* or the pasta with duck Bolognese. On the rare occasion that I do, I am equally smitten with outstanding classic pizza Margherita fresh from the wood-burning oven, seared wild salmon filet perched atop a tower of buttermilk mashed potatoes, and steak frites. My only complaint: Over the past few years the appetizers have been getting skimpier and more expensive. But don't let it deter you. Alfresco dining in the vineyards is available—and highly recommended on a warm, sunny day. Midwinter, I'm a fan of ordering a bottle of wine (always expensive here) and dining at the bar. Desserts seriously rock, so be sure to partake.

4110 Howard Lane (at St. Helena Hwy.), Napa. © 707/224-3300. www.bistrodongiovanni.com. Reservations recommended. Main courses $12–$24. AE, DC, DISC, MC, V. Sun–Thurs 11:30am–10pm; Fri–Sat 11:30am–11pm.

Ristorante Allegria ☆ NORTHERN ITALIAN   When all I really want is a quality dinner at everyday prices, I go directly to this local spot housed downtown in a beautiful historic bank. High ceilings, faux-finished walls, mood lighting, an accordion player on Mondays and Wednesdays(!), and a sectioned-off full bar create an excellent atmosphere the staff is very friendly, and you won't find a more perfectly prepared grilled salmon over Yukon gold potatoes served with baby spinach hash topped with lemon-caper aioli—especially at 17 bucks! They also make a generous and tasty Caesar salad, offer plenty of antipasti and pastas (the latter of which are not nearly as good as Don Giovanni's), and offer the likes of filet mignon with garlic-mashed potatoes and Gorgonzola compound butter to satisfy red-meat lovers. Plus, you can order their price-fixed menu of three courses plus dessert for a measly $39. You won't get the vineyard-view "wine country" dining experience—or its corresponding high prices—here, but sometimes, that's exactly what the diner ordered. Oh! And one last perk: You can pay $10 to bring and drink your own bottle of wine *and* they waive the fee if you order a bottle from the list as well.

1026 First St. (at Main St.), Napa. © 707/254-8006. www.ristoranteallegria.com. Most main courses $9–$16 lunch, $11–$22 dinner. AE, DISC, MC, V. Mon–Thurs lunch 11am–2:30pm, dinner 5–10pm; Fri–Sun 10am–11pm.

Inexpensive

Alexis Baking Company ☆ BAKERY/CAFE   Alexis (aka ABC) is a quaint, casual stop for residents and in-the-know tourists. On weekend mornings—especially Sunday, which is when you'll find me devouring their out-of-this-world huevos rancheros—the line stretches out the door. Once you order (from the counter during the week and at the table on Sunday) and find a seat, you can relax and enjoy the coffeehouse atmosphere. Start your day with spectacular pastries, coffee drinks, and breakfast goodies like pumpkin pancakes with sautéed pears. Lunch also bustles with locals who come for simple, fresh fare like grilled hamburgers with Gorgonzola, grilled-chicken Caesar salad, roast lamb sandwich with minted mayo and roasted shallots on rosemary bread, and lentil bulgur orzo salad. (Sorry fries lovers; you won't find any here.) Desserts run the gamut; during the holidays, they include a moist and magical steamed persimmon pudding. Oh, and the pastry counter's cookies and cakes beg you to take something for the road.

1517 Third St. (between Main and Jefferson sts.), Napa. © 707/258-1827. www.alexisbakingcompany.com. Main courses $5–$12 breakfast, $7–$10 lunch. MC, V. Mon–Fri 6:30am–4pm; Sat 7:30am–3pm; Sun 8am–2pm.

Sweetie Pies ☆ *Finds* CAFE/BAKERY   Simple breakfasts of granola, egg-and-cheese croissant sandwiches, quiche, and coffee are a perfect and light way to kick off each decadent day at this adorable and aptly named country bakery. But yummy pastries, decadent individual cakes, huge cookies, and lunchtime edibles like ham and fontina panini and pizzettas with mixed green salads are equal reasons to stop by and linger at one of the few tables. Got a sweet tooth? You can't go wrong with the dark chocolate and caramel ganache fudge cake or mudpie cheesecake.

520 Main St., at the south end, Napa. ℂ 707/257-7280. Breakfast snacks $2.75–$4.50; pastries $2.25–$2.75; cake $6.75; sandwiches $5.50. MC, V. Mon–Wed 6:30am–6pm; Thurs 6:30am–7pm; Fri–Sat 6:30am–8pm; Sun 7am–5pm.

Villa Corona ✿ MEXICAN   The best Mexican food in town is served in this bright, funky, and colorful restaurant hidden in the southwest corner of a strip mall behind an unmemorable sports bar and restaurant. The winning plan here is simple: Order and pay at the counter, sit at either a table inside or at one of the few sidewalk seats, and wait for the huge burritos, enchiladas, and chimichangas to be delivered to your table. Those with pork preferences shouldn't miss the carnitas, which are abundantly flavorful and juicy. My personal favorites are hard-shell tacos or chicken enchiladas with light savory red sauce, a generous side of beans, and rice. Don't expect to wash down your menudo, or anything else for that matter, with a margarita. The place serves only beer and wine. Don't hesitate to come for a hearty breakfast, too. Excellent *chilaquiles* (eggs scrambled with salsa and tortilla) and huevos rancheros are part of the package.

3614 Bel Aire Plaza, on Trancas St., Napa. ℂ 707/257-8685. Breakfast, lunch, and dinner $6–$10. MC, V. Tues–Fri 9am–9pm; Sat 8am–9pm; Sun 8am–8pm.

ZuZu ✿✿ TAPAS   A local place to the core, ZuZu lures neighborhood regulars with a no-reservation policy, a friendly cramped wine and beer bar, and affordable Mediterranean small plates, which are meant to be shared. The comfortable, warm, and not remotely corporate atmosphere extends from the environment to the food, which includes sizzling miniskillets of tangy and fantastic paella, addictive prawns with chipotle and paprika, light and delicate sea scallop seviche salad, and Moroccan barbecued lamb chops with a sweet-and-spicy sauce. Desserts aren't as fab, but with a bottle of wine and more tasty plates than you can possibly devour, who cares?

829 Main St., Napa. ℂ 707/224-8555. Reservations not accepted. Tapas $3–$13. MC, V. Mon–Thurs 11:30am–10pm; Fri 11:30am–11pm; Sat 4–11pm; Sun 4–9pm.

YOUNTVILLE
Expensive
The French Laundry ✿✿✿ CLASSIC AMERICAN/FRENCH   It's almost futile to include this restaurant, because you're about as likely to secure a reservation—or get through on the reservation line, for that matter—as you are to drive Highway 29 without passing a winery. Several years after renowned chef-owner Thomas Keller bought the place and caught the attention of epicureans worldwide (including the judges of the James Beard Awards, who named him "Chef of the Nation" in 1997), this discreet restaurant is one of the hottest dinner tickets *in the world.*

Plainly put, The French Laundry is unlike any other dining experience, period. Part of it has to do with the intricate preparations, often finished tableside and always presented with uncommon artistry and detail, from the food itself to the surface it's delivered on. Other factors are the service (superfluous, formal, and attentive) and the sheer length of time it takes to ride chef Keller's culinary magic carpet. The atmosphere is as serious as the diners who quietly swoon over the ongoing parade of bitesize delights. Seating ranges from downstairs to upstairs to seasonal garden tables. Technically, the prix-fixe menu offers a choice of nine courses (including a vegetarian menu), but after a slew of cameo appearances from the kitchen, everyone starts to lose count. Signature dishes include Keller's "tongue in cheek" (a marinated and braised round of sliced lamb tongue and tender beef cheeks) and "macaroni and cheese" (sweet butter-poached Maine lobster with creamy lobster broth and orzo with mascarpone cheese). The truth is, the experience defies description, so if you absolutely love food, you'll simply have to try it for yourself. Portions are small, but only because Keller wants his guests to taste as many things as possible. Trust me, nobody leaves hungry.

The staff is well acquainted with the wide selection of regional wines; there's a $50 corkage fee if you bring your own bottle, which is only welcome if it's not on the list. *Hint:* If you can't get a reservation, try walking in—on occasion folks don't keep their reservation and tables open up, especially during lunch on rainy days. Reservations are accepted 2 months in advance of the date, starting at 10am. Anticipate hitting redial many times for the best chance. Also, insiders tell me that fewer people call on weekends, so you have a better chance at getting beyond the busy signal.

You can now also try www.opentable.com (but it's still done 2 months in advance).

6640 Washington St. (at Creek St.), Yountville. ✆ 707/944-2380. www.frenchlaundry.com. Reservations required. 9-course chef's tasting menu or 9-course vegetable menu $210, including service. AE, MC, V. Fri–Sun 11am–1pm; daily 5:30–9pm. Dress code: no jeans, shorts, or tennis shoes; men should wear jackets; ties optional.

Redd *&&* CONTEMPORARY AMERICAN   Just before the crazy storms and floods of late 2005, chef Richard Reddington opened his own restaurant, cleverly named Redd. Though the modern and stark dining room is a wee too bland and white-on-white for my taste, the menu is definitely full-flavored. Not that I am surprised. Reddington rightfully gained major recognition while heading up the restaurant at the superfancy Auberge du Soleil resort in Rutherford. This, his first solo endeavor, definitely qualifies as one of the top three fine dining experiences in the valley. (French Laundry and Terra are the other two options.) Expect exceptional appetizers such as a delicate sashimi hamachi with edamame, cucumber, ginger, and sticky rice and a cold foie gras trio with pistachios and brioche. For entrees, the Atlantic cod with chorizo, clams, and curry sauce is a dream dish that simultaneously manages to be rich *and* light. Desserts aren't quite as celestial, but they are lovely with Meyer lemon panna cotta acidic enough to make you pucker up and rose water crème brulée that tastes just like it sounds. If your budget allows, definitely let the sommelier wine-pair the meal for you. He's bound to turn you on to some new favorites. Also, if you're looking for a lush brunch spot, this is it!

6480 Washington St., Yountville. ✆ 707/944-2222. Reservations recommended. Main courses brunch and lunch $14–$25; main courses dinner $24–$28; 5-course tasting menu $70; 9-course tasting menu $105. AE, DISC, MC, V. Mon–Thurs 11:30am–2:30pm and 5:30–9:30pm; Fri–Sat 11:30am–2:30pm and 5:30–10pm; Sun 10am–3pm and 5:30–9:30pm.

Moderate

Bistro Jeanty *&* FRENCH BISTRO   This casual, warm bistro, with muted buttercup walls, two dining rooms divided by the bar, and patio seats, is where chef Phillipe Jeanty creates seriously rich French comfort food for legions of fans. The all-day menu includes legendary tomato soup in puff pastry, foie gras pâté, steak tartare, and house-smoked trout with potato slices. No meal should start without a paper cone filled with fried smelt (it's often on the list of specials), and none should end without the crème brûlée, made with a thin layer of chocolate cream between classic vanilla custard and a caramelized sugar top. In between, it's a rib-gripping free-for-all including coq au vin; cassoulet; and juicy, thick-cut pork chop with *jus,* spinach, and mashed potatoes. Alas, quality has suffered since Jeanty has branched out to three restaurants, but when the kitchen is on it's still a fine place to sup.

6510 Washington St., Yountville. ℂ **707/944-0103**. www.bistrojeanty.com. Reservations recommended. Appetizers $8.50–$13; most main courses $15–$29. AE, MC, V. Daily 11:30am–10:30pm.

Bouchon ☆☆ FRENCH BISTRO   Perhaps to appease the crowds who never get a reservation at French Laundry, Thomas Keller opened this far more casual, but still delicious French brasserie. Along with a raw bar, expect superb renditions of steak frites, mussels meunière, grilled-cheese sandwiches, and other heavenly French classics (try the expensive and rich foie gras pâté, which is made at Bouchon). My all-time favorite must-orders: the Bibb lettuce salad (seriously, trust me on this), french fries (perhaps the best in the valley), and roasted chicken bathed in wild mushroom ragout. A bonus, especially for restless residents and off-duty restaurant staff, is the late hours, although they offer a more limited menu when the crowds dwindle.

6534 Washington St. (at Humbolt), Yountville. ℂ **707/944-8037**. www.frenchlaundry.com. Reservations recommended during the week, required on weekends. Main courses $15–$27. AE, MC, V. Daily 11:30am–12:30am.

Mustards Grill ☆☆ CALIFORNIA   Mustards is one of those standby restaurants that everyone seems to love because it's dependable and its menu has something that suits any food craving. Housed in a convivial, barn-style space, it offers 300 wines and an ambitious chalkboard list of specials. Options go from exotic offerings like smoked duck or Mongolian style pork chop with hot mustard sauce, to sautéed lemon-garlic chicken breast with mashed potatoes and fresh herbs. The menu includes something for everyone, from vegetarians to good old burger lovers, and the wine list features nothing but "New World" wines.

7399 St. Helena Hwy. (Hwy. 29), Napa. ℂ **707/944-2424**. www.mustardsgrill.com. Reservations recommended. Main courses $11–$33. AE, DC, DISC, MC, V. Mon–Thurs 11:30am–9pm; Fri 11:30am–10pm; Sat 11am–10pm; Sun 11am–9pm.

Inexpensive

Bouchon Bakery ☆ FRENCH BAKERY   In the summer of 2003, famed French Laundry chef Thomas Keller opened this adorable authentic French bakery next door to his restaurant Bouchon (see above). It ain't cheap, but that doesn't stop locals and visitors from lining up amid the storefront for the outstanding bread baked twice daily, paper-wrapped panini, killer treats (think éclairs, cookies, tarts, and more), coffee drinks, classic sandwiches, and near-perfect pastry. Grab it to go or snack at one of the garden tables, which overlook Yountville's main drag.

6528 Washington St. (between Jefferson and Yount sts.). ℂ **707/944-2253**. Pastries and sandwiches $2.25–$7. AE, MC, V. Daily 7am–7pm.

RUTHERFORD
Expensive

Auberge du Soleil ☆ *Finds* WINE COUNTRY CUISINE   There is no better restaurant view than the one at Auberge du Soleil, perched on a hillside overlooking the valley. I recommend coming during the day (request terrace seating)—especially since dinner is expensive—to join the wealthy patrons, many of whom have emerged from their uberluxury guest rooms for a casual burger or salad lunch. Although chef Robert Curry, previously at Domaine Chandon and the nearby Culinary Institute, does a fine job, there are better blow-the-bank dinners in these parts. No doubt he'll stick with seasonal local specialties. If you go for it, dress the part: The warm interior is somewhat formal.

180 Rutherford Hill Rd., Rutherford. ℂ **707/967-3111**. Reservations recommended. Main courses $19–$25 lunch, $28–$34 dinner; 4-course fixed-price dinner $79. AE, DISC, MC, V. Daily 7–11am and 11:30am–2:30pm; Sun–Thurs 6–9:30pm; Fri–Sat 5:30–9:30pm.

La Toque *☞☞* FRENCH   Renowned chef Ken Frank attracts diners to one of Wine Country's most formal dining rooms with beautifully presented five-course extravaganzas. Well-spaced tables create plenty of room to showcase the chef-owner's memorable and innovative French-inspired cuisine, which might include an incredible Indian spice–rubbed foie gras with Madras carrot purée; Alaskan King salmon with lentils and house-cured bacon; or Niman Ranch rib roast with roasted root vegetables and red wine. But don't count on it. The menu changes weekly, so you might discover a completely different, but equally delicious, menu. Should you find room and the

---

Tips **Where to Stock Up for a Gourmet Picnic**

You can easily plan your whole trip around restaurant reservations, but gather one of the world's best gourmet picnics, and the valley's your oyster.

One of the finest gourmet-food stores in the Wine Country, if not all of California, is the **Oakville Grocery Co.**, 7856 St. Helena Hwy., at Oakville Cross Road, Oakville (*✆* **707/944-8802;** www.oakvillegrocery.com). You can put together the provisions for a memorable picnic or, with at least 24 hours' notice, the staff can prepare a picnic basket for you. The store, with its small-town vibe and claustrophobia-inducing crowds, can be quite an experience. You'll find shelves crammed with the best breads and choicest cheeses in the northern Bay Area, as well as pâtés, cold cuts, crackers, top-quality olive oils, fresh foie gras (domestic and French, seasonal), smoked Norwegian salmon, fresh caviar (Beluga, Sevruga, Osetra) and, of course, an exceptional selection of California wines. The store is open daily from 9am to 6pm. There's also an espresso bar tucked in the corner (open Mon–Sat 7am–6pm; Sun 8am–6pm), offering lunch items, a complete deli, and house-baked pastries.

Another of my favorite places to fill a picnic basket is New York's version of a swank European marketplace, **Dean & DeLuca**, 607 S. St. Helena Hwy. (Hwy. 29), north of Zinfandel Lane and south of Sulphur Springs Road, St. Helena (*✆* **707/967-9980;** www.deananddeluca.com). The ultimate in gourmet grocery stores is more like a world's fair of foods, where everything is beautifully displayed and often painfully pricey. As you pace the barn-wood plank floors, you'll stumble upon more high-end edibles than you've probably ever seen under one roof. They include local organic produce (delivered daily); 300 domestic and imported cheeses (with an on-site aging room to ensure proper ripeness); shelves and shelves of tapenades, pastas, oils, hand-packed dried herbs and spices, chocolates, sauces, cookware, and housewares; an espresso bar; one hell of a bakery section; and more. Along the back wall, you can watch the professional chefs prepare gourmet take-out, including salads, rotisserie meats, and sautéed vegetables. You can also snag a pricey bottle from the wine section's 1,500-label collection. The store is open daily from 9am to 8pm (the espresso bar is open Mon–Sat at 7:30am and Sun at 9am).

extra few bucks for the cheese course, try a few delicious selections, served with walnut bread. For an additional $62 per person you can also drink well-paired wines with each course.

1140 Rutherford Rd., Rutherford. ℭ **707/963-9770**. www.latoque.com. Reservations recommended. Fixed-price menu $98. AE, MC, V. Wed–Sun 5:30–9:30pm. Closed Mon–Tues.

ST. HELENA
Expensive
Terra ✮✮✮ CONTEMPORARY AMERICAN   Terra is one of my favorite restaurants, because it manages to be humble even though it serves some of the most extraordinary food in Northern California. The creation of Lissa Doumani and her husband, Hiro Sone, a master chef who hails from Japan, is a culmination of talents brought together more than 17 years ago, after the duo worked at L.A.'s Spago. Today, the menu reflects Sone's full use of the region's bounty and his formal training in classic European and Japanese cuisine. Dishes—all of which are incredible and are served in the rustic-romantic dining room—range from understated and refined (two musttries: rock shrimp salad, or broiled sake-marinated cod with shrimp dumplings and shiso broth) to rock-your-world flavorful (petit ragout of sweetbreads, prosciutto, mushroom, and white truffle oil; or grilled squab with leek and bacon bread pudding and roasted garlic foie gras sauce). I cannot express the importance of saving room for dessert (or forcing it even if you don't). The tiramisu is to die for.

1345 Railroad Ave. (between Adams and Hunt sts.), St. Helena. ℭ **707/963-8931**. www.terrarestaurant.com. Reservations recommended. Main courses $19–$29. AE, DC, MC, V. Wed–Mon dinner starting at 6pm. Closed for 2 weeks in early Jan.

Moderate
Tra Vigne Restaurant ✮ ITALIAN   As much as I want to love everything about this famous, absurdly scenic restaurant, I can't—anymore. With lots of chef changes over the years and meals that range from barely so-so to totally rockin', it's just not the sure thing it used to be. If you sit in the Tuscany-evoking courtyard, however, you'll likely enjoy yourself regardless of whether the kitchen is on the money or missing the mark. Inside, the bustling, cavernous dining room and happening bar are fine for chilly days and eves, but they're not nearly as magical. You can also count on wonderful bread (served with house-cured olives); a menu of robust California dishes, cooked Italian-style; a daily oven-roasted pizza special; lots of pastas; and tried-and-true standbys like short ribs and fritto misto.

1050 Charter Oak Ave., St. Helena. ℭ **707/963-4444**. www.travignerestaurant.com. Reservations recommended. Main courses $15–$26. DC, DISC, MC, V. Summer daily 11:30am–10pm; winter Sun–Thurs 11:30am–9pm, Fri–Sat 11:30am–10pm.

Wine Spectator Greystone Restaurant ✮ CALIFORNIA   This place offers a visual and culinary feast that's unparalleled in the area, if not the state. The room is an enormous stone-walled former Christian Bros. winery, warmed by the festive decor and heavenly aromas. Cooking islands—complete with scurrying chefs, steaming pots, and rotating chickens—provide entertainment. The menu features creative seasonal dishes such as roasted magret of Muscovy duckling a l'orange with caramelized Italian onions, toasted pine nuts, currants, and sweet potato gnocchi; or steamed Alaskan halibut filet with young ginger, wilted Asian greens, black mushrooms, jasmine rice, and chile soy broth. I recommend that you opt for a barrage of appetizers for your table to share. You might also consider the "Lessons in Wine"—$14 to $25, which allows you to sample three 3-ounce pours of local wines such as white Rhone, pinot, or zinfandel. Although the food is serious, the atmosphere is playful—casual enough that you'll feel comfortable in jeans or shorts. If you want to ensure having a meal here, reserve far in advance (they book 60 days in advance). Personally, I prefer to stop by, have a snack at the bar, and eat big meals elsewhere.

At the Culinary Institute of America at Greystone, 2555 Main St., St. Helena. ℭ 707/967-1010. www.ciachef.edu. Reservations recommended. Temptations $9; main courses $19–$30. AE, DC, MC, V. Daily 11:15am–10pm.

Inexpensive

Market AMERICAN   In past editions I've highly recommended this upscale but cheap ode to American comfort food. But ever since the chef departed to open Cyrus, a high-end sister restaurant in Northern Sonoma County's town of Healdsburg, the food here has gone downhill (though it's incredible at Cyrus: 29 North St., Healdsburg— that's a 45-min. drive from St. Helena; ℭ 707/433-3311; 3- to 5-course menus $58–$95; www.cyrusrestaurant.com). Still, if you're in expensive St. Helena and want some casual glamour with your burger, you'll find it here with fancy stone-wall and Brunswick bar surroundings paired with clunky steak knives and simple white-plate presentations. Skip the lame chopped salad and perhaps go instead for barbecue sauce–glazed meatloaf over gravy, mashed potatoes, and carrots; or toast-it-yourself s'mores with crisp homemade graham crackers. At lunch, you can also opt for a three-course meal—a steal at a measly $15.

1347 Main St., St. Helena. ℭ 707/963-3799. www.marketsthelena.com. Most main courses $7–$19. AE, MC, V. Daily 11:30am–10pm.

Pizzeria Tra Vigne *Kids* *Value* ITALIAN   After spending a week in Wine Country, I usually can't stand the thought of another decadent wine and foie gras meal. That's when I race here for a $6.95 chopped salad, a welcome respite from gluttonous excess. Families and locals come here for another reason: Although the menu is limited, it's a total winner for anyone in search of freshly prepared, wholesome food at atypically cheap Wine Country prices. A Caesar salad, for example, costs a mere $6.95. "Piadine"—pizzas folded like a soft taco—are the house specialty and come filled with such delights as fresh rock shrimp, Crescenza cheese sauce, scallions, and deep-fried lemons. Pizzas are of the build-your-own variety, with gourmet toppings like sautéed mushrooms, fennel sausage, baby spinach, sun-dried tomatoes, and homemade pepperoni. The 14 respectable local wines come by the glass starting at a toast-worthy $5, or $18 per bottle. Dessert, at less than $4 a pop for gelato, or $6 for tiramisu, is an overall sweet deal. Kids like the pool table and big-screen TV.

At The Inn at Southbridge, 1016 Main St., St. Helena. ℭ 707/967-9999. www.travignerestaurant.com/pizzaria.htm. Pastas $8–$11; pizzas $9–$17. DC, DISC, MC, V. Daily 11:30am–9pm (Fri–Sat until 9:30pm).

Taylor's Automatic Refresher DINER   Yet another winner to slip from sublime status to buyer beware, this gourmet roadside burger shack built in 1949 still draws huge lines of tourists who love the notion of ordering at the counter and feasting alfresco. But the last few meals I had there left me knowing the $80 I coughed up for lunch for five would have been better spent at Oakville Grocery's deli. The burger, onion rings, and fries were mediocre at best, the iceberg salad was unwieldy, and only the shake left me satisfied. (How hard is it to make a great shake, after all?) Perhaps it's that the owners now have a closer eye on their San Francisco outpost, which is great, by the way. No matter. It's still the only casual burger joint in St. Helena (it also offers ahi tuna burger and various sandwiches, tacos, soups and salads) and its ever-bustling status proves everyone knows it.

933 Main St., St. Helena. ☎ **707/963-3486**. www.taylorsrefresher.com. Main courses $4–$13. AE, MC, V. Daily 10:30am–8pm (9pm in summer).

CALISTOGA
Moderate
All Seasons Café ★★ CALIFORNIA   All Seasons successfully balances old-fashioned down-home dining charm with today's penchant for sophisticated, seasonally inspired dishes. It also happens to have perhaps the best food in downtown Calistoga. Here vibrant bouquets, large framed watercolors, and windows overlooking busy Lincoln Avenue soften the look of the black-and-white checkered flooring, brick-red ceiling, and long, marble wine bar. Laid-back service belies what arrives on the plate—and the fact that they have 400-plus wines available from their adjoining wine shop (with a $15 corkage fee, buy next door and you're drinking for far cheaper than at most restaurants). But it also makes the quality of crispy skin chicken with black truffle chicken *jus* and herb-roasted monkfish with fennel nage that much more of a delicious surprise. Alas, the kitchen was a wee bit slow on my last visit, but all was forgiven when the food far surpassed my expectations.

1400 Lincoln Ave. (at Washington St.), Calistoga. ☎ **707/942-9111**. www.allseasonsnapavalley.net. Reservations recommended on weekends. Main courses $9–$11 lunch, $19–$28 dinner. DISC, MC, V. Lunch Fri–Sun noon–2:30pm; dinner Tues–Sun 6–9pm (times vary in winter, please call or go online to confirm).

Inexpensive
Wappo Bar & Bistro GLOBAL   One of the best alfresco dining venues in the Wine Country is under Wappo's jasmine-and-grapevine–covered arbor. Unfortunately, food and service are a very distant second. But much can be forgiven when the wine's flowing and you're surrounded by pastoral splendor. The menu offers a global selection, from tandoori chicken to roast rabbit with gnocchi and mustard cream sauce. Desserts of choice are black-bottom coconut cream pie and strawberry rhubarb pie.

1226 Washington St. (off Lincoln Ave.), Calistoga. ☎ **707/942-4712**. www.wappobar.com. Main courses $14–$24. AE, MC, V. Wed–Mon 11:30am–2:30pm and 6–9:30pm.

2 Sonoma Valley

A pastoral contrast to Napa, Sonoma manages to maintain a backcountry ambience, thanks to its far lower density of wineries, restaurants, and hotels. Small, family-owned wineries are Sonoma's mainstay; tastings are low-key and come with plenty of friendly banter with the winemakers. Basically, this is the valley to target if your ideal vacation includes visiting a handful of wineries along quiet woodsy roads, avoiding shopping outlets and Napa's high-end glitz, and simply enjoying the laid-back country atmosphere.

The valley is some 17 miles long and 7 miles wide, and it's bordered by two mountain ranges: the Mayacamas to the east and the Sonomas to the west. Unlike in Napa Valley, you won't find palatial wineries with million-dollar art collections or aerial trams. Rather, the Sonoma Valley offers a refreshing dose of reality, where modestly sized wineries are integrated into the community. If Napa Valley feels like a fantasyland, where everything exists to service the almighty grape and the visitors it attracts, then the Sonoma Valley is its antithesis, an unpretentious gaggle of ordinary towns, ranches, and wineries that welcome tourists but don't necessarily rely on them. The result is a chance to experience what Napa Valley must have been like long before the

Seagrams and Moët et Chandons of the world turned the Wine Country into a major tourist destination.

As in Napa, you can pick up *Wine Country Review* throughout Sonoma. It gives you the most up-to-date information on wineries and related area events.

ESSENTIALS

GETTING THERE   From San Francisco, cross the Golden Gate Bridge and stay on U.S. 101 north. Exit at Highway 37; after 10 miles, turn north onto Highway 121. After another 10 miles, turn north onto Highway 12 (Broadway), which takes you directly into the town of Sonoma.

VISITOR INFORMATION   While you're in Sonoma, stop by the **Sonoma Valley Visitors Bureau,** 453 First St. E. (© **866/996-1090** or 707/996-1090; www.sonoma valley.com). It's open Monday through Saturday from 9am to 5pm (6pm in the summer) and Sunday 10am to 5pm. An additional **Visitors Bureau** is a few miles south of the square at Cornerstone Festival of Gardens at 23570 Arnold Dr. (Hwy. 121; © **866/996-1090**); it's open daily from 9am to 4pm, 6pm during summer.

If you prefer advance information from the bureau, you can contact the Sonoma Valley Visitors Bureau to order the free *Sonoma Valley Visitors Guide,* which lists almost every lodge, winery, and restaurant in the valley.

TOURING THE SONOMA VALLEY & WINERIES

Sonoma Valley is currently home to about 40 wineries (including California's first winery, Buena Vista, founded in 1857) and 13,000 acres of vineyards. It produces roughly 25 types of wines, totaling more than five million cases a year. Unlike the rigidly structured tours at many of Napa Valley's corporate-owned wineries, on the Sonoma side of the Mayacamas Mountains, tastings are usually low-key and tours are free.

The towns and wineries covered below are organized geographically from south to north, starting at the intersection of Highway 37 and Highway 121 in the Carneros District and ending in Kenwood. The wineries tend to be a little more spread out here than they are in Napa Valley, but they're easy to find. Still, it's best to decide which wineries you're most interested in and devise a touring strategy before you set out, so you don't do too much backtracking.

I've reviewed some of my favorite Sonoma Valley wineries here—more than enough to keep you busy tasting wine for a long weekend. If you'd like a complete list of local wineries, be sure to pick up one of the free guides available at the Sonoma Valley Visitors Bureau (see "Visitor Information," above).

For a map of the wineries below, please see "The Wine Country" map on p. 269.

THE CARNEROS DISTRICT

As you approach the Wine Country from the south, you must first pass through the Carneros District, a cool, windswept region that borders the San Pablo Bay and marks the entrance to both the Napa and Sonoma valleys. Until the latter part of the 20th century, this mixture of marsh, sloughs, and rolling hills was mainly used as sheep pasture (*carneros* means "sheep" in Spanish). However, after experimental plantings yielded slow-growing, high-quality grapes—particularly chardonnay and pinot noir—several Napa and Sonoma wineries expanded their plantings here. They eventually established the Carneros District as an American Viticultural Appellation, a legally defined wine-grape growing area. Although about a dozen wineries are spread throughout the region, there are no major towns or attractions—just plenty of gorgeous scenery as you cruise along Highway 121, the major route between Napa and Sonoma.

Viansa Winery and Italian Marketplace ☆ *Finds*   The first major winery you'll encounter as you enter Sonoma Valley from the south, this sprawling Tuscan-style villa perches atop a knoll overlooking the entire lower valley. Viansa is the brainchild of Sam and Vicki Sebastiani, who left the family dynasty to create their own temple to food and wine. (*Viansa* is a contraction of "Vicki and Sam.") Here you'll find a large room crammed with a cornucopia of high-quality mustards, olive oils, pastas, salads, breads, desserts, Italian tableware, cookbooks, and wine-related gifts as well as tasting opportunities.

The winery, which does an extensive mail-order business through The Tuscan Club, has established a favorable reputation for its Italian varietals. Tastings, which cost $5 to $20 per person, are offered at the east and west end of the marketplace, and the self-guided tour includes a trip through the underground barrel-aging cellar adorned with colorful hand-painted murals. Guided tours, held at 11am and 2pm, cost $5.

Viansa is also one of the few wineries in Sonoma Valley that sells deli items—the focaccia sandwiches are delicious. You can dine alfresco under the grape trellis while you admire the bucolic view.

25200 Arnold Dr. (Calif. 121), Sonoma. ✆ **800/995-4740** or 707/935-4700. www.viansa.com. Daily 10am–5pm. Daily self-guided tours. Guided tours daily 11am and 2pm, $5.

Gloria Ferrer Champagne Caves ☆ *Finds*   When you have had it up to here with chardonnays and pinots, it's time to pay a visit to Gloria Ferrer, the grande dame of the Wine Country's sparkling-wine producers. Who's Gloria? She's the wife of José Ferrer, whose family has made sparkling wine for 5 centuries. The family business, Freixenet, is the largest producer of sparkling wine in the world; Cordon Negro is its most popular brand. That equals big bucks, and certainly a good chunk went into building this palatial estate. Glimmering like Oz high atop a gently sloping hill, it overlooks the verdant Carneros District. On a sunny day, enjoying a glass of dry brut while soaking in the magnificent views is a must.

If you're unfamiliar with the term *méthode champenoise,* be sure to take the free 30-minute tour of the fermenting tanks, bottling line, and caves brimming with racks of yeast-laden bottles. Afterward, retire to the elegant tasting room, order a glass of one of seven sparkling wines ($4–$10 a glass) or tastes of their eight still wines ($2–$3 per taste), find an empty chair on the veranda, and say, "Ahhh. *This* is the life." There are picnic tables, but it's usually too windy for them to be comfortable, and you must buy a bottle (from around $18–$40) or glass of sparkling wine to reserve a table.

23555 Carneros Hwy. (Calif. 121), Sonoma. ✆ **707/996-7256**. www.gloriaferrer.com. Daily 10am–5:15pm. Tours daily; call day of visit to confirm schedule.

SONOMA

At the northern boundary of the Carneros District along Highway 12 is the centerpiece of Sonoma Valley. The midsize town of Sonoma owes much of its appeal to Mexican general Mariano Guadalupe Vallejo, who fashioned this pleasant, slow-paced community after a typical Mexican village—right down to its central plaza, Sonoma's geographical and commercial center. The plaza sits at the top of a T formed by Broadway (Hwy. 12) and Napa Street. Most of the surrounding streets form a grid pattern around this axis, making Sonoma easy to negotiate. The plaza's Bear Flag Monument marks the spot where the crude Bear Flag was raised in 1846, signaling the end of

---

⟨Tips⟩ A Garden Detour

Garden lovers should pull over for a gander at the latest Sonoma addition, **Cornerstone Festival of Gardens,** 23570 Arnold Dr., Sonoma (© **707/933-3010; www.cornerstonegardens.com**). Modeled in part after the International Garden festival at Chaumont-sur-Loire in France's Loire Valley and the Grand Metis in Quebec, Canada, the 9-acre property is the first gallery-style garden exhibit in the United States and includes a series of 22 ever-changing gardens designed by famed landscape architects and designers. With a recently-added children's garden featuring a brightly-colored water tower surrounded by a sand moat and buckets, shovels, and plastic plumbing fittings, this is a great spot for the whole family. If you're visiting in the summer, find out about their monthly kids' programs. When you get hungry, stop by the **Market Café,** which offers light breakfast, pastries, and espresso drinks along with a seasonal lunch menu including soups, salads, and sandwiches. It's all served in nifty metal trays, perfect for carrying out to the gardens; there's also seating indoors and out in front. Another plus for those with kids: The gardens include a cleverly installed willow reed maze that's about 3 feet high and only has one entrance/exit right in front of the cafe, so if you're sitting out front and the kids get bored, you can safely let them run through the maze. If you get inspired, you can load up on loot here that will help your own garden grow—from furniture and gifts to plants, garden art, and books, as there are several interesting shops here, too. March 16 through November, the gardens are open 10am to 5pm and cost $9 general, $7.50 seniors 65 plus, $6.50 college students, $3 youth 4 to 17, and free for kids under 3 (check for locals' discounts); December through March 15, they're open 10am to 4pm and charge $5 general, $4 seniors and students, and $2 youth. You can take a self-guided tour anytime; installations are marked with descriptive plaques; 45-minute guided tours are given on Saturdays and Sundays at 11am and are included in the admission.

Mexican rule; the symbol was later adopted by the state of California and placed on its flag. The 8-acre park at the center of the plaza, complete with two ponds populated by ducks, is perfect for an afternoon siesta in the cool shade. *Note:* As this book goes to press, the pond was in the midst of a 1-year restoration, though it should be open by 2007.

Buena Vista Winery   Count Agoston Haraszthy, the Hungarian émigré who is universally regarded as the father of California's wine industry, founded this historic winery in 1857. A close friend of General Vallejo, Haraszthy returned from Europe in 1861 with 100,000 of the finest vine cuttings, which he made available to all growers. Although Buena Vista's winemaking now takes place at an ultramodern facility in the Carneros District, the winery maintains a tasting room inside the restored 1862 Press House. The beautiful stone-crafted room brims with wines, wine-related gifts, and accessories.

Tastings are $5 for four wines, $10 for a flight of three library wines. You can take the self-guided tour any time during operating hours; a "Historical Tour and Tasting" (offered daily at 11am and 2pm during high season; Mon–Fri at 2pm and Sat–Sun at 11am and 2pm during off season) details the life and times of Count Haraszthy and includes a viticultural tour and wine and food pairing. For $50, you can do a wine and cheese tasting, by appointment only; call ℭ **707/265-1460.** After tasting, grab your favorite bottle, a selection of cheeses from the Sonoma Cheese Factory, salami, bread, and spreads (all available in the tasting room), and plant yourself at one of the many picnic tables in the lush, verdant setting.

18000 Old Winery Rd. (off E. Napa St., slightly northeast of downtown), Sonoma. ℭ **800/926-1266** or 707/265-1472. www.buenavistawinery.com. Nov–May daily 10am–5pm; June–Oct 10am–5:30pm.

Sebastiani Vineyards & Winery   The name Sebastiani is practically synonymous with Sonoma. What started in 1904, when Samuele Sebastiani began producing his first wines, has in three generations grown into a small empire, producing some 200,000 cases a year. After a few years of seismic retrofitting, a face-lift, and a temporary tasting room, the original 1904 winery is now open to the public with more extensive educational tours ($5–$7.50 per person) and seminars like the Wine & Cheese ($15) and the Soil to Bottle ($25), an 80-foot S-shaped tasting bar, and lots of shopping opportunities in the gift shop. In the contemporary tasting room's mini-museum area you can see the winery's original turn-of-the-20th-century crusher and press, as well as the world's largest collection of oak-barrel carvings, crafted by bygone local artist Earle Brown. If it's merely wine that interests you, you can sample an extensive selection of wines ranging from a complimentary selection to $18 for a flight of their fancy stuff, the latter of which includes a keepsake glass. Bottle prices are reasonable, ranging from $13 to $75. A picnic area adjoins the cellars; a far more scenic spot is across the parking lot in Sebastiani's Cherryblock Vineyards. They also offer a historical

---

⟨Moments⟩ Touring the Sonoma Valley by Bike

Sonoma and its neighboring towns are so small, close together, and relatively flat that it's not difficult to get around on two wheels. In fact, if you're in no great hurry, there's no better way to tour the Sonoma Valley than by bicycle, even though there are no great bike routes (it's all along the road for the most part). You can rent a bike from the **Goodtime Bicycle Company** ☆ (ℭ **888/525-0453** or 707/938-0453; www.goodtimetouring.com). The staff will happily point you to easy bike trails, or you can take an organized excursion to Kenwood-area wineries, south Sonoma wineries, or even northern Sonoma's Russian River and Dry Creek areas. Goodtime also provides a gourmet lunch featuring local Sonoma products. If you purchase wine along the way, Goodtime will carry it for you and help with shipping arrangements. Lunch rides start at 10:30am and end around 3:30pm. The cost, including food and equipment, is $125 per person (that's a darn good deal). Rentals cost $25 a day, and include helmets, locks, everything else you'll need, and delivery and pickup to and from local hotels.

Mountain bikes, helmets, and locks are also available for rent from **Sonoma Valley Cyclery,** 20093 Broadway, Sonoma (ℭ **707/935-3377**), for $35 a day. Hybrid bikes (better for casual wine-tasting cruisers) are $25 per day, helmet and lock included.

Sonoma trolley tour at 2pm on Fridays and Saturdays (weather permitting) that takes visitors around town and through the vineyards.

389 Fourth St. E., Sonoma. © 800/888-5532 or 707/933-3200. www.sebastiani.com. Daily 10am–5pm. Tours: winter daily 11am and 3pm; summer 11am, 1pm, and 3pm, with an additional tour at noon Sat–Sun.

Ravenswood Winery   Compared to old heavies like Sebastiani and Buena Vista, Ravenswood is a relative newcomer to the Sonoma wine scene. Nevertheless, it quickly established itself as the sine qua non of zinfandel, the versatile red grape that's known in these parts for being big, ripe, juicy, and powerful. The first winery in the United States to focus primarily on zins, which make up about three-quarters of its astonishing 1 million-case production, Ravenswood underscores zins' zest with their motto, "No Wimpy Wines." But they also produce merlot, cabernet sauvignon, Rhone varietals, and a small amount of chardonnay.

The winery is smartly designed—recessed into the hillside to protect its treasures from the simmering summers. Tours ($10 per person) follow the winemaking process from grape to glass, and include a visit to the aromatic oak-barrel aging rooms. You're welcome to bring your own picnic basket to any of the tables, but if you're coming between Memorial Day and Labor Day, find out if they're giving one of their famously fun barbecues (call for details). Regardless, tastings are $5–$10, which is refundable with purchase.

18701 Gehricke Rd. (off Lovall Valley Rd.), Sonoma. © 888/NO-WIMPY or 707/933-2332. www.ravenswoodwinery. com. Labor Day–Memorial Day 10am–4:30pm; Memorial Day–Labor Day 10am–5pm. Tours by reservation only at 10:30am; with an additional 2pm tour Fri–Sun May–Oct.

GLEN ELLEN

About 7 miles north of Sonoma on Highway 12 is the town of Glen Ellen. Although just a fraction of the size of Sonoma, Glen Ellen is home to several of the valley's finest wineries, restaurants, and inns. Aside from the addition of a few new restaurants, this charming town hasn't changed much since the days when Jack London settled on his Beauty Ranch, about a mile west. Other than the wineries, you'll find few real signs of commercialism; the shops and restaurants, along one main winding lane, cater to a small, local clientele—that is, until the summer tourist season begins and traffic nearly triples on the weekends. If you haven't decided where you want to set up camp during your visit to the Wine Country, I highly recommend this lovable little rural region.

Arrowood Vineyards & Winery   Richard Arrowood had already established a reputation as a master winemaker at Château St. Jean when he and his wife, Alis Demers Arrowood, set out on their own in 1986. Their picturesque winery stands on a gently rising hillside lined with perfectly manicured vineyards. Tastings take place in the Hospitality House, the newer of Arrowood's two stately gray-and-white buildings. They're fashioned after New England farmhouses, complete with wraparound porches. Richard's focus is on making world-class wine with minimal intervention, and his results are impressive: More than one of his current releases has scored over 90 points in *Wine Spectator*. Mind you, excellence doesn't come cheap: a taste here is $5 or $10 for four limited-production wines, but if you're curious about what near-perfection tastes like, it's well worth it. *Note:* No picnic facilities are available here.

14347 Sonoma Hwy. (Calif. 12), Glen Ellen. © 707/935-2600. www.arrowoodvineyards.com. Daily 10am–4:30pm. Tours by appointment only.

Benziger Family Winery *(Finds)*   A visit here confirms that this is indeed a family winery. At any given time, two generations of Benzigers (*Ben*-zigger) may be running around tending to chores, and they instantly make you feel as if you're part of the clan. The pastoral, user-friendly property features an exceptional self-guided tour of the certified biodynamic winery ("The most comprehensive tour in the wine industry," according to *Wine Spectator*), gardens, and a spacious tasting room staffed by amiable folks. The $10, 45-minute tram tour, pulled by a beefy tractor, is both informative and fun. It winds through the estate vineyards and to caves, and ends with a tasting. *Tip:* Tram tickets—a hot item in the summer—are available on a first-come, first-served basis, so either arrive early or stop by in the morning to pick up afternoon tickets.

Tastings of the standard-release wines are $5. Tastes including several limited-production wines or reserve or estate wines cost $10. The winery also offers several scenic picnic spots.

1883 London Ranch Rd. (off Arnold Dr., on the way to Jack London State Historic Park), Glen Ellen. ℭ 888/490-2739 or 707/935-3000. www.benziger.com. Tasting room daily 10am–5pm. Tram tours daily (weather permitting) $10 adults, $5 children every half-hour, 10:30am–3:30pm.

KENWOOD

A few miles north of Glen Ellen along Highway 12 is the tiny town of Kenwood, the valley's northernmost outpost. Although Kenwood Vineyards' wines are well known throughout the United States, the town itself consists of little more than a few restaurants, wineries, and modest homes on the wooded hillsides. The nearest lodging, the luxurious Kenwood Inn & Spa (p. 315), is about a mile south of the vineyards. Kenwood makes for a pleasant half-day trip from Glen Ellen or downtown Sonoma. Take an afternoon tour of Château St. Jean (see below) and have dinner at Kenwood Restaurant (p. 319).

Kenwood Vineyards   Kenwood's history dates from 1906, when the Pagani brothers made their living selling wine straight from the barrel and into the jug. In 1970 the Lee family bought the property and dumped a ton of money into converting the aging winery into a modern, high-production facility (most of it cleverly concealed in the original barnlike buildings). Since then, Kenwood has earned a solid reputation for consistent quality with each of its varietals: cabernet sauvignon, chardonnay, zinfandel, pinot noir, merlot and, most popular, sauvignon blanc—a crisp, light wine with hints of melon.

Although the winery looks rather modest in size, its output is staggering: nearly 500,000 cases of ultrapremium wines fermented in steel tanks and French and American oak barrels. Popular with collectors is their Artist Series cabernet sauvignon, a limited production from the winery's best vineyards, featuring labels with original artwork by renowned artists. The tasting room, housed in one of the old barns, offers complimentary tastes, $2 to $5 tastings of private reserve wines, and gift items for purchase. *FYI:* The Lees no longer own the winery.

9592 Sonoma Hwy. (Calif. 12), Kenwood. ℭ 707/833-5891. www.kenwoodvineyards.com. Daily 10am–4:30pm. No tours.

Château St. Jean ⭐ *Finds*   Château St. Jean is notable for its exceptionally beautiful buildings, expansive landscaped grounds, and gourmet marketlike tasting room. Among California wineries, it's a pioneer in vineyard designation—the procedure of making wine from, and naming it for, a single vineyard. A private drive takes you to what was once a 250-acre country retreat built in 1920; a well-manicured lawn overlooking the meticulously maintained vineyards is now a picnic area, complete with a fountain and tables.

In the huge tasting room—where there's also a charcuterie shop and plenty of housewares for sale—you can sample Château St. Jean's wide array of wines. They range from chardonnays and cabernet sauvignon to fumé blanc, merlot, Johannesburg Riesling, and gewürztraminer. Tastings are $5 per person, $10 per person for reserve wines.

8555 Sonoma Hwy. (Calif. 12), Kenwood. © 800/543-7572 or 707/833-4134. www.chateaustjean.com. Tasting daily 10am–5pm. Tours 11am and 3pm. At the foot of Sugarloaf Ridge, just north of Kenwood and east of Hwy. 12.

St. Francis Winery   Although St. Francis Winery makes a commendable chardonnay, zinfandel, and cabernet sauvignon, they're best known for their highly coveted merlot. Winemaker Tom Mackey, a former high-school English teacher from San Francisco, has been hailed as the "Master of Merlot" by *Wine Spectator* for his uncanny ability to craft the finest merlot in California.

If you've visited before, but haven't been back in a while, don't follow your memory to the front door. In 2001, St. Francis moved a little farther north to digs bordering on the Santa Rosa County line. The original property was planted in 1910 as part of a wedding gift to Alice Kunde (scion of the local Kunde family) and christened St. Francis of Assisi in 1979 when Joe Martin and Lloyd Canton—two white-collar executives turned vintners—completed their long-awaited dream winery. Today the winery still owns the property, but there's new history in the making at their much larger facilities, which include a tasting room and upscale gift shop. Tastings are $5 for current releases, $10 for a reserve tasting of four wines, and $20 for a reserve tasting paired with food, served in the private reserve tasting room (by appointment). Now that St. Francis is planning more special activities, it's worthwhile to call or check their website for their calendar of events.

100 Pythian Rd. (Calif.12/Sonoma Hwy.), Santa Rosa (at the Kenwood border). © 800/543-7713, ext. 242 or 707/833-4666. www.stfranciswinery.com. Daily 10am–5pm.

WHERE TO STAY IN SONOMA VALLEY

Keep in mind that during the peak season and on weekends, most B&Bs and hotels require a minimum 2-night stay. Of course, that's assuming you can find a vacancy; make reservations as far in advance as possible. If you are having trouble finding a room, call the **Sonoma Valley Visitors Bureau** (© 866/996-1090 or 707/996-1090; www.sonomavalley.com). The staff will try to refer you to a lodging that has a room to spare but won't make reservations for you. Another option is the **Bed and Breakfast Association of Sonoma Valley** (© 800/969-4667), which can refer you to a B&B that belongs to the association. You can also find updated information on their website, **www.sonomabb.com**.

SONOMA
Very Expensive
Fairmont Sonoma Mission Inn & Spa 𝕲𝕲𝕲   As you drive through Boyes Hot Springs, you may wonder why someone decided to build a multimillion-dollar spa resort in this ordinary little town. There's no view to speak of, and it certainly isn't within walking distance of any wineries or fancy restaurants. So what's the deal? It's the naturally heated artesian mineral water, piped from directly underneath the spa into the temperature-controlled pools and whirlpools. Set on 12 meticulously groomed acres, the Fairmount Sonoma Mission Inn consists of a massive three-story replica of a California mission (well, aside from the pink paint job) built in 1927, an array of satellite wings housing numerous superluxury suites, and world-class spa facilities. It's a popular retreat for the wealthy and well known, so don't be surprised if you see a famous face (I bumped into Tiffany Amber Thiessen of "90210" in the spa dressing

Pricing Categories

Hotel listings are arranged below first by area, then by price, using the following categories: **Very Expensive,** more than $250 per night; **Expensive,** $200 to $250 per night; **Moderate,** $150 to $200 per night; and **Inexpensive,** less than $150 per night.

room during my last visit). Big changes have occurred here since Fairmont took over the resort in 2002. It has gained 60 suites, updated its spa to the tune of $25 million, and just finished a $62-million renovation, which included completely redoing the Heritage Rooms in understated country elegance. Fancier digs include more modern rooms with plantation-style shutters, ceiling fans, down comforters, and oversize bath towels. The Wine Country rooms feature king-size beds, desks, refrigerators, and huge limestone and marble bathrooms; some offer wood-burning fireplaces, too, and many have balconies or patios. For the ultimate in luxury, the opulently appointed Mission Suites are the way to go. Golfers will be glad to know the resort is also home to the nearby Sonoma Golf Club, host of the PGA championship every October.

101 Boyes Blvd., Corner of Boyes Blvd. and Calif. 12, P.O. Box 1447, Sonoma, CA 95476. (C) **800/441-1414** or 707/938-9000. Fax 707/938-4250. www.fairmont.com/sonoma. 226 units. $259–$1,259 double. AE, DC, MC, V. Valet parking is free for day use (spa-goers) and $14 for overnight guests. From central Sonoma, drive 3 miles north on Hwy. 12 and turn left on Boyes Blvd. **Amenities:** 2 restaurants; 3 large, heated outdoor pools; golf course; health club and spa (see box, "The Super Spa," on p. 312 for the complete rundown); Jacuzzi; sauna; bike rental; concierge; business center; salon; room service; babysitting; same-day laundry service/dry cleaning; free wine tasting (4:30–5:30pm). *In room:* A/C, TV, dataport, minibar, hair dryer, iron, safe, high-speed Internet access ($13 per day), free bottle of wine upon arrival.

MacArthur Place *(R)(R)*   A highly recommended alternative to the Fairmont Sonoma Mission Inn & Spa (see above) is this much smaller and more intimate luxury property and spa located 4 blocks south of Sonoma's plaza. Once a 300-acre vineyard and ranch, MacArthur Place has since been whittled down to a 5½-acre "country estate" replete with landscaped gardens and tree-lined pathways, various free-standing accommodations, and a spa and heated swimming pool and whirlpool. Most of the individually decorated guest rooms are Victorian-modern attached cottages scattered throughout the resort; all are exceedingly well stocked with custom linens, oversize comforters, and original artwork; most have flatscreen TVs. The newer suites come with fireplaces, porches, wet bars, six-speaker surround sound, and whirlpool tubs that often have shutters opening to the bedroom. Everyone has access to complimentary wine and cheese in the evening and the DVD library anytime. The full-service spa offers a fitness center, body treatments, skin care, and massages. Within the resort's restored century-old barn is Saddles, Sonoma's only steakhouse specializing in grass-fed beef, organic and sustainably farmed produce, and whimsically classy Western decor. An array of other excellent restaurants—as well as shops, wineries, and bars—is within biking distance. *Note:* All rooms are nonsmoking.

29 E. MacArthur St., Sonoma, CA 95476. (C) **800/722-1866** or 707/938-2929. www.macarthurplace.com. 64 units. Sun–Thurs $299–$525 double; Fri–Sat $349–$575 double. Rates include continental breakfast. AE, MC, V. Free parking. **Amenities:** Restaurant and bar specializing in martinis; outdoor heated pool; exercise room; full-service spa; outdoor Jacuzzi; steam room; rental bikes; concierge; room service; massage; laundry service; same-day dry cleaning. *In room:* A/C, TV/DVD, dataport, hair dryer, iron, Wi-Fi access; minibar, wet bar and coffeemaker in suites.

Expensive

Best Western Sonoma Valley Inn *(Kids)*   Perfect for the traveling family, this simple inn with recently updated rooms offers plenty for kids along for the ride. There's room to run around, plus a large, heated outdoor saltwater pool, gazebo-covered spa, and sauna to play in. The rooms come with a lot of perks, such as continental breakfast delivered to your room each morning, a gift bottle of white Sonoma Valley wine (chilling in the fridge), and satellite TV with HBO. Most rooms have either a balcony or a deck overlooking the inner courtyard. An added bonus: If you need someone to help you get the kinks out, you can book one of the two new spa rooms and have the staff book an outside company to come in and give you an on-site massage. The inn is also in a good location, just a block from Sonoma's plaza.

550 Second St. W. (1 block from the plaza), Sonoma, CA 95476. (C) **800/334-5784** or 707/938-9200. Fax 707/938-0935. www.sonomavalleyinn.com. 80 units. $114–$361 double. Rates include continental breakfast. AE, DC, DISC, MC, V. **Amenities:** Heated outdoor pool; exercise room; Jacuzzi; sauna; steam room; free Wi-Fi access. *In room:* A/C, TV, dataport, fridge, coffeemaker, hair dryer, iron, high-speed Internet.

Moderate

El Dorado Hotel *(★★)*   This 1843 mission revival building may look like a 19th-century Wild West relic from the outside, but inside it's all 21st-century deluxe. Each modern, handsomely appointed guest room has French windows and tiny balconies. Some rooms offer lovely views of the plaza; others overlook the private courtyard and heated lap pool. All rooms (except those for guests with disabilities) are on the second floor and were upgraded in 2004. The four rooms on the ground floor are off the private courtyard, and each has a partially enclosed patio. Though prices reflect its prime

---

Finds The Super Spa

The **Fairmount Sonoma Mission Inn, Spa & Country Club,** 18140 Sonoma Hwy. ((C) 800/862-4945 or 707/938-9000; www.fairmont.com/sonoma), has always been the most complete—and the most luxurious—spa in the entire Wine Country. With its recent $25-million, 43,000-square-foot facility upgrade to make the space bigger, this super spa is now one of the best in the country. The Spanish mission–style retreat offers more than 50 spa treatments, ever-popular natural mineral baths, and virtually every facility and activity imaginable. You can pamper yourself silly: Take a sauna or herbal steam, have a facial set to music, indulge in a grape-seed body wrap, relax with a massage, go for a dip in the outdoor pool, or soak away your worries in the celestial indoor mineral pool area—the list goes on and on (and, alas, so will the bill). You can also work off those wicked Wine Country meals with aerobics, weights, and cardio machines; get loose in a yoga class (all complimentary for guests); or just lounge and lunch by the pool. For non-guests, they offer personalized day spa packages, which range in price from $159 to $459 depending on what you request and include use of the pool, classes, and hot tub. If you don't mind splurging and are a fan of luxury living, you'll agree that the Fairmount Sonoma Mission Inn Spa is one of the best ways to unwind in the Wine Country.

location on Sonoma Square, this is still one of the more charming options within its price range.

405 First St. W., Sonoma, CA 95476. © **800/289-3031** or 707/996-3030. Fax 707/996-3148. www.hoteleldorado.com. 27 units. Summer $175–$195 double; winter $145–$165 double. 2 night minimum weekends and holidays. AE, MC, V. **Amenities:** Restaurant; heated outdoor pool; concierge; laundry service; dry cleaning. *In room:* A/C, flatscreen TVs, DVD/CD player, cordless phone, voice mail, dataport, fridge, hair dryer, iron, CD player.

Inexpensive

Sonoma Hotel 🐾🐾　This cute little historic hotel on Sonoma's tree-lined town plaza emphasizes 19th-century elegance and comfort. Built in 1880 by Swiss immigrant Henry Weyl, it has attractive guest rooms decorated in early California style, with French country furnishings, wood and iron beds, and pine armoires. In a bow to modern luxuries, recent additions include private bathrooms, cable TV, phones with dataports, and (this is crucial) air-conditioning. Perks include fresh coffee and pastries in the morning and wine in the evening. Its lovely restaurant, the girl & the fig (p. 316) serves California-French cuisine.

110 W. Spain St., Sonoma, CA 95476. © **800/468-6016** or 707/996-2996. Fax 707/996-7014. www.sonomahotel.com. 16 units. Summer $110–$245 double; winter $95–$195 double. 2-night minimum required for summer weekends. Rates include continental breakfast and evening wine. AE, DC, MC, V. *In room:* A/C, TV, dataport.

Victorian Garden Inn 🐾🐾　Here, proprietor Donna Lewis runs what is easily the cutest B&B in Sonoma Valley. A picket fence, a wall of trees, and an acre of gardens enclose an adorable Victorian garden brimming with violets, roses, camellias, and peonies, all shaded under flowering fruit trees. It's truly a marvelous sight in the springtime. The guest units—three in the century-old water tower and one in the main building (an 1870s Greek Revival farmhouse), as well as a cottage—continue the Victorian theme, with white wicker furniture, floral prints, padded armchairs, and claw-foot tubs. The most popular units are the Top o' the Tower and the Woodcutter's Cottage. Each has its own entrance and a garden view; the cottage boasts a sofa and armchairs set in front of the fireplace and a private deck. After a hard day of wine tasting, spend the afternoon cooling off in the pool or on the shaded wraparound porch, enjoying a mellow merlot while soaking in the sweet garden smells. You might also opt for a soak in the therapeutic hot tub, or get a massage. In the morning, they serve a "California" breakfast, including fruit, warm pastries, granola, and more. *New parents, take note:* The property recommends you leave young tots behind.

316 E. Napa St., Sonoma, CA 95476. © **800/543-5339** or 707/996-5339. www.victoriangardeninn.com. 3 units, 1 cottage. $149–$299 double. Rates include California breakfast. AE, DC, MC, V. Amenities: Outdoor pool; therapeutic hot tub; concierge; business center with free Internet access; laundry service. *In room:* A/C, fireplaces in some rooms.

GLEN ELLEN
Expensive

Gaige House Inn 🐾🐾🐾 *Finds*　Owners Ken Burnet, Jr., and Greg Nemrow run Wine Country's finest B&B. Here you'll find a level of service, amenities, and decor normally associated with four-star resorts—minus the snobbery. Every nook and cranny of the 1890 Queen Anne–Italianate building and Garden Annex is swathed with fashionable articles found during the owners' world travels. Spacious rooms offer everything you could want—firm mattresses, wondrously silky-soft Mascioni linens, and premium comforters gracing the beds; even the furniture and artwork are the kind you'd like to take home with you. All 23 rooms, artistically decorated in a plantation theme with Asian and Indonesian influences (trust me, they're beautiful), have king- or queen-size beds; four rooms have Jacuzzi tubs, one has a Japanese soaking tub, and the eight new superfancy spa garden suites have, among other delights, granite soaking tubs. For chilly country nights, fireplaces (in 17 rooms) definitely come in handy. Bathrooms are equally luxe, range in size, and are stocked with Aveda products and slippers. Attention to detail means you'll be treated to a robe I liked so much I had to buy it. For the ultimate retreat, reserve one of the suites, which have patios overlooking a stream or private gardens.

But wait, it gets better. The inn is set on a 3-acre oasis with perfectly manicured lawns and gardens, a 40-foot-long heated pool, and an inviting creek-side hammock shaded by a majestic Heritage oak. Evenings are best spent in the reading parlor, sipping premium wines. Appetizers at wine hour might include freshly shucked oysters or a sautéed scallop served ready-to-slurp on a Chinese soupspoon. Breakfast is a momentous event, accented with herbs from the inn's garden and prepared by a chef who cooked at the James Beard House in 2001.

Greg and Ken also manage two long-term rentals (private guesthouses on private estates) for those who want more privacy and fewer services.

13540 Arnold Dr., Glen Ellen, CA 95442. © 800/935-0237 or 707/935-0237. Fax 707/935-6411. www.gaige.com. 23 units. Summer $300–$595 double, $500–$595 suite; winter $195–$275 double, $325–$525 suite. Rates include evening wines. AE, DC, DISC, MC, V. **Amenities:** Large heated pool; in-room massage; free wireless Internet access. *In room:* A/C, TV/DVD, dataport, fridge in some rooms, hair dryer, iron, safe, DSL and Wi-Fi.

Inexpensive

Beltane Ranch ✦ *(Finds)* The word *ranch* conjures up a big ole' two-story house in the middle of hundreds of rolling acres, the kind of place where you laze away the day in a hammock watching the grass grow or pitching horseshoes in the garden. Well, friend, you can have all that and more at the well-located Beltane Ranch, a century-old buttercup-yellow manor that's been everything from a bunkhouse to a brothel to a turkey farm. You simply can't help but feel your tensions ease away as you prop your feet up on the shady wraparound porch overlooking the quiet vineyards, sipping a cool, fruity chardonnay while reading *Lonesome Dove* for the third time. Each room is uniquely decorated with American and European antiques; all have sitting areas and separate entrances. A big and creative country breakfast is served in the garden or on the porch overlooking the vineyards. For exercise, you can play tennis on the private court or hike the trails meandering through the 105-acre estate. The staff here is knowledgeable and helpful. *Tip:* Request one of the upstairs rooms, which have the best views.

11775 Sonoma Hwy./Hwy. 12, P.O. Box 395, Glen Ellen, CA 95442. © **707/996-6501**. www.beltaneranch.com. 5 units, 1 cottage. $140–$190 double; $220 cottage. Rates include full breakfast. No credit cards; personal checks accepted. **Amenities:** Outdoor, unlit tennis court. *In room:* No phone.

Glenelly Inn and Cottages ✦

Perhaps the best thing about this rustic retreat is its reasonable rates. But equally important, this former railroad inn, built in 1916, is positively drenched in serenity. Located well off the main highway on an oak-studded hillside, the peach-and-cream inn comes with everything you would expect from a country retreat. Long verandas offer Adirondack-style chairs and views of the verdant Sonoma hillsides; breakfast is served beside a large cobblestone fireplace; and bright units contain old-fashioned claw-foot tubs, Scandinavian down comforters, and ceiling fans (though cottages have whirlpool tubs and air-conditioning). Downsides include thin walls, the usual laugh lines that come with age, and depending on your perspective, lack of TV and phone. However, the staff understands that it's the little things that make the difference—hence the firm mattresses, good reading lights, and a simmering hot tub in a grapevine- and rose-covered arbor. All rooms are decorated with antiques and country furnishings, and have terry robes and private entrances. Top picks are the Vallejo and Jack London family suites, both with large private patios, although I also like the rooms on the upper veranda—particularly in the spring, when the terraced gardens below are in full bloom. The new free-standing garden cottages (the best option) are for those who want to splurge; they come with fireplaces, TV/VCRs, CD players, coffeemakers, and fridges.

5131 Warm Springs Rd. (off Arnold Dr.), Glen Ellen, CA 95442. (©) **707/996-6720.** Fax 707/996-5227. www.glenelly. com. 9 units. $165–$195 double/suite; $295 cottage. Rates include full breakfast. AE, DISC, MC, V. **Amenities:** Outdoor Jacuzzi; TV in common room; free Internet access at computer stations. *In room:* Wi-Fi.

KENWOOD
Very Expensive
Kenwood Inn & Spa *Inspired by the villas of Tuscany, the Kenwood Inn's honey-colored Italian-style buildings, flower-filled flagstone courtyard, and pastoral views of vineyard-covered hills are enough to make any northern Italian homesick. The friendly staff and luxuriously restful surroundings made this California girl feel right at home. What's not to like about a spacious room lavishly and exquisitely decorated with imported tapestries, velvets, and antiques, plus a fireplace, balcony (except on the ground floor), feather bed, CD player, and down comforter? With no TV in the rooms, relaxation is inevitable—especially if you book treatments at their Caudelie Vinotherapie Spa, which uses French products highlighting vine and grape seed extracts. A minor caveat is road noise, which you're unlikely to hear from your room but can be slightly audible over the tranquil pumped-in music around the courtyard and decent-size pool. Longtime guests will be surprised to find more bodies around the pool—18 guest rooms and an adjoining building joined this slice of pastoral heaven in June 2003. Anyone with a hefty credit card limit can buy complete seclusion by renting the inn's new and very private two-bedroom villa nearby.

An impressive three-course gourmet breakfast is served in the courtyard or in the Mediterranean-style dining room.

10400 Sonoma Hwy., Kenwood, CA 95452. (©) **800/353-6966** or 707/833-1293. Fax 707/833-1247. www.kenwood inn.com. 30 units. Apr–Oct $375–$700 double; Nov–Mar $350–$650 double, $800–$1,200 villa. Rates include gourmet breakfast and bottle of wine. 2-night minimum on weekends. AE, MC, V. **Amenities:** 2 heated outdoor pools; full-service spa; concierge. *In room:* Hair dryer, iron, high-speed Internet access, CD player.

WHERE TO DINE IN SONOMA VALLEY
SONOMA
Moderate
Cafe La Haye ECLECTIC Well-prepared and wholesome food, an experienced waitstaff, friendly owners, a soothing atmosphere, and reasonable prices—including a modestly priced wine list—make La Haye a favorite. In truth, everything about this cafelike restaurant is charming. The atmosphere within the small split-level dining room is smart and intimate. The vibe is small business—a welcome departure from Napa Valley's big-business restaurants. The straightforward, seasonally inspired cuisine, which chefs bring forth from the tiny open kitchen, is delicious and wonderfully well priced. Although the menu is small, it offers just enough options. Expect a risotto special; pasta such as fresh tagliarini with butternut squash, prosciutto, sage,

Pricing Categories

The restaurants listed below are classified first by town, then by price, using the following categories: **Expensive,** dinner from $50 per person; **Moderate,** dinner from $35 per person; and **Inexpensive,** dinner less than $35 per person. (**Note:** The "Very Expensive" category—dinner from $75 per person—has been omitted since no restaurants in this chapter fall under its umbrella.) These categories reflect prices for an appetizer, a main course, a dessert, and a glass of wine.

and garlic cream; and pan-roasted chicken breast, perhaps with goat cheese–herb stuffing, caramelized shallot *jus,* and fennel mashed potatoes. Meat eaters are sure to be pleased with filet of beef seared with black pepper–lavender sauce and served with Gorgonzola-potato gratin; and no one can resist the creative salads.

140 E. Napa St., Sonoma. © **707/935-5994.** Reservations recommended. Main courses $14–$24. AE, MC, V. Tues–Sat 5:30–9pm.

the girl & the fig *Finds* COUNTRY FRENCH   Well established in its downtown Sonoma digs (it used to be in Glen Ellen), this modern, attractive, and cozy eatery, with lovely patio seating, is the home for Sondra Bernstein's (the girl) beloved restaurant. Here the cuisine, orchestrated by chef de cuisine Matt Murray, is nouveau country with French nuances, and yes, figs are sure to be on the menu in one form or another. The wonderful winter fig salad contains arugula, pecans, dried figs, Laura Chenel goat cheese, and fig-and-port vinaigrette. Murray uses garden-fresh produce and local meats, poultry, and fish whenever possible, in dishes such as grilled pork chops or duck confit. For dessert, try lavender crème brûlée, a glass of Jaboulet muscat, and a sliver of one of their delicious offerings from the cheese list. Sondra knows her wines, features Rhone varietals, and will be happy to choose the best accompaniment for your meal. Looking for brunch? Head here on Sunday when it's served until 3pm.

110 W. Spain St., Sonoma. © **707/938-3634.** www.thegirlandthefig.com. Reservations recommended. Main courses $13–$24. AE, DISC, MC, V. Mon–Thurs 11:30am–10pm; Fri–Sat 11:30am–11pm; Sun 10am–10pm.

Harmony Restaurant *Finds* CONTINENTAL   The most welcome addition to Sonoma's dining scene in 2003, the Harmony Restaurant is not only a looker with its elegant Italianate dining room with dark woods, high ceilings, marble flooring, and a wall of giant doors opening to sidewalk seating and Sonoma's plaza. It also delivers in food and live entertainment. Drop in for a seasonal menu, which features hearty winter rib-grippers such as veal *osso buco* with creamy roast garlic mushroom polenta and braised greens or somewhat lighter warm-weather fare such as cumin-crusted ahi tuna with beluga lentils, roasted vegetables, and red-wine sauce. Go for sidewalk seating during warmer weather (they also have heat lamps), sit inside, or hang at the carved wood bar. Either way you'll want to face the piano when the nightly performer is tinkling the keys and singing jazz standards.

480 First St. E. (at the plaza), Sonoma. © **707/996-9779.** www.ledsonhotel.com. Reservations accepted. Entrees $19–$30. AE, DISC, MC, V. Wed–Mon 11:30am–10pm; Tues 5–10pm.

Meritage *Finds* SOUTHERN FRENCH/NORTHERN ITALIAN   Learning from the previous occupants' mistakes—that Sonoma ain't New York and shouldn't treat its customers that way—chef-owner Carlo Cavallo eliminated the big-city attitude and prices at his restaurant without diminishing style, service, or quality. The former executive chef for

Giorgio Armani, Cavallo combines the best of southern French and northern Italian cuisines (hence "Meritage," after a blend made with traditional bordeaux varieties), giving Sonomans yet another reason to eat out. The menu, which changes twice daily, is a good read: foie gras ravioli with sage truffle sauce; seafood stew with tiger prawns, manilla clams, mussels, and mixed fresh fish in a spicy tomato saffron broth; and wild boar chops in white truffle sauce with mashed potatoes. Shellfish fans can't help but love the oyster raw bar with options of fresh crab and lobster, and cocktailers revel in the new martini bar. A lovely garden patio is prime positioning for sunny brunches and lunches and summer dinners. Such edible enticement—combined with reasonable prices, excellent service, a stellar wine list, and Carlo's practiced charm—make Meritage a trustworthy option.

165 West Napa St., Sonoma. ⓒ 707/938-9430. www.sonomameritage.com. Reservations recommended. Main courses $13–$30. AE, MC, V. Mon and Wed–Fri 11:30am–9:30pm; Sat–Sun 10:30am–9:30pm.

Swiss Hotel ⓕ CONTINENTAL/NORTHERN ITALIAN   With its slanting floors and beamed ceilings, the historic Swiss Hotel, located right in the town center, is a Sonoma landmark and very much the local favorite for fine food served at reasonable prices. The turn-of-the-20th-century oak bar at the left of the entrance is adorned with black-and-white photos of pioneering Sonomans. The bright white dining room and sidewalk patio seats are pleasant spots to enjoy lunch specials such as penne with chicken, mushrooms, and tomato cream; hot sandwiches; and California-style pizzas fired in a wood-burning oven. But the secret spot is the very atmospheric back garden patio, a secluded oasis shaded by a wisteria-covered trellis and adorned with plants, a fountain, gingham tablecloths, and a fireplace. Dinner might start with a warm winter salad of radicchio and frisée with pears, walnuts, and bleu cheese. Main courses run the gamut; I like the linguine and prawns with garlic, hot pepper, and tomatoes; the filet mignon wrapped in bleu-cheese crust; and roasted rosemary chicken. The food may not knock your socks off, but it's all simply satisfying.

18 W. Spain St (at First St. W.), Sonoma. ⓒ 707/938-2884. www.swisshotelsonoma.com. Reservations recommended. Main courses lunch $8.50–$16, dinner $13–$28. AE, MC, V. Daily 11:30am–2:30pm; Sun–Thurs 5–9pm; Fri–Sat 5–10pm. (Bar daily 11:30am–2am.)

Inexpensive

Black Bear Diner ⓚⁱᵈˢ DINER   When you're craving a classic American breakfast with all the cholesterol and the fixin's (perhaps to counterbalance that wine hangover), make a beeline for this old-fashioned diner. First, it's fun, with its over-the-top bear paraphernalia, gazette-style menu listing local news from 1961 and every possible diner favorite, and absurdly friendly waitstaff. Second, it's darned cheap. Third, helpings are huge. What more could you want? Kids get a kick out of coloring books, old-timers reminisce over Sinatra playing on the jukebox, and everyone leaves stuffed on omelets, scrambles, and pancakes. Lunch and dinner feature steak sandwiches, salads, and comfort food faves like barbecued pork ribs, Cobb salad, fish and chips, and burgers—they grind their own beef. But unless you like old-school run-of-the-mill diner fare, your best bet is to dine elsewhere.

201 West Napa St. (at Second St.), Sonoma. ⓒ 707/935-6800. www.blackbeardiner.com. Main courses breakfast $5–$8.50, lunch and dinner $5.50–$17. AE, DISC, MC, V. Daily 6am–9:30pm (closing varies on weekends, depending on business).

Della Santina's ⓕⓕ TUSCAN   For those of you who just can't swallow another expensive, chichi California meal, follow the locals to this friendly, traditional Italian restaurant. How traditional? Ask father-and-son team Dan and Robert: When I last dined here, they pointed out Signora Santina's hand-embroidered linen doilies as they proudly told me about her Tuscan recipes. And their pride is merited: Every dish my party tried was refreshingly authentic and well flavored, without overbearing sauces or one *hint* of California pretentiousness. Be sure to start with traditional antipasti, particularly sliced mozzarella and tomatoes, or delicious, traditional tortellini in brodo (homemade tortellini in broth). The nine pasta dishes are, again, wonderfully authentic (gnocchi lovers, rejoice!). The spit-roasted meat dishes are a local favorite (although I found them a bit overcooked); for those who can't choose between chicken, pork, turkey, rabbit, or duck, there's a selection that offers a choice of three. Don't worry about breaking your bank on a bottle of wine, because many choices here go for under $40. Portions are huge, but be sure to save room for a wonderful dessert, like the creamy panna cotta. Though the inside's small, there's a pretty huge back patio, covered in blooming trellises, that's full practically every night in the summer (the wait's never too bad), and they've recently tented part of it, so you can eat back there in winter, too, weather permitting.

133 E. Napa St. (just east of the square), Sonoma. ☎ **707/935-0576.** www.dellasantinas.com. Reservations recommended. Main courses $10–$20. AE, DISC, MC, V. Daily 11:30am–3pm and 5–9:30pm.

Rin's Thai ☞ THAI   When valley residents or visitors get a hankering for Pad Thai, curry chicken, or *tom yum* (classic spicy soup), they head to this adorable little restaurant just off Sonoma Plaza. The atmosphere itself—contemporary, sparse, yet warm environs within an old house—is tasteful and the staff is extremely accommodating. After you settle into one of the well-spaced tables within or outside on the patio (weather permitting), go for your favorites—from satay with peanut sauce and cucumber salad or spicy red curry with a choice of pork, beef, chicken, vegetables, or seafood to yummy *larb gai salad* (minced chicken, chiles, onion, and lemon sauce) or charbroiled vegetables or ribs with chile-garlic dipping sauce. They've got it all covered, including that oh-so-sweet Thai iced tea, fried bananas with coconut ice cream, and fresh mango with sticky rice (seasonal).

139 E. Napa St. (just east of the plaza), Sonoma. ☎ **707/938-1462.** www.rinsthai.com. Reservations recommended. Main courses $7.50–$11. MC, V. Sun–Thurs 11:30am–9pm; Fri–Sat until 9:30pm.

GLEN ELLEN
Moderate

the fig café & wine bar ☞☞ NEW AMERICAN   The girl & the fig's (p. 316) sister restaurant is more casual than its downtown Sonoma sibling. But don't let the bucolic neighborhood vibe, airy environs, and soothing sage and mustard color scheme fool you. From his open kitchen, chef de cuisine Bryan Jones brings you the kind of rustic sophistication more commonly associated with urban restaurants. Consider starting with a thin-crust pizza, fried calamari with spicy lemon aioli, a cheese plate, or the signature fig and arugula salad, move on to braised pot roast with mashed potatoes or mussels in a garlic, leek, and tarragon sauce with fries, and finish with a fantastic chocolate brownie with vanilla ice cream. A perk: the "Rhone Alone" wine selections are available by the flight, glass, or bottle, free corkage.

13690 Arnold Dr. (at Madrone Rd). ☎ **707/938-2130.** www.thefigcafe.com. Reservations not accepted. Main courses $10–$17. AE, DISC, MC, V. Sun–Thurs 5:30–9pm; Fri–Sat until 9:30pm. Brunch offered Sat–Sun 9:30am–2:30pm.

Glen Ellen Inn Oyster Grill & Martini Bar ☞ CALIFORNIA   Christian and Karen Bertrand have made this place so quaint and cozy that you feel as if you're dining in their home, and that's exactly the place's charm. Garden seating is the favored choice on sunny days, but the covered, heated patio is also always welcoming. The first course from Christian's open kitchen might be a ginger tempura calamari with wasabi or a brie fondue with sourdough toast points. Main courses, which change with the seasons, range from spinach and stilton ravioli to grilled salmon with blood oranges, watercress, and lemon aioli. Other favorites include pork tenderloin with sun-dried cranberries, mozzarella, caramelized onions and polenta and utterly tender filet mignon with maytag blue cheese and garlic frites. On my last visit, the Sonoma Valley mixed-green salad, seared ahi tuna, and homemade French vanilla ice cream floating in bittersweet caramel sauce made a lovely meal. They've recently added the eponymous oyster grill and martini bar, including half-size taster martinis and, of course, oysters any way you want 'em. If that doesn't do it for you, the 550-plus selection wine list offers numerous bottles from Sonoma, as well as more than a dozen wines by the glass. *Tip:* There's a small parking lot behind the restaurant.

13670 Arnold Dr. (at O'Donnell Lane), Glen Ellen. © 707/996-6409. www.glenelleninn.com. Reservations recommended. Main courses $16–$25. AE, DISC, MC, V. Fri–Tues 11:30am–9pm (dinner from 5pm); Wed–Thurs 5:30–9pm. Closed 1 week in Jan.

Wolf House ✿ ECLECTIC   The most polished-looking dining room in Glen Ellen is elegant yet relaxed whether you're seated in the handsome dining room—smartly adorned with maple floors, gold walls, dark-wood wainscoting, and a corner fireplace—or outside on the multilevel terrace under the canopy of trees with serene views of the adjacent Sonoma Creek. The lunch menu adds fancy finishes to old favorites such as the excellent chicken Caesar salad, fresh grilled ahi tuna niçoise sandwich, or a juicy half-pound burger with Point Reyes Original Blue cheese. During dinner, skip the soggy beer-battered prawns and head straight for seared Roasted Liberty farms duck breast with wild stewed plums, cipolini onions, barley risotto, baked pears, and plum demi, or pan-roasted salmon with sweet asparagus, baby arugula salad, and sunchoke mash. The reasonably priced wine list offers many by-the-glass options as well as a fine selection of Sonoma wines. Locals love the brunch, complete with *nepalas rancheros* (chorizo, pinto beans, roasted chiles, and fried eggs), Dungeness crab cake Benedict, omelets, and brioche French toast. During my visits, service was rather languid, but well meaning.

13740 Arnold Dr. (at London Ranch Rd.), Glen Ellen. © 707/996-4401. www.jacklondonlodge.com/rest.html. Reservations recommended. Main courses brunch and lunch $8–$15, dinner $17–$32. AE, MC, V. Lunch Tues–Fri 11am–3pm; dinner Tues–Sun 5:30–9:30pm; brunch Sat 11am–3pm, Sun 10am–3pm.

KENWOOD
Moderate
Kenwood Restaurant & Bar ✿✿ CALIFORNIA/CONTINENTAL   This is what Wine Country dining should be—but often, disappointingly, is not. From the terrace of the Kenwood Restaurant, diners enjoy a view of the vineyards set against Sugarloaf Ridge as they imbibe Sonoma's finest at umbrella-covered tables. On nippy days, you can retreat inside to the Sonoma-style roadhouse, with its vibrant artwork and cushioned rattan chairs at white cloth–covered tables. Regardless of where you pull up a chair, expect first-rate cuisine, perfectly balanced between tradition and innovation, complemented by a reasonably priced wine list. Great starters are Dungeness crab cake with herb mayonnaise; superfresh sashimi with ginger, soy, and wasabi; and a wonderful Caesar salad. The main dish might be poached salmon in creamy

caper sauce or prawns with saffron Pernod sauce. But the Kenwood doesn't take itself too seriously: Great sandwiches and burgers are also available.

9900 Sonoma Hwy. (just north of Dunbar Rd.), Kenwood. ✆ **707/833-6326**. www.kenwoodrestaurant.com. Reservations recommended. Main courses $13–$30. MC, V. Wed–Sun noon–9pm.

Inexpensive

Café Citti NORTHERN ITALIAN   If you're this far north into the Wine Country, then you're probably doing some serious wine tasting. If that's the case, then you don't want to spend half the day at a fancy, high-priced restaurant. What you need is Café Citti (pronounced *Cheat*-ee), a roadside do-it-yourself Italian trattoria that is both good and cheap. You order from the huge menu board displayed above the open kitchen. Afterward, you grab a table (the ones on the patio, shaded by umbrellas, are the best on warm afternoons), and a server will bring your meal. It's all hearty, home-cooked Italian. Standout dishes are the green-bean salad, tangy Caesar salad, focaccia sandwiches, and roasted rotisserie chicken stuffed with rosemary and garlic. Wine is available by the bottle, and the espresso is plenty strong. Everything on the menu board is available to go, which makes Café Citti an excellent resource for picnic supplies.

9049 Sonoma Hwy., Kenwood. ✆ **707/833-2690**. Prices range from $7–$22. MC, V. Lunch daily 11am–3:30pm; dinner Sun–Thurs 5–8:30pm, Fri–Sat 5–9pm.

Appendix:
San Francisco in Depth

Born as an out-of-the-way backwater of colonial Spain and blessed with a harbor that would have been the envy of any of the great cities of Europe, San Francisco boasts a story as varied as the millions of people who have passed through its "Golden Gate," a strait linking the San Francisco Bay to the Pacific Ocean. It was not named for the gold rush; rather, Col. John C. Fremont named it in 1848 after "Chrysoceras," or "Golden Horn," in Constantinople.

1 The Age of Discovery

After Columbus "discovered" the New World in 1492, legends of the fertile land of California were discussed in the universities and taverns of Europe, even though no one really understood where the mythical land was. (Some evidence of arrivals in California by Chinese merchants hundreds of years before Columbus's landing has been unearthed, although few scholars are willing to draw definite conclusions.) The first documented visit by a European to Northern California was by the Portuguese explorer Juan Rodriguez Cabrillo, who circumnavigated the southern tip of South America and traveled as far north as the Russian River in 1542. Nearly 40 years later, in 1579, Sir Francis Drake landed on the Northern California coast, stopping for a time to repair his ships and to claim the territory for Queen Elizabeth of England. Another Portuguese, Sebastian Cermeño, "discovered" Punta de los Reyes (Kings' Point) in the mid-1590s. All three adventurers completely missed the narrow entrance to San Francisco Bay, either because it was enshrouded in fog or, more likely, because they simply weren't looking for it. The bay's entrance is nearly impossible to see from the open ocean.

Two more centuries passed before a European actually saw the bay that would later extend Spain's influence over much of the American West. Gaspar de Portolá, a soldier sent from Spain to meddle in a rather ugly conflict between the Jesuits and the Franciscans, accidentally stumbled upon the bay in 1769, en route to somewhere else. However, he stoically plodded on to his original destination, Monterey Bay, more than 100 miles to the south. Six years later, Juan Ayala actually sailed into San Francisco Bay while on a mapping expedition for the Spanish and immediately realized the enormous strategic importance of his find.

Colonization quickly followed. Juan Bautista de Anza and around 30 Spanish-speaking families marched through the deserts from Sonora, Mexico, arriving after many hardships at the northern tip of modern-day San Francisco in June 1776. They immediately claimed the peninsula for Spain. Their headquarters was an adobe fortress, the Presidio, built on the site of today's park with the same name. The settlers' church, a mile to the south, was the first of five Spanish missions later developed around the edges of San Francisco Bay. Although the name of the church was officially *Nuestra Señora de Dolores,* it was dedicated to St. Francis of Assisi and nicknamed San Francisco by the Franciscan priests. Later, the name applied to the entire bay.

In 1821, Mexico broke away from Spain, secularized the Spanish missions, and abandoned all interest in the natives. Freed of Spanish restrictions, California's ports suddenly opened to trade. The region around San Francisco Bay supplied large amounts of hides and tallow for transport around Cape Horn to the tanneries and factories of New England and New York. The prospect of prosperity persuaded an English-born sailor, William Richardson, to jump ship in 1822 and settle on the site of what is now San Francisco. To impress the commandant of the Presidio, whose daughter he loved, Richardson converted to Catholicism and established the beginnings of what would soon become a thriving trading post and colony. Richardson named his trading post Yerba Buena (or "good herb") because of a species of wild mint that grew there, near the site of today's Montgomery Street. (The city's original name was recalled with endless mirth 120 years later, during San Francisco's hippie era.) He conducted a profitable hide-trading business and eventually became harbormaster and the city's first merchant prince. By 1839, the place was a veritable town, with a mostly English-speaking populace and a saloon of dubious virtue.

Throughout the 19th century, armed hostilities between English-speaking settlers from the Eastern seaboard and the Spanish-speaking colonies of Spain and Mexico erupted in places as widely scattered as Texas, Puerto Rico, and along the frequently shifting U.S.-Mexico border. In 1846, a group of U.S. marines from the warship *Portsmouth* seized the sleepy main plaza of Yerba Buena, ran the U.S. flag up a pole, and declared California an American territory. The Presidio (occupied by about a dozen unmotivated Mexican soldiers) surrendered without a fuss. The first move made by the new, mostly Yankee citizenry was to officially adopt the name of the bay as the name of their town.

2 The Gold Rush

The year 1848 was one of the most pivotal in Western history, with unrest sweeping through Europe, horrendous poverty in Ireland, and widespread disillusionment about hopes for prosperity throughout Europe and the East Coast of the United States. Stories about the golden port of San Francisco and the agrarian wealth of the American West filtered east, attracting slow-moving groups of settlers. Ex-sailor Richard Henry Dana extolled the virtues of California in

Dateline

- **1542** Juan Rodriguez Cabrillo sails up the California coast.
- **1579** Sir Francis Drake lands near San Francisco, missing the entrance to the bay.
- **1769** Members of the Spanish expedition led by Gaspar de Portolá become the first Europeans to see San Francisco Bay.
- **1775** The *San Carlos* is the first European ship to sail into San Francisco Bay.
- **1776** Captain Juan Bautista de Anza establishes a presidio (military fort); San Francisco de Asis Mission opens.
- **1821** Mexico wins independence from Spain and annexes California.
- **1835** The town of Yerba Buena develops around the port; the United States tries unsuccessfully to purchase San Francisco Bay from Mexico.
- **1846–48** War between the United States and Mexico.
- **1848** Americans annex Yerba Buena and rename it San Francisco. Also, gold is discovered in Coloma, near

his best-selling novel, *Two Years before the Mast*, and helped fire the public's imagination about the territory's bounty, particularly that of the Bay Area.

The first overland party crossed the Sierra and arrived in California in 1841. San Francisco grew steadily, reaching a population of approximately 900 by April 1848, but nothing hinted at the population explosion that was to follow. Historian Barry Parr has referred to the California gold rush as the most extraordinary event to ever befall an American city in peacetime. Even without the lure of gold, San Francisco's winning combination of raw materials, healthful climate, and freedom would eventually have attracted thousands of settlers. But the gleam of the soft metal is said to have compressed 50 years of normal growth into less than 6 months. In 1848, the year gold was discovered, the population of San Francisco jumped from under 1,000 to 26,000.

If not for the discovery of some small particles of gold at a sawmill that he owned, Swiss-born John Augustus Sutter would have left a far less flamboyant legacy. Despite Sutter's wish to keep the discovery quiet, his employee, John Marshall, leaked word of the discovery to friends. It eventually appeared in local papers, and smart investors on the East

Coast took immediate heed. The rush did not start, however, until Sam Brannan, a Mormon preacher and famous charlatan, ran through the streets of San Francisco shouting, "Gold! Gold in the American River!" (Brannan, incidentally, bought up all the harborfront real estate he could and cornered the market on shovels, pick-axes, and canned food just before making the announcement that was heard around the world.)

A world on the brink of change responded almost frantically. The gold rush was on. Shop owners hung GONE TO THE DIGGINGS signs in their windows. Flotillas of ships set sail from ports throughout Europe, South America, Australia, and the East Coast, sometimes nearly sinking with the weight of mining equipment. Townspeople from the Midwest headed overland, and the social structure of a nation was transformed almost overnight. Not since the Crusades of the Middle Ages had so many people mobilized in so short a time. Daily business stopped; ships arrived in San Francisco, and their crews almost immediately deserted. News of the gold strike spread like a plague through every discontented hamlet in the known world.

Although other settlements were closer to the gold strike, San Francisco was the famous name and where gold-diggers

Sacramento. San Francisco's population swells from about 900 to 26,000.

- **1851** Lawlessness becomes acute before attempts to curb it.
- **1869** The transcontinental railroad reaches San Francisco.
- **1873** Andrew S. Hallidie invents the cable car.

- **1906** The Great Earthquake strikes, and the resulting fire levels the city.
- **1915** The Panama-Pacific International Exposition celebrates San Francisco's restoration and the completion of the Panama Canal.
- **1936** The Bay Bridge is completed.
- **1937** The Golden Gate Bridge is completed.

- **1945** The United Nations Charter is drafted in San Francisco and adopted by the representatives of 50 countries.
- **1950** The Beat Generation moves into the bars and cafes of North Beach.
- **1967** A free concert in Golden Gate Park attracts 20,000 people, ushering in the Summer of Love and the hippie era.

disembarked. Tent cities sprang up, and demand for virtually everything skyrocketed. Although some miners actually found gold, smart merchants discovered more enduring business in servicing the needs of the thousands of miners who arrived ill-equipped and ignorant of the lay of the land. Prices soared. Miners, faced with staggeringly inflated prices for goods and services, barely turned a profit after expenses. Most prospectors failed, many died of hardship, and others committed suicide at the alarming rate of 1,000 a year. Yet despite the tragedies, graft, and vice associated with the gold rush, within mere months San Francisco had been forever transformed from a tranquil Spanish settlement into a roaring, boisterous boomtown.

3 Boomtown Fever

By 1855, most of California's surface gold had already been panned out, leaving only the richer but deeper veins of ore, which individual miners couldn't retrieve without massive capital investments. Despite that, San Francisco had evolved into a vast commercial magnet, sucking into its warehouses and banks the staggering riches that overworked newcomers had dragged, ripped, and distilled from the rocks, fields, and forests of western North America.

Investment funds poured into more than mining, however. Speculation on the newly established San Francisco stock exchange could make or destroy an investor in a single day, and several noteworthy writers (including Mark Twain) were among the young men forever influenced by the boomtown spirit. The American Civil War left California firmly in the Union camp, ready, willing, and able to receive hordes of disillusioned soldiers fed up with the internecine warmongering of the Eastern seaboard. In 1869, the transcontinental railway linked the Eastern and Western seaboards of the United States, ensuring the fortunes of the barons who controlled it. The railways shifted economic power bases, however, as cheap manufactured goods from the East undercut the costly articles brought on ships that sailed or steamed around the tip of South America. The "Big Four"—iron-willed capitalists Leland Stanford, Mark Hopkins, Collis P. Huntington, and Charles Crocker—almost completely controlled ownership of the newly formed Central Pacific and Southern Pacific railroads, and their ruthlessness was legendary. (Much of the bone-crushing railway labor

- **1974** BART's high-speed transit system opens a tunnel linking San Francisco with the East Bay.
- **1978** Harvey Milk, a city supervisor and America's first openly gay politician, is assassinated, along with Mayor George Moscone, by political rival Dan White.
- **1989** An earthquake registering 7.1 on the Richter scale hits San Francisco just before a World Series baseball game, as 100 million watch on TV; the city quickly rebuilds.
- **1991** Fire rages through the Berkeley and Oakland hills, destroying 2,800 homes.
- **1993** Yerba Buena Center for the Arts opens.
- **1995** The new San Francisco MOMA opens.
- **1996** Former Assembly Speaker Willie Brown is elected mayor of San Francisco.
- **1998** El Niño deluges San Francisco with its second-highest rainfall in history.
- **2000** Pacific Bell Park (later renamed AT&T Park) opens as the new home of the San Francisco Giants baseball team with an exhibition

was done by low-paid Chinese newcomers, most of whom arrived in overcrowded ships at San Francisco ports.) As the 19th century came to a close, civil unrest became more frequent as the monopolistic grip of the railways and robber barons became more obvious. Adding to the discontent were the uncounted thousands of Chinese immigrants who fled starvation and unrest in Asia at rates rivaling those of the Italians, Poles, Irish, and British.

During the 1870s, the flood of profits from the Comstock Lode in western Nevada diminished to a trickle, a cycle of droughts wiped out part of California's agricultural bounty, and local industry struggled to survive the flood of manufactured goods coming by rail from well-established East Coast and Midwestern factories. Often, discontented workers blamed their woes on the now-unwanted hordes of Chinese workers who, by preference and for mutual protection, had congregated in teeming all-Asian communities.

Despite these downward cycles, the city enjoyed bouts of prosperity around the turn of the 20th century, thanks to the Klondike gold rush in Alaska and the Spanish-American War. Accustomed to making a buck off gold fever, San Francisco positioned itself as a point of embarkation for supplies bound for Alaska.

4 The Great Fire

On the morning of April 18, 1906, San Francisco changed for all time. The city has never experienced an earthquake as destructive as the one that hit at 5:13am; scientists estimate its strength at 8.1 on the Richter scale. All but a handful of the city's 400,000 inhabitants lay fast asleep when the ground went into a series of convulsions. As one eyewitness put it, "The earth was shaking . . . it was undulating, rolling like an ocean breaker." The quake ruptured every water main in the city and simultaneously started a chain of fires that rapidly fused into one gigantic conflagration. The fire brigades were helpless, and for 3 days San Francisco burned.

The final damage stretched across a path of destruction 450 miles long and 50 miles wide. The earthquake and subsequent fire so decisively changed the city that post-1906 San Francisco bears little resemblance to the town before the quake. Out of the ashes rose a bigger, healthier, and more beautiful town, although latter-day urbanologists regret that the rebuilding that followed the San Francisco earthquake did not have a more

game against the Milwaukee Brewers.
- **2003** Debonair Gavin Newsome is elected mayor of San Francisco.
- **2004** Mayor Newsome's permission of gay marriages garners national attention before

it's stopped by governmental higher-ups.
- **2006** San Francisco Giants outfielder Barry Bonds hits his 715th home run on May 28, passing Babe Ruth for second on the all-time home run list.

enlightened plan. So eager was the city to rebuild that the old, somewhat unimaginative gridiron plan was reinstated, despite the opportunities for more daring visions afforded by the quake's aftermath.

In 1915, in celebration of the opening of the Panama Canal and to prove to the world that San Francisco was restored to its full glory, the city was host to the Panama-Pacific International Exhibition, a world's fair that introduced hundreds of thousands of visitors to the city's unique charms. The frenzy of boosterism, however, reached its peak during the years just before World War I, when investments and civic pride might have reached an all-time high.

5 The Great Depression & World War II

The Great Depression hit San Francisco as it did the rest of the country. To alleviate some of the sting, the federal government created the Works Progress Administration (WPA) program in the late 1930s to provide work for artists during lean years. It not only supplied local artists with funds to create public murals, many of which still exist today and can be viewed at Coit Tower and Golden Gate Park's Beach Chalet, it also documented San Franciscan culture and landscape as well as provided citizens with at least a few pictures that were prettier than the current state of affairs.

The Japanese attack on Pearl Harbor on December 7, 1941, mobilized the U.S. into a massive war machine, with many shipyards strategically positioned along the Pacific Coast, including San Francisco's. Within less than a year, several shipyards were producing up to one new warship per day, employing hundreds of thousands of people working round-the-clock. Workers flooded the city from virtually everywhere, forcing an enormous boom in housing.

After the hostilities ended, many soldiers remembered San Francisco as the site of their finest hours and returned to live there permanently. The economic prosperity of the postwar years enabled massive enlargements of the city, including freeways, housing developments, a booming financial district, and pockets of counterculture enthusiasts, such as the beatniks, gays, and hippies.

6 The 1950s: The Beats

San Francisco's reputation as a rollicking place where anything goes dates from the Barbary Coast days when gang warfare, prostitution, gambling, and drinking were major pursuits, and citizens took law and order into their own hands. Its more modern role as a catalyst for social change and the avant-garde began in the 1950s. A group of young writers, philosophers, and poets challenged the materialism and conformity of American society by embracing anarchy and Eastern philosophy, expressing their notions in poetry. They adopted a uniform of jeans, sweaters, sandals, and berets, called themselves "Beats," and hung out in North Beach, where rents were low and cheap wine was plentiful. *San Francisco Chronicle* columnist Herb Caen, to whom they were totally alien, dubbed them "beatniks" in his column.

Allen Ginsberg, Gregory Corso, and Jack Kerouac had begun writing at Columbia University in New York, but it wasn't until they came west and hooked up with Lawrence Ferlinghetti, Kenneth Rexroth, Gary Snyder, and others that the movement gained national attention. The bible of the Beats was Ginsberg's "Howl," which he first read at the Six Gallery on October 13, 1955. By the time he finished reading, Ginsberg was crying, the audience was chanting, and his fellow poets were announcing the arrival of an epic bard. Ferlinghetti published "Howl," which was deemed obscene, in 1956. A trial followed, but the court found that the poem had redeeming social value, reaffirming the right of free expression. Another major Beat work, Kerouac's *On the Road*, was published in 1957 and instantly became a bestseller. (He had written it as one long paragraph in 20 days in 1951.) The freedom and sense of possibility the book conveyed became the bellwether for a generation.

While the Beats gave poetry readings and generated controversy, two clubs in North Beach were also making waves, notably the hungry i and the Purple Onion, where everyone who was anyone or became anyone on the entertainment scene appeared. Mort Sahl, Dick Gregory, Lenny Bruce, Barbra Streisand, and Woody Allen all worked there. Maya Angelou appeared as a singer and dancer at the Purple Onion. The cafes of North Beach—Vesuvio, Caffè Trieste, Caffè Tosca, and Enrico's Sidewalk Cafe—were the center of bohemian life in the '50s. When the tour buses started rolling in, rents went up, and Broadway became a sex-club strip in the early 1960s. Thus ended an era, and the Beats moved on— the alternative scene eventually shifting to Berkeley and the Haight.

7 The 1960s: The Haight

The torch of freedom passed from the Beats and North Beach to the hippies and Haight-Ashbury, but it was a radically different torch. The hippies replaced the Beats' angst, anarchy, negativism, nihilism, alcohol, and poetry with love, communalism, openness, drugs, rock music, and a back-to-nature philosophy. Although the scent of marijuana wafted everywhere—on the streets, in the cafes, in Golden Gate Park—the real drugs of choice were LSD (a tab of good acid cost $5) and other hallucinogenics. Timothy Leary experimented with its effects and exhorted youth to "turn on, tune in, and drop out." Instead of hanging out in coffeehouses, the hippies went to concerts at the Fillmore or the Avalon Ballroom to dance. The first Family Dog Rock 'n' Roll Dance and Concert, "A Tribute to Dr. Strange," was at the Longshoremen's Hall in 1965. It featured Jefferson Airplane, the Marbles, the Great Society, and the Charlatans. At the event, the first major happening of the 1960s, Ginsberg led a snake dance (a group advancing in a single-file serpentine path) through the crowd. In January 1966, Longshoremen's Hall was the site of the 3-day Trips Festival, organized by rock promoter Bill Graham. The climax was the Ken Kesey and the Merry Pranksters Acid Test show, which used five movie screens, psychedelic visions, and the sounds of the Grateful Dead and Big Brother and the Holding Company. The "be-in" followed in the summer of 1966 at the polo grounds in Golden Gate Park, when an estimated 20,000 heard Jefferson Airplane perform and Ginsberg chant, while the Hell's Angels acted as unofficial police. During the Summer of Love, in 1967, thousands of young people streamed into the city in search of drugs and sex.

One way that the '60s Haight scene was very different from the '50s Beat scene was that the hippies were much younger than the Beats had been, constituting the first youth movement to take over the nation. (They also became the first generation of young, independent, and moneyed consumers to be courted by corporations.)

Ultimately, the Haight and the hippie movement deteriorated from love and flowers into drugs and crime, drawing a fringe of crazies like Charles Manson and leaving a legacy of sex, drugs, violence, and consumerism. As early as October 1967, the "Diggers," who had opened a free shop and soup kitchen in the Haight, symbolically buried the dream in a clay casket in Buena Vista Park.

The end of the Vietnam War and the resignation of President Richard Nixon took the edge off politics. The last fling of the mentality that had driven the 1960s occurred in 1974, when the Symbionese Liberation Army kidnapped newspaper heiress Patty Hearst from her Berkeley apartment and took her on a bank-robbing spree before surrendering in San Francisco.

8 The 1970s & 1980s: Gay Rights

The homosexual community in San Francisco developed at the end of World War II, when thousands of military personnel returned to the United States via San Francisco. A substantial number of those men were homosexual and decided to stay in the city. A gay community grew up along Polk Street between Sutter and California. Later, the larger community moved into the Castro District, where it remains today.

The gay political-protest movement is usually dated from the 1969 Stonewall raid in Greenwich Village. Although the political movement started in New York, California had already given birth to two major organizations for gay rights: the Mattachine Society, founded in 1951 by Henry Hay in Los Angeles; and the Daughters of Bilitis, a lesbian organization founded in 1955 in San Francisco.

After Stonewall, the Committee for Homosexual Freedom was created in the spring of 1969 in San Francisco and a Gay Liberation Front chapter was organized at Berkeley. In the fall of 1969, Robert Patterson, a columnist for the *San Francisco Examiner,* referred to homosexuals as "semi males," "drag darlings," and "women who aren't exactly women." On October 31 at noon, a group began a peaceful picket of the *Examiner.* Peace reigned until someone threw a bag of printer's ink from an *Examiner* window. Things got violent and, eventually, the police moved in to clear the crowd, clubbing people as they went. The remaining picketers retreated to Glide Methodist Church, then marched on city hall. Unfortunately, the mayor was away. Unable to air their grievances, the picketers started a sit-in that lasted until 5pm, when they were ordered to leave. Most did, but three remained and were arrested.

Later that year, at an anti-Thanksgiving rally, gays protested against several national and local businesses: Western and Delta airlines (the former for firing lesbian stewardesses, the latter for refusing to sell a ticket to a young man wearing a Gay Power button); radio station KFOG, for its antihomosexual broadcasting; and some local gay bars for exploitation. On May 14, 1970, a group of gay and women's liberationists invaded the convention of the American Psychiatric Association in San Francisco to protest the reading of a paper on aversion therapy for homosexuals, forcing the meeting to adjourn.

The rage against intolerance was appearing on all fronts. At the National Gay Liberation conference in August 1970 in the city, Charles Thorp, chairman of the San Francisco State Liberation Front, called for militancy and issued a challenge to come out with a rallying cry of "Blatant is beautiful." He also argued for the use of what he felt was the more positive, celebratory term *gay* instead of *homosexual,* and decried the fact that homosexuals were kept in their place at the three Bs: the bars, the beaches, and the baths. As the movement grew in size and power, debates on strategy and tactics occurred, most dramatically between those gays who wanted to withdraw into separate ghettos, and those who wanted to enter mainstream society. In the end, the movement concentrated on integration and civil rights, not separatism. Gays elected politicians who were sympathetic to their cause and celebrated their new identity by establishing National Gay Celebration Day and Gay Pride Week, the first of which was celebrated in June 1970, when 1,000 to 2,000 marched in New York, 1,000 in Los Angeles, and a few hundred in San Francisco.

By the mid-1970s, the gay community craved a more central role in city politics. Harvey Milk, owner of a camera store in the Castro, decided to run for the board of supervisors. He won, becoming the first openly gay person to hold a major public office. He and liberal mayor George Moscone developed a gay rights agenda, but in 1978 they were both shot and killed by former supervisor Dan White, after Moscone refused White's request for reinstatement. White, a former police officer, had consistently opposed Milk's and Moscone's more liberal policies. At his trial, White successfully pleaded temporary insanity caused by additives in his fast-food diet. The media dubbed it the "Twinkie defense," but the murder charges against White were reduced to manslaughter. On that day, angry and grieving, the gay community rioted, overturning and burning police cars in a night of rage. To this day, a candlelight memorial parade is held on November 27. Milk's martyrdom was both a political and a practical inspiration for gay candidates across the country.

The emphasis in the gay movement shifted abruptly in the 1980s, when the AIDS epidemic struck the community. AIDS has had a dramatic impact on the Castro: While it's still a thriving and lively community, it's no longer the constant party it once was. The hedonistic lifestyle that had played out in the discos, bars, baths, and streets changed as the seriousness of the epidemic sank in and the number of deaths increased. Political efforts by gays have shifted away from enfranchisement and toward demands for social services and research money to deal with the AIDS crisis. Despite its difficulties, the gay community in San Francisco is still thriving. And let's not forget the hullabaloo around gay marriage, which Mayor Gavin Newsome legalized for a moment in early 2004 until higher-ranking governmental officials put a stop to it.

9 The Big One, Part Two

Compared to previous decades, the 1980s may have arrived in San Francisco with a whimper, but they went out with quite a bang. At 5:04pm on Tuesday, October 17, 1989, as more than 62,000 baseball fans filled Candlestick Park for the third game of the World Series—and the Bay Area commute moved into its heaviest flow—an earthquake of magnitude 7.1 struck. Within the next 20 seconds, 63 lives were lost, $10 billion in damage occurred, and the entire Bay Area community was reminded of its humble insignificance. Centered about 60 miles south of San Francisco in the Forest of Nisene Marks, the deadly temblor was felt as far away as San Diego and Nevada.

Although scientists had predicted an earthquake on this section of the San Andreas Fault, certain structures built to withstand such an earthquake failed miserably. The most catastrophic event was the collapse of the elevated Cypress Street section of Interstate 880 in Oakland; the upper level of the freeway pancaked onto the lower level, crushing everything between them with such force that cars were reduced to inches. Other heavily

Politics of the City Today

Shaken but not stirred by the Loma Prieta earthquake in 1989, San Francisco witnessed a spectacular rebound during the 1990s. The seaside Embarcadero, once plagued by a horrendously ugly freeway overpass, was revitalized by a multimillion-dollar face-lift, complete with palm trees, a cable-car line, wide cobblestone walkways, new restaurants, and a skating, biking, and walking promenade. SoMa, the once-shady neighborhood south of Market Street, exploded with new development and became home to the Museum of Modern Art; the beautiful and attraction-packed Yerba Buena Gardens; uberluxurious hotels; a slew of hip clubs, cafes, and condos; a new baseball stadium; and, most influential, dot-com companies. Plus, the tourist and shopping mecca Union Square got a gussied-up central plaza. But what comes up must come down.

When the Internet industry bubble burst, which was evident by spring 2000, it left serious damage to San Francisco. Contrary to the previous years' soar in population, rental and housing prices, and salaries, it was unemployment, commercial space availability, and dismal economic forecasts that were hitting new highs.

San Francisco definitely bore the brunt of the recent economic hiccup, but, not surprisingly, the city founded on the boom-and-bust mentality of gold seekers survived the experience just fine. New businesses slowly filled the dot-com office spaces, the Ferry Building Marketplace and its Farmers Market became the city's gastronomic Disneyland, and waiters who fled the restaurant industry for high-tech jobs returned to the dining rooms and resurrected the recognized importance of excellent service with them.

Of course, San Francisco still has typical big-city problems. Homelessness and panhandling have gone largely ignored. Visitors new to the city will be

damaged structures included the San Francisco–Oakland Bay Bridge, shut down for months when a section of the roadbed collapsed; San Francisco's Marina District, where several multimillion-dollar homes collapsed on their weak, shifting bases of landfill and sand; and the Pacific Garden Mall in Santa Cruz, which was devastated.

At least 3,700 people were reported injured and more than 12,000 were displaced. More than 18,000 homes were damaged and 963 others destroyed. Although fire raged in the city and water supply systems were damaged, the major fires in the Marina District were brought under control within 3 hours.

After the rubble finally settled, it was unanimously agreed that San Francisco and the Bay Area had pulled through miraculously well—particularly when the quake was compared with the recent earthquake in Kobe, Japan, which had killed thousands and displaced an entire city. After the quake, a feeling of esprit de corps swept the city as neighbors helped each other rebuild and donations poured in from all over the world. Although over a decade has passed, San Francisco is still feeling the effects of the quake, most noticeably during rush hour as commuters take a variety of detours to circumvent freeways that were damaged or destroyed and are still under construction.

surprised by its dirtiness in some areas. Those with enough funds to buy a spacious home in most parts of the U.S. can't afford a one-bedroom condo here. Rental units are still expensive enough to have changed the city's demographics: Artists, young transplants, and others seeking an alternative lifestyle can no longer afford to move here and sustain their lifestyle. Parking is beyond a nightmare. Public transportation is embarrassingly inefficient. Congestion and impatient drivers make cruising the town an anxiety-ridden and very slow ride.

But the city's in good spirits—especially since electing Mayor Gavin Newsome in 2003. After barely settling into office, the young (and media-savvy) mayor created controversy and heightened Bay Area pride by allowing gay marriages. It didn't take long to be overruled by the higher-ups. But not before Mayor Newsome won the respect of locals, many of whom see alternative lifestyles and equal rights as trademark San Francisco, at least in theory if not in practice.

As a whole, San Francisco is doing just fine. Its symphony is in the black, restaurants' cheaper prices (lowered during harder times) and new exciting destination haunts woo locals to dine out, and though many of the once instantly rich residents lost it all in the stock market, many argue it's been a good thing for the city. We needed a little reality, not to mention elbow-room for those making under six figures.

Anyone who remembers the old, liberal, truly progressive, and funky San Francisco knows those days are long behind us. But even without the hard-core alternative edge, San Francisco rightfully retains its title as Americans' favorite city destination.

10 The 1990s: The New Gold Rush

During the early 1990s, nothing earth-shattering took place in San Francisco. The nationwide recession influenced the beginning of the decade, and the quiet rumblings of the new frontier in Silicon Valley escaped much notice. By the middle of the decade, however, San Francisco and the surrounding areas had discovered a new kind of gold rush—the Internet industry.

Not unlike the gold fever of the 1800s, people flocked to the Western shores to strike it rich—and they did. In 1999, local media reported that every day 64 Bay Area residents were gaining millionaire status.

Real estate prices went into the stratosphere, and the city's gentrification financially squeezed out many of those residents who didn't mean big business (read: many of the alternative types, the elderly, and minorities who made the city colorful). New businesses popped up everywhere—especially in the SoMa area, where startup companies jammed warehouse spaces to the rafters. As the most popular posteducation destination for MBAs and the leader in the media of the future, San Francisco no longer opened its Golden Gate to everyone looking for the legendary alternative lifestyle—unless they could afford a $1,000 studio apartment and $20-per-day fees to park their cars.

The new millennium was christened with bubbly in hand, foie gras and caviar in mouth, and seemingly everyone in the money. New restaurants charging $35 per entree were all the rage, hotels were renovated, the new bayfront ballpark was packed, and stock market tips were as plentiful as million-dollar SoMa condos and high-rises. San Franciscans were too busy raking in the dough and working and playing hard to heed the writing on the wall.

11 The New Millennium: A Reality Check

The new millennium started off well enough. The initial fallout in the market and the stability of previously well-funded companies was expected; everyone cashing in on the new economy knew the situation was too good to be true. Venture capitalists began holding onto their funding with both hands rather than doling it out freely to anyone with an idea and a ".com" suffix. The business community figured the scale was finally balancing, with sound companies outweighing the less-concrete ideas on the bandwidth bandwagon.

By mid-2000, investors began to shy away from companies with high valuations and no profits. The billions of dollars of funding that poured into the Bay Area had dried up. Dot-com obituaries and layoff notifications grew longer and grimmer, until finally, by early 2001, it seemed the entire industry had collapsed.

The events of the September 11, 2001, terrorist attacks, coupled with the recent war and economic uncertainty, made matters that much worse. The tourist industry disappeared for a while, business travel dropped off, hotels were nearly empty, and restaurant closings were announced almost daily.

It's been a wild ride since the late 1990s, during which time the city was too crowded, too successful, too rich, and becoming too ruthless. After the burst of the dot-com bubble, September 11, 2001, and the continued economic downturn, we denizens became more humble, more appreciative and supportive, even more in love with our comfortable, friendly, and provincial city.

Over the past 3 years, The City by the Bay has rebounded. New restaurants ranging from neighborhood haunts to big-bucks formal affairs opened to great fanfare, new hotels constructed from the ground up instantly demanded—and got—nightly rates that top many people's mortgages, and home sales continue to have analysts scratching their heads and asking when the proverbial bubble will burst. It's likely that for San Franciscans, the answer is never: With such stunning surroundings and a truly exceptional quality of life, most residents feel that even during the darkest days of stupendous home prices and salaries that cannot support them, we are truly blessed.

Index

See also Accommodations and Restaurant indexes, below.

FRI - Alcatraz/wharf

SAT. -

SUN. -

MON. -

TUES. -

THE NEW TRAVELOCITY GUARANTEE

EVERYTHING YOU BOOK WILL BE RIGHT, OR WE'LL WORK WITH OUR TRAVEL PARTNERS TO MAKE IT RIGHT, RIGHT AWAY.

*To drive home the point,
we're going to use the word "right" in every single sentence.*

Let's get right to it. Right to the meat! Only Travelocity guarantees everything about your booking will be right, or we'll work with our travel partners to make it right, right away. Right on!

Here's a picture taken smack dab right in the middle of Antigua, where the guarantee also covers you.

The guarantee covers all but one of the items pictured to the right.

For example, what if the ocean view you booked actually looks out at a downright ugly parking lot? You'd be right to call – we're there for you. And no one in their right mind would be pleased to learn the rental car place has closed and left them stranded. Call Travelocity and we'll help get you back on the right track.

Now, you may be thinking, "Yeah, right, I'm so sure." That's OK; you have the right to remain skeptical. That is until we mention help is always right around the corner. Call us right off the bat, knowing that our customer service reps are there for you 24/7. Righting wrongs. Left and right.

Now if you're guessing there are some things we can't control, like the weather, well you're right. But we can help you with most things – to get all the details in righting,* visit **travelocity.com/guarantee**.

Sorry, spelling things right is one of the few things not covered under the guarantee.

I'd give my right arm for a guarantee like this, although I'm glad I don't have to.

travelocity
You'll never roam alone.

05 Travelocity.com LP. UST F2 205547A 250

IF YOU BOOK IT, IT SHOULD BE THERE.

Only Travelocity guarantees it will be, or we'll work with our travel partners to make it right, right away. So if you're missing a balcony or anything else you booked, just call us 24/7. 1-888-TRAVELOCITY.

***⁂** travelocity

You'll never roam alone.

My San Francisco

by Erika Lenkert

AS A NATIVE SAN FRANCISCAN BORN TO A JAZZ SINGER DURING THE
Summer of Love, I have a different relationship with the City By the Bay than most residents. In my Cole Valley–raised eyes, the city is more conservative and segregated and not nearly as ethnically or professionally diverse or funky and homespun as it once was. Of course, most longtime residents have similar complaints after watching their hometowns evolve and gentrify. But if one thing has refreshed my appreciation for this city, it has been living for the past four years in the bucolic Napa Valley.

Maybe San Francisco is a little slicker and more commercial than it used to be. But its undeniable beauty still hits me every time I drive over the Bay or Golden Gate bridges. I no longer take San Francisco's worldliness for granted. I come regularly for outstanding ethnic food, decent fashions, museum exhibitions, indie films, affordable manicures, and to mingle with a population more diverse than the one I've found in Napa. San Francisco may no longer be the groovy (or affordable) place that once inspired America's disillusioned youth to gather in celebration of peace, love, drugs, music, and sex. But one visit to the Haight Ashbury, Castro, or Mission districts; one night in a great restaurant; or one stroll through Golden Gate Park confirms that my ever-evolving city is still as much defined by its lively character as it is by its hills. These photos offer a glimpse of the San Francisco I love.

© Garry Gay/Alamy

Frommer's®
San Francisco